ADVANCED
ANSI COBOL WITH
STRUCTURED PROGRAMMING

Advanced
ANSI COBOL with
Structured Programming

FOR VS COBOL II™ AND
MICROSOFT™ MICRO FOCUS™ COBOL

Second Edition

Gary DeWard Brown

John Wiley & Sons, Inc.

New York Chichester Brisbane Toronto Singapore

CICS, CISC/ESA, DB2, IBM, MVS, MVS/ESA, MVS/XA, OS/2, SAA System/370, System/390, and VS COBOL II are registered trademarks of International Business Machines Corporation.
Micro Focus, ANIMATOR, and Micro Focus COBOL/2 are registered trademarks of Micro Focus Limited.
Microsoft, MS, MS-DOS, and Windows are all registered trademarks of Microsoft Corporation.

Library of Congress Cataloging-in-Publication Data
Brown, Gary DeWard.
    Advanced ANSI COBOL with structured programming : for VS COBOL II
and Microsoft Micro Focus COBOL / Gary DeWard Brown.
        p.   cm.
    Rev. ed. of: Advanced ANS COBOL with structured programming.
c 1977.
    ISBN 0-471-54786-7 (paperback)
    1. COBOL (Computer program language) 2. Structured programming.
I. Brown, Gary DeWard. Advanced ANS COBOL with structured
programming. II. Title.
QA76.73.C25B76 1992
005.13'3–dc20   91-32450

Printed in the United States of America

10 9

Preface

Often the worst days in your life are the first few days on a new job. Everyone in the company knows what they are supposed to be doing, and you can't even find the coffee machine. This book eases the transition from general programming training to the programming done in business applications using COBOL.

COBOL is used more widely by professional programmers than any other programming language. COBOL has been extremely successful for three decades. Each year some new language or concept, such as PL/I, fourth-generation languages, or CASE (Computer-Aided Software Engineering), is supposed to make COBOL obsolete. And yet it continues to be as alive and successful as ever.

COBOL was the first major programming language to address the needs of business data processing, and it is ideally suited to business applications. It contains many innovations, the most successful of which is the requirement that all data be described in a discrete, separate process, rather than defining data implicitly.

COBOL was given an English-language syntax with the implicit assumption that it would be easy for nonprogrammers to use. This didn't happen—nonprogrammers don't use COBOL. They *do* use BASIC, Pascal, Lotus 1-2-3, and D-BASE IV extensively, none of which have English-language syntax. Meanwhile, COBOL has come to be viewed as a very difficult language whose use is limited to professional programmers. And yet, the English-language syntax did have an important benefit. It made COBOL programs relatively easy to read. Since about 80 percent of today's programming effort is in maintenance, this is extremely important.

COBOL is the most untraditional of all the major programming languages. COBOL was the first language designed by a committee and the first to become an ANSI (American National Standards Institute) standard. It reflects both the good and bad results from this. The good is that is makes COBOL a standard language. The bad is that the language evolves very slowly. The COBOL 85 standard replaced the COBOL 74 standard only after extensive controversy, injured egos, and threats of lawsuits.

One of the main weaknesses of COBOL was the difficulty in modularizing by writing subroutines and functions. The new standard makes writing subroutines (subprograms) easier, and ANSI Standard ANSI X3.23a = 1989, *Programming Language—Intrinsic Function Module for COBOL* recently gave intrinsic functions to COBOL as described in Appendix D. These are now implemented in Microsoft COBOL. (Microsoft COBOL also has a library of subprograms for terminal I/O.) The result is that the COBOL culture does not share code across the industry. Any sharing is usually within a company. In contrast to a language like C, where many programmers purchase more code than they write, most COBOL programmers write their applications from scratch, or they use a similar application within the company as a prototype and then modify it. Since purchased software is usually extremely cost-effective, this has been an expensive omission. (Of course, locating, evaluating, installing, testing, and modifying external software is no panacea either.)

The next step in COBOL evolution will likely be toward object-oriented programming. Despite the excitement about object-oriented programming, there remains little empirical evidence that proves it is "better." Given the time it takes to change the COBOL standard and the difficulty of retraining programmers, COBOL is unlikely to become object-oriented in the next few years. COBOL has many technical problems in becoming object-oriented, but even more difficult cultural ones.

Unfortunately, each new COBOL standard renders portions of the old standard obsolete, often requiring a conversion in order to run under the new standard. The conversion to COBOL 85 cost some companies millions of dollars. You don't have to move very high up the corporate ladder to find the request to spend millions on a conversion required by a "standard" ranking somewhere in popularity below a hostile takeover.

Most other computer languages use the same vocabulary, but COBOL is different. For example, a "variable" is an "identifier" in COBOL. This has reinforced the cultural gap between COBOL and non-COBOL programmers. COBOL programmers who are otherwise tolerant have total disdain for someone who calls an identifier a variable. This cultural wall has been unfortunate for data processing. It restricts the flow between COBOL and non-COBOL programmers, along with the attendant ideas. Besides the occasional satisfaction of a good put-down, it has no advantage.

GARY DEWARD BROWN

December 1991
Los Angeles, California

About the Author

Gary DeWard Brown is currently a data processing consultant and writer. He is the author of seven other data processing books published by John Wiley & Sons, including *System 370/390 Job Control Language*; *System/370 Job Control Language*; *System/360 Job Control Language*; *Surviving with Financial Application Packages for the Computer*; *Beyond COBOL: Survival in Business Applications Programming*; *Advanced ANS COBOL with Structured Programming*; and *FORTRAN to PL/I Dictionary, PL/I to FORTRAN Dictionary*. Brown's *System/370 Job Control Language* has sold over 400,000 copies.

Mr. Brown was a co-founder of Crwth Computer Courseware, where he was its principal author. He designed and wrote its authoring/presentation system: Crwth Format. Mr. Brown began his programming career with Douglas Aircraft as a scientific programmer. He worked for the Rand Corporation for several years and has also been an instructor in comparative programming languages for UCLA's Engineering College. Mr. Brown has worked in many phases of computing, including scientific applications, systems programming, business applications programming, PC and cross-system interactive systems, and training.

Mr. Brown graduated with the BS in Engineering from the University of Wyoming and an MBA from UCLA. He resides in Los Angeles with his wife Lolly and children Hillary and Lindsay.

Contents

1

Introduction

I. THE BOOK'S INTENT

More people learn COBOL each year, adding to the number of active COBOL programmers. This book is for people who know the basics of programming and want to learn COBOL quickly without wasting time rehashing basic programming techniques. Having advanced beyond the introductory programming manual, they need a book that touches only lightly on the basics of computing, but goes into detail on both programming techniques and the COBOL statements. The book assumes you are familiar with computers, computer applications, and a programming language, not necessarily COBOL. The book describes the COBOL statements in enough detail to enable someone familiar with programming to learn COBOL.

The book is intended to make the programmer a master of COBOL programming skills. This may help to solve some programming problems, but not all. The book cannot help with the difficult problems of dealing with an uncooperative customer, fighting an unreliable computer system, or designing a computer solution to a problem not worth a solution. But the book should give you confidence in your technical programming skills, making it possible to face the other more difficult problems with this confidence.

In addition to the advanced COBOL features, such as the SORT verb, pointers and addresses, tables, subprograms, and character-string manipulation, the book describes programming techniques with structured programming. Advanced programming does not imply that programming be clever, obscure, or difficult. On the contrary, it implies that it be simple, concise, and clear. Programming style can also contribute to simplicity, conciseness, and clarity. Although style is partly a matter of personal taste, Chapter 2 develops a set of objective criteria that leads to the style used throughout this book.

The book covers three versions of COBOL:

- The 1985 version of the American National Standard Programming Language COBOL, ANSI X3.23-1985.[1] The book covers all the standard except for the Report Writer and Communications facility, because they are not in the IBM VS COBOL II compiler. (They are in Microsoft COBOL.)

1

- The IBM VS COBOL II compiler through Version 3 for the MVS/ESA operating system.[2] MVS/ESA—Multiple Virtual System/Enterprise Systems Architecture—is IBM's main operating system for the mainframe. Except for the Report Writer and Communications facility, it is essentially the same as the ANSI Standard. The book includes information from the *VS COBOL II Programmer's Guide*[3] at the appropriate places in the text. The book introduces MVS Job Control Language (JCL)[4,5] because it is essential to VS COBOL II and MVS is IBM's most widely used operating system.
- The Microsoft ® COBOL compiler[6] under DOS or OS/2 on the PC. (Microsoft COBOL is the same as Micro Focus COBOL/2®[7].) The Microsoft COBOL compiler is a superset of both the ANSI Standard and VS COBOL II. The book covers the subset that is included in VS COBOL II.

Several statements and facilities in the ANSI Standard are obsolete, to be removed in the next revision. These include items that were bad ideas, such as the ALTER GO TO, or are no longer useful, such as checkpoint/restart, because they are now specified externally with operating system commands. Obsolete items are put in Appendix C to discourage their use. The exception is the COBOL debugging module. Debugging is always useful, absolutely necessary, and easily removed should the standard change. Punched cards are not mentioned because they are obsolete.

The book assumes you will write applications in one of the following environments:

- Development and production on an IBM mainframe computer.
- Production to run on both the IBM PC and mainframe computers.
- Development on an IBM PC with production on an IBM mainframe computer. Chapter 26 discusses this in some detail.

The last item is likely to become the typical environment. It allows the programmer to make the most effective use of both the PC and mainframe. Nothing can touch the mainframe computer for large-volume, batch production runs. Nothing can touch the PC for interactive computing, fast compilation, and development. Because almost all mainframes run close to capacity, there is a strong incentive to move as much to a PC as possible.

II. USE OF THIS BOOK

The language features are described with examples—not long examples illustrating applications, but short examples illustrating language features. Applications are important, but as examples they are too long and involved to hold your interest. A few complete programs are included to show how all the COBOL statements look when they are put together in a complete program.

First, criteria are developed to evaluate programming techniques and language features. The basic COBOL statements come next, and the COBOL statements for structured programming are introduced. The advanced COBOL features follow. To use the book as a textbook, read the chapters in sequence and work the exercises. If you are an experienced programmer, you may wish to choose selected chapters after reading Chapters 2 through 5.

The ANSI Standard and Microsoft COBOL notation show optional clauses with braces and brackets, whereas IBM uses arrows. Rather than having you decipher a notation, this book just shows the statements as they are written. If there are several forms or options, you are shown each form. This lets you see how it is coded, without the distraction of braces, brackets, lines, and other items not coded. A dashed line indicates that one of several items may be coded, with the items listed above the dashed lines. Comments that describe the statements are set off in brackets. Language statements are in uppercase letters; lower-case italic/type denotes generic terms, such as *name* or *value*.

```
      INPUT
      OUTPUT
OPEN _____ file-name
```
   [*Explanations are in this typeface. You could code this statement in two ways. You choose the file-name .*]
```
OPEN OUTPUT OUT-FILE      [Or.]      OPEN INPUT IN-FILE
```

COBOL now allows statements to be written in upper or lower case. The book shows the COBOL statements in upper case, because that is how most people are used to seeing them.

```
OPEN INPUT IN-FILE      [is the same as]      open input in-file
```

The vocabulary used to describe COBOL differs from that used with other languages such as FORTRAN, C, and PL/I. This book generally tries to avoid any specialized vocabulary, but a major difference in COBOL is the vocabulary. Since the COBOL vocabulary is an important part of the COBOL culture, you need to acquaint yourself with the following COBOL terms that are used throughout the book.

- *Data item*. A unit of data used by the COBOL program. Note that literals are not considered data items.
- *Name*. A part of a COBOL definition or operation. For example, the statement MOVE A TO B is composed of four names: MOVE is the verb, A and B are identifiers, and TO is a keyword.
- *Data name*. A user-defined word that names a data item. You must describe it in a data description entry in the Data Division.
- *Elementary item*. A data item described as not being further logically subdivided. For example, the month might be an elementary item in a date. An elementary data item in COBOL is any item that has a PIC, COMP-1, or COMP-2 clause. COMP-1 and COMP-2 are not in the ANSI Standard.
- *Identifier*. A data name, followed as required by the syntactically correct combination of qualifiers, subscripts, and indices necessary to reference a data item uniquely. Other languages call an identifier a *variable*. For example, the

data name of a table might be MONTHS. An identifier would be MONTHS(1), which would refer to the first month of the table.

- *Numeric literal.* A literal composed of one or more numeric characters that also may contain a decimal point, an algebraic sign, or both. For example, 2 and 3.1416 are numeric literals. The decimal point must not be the rightmost character. The algebraic sign, if present, must be the leftmost character. An *integer* is a numeric literal without a decimal point. Other languages call a numeric literal a *numeric constant.*

- *Nonnumeric literal.* A character string bounded by quotation marks. Other languages call it an alphanumeric or character literal. For example, "THE END" is a nonnumeric literal.

- *Figurative constant.* A figurative constant is a COBOL word that denotes a constant. For example, the word HIGH-VALUE represents the highest value of a character in the computer's collating sequence.

- *Table.* A set of logically consecutive items of data defined in the Data Division with the OCCURS clause. Other languages call a table an *array.*

An *item* may be either a literal or identifier of a data type appropriate to the context. Thus, the general form of a statement may be given as

        MOVE   *item*   TO   *identifier*

The following MOVE statements are then valid:

        MOVE 2 TO X   [*Numeric literal moved to an identifier.*]
        MOVE "A" TO Y   [*Nonnumeric literal moved to an identifier.*]
        MOVE W TO Z   [*Identifier moved to another identifier.*]

But the following statement is invalid:

        MOVE W TO 2   [*Can't move an identifier to a literal.*]

You may notice that many examples use short, meaningless names, such as ADD Y TO X, despite the book's urging you to use meaningful names. The reason for this apparent contradiction is to emphasize the statement rather than the data. A statement such as ADD 2 TO CITY-POPULATION might evoke thoughts about cities and their populations, distracting from the operation of the ADD.

COBOL often allows several alternative ways to code the same thing, such as A OF B or A IN B. This book generally describes only one of the forms. Additionally, COBOL has several optional words that may be omitted, such as (A IS = B) or (A = B), and the book ignores some optional words. These omissions simplify the language descriptions by giving you a single form for coding the language statements that works. Because all the redundant ways of coding statements are not described, the book is not a complete reference manual. Instead, it is more a manual for learning COBOL programming. The emphasis is on simplifying language features and not on giving all the possible ways of coding them.

III. INTRODUCTION TO COBOL

COBOL differs from most programming languages. It is based on English, which is not unusual, but it is designed especially for business applications, and this is unusual. COBOL programs are highly structured in that they are divided into four divisions.

The first division, entitled the Identification Division, names the program and contains optional comments that identify the program's author and describe when it was written and what it does.

The second division, entitled the Environment Division, describes those aspects of the program that depend on the physical characteristics of a specific computer. It describes each file used by the program and additionally associates the internal file name with an external Job Control Language statement or file.

The third division, entitled the Data Division, describes all the data used in the program. You must explicitly describe each data item. COBOL is designed to process files, and the data descriptions take the form of a record structure. For example, the file might contain lines having the format shown in Figure 1.1.

You write the data description entries describing this record as follows:

```
01  INPUT-RECORD.
```
        [*Names the record.*]
```
    05  PERSON-NAME              PIC X(25).
```
        [*Specifies 25 alphanumeric characters of data.*]
```
    05  FILLER                  PIC X.
```
        [*Specifies one alphanumeric character.* FILLER *indicates that the item is not given a name.*]
```
    05  PERSON-SALARY           PIC 999V99.
```
        [*Specifies a five-digit number with two places to the right of the assumed decimal point. The 12555 on the line is treated as 125.55.*]

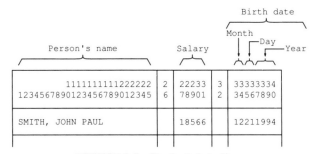

FIGURE 1.1   Typical data line.

```
05  FILLER                        PIC X.
```
[*Specifies one alphanumeric character. The item is not given a name.*]
```
05  PERSON-BIRTH-DATE.
```
[*Names a group item, which is further subdivided.*]
```
    10  MONTH                     PIC 99.
```
[*Specifies two numeric digits.*]
```
    10  DAYS                      PIC 99.
```
[*Specifies two numeric digits.*]
```
    10  YEAR                      PIC 9(4).
```
[*Specifies four numeric digits.*]

The record enables the data to be treated as a unit, and yet you can still refer to each individually named item of data that it contains. You also describe independent elementary items and tables in this record form:

```
77  FLAG-A                        PIC X.
```
[*Elementary item. It is called a noncontiguous elementary item because it is not part of a data structure.*]
```
01  CITY.
```
[*CITY names a data structure composed of several data items.*]
```
    05  POPULATION                PIC X(5)
                                  OCCURS 100 TIMES.
```
[*POPULATION is a table containing 100 elements, and each element contains five characters.*]

The several COBOL classes and categories of data are as follows. The VALUE clause assigns initial values to data items as shown.

• *Numeric class.* You can perform arithmetic operations on this class of data.

```
77  ITEM-A                        PIC S999V99 VALUE 1.
```
[*External decimal number. The data contains numeric data in character form, and you can perform arithmetic operations on it.*]
```
77  ITEM-B                        PIC S999V99 BINARY VALUE 1.
```
[*Binary data.*]
```
77  ITEM-C                        PIC S999V99 PACKED-DECIMAL
                                  VALUE 1.
```
[*Numeric packed decimal data.*]
```
77  ITEM-D COMP-1                 VALUE 0.1E+1.
```
[*Numeric single-precision floating-point data.*]
```
77  ITEM-E COMP-2                 VALUE 0.1E+1.
```
[*Numeric double-precision floating-point data.*]

• *Alphanumeric class.* You cannot perform arithmetic operations on this class of data.

```
77  ITEM-F                        PIC X(3) VALUE "AB1".
```
[*Alphanumeric data.*]
```
77  ITEM-G                        PIC $9,999.99.
```

[*Numeric edited data. Edits numeric data for display.*]

```
77  ITEM-H                          PIC XX/XX/XX.
```

[*Alphanumeric edited data. Edits alphanumeric data for display.*]

- *Alphabetic class.* You cannot perform arithmetic operations on this class of data.

```
77  ITEM-I                          PIC A(3) VALUE "ABC".
```

[*Alphabetic data.*]

Another numeric form, the *index,* can only refer to table elements, and is described along with the table.

```
01  CITY.
    05  POPULATION                  PIC X(5)
                                    OCCURS 100 TIMES
                                    INDEXED BY X-POP.
```

[X-POP *is defined as the index, and you can use it to index the POPULATION table.*]

There is also a Double-Byte Character Set (DBCS) used for Japanese Kanji and graphics (described in Chapter 22), and a pointer form for containing storage addresses (described in Chapter 23).

The fourth division, termed the Procedure Division, contains the executable program statements. The statements are a rigid subset of English.

```
MOVE A TO B              [A is stored in B.]
ADD 1 TO A               [1 is added to A.]
COMPUTE C = D * E / F
                         [The value of D times E divided by]
                         [F is stored in C.]
```

COBOL doesn't check for the beginning of a sentence by context, but by recognizing one of its reserved words, such as MOVE, ADD, and COMPUTE in the previous examples. There is no statement termination punctuation, and so it recognizes the end of the statement only when it encounters a key word that begins a new statement. Because of this, all COBOL language words are reserved. You cannot use MOVE, ADD, and COMPUTE as data items, because they are part of COBOL statements.

Each COBOL *statement* begins with a reserved-word verb and performs some operation. You can collect a group of statements into what COBOL calls a sentence. A COBOL *sentence* contains one or more statements and ends with a period. You can use a sentence in conditional statements, such as the IF, to execute several statements based on the condition. The following example shows this.

```
IF A = B
   THEN MOVE C TO D     [These two statements are executed if A equals B.]
        MOVE E TO F
```

```
ELSE MOVE G TO H      [These two statements are executed if A does not equal B.]
     MOVE I TO J.
     [The period terminates the sentence.]
```

In the previous version of COBOL, the period was the only way of collecting statements in conditional statements. It was very unsatisfactory, especially in nested IF/THEN/ELSE statements. The period is still valid, but COBOL 85 eliminates the need for it by providing explicit scope terminators. The above is better coded as follows.

```
IF A = B
   THEN MOVE C TO D      [These two statements are executed if A equals B.]
        MOVE E TO F
   ELSE MOVE G TO H      [These two statements are executed if A does not equal B.]
        MOVE I TO J
END-IF
   [The END-IF terminates the IF statement.]
```

All COBOL conditional statements have *explicit scope terminators* similar to the END-IF above. The explicit scope terminator is better than using sentences and periods, and this book uses them exclusively.

The DISPLAY statement displays the value of alphanumeric literals and numeric and alphanumeric data items on the standard output file — either a terminal or printer.

```
DISPLAY ITEM-A
   [Displays the contents of ITEM-A.]
DISPLAY "THE VALUE IS: ", ITEM-B
   [Displays "THE VALUE IS: ", followed by the contents of ITEM-B.]
```

COBOL files, also termed *data sets* in MVS, must be described explicitly by a series of entries in the Environment and Data Divisions. You must open files before you can read or write them, and you should close them when processing is complete. (The system automatically closes any files that are open when the program terminates.)

```
OPEN INPUT IN-FILE       [IN-FILE is opened for input.]
OPEN OUTPUT OUT-FILE     [OUT-FILE is opened for output.]
CLOSE IN-FILE            [IN-FILE is closed.]
```

COBOL input/output is record-oriented; that is, each READ or WRITE transmits one logical record. (The operating system may group several records together in a block to transmit them as a physical unit between the I/O device and the computer's memory.) For example, the INPUT-RECORD defined earlier is read and written as shown in the following example. In the example, the AT END phrase in the READ statement contains an imperative statement to be executed if there is no record to be read.

```
READ IN-FILE INTO INPUT-RECORD
```
   [*A record is read into* INPUT-RECORD.]
```
AT END MOVE SPACES TO INPUT-RECORD
```
   [SPACES *is a figurative constant that assumes the value of literal blank characters
   equal to the length of the item to which it is moved. The program moves spaces to*
   INPUT-RECORD *if there is no record to read.*]
```
NOT AT END WRITE OUT-REC FROM INPUT-RECORD
```
   [*If a record is read successfully, the* WRITE *statement writes it from* INPUT-RECORD.]
```
END-READ
```
   [*This terminates the* READ *statement*.]

In COBOL, an *imperative statement* is one that either specifies an unconditional action or is a conditional statement that is terminated by its explicit scope terminator. This is another reason for using explicit scope terminators: You can use a conditional statement anywhere an imperative statement is allowed. In this book, all statements are made imperative statements so that they can be placed anywhere.

COBOL I/O transmits data without conversion. Once a string of digits is read, you could check the numeric digits for validity and then convert them from character to a more efficient numeric form by moving them to a numeric data item.

```
MOVE PERSON-SALARY TO   numeric-data-item
```

COBOL can also label executable statements and branch to the statement with a GO TO statement. Labels in COBOL are termed *procedure names*. Labels must begin in column 8 and be terminated by a period. Statements must begin in column 12 or beyond.

```
A10-INITIALIZE.
    MOVE A TO B
```

In COBOL, labels name a group of statements to be executed as a unit by the PERFORM statement. The PERFORM statement names a procedure and executes all the statements following the procedure name, up to the next procedure name. Such a collection of statements is termed a *paragraph*. You usually organize COBOL programs as a collection of paragraphs invoked by PERFORM rather than using GO TOs to thread control through the statements.

```
PERFORM A10-INITIALIZE
```
   [*Executes all the statements following* A10-INITIALIZE *up to the next paragraph name,
   and then returns control to the next executable statement following the* PERFORM.]
```
PERFORM A20-READ-FILE
```
   [*Executes all the statements in the* A20-READ-FILE *paragraph*.]

Execution continues sequentially, and so the paragraphs invoked must not immediately follow the invoking statements, or control will flow through them again.

```
A10-INITIALIZE.
    OPEN INPUT IN-FILE          [Invoked by
    MOVE 0 to IN-COUNT            PERFORM A10-INITIALIZE.]
```

[*COBOL requires that each paragraph end with a period. Since the period is not otherwise needed, this book places it on a separate line at the end of the paragraph. This makes it stand out and helps to mark the end of the paragraph. The alternative, remembering to code a period on the last statement within the paragraph, is easy to forget.*]

```
A20-READ-FILE.
    READ IN-FILE INTO INPUT-RECORD
       AT END                              [Invoked by
          MOVE SPACES TO INPUT-RECORD        PERFORM A20-READ-FILE.]
          IF INPUT-RECORD NOT = SPACES
             THEN ADD 1 TO IN-COUNT
          END-IF
       END-READ
```

This is the essence of COBOL and should give enough background for the next chapter, which develops a set of criteria for developing good programming style. These criteria are then applied throughout the remainder of the book in describing the COBOL statements.

REFERENCES

1. "American National Standard for Information Systems—Programming Language—COBOL," ANSI X3.23-1985, New York; American National Standards Institute, Inc., 1985.

2. "VS COBOL II Application Programming Language Reference," Order No. GC26-4047, San Jose, CA: IBM Corporation, 1989.

3. "VS COBOL II Application Programming Guide for MVS and CMS," Order No. SC26-4045, San Jose, CA: IBM Corporation, 1989.

4. "MVS/ESA JCL Reference," Order No. GC28-1654, Poughkeepsie, NY: IBM Corporation, 1991.

5. Gary Brown, System/370/390 Job Control Language, New York: John Wiley& Sons, 1991.

6. "Microsoft® COBOL Optimizing Compiler Version 3.0 for MS® OS/2 and MS-DOS®," Microsoft Corporation, 1988.

7. "Micro Focus COBOL/2™," Palo Alto, CA: Micro Focus Inc., 1991.

2

Criteria

I. RATIONALE FOR RULES AND GUIDELINES

The criteria developed here are used throughout the book, and lead to several rules and guidelines for style. A *rule* is something there is every reason to observe, and no valid reason not to. Indenting nested IF statements is a rule. A *guideline* has valid reasons for being followed, but exceptional instances for not being followed. Eliminating the GO TO statement is a guideline.

Some rules and guidelines must be ambiguous. Everyone agrees that IF statements should not be nested to too deep a level, but we can argue how deep. Either there is no precise definition, or it would take so many words to state the rule as to be useless. In these instances, we shall resort to the reasonable-person rule. In a court of law, this rule states that if a reasonable person would find something wrong, it is wrong.

Frequently we find ourselves objecting to something with feelings like those expressed in the childhood ditty:

> *I do not like thee, Doctor Fell;*
> *The reason why, I cannot tell;*
> *But this I know and know full well,*
> *I do not like thee, Doctor Fell.*

Rules give us words to express why we feel as we do about something. Rules are often said to detract from creativity, but creativity is hard to suppress. The poet Homer followed precise rules of meter and rhyme, but that didn't suppress his creativity in writing the *Iliad* and the *Odyssey*. Good rules are not a panacea, but they help.

At first glance, this chapter may appear to be reinventing the wheel. In fact, it does even less; it simply suggests that we use the wheel. None of the criteria developed in this chapter are new. A selected reading list is given at the end of the chapter, but many of the criteria have been with us since sabre-toothed tigers stopped being a menace.

II. THE ENVIRONMENT

The COBOL programming environment is that of production computing for commercial applications. Production programs have a relatively long life, are perhaps more input/output-oriented than computation-oriented, and more logical than algorithmic. There is often a separation of effort in design, programming, running, maintenance, and even documentation, with different people working on different parts. This makes communication vital. It is this environment for which the programming criteria are derived, and the goal is to improve program maintenance, correctness, reliability, and efficiency.

Too often, "programming techniques" are concerned only with the efficiency and implementation of individual language statements. But the life of such knowledge is short, and what was avoided with old compilers may be encouraged with new ones. The short half-life of COBOL compilers makes it hard to generalize about the efficiency or correctness of individual language statements. Someone's writing a bad compiler shouldn't change good programming techniques.

III. THE RULES AND GUIDELINES

We often fail to appreciate just how hard programming is. Is the following COBOL statement correct?

```
COMPUTE X = Y / Z
```

Y or Z might not have been assigned values; Z might contain zero; the identifiers might be of improper data types; they might be undefined; or the names might be reserved words. Precision might be lost, an underflow or overflow might occur, the statement may be in the wrong columns, or blanks may not have been properly inserted. The statement might be at the wrong place in the program, or we may have actually wanted Y * Z. These are only the obvious errors from a single statement containing no logic. Programs consist of hundreds of statements with logic and interaction, and systems contain thousands of statements. Each statement is like a moving part in a machine, and if a part fails, the entire system may fail. Additionally, the job control language and the interaction with the operating system can be more complex than the programming language. Programming is a difficult undertaking in which nothing is trivial. This leads to the first and most important rule.

Simplify.

Simplifying programs makes them easier to design, maintain, understand, document, and run. Begin simplifying in the design, because simplicity lost here cannot be regained. Simplicity may not always be possible, but we can always eliminate needless complexity.

We tend to regard complexity highly, because it is human nature to hold in awe that which we do not comprehend. But accomplishment comes from making things simple rather than complex. Even in science, the great ideas are simple. Sir Isaac Newton expressed three classic laws of physics with a fraction of the complexity found in the 1040 income tax forms. Were he alive today, surely he too would have an accountant prepare his income tax returns.

The techniques of good expository writing in English also apply to programming. Many of the following rules are borrowed from Strunk and White's *The Elements of Style* and George Orwell's essay on "Politics and the English Language." The essence of good expository writing is to decide what you want to say, and then to say it as simply, concisely, and clearly as possible. This is also the essence of good programming.

Many simple programming techniques appear difficult because they are unfamiliar. A binary search is difficult in COBOL only if you are unfamiliar with the SEARCH statement. A goal of this book is to make all COBOL statements familiar by describing them and giving examples of their use.

Eliminate the unnecessary.

That which is eliminated does not need to be designed, programmed, documented, and maintained, and costs nothing to run. Never use a long word where a short one will do, such as PICTURE for PIC. Omit unused paragraph names, because they can distract and confuse. A single discounted cash flow subprogram written to be used by many will save effort and likely be both more reliable and more efficient than separate subprograms written for several individual applications.

Eliminating the unnecessary also simplifies. Notice the apparent difference in complexity in the following two descriptions that produce identical results.

```
77  X PICTURE S999999V99 USAGE IS COMPUTATIONAL VALUE IS ZERO.
77  X PIC S9(6)V99 COMP VALUE ZERO.
```

Neither statement is comprehensible to someone unfamiliar with COBOL, but the first appears more complex. PIC for PICTURE and COMP for COMPUTATIONAL become as familiar to COBOL programmers as are Dr. for doctor, Ms. for Miss/Mrs., and COBOL for COmmon Business-Oriented Language.

Eliminate useless repetition. Useless repetition occurs in many ways. For example, data entered into a system may be used in several programs. By validating the data only once as it enters the system rather than each place it is used in a program, we save our effort, save the computer's resources, and make the system easier to change. Useless repetition often creeps in under the guise of flexibility. Many people feel that it is good to provide a variety of ways in which to do something. They are like the old farmer who is asked for directions back to the main road. He doesn't realize that by describing several alternatives, he is making us more lost.

COBOL often gives the appearance of having been designed by the same old farmer. The following statements all add 1 to an identifier.

```
COMPUTE VARIABLE = VARIABLE + 1
ADD 1 TO VARIABLE
ADD 1 TO VARIABLE GIVING VARIABLE
SUBTRACT -1 FROM VARIABLE
```

```
SUBTRACT -1 FROM VARIABLE GIVING VARIABLE
SET INDEX-VARIABLE UP BY 1
```

Each statement has its own options and operates on limited data types. What is essentially simple becomes complex with the many ways in which it can be done. You are forced to make an unnecessary choice and then worry whether it was the correct one.

   Clarify. Write to be read by others.

Programs are read more frequently than they are written. Even a program's author writes a program only once and then reads it many times during debugging. It follows that it is more important that programs be easily read than that they be easily written. Programs are also likely to be read by someone other than the program's author. Often, programs are considered to be readable if someone who understands what the program is to do can understand how the code accomplishes it. This is the absolute minimum in readability. The goal should be to go beyond this to write programs so that someone can understand what the program is to do from reading the code.

   Programmers often sacrifice clarity to optimize at the detail level, where the results are rarely measurable. Efficiency should come from the design and not during debugging or production. Programs cost little to change during design but are expensive to change once they have been coded, and it is risky to modify a correct program. Any significant inefficiency is usually localized to a few areas. Avoid cleverness when it is at the expense of clarity.

   One way to clarify is to avoid ambiguity. For example, the statement MULTIPLY A BY B is ambiguous, because it is not apparent where the result is stored. Surprisingly, it is stored in B. The statement COMPUTE B = B * A avoids the ambiguity. Few people remember the hierarchy of logical and arithmetic operations. In what order will the following operations be performed?

```
IF A = B OR C = D AND E = F...
```

Use parentheses to show the hierarchy and remove the ambiguity.

```
IF (A = B) OR ((C = D) AND (E = F))...
```

   Clarify the sequence of execution; things that hide it are bad. This rule is the basis for structured programming. To understand the sequence of instructions at any point in a program, we must know where control came from and where it is going. A good way to clarify the flow of control is to have a single entry and exit in each functional unit of code. This eliminates the threading in and out of statements with a GO TO. For example, if control can reach a paragraph by sequential execution, falling through from the previous paragraph, and by a PERFORM or GO TO, it is difficult to tell where we came from. The following code is typical.

```
A.  IF NOT a-condition  THEN GO TO B.
    a-statements.
```

```
B.    IF NOT b-condition  THEN GO TO C.
      b-statements.
      GO TO D.
C.    c-statements.
D.    d-statements.
```

The code is intertwined and hard to follow. How do we get to D? Under what conditions do we execute C? Is the above a complete unit, or might C be the target of a PERFORM or GO TO from somewhere else? Now examine the way the above coding reads when we eliminate the unnecessary GO TOs.

```
A.    IF a-condition
           THEN a-statements
      END-IF
      IF b-condition
           THEN b-statements
           ELSE c-statements
      END-IF
      d-statements
```

Now it is clear that paragraph A is a unit and that the *d-statements* are always executed. The *c-statements* cannot be the target of a PERFORM or GO TO, and we get to the *c-statements* when *b-condition* is false.

Weinberg, in his book *The Psychology of Computer Programming*, points out that a linear sequence is easier to follow than a nonlinear one. A program containing many GO TOs is hard to follow, because you must keep track of all the possible paths and flip back and forth in a listing.

The GO TO is not all bad. It does make it clear where control is going. It is bad only in that it clouds where control came from and distracts the reader by breaking the linearity of the program.

Eliminating unnecessary GO TOs is good, but it does not ensure that the flow of control is clear. The following example also hides the sequence of execution.

```
IF COST IS EQUAL TO ZERO MOVE ZERO TO PAGE-A, MOVE 1 TO
NEW-LINE, ELSE PERFORM MAX-SIZE, IF COST IS GREATER THAN
ZERO PERFORM ZERO-COST, ELSE PERFORM BIG-COST.
```

It reads well as an English sentence, but it is difficult to read as a sequence of discrete steps. It is better written as follows:

```
IF COST = 0
    THEN MOVE 0 TO PAGE-A
         MOVE 1 TO NEW-LINE
    ELSE PERFORM MAX-SIZE
         IF COST > 0
             THEN PERFORM ZERO-COST
             ELSE PERFORM BIG-COST
         END-IF
    END-IF
```

Now the logical sequence is clear. Computer programs are not read for their contribution to the literature of the English language but to understand the logic and computations within the program. English is not even the first language of many who program in COBOL. The previous example shows how programs can be made clear by proper indentation. Programs are also more readable and easier to change if a single statement is contained on a line. If a line must be continued, break the statement at a point where it is obvious that it is continued, and indent the continuation. Thus, we express the logic and continuation of statements by indentation.

Nested IFs were often avoided in the past, but they are good if written so that the intent is clear. The following statement is a nested IF, and it is clear:

```
IF A = B
    THEN MOVE C TO D
        MOVE X TO Y
        IF E = F
            THEN PERFORM M
                IF G = H
                    THEN PERFORM Z
                    ELSE PERFORM X
                END-IF
            END-IF
    END-IF
```

Explicit scope terminators were added to COBOL 85 to aid with such things as nested IFs. It is better to use explicit scope terminators than to rely on the period to terminate the statements. For example, the following statement is terminated with a period and does not execute as it reads:

```
IF A = B
    THEN MOVE 1 TO X
        IF C = D
            THEN PERFORM U
            ELSE PERFORM V
        PERFORM W.
```

The PERFORM W is a part of the last ELSE clause. The END-IF to terminate the IF/THEN/ELSE solves the problem:

```
IF A = B
    THEN MOVE 1 TO X
        IF C = D
            THEN PERFORM U
            ELSE PERFORM V
        END-IF
        PERFORM W
    END-IF
```

Avoid nesting to a level at which the indentation forces statements beyond column 72. THEN clauses nested to several levels are usually clear, but ELSE clauses can cause problems, as shown in the following example.

```
IF A = B
   THEN MOVE 1 TO X
        IF C = D
           THEN PERFORM U
                IF E = F
                   THEN PERFORM V
                        PERFORM W
                   ELSE PERFORM M
                END-IF
           ELSE PERFORM N
                MOVE X TO Y
        END-IF
   ELSE PERFORM P
END-IF
```

Each ELSE clause has a corresponding THEN clause, and these clauses are hard to pair up if the ELSE does not immediately follow the THEN. A little astigmatism on the part of the readers, and they would be lost. Nested IFs are good if not nested too deeply and if the corresponding ELSE clause is kept close to its THEN clause.

Keep the major logic and organization as visible and at as high a level as possible.

This makes programs easier to follow and change. A good way to do this is to use the PERFORM statement:

```
MOVE "N" TO EOF-MASTER
PERFORM READ-MASTER UNTIL EOF-MASTER = "Y"
```

These statements tell us where we are reading the master file, that it is read within a loop, and that the loop terminates when EOF-MASTER is set to "Y", probably by detecting the end of file. It clearly indicates the start of the read loop (the beginning of paragraph READ-MASTER), and the end of the loop (the end of paragraph READ-MASTER).

Make the program *modular* by organizing it into distinct functional parts. Invoke the modules with PERFORM statements. This aids in quickly finding your way into a program by giving the equivalent of a table of contents for program execution. It also divides the program into smaller parts that can be readily digested, and it eases maintenance, because you can identify the beginning and end of a functionally related part of the program. Additionally, it reduces the interaction, or at least keeps the interacting components together. There is no firm rule on the maximum size of such a functional unit of code or module, but 50 lines of code is a reasonable limit. It is comprehensible and will fit on a single page. (However, the use of computer terminals is making the concept of a page irrelevant.)

In psychology, breaking up long items into shorter parts is termed *chunking*. The term may be unfamiliar, but the practice is not; we do it constantly without giving it much thought. The number 12135550911 becomes relatively easy to remember and comprehend as 1-(213) 555-0911. Dividing a complex program into digestible components makes it much more manageable.

Convey as much useful information in the coding as possible.

COBOL is largely self-documenting and is made more so by selecting meaningful names. For example, the paragraph name READ-LOOP conveys more information than A1. A10-READ-LOOP conveys even more information, because it indicates its location relative to other names if the names are placed in sequential order within the program. By conveying useful information, we lead the reader through the code. Consider the following two examples that show alternative ways to code a loop.

```
    SET K TO 1.
A20-MAX.
    several-statements
    SET K UP BY 1
    IF K NOT > 20 GO TO A20-MAX
```

Not until after plowing through many statements to discover a GO TO back to the start do we discover that it is a loop. The following is a better way to code the loop.

```
    PERFORM A20-MAX
            VARYING K FROM 1 BY 1
            UNTIL K > 20
    ■ ■ ■
A20-MAX.
    several-statements.
```

Now it is clear that a loop controlled by K is repeated 20 times. However, the loop is still bad, because the statements comprising the loop do not immediately follow the statement controlling them. In this case, it would be better to use an in-line PERFORM so that the statements can be placed within the loop:

```
    PERFORM VARYING K FROM 1 BY 1
            UNTIL K > 20
        several-statements
    END-PERFORM
```

Keep the reader in context.

Things are easier to understand when they are in context. The context consists of the surrounding items that, by their presence, tell us something about the item. In the following example, a single word of context is enough to give the word *beagle* three different meanings and, in one case, enough to indicate a spelling error.

Beagle—dog (a breed of dogs)

Beagle—Darwin (the ship upon which Darwin sailed)

Beagle—hawk (a misspelling of eagle)

The first step in making a program understandable is to put the reader in context. A short narrative at the start of the program should tell what the program does, what goes into it, and what comes out of it. Place related items together so that each item contributes to the understanding of the others. Isolating related items also makes them easier to change. Weinberg terms this *locality*, and he also notes that programs are easier to understand if the related items are kept on the same page of the source listing.

Write programs to be changed.

Change is constant for most programs. In theory, programs are written from a complete set of specifications, and when the programs perform according to the specifications, the job is complete. In practice, it rarely works like this. Specifications are written when the least amount is known about the program, and no specifications can be complete enough to account for all contingencies. Programs evolve during the implementation. The budget might be cut, requiring a less elaborate program. In a personnel program, new legislation could require the addition of new information and the exclusion of old information. A new personnel director might want a different set of reports. This evolution does not end when the program is placed in production but continues over its entire life. Information produced by programs acts as a catalyst, generating a desire for more or different information. After the people have worked with the program for a while, they may begin to understand what they really want. Programming is an iterative process.

Maintenance often costs more than development, because a surprising number of items can change. The number of departments and locations within a company can certainly change, but we might forget that the number of states can also change (viva the Virgin Islands!). And, of course, the calendar changes each year. About the only things unlikely to change are the number of months in a year (unless the Aztecs stage a comeback) and physical measurements (until the United States switches to the metric system).

Facilitating change is very important in the design of data. As a simple example, you should never store a person's age in a data record. This would require updating the record on the person's birthday and, if nothing else, might present some difficult job scheduling problems. It would be better to store the person's date of birth and then write a subprogram to compute the person's age given the person's birth date and the current date as parameters.

We can make programs easier to change by making data and data descriptions drive the program wherever possible. If a table may change, read it in from a file on disk rather than building it into the program. Then we can make the change in the external data without disturbing the program. Make all items that are likely to change be parameters.

Be definitive.

Regardless of what a comment says, a program will do as directed by the statements. The statements themselves should serve as the documentation where possible, eliminating a separate documentation effort and the possibility that it will be incorrect or outdated. Experienced maintenance programmers know that program flow charts, while a fine tool for design, are difficult to draw and are rarely kept up to date. Documentation that isn't trusted isn't used.

Use comments when the language statements do not make clear what will be done, but never when the statements themselves are clear. Comments are easily confused with language statements in COBOL. Indent or set off the comment so that it does not hide or blend in with the statements. Thus, we should use only as many comments as necessary and not let them obscure the code.

Write the program to minimize the need for comments. Use comments where necessary, but do not use them to state the obvious or as an expedient to make up for writing obscure code. In the following, the comment just restates what the statement does. It doesn't tell us what we really need to know—why the year is being divided by 4.

```
*   Divide LAST-YR by 4.
       DIVIDE LAST-YR BY 4 GIVING A-NUM REMAINDER LEAP-FLAG
```

Better is

```
*   Determine if LAST-YR is a LEAP YEAR.  If so, LEAP-FLAG
*   contains ZERO.
         DIVIDE LAST-YR BY 4 GIVING A-NUM REMAINDER LEAP-FLAG
```

Do not mislead, surprise, or confuse.

Human beings have difficulty in noticing the unexpected. We have all seen examples such as the following.

PARIS IN THE

THE SPRING.

Because we do not expect to find the extra THE, we do not see it. Computers lack this tolerance for ambiguity, and this causes problems in our communicating with them. An example of surprising and confusing the reader is to use a variable named DAYS to contain units of months. Exceptions can make programs complex and difficult to follow, and they can contribute heavily to maintenance problems. Eliminate exceptions where possible. Failing this, comment them as exceptions, giving the reason and explaining how they are handled.

Much of the surprise and confusion in programming comes from inconsistency. Weinberg terms this the principle of *uniformity*. For example, in COBOL, you must READ a *file-name*, but WRITE a *record-name*. This is inconsistent, and as a result it is easy to confuse the two. Rules, standards, and a confidence in your tools, techniques, and abilities all lead to consistency.

Avoid complex logical expressions, such as those combining NOT with OR or those with double negatives. In the following example, it is not immediately apparent that STOP RUN is always executed

```
IF (SALARY NOT = 0) OR
   (SALARY NOT = 1)
     THEN STOP RUN
END-IF
```

Do not force small incompatibilities for small improvements. It sometimes seems as if a cavalier attitude, rather than necessity, is the mother of incompatibility. Often it is better to live with bad features than to undergo the slow torture of minor, incompatible improvements.

Check for errors where they can occur, on the assumption that things will go wrong.

One of the frustrating aspects of computer programming is that a program may run correctly hundreds of times and then erupt with an error. This inevitably happens, and we should design and program for it. You do this by checking for errors, recovering if possible, and printing error messages. For example, when you read a table, check for the table exceeding the internal table size. If you divide by a variable, check for zero divide. Validate all raw input data. Do not assume that things have gone correctly. For example, we might think that there is no need to check the sequence of a master file because it is kept in sort order. We forget that the sort key may be updated, an unsorted file may be inadvertently read, or any of a hundred other things may go wrong.

Once you detect an error, print a clear, concise message describing the error. Make error messages relevant and direct them to the person who will read them. The message "TABLE OVERFLOW--ABEND" is ambiguous if the program has more than one table. ABEND means "evening" in German, but little else to nonprogrammers. The error message should describe what went wrong, the transaction or data involved, the action taken within the program, and any action that must be taken outside the program.

Break any of these rules rather than do anything outright barbarous.

This is just to say that rules must not stop us from thinking.

IV. SUMMARY

This concludes the set of criteria. Before applying them to the COBOL language features and to structured programming, reread them carefully.

- Simplify.
- Eliminate the unnecessary.
- Clarify. Write to be read by others.
- Keep the major logic and organization as visible and at as high a level as possible.
- Convey as much useful information in the coding as possible.
- Keep the reader in context.
- Write programs to be changed.
- Be definitive.
- Do not mislead, surprise, or confuse.
- Check for errors where they can occur, on the assumption that things will go wrong.
- Break any of these rules rather than do anything outright barbarous.

EXERCISES

1. Critique one of the following computer languages using the criteria developed in this chapter.

ALGOL	PL/I
COBOL	C
APL	Pascal
FORTRAN	BASIC
Assembler Language	RPG

2. Write a paper suggesting additions, deletions, or a complete new set of criteria if you disagree with those in this chapter.

3. Write a paper critiquing the computer's operating system or job control language with which you are familiar, using the criteria developed in this chapter.

ADDITIONAL READINGS

Kernighan, Brian W., and P. J. Plauger, *The Elements of Programming Style,* New York: McGraw-Hill, 1974.

Ledgard, Henry F., *Programming Proverbs,* Rochelle Park, NJ: Hayden Book Company, 1975.

Orwell, George, *A Collection of Essays,* Garden City, NY: Doubleday, 1954.

Strunk, William, Jr., and E. B. White, *The Elements of Style,* Revised Edition, New York: Macmillan , 1959.

Shneiderman, Ben, *Software Psychology. Human Factors in Computer and Information Systems,* Cambridge, MA: Winthrop Publishers, 1980.

Weinberg, Gerald M., *The Psychology of Computer Programming,* New York: Nostrand Reinhold, 1971.

3

General Language Rules

The general language rules are explained here in light of the criteria developed in the preceding chapter. Several techniques for coding are described and then used throughout the remainder of the book. At the end of the chapter, these techniques are applied to a complete COBOL program to illustrate their use and preview what a complete COBOL program looks like.

I. COBOL CHARACTER SET

The characters A through Z, a through z, and blank are alphabetic; 0 through 9 are numeric; and + - * / = $, ; . " ( ) ❯ ❮ : are special. The quotation (") delimits character strings. The upper- and lower-case characters are equivalent, except when they appear in a character string:

```
MOVE "THE END" TO A    [Same as]         move "THE END" to a
MOVE "The end" TO A    [Not the same as]  MOVE "THE END" TO A
```

Note that on the mainframe, the character set is EBCDIC; on other computers, such as the PC, it is ASCII.

II. STATEMENT FORMAT

The COBOL statement format was designed for punched cards (found today in museums) and must be coded in certain columns:

- 1 to 6 contain an optional sequence number.
- 7 indicates the continuation of literals. Also used for comments, debugging statements, and page ejects (form feeds).
- 8 to 12 is termed the *A-area*. Procedure names begin in this area. Column 8 is termed the *A margin*.
- 12 through 72 are termed the *B area*. Statements begin in this area. Column 12 is termed the *B margin*.

FIGURE 3.1   Cobol coding form.

- 73 through 80 are available for program identification. These often contain sequence numbers. Figure 3.1 shows the COBOL coding form.

The sequence numbers in columns 1 to 6 have no effect on the program and in the old days served to help put back together a card deck if it was dropped. This problem disappeared with the punched card, and today the sequence number is used for change control, if at all. Many installations use change control systems that maintain their own sequence numbers, and there may be no need to code the COBOL sequence numbers at all. Sequence numbers are omitted in this book.

```
LABEL-A.                    [Begins in the A margin.]
      MOVE C TO D           [Begins in the B margin.]
```

A. Continuation

If a statement exceeds one line, continue the statement on the next line in column 12 or beyond. The last character of the line being continued is assumed to be followed by a space. For readability, break the statement where it is obvious that it is continued, and indent the continuation.

```
COMPUTE A = (VAR + 27.6 -
   VAL) / (HOMES -
   RENT)
```

You can also break a line in any column. Code a hyphen (-) in column 7 of the next line, and continue in column 12. The continuation follows the last nonblank character of the first line. For example, you could also continue the above by coding

```
1        2        3        4        5        6        7
789012345678901234567890123456789012345678901234567890123456789012
    COMPUTE A = (VAR + 27
-   .6 - VAL) / (HOMES - RENT)
```

To continue an alphanumeric literal, code the literal through column 72, code a hyphen in column 7 of the next line, code a quotation in column 12 or beyond, and continue the literal.

```
1        2        3        4        5        6        7
789012345678901234567890123456789012345678901234567890123456789012
    MOVE "THIS IS THE WINTER OF OUR DISCONTENT.  SUMMERS ARE WORS
-     "E." TO A
```

Avoid continuing alphanumeric literals wherever possible, because it increases the chance for error. The previous statement is better written as follows:

```
 1       2       3       4       5       6       7
789012345678901234567890123456789012345678901234567890123456789012
    MOVE
    "THIS IS THE WINTER OF OUR DISCONTENT.  SUMMERS ARE WORSE".
      TO -A
```

B. Blanks and Separators

Blanks in COBOL separate items. Place at least one blank wherever you might expect a blank in an English sentence. You can code multiple blanks wherever a single blank may appear.

```
        COMPUTE    A = 1.3     + FIVE
[Or]
        COMPUTE A = 1.3 + FIVE
```

The following characters also separate items, depending on the context. Note that in this book, a lower-case *b* indicates a blank.

Separator	Rules
,b	Follow a comma with one or more blanks.
.b	Follow a period with one or more blanks.
;b	Follow a semicolon with one or more blanks.
(	Left parentheses need not be preceded or followed by blank.
)	Right parentheses need not be preceded or followed by blank.
:	Colon need not be followed by blank.
b"	Precede an opening quotation mark with one or more blanks.
"b	Follow a closing quotation mark with one or more blanks.
b = =	Opening pseudo text delimiter must be preceded by blank.
= = b	Closing pseudo text delimiter must be followed by blank.

C. Formatting the Listing

The careful insertion of blank lines and page ejects (form feeds) makes the source listing easier to read. You can insert blank lines anywhere in a source module for clarity. Although not in Microsoft COBOL or the ANSI Standard, VS COBOL II has SKIP1, SKIP2, and SKIP3 commands to skip one, two, or three lines. You code them in column 12 or beyond with no punctuation. They aren't needed. If you want to skip lines, just leave blank lines in the source.

To cause a page eject in the listing, code a slash (/) in column 7. The remainder of the line can contain comments, which are listed on the first line of the next page.

```
 1       2       3       4       5       6       7
789012345678901234567890123456789012345678901234567890123456789012 /
/ANY COMMENTS CAN GO ON THIS LINE.
```

VS COBOL II provides an EJECT statement, which is not itself listed but causes a page eject where it appears in the source listing. EJECT has no punctuation and begins in column 12 or beyond.

```
EJECT
```

EJECT and SKIP*n* are carried over from older IBM compilers. The ANSI Standard now provides the same facility—but implemented differently. It is best to not use EJECT or SKIP*n*, because IBM may someday drop support for them.

III. COBOL STATEMENTS

A. Statements

A COBOL statement begins with an English verb, such as COMPUTE, ADD, and MOVE. The rest of the statement may consist of item names, separators (usually the blank), key words, and sometimes optional words. There is no statement terminator in COBOL. The result of this is that COBOL only knows where a statement begins by recognizing the verb that begins the statement. For this reason, all COBOL words are reserved and cannot be used for data names.

A line may contain a whole statement, part of a statement, or several statements:

```
MOVE X TO Y    MOVE V TO W MOVE M TO N
```

Or

```
MOVE X TO
Y    MOVE V TO W MOVE M
TO N
```

Code a single statement per line to make the statements easier to read and the program easier to change:

```
MOVE X TO Y
MOVE V TO W
MOVE M TO N
```

B. Sentences

One or more statements terminated by a period is termed a *sentence* in COBOL. The following is a sentence containing three statements:

```
MOVE X TO Y
MOVE V TO W
MOVE M TO N.
```

The choice of a period to delimit a sentence was an attempt to emulate English, but it didn't work very well. It was ambiguous, because numeric literals also contain periods as decimal points, so that you must be careful to write 2 or 2.0 rather than 2., which would delimit a sentence. The period as a delimiter also didn't work well for nesting statements, which is a serious drawback when trying to do structured programming. COBOL 85 provides explicit scope terminators to mark the end of conditional statements, and you no longer need the period except to end a paragraph. The practice today is to code the period only after the last statement in a paragraph. This book places the period on a separate line, which makes modifications easier and marks the end of a paragraph.

C. Clauses and Phrases

COBOL also has what it terms *clauses* and *phrases*. A *clause* consists of the words in a definition that specify attributes, and are often optional. The VALUE in the definition of THE-AGE below is a clause:

```
01 THE-AGE                       PIC S9(3) VALUE 21.
```

A *phrase* is a subpart of a COBOL statement and may or may not be optional. For example, THEN is a phrase in the IF statement:

```
IF A = B
   THEN MOVE X TO Y
END-IF
```

D. Separators

You can code a separator comma (comma followed by one or more spaces) wherever a blank can be placed. The comma and semicolon are also interchangeable as separators. Thus, you can separate a series of items with blanks, commas and blanks, or semicolons and blanks. The choice is a matter of personal preference.

```
ADD A B C TO D        [Same as]    ADD A, B, C TO D
                      [Same as]    ADD A; B; C TO D
```

Likewise, you can separate statements with commas and blanks or semicolons and blanks. However, don't use commas and semicolons, because they can only cause problems.

```
MOVE A TO B, MOVE C TO D   [Same as]    MOVE A TO B; MOVE C TO D
```

Better as

```
MOVE A TO B
MOVE C TO D
```

IV. WORDS

A COBOL word consists of 1 to 30 characters. The characters may be 0 to 9, A to Z, a to z, or the hyphen (-). The hyphen must not be the first or last character, but all other characters may appear in any position. (-X and X- are invalid, but X-X is valid.) COBOL names that identify procedures and data must be COBOL words that conform to these rules.

V. NAMES

You must name paragraphs and sections, which are termed *procedure names*. Section names must be unique, and paragraph names must be unique within a section. Begin the procedure names in columns 8 to 12, and end them with a period:

```
A10-INITIALIZE.
```

Statements may appear on the same line as the procedure name, provided that they begin in column 12 or beyond and are separated from the name and its period. However, the procedure stands out more when the name is on a line by itself.

```
[Correct, but not as clear:]              [Better coded as]
A20-END.   MOVE 16 TO RETURN-CODE.        A20-END.
                                             MOVE 16 TO RETURN-CODE
```

Make each procedure contain a functionally related unit of code. The procedure name marks the start of such a functional unit, and the name should indicate what the procedure does. You can make the procedure easier to locate in the listing by preceding the procedure name with characters or numbers that indicate its position relative to other procedure names.

```
B10-INITIALIZE.
    PERFORM A20-ZERO              [A20 should precede B10 in the listing.]
    .
B20-READ-MASTER.                  [B20 should follow B10.]
    PERFORM Z10-TERMINATE         [Z10 would be much further down in the listing.]
    .
```

Data names are also 1 to 30 characters (A to Z, a to z, 0 to 9, -), and the hyphen must not be the first or last character. Data names must be unique within a program or subprogram.

```
77  TOTAL-AMOUNT                  PIC X.
01  EOF-INPUT                     PIC X.
```

Select data names that describe their contents. For example, COUNTER only tells us that something is counted. PAGE-COUNT tells us what is counted, REPORT-6-PAGE-COUNT tells for which report pages are counted, and RPT-6-PAGE-NO conveys the same information by using shorter words and abbreviations.

VI. COMMENTS

Write comments one per line by coding an asterisk (*) in column 7, and the comments in the remaining columns of the line.

```
    1         2         3         4         5         6         7
78901234567890123456789012345678901234567890123456789012345678901234567890123456789012
* ASTERISK IN COLUMN 7.
* COMMENTS IN REMAINING COLUMNS OF LINE.
```

Indent the comment or set it off if it might hide or obscure the statements. You might write the comments in lower case to make them distinct from the COBOL statements.

```
  A10-INITIALIZE.
  ***************************************************
  * Enclosing the comment in asterisks sets it off. *
  ***************************************************
      OPEN INPUT FILE-IN
  *            This comment is indented to set it off.
      DISPLAY "FILE OPENED."
  **** Exit
```

You can place comments anywhere within a program. The ANSI Standard does not allow them before the Identification Division header, but VS COBOL II and Microsoft COBOL do, as long as they follow any compiler control statements.

VII. SPECIAL WORDS

A. Abbreviations and Synonyms

Several long COBOL reserved words can be abbreviated, such as PIC for PICTURE and THRU for THROUGH. This book generally uses the abbreviation rather than the long form. You can write most words that can be singular or plural either way: ZERO or ZEROS, SPACE or SPACES, and so on. Likewise you can interchange IS/ARE and OF/IN: DAY OF MONTH or DAY IN MONTH.

B. Reserved Words

All COBOL defined words are reserved and cannot be used as procedure names or data names. Appendix A lists COBOL reserved words. New reserved words are constantly added as COBOL is expanded, and a program that compiles properly today may not compile properly tomorrow. This is an inherent and frustrating part of the COBOL language.

There are over 500 COBOL reserved words, including such common words as TIME, DATE, and ADDRESS, and no one remembers them all. No reserved word currently begins with a numeric character or the letters X and Y, or contains two consecutive hyphens. Thus, 9TOTAL-AMOUNT, XTOTAL-AMOUNT, and TOTAL--AMOUNT would be relatively safe in never being reserved words, but this technique results in ugly names. Perhaps the best technique is to select meaningful names and then, if in doubt, check the name in Appendix A.

C. Optional Words

COBOL has optional words whose sole purpose is to improve readability. IS is such a word and is always optional.

```
IF A = B THEN ...
```

Same as

```
IF A IS = B THEN ...
```

Same as

```
IF A IS EQUAL TO B THEN ...
```

Optional words make statements more like English language sentences, which may or may not be good. However, they also make programming harder. You must remember the valid optional words, as not just any word will do, and remember where the optional words may be placed. This book gives a single form for coding each statement and ignores some optional words.

D. Figurative Constants

COBOL has several figurative constants that assume the value of an alphanumeric or numeric literal when used. Their advantage is that they assume the appropriate attributes for the data type depending on the context in which they are used. For example, ZEROS assumes the value of a numeric zero or zero characters, depending on the context. When used as an alphanumeric literal, ZEROS represents the character literal "000...0" whose length is that required by the operation. COBOL provides the following figurative constants.

- ZEROS (or ZERO or ZEROES). ZEROS assumes the value of an arithmetic zero or one or more zero characters.
- SPACES (or SPACE). One or more blank characters.

- HIGH-VALUES (or HIGH-VALUE). One or more characters having the highest value in the collating sequence. You can only use HIGH-VALUES as alphanumeric data, not as numeric data.
- LOW-VALUES (or LOW-VALUE). One or more characters having the lowest value in the collating sequence. You can only use LOW-VALUES as alphanumeric data, not as numeric data.
- QUOTES (QUOTE also permitted). Represents one or more of the quotation character ("). This is also the standard in VS COBOL II, unless the APOST compiler option is used, which causes QUOTES to represent an apostrophe (') rather than a quotation. Note that although QUOTES represents a quotation character, you cannot code it in a character string. That is, "THE QUOTE." appears as shown, not as "THE "."".
- NULLS (NULL also permitted). Not in the ANSI Standard. It represents a null value in storing addresses.
- ALL "*characters*". ALL repeats the *characters* as often as required by the context in which it appears. You can also precede any of the foregoing with ALL. That is, ALL ZEROS is identical to ZEROS.

```
ALL "AB"              [Same as]              "ABABAB...AB"
```

ALL is an obsolete item in the ANSI Standard when associated with a numeric item with a length greater than one. The reason is that characters may have to be truncated when moved to a numeric item, and the results are often unexpected. For example, suppose you have a numeric item described as

```
01  A                      PIC 99V99.
```

You might then use ALL to move a literal to it, with surprising results. The involved explanation for the results is the reason ALL was made an obsolete item when used this way.

```
MOVE ALL "1" TO A        [A contains 11.00.]
MOVE ALL "12" TO A       [A contains 12.00.]
MOVE ALL "123" TO A      [A contains 31.00.]
MOVE ALL "1234" TO A     [A contains 34.00.]
MOVE ALL "12345" TO A    [A contains 45.00.]
```

E. Special Registers

COBOL has several built-in registers, either used by statements or providing an interface to the operating system.

- DEBUG-ITEM. Used in the Debug Module. It is described in Chapter 18 and is defined as

```
01  DEBUG-ITEM.
    02  DEBUG-LINE.                PIC X(6).
    02  FILLER                     PIC X VALUE SPACE.
    02  DEBUG-NAME                 PIC X(30).
    02  FILLER                     PIC X VALUE SPACE.
    02  DEBUG-SUB-1                PIC S9(4) SIGN LEADING SEPARATE.
    02  FILLER                     PIC X VALUE SPACE.
    02  DEBUG-SUB-2                PIC S9(4) SIGN LEADING SEPARATE.
    02  FILLER                     PIC X VALUE SPACE.
    02  DEBUG-SUB-3                PIC S9(4) SIGN LEADING SEPARATE.
    02  FILLER                     PIC X VALUE SPACE.
    02  DEBUG-CONTENTS             PIC X(n).
```

- LINAGE-COUNTER. Used in the LINAGE clause of the File Description entry. It is described in Chapter 13 and has the same definition as the LINAGE clause.
- LINE-COUNTER. Used by the report writer, and is not in VS COBOL II.
- PAGE-COUNTER. Used by the report writer, and is not in VS COBOL II.

The following special registers are not a part of the ANSI Standard but are provided in VS COBOL II and Microsoft COBOL.

- ADDRESS OF *record*. Obtains storage address of an item for POINTER data. It is described in Chapter 23 and implicitly defined for each record in the Linkage Section.
- LENGTH OF *item*. Obtains the length of a numeric data item. It is described in Chapter 7 and is defined as PIC 9(9) BINARY.
- RETURN-CODE. Returns a completion code to the operating system when the run terminates. RETURN-CODE is described in Chapter 13 and is defined as

```
01  RETURN-CODE                PIC S9(4) BINARY VALUE ZERO.
```

To set a return code, just move a value to the RETURN-CODE:

```
    MOVE 16 TO RETURN-CODE
```

- SORT-CONTROL. Contains the *ddname* (see Chapter 16) of a data set containing the sort control statement. It is described in Chapter 21 and is defined as

```
01  SORT-CONTROL               PIC X(8) VALUE "IGZSRTCD".
```

- SORT-RETURN. Sets the return code for a sort. It is described in Chapter 21 and is defined as

```
01  SORT-RETURN                PIC S9(4) BINARY VALUE ZERO.
```

- SORT-CORE-SIZE. Sets the number of bytes of memory for the sort. It is described in Chapter 21 and is defined as

```
01  SORT-CORE-SIZE              PIC S9(8) BINARY VALUE ZERO.
```

- SORT-FILE-SIZE. Estimates the number of records to be sorted. It is described in Chapter 21 and is defined as

```
01  SORT-FILE-SIZE              PIC S9(8) BINARY VALUE ZERO.
```

- SORT-MESSAGE. Specifies the ddname of a data set that the sort program is to use in place of the SYSOUT data set. It is described in Chapter 21 and is defined as

```
01  SORT-MESSAGE                PIC X(8) VALUE "SYSOUT".
```

- SORT-MODE-SIZE. Estimates the most-frequent record length of variable-length records for sorting. It is described in Chapter 21 and is defined as

```
01  SORT-MODE-SIZE              PIC S9(5) BINARY VALUE ZERO.
```

- TALLY. An identifier that may be used to store numeric values. It is defined as

```
01  TALLY                       PIC 9(5) BINARY VALUE ZERO.
```

TALLY is also in Microsoft COBOL, but not when you specify the VSC2 option for compatibility with VS COBOL II. Because of this and because TALLY isn't in the ANSI Standard, don't use it.

- WHEN-COMPILED. Contains the compilation date. It is defined as

```
01  WHEN-COMPILED               PIC X(16).
```

The date is stored in the form "mm/dd/yyhh.mm.ss"; in Microsoft COBOL, it is PIC X(20) and is in the form "mm/dd/yyhh.mm.ss" for the VSC2 compiler option or "hh.mm.ssmmm dd, yyyy" for the OSVS compiler option. For example,

```
01  WHEN-COMPILED               PIC X(16).
```

might contain "02/20/9214.35.00"; this indicates that the listing was compiled at 2:35 P.M. on February 20, 1992.

- SHIFT-IN and SHIFT-OUT. Use to specify unprintable DBCS (Double-Byte Character Set) characters. They are described in Chapter 22 and are defined as follows:

```
01  SHIFT-IN                    PIC X(1) VALUE X"OF".
01  SHIFT-OUT                   PIC X(1) VALUE X"OF".
```

VIII. PROGRAM ORGANIZATION

COBOL programs are divided into four divisions, each beginning with a header:
IDENTIFICATION DIVISION, ENVIRONMENT DIVISION, DATA DIVISION,
and PROCEDURE DIVISION. The Identification Division contains comments
identifying the program, author, and date written. The Environment Division
describes the computer, the I/O devices, and the access methods to be used. The
Data Division describes all the data, and you must explicitly describe all data
items. The Procedure Division contains the executable program statements.

You can group together COBOL statements into a sentence and terminate it
with a period. You group together sentences into paragraphs that begin with a
label—a paragraph name. All the sentences that follow belong to that paragraph
up to the next paragraph name. The Procedure Division is usually composed
of paragraphs that are invoked by the PERFORM statement.

COBOL also provides subprograms (called subroutines in other languages),
which are invoked by the CALL statement. You share data between the calling program and the subprogram by including the data as parameters (called
arguments in other languages) in the CALL statement.

With COBOL 85, you can also nest one program inside another. That is,
you can place one PROCEDURE DIVISION inside another. There may be uses
for this, but it is difficult to think of one.

The following are suggestions for writing programs:

- Begin the program with comments that summarize the program's purpose.
  Describe the program in enough detail to give a reader the proper background
  for reading the program. Generally a few paragraphs will do. Add comments
  if the program is changed during production so that the reader has a record
  of the major changes made, the date, and who made them.

- Organize the program into paragraphs, and invoke them with PERFORM statements. This gives the equivalent of a table of contents to the program, as
  shown in the following example. Notice how the following few statements
  give the reader a good idea of what the program is to do and the order in
  which it is done:

```
PROCEDURE DIVISION.
A10-BEGIN.
    PERFORM B10-INITIALIZATION
    PERFORM C10-READ-IN-TABLES
    MOVE LOW-VALUES TO RECORD-KEY
    PERFORM D10-READ-MASTER-FILE UNTIL RECORD-KEY = HIGH-VALUES
    PERFORM E10-WRAPUP
    STOP RUN

    .
```

- Make each main paragraph be a functionally related unit of code, such as
  initialization or record selection. Make the beginning and ending of each such
  unit stand out. How you do it is a matter of taste. The following example
  illustrates one method:

```
D10-READ-MASTER-FILE.
********************************************************************
* PROCEDURE TO READ AND SELECT RECORDS.                           *
*      Records with RECORD-TYPE = "F" selected and displayed.     *
* IN:  IN-FILE open.                                              *
*      SS-NAME contains person's name.                            *
* OUT: RECORD-KEY contains HIGH-VALUES.                           *
*      All records in IN-FILE read.  Records with                *
*        RECORD-TYPE = "F" displayed.                             *
********************************************************************
      MOVE LOW-VALUES TO RECORD-KEY
      PERFORM UNTIL RECORD-KEY = HIGH-VALUES
        MOVE LOW-VALUES TO RECORD-TYPE
        PERFORM UNTIL (RECORD-KEY = HIGH-VALUES) OR
                      (RECORD-TYPE = "F")
          READ IN-FILE INTO IN-RECORD
            AT END
              MOVE HIGH-VALUES TO RECORD-KEY
            NOT AT END
              DISPLAY "RECORD-KEY = ", RECORD-KEY
          END-READ
        END-PERFORM
      END-PERFORM

**** Exit
```

• Whenever there are several related items in a statement, code each of them
  on a separate line.

```
      OPEN INPUT FILE-A,
                 FILE-B,
                 FILE-C
```

• Organize the listing to help the reader. Use blank lines or lines of asterisks
  to set off paragraphs. Use a page eject (a slash in column 7) to begin a
  major part of the program. Place as much related information on a page as
  possible without crowding or awkward page breaks. It works out nicely if
  the functional units of code are limited to about 50 lines. But since there is
  no logical connection between what you are coding and the page size, this
  is not a firm rule. Save the reader from having to flip pages back and forth
  to follow the logical flow by placing the paragraphs of the program in the
  sequence in which they execute.

The statements in a COBOL program must be in the following order.

```
IDENTIFICATION DIVISION.
    PROGRAM-ID.  program-name .
```

```
ENVIRONMENT DIVISION.
CONFIGURATION SECTION.
INPUT-OUTPUT SECTION.
     SELECT file-name ASSIGN TO ddname .
     [Associates the file with JCL statements that specify the I/O device.]
DATA DIVISION.
FILE SECTION.
     [You describe all files here.]
FD   file-name
     [You code the FD to describe each file.]
     RECORD CONTAINS integer CHARACTERS.
01   record-name                      PIC X(record-length ).
     [This is the record-area. The records placed here describe the preceding FD's records.]
WORKING-STORAGE SECTION.
     [You describe the data items here.]
01   J.
     [J  is a record.]
   05   K                             PIC X(1).
     [Alphanumeric elementary item.]
   05   L.
     [L is a group item.]
       10   M                         PIC S9.
          [External decimal number elementary item.]
       10   N                         PIC X(4).
          [Alphanumeric elementary item.]
PROCEDURE DIVISION.
  [Program statements of the main body follow this.]
A10-BEGIN.
  [The Procedure Division is composed of paragraphs or sections.]
     OPEN INPUT file-name
     MOVE "N" TO K
     MOVE ZERO TO M
     PERFORM A10-READ-FILE UNTIL K = "Y"
     CLOSE file-name
     STOP RUN

        .
**** End of program execution.
A10-READ-FILE.
     READ file-name INTO J
       AT END
          MOVE "Y" TO K
          DISPLAY "END OF FILE"
       NOT AT END
          COMPUTE A = B + C - D * E / C ** B
          ADD 1 TO M
     END-READ
```

```
**** Exit
END PROGRAM program-name .
```

The many required statements give even simple COBOL programs a formidable look, but writing them soon becomes automatic. They do help in reading programs, because you know where to look to find things. A quick look at the Input-Output Section tells which files are used, and the Data Division describes all the data used in the program. The next chapter describes each of the basic COBOL statements in detail.

EXERCISES

1. What problems can the reserved words of COBOL cause?

2. Tell which of the following COBOL names are incorrect, and why.

```
FORMULA                   Z
2HOT                      NOT-HER
PROGRAM-ID                7UP
OH*                       UP-OR-DOWN
W-                        EITHER/OR
UP                        TO H24
NOW--OR-LATER             -TO-HERE
TEXT                      MEET-ME @4
F-117                     AVERAGE-AMOUNT-OF-DOLLARS-REMAINING
HUT_16
HASN'T
```

3. Explain the syntax errors in the following statements.

```
A1.  COMPUTE A = B * C.
MOVE ZERO TO A.
     IF (B=C) THEN GO TO A1.
     MOVE 1 TO X(1,2).
     **** BEGIN COMPUTATIONS
START-IT.
     MOVE X
     TO Y, MOVE V
     TO W
     ADD A, B C TO D.
     ADD E,F,G TO H.
NEW-PART
     ADD I,J TO K.
     ADD X(1) TO Y.
     COMPUTE A = B+C.
     MOVE STRING TO X.
```

4

Basic COBOL Statements

The basic COBOL statements are presented here so that they will be familiar to you in the next chapter on structured programming. The experienced programmer should also read this chapter because, while the statements may be familiar, the style in which they are coded may not be.

I. THE MOVE STATEMENT

The MOVE statement assigns the value of an item to an identifier. If necessary, COBOL converts the item to the data type of the identifier.

```
MOVE item TO identifier
MOVE 6 TO A
MOVE "CHARACTERS" TO B
MOVE C TO D
```

You can assign a single item to several identifiers:

```
MOVE 0 TO REC-IN,          [Same as]    MOVE 0 TO REC-IN
          REC-SELECTED,                  MOVE 0 TO REC-SELECTED
          REC-IGNORED                    MOVE 0 TO REC-IGNORED
```

You can move corresponding elements of records by appending CORRESPONDING, abbreviated CORR, to the MOVE:

```
01  A.
    05  X                        PIC X.
    05  Y                        PIC X.
    05  V                        PIC X.
01  B.
    05  V                        PIC X.
    05  W                        PIC X.
    05  X                        PIC X.
    ▪ ▪ ▪
    MOVE CORR A TO B    [Same as]    MOVE X OF A TO X OF B
                                     MOVE V OF A TO V OF B
```

38

Notice that the data items on the right in the preceding example are *qualified*. When two records have elements with the same names, you must qualify the element names with the record name so that COBOL can know which element is meant. In the example, you must write element X as X OF A or X OF B to distinguish the element. You can also code CORR with the ADD and SUBTRACT statements, as described in the next section. CORR is described more completely in Chapter 8.

The MOVE statement can either move single items (an *elementary move*) to an indentifier or move one group of items (*a group move*) to another group. The following is an example of a group move:

```
01  A.
    05  B                       PIC X.
    05  C                       PIC X(100).
01  D.
    05  E                       PIC S9(4).
    05  F                       PIC X(50).
    05  G                       PIC S9(4).
    ■ ■ ■
    MOVE D TO A
```

> [*52 bytes from* D *are moved to* A, *and the remaining 49 bytes of* A *are padded on the right with blanks.*]

In a group move, COBOL moves the bytes from the sending field to the receiving field without conversion. If the receiving field is shorter than the sending field, COBOL truncates the bytes. If the receiving field is longer, COBOL pads the field with blanks on the right. (If you code JUST LEFT, which left-justifies the data and is described in Chapter 7, for the receiving field, COBOL pads on the left.)

In Microsoft and the ANSI Standard, the results are undefined when the sending and receiving items overlap. VS COBOL II performs an overlapping move but issues a warning message, because overlapping moves is bad practice and is usually an accident.

```
01  A.
    05  B                       PIC X.
    05  C                       PIC X VALUE "X".
    05  D                       PIC X(99).
    ■ ■ ■
    MOVE C TO A
```

> [*Warning, because* C *is contained in* A.]

II. ARITHMETIC STATEMENTS

The COMPUTE statement evaluates an arithmetic expression on the right of the equal sign and assigns it to the identifier on the left. Conversion will occur if necessary to evaluate the expression or assign its value to the identifier. An *arithmetic expression* is either a single item or several items operated on by the arithmetic operations (+ - * / **). A, A + D, and A + B * 2 are arithmetic expressions.

```
COMPUTE identifier  = arithmetic-expression
COMPUTE A = B * 2
COMPUTE A = B + C / D
```

You can also code multiple receiving fields:

```
COMPUTE A, B = C + D          [Same as]        COMPUTE A = C + D
                                               COMPUTE B = C + D
                             [Or]              COMPUTE A = C + D
                                               MOVE A TO B
```

Parentheses specify the order in which the operations are to be performed. Those within inner parentheses are performed first:

```
COMPUTE X = (A + (B - C) * D / E) ** 2
```

The spaces in the COMPUTE statement are important, and the rules for placement are as follows:

- One or more spaces before and after the equal sign: A = B but not A=B
- One or more spaces before and after the arithmetic operators + - * / and **. A + B but not A+B

Note that the simplest form of the COMPUTE is identical to the MOVE:

```
COMPUTE A = B             [Same as]            MOVE B TO A
```

COBOL also has ADD, SUBTRACT, MULTIPLY, and DIVIDE statements, which perform the arithmetic operations implied by their names. They are redundant to COMPUTE, and their advantage is that they are perhaps more readable to someone unfamiliar with algebra. You needn't use them, but the ADD statement is convenient for adding an item to an identifier.

```
ADD item TO identifier        [Same as]        COMPUTE identifier  =
                                                        identifier+ item
ADD 1 TO A                                      COMPUTE A = A + 1
ADD B TO C                                      COMPUTE C = C + B
```

You need ADD and SUBTRACT to perform corresponding operations on records with the CORR phrase, because COMPUTE cannot have the CORR phrase. You need DIVIDE to compute the remainder from a division. The following forms of ADD, SUBTRACT, MULTIPLY, and DIVIDE are permitted. The equivalent COMPUTE statement indicates the operation performed.

```
ADD A TO B                  [Same as]    COMPUTE B = B + A
ADD A, B GIVING C                        COMPUTE C = A + B
ADD A, B, C TO D                         COMPUTE D = D + A + B + C
ADD A, B, C TO D, E                      COMPUTE D = D + A + B + C
                                         COMPUTE E = E + A + B + C
ADD A, B, C GIVING D                     COMPUTE D = A + B + C
ADD A, B, C GIVING D, E                  COMPUTE D = A + B + C
                                         COMPUTE E = A + B + C


SUBTRACT A FROM B      [Same as]         COMPUTE B = B - A
SUBTRACT A, B, C FROM D                   COMPUTE D = D - A - B - C
SUBTRACT A, B, C FROM D, E               COMPUTE D = D - A - B - C
                                         COMPUTE E = E - A - B - C
SUBTRACT A FROM B GIVING C               COMPUTE C = B - A
SUBTRACT A, B, C FROM D                   COMPUTE E = D - A - B - C
  GIVING E
SUBTRACT A, B, C FROM D                   COMPUTE E = D - A - B - C
  GIVING E, F                            COMPUTE F = D - A - B - C


DIVIDE A INTO B        [Same as]         COMPUTE B = B / A
DIVIDE A INTO B, C                       COMPUTE B = B / A
                                         COMPUTE C = C / A
DIVIDE A INTO B GIVING C                 COMPUTE C = B / A
DIVIDE A INTO B                          COMPUTE C = B / A
  GIVING C, D                            COMPUTE D = B / A
DIVIDE A BY B GIVING C                    COMPUTE C = A / B
DIVIDE A BY B GIVING C, D                COMPUTE C = A / B
                                         COMPUTE D = A / B
MULTIPLY A BY B        [Same as]         COMPUTE B = A * B
MULTIPLY A BY B, C                       COMPUTE B = A * B
                                         COMPUTE C = A * C
MULTIPLY A BY B GIVING C                 COMPUTE C = A * B
MULTIPLY A BY B                          COMPUTE C = A * B
  GIVING C, D                            COMPUTE D = A * B
```

The CORR phrase option in the ADD and SUBTRACT statements causes the operation to be performed on corresponding elements of records. Note that CORR can't be used with GIVING.

```
01  A.
    05  X                      PIC 9.
    05  Y                      PIC 9.
    05  V                      PIC 9.
01  B.
    05  V                      PIC 9.
    05  W                      PIC 9.
```

```
05  X                              PIC 9.
■ ■ ■
ADD CORR A TO B          [Same as]    ADD X OF A TO X OF B
                                      ADD V OF A TO V OF B
SUBTRACT CORR B FROM A   [Same as]    SUBTRACT X OF B FROM X OF A
                                      SUBTRACT V OF B FROM V OF A
```

COMPUTE is simpler to write and often makes the computation easier to understand than the other statements. Consider the following two statements:

```
MULTIPLY M BY C GIVING E
MULTIPLY C BY E
```

Do the two statements represent a single computation? What is being computed? Now look at the same equation written with the COMPUTE statement.

```
COMPUTE E = M * C ** 2
```

The COMPUTE makes it easy to see that this is Einstein's famous equation, $e = mc^2$. COMPUTE also keeps track of any intermediate results and, in VS COBOL II compilers, gives more accuracy by extending the precision to 30 digits if necessary. However, the intermediate results are more difficult to keep track of in long COMPUTE statements, especially those with divisions. It may be better to break up the COMPUTE and define a data item of the desired precision to control the intermediate results.

```
COMPUTE A = B * (C / D) * E
```

Perhaps better as

```
77  TEMP                         PIC S9(5)V9(6) PACKED-DECIMAL.
■ ■ ■
COMPUTE TEMP = C / D
COMPUTE A = B * TEMP * E
```

A. Order of Phrases

For reference, the various phrases described below must be coded in the following order:

```
DIVIDE/ADD/SUBTRACT/MULTIPLY/DIVIDE    COMPUTE ROUNDED =
GIVING                                 ON SIZE ERROR
ROUNDED                                NOT ON SIZE ERROR
REMAINDER (DIVIDE only)                END-COMPUTE
ON SIZE ERROR
NOT ON SIZE ERROR
END-verb
```

For example:

```
DIVIDE A INTO B
  GIVING C ROUNDED
  REMAINDER D
  ON SIZE ERROR
      MOVE ZERO TO B
  NOT ON SIZE ERROR
      MOVE ZERO TO A
  END-DIVIDE
```

B. The ROUNDED **Phrase**

The final results in arithmetic statements are normally truncated if their precision is greater than that of the identifiers to which they are assigned. Thus, if a resulting identifier has precision of PIC S999, a result of 22.9 is truncated to 22, and a −6.1 is truncated to −6. The ROUNDED phrase rounds the final results rather than truncating them and can be used in the COMPUTE, ADD, SUBTRACT, MULTIPLY, and DIVIDE statements. A 22.9 is rounded to 23, and a −6.1 is rounded to −6. COBOL rounds a value whose rightmost digit is 5 up in absolute magnitude, so that 1.5 is rounded to 2 and −1.5 is rounded to −2. ROUNDED has no affect on COMP-1 and COMP-2 floating-point numbers and is ignored. You code the ROUNDED phrase as follows:

```
COMPUTE A ROUNDED = B + C
ADD A TO B ROUNDED
ADD A TO B GIVING C ROUNDED
SUBTRACT C FROM D ROUNDED
MULTIPLY F BY G ROUNDED
DIVIDE H BY I GIVING J ROUNDED
```

If there are multiple receiving fields, you can code ROUNDED for each:

```
MULTIPLY F BY G GIVING H ROUNDED,
                    I ROUNDED
COMPUTE A ROUNDED, B ROUNDED = X / Y
```

Rounding gives more accurate results than does truncation. This is especially important when repetitive operations are performed on numbers. Suppose that in a report, dollars and cents are to be summed, but the numbers are to be printed in units of whole dollars. A common error is to sum the rounded or truncated numbers, as shown in the following columns representing the report:

Full Accuracy	Rounded	Truncated
10.00	10	10
10.50	11	10
10.60	11	10
10.10	10	10
10.60	11	10
51.80	53	50

Summing the rounded or truncated numbers gives a wrong total that appears correct in that the individual numbers do sum to the total, even though this total is wrong. The correct total is 51.80, which is 52 if rounded or 51 if truncated. When many numbers are summed, the results can be off considerably. Always compute the sum with the full precision and then round or truncate this sum, as shown in the following columns:

Full Accuracy	Rounded	Truncated
10.00	10	10
10.50	11	10
10.60	11	10
10.10	10	10
10.60	11	10
51.80	52	51

This gives the correct totals. Unfortunately, the totals appear wrong, because the individual numbers do not equal the total when summed. Reports lose their credibility when someone cannot add a column and obtain the same total printed by the computer. The choice between correct totals that appear wrong and incorrect totals that appear correct is not a happy one. You should choose the correct totals even at the cost of appearing wrong. Avoid the problem by printing the dollars and cents, even though the cents might not be of interest. Whenever possible, avoid either truncating or rounding.

C. The SIZE ERROR **Phrase**

A *size error* occurs when the magnitude of a result exceeds the size of the identifier into which it is to be stored. You can append the ON SIZE ERROR phrase to an arithmetic statement to execute imperative statements if a size error occurs. Division by zero always causes a size error. You can code SIZE ERROR for the COMPUTE, ADD, SUBTRACT, MULTIPLY, or DIVIDE statements.

```
ADD A TO B
  ON SIZE ERROR imperative-statements.
COMPUTE A = B / C
  ON SIZE ERROR imperative-statements.
ADD A TO B
  ON SIZE ERROR MOVE C TO D.
COMPUTE A = B / C
  ON SIZE ERROR MOVE C TO D
               MOVE E TO F.
```

In the above, the period delimits a sentence. This works, but there is a better way. Don't code the periods; end the statement containing the ON SIZE

ERROR with the appropriate END scope terminator (END-COMPUTE, END-ADD, and so forth). The preceding example is better coded as

```
ADD A TO B
  ON SIZE ERROR
      imperative-statements
END-ADD
COMPUTE A = B / C
  ON SIZE ERROR
      imperative-statements
END-COMPUTE
ADD A TO B
  ON SIZE
      ERROR MOVE C TO D
END-ADD
COMPUTE A = B / C
  ON SIZE ERROR
      MOVE C TO D
      MOVE E TO F
END-COMPUTE
```

An *imperative statement* is one that specifies no conditional actions. An imperative statement may also consist of a sequence of imperative statements. Any conditional statement that is delimited by its explicit scope terminator is an imperative statement. Thus, the following is permitted:

```
COMPUTE A = B / C
  ON SIZE ERROR
      IF C = 0
          THEN DISPLAY "ZERO DENOMINATOR"
          ELSE
           DISPLAY "NUMERATOR TOO BIG OR DENOMINATOR TOO SMALL"
      END-IF
END-COMPUTE
```

You can also specify statements to execute if no size error occurs, by coding the NOT ON SIZE ERROR clause. You can code it following the ON SIZE ERROR or by itself:

```
ADD A TO B
  NOT ON SIZE ERROR
      imperative-statements
END-ADD
COMPUTE A = B / C
  ON SIZE ERROR
      imperative-statements
  NOT ON SIZE ERROR
      imperative-statements
END-COMPUTE
```

If there is no SIZE ERROR phrase and a size error occurs, VS COBOL II truncates the results. (Microsoft COBOL and the ANSI Standard leave the result undefined.) When ON SIZE ERROR occurs, the result of the operation is not stored in the resultant identifier. When the ROUNDED phrase is specified, the rounding occurs before the check is made for a size error.

```
COMPUTE A ROUNDED = B + C * D
  ON SIZE ERROR
      MOVE ZERO TO A
END-COMPUTE
```

If SIZE ERROR is coded for ADD or SUBTRACT CORR, a size error on any of the data items causes the appropriate SIZE ERROR statements to be executed. However, COBOL executes them only once, after all the corresponding operations are done.

D. The REMAINDER **Phrase**

The DIVIDE GIVING statement with the REMAINDER phrase computes a remainder. (You can't use REMAINDER with COMP-1 or COMP-2 floating-point data.)

```
DIVIDE A INTO B GIVING C REMAINDER D
```

If A contains 6 and B contains 17, D would contain the remainder 5. REMAINDER must follow ROUNDED if it is present:

```
DIVIDE A INTO B GIVING C ROUNDED REMAINDER D
```

The following is illegal:

```
DIVIDE A INTO B GIVING C REMAINDER D ROUNDED
```

III. ARITHMETIC OPERATIONS

The *arithmetic operations* are + for add, – for subtract, * for multiply, / for divide, and ** for raise to power. You usually code them in COMPUTE and IF statements. Precede and follow them by one or more spaces. COBOL converts the items within the expression to a common base if necessary.

```
COMPUTE X = A + B - C / D ** 2
IF (A + B) = (C - 1)
    THEN PERFORM B10-ZERO-TABLE
END-IF
```

You can precede an arithmetic expression with a plus or minus sign as a prefix, termed a *unary operator*. (A unary sign indicates the sign of the item, not a subtraction or addition. Note that it must also be preceded and followed by a space.) COBOL interprets the following statement as X plus a minus Y:

```
COMPUTE W = X + - Y
```

IV. CONDITIONAL OPERATIONS

The following conditions, including the relational condition, the sign condition, the class condition, and the condition-name condition, can appear only in the IF, PERFORM, EVALUATE, and SEARCH statements. (SEARCH is described in Chapter 9.)

A. Relational Conditions

<	Less than.
NOT <	Not less than, same as greater than or equal to.
>	Greater than.
NOT >	Not greater than, same as less than or equal to.
=	Equal.
NOT =	Not equal.

You can also write the relational conditions in long form, such as IS EQUAL TO for = and IS GREATER THAN OR EQUAL TO for >=. Some might argue that the long forms are easier to understand, but the >= form is clearer to most people who program.

Precede and follow relational conditions with one or more spaces. You can compare identifiers, literals, and arithmetic expressions.

```
IF A = B
   THEN ADD 1 TO C
END-IF
IF (X * Y + Z) = 2
   THEN ADD 1 TO D
END-IF
```

B. The Sign Condition

The *sign condition* tests for positive, negative, or zero values. It is completely redundant to the relational conditions and need never be used.

IF X IS POSITIVE	[*Same as*]	IF X > ZERO
IF X IS NOT POSITIVE		IF X <= ZERO
IF X IS NEGATIVE		IF X < ZERO
IF X IS NOT NEGATIVE		IF X >= ZERO
IF X IS ZERO		IF X = ZERO

C. Class Conditions

A *class condition* tests whether an identifier contains only numeric or alphabetic data.

1. The NUMERIC *Condition*

The NUMERIC condition is true if the identifier contains only the digits 0 to 9, with or without a + or - sign. You can only test identifiers declared as alphanumeric (USAGE DISPLAY) or PACKED-DECIMAL numeric for NUMERIC, not alphabetic characters declared as PIC A. (PIC 999 or PIC XXX, but not PIC AAA.) There is no class test for floating-point.

```
IF identifier  IS NUMERIC ...
IF identifier  IS NOT NUMERIC ...

IF X IS NOT NUMERIC
   THEN MOVE B TO C
END-IF
```

For USAGE DISPLAY external decimal numbers, the data is considered numeric if it is unsigned or has an operational sign carried with the rightmost digit. However, COBOL does not consider them to be numeric if the characters plus (+) or minus (-) are present unless you code the SIGN clause, described in Chapter 6.

2. The ALPHABETIC *Condition*

The ALPHABETIC test is true if the identifier contains only the characters A to Z, a to z, and blank. ALPHABETIC-UPPER tests for A to Z and blank. ALPHABETIC-LOWER tests for a to z and blank. ALPHABETIC can test only alphanumeric or alphabetic identifiers (USAGE DISPLAY) described as PIC A or X (that is, PIC AAA or PIC XXX, but not PIC 999).

```
IF identifier  IS ALPHABETIC ...
IF identifier  IS NOT ALPHABETIC ...
IF identifier  IS ALPHABETIC-UPPER ...
IF identifier  IS NOT ALPHABETIC-LOWER ...
IF X IS ALPHABETIC
   THEN MOVE B TO C
END-IF
```

D. Condition-Name Conditions

Condition names are another redundant language feature that allows you to specify some of the logic in the data descriptions, and which may or may not make programs easier to read. (This feature is perhaps the only part of COBOL that comes close to being object-oriented.) *Condition-names* are level 88 data items defined for an elementary item and assigned a value. Testing the condition name is the same as testing the data item for the value. The following example illustrates a condition name:

```
01 THING                        PIC X.
   88  THING-IS-BIG             VALUE "Y".
   ■ ■ ■
   IF THING-IS-BIG    [Same as]     IF THING = "Y"
      THEN MOVE C TO D                 THEN MOVE C TO D
   END-IF                           END-IF
```

One might argue that the example on the left is clearer. But one could also argue that it can't be understood without flipping back to the data description to see what the level 88 data item contains. The example on the right allows you to see directly what operation is performed.

You can assign each condition name to a value, a range of values, several single values, or some combination of these. Within a record, level 88 denotes a condition name and cannot be used for other than this.

```
01  SOMETHING                   PIC S9(6) PACKED-DECIMAL.
    88  FEW                      VALUE 1.
    88  LOTS                     VALUE 1 THRU 10.
    88  MANY                     VALUE 1, 3.
    88  MYRIAD                   VALUE 1, 3, 9 THRU 16, 17,
                                       25 THRU 50.

    ■ ■ ■
    IF FEW              [Same as]     IF SOMETHING = 1
       THEN MOVE C TO D                 THEN MOVE C TO D
    END-IF                           END-IF
    IF NOT LOTS                      IF (SOMETHING < 1) OR
       THEN MOVE C TO D                 (SOMETHING > 10)
    END-IF                              THEN MOVE C TO D
                                     END-IF
```

The COBOL SET statement sets an identifier to a value that is true for a condition name. For example, you could code

```
    SET FEW TO TRUE       [SOMETHING is set to 1.]
    SET LOTS TO TRUE      [SOMETHING is set to 1. If there are several values, the first
                           value is set.]
```

You can also list several condition names in one SET. The effect is as if several SET statements had been written:

```
    SET MANY, MYRIAD TO TRUE    [Same as]   SET MANY TO TRUE
                                            SET MYRIAD TO TRUE
```

You can also define condition names for group items in a record, but the value must be an alphanumeric literal or a figurative constant. Assigning condition names for group items does not preclude defining condition names for elementary items. However, the elementary items must all be USAGE DISPLAY.

```
01  DATE-REC.
    88  NEW-YEAR               VALUE "940101".
    05  YEAR                   PIC XX.
        88  THIS-YEAR          VALUE "94".
    05  MONTH                  PIC XX.
    05  DAYS                   PIC XX.
```

You can assign condition names to table elements, and you must subscript the condition name when used.

```
05  ARRAY-A                    PIC X
                               OCCURS 10 TIMES.
    88  YES                    VALUE "Y".
    ■ ■ ■
    IF YES(3) THEN ...    [Same as]    IF ARRAY-A(3) = "Y" THEN ...
```

Condition names make COBOL programs easier to read as English sentences, but harder to read to understand what is happening in the program. They are convenient for testing several values. They may also make it easier to change the program, because the change can be made in a single place in the Data Division rather than in several places throughout the program.

E. Logical Operations

The *logical operations,* also termed *Boolean operations,* can connect the relational, sign, class, and condition-name conditions. They consist of the AND, OR, and NOT.

1. *Logical* AND

If X and Y are both true, then X AND Y has the value true. If either X or Y or both are false, then X AND Y has the value false.

```
    IF (X = 1) AND (Y = 0)
        THEN PERFORM X10-DONE
            [The THEN clause executes only if X equals 1 and Y equals 0.]
    END-IF
```

2. *Logical* OR

If either X or Y or both are true, then X OR Y has the value true. If both X and Y are false, then X OR Y has the value false.

```
    IF (X = 1) OR (Y = 0)
        THEN PERFORM X10-DONE
            [The THEN clause executes if X equals 1 or if Y equals 0.]
    END-IF
```

3. *Logical* NOT

If X is true, then NOT X has the value false. If X is false, then NOT X has the value true.

```
IF NOT ((X = 1) AND (Y = 2))
    THEN PERFORM X10-DONE
        [The THEN clause executes if X is not equal to 1 or if Y is not equal to 2.]
    END-IF
```

4. *Implied Relations*

If the same item is compared to several other items connected by AND, OR, or NOT, you needn't write the full relational condition for each item; it is implied:

```
A < B OR > C               [Same as]        (A < B) OR (A > C)
A NOT = B OR > C                            (A NOT = B) OR (A > C)
A = B OR > C AND < D                        (A = B) OR
                                           ((A > C) AND (A < D))
```

You can also imply the relational condition itself:

```
A = B OR C                 [Same as]        (A = B) OR (A = C)
A = B AND C AND D                           (A = B) AND (A = C) AND
                                           (A = D)
```

In these simple forms, the implied relations improve readability, but they quickly become confusing when used to excess. The following is unclear, because it is not apparent that the last relational operator (>) applies to D:

```
A = B AND > C OR D         [Same as]        (((A = B) AND (A > C)) OR
                                           (A > D))
```

The NOT is especially troublesome. COBOL treats it as part of the relational condition if it precedes the <, =, or >. To be safe, avoid implied conditions containing the NOT.

Complex logical conditions are often a source of error. For example, are the following two logical expressions equivalent?

```
NOT (A = B OR A = C)                        (A NOT = B) OR (A NOT = C)
```

It is not obvious that they are different. The first expression is true only if A is not equal to either B or C. The second expression is true either if A is not equal to B or if A is not equal to C. Avoid complex logical expressions, double negatives, and NOT in combination with OR. For example, NOT (A NOT = B) is better written as A = B. Use a decision table to decipher particularly complex conditional statements. The following decision table shows that the previous two expressions are not equivalent:

	Possible Conditions:
A = B	Yes No Yes No
A = C	Yes Yes No No
	Value of
NOT (A = B OR A = C)	False False False False
	Value of
(A NOT= B) OR (A NOT= C)	False True True True

If you must write a decision table to decipher a logical expression, the expression is not very readable. Try not to write logical expressions that require a decision table to be understood. Recast the logical expression or rewrite it with nested IFs to make it clearer.

[*Unclear:*]
```
    IF NOT (A = B OR C)
        THEN do something
    END-IF
```

[*Better as*]
```
    IF A = B OR C
        THEN CONTINUE
            ELSE do something
        END-IF
```
[*Or*]
```
        IF A NOT = B AND A NOT = C
            THEN do something
        END-IF
```
[*Or*]
```
        IF A NOT = B
            THEN IF A NOT = C
                    THEN do something
                END-IF
        END-IF
```

F. Conditional Expression

A *conditional expression* consists of a relational, sign, class, or condition name condition, or several relational, sign, class, or condition-name conditions, connected by the AND, OR, or NOT logical operations. For example, A = B AND C = 6.

G. Hierarchy of Operations

The following hierarchy list specifies the order, from highest to lowest, in which operations are performed.

Highest:	Unary operator (sign as prefix)	+ B or - C
	Exponentiate	A ** B
	Multiply, Divide	A * B / C
	Add, Subtract	A + B - C
	Relational, sign, class, condition-name	
	conditions	A > B
	Logical NOT	NOT (A > B)
	Logical AND	A AND B
Lowest	Logical OR	A OR B

COBOL evaluates operations having equal hierarchy from left to right.

```
A * B * C            [Same as]      (A * B) * C
A + B - C ** D       [Same as]      (A + B) - (C ** D)
```

Parentheses override the hierarchy. They specify the hierarchy of operations explicitly so that you do not have to remember the foregoing rules. Since there is no question of the hierarchy of operations when parentheses are used, use them to lessen the chance for error.

```
[Unclear: ]                         [Better  as]
    IF A + B * D = 2 OR A > 6           IF ((A + (B * D)) = 2) OR
       THEN ADD 1 TO X                     (A > 6)
    END-IF                                 THEN ADD 1 TO X
                                        END-IF
```

V. **THE** GO TO **STATEMENT**

The GO TO statement transfers control to the first executable statement in the named procedure:

```
A10-START.
    GO TO X10-END-IT-ALL

    .

X10-END-IT-ALL.
    GO TO A10-START
```

Structured programming has given the GO TO bad press, most of it deserved. However, the GO TO is not all bad, and one need not be fanatical about it. You can use it, but don't transfer backward or intertwine the code with GO TOs, because this makes the logical flow hard to follow. Intertwining occurs when the path of one GO TO crosses the path of another, as shown in the following two examples.

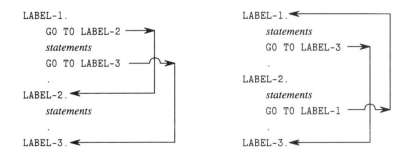

GO TOs should not exit from a paragraph to several different points outside the paragraph, because this also obscures the logical flow by forcing the reader to follow the various paths. The following example illustrates this:

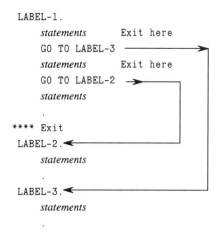

The GO TO DEPENDING ON statement transfers to one of several procedures depending on the contents of a numeric elementary data item:

```
GO TO procedure, procedure, ..., procedure
      DEPENDING ON identifier
MOVE 2 TO CASE
GO TO A10-START,          [Same as]       GO TO B30-CONTINUE
      B30-CONTINUE,
      B50-DONE
   DEPENDING ON CASE
```

If CASE contains a value other than 1, 2, or 3, the GO TO DEPENDING ON is ignored, and execution continues with the next executable statement. VS COBOL II allows 255 labels in the GO TO DEPENDING ON.

The GO TO DEPENDING ON statement provides a little of the *Case* function of structured programming. However, the EVALUATE statement, described later in this chapter, is far superior. There is little reason to use GO TO DEPENDING ON.

VI. PERFORM **STATEMENTS**

For reference, code the phrases in the PERFORM in the following order:

```
PERFORM
procedure   THRU procedure
WITH TEST
VARYING/FROM/BY/UNTIL       [Only one]
AFTER/FROM/BY/UNTIL         [Several ]
END-PERFORM
```

A. **Execution of Procedures**

The PERFORM statement is a brilliant concept that selectively executes groups
of statements. It permits a program to be organized into functional units that
are invoked with the PERFORM statement. It is especially useful for invoking
functional units from several points within a program to save having to code
the same function in several places.

Code the *out-of-line* PERFORM as follows:

```
PERFORM procedure
```

The out-of-line PERFORM may invoke either a paragraph or section. A paragraph consists of a paragraph name and all following statements up to the next
paragraph name. A section is a collection of paragraphs that begins with a
SECTION name and includes all paragraphs up to the next section.

```
A10-A SECTION.
A20-B.
    MOVE A TO B     [Paragraph]
    .
                                    [Section]
A30-C.
    MOVE D TO E     [Paragraph]
    .
B10-A SECTION.
```

  PERFORM transfers control to the first executable statement in the procedure.
Control returns to the next executable statement following the PERFORM after
the last statement in the procedure executes. The last statement in a procedure is the one preceding the next procedure name. This is a rather passive
way of indicating the end of a procedure, especially if the next procedure is
on the following page. Use a comment to highlight the end of a procedure
invoked by a PERFORM. This tells the reader that control is expected to return to

the invoking PERFORM rather than continuing on to the next procedure, as would
occur if the procedure were the target of a GO TO:

```
    PERFORM B10-ONE
    MOVE A TO B
    ■ ■ ■
 B10-ONE.
    MOVE 1 TO A
    COMPUTE B = C + D
      .
**** Exit
 B20-TWO.
```

The previous statements execute in the following sequence:

```
    PERFORM B10-ONE
    MOVE 1 TO A
    COMPUTE B = C + D
    MOVE A TO B
```

The out-of-line PERFORM operates as a GO TO, transferring control to the first
executable statement in the procedure. At the end of the procedure COBOL
executes another GO TO to transfer back to the next executable statement following the PERFORM. PERFORM operates as follows:

```
    PERFORM B10-ONE
       [Operates as GO TO B10-ONE.]
    MOVE A TO B
       ■ ■ ■
 B10-ONE.
    MOVE 1 TO A
    COMPUTE B = C + D
       [The end of the paragraph operates as a GO TO statement-following-the-PERFORM.]
      .
**** Exit
   [The comment has no effect.]
 B20-TWO.
    [This paragraph name marks the end of the preceding paragraph.]
```

Sometimes you need a GO TO to transfer to the end of the procedure, requiring another procedure name. But the GO TO would transfer out of the first
procedure, and control would not return following the PERFORM, as shown in
the following example:

```
    PERFORM B10-ONE
    ■ ■ ■
 B10-ONE.
    READ IN-FILE INTO IN-RECORD
      AT END GO TO B20-TWO
    END-READ
```

```
    MOVE IN-RECORD TO OUT-RECORD
        .
**** Exit
 B20-TWO.
```

If the GO TO is executed, control will not return following the PERFORM, but will continue sequentially in paragraph B20-TWO. You can solve this problem with the PERFORM THRU, which names a first and last procedure to specify a range of procedures to execute.

```
    PERFORM first-procedure THRU last-procedure
```

Execution begins with the first executable statement in *first-procedure,* and control returns following the PERFORM when the last statement in *last-procedure* executes. The *first-procedure* must precede *last-procedure* in the program. We can now code the following:

```
    PERFORM B10-ONE THRU B10-ONE-EXIT
    ■ ■ ■
 B10-ONE.
    READ IN-FILE INTO IN-RECORD
      AT END GO TO B10-ONE-EXIT
    END-READ
    MOVE IN-RECORD TO OUT-RECORD
        .
 B10-ONE-EXIT.  EXIT.
**** End of B10-ONE.
```

EXIT is a special null statement used to terminate a range of procedures. EXIT is not required, just a good practice, and any sequential range of procedures can be executed. The following example executes the C10-FIRST paragraph and then the C20-SECOND paragraph.

```
    PERFORM C10-FIRST THRU C20-SECOND
    ■ ■ ■
 C10-FIRST.
    MOVE 1 TO A
    COMPUTE B = C + D
        .
**** Exit
 C20-SECOND.
    MOVE B TO C
    COMPUTE D = A - B
        .
**** Exit
```

Note that the PERFORM C10-FIRST THRU C20-SECOND is equivalent to

```
    PERFORM C10-FIRST
    PERFORM C20-SECOND
```

This is better, because the goal is to isolate functionally related code, and invoking different ranges of procedures makes it unclear where the functionally related code begins and ends. Are C10-FIRST and C20-SECOND separate units, or are they part of a single unit? One cannot tell.

The procedure specified in the THRU clause may optionally contain only an EXIT statement. There is less chance for confusion if the THRU clause names an EXIT statement, which must be the only statement in its procedure. That is, you must precede and follow it with procedure names. If an EXIT statement is executed without being named in a PERFORM, execution continues with the procedure following the EXIT. Always use EXIT to terminate procedures invoked by the PERFORM THRU so that it is apparent that the several procedures constitute a unit. Also include the word EXIT in the procedure name to show that it is an EXIT:

```
      PERFORM C10-FIRST THRU C20-FIRST-EXIT
      ■ ■ ■
C10-FIRST.
      READ IN-FILE INTO IN-RECORD
        AT END GO TO C20-FIRST-EXIT
      END-READ
      MOVE IN-RECORD TO OUT-RECORD
      MOVE SPACES TO IN-RECORD

C20-FIRST-EXIT.   EXIT.
```

Any procedures invoked by a PERFORM execute in sequence if they are encountered during normal execution, but avoid this because it makes the program hard to follow. The following example illustrates this.

```
      PERFORM B10-ONE THRU B30-THREE-EXIT.
        [Control returns to the next statement.]
B10-ONE.   MOVE 1 TO A.        [This is the next statement.]
B20-TWO.   MOVE 1 TO B.
B30-THREE-EXIT.   EXIT.
B40-FOUR.   MOVE 1 TO C.
```

These statements execute in the following sequence:

```
      PERFORM B10-ONE THRU B30-THREE-EXIT.
B10-ONE.   MOVE 1 TO A.
B20-TWO.   MOVE 1 TO B.
B30-THREE-EXIT.   EXIT.
B10-ONE.   MOVE 1 TO A.
B20-TWO.   MOVE 1 TO B.
B30-THREE-EXIT.   EXIT.
B40-FOUR.   MOVE 1 TO C.
```

To reiterate, if you invoke a procedure with a PERFORM, don't also execute it by letting control fall through from the preceding procedure. Although the GO TO can transfer out of the range of statements being invoked by the PERFORM, this leads to confusion and you should avoid it. Use the GO TO to transfer out of a procedure only when the flow of control must be broken. For example, use it when you terminate a loop early or when the run terminates because of an error.

B. In-Line PERFORM

The *in-line* PERFORM consists of a PERFORM statement followed by any imperative statements and terminated by an END-PERFORM. (Remember that an imperative statement can be a conditional statement, as long as it is terminated with its END scope terminator.)

```
PERFORM
    imperative-statements
END-PERFORM
```

The in-line PERFORM becomes more interesting when it is used for loops.

C. Execution of Loops

The PERFORM also implements loops. The simplest loop is to PERFORM a procedure some number of times:

```
PERFORM integer TIMES
    imperative-statements
END-PERFORM


PERFORM procedure integer TIMES
PERFORM first-procedure THRU last-procedure integer TIMES
```

The loop executes *integer* times. The *integer* may be a numeric integer literal or identifier. If *integer* is zero or negative, the *procedure* is not performed. Once PERFORM is executed, changes in the value of an identifier *integer* have no effect on the number of times the loop executes.

```
77  A                          PIC S9(4) BINARY.
    ■ ■ ■
    MOVE 6 TO A
    PERFORM A TIMES
      ADD 1 TO A
    END-PERFORM
```
  [*The* ADD *statement executes 6 times, even though the value of* A *is changed within the loop.*]
```
    PERFORM A60-ZERO-TABLE TABLE-SIZE TIMES
```
  [A60-ZERO-TABLE *executes 10 times, even if a new value is assigned to* TABLE-SIZE *in the* A60-ZERO-TABLE *paragraph.*]

The PERFORM UNTIL executes a procedure until a specified condition is met. The WITH TEST BEFORE or AFTER phrase tells whether to test the condition before or after executing the loop.

```
                        AFTER
                        BEFORE
PERFORM WITH TEST _____ UNTIL condition
    imperative-statements
END-PERFORM


PERFORM procedure  WITH TEST BEFORE UNTIL condition
    [The WITH TEST BEFORE is a Do While in structured programming terminology.]
PERFORM first-procedure  THRU last-procedure  WITH TEST AFTER
        UNTIL condition
    [The WITH TEST AFTER is a Do Until in structured programming terminology. If the
    condition is true when PERFORM is executed, the procedure is not performed.]


PERFORM A10-TEST WITH TEST AFTER UNTIL END-FLAG = "Y"
```

If you omit the WITH TEST phrase, WITH TEST BEFORE is assumed:

```
PERFORM WITH TEST BEFORE UNTIL condition
```

Same as

```
PERFORM UNTIL condition
```

In the following example, PERFORM UNTIL is used to read in a file until a desired record is selected or until an end-of-file is encountered. Note that the WITH TEST AFTER is used, so that the loop is performed at least once. (Assume that IN-RECORD-KEY and IN-RECORD-TYPE are WORKING-STORAGE data items within IN-RECORD.)

```
PERFORM WITH TEST AFTER
        UNTIL (IN-RECORD-KEY = HIGH-VALUES) OR
              (IN-RECORD-TYPE = "A")
    READ IN-FILE INTO IN-RECORD
      AT END MOVE HIGH-VALUES TO IN-RECORD-KEY
    END-READ
END-PERFORM

**** Exit
```

The PERFORM VARYING can loop while incrementing a control identifier. You often use this type of loop to manipulate tables:

```
PERFORM WITH TEST BEFORE [or AFTER]
        VARYING subscript  FROM start  BY increment
        UNTIL condition
PERFORM procedure  WITH TEST BEFORE [or AFTER]
        VARYING subscript  FROM start  BY increment
```

```
                UNTIL condition
      PERFORM first-procedure THRU last-procedure
                WITH TEST BEFORE [or AFTER]
                VARYING subscript  FROM start  BY increment
                UNTIL condition
```

The *subscript* is a numeric identifier or index that is incremented each time through the loop. (Subscripts and indexes are described in detail in Chapter 9.) The *subscript* is set to the value of *start* at the beginning of the loop. COBOL evaluates the UNTIL condition at the place specified and, if the condition is true, terminates the loop. If the condition is not true, the *increment* is added to *subscript* and the loop continues another iteration. At the end of the loop, *subscript* contains the value it had when the UNTIL condition became true. (If the condition is true at the start of the loop, *subscript* contains the value of *start*.)

You would usually code the *condition* for a loop as shown here:

```
PERFORM WITH TEST BEFORE [or AFTER]
        VARYING subscript  FROM start  BY increment
        UNTIL subscript  > end
```

The *start, increment,* and *end* may be numeric identifiers, literals, or indexes:

- *start* is the first value that *subscript* is to assume within the loop.
- *increment* is a value added to *subscript* at the end of each pass through the loop.
- *end* is the last value that *subscript* is to assume within the loop.

In the following example, the loop executes 10 times, with IX assuming values from 1 to 10. IX contains 11 at the end of the loop.

```
PERFORM WITH TEST BEFORE
        VARYING IX FROM 1 BY 1
        UNTIL IX > 10
   MOVE ZEROS TO TABLE-1(IX)
END-PERFORM
```

Valid values for an index are from 1 to the size of the table—that is, it cannot exceed the bounds of the table. However, the loop can increment or decrement the index to be one more or less than this because this is necessary to terminate the loop. For example, consider the following loop to zero out a table of 30 elements:

```
01 A-TABLE.
   05  TAB-VALS            PIC S9(4)
                           OCCURS 30 TIMES
                           INDEXED BY TAB-X.
   ■ ■ ■
```

```
PERFORM VARYING TAB-X FROM 1 BY 1 UNTIL TAB-X > 30
   MOVE ZEROS TO TAB-VALS(TAB-X)
END-PERFORM
```

To terminate the loop, TAB-X is allowed to contain 31. However, according to the ANSI Standard, this is an invalid value and is undefined. Fortunately, both VS COBOL II and Microsoft COBOL have no problem with values greater than the maximum size of tables. You could test TAB-X outside the loop to see whether it contained 31.

The *increment* may be positive or negative. If negative, *subscript* is decremented, and you should code the UNTIL phrase as UNTIL *subscript* < *end*. The following statement executes the loop 100 times, with IX assuming values from 100 to 1 within the loop. At the end of the loop, IX contains 0. A value of 0 for an index is undefined in the ANSI Standard and Microsoft COBOL; therefore, IX may contain garbage. Don't depend on its value if the final value may be zero—use an identifier rather than an index as a subscript.

```
PERFORM WITH TEST BEFORE
        VARYING IX FROM 100 BY -1
        UNTIL IX < 1
```

The UNTIL phrase may be any conditional expression. For a WITH TEST BEFORE, the loop is not executed if the UNTIL condition is true. The following loop is not executed, because START-IT is greater than 10:

```
MOVE 11 TO START-IT
PERFORM WITH TEST BEFORE
        VARYING IX FROM START-IT BY 1
        UNTIL IX > 10
```

But the loop executes once if a WITH TEST AFTER is used:

```
MOVE 11 TO START-IT
PERFORM WITH TEST AFTER
        VARYING IX FROM START-IT BY 1
        UNTIL IX > 10
```

At the end of the loop, execution continues with the next executable following the PERFORM (for an out-of-line PERFORM) or the END-PERFORM (for an in-line PERFORM). The *subscript* contains the next value greater than *end* (or less than *end* if *increment* is negative). In the following example, the loop executes with IX containing values of 1 to 10. At the termination of the loop, IX will contain 11.

```
PERFORM WITH TEST BEFORE
        VARYING IX FROM 1 BY 1 UNTIL IX > 10
```

If *increment, end,* and *subscript* are identifiers and you change their values within the loop, it will affect the number of times the loop is performed. Changing the value of *start* within the loop has no effect on the loop.

The ANSI Standard requires that an in-line or out-of-line PERFORM execute at least one statement, but VS COBOL II and Microsoft COBOL don't have this requirement. For some things, such as searching an alphanumeric item to find the first nonblank character, all you want to do is perform the loop without executing a statement. Examples of this are given in Chapter 20. The choice of whether to use an in-line or out-of-line loop depends on the following:

- Use an out-of-line loop when the statements within the loop can be invoked from more than one place in the program.
- Use an out-of-line loop when the loop contains a large number of statements. (What constitutes a large number is a matter of choice.)
- For most other situations, use an in-line loop. It is easier to read because the statements are placed directly in the line of flow in the source.

You can nest the out-of-line PERFORM to seven levels. You can code one VARYING and several AFTER phrases for nested loops. The last AFTER varies most rapidly. Since tables can have seven dimensions, there can be as many as six AFTER clauses. The AFTER/FROM/BY phrase cannot be coded in an in-line PERFORM. It is permitted only in an out-of-line PERFORM.

```
PERFORM paragraph-name  WITH TEST BEFORE  [or AFTER]
        VARYING subscript-1  FROM start-1 BY increment-1
          UNTIL condition-1
        AFTER subscript-2  FROM start-2 BY increment-2
          UNTIL condition-2
        AFTER subscript-3  FROM start-3 BY increment-3
          UNTIL condition-3
        ⋮
        AFTER subscript-7  FROM start-7 BY increment-7
          UNTIL condition-7
```

The *start* values are set for each *subscript,* and then each UNTIL condition is tested to see whether the loop should be performed. The loop is performed with the *subscript* in the last AFTER varying the most rapidly, as shown in the following example.

```
PERFORM A10-ZERO-TABLE WITH TEST BEFORE
        VARYING IX FROM I BY 1 UNTIL IX > 5
          [This varies last.]
        AFTER IY FROM 1 BY 1 UNTIL IY > 4
          [This varies next.]
        AFTER IZ FROM 1 BY I UNTIL IZ > 8
          [This varies first.]
        ⋮
```

```
A10-ZERO-TABLE.
    MOVE ZERO TO TABLE-A( IX, IY, IZ)
    .
**** EXIT
```

The loop is performed 160 times, with the subscripts varying as shown.

```
IX = 1, IY = 1, IZ = 1 to 8
IX = 1, IY = 2, IZ = 1 to 8
   :
IX = 1, IY = 4, IZ = 1 to 8
IX = 2, IY = 1, IZ = 1 to 8
   :
IX = 5, IY = 4, IZ = 1 to 8
```

At the end of a PERFORM with AFTER phrases, the VARYING *subscript* will contain the value that caused the UNTIL condition to be true. All the AFTER *subscripts* will contain their appropriate *start* values.

The AFTER/FROM/BY/UNTIL phrase can only appear in an out-of-line PERFORM. It cannot appear in an in-line PERFORM. The following is in error:

```
PERFORM WITH TEST BEFORE                              [Invalid]
        VARYING IX FROM I BY 1 UNTIL IX > 5
        AFTER IY FROM 1 BY 1 UNTIL IY > 4
        AFTER IZ FROM 1 BY I UNTIL IZ > 8
    MOVE ZERO TO TABLE-A( IX, IY, IZ)
END-PERFORM                                           [Invalid]
```

To perform in-line operations on multi-dimensional tables, you can nest the PERFORM statements within the loop. Such loops can be nested to any level. This also makes clear the order in which the indexes are to be varied. The embedded PERFORM must perform statements totally included in or totally excluded from the range of statements in the original PERFORM. The following example will do what the preceding one was intended to do:

```
PERFORM WITH TEST BEFORE
        VARYING IX FROM 1 BY 1 UNTIL IX > 5
    PERFORM WITH TEST BEFORE
            VARYING IY FROM 1 BY 1 UNTIL IY > 4
        PERFORM WITH TEST BEFORE
                VARYING IZ FROM 1 BY 1 UNTIL IZ > 8
            MOVE ZERO TO TABLE-A( IX, IY, IZ)
        END-PERFORM
    END-PERFORM
END-PERFORM
```

VII. IF **STATEMENTS**

The IF statement evaluates a conditional expression and, depending on the outcome, executes statements. The general form of the IF statement is as follows:

```
IF conditional-expression
    THEN imperative-statements
    ELSE imperative-statements
END-IF
```

You can also write the IF statement without the END-IF if you terminate it with a period. However, things get very messy when you try to nest IF statements in this form.

```
IF conditional-expression
    THEN imperative-statements
    ELSE imperative-statements.
```

A common COBOL error before the implementation of the END-IF was to misplace a period in a conditional statement. The following example illustrates the dangers. The statements on the right are indented to show how the statements on the left are executed. (The indentation, of course, has no effect on the way in which the statements execute.)

```
[As coded:]                          [As executed:]
    IF A = B                             IF A = B
       THEN MOVE 100 TO A.                  THEN MOVE 100 TO A.
            ADD 2 TO B.               ADD 2 TO B.
```

It is much better to use the END-IF form. For example, the following is a typical error that results in an error message because the compiler now sees that the END-IF doesn't terminate anything.

```
IF A = B
   THEN MOVE 100 TO A.
        ADD 2 TO B.
END-IF
```

The THEN *statements* execute if the *conditional-expression* is true, and the ELSE *statements* execute if it is false.

```
IF A > B
   THEN MOVE 1 TO A
           [Executed if A is greater than B.]
   ELSE MOVE 0 TO A
           [Executed if A is not greater than B.]
END-IF
```

Although it isn't required, you should always indent the IF statement to show the flow of logic. There are various ways of doing this. Some people prefer to indent the IF statement as follows:

```
IF condition
THEN
    imperative-statements
ELSE
    imperative-statements
END-IF
```

The THEN keyword is optional, and some people prefer to write the IF this way:

```
IF condition
imperative-statements
ELSE
imperative-statements
END-IF
```

It is a matter of personal choice—or company standards.

The ELSE portion of the IF statement is optional, and if it is omitted, the THEN statements are skipped if the condition is false.

```
IF A = B
    THEN MOVE 0 TO A
END-IF
```

A common error is to forget to include an END-IF statement delimiter. The result will be no compilation error, but the meaning of the statements will change. For example:

```
IF A = B
    THEN MOVE 0 TO A
    ELSE MOVE 2 TO A
    [Missing END-IF here.]
MOVE A TO B
■ ■ ■
```

The statements are interpreted as

```
IF A = B
    THEN MOVE 0 TO A
    ELSE MOVE 2 TO A
        MOVE A TO B
        ■ ■ ■
```

You can nest IF statements to any level. However, do not nest to a level that forces statements beyond column 72. It is best to keep the ELSE clauses close to their corresponding THEN clauses. (You can do this by placing some of the inner code in a separate paragraph and executing it with a PERFORM.) Again, always indent to show the logical flow. Note also that a separate END-IF is required for each IF.

```
IF A = B
   THEN IF X = Y
           THEN MOVE 0 TO A
           ELSE MOVE 1 TO A
        END-IF
   ELSE IF X > Y
           THEN MOVE 2 TO A
           ELSE MOVE 3 TO A
        END-IF
END-IF
```

You can nest THEN clauses to several levels with the meaning remaining clear, as shown in the following example.

```
IF A = B
   THEN ADD 1 TO C
        IF C = D
           THEN PERFORM A10-START
                IF E = F
                   THEN IF G = H
                           THEN MOVE X TO Y
                                IF I = J
                                   THEN PERFORM A20-NEXT
                                END-IF
                        END-IF
                END-IF
        END-IF
END-IF
```

Now suppose you have this requirement:

```
IF condition
   THEN do nothing
   ELSE imperative-statements
END-IF
```

The THEN clause must contain at least one statement. Thus, you cannot code the following:

```
IF condition
   THEN                           [Must be a statement here.]
   ELSE imperative-statements
END-IF
```

One way to accomplish this is to place a NOT in front of the condition and place the statements in the THEN phrase:

```
IF NOT condition
    THEN imperative-statements
END-IF
```

The NOT makes logical expressions more difficult to read. You can use the CONTINUE, COBOL's null statement. It does nothing, but serves the requirement for a statement being present. Here is the foregoing example with CONTINUE:

```
IF condition
    THEN CONTINUE
    ELSE imperative-statements
END-IF
```

COBOL also has a NEXT SENTENCE statement, which was often used in previous COBOL versions. You can only place a NEXT SENTENCE in an IF statement that has no END-IF. It acts as a branch to the start of the next sentence—the next statement following a period. Here is an example:

```
IF A = C
    THEN IF B = D
            THEN COMPUTE A = A / B
            ELSE NEXT SENTENCE
                    [Branches to ADD statement.]
    ELSE IF A = D
            THEN COMPUTE A = A * B
            ELSE NEXT SENTENCE.
                    [Branches to ADD statement.]
    ADD 1 TO A
    [This is the first statement following the period.]
```

Since it is easy to overlook a period, NEXT SENTENCE led to many errors. With the CONTINUE statement in COBOL 85, there is no reason now to use NEXT SENTENCE.

Each THEN or ELSE can execute several statements; simply list them without periods. Several statements executed as a group are termed a *statement-group*.

```
IF A = B
    THEN MOVE 100 TO A
         MOVE 200 TO B
END-IF
IF C = D THEN MOVE 100 TO E
                MOVE 200 TC F
            ELSE MOVE 1 TO A
                ADD 2 TO B
                PERFORM A60-READ-FILE
END-IF
```

You will often control the logic within a program by using flags. Define such flags as PIC X, and use values for the flags that describe their meaning, such as "Y" for yes and "N" for no. The following example executes one statement the first time it is encountered and another statement from then on:

```
77  FIRST-TIME                    PIC X VALUE "Y".
■ ■ ■
    IF FIRST-TIME = "Y"
       THEN PERFORM A10-INITIALIZE
            MOVE "N" TO FIRST-TIME
       ELSE PERFORM A10-NORMAL
    END-IF
```

VIII. THE EVALUATE STATEMENT

The EVALUATE statement is a *Case* statement in structured programming terminology. It tests for several conditions and executes different statements for each condition. The simplest form of EVALUATE is

```
EVALUATE expression
   WHEN value
      imperative-statements
   WHEN value
      imperative-statements
          ⋮
   WHEN value
      imperative-statements
END-EVALUATE
```

Here is an example:

```
EVALUATE A / B
   WHEN 1
     PERFORM A10-FIRST
       [Executed if A / B equals 1.]
   WHEN ZERO
     PERFORM A10-ZERO
       [Executed if A / B equals 0.]
   WHEN -1
     PERFORM A10-NEGATIVE
       [Executed if A / B equals -1.]
END-EVALUATE
```

EVALUATE is extremely handy for organizing the overall logic of a program and performing the appropriate actions.

The expression following the EVALUATE is called the *selection subject*. (VS COBOL II allows 256 WHEN clauses and 64 selection subjects.) It can be a literal, an identifier, or an expression of the proper data type. The values following the WHEN phrase are called the *selection objects*. They can be literals, identifiers, or arithmetic expressions, as long as they have a data type that can be compared with the result of the selection subject following the EVALUATE.

```
EVALUATE A * B * C
     [The selection subject is a numeric expression.]
  WHEN AVERAGE-COST
     [Therefore, AVERAGE-COST must be a numeric identifier.]
       imperative-statements
  WHEN D / E
     [D / E is valid, because it is an arithmetic expression, whose data type can
       be compared to A * B * C.]
     imperative-statements
     ⋮
END-EVALUATE
```

Rather than a single value, the selection objects following the WHEN can be a range of values specified with the THROUGH keyword, abbreviated THRU:

```
WHEN 12 THRU 21
WHEN SIZE-SMALL THRU SIZE-BIG
WHEN A * B THROUGH (A * 2) * B
```

COBOL examines each WHEN phrase in turn, and if the value of the subject expression equals a single value or falls within a range of values, it executes the statements following that WHEN phrase. Control then resumes with the next statement following the END-EVALUATE. Only one WHEN phrase is executed. The following example illustrates this:

```
EVALUATE PERSON-AGE
  WHEN 15
    CONTINUE
  WHEN 13 THRU 19
    ADD 8 TO FEEDING-COST
  WHEN 20 THROUGH 29
    SUBTRACT 2 FROM FEEDING-COST
END-EVALUATE
```

If PERSON-AGE contains 15, execution immediately resumes following the END-EVALUATE. You can use the CONTINUE null statement to perform no action for WHEN phrases. Even though 15 would be true for the second WHEN, it is never reached, because the previous WHEN executes.

If you want to select any of several discrete values, you can code several WHEN phrases in succession. Stacking the WHEN phrases in front of the imperative statements causes COBOL to treat them as if they were all connected by logical ORs. The following example adds 10 to FEEDING-COST if PERSON-AGE contains 11, 13, or 19. A value of 20 is added if PERSON-AGE contains 12, 14 through 18, or 20.

```
EVALUATE PERSON-AGE
   WHEN 11
   WHEN 13
   WHEN 19
       ADD 10 TO FEEDING-COST
   WHEN 12
   WHEN 14 THRU 18
   WHEN 20
       ADD 20 TO FEEDING-COST
END-EVALUATE
```

If no WHEN is selected, execution continues following the END-EVALUATE. You can place a WHEN OTHER phrase last as a catchall to execute statements if none of the previous WHEN phrases executes. Here is the simplest example:

```
EVALUATE A / B
   WHEN ZERO
      ADD 1 TO C
   WHEN OTHER
      ADD 2 TO C
END-EVALUATE
```

This simplest form acts as IF/THEN/ELSE statement:

```
IF A / B = ZERO
   THEN ADD 1 TO C
   ELSE ADD 2 TO C
END-IF
```

You can also precede a selection object in a WHEN phrase with the NOT. The following would catch all values except 15 through 21.

```
WHEN NOT 15 THRU 21
```

There can be several selection subjects, separated from each other by the keyword ALSO. There must be a corresponding number of selection objects on each WHEN, also separated by ALSO. The following illustrates this:

```
EVALUATE PERSON-AGE ALSO PERSON-INCOME ALSO PERSON-STATE
   WHEN 21 ALSO 100000 ALSO "CA"
```
      [If PERSON-AGE *equals 21,* PERSON-INCOME *equals 100000, and*
      PERSON-STATE *equals* "CA", *COBOL executes this WHEN phrase.*
      If any of the comparisons is not true, it goes to the next WHEN.*]*

■ ■ ■

Note that any NOT applies to only a single value or range. For example, WHEN NOT 21 ALSO 100000 is not the same as WHEN NOT 21 ALSO NOT 100000.

Code the keyword ANY in place of any selection object following the WHEN if you want to ignore a particular comparison.

```
WHEN 21 ALSO 100000 ALSO ANY
    [This selects if PERSON-AGE equals 21 and PERSON-INCOME equals
    100,000. Any value of PERSON-STATE is accepted.]
```

So far, we have used EVALUATE to compare expressions as selection subjects to identifiers or literals as expression objects. You can reverse this to use logical expressions following the WHEN as selection objects. You then place TRUE or FALSE as the selection subjects following the EVALUATE to tell what value of the logical expressions you want to select. The advantage is that the WHEN can test different identifiers. The following example illustrates this:

```
EVALUATE TRUE
    WHEN PERSON-AGE = 21
        PERFORM A10-FIRST
    WHEN PERSON-INCOME > 100000
        PERFORM A20-SECOND
END-EVALUATE
```

Notice that this is the same as coding

```
EVALUATE FALSE
    WHEN PERSON-AGE NOT = 21
        PERFORM A10-FIRST
    WHEN PERSON-INCOME <= 100000
        PERFORM A20-SECOND
END-EVALUATE
```

Any logical expression that you can code in an IF statement can be coded with this form of the EVALUATE. The expressions needn't compare the same identifiers. You can also compare multiple expressions using the ALSO keyword. Each WHEN phrase must contain the same number of logical expressions as there are selection subjects following the EVALUATE:

```
EVALUATE TRUE ALSO FALSE
    WHEN ZIP-CODE IS NUMERIC ALSO PERSON-STATE = "CA"
        [This WHEN phrase executes if ZIP-CODE is numeric and the
        PERSON-STATE does not contain "CA".]
        PERFORM A10-FIRST
    WHEN ANY ALSO PERSON-STATE = "NY"
        [This WHEN phrase executes if PERSON-STATE contains NY. Notice that
        ANY can also be used in place of an expression.]
        PERFORM A20-SECOND
```

■ ■ ■

You can also place the logical expressions as the selection subjects following the EVALUATE and code TRUE or FALSE as the selection objects following the WHEN. This is a simple way of writing a decision table.

```
EVALUATE PERSON-STATE = "CA" ALSO PERSON-AGE > 21
    WHEN TRUE ALSO TRUE
        [PERSON-STATE = "CA" and PERSON-AGE greater than 21.]
      imperative-statements
    WHEN TRUE ALSO FALSE
        [PERSON-STATE = "CA" and PERSON-AGE less than or equal to 21.]
      imperative-statements
    WHEN FALSE ALSO TRUE
        [PERSON-STATE NOT = "CA" and PERSON-AGE greater than 21.]
      imperative-statements
    WHEN FALSE ALSO FALSE
        [PERSON-STATE NOT = "CA" and PERSON-AGE less than or equal to 21.]
      imperative-statements
END-EVALUATE
```

Note that in this example, all cases are accounted for and there would be no need for a WHEN OTHER. You could code one, but it would never execute.

And finally, you can mix and match:

```
EVALUATE FALSE ALSO A * B
    WHEN D > E ALSO 12 THRU 24
    [This WHEN phrase executes when D > E and A * B has a value of 12 through
    14.]
```
    ■ ■ ■

IX. SCOPE TERMINATORS

Each of the following conditional statements has an associated *explicit scope terminator*. Several of these statements are described later.

ADD	END-ADD	READ	END-READ
CALL	END-CALL	RETURN	END-RETURN
COMPUTE	END-COMPUTE	REWRITE	END-REWRITE
DELETE	END-DELETE	SEARCH	END-SEARCH
DIVIDE	END-DIVIDE	START	END-START
EVALUATE	END-EVALUATE	STRING	END-STRING
IF	END-IF	SUBTRACT	END-SUBTRACT
MULTIPLY	END-MULTIPLY	UNSTRING	END-UNSTRING
PERFORM	END-PERFORM	WRITE	END-WRITE

COBOL can also assume necessary scope terminators for you. These are termed *implicit scope terminators*. Implicit scope terminators are assumed as follows.

A *period* terminates any unterminated statements. For example:

```
PERFORM 10 TIMES      [Same as]   PERFORM 10 TIMES
  IF F = G                          IF F = G
    THEN MOVE H TO I.                 THEN MOVE H TO I
                                     END-IF
                                   END-PERFORM
```

Note that the following would result in an error:

```
PERFORM 10 TIMES      [Same as]   PERFORM 10 TIMES
  IF F = G                          IF F = G
    THEN MOVE H TO I.                 THEN MOVE H TO I
  END-IF                           END-IF
END-PERFORM                        END-PERFORM
                                   END-IF
                                   END-PERFORM
                                   [The second END-IF and END-PERFORM
                                   don't close anything.]
```

Periods can often result in an undetected error. For example, suppose you coded the following:

```
IF F = G                  [Executed as]   IF F = G
    THEN MOVE H TO I                        THEN MOVE H TO I
         MOVE J TO K.                             MOVE J TO K
         MOVE L TO M                       END-IF
                                           MOVE L TO M
```

The unintended period terminates the IF statement with no error message. This type of error is extremely easy to make and difficult to detect. It is one reason it is best never to use periods except at the end of a paragraph.

Since each paragraph must end with a period, COBOL assumes implicit scope terminators as needed at the end of a paragraph.

COBOL assumes implicit scope terminators when statements are nested and an explicit scope terminator for the outside statement is encountered. For example:

```
PERFORM 10 TIMES      [Same as]   PERFORM 10 TIMES
  IF F = G                          IF F = G
    THEN MOVE H TO I                  THEN MOVE H TO I
END-PERFORM                        END-IF
                                   END-PERFORM
```

This can also easily lead to errors, such as the following:

```
PERFORM 10 TIMES      [Executed as]   PERFORM 10 TIMES
  IF F = G                              IF F = G
```

```
        THEN MOVE H TO I                THEN MOVE H TO I
   MOVE J TO K                              MOVE J TO K
   END-PERFORM                         END-IF
                                    END-PERFORM
```

A new phrase will also cause an implicit scope terminator to be assumed when nesting, as shown in the following example:

```
READ IN-FILE INTO IN-REC   [Same as]  READ IN-FILE INTO IN-REC
   AT END                                AT END
      IF A = B                              IF A = B
         THEN MOVE C TO D                      THEN MOVE C TO D
             MOVE E TO F                           MOVE E TO F
   NOT AT END                               END-IF
      MOVE G TO H                        NOT AT END
END-READ                                    MOVE G TO H
                                      END-READ
```

The one exception to this is in nested IF statements. ELSE phrases are applied as appropriate to matching THEN phrases, as shown in the following example:

```
IF A = B               [Same as]   IF A = B
   THEN MOVE C TO D                    THEN MOVE C TO D
       IF E = F                            IF E = F
          THEN MOVE G TO H                    THEN MOVE G TO H
          ELSE MOVE I TO J                    ELSE MOVE I TO J
       ELSE MOVE K TO L                    END-IF
   END-IF                              ELSE MOVE K TO L
                                    END-IF
```

Implicit scope terminators save coding but are a major source of error, which is not a wise tradeoff. Eliminate them all by always coding explicit scope terminators.

The language statements described in this chapter are the core of COBOL. The next chapter describes how they are used for structured programming.

EXERCISES

1. What will the identifiers A, B, C, and D contain after each of the following statements has been executed? Assume that each identifier has a precision of S9(4).

```
MOVE 1 TO A, B
COMPUTE B = A + 1
ADD B TO A
MULTIPLY B BY A
DIVIDE A BY 5 GIVING C REMAINDER D
```

2. Place parentheses around the following expressions to indicate the hierarchy of operations. Also insert blanks where necessary.

```
1/2* A* T** 2
A** B-2/Y-D
A+2* C** 2/B+6* 4
A+B=ZERO OR NOT A NOT=1 AND B > A*10-6
```

3. The following statements each contain an actual or an almost certain potential error. Find each error.

```
MULTIPLY A BY 2
ADD "125" TO B
DIVIDE BUDGET-REMAINING BY PERIODS-REMAINING
MOVE ZERO TO A, B.   C
COMPUTE A = B * C ROUNDED
IF A = 2 = C
   THEN ADD 1 TO A
END-IF
```

4. The following table contains paragraph names and associated values of the identifier SWITCH-A. Perform the proper paragraph name as given by the value of SWITCH-A, first using IF statements and then an EVALUATE statement.

Value of SWITCH-A	Paragraph Name
1	START-IT
2	FINISH-IT
3	CONTINUE-IT
4	PROCEED-TO

5. Use IF statements to set the identifier ANS to the appropriate value based on the conditions given. Then do the same using an EVALUATE statement.

Value of ANS	Condition
0	If X equals zero.
−1	If X is negative and Y is not greater than zero.
−2	If both X and Y + Z are greater than 22.
100	If X equals 1 and Y equals 1, or if half of Y + Z equals 1.
200	All other conditions.

6. Rewrite the following IF statement using condition names.

```
01  X                          PIC S9(5).
    ▪ ▪ ▪
    IF (X = 1) OR
       ((X NOT < 20) AND (X NOT > 30)) OR
```

```
      (X = 50 OR 60 OR 61)
      THEN ...
  END-IF
```

7. Write decision tables to show whether the following IF statements are true or false for all possible conditions.

```
  IF (X = 1 AND NOT Y = 1) OR
     NOT (X = 0 OR Y = 1)
       THEN ...
  END-IF
  IF (X NOT = 1 OR Y NOT = 1) OR
     NOT (X = Y)
       THEN ...
  END-IF
```

8. What values will X assume within the following loops?

```
  PERFORM LOOP1 VARYING X FROM -10 BY 3 UNTIL X > 6
  PERFORM LOOP2 VARYING X FROM 1 BY 1 UNTIL X > 1
  MOVE 4 TO Y
  PERFORM WITH TEST BEFORE VARYING X FROM 1 BY 1
          UNTIL (X > 10) OR (Y NOT > 0)
    PERFORM VARYING X FROM -3 BY -2 UNTIL X < -7
      imperative-statements
    END-PERFORM
  END-PERFORM
```

9. Assume that DY, MO, and YR contain the day, month, and year of a start date, and that DUR contains a duration in days. Assuming 30 days per month, use IF and COMPUTE statements to compute the end date from the start date and the duration, and store the results back in DY, MO, and YR.

10. Assume that the day, month, and year of a start date are contained in S-DY, S-MO, and S-YR, and the end date in E-DY, E-MO, and E-YR. Write the statements necessary to store the exact duration in days in DUR, assuming 30 days per month.

11. An equation is given as $Y = (X - 1)/(X^2 + 1)$. Write the statements necessary to evaluate the equation for values of X ranging from -6 to 10 by steps of 0.5.

12. Rewrite the following statements without using the GO TO statement but using instead the IF, EVALUATE, or PERFORM statements.

```
      MOVE 1 TO X.
LOOP1.  MOVE ZERO TO A(X).
      ADD 1 TO X.
```

```
      IF X < 10 THEN GO TO LOOP1.
      IF B > 6 THEN GO TO NEXT1.
      IF B < ZERO THEN GO TO NEXT1.
      IF C = ZERO THEN GO TO NEXT1.
      IF B > 3 THEN GO TO NEXT2.
      MOVE ZERO TO D.
      ADD 1 TO B.
      GO TO NEXT3.
NEXT1.  MOVE ZERO TO E.
      IF X + Y > 0 THEN GO TO NEXT3.
      ADD 1 TO G.
      GO TO NEXT3.
NEXT2.   ADD 1 TO G.
      GO TO NEXT4.
NEXT3.   ADD 1 TO F.
NEXT4.
```

13.   The following IF statement has been coded.

```
IF XX NOT = ZERO AND ZZ = 1 AND XX NOT = 1 OR XX NOT = 2
   THEN PERFORM FINI
END-IF
```

Tell whether the FINI paragraph will be executed, based on the following combinations of values of XX and ZZ.

XX	YY
0	0
0	1
0	2
0	3
1	0
1	1
1	2
1	3

14.   What combinations of values will X, Y, and Z have in the loop?

```
PERFORM LOOP1 WITH TEST BEFORE
        VARYING X FROM 1 BY 2 UNTIL X > 4
        AFTER Y FROM 0 BY -1 UNTIL Y < -1
        AFTER Z FROM 2 BY 3 UNTIL Z > 7
```

5

Structured Programming

This book takes a wide view of structured programming as a way of organizing our thoughts and programs to achieve correct and easily modifiable programs. This is done by applying the criteria in Chapter 2 along with the structured programming constructs to show the purpose of a program by its form. *Structured Programming*, in its most limited definition, consists of a few constructs that specify the flow of control of the program.

The terms *top-down design* and *structured programming* are closely related. Top-down design, sometimes termed *stepwise refinement*, consists of identifying the major functions of a program and decomposing these functions into smaller and smaller functional units until the lowest level is specified. You write the program in the same order, with the highest level written first. This gives discipline to the design and ensures that the most important part of the program, its overall design, is coded first. It also serves to organize the program into digestible components consisting of functionally related parts that reflect the original design concept. Top-down design boils down to worrying about designing the forest before you plant the trees.

Lest one accept top-down design without question, *object-oriented programming* is just the opposite. Object-oriented programming argues that top-down design has two major problems. First, it is difficult to adapt to changing needs. This is often reflected in statements like "Well, if they would just tell us what they want and freeze the design, we could build the thing." Object-oriented programming enthusiasts argue quite correctly that this will never happen, because all needs are dynamic and constantly change. The second criticism of top-down is that it does not produce reusable code. All designs and programs become unique to the application, and one of the most cost-effective techniques, the reuse of code, is forgone.

Object-oriented programming advocates would say that you should start by designing ways to plant trees because you can then build any kind of forest. Besides, the customer probably didn't want a forest anyway—just a grove of trees. Object-oriented programs concentrate on the data first, and then incorporate the functions that operate and manipulate the data as an inherent part of data definition. The only thing in COBOL that is at all similar is a level 88 data item, in which conditional operations are defined in the data. Object-oriented programming would extend this so that if a date were defined, operations on the date would be a part of the date definition. This would include such things as determining if a year were a leap year, converting to other date formats, or calculating elapsed days or years between two dates. All programmers could then use these common routines.

With object-oriented programming, the design focuses on the lower level to develop general-purpose routines. These can then be put together at a higher level for many different purposes. By including the concept of inheritance, whereby the operations on the data can be inherited and modified, the programs then in theory become much more flexible. For example, if a routine were included to compute the elapsed days between two dates, you could inherit this routine and modify it to exclude weekends and holidays.

Of course, neither top-down nor object-oriented is likely the last word in programming. It is easy to see object-oriented as a strategic concept for a company in designing data and the common routines to operate on the data. Then top-down might be used tactically to design applications using the routines that resulted from the object-oriented design. Adherence to either top-down or object-oriented should not be an excuse for not thinking.

COBOL is not an object-oriented language. However, many of the concepts of object-oriented programming can be used, such as defining a set of common routines to operate on data items when the data items are defined.

Structured programming is inherent in both top-down and object-oriented design. This book deals with programming in COBOL rather than design, and so the focus is on structured programming, not top-down or object-oriented design. The major advantages of structured programming are that it gives form, order, uniformity, and discipline to programs and simplifies their logical flow. Another side benefit of structured programming is that it has changed the emphasis from *clever* programming to *clear* programming, where it properly belongs.

Structured programming consists of three primitive forms or constructs that have been mathematically proved to be the minimum required to code all program logic. Because these three constructs can be proved mathematically to be the minimum required, they enable a program to be mathematically proved logically correct. However, proving programs to be mathematically correct is not practical and has little relevance to most programming. Also, it does not logically follow that because these three constructs are the minimum required to write a program, they are the only ones needed. View them as guidelines and not rules, because they are not always the most direct means of programming, and use them only if they clarify the sequence of execution.

I. SEQUENTIAL EXECUTION OF STATEMENTS

Sequential execution is the most elementary of the three constructs and is shown in Figure 5.1.

```
ADD X TO Y
PERFORM C10-TOTALS
COMPUTE B = C + D * E
```

FIGURE 5.1 Sequential execution.

II. THE *If/Then/Else* CONSTRUCT

The *If/Then/Else* construct executes one or the other of two blocks of code based on the results of a conditional test. Figure 5.2 shows this.

```
IF A = B
   THEN ADD X TO Y
        MOVE 2 TO Z
   ELSE COMPUTE B = C + D * E
        ADD 1 TO X
END-IF
```

Either the *Then* or the *Else* may be null. In COBOL, the THEN must always be present (you may use the CONTINUE statement), but you may omit the ELSE. Figure 5.3 shows this.

```
IF A = B
   THEN CONTINUE
            [CONTINUE is a null statement used here to fulfill the requirement that there
             be a THEN phrase. The THEN phrase must contain a statement; you can't code
             just THEN.]
   ELSE COMPUTE B = C + D * E
        ADD 1 TO X
END-IF
IF A = B
   THEN ADD X TO Y
        MOVE 2 TO Z
END-IF
```

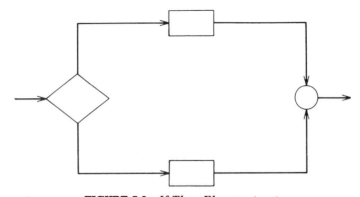

FIGURE 5.2 *If Then Else* construct.

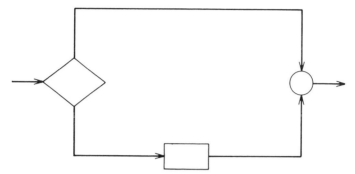

FIGURE 5.3 *If Then* **construct.**

A single IF statement nested to great depth is hard to follow, and indenting to show the logical flow can soon force the coding beyond column 72. Keep each ELSE close to its related THEN. You can make inner groups be separate paragraphs with the IF statement performing them. The PERFORM statement makes COBOL a convenient language for structured programming.

The IF statement tests a condition, or several conditions connected by AND, OR, or NOT. Try to prevent such logical expressions from becoming too complex. As in English, avoid double negatives. NOT in combination with OR is usually written incorrectly. Be careful not to confuse AND with OR. Structure the logical expression to show the relationship.

```
IF ((THE-AGE > 35) OR
   ((THE-WEIGHT > 110) AND (THE-HEIGHT > 5)) OR
   (THE-EYES = "BLUE"))
        AND
   (THE-NAME = "SMITH")
   THEN PERFORM A30-SELECT-PERSON
END-IF
```

Sometimes a logical expression is clearer if it is written as a nested IF. Each nested IF acts as if it were an AND applied to the previous IF.

```
IF (X = 1) AND
   (Y = 1)
   THEN PERFORM B10-LAST
END-IF
```

Same as

```
IF X = 1
   THEN IF Y = 1
           THEN PERFORM B10-LAST
        END-IF
END-IF
```

Logical expressions are usually the hardest part of a computer program to read. They can become so complex that you must write a decision table to understand them. Sometimes it is more straightforward to use the EVALUATE statement than to use the IF. Try to break up long logical expressions into shorter ones that can be more easily understood. Use parentheses, indentation, implied logical operations, and nested IF statements to accomplish this. The following example illustrates an IF statement that is hard to read and recasts it to be more readable:

```
IF THE-SEX = "M" AND ((THE-AGE > 20 AND THE-AGE < 30) AND
(THE-WEIGHT > 90 AND THE-WEIGHT < 150) AND (THE-HEIGHT > 5 AND
THE-HEIGHT < 6)) OR THE-WEALTH > 1000000 THEN PERFORM
B10-SELECT-PERSON
END-IF
```

Much clearer as

```
IF THE-SEX = "M"
   THEN IF ((THE-AGE > 20 AND < 30) AND
            (THE-WEIGHT > 90 AND < 150) AND
            (THE-HEIGHT > 5 AND < 6))
                    OR
            (THE-WEALTH > 1000000)
            THEN PERFORM B10-SELECT-PERSON
         END-IF
END-IF
```

III. THE *Do While* CONSTRUCT

The *Do While* construct repeats an operation while a condition is true. Figure 5.4 shows this. The PERFORM WITH TEST BEFORE does this in COBOL. Note that if the condition is true when the PERFORM is encountered, the PERFORM statements are skipped.

```
PERFORM WITH TEST BEFORE UNTIL EOF-IN = "Y"
    imperative-statements
END-PERFORM
```

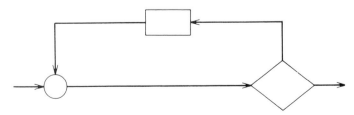

FIGURE 5.4 *Do While* **construct.**

Any form of the PERFORM is valid.

```
PERFORM WITH TEST BEFORE
        VARYING I FROM 1 BY 1
        UNTIL IX > 10
```

Although these three constructs are the minimum required to perform all logical operations, two additional structured programming constructs are provided for convenience.

IV. **THE** *Do Until* **CONSTRUCT**

The *Do Until* is identical to the *Do While,* except that the operation is always performed at least once. Figure 5.5 shows this. The PERFORM WITH TEST AFTER is the COBOL form of the *Do Until.*

```
PERFORM WITH TEST AFTER UNTIL EOF-FLAG = "Y"
    imperative-statements
END-PERFORM
```

Note that COBOL assumes the WITH TEST AFTER if no WITH TEST phrase is coded. The foregoing PERFORM is the same as

```
PERFORM UNTIL EOF-FLAG = "Y"
```

V. **THE** *Case* **CONSTRUCT**

The *Case* construct executes one of several groups of statements, depending on a value. Figure 5.6 shows this. The EVALUATE statement is the COBOL form of the *Case.* If you want to test a single identifier for several possible values, you usually code the EVALUATE as shown here.

```
EVALUATE THE-X
    WHEN "A"
      PERFORM C20-MAX
```

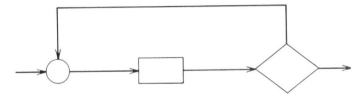

FIGURE 5.5 *Do Until* **construct.**

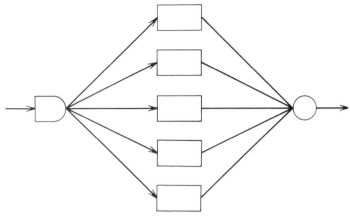

FIGURE 5.6 *Case* **construct.**

```
WHEN "B"
   PERFORM C20-MIN
WHEN "C"
   PERFORM C20-AVG
WHEN OTHER
   PERFORM C20-ERROR
END-EVALUATE
```

If, instead, you want to test for one of several conditions, you usually code the EVALUATE as follows:

```
EVALUATE TRUE
   WHEN THE-X <= "A"
      PERFORM C20-MAX
   WHEN THE-X >= "Z"
      PERFORM C20-MIN
   WHEN SOMETHING-ELSE = "C"
      PERFORM C20-AVG
   WHEN OTHER
      PERFORM C20-ERROR
END-EVALUATE
```

VI. BREAKING OUT OF LOOPS AND PARAGRAPHS

There is one major problem associated with the flow of control not covered by the structured programming constructs—how to quit in the middle of a block of code. This can occur inside a nested IF or other conditional statement, inside a paragraph, or inside a loop. A typical example is to read a file and terminate at the end-of-file. The following functional need occurs in almost every program:

paragraph-label.
```
    READ IN-FILE INTO IN-REC
        AT END want-to-quit-paragraph
    END-READ
```
many-statements-to-process-record
       .

```
**** Exit
```

This leads to a more general need to be able to exit from a paragraph or loop anywhere within it, such as the following:

paragraph-name.
  statements
```
    IF condition
        THEN want-to-exit-paragraph
    END-IF
```
remainder-of-statements
       .

```
**** Exit
```

Conditional statements such as the IF can do this by executing the remaining statements in the procedure as a statement group. However, this is often awkward and results in nesting statements to several levels:

paragraph-name.
  statements
```
    IF NOT condition
        THEN remainder-of-statements
    END-IF
```
       .

```
**** Exit
```

Alternatively, you can use the NEXT SENTENCE statement to skip to the end of the sentence—just past the next period. However, one misplaced period and things fall apart. This is like leaving time bombs in a program and is not recommended:

paragraph-name.
  statements
```
    IF condition
        THEN NEXT SENTENCE
    END-IF
```
statements   *[Any period in these statements would result in an error.]*
       .

```
**** Exit
```

Often the simplest and most straightforward way of breaking out of conditional statements or a paragraph is to use a GO TO:

```
paragraph-name.
    statements
    IF condition
        THEN GO TO label
    END-IF
    remainder-of-statements
     .
label.  EXIT.
```

Just remember to perform such a paragraph with a PERFORM THRU:

```
PERFORM paragraph-name  THRU label
```

The same thing often occurs within loops where you want to jump to the end of the loop and continue or break out of the loop:

```
PERFORM UNTIL condition
    statements
    IF first-condition
        THEN want-to-branch-to-end-of-loop-and-continue
    END-IF
    more-statements
    IF second-condition
        THEN want-to-break-out-of-loop
    END-IF
    remainder-of-statements
END-PERFORM
```

Again, you might be able to use IF statements to do this, but it gets very awkward:

```
PERFORM UNTIL condition
    statements
    IF first-condition
        THEN CONTINUE
        ELSE more-statements
            IF second-condition
                THEN set-condition-to-end-loop
                ELSE remainder-of-statements
            END-IF
    END-IF
END-PERFORM
```

You can use a GO TO to break out of a loop. However, you can't use a GO TO to continue an in-line loop, because you can't place a label between PERFORM and END-PERFORM. Sometimes the best way is to separate some of the code into paragraphs and PERFORM it. The following illustrates a GO TO to break out of a loop and a PERFORM to continue it.

```
PERFORM UNTIL condition
    statements
    IF first-condition
        THEN CONTINUE
        ELSE PERFORM A10-MORE-STATEMENTS
            IF second-condition
                THEN GO TO A10-BREAK-LOOP
                ELSE PERFORM A10-REST-OF-STATEMENTS
            END-IF
    END-IF
END-PERFORM
   .
A10-BREAK-LOOP.
   ■ ■ ■
A10-MORE-STATEMENTS.
    more-statements
   .
**** Exit
A10-REST-OF-STATEMENTS
    remainder-of-statements
   .
**** Exit
```

Using a GO TO and placing code in a paragraph to solve logic problems is not desirable. But do it if the alternatives are less desirable.

The GO TO is also useful for branching to an error exit when a catastrophic error is encountered that breaks the main line of the program. You can use nested IFs, with the THEN clause as the error routine and the ELSE clause as the remainder of the program. However, this is needlessly complex and holds the least interesting code, the error termination, in front of the reader, forcing him or her to look elsewhere for the remainder of the program. It is better to terminate a program with a GO TO.

```
IF error-condition
    THEN GO TO Z10-ERROR-ROUTINE
END-IF
```

VII. WRITING STRUCTURED PROGRAMS

Flags often control the logic in structured programming, although they can be confusing and lead to errors. But generally they contribute less confusion and errors than would the GO TOs that they replace. Use consistent values for each flag, such as "Y" and "N" for yes and no or "T" and "F" for true and false. Define each flag as PIC X to permit such symbolic values to be assigned to it.

Do not reuse a flag for different purposes to conserve storage, because the confusion and error potential outweigh the minimal storage savings. When a flag has a single purpose, the cross-reference listing or a global search with a text editor will show wherever that purpose is tested. A common error with flags is to forget to assign initial values to them. Set the flag just before its use to ensure that it has a proper initial value. Then the reader need not check elsewhere in the program to find the last place it was assigned a value.

The next example illustrates the advantages of structured programming in a rather long example. Assume that an input file IN-FILE with a Working-Storage record IN-REC is to be copied to OUT-FILE with a Working-Storage record OUT-REC. A transaction file TRANS-FILE with a Working-Storage record TRANS-REC identical in format to IN-REC is to be read. If a transaction record matches an input record, the input record is displayed and deleted—not written out. If an input record is not matched by a transaction record, the input record is to be displayed and written out. Any transaction records not matching an input record are also to be displayed.

This sounds simple, but the logic is involved. The limiting cases must also be considered, where there may be no input or transaction records. For simplicity, we shall assume that the input and transaction files are in proper sort order, and we shall show only the Procedure Division statements. We shall also omit such niceties as printing the number of records read and written.

We will need flags to indicate an end-of-file for the input and transaction files. Rather than defining a separate flag, we shall use the record item itself and set it to HIGH-VALUES when an end-of-file is encountered. (This requires that the record be defined in the Working-Storage Section; you cannot define it in the File Section.) Besides eliminating a separate flag, this simplifies the logic. The comparison of the input record against the transaction record works properly when either record has been set to HIGH-VALUES for an end-of-file. The technique of setting a record to HIGH-VALUES to indicate an end-of-file often simplifies the logic of matching files. The nonstructured programming example is shown first, using GO TOs.

```
PROCEDURE DIVISION.
START-PROGRAM.
    DISPLAY "BEGINNING TEST PROGRAM"
    OPEN INPUT IN-FILE
              TRANS-FILE,
         OUTPUT OUT-FILE
    MOVE LOW-VALUES TO TRANS-REC
    .
A10-READ-NEXT.
    READ IN-FILE INTO IN-REC
      AT END DISPLAY "EOF IN"
            GO TO A70-PURGE-TRANS
    END-READ
```

```
      IF TRANS-REC = LOW-VALUES
         THEN GO TO A40-READ-TRANS
      END-IF
          .
A20-CHECK-FOR-DELETE.
      IF TRANS-REC < IN-REC
         THEN DISPLAY "TRANSACTION IGNORED: ", TRANS-REC
            GO TO A40-READ-TRANS
      END-IF
      IF TRANS-REC = IN-REC
         THEN DISPLAY "DELETING: ", IN-REC
            MOVE LOW-VALUES TO TRANS-REC
            GO TO A10-READ-NEXT
      END-IF
          .
A30-WRITE-OUT.
      WRITE OUT-REC FROM IN-REC
      DISPLAY "WRITING: ", IN-REC
      GO TO A10-READ-NEXT
          .
A40-READ-TRANS.
      READ TRANS-FILE INTO TRANS-REC
        AT END MOVE HIGH-VALUES TO TRANS-REC
              DISPLAY "EOF TRANS"
              GO TO A30-WRITE-OUT
      END-READ
      GO TO A20-CHECK-FOR-DELETE
          .
A70-PURGE-TRANS.
      IF TRANS-REC = HIGH-VALUES
         THEN GO TO A90-DONE
      END-IF
          .
A80-SKIP-TRANS.
      READ TRANS-FILE INTO IN-REC
        AT END GO TO A90-DONE
      END-READ
      DISPLAY "TRANSACTION IGNORED: ", TRANS-REC
      GO TO A80-SKIP-TRANS
          .
A90-DONE.
      DISPLAY "END OF PROGRAM"
      CLOSE IN-FILE,
           TRANS-FILE,
           OUT-FILE
      STOP RUN
          .
END PROGRAM TESTPGM.
```

Now we shall write the program using structured programming. The first step in writing a structured program is to step back and think about what the program is to do, without getting immersed in the details of programming.

Before starting the code, let us specify the program in more detail.

Many programmers use pseudocode to express the design. You can use English, the structured programming constructs, an idealized COBOL, or whatever helps you to express what the program is to do. The pseudocode is often better for designing a program than is a flow chart. The basic approach will be to read an IN-FILE record and then read all TRANS-FILE records until we get one that is equal to or greater than the IN-FILE record. We'll ignore any TRANS-FILE records less than the IN-FILE record. If a TRANS-FILE record matches the IN-FILE record, we'll display the IN-FILE record as deleted. Otherwise, we'll write it out.

We begin the main program logic by reading each IN-FILE record until there are no more. That is, until the EOF (end-of-file) is reached. This is expressed in pseudocode as

Do Until EOF IN-FILE
   Read an IN-FILE *record*

We need a *Do Until* rather than a *Do While*, because we must go through the loop to read a record before we can tell if we have reached EOF.

Now, let us take the next step in detail. After each IN-FILE record is read, we want to read TRANS-FILE records while they are less than the IN-FILE record. We need a *Do While*, because we don't want to read any IN-TRANS records if we already have one that is greater than or equal to the IN-FILE record. However, we have to "prime the pump" by making sure we read a TRANS-FILE record the first time. We could read it before entering the loop, but it would be simpler to preset a condition so that the *Do While* is executed the first time. We can do this by moving LOW-VALUES to the TRANS-FILE record to make it less than any IN-FILE record.

Move LOW-VALUES *to* TRANS-FILE *record*
Do Until EOF IN-FILE
   Read an IN-FILE *record*
   Do While not EOF TRANS-FILE *and* TRANS-FILE *record* ‹ IN-FILE *record*
      Read TRANS-FILE *record*

Now we have either an EOF or a record for the TRANS-FILE. If there is a record and it is less than the IN-FILE record, we display that we are ignoring it and continue the *Do While* loop. If there is a TRANS-FILE EOF or the TRANS-FILE record is equal to or greater than the IN-FILE record, we do nothing and let the *Do While* loop terminate.

Move LOW-VALUES *to* TRANS-FILE *record*
Do until EOF IN-FILE

```
Read an IN-FILE record
Do while not EOF TRANS-FILE and TRANS-FILE record < IN-FILE record
   Read TRANS-FILE record
     Not at end
        If TRANS-FILE record < IN-FILE record
           Then Display < TRANS-FILE record
        End If
     End Read
End Do While
```

Let's not worry about the exceptional cases of an EOF condition yet, and assume that when we drop through the *Do While*, we have both an IN-FILE and a TRANS-FILE record. The possibilities are now the following:

- The TRANS-FILE equals the IN-FILE record. We display that we are deleting the IN-FILE record and continue the *Do Until* loop.
- The TRANS-FILE record is greater than the IN-FILE record. We write the IN-FILE record and continue the *Do Until* loop.
- The TRANS-FILE record is less than the IN-FILE record. This can't happen, because the *Do While* continues until this condition is no longer true. Thus, there are only two conditions to test.

We can now add an *If* statement to handle the two possible situations.

```
Move LOW-VALUES to TRANS-FILE record.
Do Until EOF IN-FILE
   Read an IN-FILE record
   Do While not EOF TRANS-FILE and TRANS-FILE record < IN-FILE record
        Read TRANS-FILE record
          Not at end
             If TRANS-FILE record = IN-FILE record
                Then Display TRANS-FILE record
             End If
          End Read
   End Do While
   If TRANS-FILE record = IN-FILE record
      Then Display deleting IN-FILE record
      Else Display writing IN-FILE record
           Write IN-FILE record into OUT-FILE
   End If
End Do Until
```

Now, let's think about the exceptional cases, such as end-of-file. We'll consider the EOF for IN-FILE first. When we reach EOF for IN-FILE and end the *Do Until* loop, could there still be records left in TRANS-FILE?

There could, so we need to force all the TRANS-FILE records to be read when IN-FILE reaches EOF. The simplest way to do this is to move HIGH-VALUES to the IN-FILE record when it reaches EOF. This makes the TRANS-FILE record always less than the IN-FILE record so that the *Do While* continues until TRANS-FILE also reaches EOF.

If we initialize the IN-FILE record to LOW-VALUES, we can test it for HIGH-VALUES to determine if there is an end-of-file. The use of LOW-VALUES for the initial condition and HIGH-VALUES for the final condition is a common practice in reading sequential files. The LOW-VALUE and HIGH-VALUES don't disturb any test for the records being in sequence. This method does depend on LOW-VALUES and HIGH-VALUES not being legitimate values within the actual records.

We also need to consider what the conditions are when we drop through the *Do While*. The conditions are as follows:

- EOF IN-FILE, EOF TRANS-FILE. The IN-FILE record will contain HIGH-VALUES. We don't want to do anything, and the *Do Until* loop will terminate.
- EOF IN-FILE, TRANS-FILE record. This can't occur because an IN-FILE EOF forces the *Do While* to continue until TRANS-FILE also reaches EOF.
- EOF TRANS-FILE, IN-FILE record. We need to write out the IN-FILE record.
- TRANS-FILE record, IN-FILE record. If the records are equal, we display that we are deleting the IN-FILE record. Otherwise we write the IN-FILE record.

We can now modify the *If* statement following the end of the *Do While* to handle the possible conditions.

```
Move LOW-VALUES to TRANS-FILE record, IN-FILE record
Do Until IN-FILE record = HIGH-VALUES
   Read an IN-FILE record
     At end
        Move HIGH-VALUES to IN-FILE record
   End Read
   Do While Not EOF TRANS-FILE and TRANS-FILE record < IN-FILE  record
     Read TRANS-FILE record
       Not at end
          If TRANS-FILE record < IN-FILE  record
             Then Display TRANS-FILE record
          End  If
     End  Read
   End Do While
   If IN-FILE record = HIGH-VALUES
     Then  Continue
     Else If TRANS-FILE record = IN-FILE  record
```

> *Then Display deleting* IN-FILE *record*
> *Else Display writing* IN-FILE *record*
>   *Write* IN-FILE *record into* OUT-FILE
>   *End If*
> *End If*
> *End Do Until*

Now let's consider what happens when we reach EOF for TRANS-FILE. We could still have records in IN-FILE, but these will be read and written properly. We can simplify the code by also moving HIGH-VALUES to TRANS-FILE when it reaches EOF and testing for this as the EOF condition:

> *Do While* TRANS-FILE *record Not* = HIGH-VALUES *and*
>   TRANS-FILE *record* ‹ IN-FILE *record*

We don't need the "TRANS-FILE *record Not* = HIGH-VALUES." When TRANS-FILE equals HIGH-VALUES, the "TRANS-FILE *record* < IN-FILE *record*" terminates the loop. We can simplify it to

> *Do while* TRANS-FILE *record* ‹ IN-FILE *record*

The pseudocode now becomes

Move LOW-VALUES *to* TRANS-FILE *record,* IN-FILE *record*
Do until IN-FILE *record* = HIGH-VALUES
    Read an IN-FILE *record*
      At end
          Move HIGH-VALUES *to* IN-FILE *record*
    End Read
    Do while TRANS-FILE *record* ‹ IN-FILE *record*
        Read TRANS-FILE *record*
          At end
              Move HIGH-VALUES *to* TRANS-FILE *record*
          Not at end
              If TRANS-FILE *record* ‹ IN-FILE *record*
                  Then Display TRANS-FILE *record*
              End If
        End Read
    End Do While
    If IN-FILE *record* = HIGH-VALUES
        Then Continue
        Else If TRANS-FILE *record* = IN-FILE *record*
                  Then Display deleting IN-FILE *record*
                  Else Display writing IN-FILE *record*
                        Write IN-FILE *record into* OUT-FILE
                  End If
    End If
End Do Until

The nested *If* statement executed when we drop through the *Do While* is needlessly complex. Since we are testing for several conditions, it really should be a *Case* construct. We can replace the nested *If* with the COBOL EVALUATE statement.

```
Evaluate true
   When IN-FILE record = HIGH-VALUES
      Continue
   When TRANS-FILE record = IN-FILE record
      Display deleting IN-FILE record
   When other
      Display writing IN-FILE record
      Write IN-FILE record into OUT-FILE
End Evaluate
```

Our pseudocode now becomes

```
Move LOW-VALUES to TRANS-FILE record, IN-FILE record
Do until IN-FILE record = HIGH-VALUES
   Read an IN-FILE record
    At end
         Move HIGH-VALUES to IN-FILE record
   End Read
   Do while TRANS-FILE record < IN-FILE record
      Read TRANS-FILE record
       At end
            Move HIGH-VALUES to TRANS-FILE record
       Not at end
            If TRANS-FILE record < IN-FILE record
                 Then Display TRANS-FILE record
            End If
      End Read
   End Do While
   Evaluate true
      When IN-FILE record = HIGH-VALUES
         Continue
      When TRANS-FILE record > IN-FILE record
        Display writing IN-FILE record
        Write IN-FILE record into OUT-FILE
      When other
          Display deleting IN-FILE record
   End Evaluate
End Do Until
```

What happens if there are no IN-FILE records? We set the IN-FILE record to HIGH-VALUES, which forces the *Do While* to continue until TRANS-FILE also reaches EOF and we store HIGH-VALUES in its record.

What happens if there are no TRANS-FILE records? We set the TRANS-FILE record to HIGH-VALUES, which prevents it from executing again. In the EVALUATE statement, the HIGH-VALUES in the TRANS-FILE record will always be greater than the IN-FILE record, which forces the IN-FILE record to be written. Thus, we continue reading all the IN-FILE records and writing them out.

What happens when we reach EOF on both the IN-FILE and the TRANS-FILE? The *Do Until* immediately terminates.

What happens if the IN-FILE or the TRANS-FILE records are not in the same ascending sort order? The program will not work properly, and so we might think about checking the sort order of these two files. If we wanted to do this, we would add it to our pseudocode as follows.

```
Read an IN-FILE record
  At end
      Move HIGH-VALUES to IN-FILE record
  Not at end
      If IN-FILE record < last IN-FILE record
          Then Display error message
               Terminate program
          Else Move IN-FILE record to last IN-FILE record
        End If
  End Read
```

We would need to initialize the *last* IN-FILE *record* by moving LOW-VALUES to it at the start of the program. We would also want the same sequence checking for TRANS-FILE.

What happens if there are duplicate records in either file? Duplicate IN-FILE records are deleted or written properly. Duplicate TRANS-FILE records will be displayed, which is probably what we would want. The specifications did not tell us what to do in the event of duplicates, and we might want to resolve this before writing the program—perhaps printing an error message. However, for now the program is probably handling duplicates properly. If we wanted to check for duplicate records, we could change the pseudocode as follows:

```
Read an IN-FILE record
  At end
      Move HIGH-VALUES to IN-FILE record
      If IN-FILE record < last IN-FILE record
        Then Display error message
               Terminate program
        Else if IN-FILE record = last IN-FILE record
               Then Display error message
               ELSE Move IN-FILE record to last IN-FILE record
            End If
        End If
  End Read
```

Now we can begin thinking about the code. The *Do Until* in COBOL is a PERFORM WITH TEST AFTER. The *Do While* is a PERFORM WITH TEST BEFORE, but instead of coding *Do While* TRANS-FILE *record* < IN-FILE *record*, we must PERFORM UNTIL TRANS-FILE *record* >= IN-FILE record:

> *Do While* TRANS-FILE *record* < IN-FILE *record*

becomes

> PERFORM WITH TEST BEFORE UNTIL TRANS-FILE *record* >= IN-FILE *record*

We'll assume the record area for IN-FILE and IN-TRANS are IN-REC and TRANS-REC. We can now make the minor changes in the pseudocode to turn it into true COBOL code. We need to open and close the files and perhaps use DISPLAY to note the progress of the program. To simplify the program structure, we can PERFORM the update as a paragraph. The COBOL program is then as follows:

```
PROCEDURE DIVISION.
START-PROGRAM.
    DISPLAY "BEGINNING TEST PROGRAM"
    OPEN INPUT IN-FILE,
             TRANS-FILE,
        OUTPUT OUT-FILE
    MOVE LOW-VALUES TO IN-REC, TRANS-REC
    PERFORM A10-READ-IN-FILE WITH TEST AFTER
            UNTIL IN-REC = HIGH-VALUES
    DISPLAY "END OF PROGRAM"
    CLOSE IN-FILE,
          TRANS-FILE,
          OUT-FILE
    STOP RUN

**** Exit
 A10-READ-IN-FILE.
    READ IN-FILE INTO IN-REC
      AT END
        MOVE HIGH-VALUES TO IN-REC
    END-READ
    PERFORM WITH TEST BEFORE UNTIL TRANS-REC >= IN-REC
      READ TRANS-FILE INTO TRANS-REC
        AT END
          MOVE HIGH-VALUES TO TRANS-REC
        NOT AT END
          IF TRANS-REC < IN-REC
            THEN DISPLAY "TRANSACTION IGNORED:", TRANS-REC
          END-IF
      END-READ
```

```
      END-PERFORM
      EVALUATE TRUE
        WHEN IN-REC = HIGH-VALUES
          CONTINUE
        WHEN TRANS-REC = IN-REC
          DISPLAY "DELETING:", IN-REC
        WHEN OTHER
          DISPLAY "WRITING: ", IN-REC
          WRITE OUT-REC FROM IN-REC
      END-EVALUATE

**** Exit
  END PROGRAM TESTPGM.
```

The nonstructured program contains 32 COBOL verbs and 8 paragraph names. The structured program contains only 21 COBOL verbs and 2 paragraph names. Our goal was not to write the program with the fewest statements, but simple, clear programs will generally lead to this. But which is the most efficient? Chapter 25 discusses efficiency, but for now let us assume that the efficiency will be about equal unless the compiler generates atrocious code.

If nothing else, there are two things that you should get out of structured programming. First, you should step back and think about what you want to program without getting immersed in the detail. Call this top-down design, stepwise refinement, or simply not worrying about where the trees go until you have planned the forest—it is an essential discipline in programming. Second, you should write the program in the simplest, clearest possible way.

This completes the discussion of structured programming. The next chapters delve into the COBOL data types and data storage.

EXERCISES

1. Develop a set of rules for using GO TO statements.

2. What changes do you believe should be made to COBOL to enhance its use for structured programming?

3. Write a paper on what, if anything, you believe makes structured programming a better way to program.

4. Write a paper discussing and evaluating one of the following:

   Structured walk-throughs

   Chief programming teams

   Modular programming

   HIPO charts, a method of charting programs as a replacement for flow charts; HIPO charts were popular in the 1970s

   Object-oriented programming

   Object-oriented design

   CASE (Computer-Aided Software Engineering) tools

5. The following is an excerpt from a typical nonstructured program. Rewrite it as a structured program.

```
START-IT.   READ IN-FILE INTO REC-IN AT END GO TO DONE.
    IF REC-TYPE = " " GO TO DONE.
    IF REC-TYPE = "A" GO TO GO-ON.
    IF REC-TYPE = "B" GO TO START-IT.
    IF REC-TYPE = "C" GO TO GO-ON.
    GO TO START-IT.
GO-ON.  MOVE 1 TO IX.
    IF REC-NAME (IX) = SPACES GO TO START-IT.
STORE-NAME.  MOVE REC-NAME (IX) TO SAVE-NAME (IX).
    MOVE 1 TO IY.
STORE-POP.  IF REC-POP (IX, IY) = SPACES GO TO MORE-NAMES.
    MOVE REC-POP (IX, IY) TO SAVE-POP (IX, IY).
    ADD 1 TO IY.
    IF IY < 11 GO TO STORE-POP.
MORE-NAMES.  ADD 1 TO IX.
    IF IX < 21 GO TO STORE-NAME.
    MOVE REC-NO TO SAVE-NO.
    GO TO START-IT.
DONE.
```

■ ■ ■

6. Assume that you are attending a symposium on programming techniques. One speaker claims to have a new composite technique that improves programmer productivity, as measured by code produced per day, by an order of magnitude. His method is to use structured, top-down design while regressing stepwise using interactive meditation. This is augmented with the power of positive thinking, organized into on-line, modular programming teams with frequent work breaks while everyone faces east, links arms with others, and slowly repeats a mystic Hindu chant.

- Assuming that you have some doubts about the productivity claims, what questions would you ask to dispute or verify the claims?
- Assume that the claim of a tenfold improvement in the ability of programmers to write programs is true. What are the possible outcomes of each programmer being able to write 10 times the amount of code that he or she can produce today?

7. The last two examples in this chapter are a nonstructured and structured program to update a file. Make the following changes to both programs and discuss the difficulty of making the changes.

- Check the IN-FILE and TRANS-FILE for ascending sort order.
- Check the IN-FILE and TRANS-FILE for duplicate records.

- Count the IN-FILE and TRANS-FILE records read and the number of records written.
- If three consecutive TRANS-FILE records do not match an IN-FILE record, print an error message and continue.
- If there are no IN-FILE records, or if there are no TRANS-FILE records, print an error message and continue.

ADDITIONAL READINGS

Russell M. Armstrong, *Modular Programming in COBOL*, New York: John Wiley & Sons, 1973.

Joel D. Aron, *The Program Development Process*, Reading, MA: Addison-Wesley, 1974.

"Chief Programmer Teams Principles and Procedures," Report No. FSC 715108, Gaithersburg, MD: IBM Corporation, 1971.

Peter Coad, Edward Yourdon, *Object-Oriented Analysis*, Englewood Cliffs, NJ: Prentice Hall, 1990.

Brad Cox, *Object-Oriented Programming: An Evolutionary Approach*, Reading, MA: Addison-Wesley, 1986.

O. J. Dahl, E. W. Dijkstra, C. A. R. Hoare, *Structured Programming*, London: Academic Press Ltd, 1972.

Edsger W. Dijkstra, *A Discipline of Programming*, Englewood Cliffs, NJ: Prentice Hall, 1976.

"HIPO—A Design Aid and Documentation Technique," Order No. GC20-1851, White Plains, NY: IBM Corporation, 1974.

"Improved Programming Techniques Management Overview," White Plains, NY: IBM Corporation, August 1973.

Clement L. McGowan and John R. Kelly, *Top-Down Structured Programming Techniques*, New York: Petrocelli/Charier, 1975.

Bertrand Meyer, *Object-oriented Software Construction*, Hemel Hempstead, Hertfordshire, England: Prentice Hall International Ltd., 1988.

H. D. Mills, "Top Down Programming in Large Systems," *Debugging Techniques in Large System*, Englewood Cliffs, NJ: Prentice Hall, 1971, pp. 41-55.

Glenford J. Myers, *Reliable Software Through Composite Design*, New York: Petrocelli/Charter, 1975.

Niklaus Wirth, "Programming Development by Step-wise Refinement," *Communications of the ACM*, Vol. 14, No. 4 (1971), pp. 221-227.

Edward Yourdon, *Techniques of Program Structure and Design*, Englewood Cliffs, NJ: Prentice Hall, 1975.

6

Numeric Data

The ANSI Standard does not specify the internal form of numeric data and the precision of intermediate results. This chapter describes the numeric data types for VS COBOL II and Microsoft COBOL.

The numeric data types consist of BINARY or COMP (binary), COMP-1 (single-precision floating-point), COMP-2 (double-precision floating-point), PACKED-DECIMAL, and DISPLAY (called *external decimal numbers* and containing numbers as character data). For numeric data, the PIC character string can contain only 9, P, S, and V. The data types have different characteristics and uses and are described later in this chapter. PACKED-DECIMAL is usually the most convenient form for monetary data. COMP-1 and COMP-2 floating-point-types are in VS COBOL II and Microsoft COBOL. You will seldom use them in COBOL, and the following discussion does not apply to them.

You write numeric literals as decimal numbers with an optional decimal point. The numbers may be signed plus ($+$) or minus ($-$) or remain unsigned (assumed positive).

```
23   175.925   -.00973   +16
MOVE 23 TO A
COMPUTE B = C / 176.925
```

Numeric literals cannot end with the decimal point, because COBOL would confuse it with the period that ends a sentence.

2 or 2.0, but not 2.

You describe elementary numeric data items with a level number, a name, a PICTURE clause (abbreviated PIC), and the data type (BINARY, PACKED-DECIMAL, or DISPLAY).

nn   *identifier-name*   PIC *string   data-type*.

Note that the period at the end of each data description is required. For example,

```
01  STATE-POPULATION              PIC S999V99 PACKED-DECIMAL.
```

The *nn* level may be 01 through 46. Level 01 specifies either a group or an elementary data item. Levels 02 through 46 specify group or elementary items that are part of a lower level. There are also three special levels: 66, 77, and 88. Level 66 renames data items (described in Chapter 8), level 77 defines an elementary data item, and level 88 defines a condition-name entry (described in Chapter 4). Chapter 8 describes the levels in more detail.

The PIC clause specifies the precision with the number of digits to the left and right of the decimal point. The form is PIC S99...9V99...9, where S indicates a signed number, each 9 represents a decimal digit, and the V specifies the assumed decimal point. Therefore, S9V999 can contain numbers such as −0.007, 9.265, and 3.000. If you omit the V, the decimal point is assumed on the right, so that S99 and S99V are equivalent. The V does not count in determining the length of a data item. The S also does not count in determining the length unless the SIGN IS LEADING SEPARATE clause, discussed in a following section, is coded.

If the S is omitted, the number is unsigned and treated as positive. Except for a number that is always positive, such as a length, code the S to make the number signed. (Negative numbers were heretical during the Middle Ages, but became accepted at the start of the seventeenth century.) Unsigned numbers can give surprising results. The following statements make it appear as if −1 + 1 equals 2:

```
77  X                             PIC 999 PACKED-DECIMAL.
    ▪ ▪ ▪
    MOVE ZERO TO X      [X contains 0.]
    SUBTRACT 1 FROM X   [X contains 1 because the minus sign is lost.]
    ADD 1 TO X          [X contains 2.]
```

As an extra bonus, VS COBOL II PACKED-DECIMAL signed numbers are more efficient than unsigned numbers.

If there are many 9's, they become tedious to write. Instead, code a single 9 and follow it with the number of 9's enclosed in parentheses. This is preferable, because you can tell at a glance the number of digits to the left and right of the decimal point.

```
    S9(5)        [Same as]      S99999
    SV9(4)       [Same as]      SV9999
    S(6)V9(8)    [Same as]      S999999V99999999
```

The maximum number of digits that can be contained in a numeric data item is 18.

You can specify that the decimal point lies outside the number. This allows you to represent very large or small numbers with only a few digits of storage.

Code a P to the left or right of the 9's to specify the position of the decimal point when it lies outside the number. You can omit the V. For example, SP(5)9(4) permits you to represent the number .000001234 with four digits. The following example specifies a data item that contains only three digits, such as 213, but is treated as if it had the value .0000213:

```
77  A                       PIC SP(4)999 PACKED-DECIMAL.
```

Place the P's on the right to specify that the decimal point is to the right of the number. The following example specifies a data item that contains only three digits, such as 213, but is treated as if it had the value 21,300,000.

```
77  A                       PIC S999P(5) PACKED-DECIMAL.
```

The total number of digits, including those specified by the P's, cannot exceed 18. The P's conserve file and memory storage, but often the savings are not worth the extra effort and potential confusion. The P doesn't count in determining the storage length of the data item.

You can write PIC in its long form as PICTURE or PICTURE IS. You can code USAGE in front of the type of data: PACKED-DECIMAL or USAGE PACKED-DECIMAL. The guideline of never using a long word when a short one will do makes the last description preferable in the following:

```
77  A     PICTURE S99999 USAGE PACKED-DECIMAL.
77  A     PICTURE IS S99999 USAGE PACKED-DECIMAL.
77  A     PIC S9(5) PACKED-DECIMAL.
```

The VALUE clause assigns initial values to data items. A data item has no predictable value unless you assign it an initial value or store a value into it.

```
77  X                       PIC S9(5) PACKED-DECIMAL VALUE 0.
```
   [X is initialized with a value of zero.]

Plan the number of digits to carry in data items. Larger numbers require more memory and I/O storage, and you should not be wasteful. But smaller numbers may not allow room for growth, and one way to minimize change is to provide for growth. For example, a company with $50,000 in sales might require a data item of S9(5)V99 today, but what happens if sales grow to over $100,000? Inflation alone could see to this in a depressingly short time. If there is no physical limit on the size of a number, define the item to contain the largest number expected plus at least one digit for safety.

Keep the numeric precision consistent, even if some numbers are defined to be larger than necessary. Arithmetic operations are more efficient if all the numbers have the same precision. Generalized subprograms are also easier to write when all the potential applications have the same precision. For example, if the total revenue of a company is $100,000, but the largest revenue of a division is only $10,000, describe all revenue data items as S9(7)V99 for consistency and safety.

Data items containing dollar amounts should provide two digits to the right of the decimal point (V99) to carry the cents, even if only whole dollar amounts are wanted. Carry the cents to prevent rounding errors and to guard against a future requirement of carrying cents.

I. PACKED-DECIMAL **NUMBERS**

You can code PACKED-DECIMAL as COMP-3 in VS COBOL II and Microsoft COBOL. (This was the only way of coding it in old IBM compilers.) PACKED-DECIMAL is now the ANSI Standard and you should use it.

```
01   A                          PIC S9(5)V99 PACKED-DECIMAL.
```

The computer stores PACKED-DECIMAL numbers with each group of four binary digits representing a single decimal digit. For example, 0000 represents 0, 0001 represents 1, 0100 represents 4, and 0001 0100 represents 14. Each digit occupies one-half byte, as does the sign. Therefore, S99V9 occupies one and one-half bytes for the digits and one-half byte for the sign, for a total of two bytes. To determine the number of storage bytes for a number, count the number of digits, add 1 for the sign, round up to the next even number if necessary, and divide by 2. Both S9(6)V9(2) and S9(6)V9(3) occupy five bytes.

VS COBOL II deals more efficiently with signed numbers that occupy an integral number of bytes. Specify an odd number of digits so that the number with its sign will occupy an integral number of bytes. S9(4) wastes one-half byte; S9(5) occupies the same three bytes and is more efficient.

PACKED-DECIMAL numbers may contain up to 18 digits and should be used for most numeric data, except internal counters and subscripts. They are relatively efficient in both storage and computations, and they allow a wide range of numbers with integral precision. PACKED-DECIMAL numbers are somewhat less efficient for computations than BINARY numbers. However, they are more flexible. They are also more efficient for input/output, because they do not require alignment, which results in messy slack bytes, described in Chapter 8. PACKED-DECIMAL is especially useful for monetary data.

Assign initial values with the VALUE clause:

```
77   X                          PIC S9(5) PACKED-DECIMAL
                                VALUE 23.
```

     [X *is initialized with a value of 23.*]

PACKED-DECIMAL numbers carry the sign in the rightmost four bits. A plus sign is a hexadecimal C, a minus a D, and an unsigned number is represented by an F. The ANSI Standard provides for four separate codes for a plus sign and three for a minus. Obviously, this takes considerably more time for the computer to determine whether a number is positive or negative than if a single code specified the plus and minus sign. In VS COBOL II, you can specify the NUMPROC(STD) compiler option, described in Chapter 17, if your program keeps the plus and minus signs with a single code each. Unless you are reading data generated by an old compiler, you should use this compiler option to save execution time.

II. BINARY **NUMBERS**

BINARY (or COMP) numbers are stored internally in a computer word, half-word, or double word as a group of binary digits (bits) representing the number to the base 2. For example, 101 represents 5 and 1110 represents 14. Binary numbers are the most efficient numbers for arithmetic computations, because computers are binary machines. However, in VS COBOL II they are poor as data in I/O records, because their alignment can cause problems, as described in Chapter 8. You should use them for internal counters and subscripts.

```
77  A                           PIC S9(4) BINARY.
```

The number of bytes needed to contain the value depends on the number of digits as follows:

1 to 4	Half-word or two bytes.
5 to 9	Full word or four bytes.
10 to 18	Two full words or eight bytes. (This is less efficient than half-words or full words. The data is stored as packed decimal.)

The VALUE clause assigns initial values to data items.

```
77  X                           PIC S9(4) BINARY VALUE 100.
```
   [X *is initialized with a value of 100.*]

III. EXTERNAL DECIMAL NUMBERS

A. Describing External Decimal Numbers

External decimal numbers are also termed USAGE (or just DISPLAY) numbers, *zoned decimal* numbers, and *numeric field data*. You use these for source input and printed output. They consist of character data that contains only numeric digits, one digit per byte in storage. You can treat the data as alphanumeric and print it without conversion. You can perform arithmetic operations on external decimal numbers; COBOL converts the external decimal number to packed decimal for the arithmetic computations. External decimal numbers are inefficient for computations. Limit arithmetic computations on them to such simple operations as incrementing a page number.

External decimal number items can contain 1 to 18 numeric digits and are described as follows.

```
77   A                        PIC S999V99.
```

Their data type is DISPLAY. However, DISPLAY is assumed if no type is coded. The following three forms are identical; all contain five characters.

```
77   B                        PIC S9(5).
77   B                        PIC S9(5) DISPLAY.
77   B                        PIC S99999 USAGE DISPLAY.
```

The VALUE clause assigns initial values to data items.

```
77   X                        PIC S9(5) VALUE 6.
     [X contains the digits "00006".]
```

External decimal numbers must always have leading zeros, not leading blanks. You can also treat external decimal numbers as alphanumeric data. The statements that operate on alphanumeric data, such as INSPECT, STRING, and UNSTRING, may also operate on it.

If the number is signed (denoted by a leading S), the operational sign is carried in the left half of the rightmost byte. The S does not count as a character position; both S999V9 and 999V9 occupy four character positions.

The same NUMPROC(STD) compiler option discussed for PACKED-DECIMAL numbers also applied to external decimal numbers and can save execution time for most applications.

B. The SIGN Clause

Before the current ANSI Standard, COBOL expected the minus sign to be overpunched over the rightmost column when external decimal numbers were read. This dated back to when the standard data entry device was a keypunch, and one could punch two characters in the same column. Today, a terminal is the standard input device, and it doesn't have the facility for overpunching. You can still type the character that corresponds to the digit with the plus or minus sign overpunched. The sign is contained in the left half-byte of the rightmost digit. It is a hexadecimal F, written X"F", if the number is unsigned, an X"C" if positive signed, and an X"D" if negative signed. Thus, an unsigned number will have X"F0" to X"F9" as the rightmost digit, which are the EBCDIC characters 0 to 9. A signed number will have X"C0" to X"C9" if positive and X"D0" to X"D9" if negative. X"C1"to X"C9" are the EBCDIC characters A to I, and X"D1" to X"D9" are the EBCDIC characters J to R. (As for the zeroes, X"C0" is an EBCDIC left brace {, and X"D0" is a right brace }.) So, if you wanted to enter a −21, you could type 2J. This is a bad way to enter numbers. It is much better to enter the number as people expect to see it (−21). The SIGN clause is one way around this problem. Another solution is to *de-edit* the number, as described later in this section.

COBOL has a SIGN clause, which permits a sign to be coded in a fixed position in the field for a DISPLAY data item.

```
77  X                          PIC S9(4) SIGN IS LEADING.
```
   [*X occupies four character positions. The* S *in the* PIC *does not count in determining the size of the data item. The sign is assumed to be typed over the leading numeric digit.*]
```
77  X                          PIC S9(4) SIGN IS TRAILING.
```
   [*The same, but the sign is assumed to be typed over the trailing digit. Note that this is the default if the* SIGN *clause is omitted.*]
```
77  X                          PIC S999
                               SIGN IS LEADING SEPARATE.
```
   [*X occupies four character positions. The sign is assumed to be a separate leading character, and the* S *in the* PIC *clause counts in determining the length of the data item. A sign (+ or −) must be present in the leading position. The number can participate in arithmetic operations even though it contains a nonnumeric character (+ or −).*]

■ ■ ■
```
MOVE -14 TO X
```
   [*X contains* "-014".]
```
MOVE 14 TO X
```
   [*X contains* "+014".]
```
77  Y                          PIC S999
                               SIGN IS TRAILING SEPARATE.
```
   [*Y occupies four character positions.*]

■ ■ ■
```
MOVE 23 TO Y
```
   [*Y contains* "023+".]
```
MOVE -23 TO Y
```
   [*Y contains* "023-".]

If data is moved to an item with the SIGN clause and conversion is necessary, COBOL inserts the sign in the proper position. If data is moved to an item with the SIGN clause without conversion, no sign is set, and the job terminates if you perform arithmetic operations on the number. This can occur in a group move or when you read data into the item.

C. De-Editing Edited External Decimal Numbers

As described in Chater 13, you can edit external decimal numbers to insert various nonnumeric characters for display. For example, you can edit the external decimal number "00234480P" to become " -23,448.07". The blank, comma, and period are nonnumeric characters that make the number easy to read for humans. Unfortunately, the computer doesn't accept these nonnumeric characters when it performs computations. To get rid of them, move the edited decimal number to a numeric or other external decimal item. For example, if the field HOURLY-RATE contained "$22,456.23", you could de-edit it as follows:

```
77   NUM-ITEM                          PIC S9(9)V9(2) PACKED-DECIMAL.
     ■ ■ ■
     MOVE HOURLY-RATE TO NUM-ITEM
```

[NUM-ITEM *will contain the packed decimal digits in hexadecimal as* "00002245623C" *where the C indicates a positive number.*]

NUM-ITEM will contain the numeric value and can participate in arithmetic operations. (HOURLY-RATE could not participate in numeric operations, because it contains nonnumeric data.)

IV. COMP-1 and COMP-2 **FLOATING-POINT NUMBERS** (Not in ANSI Standard)

COMP-1 and COMP-2 floating-point numbers, normally used in scientific computations, are rarely used in COBOL. Numbers in scientific computations are often derived from physical measurements that have limited precision. This contrasts with the integral units common in commercial computations, such as dollars and cents. For example, a bicycle might cost exactly $122.98, but the weight might be 21, 21.3, 21.332, or 21.33186 pounds, depending on the accuracy of the scale.

The computer stores floating-point numbers in a computer word in two parts. One part represents the significant digits of the number. The other part represents the exponent that determines the magnitude of the number. This corresponds to scientific notation, where, for example, 0.25E-5 represents 0.0000025 and -0.25E5 represents -25,000. This notation allows a wide range of numbers to be used in arithmetic computations without losing significant digits of precision.

To add or subtract numbers expressed in this notation, the system must normalize them to the same power of 10. For example, 6E4 + 8E2 would be normalized to .06E2 + 8E2 to equal 8.06E2. To multiply numbers, the exponents are added, so that 6E4 * 8E2 equals 48E6. To divide two numbers, the exponent of the denominator is subtracted from that of the numerator, so that 6E4 / 8E2 equals 0.75E2. Thus, to calculate the time in seconds that it takes light traveling at 11,800,000,000 inches per second to pass through a film 0.0001 inches thick, the computation is done as 1.0E-4 / 1.18E10 to equal 0.847E-14. Computers have special floating-point hardware to do such computations efficiently, and you need not worry about normalizing the numbers.

Floating-point numbers are not precise; their precision is limited to some number of significant digits. For example, a computation such as 0.1 + 0.1 may yield a result of 0.19999 when expressed in floating-point, rather than exactly 0.2. This is acceptable in scientific computations, where answers are given plus or minus some tolerance, but it can be inappropriate for business applications, where numbers must balance to the penny. Since 0.1 + 0.1 may result in 0.19999 rather than 0.2, never compare floating-point numbers solely for equality. Nor should you use them for counters.

Write a floating-point literal as a decimal number, followed by an E, followed by an exponent. You can sign both the number and the exponent.

```
2E0    -9E0    15.3E5    2.2E-1
```

COMP-1 single-precision numbers occupy a full word of four bytes. The maximum magnitude is from 10^{-78} to 10^{+75}, and the number has at least six decimal digits of precision. COMP-2 double-precision numbers occupy a double word of eight bytes. The maximum magnitude is from 10^{-78} to 10^{+75}, and the number has at least 16 decimal digits of precision. You specify floating-point data items as COMP-1 (single-precision) or COMP-2 (double-precision). Don't code a PIC clause. You can also code COMP-1 and COMP-2 as COMPUTATIONAL-1 and COMPUTATIONAL-2. The following two descriptions are equivalent.

```
77   A COMPUTATIONAL-1.        [Same as]        77   A COMP-1.
77   B COMPUTATIONAL-2.                         77   B COMP-2.
```

You can assign initial values to data items:

```
77   X COMP-2                          VALUE 1.26E+3.
```

The value can only be a floating-point literal or ZERO. You can use floating-point data wherever numeric data is allowed, with the few exceptions noted where appropriate in this book.

V. DATA CONVERSION AND PRECISION

Conversion occurs automatically when arithmetic operations are performed on numeric data of different types. This can occur both in arithmetic statements, such as COMPUTE and ADD, and in relational expressions, such as those in the IF statement. The arithmetic statements also result in conversion if the resultant identifier differs from the data type of the data being stored. COBOL converts the data to a common numeric type to perform the operations, according to the following hierarchy:

```
[Highest:]  COMP-2
            COMP-1
            PACKED-DECIMAL
            DISPLAY
               [COBOL converts external decimal numbers to PACKED-DECIMAL for computa-
               tions.]
[Lowest:]   BINARY
```

In the statement COMPUTE A = B + C + D, if A and B are BINARY, C is PACKED-DECIMAL, and D is COMP-1, COBOL converts B and C to COMP-1 for the arithmetic operation. COBOL then converts this intermediate result to BINARY and stores it in A.

You can convert numeric data to alphanumeric data by moving it to an alphanumeric data item. If the data item is an external decimal number, COBOL aligns the number on the decimal point and sets the sign. If the numeric data is copied to a PIC X alphanumeric data item, the numeric data is converted to character, left-justified, with the decimal point and any sign removed.

```
77  Y                           PIC X(3).
    ■ ■ ■
    MOVE 22 TO Y      [Y contains "22 ".]
    MOVE -2.1 TO Y    [Y contains "21 ".]
    MOVE 2345 TO Y    [Y contains "234".]
```

You convert alphanumeric data to numeric by moving it to a numeric data item. (You can't convert data defined as alphabetic PIC A to numeric.) You can convert data contained in a PIC X item to numeric only if it contains the characters 0 to 9. (The SIGN clause, described earlier, further allows the item to contain a + or – in a leading or trailing position.) You can convert only integers to alphanumeric (PIC S99V but not S99V9).

```
77  Y                           PIC S999V.
    ■ ■ ■
    MOVE "023" TO Y   [Y contains a numeric 23.]
```

Alphanumeric data cannot appear in arithmetic expressions. Conversion also takes computer time, and excessive conversions can make a program run slowly.

Arithmetic precision can be lost during conversion in the low-order digits. In an assignment statement, precision can be lost in both the high- and low-order digits if the data item to which the data is being assigned cannot contain the number being assigned. You can detect the loss of high-order digits by the ON SIZE ERROR phrase, but you can't detect the loss in low-order digits. The following example illustrates how high- and low-order digits are lost.

```
77  X                           PIC S99V99 PACKED-DECIMAL.
    ■ ■ ■
    MOVE 123.456 TO X   [X contains 23.45.]
```

In the absence of a ROUNDED phrase in arithmetic operations, low-order digits of precision are lost by truncation, not rounding. For example, if the number 1.999 is stored in a data item of precision S9V99, COBOL truncates the number to 1.99. The ROUNDED phrase in the arithmetic statements rounds a number rather than truncating it. Values whose rightmost digit is less than 5 are rounded down in absolute magnitude, and values whose rightmost digit is 5 or greater are rounded up in absolute magnitude. Thus, 1.995 is rounded to 2.00.

When there is more than one arithmetic operation performed in a single statement, COBOL must carry intermediate results. For example, in COMPUTE X = (A * B) / C, the A * B is first evaluated and held as an intermediate result. This intermediate result is then divided by C, and the intermediate result from this is stored in X.

Loss of precision and overflow in intermediate results are a common source of error. A grade-school student would give the correct result of the expression 6 * (2 / 4) as 3, but VS COBOL II evaluates it as 0. The 2 / 4 yields an intermediate result of precision PIC S9, the 0.5 is truncated to zero to store the intermediate result, and 0 times 6 yields 0. (The ANSI Standard leaves the result undefined. The result is 3 in Microsoft COBOL.) The precision of VS COBOL II intermediate results shown for the arithmetic operations in the following examples are given by iVd. The i signifies the number of decimal digits to the left of the decimal point and d the number of digits to the right.

- Add, subtract:

  $i_1Vd_1 + i_2Vd_2$ yields $(max(i_1, i_2) + 1)Vmax(d_1, d_2)$
  99V9 + 9V999 yields precision of 9(3)V9(3)
  99.9 + 9.999 equals 109.899

- Multiply:

  $i_1Vd_1 * i_2Vd_2$ yields $(i_1 + i_2)V(d_1 + d_2)$
  99V9 * 9V999 yields precision of 9(3)V9(4)
  99.9 * 9.999 equals 998.9001

- Divide:

  i_1Vd_1/i_2Vd_2 yields $(i_1 - d_2)Vmax(d)$
  $max(d)$ is the maximum of d_1, d_2, the d of the data item into which the result is stored, or the d of other intermediate results.
  99V9 / 9V999, final result of 99V9, yields precision of 9(5)V9(3)
  99.9 / 0.001 equals 99900.000
  99V9 / 9V999, final result of 99V9(4), yields precision of 9(5)V9(4)
  00.1 / 3.000 equals 00000.0333

- Exponentiate:

  If exponent has decimals, both the number and the exponent are converted to floating-point for the calculation.
  If both item and exponent are integer literals:
  $i * * n$ yields i set to actual number of digits that result.
  25 * * 2 equals 625.
  If item is identifier and exponent is integer literal:
  $i_1Vd_1 * * n$ yields i set to actual number of digits that result and $max(d)$ decimal places.
  $max(d)$ is the maximum of d_1, the d of the data item into which the result is stored, or the d of other intermediate results.
  99V9 * * 2 yields precision of 9(3)V9.
  25.3 * * 2 equals 0640.0.

If the exponent is an integer identifier:

$i_1 V d_1 * * n$ yields $(i_1 \times n) + (n - 1)V(d_1 \times n)$
99V9 $* *$ 2 yields precision of 9(5)V99.
25.3 $* *$ 2 equals 00640.09.

Except for floating-point numbers, VS COBOL II carries as many as 30 digits of precision in intermediate results. High-order precision is lost only if the intermediate results require more than 30 digits, and the compiler will issue a warning if it is possible for this to occur. BINARY numbers are converted to PACKED-DECIMAL if the intermediate results require more than 18 digits.

Addition and subtraction generally cause no problems. Multiplication can cause a problem if the result can exceed 30 total digits of precision—unlikely in commercial applications. Division causes the most problems. The result can exceed 30 total digits of precision when a very large number is divided by a very small number. A more likely error is loss in precision caused by a division resulting in a fraction. We have seen how 6 * (2 / 4) yields zero. We could obtain the correct result by any or the following.

- Coding 6 * (2 / 4.0) to force the intermediate result to be carried to one decimal place.
- Defining the final result to have a decimal precision of V9 to force the intermediate result to be carried to one decimal place.
- Coding (6 * 2) / 4 to perform the division last. This method is preferable unless the result of the multiplication could exceed 30 total digits of precision. This works equally well for (6 * 1) / 3, whereas the two previous methods would give a result of 1.8.
- Define a data item to contain the intermediate result and perform the operation in parts:

```
77  TEMP                       PIC S9(4)V9(5) PACKED-DECIMAL.
    ■ ■ ■
    COMPUTE TEMP = 6 * 2
    COMPUTE FINAL-RESULT = TEMP / 4
```

Be careful with division and, whenever possible, perform the division last in a series of computations. An expression such as X * (Y / Z) may lose precision, and you should change it to (X * Y) / Z. Except for logical expressions, numeric computations are perhaps the most common source of error. Errors in loss of precision are especially hard to find, because a program runs as expected, but the numbers computed may be off slightly. Always hand-calculate critical computations to check the precision.

VI. NUMERIC DATA IN APPLICATIONS

You often encounter the following numeric data types in COBOL applications.

- Percentages. Divide percentages by 100 for storage so that you can use them directly in applications. Store percentages as PIC S9V999 PACKED-

DECIMAL data items. (That is, carry 50 percent as 0.500.) Three decimal places permits percentages accurate to $\frac{1}{8}$ percent.
- Dollar amount. Always carry dollar amounts in dollars in cents as PIC S9(n)V99 PACKED DECIMAL, even if only whole dollars are to appear in reports. Make dollar amounts signed so that you can carry debits and credits.
- Hours. If hours are used in calculations, keep them as PIC S9(n)V99 PACKED-DECIMAL data items rather than separately as hours and minutes. The two decimal digits are accurate to the minute, which is sufficient for most business applications. The following statement converts hours and minutes to a decimal number:

```
COMPUTE time = hours + minutes  / 60
```

- Salary. Although salary is often given in an amount per year, month, week, or day, you must often convert it to an hourly rate for internal use. Carry dollars to 3 or 4 decimal places. (Union contracts sometimes quote hourly rates as low as $\frac{1}{8}$ cent.)

This concludes the discussion of numeric data. The next chapter describes alphanumeric data, which have entirely different properties, operations, and problems.

EXERCISES

1.   Select the data types that would be best for the following uses, and describe why they would be best.

A count of the input records read from a file.
The population of states contained within a record.
Computing rocket trajectories.
Computing the interest on a house loan.
Reading numbers in from an input line.

2.   The equation for a future amount invested at i percent per year for n years is

$$future\ amount = investment \left(1 + \frac{i}{100}\right)^n$$

Write the statements necessary to compute the future amount of 10-year investments ranging from $100 to $102 by increments of 5 cents at an interest rate of $7\frac{1}{4}$ percent.

3.   Assume the following items are declared.

```
77  A                          PIC S9(6)V999.
77  B                          PIC S9(3)V99 PACKED-DECIMAL.
77  C                          PIC S9(4) BINARY.
77  D                          COMP-1.
77  E                          COMP-2.
```

Describe the conversion that will be done in each of the following statements.

```
COMPUTE E = A *  D
COMPUTE A = D *  B *  C
ADD 1 TO C
MOVE B TO A
```

4. Assume that the following data items are described:

```
77  A                          PIC S9(4) BINARY.
77  B                          PIC S9(6)V9(3) PACKED-DECIMAL.
77  C                          PIC S9(3) PACKED-DECIMAL.
```

Show the results of the following statements.

```
COMPUTE A = 3.5
COMPUTE A ROUNDED = 3.5
COMPUTE B = 1254.6 *  3.3235 / 6.43229 + 12.1136
MOVE 12.211 TO B
COMPUTE B = B / 4.395 *  6.4 + 7.1135
COMPUTE A = (12 + .1) / 7
COMPUTE A = (12 / 7) + .1
```

5. The IRS has called you in to do some programming. It feels that it has not been getting a fair shake from the taxpayers. It has decided to pay off the national debt by billing each taxpayer his or her share. You are told that the national debt is $1,627,260,497,937.12. The IRS insists that the national debt be paid off to the penny. The share for each person is to be paid in the proportion of his or her personal income tax to the total income tax. Under these circumstances, is it possible to pay off the national debt to the penny? Assume that there are 107,916,412 taxpayers. Under the worst possible circumstances, assuming that you round, how much over or under might you collect? If you truncate, how much over or under might you collect?

7

Character Data

I. DEFINING CHARACTER DATA

Character data consists of a string of characters. The names of people, their street addresses, and the words on this page all constitute character data. *Character data* is not a COBOL term, but is a convenient term for describing data in character form. Character data is also termed *character string* and *text* data in other languages. In COBOL, data described as DISPLAY constitutes character data.

COBOL defines three *classes* of character data: alphanumeric (PIC X), numeric (PIC 9), and alphabetic (PIC A). *Alphanumeric* data can consist of any of the characters in the COBOL character set, including alphabetic and numeric characters. *External decimal numbers,* described in Chapter 6, consist of the digits 0 to 9. Since they contain only numeric digits, they can participate in arithmetic operations. *Alphabetic* data can contain only the characters A to Z, a to z, and blank. You rarely need it, both because alphanumeric data serve better and because data containing only alphabetic characters are rare. Even people's names, such as "O'Reilly", require alphanumeric data items.

The PIC and DISPLAY clauses specify three types of data: alphanumeric, alphabetic, and external decimal numbers. Throughout this book, the term DISPLAY indicates that the data items may be any of these three. However, the examples don't code DISPLAY, because it defaults if omitted.

COBOL further divides the alphanumeric class of data into three *categories:* numeric edited, alphanumeric edited, and alphanumeric. Numeric edited data, such as "$33,425.37 CR" for a credit, and alphanumeric edited data, such as "12/21/95" for a date, contain special edit characters coded in the PIC clause. They are generally used for printing and are discussed in Chapter 13. Group items may also be operated on as character data, and the group item is treated as if it contained all alphanumeric data. Table 7.1 summarizes the classes and categories of COBOL character data.

You write alphanumeric literals by enclosing the characters in quotation marks ("). VS COBOL II provides the APOST compiler option, described in

TABLE 7.1 COBOL Character Data

Level of Item	Class	Category
Elementary	Alphabetic External decimal Alphanumeric	Alphabetic External decimal Numeric edited Alphanumeric edited Alphanumeric
Group	Alphanumeric	Alphabetic Numeric Numeric edited Alphanumeric edited Alphanumeric

Chapter 17, to let you use an apostrophe (') instead. Microsoft COBOL allows either the quotation (") or apostrophe (') to be used, as long as the same character is used at the beginning and end of a string.

```
"AT"  "FIVE"  "ME TO"
```

VS COBOL II allows nonnumeric literals to be a maximum of 160 characters long. Specify a double quotation character (") by coding two consecutive quotation marks:

```
"""WHERE IS IT?"""          [Becomes]          "WHERE IS IT?"
```

The number of X's in the PIC clause specifies the length of alphanumeric data items: PIC XX...X or X(integer). The *integer* is the number of characters that the data item is to contain; it may be a maximum of 249 in VS COBOL II.

```
01   data-name                        PIC X(integer ).
```

Or:

```
01   data-name                        PIC XXX...X.
```

You may also explicitly describe the data type as DISPLAY, USAGE DISPLAY, or USAGE IS DISPLAY. In the following example, B contains 12 characters, C contains three characters, and D contains 4 characters.

```
01  B          PIC X(12) DISPLAY.          [Or]     01  B     PIC X(12).
01  C PICTURE XXX USAGE DISPLAY.           [Or]     01  C     PIC X(3).
01  D PICTURE XXXX USAGE IS DISPLAY.       [Or]     01  D     PIC X(4).
```

You describe alphabetic data items the same as alphanumeric items, except that you code an A rather than an X.

```
01   W     PIC AAAA.                    [Or]    01   W     PIC A(4).
```

The PIC clause may contain A or 9 in combination with X, but COBOL treats the item as if it were all X's.

```
01   Y     PIC XXAA9.                   [Same as]    01   Y     PIC XXXXX.
```

Give alphanumeric data items initial values by appending the VALUE clause to the description. The following example initializes Bwith the characters "ABCD":

```
01   A                     PIC X(4) VALUE "ABCD".
```

If too few characters are specified, COBOL pads the string out on the right with blanks. If too many characters are specified, the description is in error.

```
01   B                     PIC X(4) VALUE "1".
     [B contains "1bbb".]
01   C                     PIC X(4) VALUE "VWXYZ".
     [C is in error.]
```

A.   The JUSTIFIED Clause

If you want data stored right-justified in a DISPLAY elementary data item, you can code the JUSTIFIED RIGHT clause, abbreviated JUST RIGHT or merely JUST. You cannot code it for numeric, numeric edited, or alphanumeric edited items.

```
01   A                     PIC X(6) JUST RIGHT.
■ ■ ■
    MOVE "AB" TO A     [A contains "bbbbAB".]
```

If a sending item is longer than a JUST RIGHT receiving item, COBOL truncates the leftmost characters; if shorter, it pads the data on the left with blanks.

```
    MOVE "ABCDEFGH" TO A     [A contains "CDEFGH".]
```

JUST RIGHT has no effect on any initial value set by VALUE:

```
01   A                     PIC X(6) JUST RIGHT VALUE "AB".
     [A contains "ABbbbb", not "bbbbAB".]
```

B. The BLANK WHEN ZERO **Clause**

BLANK WHEN ZERO causes blanks to be stored in an elementary identifier when it has a zero value. You can use it for a DISPLAY item that is either numeric or numeric edited (but not for floating-point).

```
01  A                          PIC S9(4)V99 BLANK WHEN ZERO.
    ▪ ▪ ▪
    MOVE ZERO TO A     [A contains all blanks.]
```

C. Hexadecimal Literals (Not in ANSI Standard)

You can write hexadecimal (hex) literals as follows:

VS COBOL II: Microsoft COBOL:

X"*hex-digits*"   H"*hex-digits*"

There must be two hex digits per byte, and you can specify a maximum of 320 digits in VS COBOL II and 8 digits in Microsoft COBOL:

X"C1C2C3" is the same as "ABC" in VS COBOL II.

H"414243" is the same as "ABC" in Microsoft COBOL.

II. SPECIFYING YOUR OWN CHARACTER SET WITH ALPHABET

By default, the character set will be EBCDIC for the mainframe and ASCII for the PC. In the Environment Division, in the SPECIAL-NAMES paragraph, you can code the ALPHABET clause to specify another character set:

```
ENVIRONMENT DIVISION.
CONFIGURATION SECTION.
SOURCE-COMPUTER.  computer-name.
OBJECT-COMPUTER.  computer-name.
SPECIAL-NAMES.
    ALPHABET alphabet-name IS character-set

    .
```

The *alphabet-name* is a name you choose to call the character set. The *character-set* can be one of the following:

STANDARD-1	For ASCII-encoded files
STANDARD-2	For ISO y-bit encoded files
EBCDIC	For EBCDIC—the default for VS COBOL II
ASCII	Microsoft COBOL only; for ASCII—the default.
NATIVE	The computer's native mode; this is the default if you omit CODE-SET (see Chapter 12).

If none of these satisfy you, you can devise your own character set and specify it by coding the *character-set* as:

```
ALPHABET alphabet-name IS literal
                          literal THRU literal
```

The *literal* is the character wanted. You can code a single character literal ("Z") or an unsigned decimal representation of the character you want with a value from 1 to 255. For example, an EBCDIC "Z" is a hex "E9", which is decimal 234. If the entire character set consisted of S through Z, you could code

```
ALPHABET alphabet-name IS 227 THRU 234.
```

or

```
ALPHABET alphabet-name IS "S" THRU "Z".
```

The collating sequence of the character set depends on the order in which you specify the codes. For example, if you code

```
ALPHABET alphabet-name IS "A", "Z" THRU "S".
```

the collating sequence from low to high is: A Z Y X W V U T S. Thus, you can make the collating sequence be whatever you want it. The first character specified is associated with the figurative constant LOW-VALUES and the last character with HIGH-VALUES. If two or more characters are to have same position in the collating sequence, code them as

```
literal ALSO literal ALSO literal  ... ALSO literal
```

The following example establishes an alphabet named VOWELS:

```
SPECIAL-NAMES.
    ALPHABET VOWELS IS "A", "E", "I", "O", "U"
```

III. DEFINING FIGURATIVE CONSTANTS: SYMBOLIC CHARACTERS CLAUSE

The normal figurative constants that can be used with character data are ZEROS, SPACES, HIGH-VALUES, LOW-VALUES, QUOTES, and ALL. You can also define your own figurative constants with the SYMBOLIC CHARACTERS clause. You code it in the Environment Division in the SPECIAL-NAMES paragraph as follows:

```
ENVIRONMENT DIVISION.
■ ■ ■
```

```
SPECIAL-NAMES.
    SYMBOLIC CHARACTERS name-1, name-2, ..., name-n
        ARE integer-1, integer-2, ..., integer-n.
```

Each *name* is a unique user-defined word that must contain at least one alphabetic character: 9999A but not 9999. There must be an *integer* corresponding to each *name*. The *integer* is the ordinal position (1 to *n*) of the character in the character in the character set. For example, an EBCDIC dash or minus sign is a hex X"60", which is 96 in decimal. But since the first EBCDIC character is X"00", the ordinal position of the minus is 97. Here is how it could be defined:

```
    SYMBOLIC CHARACTERS A-DASH IS 97.
```

Now you could treat A-DASH as a figurative constant:

```
    MOVE ALL A-DASH TO A-LINE
    [A-LINE would be filled with dashes.]
```

If you use the ALPHABET clause to specify your own alphabet, you can assign a symbolic name to one of these characters. Code the *integer* as the ordinal position (1 - *n*) of the character in the alphabet, and follow *integer* with IN *alphabet-name* to name the alphabet.

```
SPECIAL-NAMES.
    ALPHABET alphabet-name IS literal, literal, ...
    SYMBOLIC CHARACTERS name IS integer IN alphabet-name
        .
```

Here's an example that creates an alphabet named DIGITS for the numeric digits and assigns the symbolic name UNITY to the second digit (1) and the symbolic name TRINITY to the fourth digit (3).

```
SPECIAL-NAMES.
    ALPHABET DIGITS IS "0" THRU "9"
    SYMBOLIC CHARACTERS
            UNITY IS 2 IN DIGITS,
            TRINITY IS 4 IN DIGITS
        .
```

IV. OPERATING ON CHARACTER DATA

A. Moving Character Data

The MOVE statement can move alphanumeric identifiers and literals to other alphanumeric identifiers. The following example sets K to "12345":

```
01  K                           PIC X(5).
01  L                           PIC X(5) VALUE "12345".
■ ■ ■
    MOVE L TO K         [Or]         MOVE "12345" TO K.
```

In the MOVE statement, COBOL pads identifiers on the right (unless they are declared JUST RIGHT) with blanks if they are assigned a smaller item; it truncates longer items on the right (again, unless they are declared JUST RIGHT):

```
01  B                          PIC X(4).
    ■ ■ ■
    MOVE "AB" TO B          [B contains "ABbb".]
    MOVE "ABCDEF" TO B      [B contains "ABCD".]
```

To repeat a literal to fill an item, precede the literal with ALL:

```
01  Z                          PIC X(6) VALUE ALL "1".
        [Z contains "111111".]
    ■ ■ ■
    MOVE ALL "A" TO Z    [Z contains "AAAAAA".]
```

B. Reference Modification

COBOL allows you to refer to substrings of character data by giving the starting character position and the length. The general form for this *reference modification* is:

    identifier(starting-character:length)

Both the *starting-character* and *length* must be arithmetic expressions. The *starting-character* is the starting character position (the first character is 1), and must result in a value from 1 to the length of the identifier. The *length* must result in a positive, nonzero value. For example:

```
01  A                          PIC X(6) VALUE "ABCDEF".
01  B                          PIC X(6).
■ ■ ■
    MOVE A(3:2) TO B      [Acts as]    MOVE "CD" TO B
```

The *length* is optional. If omitted, COBOL assumes a length from the *starting-character* to the rightmost character. Note that you must always code the colon, even if the length is omitted.

```
    MOVE A(2:) TO B       [Acts as]    MOVE "BCDEF" TO B
                          [Same as]    MOVE A(2:5) TO B
```

Except when restricted in specific statements, you can use reference modification wherever you can use an alphanumeric identifier. For example:

```
    MOVE SPACES TO B
    MOVE "XY" TO B(3:2)      [B now contains "bbXYbb".]
    MOVE A(3:2) TO B(1:2)    [B now contains "CDXYbb".]
```

C. LENGTH OF **Special Register (Not in ANSI Standard)**

The LENGTH OF special register obtains the number of bytes occupied by an identifier—that is, the identifier's length. You write it as

```
LENGTH OF identifier
```

For example:

```
01  A                          PIC X(10).
01  B                          PIC S9(4) BINARY.
    ■ ■ ■
    MOVE LENGTH OF A TO B       [Moves 10 to B.]
    MOVE LENGTH OF A(3:) TO B   [Moves 8 to B.]
    MOVE LENGTH OF B TO B       [Moves 2 to B.]
```

For variable-length tables (described in Chapter 9), LENGTH OF gives the current length of the table. Suppose you have the following:

```
01  ARRAY-A.
    05  A                      OCCURS 100 TIMES
                               DEPENDING ON LEN-A
                               PIC X(4).
01  LEN-A                      PIC S9(4) BINARY.
    ■ ■ ■
    MOVE LENGTH OF ARRAY-A TO AN-ITEM
        [Contents of AN-ITEM are undefined, because no value has been stored in LEN-A to
        specify the length of the table.]
    MOVE 10 TO LEN-A
    MOVE LENGTH OF ARRAY-A TO AN-ITEM
        [AN-ITEM contains 40, because ARRAY-A has 10 elements of 4 bytes each.]
    MOVE 100 TO LEN-A
    MOVE LENGTH OF ARRAY-A TO AN-ITEM
        [AN-ITEM contains 400, because ARRAY-A has 100 elements of 4 bytes each.]
```

D. Comparing Character Data

Relational conditions, such as those in the IF statement, can compare two character strings. COBOL compares the two strings character by character from left to right according to the collating sequence of the character set. Chapter 21 shows the collating sequence of the EBCDIC and ASCII character sets.

In the relational condition, if the strings are of unequal length, COBOL pads the shorter with blanks on the right to equal the length of the longer string for the comparison. The following example compares the characters "ABCD" with "23bb".

```
01  X                             PIC X(4) VALUE "ABCD".
    ■ ■ ■
    IF X = "23" ...
```

You can test alphanumeric and alphabetic PIC A items to determine if they contain only the alphabetic characters A to Z, a to z, or blank.

```
IF identifier  ALPHABETIC THEN ...
IF identifier  NOT ALPHABETIC THEN ...
IF identifier  ALPHABETIC-UPPER THEN ...
IF identifier  NOT ALPHABETIC-LOWER THEN ...
```

You can also test alphanumeric and external decimal number items to determine if they contain only the numeric characters 0 to 9.

```
IF identifier  NUMERIC THEN ...
IF identifier  NOT NUMERIC THEN ...
```

Table 7.2 summarizes the tests that may be made on alphanumeric, alphabetic, and external decimal numbers.

COBOL also allows you to define your own classes of data in the SPECIAL-NAMES paragraph of the Environment Division. For example, suppose we want to define a class named ODD-NUM for odd numeric characters. We write the SPECIAL-NAMES paragraph with a CLASS clause as

```
SPECIAL-NAMES.
    CLASS ODD-NUM IS "1", "3", "5", "7", "9".
    ■ ■ ■
01  THE-DATA                      PIC X(6).
    ■ ■ ■
    IF THE-DATA(6:1) ODD-NUM THEN ...
    IF THE-DATA(6:1) NOT ODD-NUM THEN ...
```

TABLE 7.2 Alphabetic and Numeric Tests

Type of Item	Permissible Tests
PIC A	ALPHABETIC
	ALPHABETIC-UPPER
	ALPHABETIC-LOWER
PIC X	ALPHABETIC
	NUMERIC
PIC 9	NUMERIC

The general form of the CLASS clause is

```
SPECIAL-NAMES.
    CLASS class-name IS literal, literal,
              literal THRU literal, literal, ...
```

The *literal* is usually a single-character literal, such as "1" or "%", or multiple characters, such as "13579", that are treated as if the characters had been written separately. The aforementioned CLASS clause could also have been written as

```
CLASS ODD-NUM IS "13579".
```

The *literal* cannot be a symbolic character, such as SPACE. The *literal* can also be an integer that represents the EBCDIC or ASCII character code. For example, the EBCDIC numeric code for a "%" is 108.

```
CLASS class-name IS 108, ...
```

In EBCDIC, this is the same as

```
CLASS class-name IS "%", ...
```

However, in ASCII, a 108 is a "1", so that the foregoing in ASCII is the same as

```
CLASS class-name IS "1", ...
```

You cannot use the *class-name* test for external decimal numbers (PIC 9).

V. CHARACTER DATA IN APPLICATIONS

Always keep character and text data as PIC X and not PIC A. Very few data items are truly alphabetic. For example, names often are hyphenated or contain apostrophes. The main problem with text fields is determining their maximum length. The following are only suggestions.

   Names. Nothing is more insulting than to receive computer-generated output in which your name is truncated. Allow plenty of room in storing names.

- Last name: 20 characters. According to the Guinness *Book of World Records,* Featherstonehaugh is the longest English name. However, hyphenated last names after marriage are becoming more common today. The 20 characters should allow for non-English and foreign names.
- First name: 15 characters. Christopher is the longest of the common given names. The 15 characters provide a margin for this.

- Middle name: 20 characters. The middle name is often a family name. If you store only the middle initial, you need only a single character.

Address. The following items are usually required for addresses in the United States and most foreign addresses. Allow plenty of room, because it can be extremely offensive to truncate a company, city, or nation name.

- Company name: 50 characters. *The Atchison Topeka and Santa Fe Railroad Company* is the longest of the Fortune 500 names. The names of law firms go on forever.
- Division name: 50 characters. Same as the company name.
- Street address: 40 characters. The longest street name I have encountered is my own: *Mandeville Canyon Road.* Leave some room for street number and room, suite, or apartment number.
- City: 23 characters. *Southampton Long Island* is the longest name in the United States. Fortunately, *El Pueblo de Nuestra Señora la Reina de los Angeles de Porciuncula* can be abbreviated L.A. (Wales has longer names, and allow more if you want to avoid offending the Welsh.)
- State: 14 characters for United States (the *Carolina*s) or 21 to include Canada (*Northwest Territories*) if name is spelled out or foreign addresses are needed. Allow 2 characters if you need only the post office code for U.S. states.
- Zip Code: 9 characters. The U.S. ZIP+4 code is the longest of any country.
- Country: 30 characters. *St. Vincent and the Grenadines* is the longest name not usually abbreviated. A full 37 characters are required for the *Democratic People's Republic of Yemen* (and *Korea*). (However, People's Republics are becoming an endangered species.) The *Russian Soviet Federated Socialist Republic* is 43 characters, but its name may go the way of Leningrad and Stalingrad. The longest name of a member of the UN requires 38 characters: *Byelorussian Soviet Socialist Republic.* (Socialist Republics also are on the endangered list.)

This covers the basics of character data. Chapter 20 describes other COBOL statements that operate on data and advanced character manipulation. The discussion is delayed until this chapter, because it makes extensive use of the subprograms described in Chapter 19. Meanwhile, the next chapter explains how records and data structures are described.

EXERCISES

1. Show what these identifiers will contain when initialized as follows.

```
01  A                     PIC X(6) VALUE ZEROS.
01  B                     PIC X(6) VALUE "MARYQUOTES".
01  C                     PIC X(3) VALUE "ABC".
01  D                     PIC X(6) VALUE ALL "12".
01  E                     PIC X(8) JUST RIGHT VALUE "123".
01  F                     PIC X(6) VALUE "ABC".
01  G                     PIC X(8) VALUE ALL ZEROS.
```

2. Define an identifier named TEXT-A containing 20 characters and an identifier named STATE containing four characters. Write the statements necessary to move the data in STATE to TEXT-A, right-justifying it with leading blanks.

3. Define an alphabet named HAWAIIAN-ALPHABET. It is to contain only the vowels A, E, I, O, U, and the consonants H, K, L, M, N, P, and W. Also define a class name of HAWAIIAN for the same characters. Test the variable named CITY-NAME to see if it contains only HAWAIIAN characters.

4. Using IF statements, examine a variable named THE-NUM defined as PIC S9(5) and set it to blanks if it contains zero. This is to do functionally the same as if you had defined THE-NUM with BLANK WHEN ZERO.

5. Define symbolic parameters named DOLLAR for "$" and POUND-STERLING for "£". Assume that you are doing this only for the PC. The ASCII code for the £ is 156.

6. Assume that you must display numbers of precision S9(5), and you want negative numbers to be enclosed in parentheses. Positive numbers are to appear without parentheses. Define an identifier containing seven characters. Store the number in character positions 2 through 6. Place the parentheses in character positions 1 and 7 if the number is negative. Thus, 23 would appear as "bbbb23b" and -23 as "(bbb23)".

Repeat this, but let the left parenthesis float so that -23 prints as "bbb(23)".

8

Data Descriptions and Records

For reference, you code the clauses in a data description in the order shown. Several clauses are described in other chapters.

```
level
data-name  [or  FILLER]
REDEFINES
EXTERNAL  [or  COMMON]
PIC
USAGE
SIGN
OCCURS
   DEPENDING ON
   ASCENDING [or  DESCENDING] KEY
   INDEXED BY
SYNCHRONIZED
JUSTIFIED
BLANK WHEN ZERO
VALUE
```

I. WRITING DATA DESCRIPTIONS

You can allocate storage for elementary items, for records, and for tables. You must explicitly describe all data items. COBOL does not automatically set storage to zero or blanks, and you must initialize each data item or assign a value to it before using it in computations. You write data descriptions as follows:

nn data-name   PIC *character-string* USAGE *clause* .
  [*nn is the level number. Note that you must always terminate the description with a period.*]

* *level-number.* One or two numeric digits specifying the level. The levels can be 01 to 49 (or 1 to 49), 66, 77, and 88.

- *data-name*. A name containing 1 to 30 characters: 0 to 9, A to Z or a to z, or the hyphen. The hyphen cannot be the first or last character. The name must begin in column 12 or beyond. Level numbers 01 and 77 names must be unique. Omit the name, or code FILLER as the data name, to indicate an unnamed item.
- *character-string*. Characters specifying the length or precision of the data item. For example, X(10) specifies 10 characters, and S999V99 specifies a signed number with three digits to the left and two to the right of the assumed decimal point. The maximum length of the character string is 30 characters.
- USAGE clause. Specifies the representation of the data. You can code BINARY, COMP-1 (single-precision floating-point), COMP-2 (double-precision floating-point), PACKED-DECIMAL, or DISPLAY (external decimal numbers, alphanumeric, or alphabetic). Don't code PIC for COMP-1 and COMP-2. The keyword USAGE is optional.

You can code only a single data description entry on a line, but you may continue it onto other lines. You can use the following level numbers:

- 01. Used for record names; must begin in columns 8 to 11. Aligned on a double-word boundary in VS COBOL II.
- 02 to 49. Used for levels within a record; may begin in column 8 or beyond.
- 66. Used for renaming groups of items within a record; may begin in column 8 or beyond.
- 77. Used for noncontiguous elementary data items—those not a part of a record. Aligned on a full-word boundary in VS COBOL II; must begin in columns 8 to 11.
- 88. Used for condition names that assign a logical value to the contents of a data item; may begin in column 8 or beyond. Described in Chapter 4.

The data descriptions may appear in any of the three sections within the Data Division. The File Section describes I/O records; the Working-Storage Section describes elementary items, records, and tables; and the Linkage Section describes subprogram parameters:

```
DATA DIVISION.
FILE SECTION.
FD [or SD] record-descriptions .
01 record-name .
```

You follow each File Description (FD) and Sort Description (SD) entry with a data description describing the record. This area for describing records is termed the *record area*. COBOL doesn't allocate storage for the record descriptions, and aside from level 88 condition names, you cannot assign initial values. The *record-name* describes the format of the record within the input or output buffer. The record length must equal the logical record length.

```
WORKING-STORAGE SECTION.
77   data-name                        PIC ...
01   data-name.
```

COBOL allocates storage to any level 77 items, and you can assign them initial values. They can appear before or after any level 01 descriptions. Level 77 items are a redundant COBOL feature. It makes no difference whether you code a level 01 or 77 item:

```
77   AN-ITEM                          PIC X(4) VALUE "ABCD".
```

Identical to

```
01   AN-ITEM                          PIC X(4) VALUE "ABCD".
```

You describe all subprogram parameters within a subprogram in the Linkage Section. COBOL doesn't allocate them storage, and aside from level 88 condition names, you cannot assign them initial values. They are associated with the data passed in the parameters of the calling program.

```
LINKAGE SECTION.
77   data-name                        PIC ...
01   data-name.
```

II. DESCRIBING RECORDS

A *record* is a hierarchical collection of related data items, which may be of different data types. You describe I/O records as records. For example, a record describing a person might include the person's name and date of birth. Some items might be group items, as for example the date of birth that consists of a month, a day, and a year. The following example shows how such a record is described. The two records below are identical. Notice how aligning the PIC clauses makes the hierarchical relationship easier to understand.

```
01   PERSON.
02   THE-NAME PIC X(25).
     02   BIRTH-DATE.
     03   MONTH PIC X(9).
03   DAYS PIC S99 PACKED-DECIMAL.
         03   YEAR PIC S9(4).
```

Same as

```
01   PERSON.
     02   THE-NAME              PIC X(25).
     02   BIRTH-DATE.
         03   MONTH             PIC X(9).
         03   DAYS              PIC S99 PACKED-DECIMAL.
         03   YEAR              PIC S9(4).
```

A. Level Numbers

The record name, PERSON in the previous example, must be level number 01, and all succeeding items within the record must have level numbers greater than 01. The level numbers need not be consecutive, as they serve only to indicate the relative hierarchy of the record. For example, the following record is identical to the previous two.

```
01  PERSON.
    05  THE-NAME                 PIC X(25).
    05  BIRTH-DATE.
        10  MONTH                PIC X(9).
        10  DAYS                 PIC S99 PACKED-DECIMAL.
        10  YEAR                 PIC S9(4).
```

Increment the levels by a number such as 5 to leave room for subdividing items if later required. Level numbers must be consistent. The following example illustrates this requirement.

```
    [Incorrect: ]               [Correct: ]
    01                          01
        05                          05
            10                          10
        06                          05
```

Items within a record that are not further subdivided are elementary items. They must contain the PIC clause (except for COMP-1 and COMP-2). In the previous record, THE-NAME, MONTH, DAYS, and YEAR are elementary items. The group items subdivided into elementary items are referred to by their names. For example, the entire record is referred to by its name, PERSON in the previous example.

B. Scope of Names

The record name must be unique, but the group and elementary names need not be unique, as long as they can be qualified to make them unique. The same names may appear in other records or within the same record. For example, the PERSON might also have a college graduation date that has a MONTH, DAYS, and YEAR.

```
    05  GRADUATION.
        10  MONTH                PIC X(9).
        10  DAYS                 PIC S99 PACKED-DECIMAL.
        10  YEAR                 PIC S9(4).
```

Now you must qualify the data names to make them unique. You qualify data names by writing them in the hierarchy, from highest level number to lowest,

separated by the word OF or IN. MONTH OF GRADUATION refers to the month
in the graduation date rather than that in the birth date. You can also give the
full hierarchy of data names. You can write MONTH OF BIRTH-DATE as MONTH
OF BIRTH-DATE OF PERSON. You need qualify data names only enough to
make them unique. The following two structures illustrate this.

```
01  A.                                01  J.
     05  B.                                05  K.
          10  V     PIC X.                       10  X     PIC X.
          10  W     PIC X.                       10  W     PIC X.
```

The name B is unique and can be written as B or as B OF A. The name V
is unique and can be written as V, V OF B, V OF A, or V OF B OF A. The
name W is not unique and must be written as W OF B, W OF A, or W OF B
OF A to identify the W in the A record. Unfortunately, this can lead to long
data names, and so, where possible, make the data names unique to avoid long
qualifications.

C. FILLER

The special data name FILLER describes data items in a record that need no
name, such as text within a print line. This saves having to make up a name
that will never be used. FILLER must be an elementary item and contain the
PIC clause. It is often used to pad out records to increase their size. You may
assign FILLER an initial value.

```
01  HEADER.
     05  FILLER                    PIC X(6) VALUE "DATE".
     05  A-DATE.
          10  MONTH                PIC XX.
          10  FILLER               PIC X VALUE "/".
          10  DAYS                 PIC XX.
          10  FILLER               PIC X VALUE "/".
          10  YEAR                 PIC XX.
```

You can also omit FILLER, so that the foregoing is identical to:

```
01  HEADER.
     05                            PIC X(6) VALUE "DATE".
     05 A-DATE.
          10  MONTH                PIC XX.
          10                       PIC X VALUE "/".
          10  DAYS                 PIC XX.
          10                       PIC X VALUE "/".
          10  YEAR                 PIC XX.
```

D. The USAGE Clause

You can code the USAGE data types BINARY, COMP-1, COMP-2, and PACKED-DECIMAL at the group item level to apply to all data items within the group. However, avoid this, because it is easy to mistake the elementary items for external decimal numbers when they are specified to be another data type at the group level. The example on the right makes it clearer that Y and Z are BINARY:

```
05  X BINARY.           [Same as:]   05  X.
      10  Y   PIC S9(5).                   10  Y    PIC S9(5) BINARY.
      10  Z   PIC S9(5).                   10  Z    PIC S9(5) BINARY.
```

E. The VALUE Clause

You can also code the VALUE clause at the group level if all the group items are alphanumeric data items (DISPLAY). The VALUE at the group level must be a figurative constant or a nonnumeric literal. COBOL initializes the group area without regard to the elementary item data types, as if they were all PIC X. The items within the group cannot contain the VALUE, JUST, or SYNC clauses.

```
01  X VALUE SPACES.     [Same as]   01  X.
      05  Y   PIC X(3).                    05  Y    PIC X(3) VALUE SPACES.
      05  Z   PIC X(2).                    05  Z    PIC X(2) VALUE SPACES.
```

III. RECORD ALIGNMENT AND THE SYNC CLAUSE

COBOL does not automatically align BINARY, COMP-1, and COMP-2. If the numbers are not properly aligned, VS COBOL II moves the numbers to a work area to perform arithmetic operations, which may be inefficient. The SYNCHRONIZED clause, abbreviated SYNC, is an option that can be coded for elementary items to align data on the proper word boundary. (VS COBOL II and Microsoft COBOL, but not the ANSI Standard, permit SYNC to be coded for a level 01 item. This acts the same as if all elementary items within it had SYNC coded.) Numbers are unaligned if SYNC is omitted. If SYNC is used for a table, each table element is aligned. SYNC aligns only BINARY, COMP-1, and COMP-2 data items. VS COBOL II aligns data types as follows:

BINARY S9 to S9(4)	Half-word
BINARY S9(5) to S9(18)	Full word
COMP-1	Full word
COMP-2	Double word or eight bytes
All else	Byte boundary, no need for SYNC

VS COBOL II aligns the level number 01 for each record on a double-word boundary. It also aligns the first item in the Data Division on a double-word boundary. It aligns level number 77 items on a full-word boundary.

SYNC is in the ANSI Standard, but the standard leaves the actual synchronization computer-dependent. If you use the IBMCOMP system directive in Microsoft
COBOL, it will assume the same alignment as VS COBOL II.

When data items within a record are aligned, some wasted space, termed
slack bytes, may result. For example, suppose a VS COBOL II data item
aligned on a double word is followed by an item aligned on a full word, and
then followed by an item aligned on a double word. The result is a full word
of 4 slack bytes. Count these slack bytes in determining the size of a record.
The record in the following example is 32 bytes in length.

```
01   A.
     05   B COMP-2 SYNC.
          [Aligned on a double word.]
     05   C                          PIC X(2).
     [Two slack bytes inserted here.]
     05 D                            PIC S9(5) BINARY SYNC.
          [Aligned on a full word.]
     05   E                          COMP-1 SYNC.
          [Aligned on a full word.]
     [Four slack bytes inserted here.]
     05   F                          COMP-2 SYNC.
          [Aligned on a double word.]
```

Slack bytes are confusing. You can avoid them by placing all the double-word
alignment items first in the record, followed by all the full-word alignment
items, followed by all the half-word alignment items, followed by all the remaining items. Another alternative is to not code SYNC and live with whatever
efficiency penalty results for computations. A final alternative is to not use
BINARY, COMP-1, or COMP-2 items in records.

IV. DOCUMENTING RECORDS

Documenting records, especially those describing I/O records, is perhaps the
most important of all program documentation. You can read a program and
understand the computations done on the data from the statements, but unless
you understand the data, the program will have little meaning. There are many
ways to document records, and many installations have detailed standards. The
following are suggestions.

Document the records with comments, placing them on the right side of the
page so that they do not distract from the data descriptions. The data descriptions describe the form of the data, and the comments describe its meaning.
Include the following in the comments:

• A short description of each data item.
• The meaning of values within the item. This applies mainly to flags and codes.

```
      05  FLSA                    PIC X.
*         Exemption code.
*            E - Exempt.
*            N - Nonexempt.
      05  THE-STATUS              PIC X.
*         Marital status.
*            M - Married.
*            S - Single.
```

You should include three other items for I/O records. Some compilers provide the last two items automatically, saving you this tedious work.

- A short description of the file.
- The record length in bytes. The reader will want to know this, and here is the best place to document it.
- The relative byte location of each data item. You need this to specify the sort fields for external sort and to locate data items in a file dump. You must do this anyway to compute the record length, and it is little extra effort to document it at the same time. Place the relative byte locations in a comment following the item. If you must insert a field, all the following relative byte locations must be recomputed. Some compilers compute the relative byte locations and print them on the source listing, obviating the need for the relative byte locations.

   Give the level 01 items a short name and append this name to all items within the record. This way, it is apparent which record they belong to when they are used in the program.

```
******** PAY is the master payroll file.
******** Record length is 400 bytes.
  01  PAY.
      05  PAY-NAME                PIC X(25).
*         Name of person.         Bytes 1-25.
      05  PAY-CODE                PIC X.
*         Type of pay.            Byte 26.
*            H - Hourly.
*            S - Salaried.
      05  PAY-SALARY              PIC S999V99.
*         Hourly rate.            Bytes 27-31.
```

   Documentation of this type is easy to maintain, because it is right there to change when the record description is changed. Keep all the I/O records in a COPY library, as described in Chapter 18, so that all programs using the file will automatically include the file documentation. All the file documentation then exists in one place and is fully descriptive.

V. RECORD OPERATIONS

A. Group Items

You can operate on elementary items within a record the same as any data item, although the data names may have to be qualified to make them unique. Group items named in expressions are treated as elementary alphanumeric data items. Group item names can appear only in nonarithmetic expressions, such as the IF, MOVE, and INSPECT statements. (They may also appear in arithmetic operations that contain the CORR phrase, but this is a different type of operation described below.) The following example illustrates the treatment of group items in expressions.

```
01  Y.
    05  B                           PIC S9(7) PACKED-DECIMAL.
    05  C.
        10  D                       PIC X(10).
        10  E                       PIC S99.
    ■ ■ ■
MOVE SPACES TO Y
```

> [*Blanks are moved to the entire record without conversion, just as if* Y *had been declared as an elementary data item with* PIC X(16). *Note that this moves blanks into* B *and* E, *which are described as numeric items. An error will occur if they are used in an arithmetic expression, because they contain invalid data.*]

```
MOVE ZEROS TO Y
```

> [*Sixteen zero characters are moved to* Y. *This also moves character data into the* PACKED-DECIMAL *identifier* B, *and a data exception will occur if* B *is used in an arithmetic expression. However,* E *now contains valid data.*]

The IF statement can test group or elementary items. It treats a group item as an elementary alphanumeric data item.

```
        IF Y = SPACES THEN  ...         [Y is considered to be PIC X(16).]
```

B. The CORRESPONDING Phrase

You can code the CORRESPONDING phrase, abbreviated CORR, with the MOVE, ADD, and SUBTRACT statements to cause only elements whose qualified names are the same to participate in an operation.

```
    MOVE CORR group-name-1  TO group-name-2
    ADD CORR group-name-1  TO group-name-2
    SUBTRACT CORR group-name-1  FROM group-name-2
```

All elementary items that have the same name and qualification, up to but not including the group names, participate in the operation. The elementary items need not be in the same order or be of the same data types. COBOL will convert items of different data types.

```
01  DATES.
    05  START-DATE.
        10  MONTH                    PIC XX.
        10  DAYS                     PIC S999 PACKED-DECIMAL.
        10  YEAR                     PIC S99.
        10  CENTURY                  PIC S9999.
    05 DAYS-IN-YEAR                  PIC S999.
    05  END-DATE.
        10  YEAR                     PIC S99.
        10  MONTH                    PIC S99.
        10  DAYS                     PIC S99.
    05  YRNDAY.
        10  DAYS-IN-YEAR             PIC S999.
    ■ ■ ■
MOVE CORR START-DATE TO END-DATE
```

Same as

```
MOVE MONTH OF START-DATE TO MONTH OF END-DATE
MOVE DAYS OF START-DATE TO DAYS OF END-DATE
MOVE YEAR OF START-DATE TO YEAR OF END-DATE
```

Elementary item names must have the same qualification to participate in the operation. CENTURY does not participate because it is not an elementary item in END-DATE, and DAYS-IN-YEAR does not participate because its fully qualified names do not match. If the group names contain tables, the tables are ignored. Any FILLER is likewise ignored.

```
01  SOMETHING.
    05  B                            OCCURS 20 TIMES.
        10  C                        PIC X.
        10  D                        PIC X.
    05  FILLER                       PIC X.
    05  E                            PIC X.
```

If SOMETHING were named in a CORR operation, table B and the FILLER would not participate. The group names may be tables or belong to tables, in which case they must be subscripted or indexed. The following statement would be valid for the previous record:

```
MOVE CORR B(1) TO X
```

With a good compiler, the CORR phrase is neither more nor less efficient than individual MOVES, ADDS, and SUBTRACTS. The CORR phrase can make

programs easier to change, especially when corresponding elements are likely
to be added or deleted from records. You can make a single change to the data
descriptions rather than the statements scattered throughout the program.

However, CORR has disadvantages. It may not be obvious, when a data
description is changed, that the execution of Procedure Division statements that
have a CORR phrase may be changed too. In practice, CORR always seems to be
less useful than it would seem—usually because different names always seem
to have already been chosen for the file descriptions your program is using.
And finally, the coding effort you save by using CORR is often more than offset
by having to qualify all the items (MONTH OF START-DATE) because they do
not have unique names.

VI. INITIALIZING RECORDS

A. Initializing Data Items

When a record is used to create an output record, it must first be initialized,
generally by moving spaces to the alphanumeric fields and zeros to the numeric
fields. Consider the following record to be initialized:

```
01  A.
    05  B                       PIC X(10).
    05  C                       PIC S9(5) PACKED-DECIMAL.
    05  D                       PIC X(3).
    05  E                       PIC S9(5) PACKED-DECIMAL.
```

You can initialize the record by coding VALUE clauses to assign initial values
to the elementary items:

```
01  A.
    05  B                       PIC X(10) VALUE SPACES.
    05  C                       PIC S9(5) PACKED-DECIMAL
                                VALUE ZERO.
    05  D                       PIC X(3) VALUE SPACES.
    05  E                       PIC S9(5) PACKED-DECIMAL
                                VALUE ZERO.
```

You can also initialize a record by moving values to the elementary items:

```
MOVE SPACES TO B, D
MOVE ZEROS  TO C, E
```

The easiest way to initialize a record is to move SPACES to the record as a
group item and then move ZEROS to the numeric items.

```
MOVE SPACES TO A
MOVE ZEROS TO C, E
```

B. The INITIALIZE Statement

The INITIALIZE statement saves you having to write several MOVE statements
to initialize data. You write it as

```
INITIALIZE data-name
```

INITIALIZE moves SPACES to all alphabetic, alphanumeric, and alphanumeric
edited items; it moves ZEROS to all numeric and numeric edited items. For
example, the record A at the beginning of this section can be initialized as
follows:

```
INITIALIZE A           [Same as]      MOVE SPACES TO B, D
                                      MOVE ZEROS  TO C, E
```

The *data-name* cannot contain a RENAMES clause or be an index. However, it
can be an indexed data item.
   You can also add the REPLACING clause to the INITIALIZE statement to
restrict the initialization to specific types of data and assign values other than
SPACES and ZEROS.

```
                                    NUMERIC
                                    ALPHABETIC
                                    ALPHANUMERIC
                                    NUMERIC-EDITED
                                    ALPHANUMERIC-EDITED
           INITIALIZE data-name REPLACING _____ BY value
```

The *value* can be an identifier or literal. It must be of a compatible data type
with the *data-name*. For example:

```
INITIALIZE A REPLACING NUMERIC BY 10
```

Same as

```
MOVE 10 TO C, E
```

You can also write several phrases following REPLACING, but you must use a
different category each time. Note also that you code REPLACING only once.

```
INITIALIZE A REPLACING NUMERIC BY 2
                       ALPHANUMERIC BY ALL "X"
```

Same as

```
MOVE 2 TO C, E
MOVE ALL "X" TO B, D
```

When you use the REPLACING for a group item, only elementary items within the group that match the type are initialized. If you use REPLACING for an elementary item and it doesn't match the type, nothing is initialized.

```
INITIALIZE C REPLACING ALPHANUMERIC BY ALL "X"
    [This statement is ignored.]
```

Chapter 9 describes how to assign initial values to tables.

VII.   REDEFINITION OF STORAGE

A.   The REDEFINES Clause

The REDEFINES clause assigns different data names and descriptions to the same storage by redefining one data item to occupy the same storage as another. The general form of writing the REDEFINES clause is:

nn redefining-item REDEFINES *redefined-item*   PIC ...

In the following example, B redefines A to occupy the same storage location.

```
01  OUT-REC.
    05  A                       PIC S9(5) PACKED-DECIMAL.
    05  B REDEFINES A           PIC X(3).
```

The level number of the redefining item, the item to the left of the REDEFINES, must be the same as the level of the redefined item, and they cannot be level 66 or 88. The redefining item can be a data name or FILLER. The redefining item can also be a structure.

```
01  OUT-REC.
    05  AX                      PIC S9(5) PACKED-DECIMAL.
    05  NEW-AX REDEFINES AX     PIC A(3).
            [It is given a name here.]
    05  FILLER REDEFINES AX.
            [It can also be FILLER. ]
        10  FIRST-2             PIC X(2).
        10  NEXT-1              PIC X.
    05      REDEFINES AX.
        [Or you needn't give it a name.]
        10  FIRST-1             PIC X.
        10  NEXT-2              PIC X(2).
```

Don't qualify the redefined item following the REDEFINES, even if the name is not unique. COBOL doesn't need the qualification, because it knows which item you mean from where you place the redefining item containing the REDEFINES.

The redefining item must follow the redefined item, with no intervening nonredefined items. Note that the same area can be redefined more than once.

```
[Incorrect: ]                                [Correct: ]
77   A                PIC X(10).             77   A                PIC X(10).
77   B                PIC X(10).             77   B REDEFINES A PIC X(10).
77   C REDEFINES A PIC X(10).                77   C REDEFINES A PIC X(10).
```

The ANSI Standard doesn't let a redefined item contain a REDEFINES. VS COBOL II and Microsoft COBOL do. For them, you could code the following for C in the previous correct example.

```
                         77   C REDEFINES B PIC X(10).
```

For a level 01 item, the length of the redefined item can be shorter or longer than the redefining item. (However, the redefining item must not be longer than the redefined item if the redefined item is declared EXTERNAL, as described in Chapter 18.)

```
01   A                                    PIC X(10).
01   B REDEFINES A                        PIC X(2).
        [It can be shorter.]
01   C REDEFINES A                        PIC X(20).
        [It can also be longer.]
```

However, if the level is not 01 or the redefined item is declared EXTERNAL, the redefining item must be equal to or shorter than the redefined item.

```
01   A.
     05   B                              PIC X(10).
     05   C REDEFINES B                  PIC X(10).
          [It can be the same.]
     05   D REDEFINES B                  PIC X(2).
          [It can be shorter.]
     05   E REDEFINES B                  PIC X(20).   [Invalid]
          [It can't be longer.]
```

The REDEFINES clause must immediately follow the data name.

```
[Incorrect: ]                             [Correct ]:
77   B     PIC X(5) REDEFINES A.          77   B REDEFINES A      PIC X(5).
```

The redefined item can contain a VALUE clause, but the redefining item cannot—unless it is a level 88 item. The redefining item may contain the SYNC clause, as long as the synchronization does not cause the redefining item to extend beyond the redefined item, when this is not allowed.
   Incorrect:

```
77   A                                    PIC S9(5) BINARY.
77   B REDEFINES A                        PIC S9(5) BINARY VALUE 10.
```

Correct:

```
77  A                           PIC S9(5) BINARY VALUE 10.
77  B REDEFINES A               PIC S9(5) BINARY.
```

Although level 88 items cannot be redefined, both the redefining item and the redefined item may have level 88 condition names.

```
77  A                           PIC S9(5) BINARY SYNC VALUE 10.
88  BIG-A                       VALUE 200.
77  B REDEFINES A               PIC S9(5) BINARY.
88  BIG-B                       VALUE 100.
```

Redefinition can conserve memory storage by allowing the same storage to be reused for different purposes. You must use it for only one purpose at a time. Avoid redefinition, because it leads to confusion and errors. Redefinition is best when used to overlay data of one type with another for files that contain more than one record type. Each record can contain a flag that specifies the record type, and you can interrogate the flag to determine which redefinition item describes the record. (REDEFINES cannot be used for 01 level items in the record area of the File Section as described in Chapter 12. There, you implicitly redefine level 01 records by placing one after the other.) The following example illustrates a record with a field that may contain two data types.

```
01  REC.
    05  REC-TYPE                PIC X.
    05  REC-CHAR                PIC X(4).
    05  REC-NUM REDEFINES REC-CHAR PIC S9(7) PACKED-DECIMAL.
```

This record might contain alphanumeric data, referred to by REC-CHAR, or a packed decimal number, referred to by REC-NUM, depending on the value contained in REC-TYPE. Redefinition also allows data of one type to be stored in a data item of another type without conversion.

```
    MOVE "ABCD" TO REC-CHAR     [REC-NUM also contains "ABCD".]
```

You can also redefine tables to occupy the same storage.

```
01  TABLE-A.
    05  LEVEL-1                 OCCURS 100 TIMES.
        10  X                   PIC S9(5) PACKED-DECIMAL
                                OCCURS 50 TIMES.
01  TABLE-B REDEFINES TABLE-A.
    05  LEVEL-1                 OCCURS 100 TIMES.
        10  Y                   PIC X(3)
                                OCCURS 50 TIMES.
```

The redefined item cannot itself contain an OCCURS clause. However, the redefined item may be subordinate to an item containing an OCCURS clause, but not an OCCURS DEPENDING ON clause. This means that table elements can be redefined.

```
01   TABLE-A.
     05   LEVEL-1                    OCCURS 100 TIMES.
          10   X                     OCCURS 50 TIMES.
               15   Y                PIC S9(5) PACKED-DECIMAL.
               15   Z REDEFINES Y    PIC X(2).
```

An OCCURS DEPENDING ON clause cannot be coded for a redefining item, for a redefined item, or for any item subordinate to them.

B. The RENAMES Clause

The REDEFINES clause just described redefines one record over the same storage area as another. In contrast, the level 66 RENAMES clause allows a single data name to rename a series of data items within a record. There are two forms:

```
66   data-name-1   RENAMES data-name-2 .
```
   [*data-name-1 simply renames data-name-2. This is not particularly useful.*]
```
66   data-name-1   RENAMES data-name-2   THRU data-name-3 .
```
   [*data-name-1 renames all items from data-name-2 through data-name-3.*]

The following example illustrates the RENAMES clause:

```
01   A.
     05   B.
          10   C                     PIC X(3).
          10   D                     PIC X(4).
     05   E                          PIC X(5).
     05   F.
          10   G                     PIC X(6).
          10   H                     PIC X(7).
66   W                               RENAMES C.
```
          [*W is just another name for C.*]
```
66   X                       RENAMES B.
```
          [*X is a group item containing 7 characters and is just another name for B.*]
```
66   Y                       RENAMES B THRU G.
```
          [*Y is a group item containing 18 characters. It consists of the storage of the C, D, E, and G data items.*]

You cannot use *data-name-1* as a qualifier (C OF X is invalid). You can only qualify it with the record name within which it renames items (W OF B is valid). If an elementary item is renamed, the level 66 item assumes the attributes of the item renamed. When group items are renamed, the level 66 item is also a group item.

The level number 66 RENAMES clause must immediately follow the last item in the record description, and you can code several RENAMES clauses for a single record. You cannot rename level numbers 01, 66, 77, and 88 items, but you can rename both elementary items and group items within a record. If the RENAMES *data-name-1* THRU *data-name-2* form is used, *data-name-2* must follow *data-name-1* in the record, and it may be subordinate to it. You cannot rename items that contain an OCCURS clause or are subordinate to an item containing an OCCURS clause. This means that an element of a table cannot be the subject of the RENAMES.

Records contain a single instance of related data. The next chapter describes tables, which allow many instances of such data to be contained.

EXERCISES

1. Assume that a record is to contain an employee's name, social security number, age, date of birth, annual salary, and number of dependents. Define and document the record to contain this information. Define the name so that you can retrieve the initials and the last name.

2. Assume that you are being passed a transaction generated by the computer. Each 80-character line contains 10 fields of 8 characters each. The first character of each field describes the data contained in the remaining 7 characters of the field. The fields are as follows:

First Character	Remainder of Field
1	7 characters
2	3 characters, left justified
3	4 characters, right justified
4	7-digit number
5	2 numbers, one with 3 digits and one with 4 digits
6	5-digit number, left justified, with 2 positions to right of assumed decimal point

Define a record to contain this record and allow you to manipulate it. Edit the numeric data to ensure its validity for COBOL.

3. Assume that an old program is run on a new computer, and it terminates with an error. Fortunately, it tells you the statement number at which it terminated. It terminated in the second of the following two statements:

```
MOVE SPACE TO FIRST-BYTE
MOVE LEFT-PART TO RIGHT-PART
```

Next, you look in the Data Division and find the following record:

```
01  BIG-TABLE.
    05  WHAT-IT-CONTAINS          PIC X(200).
```

```
    05  REDEFINE-IT REDEFINES WHAT-IT-CONTAINS.
        10  FIRST-BYTE              PIC X.
        10  RIGHT-PART              PIC X(199).
01  LEFT-PART REDEFINES BIG-TABLE  PIC X(199).
```

What was the programmer attempting to do? Why might it be failing on the new computer? Is this a good programming practice?

4. Two records are defined as follows:

```
01  ONE.
    02  A.
        03  B                      PIC X(3).
        03  C                      PIC S999 PACKED-DECIMAL.
        03  D.
            04  E                  PIC S9(6) PACKED-DECIMAL.
            04  F                  PIC X(2).
    02  G                          PIC X(6).
    02  H                          PIC X(6).


01  TWO.
    02  J.
        03  D                      PIC X(3).
        03  C                      PIC S9(3) PACKED-DECIMAL.
        03  Q.
            04  E                  PIC S9(6) PACKED-DECIMAL.
            04  F                  PIC X(2).
    02  R                          PIC X(6).
    02  S                          PIC X(6).
```

Note the elements that participate in the following statements.

```
MOVE TWO TO ONE
MOVE CORR TWO TO ONE
MOVE CORR J TO A OF ONE
MOVE S TO G
```

5. Use the INITIALIZE statement to initialize the records in Problem 4 with values as follows:
  ONE: Initialize nonnumeric identifiers to blank and numeric identifiers to 0.
  TWO: Initialize nonnumeric identifiers to all "-" and numeric identifiers to 1.

9

Tables

For quick reference, the various phrases used in defining tables are coded in the following order:

PIC/USAGE (Can be in any position.)

OCCURS

DEPENDING ON

ASCENDING/DESCENDING KEY

INDEXED BY

A *table,* also termed an *array,* is an arrangement of elements in one or more dimensions. Tables, powerful data processing tools, are much more common than one might expect. You can express the United States as a table containing 50 states as elements. The calendar can be represented as a table containing 12 months as table elements. Such a table has one *dimension;* that is a single sequence of elements. The range of elements constitutes the *bounds* of the table; the bounds of the calendar table are 1 to 12.

Tables may have more than one dimension. A table with two dimensions is termed a *matrix,* with the first dimension referred to as the *row,* and the second dimension as the *column.* The seats of an auditorium are elements of a matrix, with rows and columns. COBOL tables may have a maximum of seven dimensions. We might make the auditorium table a three-dimensional table, with the third dimension representing the auditorium within the city. If we allow for 100 rows, 75 columns, and 10 auditoriums in the city, the table would have $100 \times 75 \times 10$ or 75,000 table elements representing auditorium seats.

To refer to a specific element, the table is *subscripted.* If the three-dimensional auditorium table is named SEAT, we can refer to the twelfth seat in the fifth row of the third auditorium as SEAT(5, 12, 3). The subscript may be an integer literal, an integer elementary data item, or a special data item called an *index,* which is described later in this chapter.

An important property of tables is their ability to hold several records in storage for computations. Suppose that a file contains numbers that are to be printed in a column of a report, with 50 lines per page. Now suppose that the sum of the numbers on each page is to be printed at the top of the page before the numbers themselves are printed. We can read 50 numbers into a table, sum the elements of the table, and print this total at the top of the page. Then we can print the 50 numbers from the table.

Now suppose that 100 numbers are to be printed in two columns on a page, with the first 50 numbers in the left column and the next 50 numbers on the right. We could define a table of 100 elements to contain the page. However, it is easier to define a two-dimensional table with the first dimension representing the line on the page (1 to 50), and the second representing the column (1 or 2).

Furthermore, suppose that the first page of the report is to contain the total of all numbers in the report. We can define a three-dimensional table, with the first dimension representing the line on the page, the second dimension the column, and the third dimension the page of the report. By storing the entire report in a table, we can sum the numbers to print the total first, and then print the numbers from the table. A 100-page report would have $100 \times 2 \times 50$ or 10,000 table elements.

The use of tables may also reduce the number of statements required, which in turn may save coding time and internal storage. But what is more important, it is easier to comprehend a few statements than many. As an example illustrating the benefits of a table, we'll use a record containing the population of the 50 states described without the use of a table:

```
01  POPULATION-COUNT              PIC S9(11) PACKED-DECIMAL.
01  STATES.
    05  ALABAMA                   PIC S9(11) PACKED-DECIMAL.
    05  ARKANSAS                  PIC S9(11) PACKED-DECIMAL.
    :
    05  WYOMING                   PIC S9(11) PACKED-DECIMAL.
```

To compute the total population of all states, we would code the following:

```
MOVE ZERO TO POPULATION-COUNT
ADD ALABAMA TO POPULATION-COUNT
ADD ARKANSAS TO POPULATION-COUNT
:
ADD WYOMING TO POPULATION-COUNT
```

Now suppose that we wish to determine the largest and smallest populations of the states. This would require the following:

```
77  MIN                          PIC S9(11) PACKED-DECIMAL.
77  MAX                          PIC S9(11) PACKED-DECIMAL.
    ■ ■ ■
MOVE ZERO TO MAX
MOVE 99999999999 TO MIN
```

```
IF ALABAMA < MIN
    THEN MOVE ALABAMA TO MIN
END-IF
IF ALABAMA > MAX
    THEN MOVE ALABAMA TO MAX
END-IF
  :
```

This would be tedious to code, and if California were to be split into two states or the Virginias were to be reunited, the program would require several changes. We can reduce the amount of coding, make the operations more understandable, and allow for change by making the state populations a table. You specify a table with the OCCURS clause:

```
01  STATES.
    05  NO-STATES             PIC S9(4) BINARY VALUE 50.
    05  POPULATION            OCCURS 50 TIMES
                              INDEXED BY IX
                              PIC S9(11) PACKED-DECIMAL.
           [POPULATION is described as a table with 50 elements.]
```

The population is then summed and the minimum and maximum are computed as follows:

```
MOVE ZERO TO POPULATION-COUNT, MAX
MOVE 99999999999 TO MIN
PERFORM VARYING IX FROM 1 BY 1 UNTIL IX > NO-STATES
    [IX is used as a subscript to refer to individual elements of the table.]
    ADD POPULATION(IX) TO POPULATION-COUNT
    IF POPULATION(IX) < MIN
        THEN MOVE POPULATION(IX) TO MIN
    END-IF
    IF POPULATION(IX) > MAX
        THEN MOVE POPULATION(IX) TO MAX
    END-IF
END-PERFORM
```

Now if a new state is added, you can make the change in the Data Division rather than the Procedure Division.

I. FIXED-LENGTH TABLE DESCRIPTIONS

A. The OCCURS Clause

You describe fixed-length tables by appending the OCCURS n TIMES clause to the data description. The n, an integer literal greater than zero, specifies the table size. You cannot code the OCCURS clause for 01, 66, 77, or 88 level data items. In the following example, A-TABLE is described as a single-dimensional table containing 30 elements:

```
01  SOMETHING.
    05  A-TABLE                    OCCURS 30 TIMES
                                   PIC S9(3) PACKED-DECIMAL.
```

Note the following is invalid, because OCCURS cannot be coded for the 01 level.

```
01  SOMETHING                      OCCURS 30 TIMES    [Invalid]
                                   PIC S9(3) PACKED-DECIMAL.
```

Note also that OCCURS can be coded for a group item or an elementary data item.

```
01  SOMETHING.
    05  A-TABLE                    OCCURS 30 TIMES
                                   PIC S9(3) PACKED-DECIMAL.
    05  B-TABLE                    OCCURS 30 TIMES.
        10  THING-1                PIC X(4).
        10  THING-2                PIC X(4).
```

COBOL tables may have from one to seven dimensions. (Microsoft COBOL allows sixteen.) You describe multidimensional tables as records, with each dimension specified by a lower-level item. The following example describes Y as a 2 by 10 by 20 table:

```
01  A-RECORD.
    05  LEVEL-1                    OCCURS 2 TIMES.
        10  LEVEL-2                OCCURS 10 TIMES.
            15  Y                  OCCURS 20 TIMES
                                   PIC S9(3) PACKED-DECIMAL.
```

You don't need to give names to levels where you have no use for the name. You could code the foregoing as

```
01  A-RECORD.
    05                             OCCURS 2 TIMES.
        10                         OCCURS 10 TIMES.
            15  Y                  OCCURS 20 TIMES
                                   PIC S9(3) PACKED-DECIMAL.
```

B. Initializing Tables

Individual elements of a table can all be assigned the same initial value. The following example initializes each element of the table to zero:

```
01  A-RECORD.
    05  A-TABLE                    OCCURS 100 TIMES
                                   PIC S9(5) PACKED-DECIMAL
                                   VALUE 0.
```

If the elements are each to contain different values, you can either move values to the elements or use the INITIALIZE statement. Alternatively, you can describe a record containing several data items with initial values and then redefine the record as a table. The following is an example of this.

```
01  A-RECORD.
    05  FILLER                  PIC S9(5) PACKED-DECIMAL
                                VALUE 2.
    05  FILLER                  PIC S9(5) PACKED-DECIMAL
                                VALUE 3.
    05  FILLER                  PIC S9(5) PACKED-DECIMAL
                                VALUE 6.
01  Y REDEFINES A-RECORD.
    05  A-TABLE                 OCCURS 3 TIMES
                                PIC S9(5) PACKED-DECIMAL.
```

You can also use INITIALIZE to initialize a table, as shown in the following example. Note that indexes and FILLER data items are not initialized.

```
01  RECORD-OUT.
    05  SCHOOL                  PIC X(25).
    05  FILLER                  PIC X(10).
    05  CHILDREN                OCCURS 600 TIMES
                                INDEXED BY IX.
        10  AGES                PIC S9(3) PACKED-DECIMAL.
        10  NAMES               PIC X(25).
■ ■ ■
INITIALIZE RECORD-OUT REPLACING ALPHANUMERIC BY SPACES
                      NUMERIC BY ZEROS
```

Same as

```
INITIALIZE RECORD-OUT
```

Same as

```
MOVE SPACES TO SCHOOL OF RECORD-OUT
PERFORM VARYING IX FROM 1 BY 1 UNTIL IX > 600
  MOVE ZERO TO AGES OF CHILDREN OF RECORD-OUT(IX)
  MOVE SPACES TO NAMES OF CHILDREN OF RECORD-OUT(IX)
END-PERFORM
```

You can use INITIALIZE for a table that contains an OCCURS clause, but not an OCCURS DEPENDING ON. That is, you can't use INITIALIZE for a variable-length table.

You can initialize a complete table only by specifying a group item that contains the complete table. In the previous table, both of these would be invalid because they are not group items containing the entire table:

```
INITIALIZE CHILDREN      [Invalid]
INITIALIZE AGES          [Invalid]
```

C. Initializing Complex Structures

If the record is to be initialized from several places within the program, you can place the initialization in a paragraph and then perform it. Now consider the following record. The 600 elements of INCREMENT-VALUE are to be set to values of 1 to 600, and the elements of DECREMENT-VALUE are to be set to values of 600 to 1, as shown.

```
01  RECORD-OUT.
    05  INCREMENTS                    OCCURS 600 TIMES
                                      INDEXED BY IX.
        10  INCREMENT-VALUE           PIC S9(3) PACKED-DECIMAL.
        10  DECREMENT-VALUE           PIC S9(3) PACKED-DECIMAL.
77  DEC-NO                            PIC S9(3) PACKED-DECIMAL.
    ■ ■ ■
    MOVE 600 TO DEC-NO
    PERFORM VARYING IX FROM 1 BY 1 UNTIL IX > 600
      SET INCREMENT-VALUE(IX) TO IX
      MOVE DEC-NO TO DECREMENT-VALUE(IX)
      SUBTRACT 1 FROM DEC-NO
    END-PERFORM
```

We can initialize the table in a loop, but if the record had to be reinitialized many times, this would be wasteful. A more efficient way to accomplish this, at some cost in storage, is to define a new record that contains the same number of characters as the record to be written. We can initialize the original record only once and move it to the new record. Then, whenever we wish to initialize the original record, we move the new record to it. This also works well when initial values are assigned to the first record or when you compute the initialization values within the program.

```
01  ZERO-IT                          PIC X(2400).
        [Same size as RECORD-OUT.]
    ■ ■ ■
    MOVE 600 TO DEC-NO
    PERFORM VARYING IX FROM 1 BY 1 UNTIL IX > 600
      SET INCREMENT-VALUE(IX) TO IX
      MOVE DEC-NO TO DECREMENT-VALUE(IX)
      SUBTRACT 1 FROM DEC-NO
    END-PERFORM
    MOVE RECORD-OUT TO ZERO-IT
```

This initializes the record and saves a copy of it in ZERO-IT. Now you can initialize the record very efficiently by moving ZERO-IT back to it:

```
MOVE ZERO-IT TO RECORD-OUT
```

D. Subscripting Tables

In the table just defined, Y must be subscripted to refer to a specific element. The subscripts correspond to the order of the OCCURS clauses. Y(2, 10, 20) refers to the last element in the table. COBOL stores tables in row-major order, with the rightmost subscript increasing most rapidly. Thus, the elements of the Y table are stored in the order Y(1, 1, 1), Y(1, 1, 2), ..., Y(1, 1, 20), Y(1, 2, 1), ..., Y(2, 10, 20). VS COBOL II limits the elements of a table to 16,777,215 bytes.

You can describe group items as tables. The following record describes 50 states, 5 rivers within each state, 20 counties within each state, and 10 cities within each county:

```
01  NATION.
    05  STATE                      OCCURS 50 TIMES.
        10 STATE-NAME              PIC X(25).
        10 RIVER                   OCCURS 5 TIMES
                                   PIC X(25).
        10 COUNTY                  OCCURS 20 TIMES.
            15 CITY                OCCURS 10 TIMES.
                20 CITY-NAME       PIC X(25).
                20 CITY-SIZE       PIC S9(7) PACKED-DECIMAL.
```

You write the subscripts after the last qualifier name of a record:

```
STATE(1) or STATE OF NATION(1)
```
  [*Refers to the first* STATE *group item.*]
```
COUNTY(2, 3)
```
  [*Refers to the third* COUNTY *of the second* STATE *group item.*]
```
RIVER OF STATE(2, 3)
```
  [*Refers to the third* RIVER *element of the second* STATE *group item.*]
```
CITY-NAME OF CITY OF COUNTY OF STATE OF NATION(4, 3, 2)
```
  [*Refers to the* CITY-NAME *element of the second* CITY *group item of the third* COUNTY *group item of the fourth* STATE *group item.*]

Subscripts must be positive, nonzero integer literals or elementary data items that lie within the bounds of the table. That is, their value can range from 1 to the maximum table size. VS COBOL II literals are slightly more efficient than identifiers as subscripts, and the most efficient data type for subscripts in VS COBOL II is PIC S9(4) BINARY. The subscript may be qualified but not subscripted. That is, A(J OF K) is valid, but A(I(J)) is not.

When a data item is subscripted, there must always be the same number of subscripts as there are dimensions in the table; that is, the same number of subscripts as there are OCCURS clauses:

```
A(I, J, K)
```
   [Blanks required following the commas, as shown.]

E. Table Indexes

In addition to integers and elementary data items, a subscript can be an *index*, which is a special data type used only to refer to table elements just as are subscripts. As such, they are generally more efficient as subscripts than are elementary data items. You describe indexes with the INDEXED BY phrase of the OCCURS clause. The following example describes BX as an index for table B.

```
01  A.
    05  B                         OCCURS 10 TIMES
                                  INDEXED BY BX
                                  PIC S9(3) PACKED-DECIMAL.
```

The index defined for a table can be used only to index that table. BX above can be used only to index the A table. (VS COBOL II allows an index to be used for any table.) You can use indexes in combination with literals or elementary data items. For example, if B were a three-dimensional table, you could code:

```
MOVE B(index, identifier, integer) TO ...
```

Arithmetic statements, such as ADD and COMPUTE, cannot operate on indexes. An index is a four-byte binary item. You can define several indexes for each dimension of a table, and only those defined can be used to index that dimension of the table. The general form of the INDEXED phrase is as follows.

```
INDEXED BY index-1, index-2, ..., index-n
```

VS COBOL II permits 12 indexes to be defined for a single item. The *indexes* are any unique, valid COBOL name with at least one letter alphabetic, and they are defined as indexes for only that dimension of the table. The following example shows the specification of two indexes for each level of a three-dimensional table.

```
01  A.
    05  B                         OCCURS 4 TIMES
                                  INDEXED BY BX1, BX2.
        10  C                     OCCURS 6 TIMES
                                  INDEXED BY CX1, CX2.
            15  D                 OCCURS 10 TIMES
                                  INDEXED BY DX1, DX2
                                  PIC S9(3) PACKED-DECIMAL.
```

Note that INDEXED BY must follow the OCCURS clause. You can code them
before or after any PIC clause.

```
[Correct: ]                              [Incorrect: ]
15  D PIC X(4) OCCURS 10 TIMES           15  D PIC X(4) INDEXED BY DX
            INDEXED BY DX.                       OCCURS 10 TIMES.
15  E OCCURS 10 TIMES                    15  E INDEXED BY EX
       INDEXED BY EX PIC X(4).                   OCCURS 10 TIMES PIC X(4).
```

F. Relative Indexing

You can code both indexes and elementary data items plus or minus an integer
literal. This is termed *relative indexing*. Notice that you must leave a space
before and after the plus or minus:

   table (*data-name* ± *integer, ...*)

(If either the *data-name* or *identifier* is signed, they must be positive.) The
following indexes are then valid for array D:

```
D(BX1 + 2, CX1 - 3, DX1)
```

If BX1 was set to 1, CX1 to 6, and DX1 to 7, the previous item would be the
same as D(3, 3, 7). You can only code plus or minus an integer literal; not
plus or minus an elementary data item or another index. In VS COBOL II, the
integer cannot be greater than 32,765.

G. Index Data Items

An index data item is an index that is not associated with any table. You can
use them only to save the values of other indexes. They are described by:

```
nn   index-name                      INDEX.
```

For example:

```
01  AN-INDEX                         INDEX.
```

The *index-name* is any unique, valid COBOL name. Index data items can
contain only index values.

```
SET AN-INDEX TO 1    [Invalid. Not set to an index value.]
SET AN-INDEX TO IX   [Valid if IX is an index.]
```

Index data items cannot themselves be used to index a table. You can manipulate indexes and index data items only with the SET and SEARCH statements,
in relational conditions such as in a PERFORM VARYING, and in the USING
phrase. Index data items also participate in a group move with the MOVE state-

ment, but you can move them only to other index data items. You cannot name an elementary index data item in a MOVE.

```
MOVE AN-INDEX TO A-NUM      [Invalid. Index item can't be named in a MOVE. ]
```

H. The SET Statement

The SET statement manipulates indexes and has the following form:

```
SET index-1, index-2, ..., index-n TO item
```

You can set one or more *indexes* to an *item*. The *item* may be an integer numeric literal or identifier, another index, or an index data item. Numeric literals must be positive nonzero integers.

```
SET IX1 TO 10
SET IX1, IX2 TO IX3
```

You cannot use the MOVE statement for indexes; you use the SET statement instead. You can also set one or more integer numeric identifiers to the current value of an index.

```
SET identifier-1, identifier-2, ..., identifier-n TO index
SET A, B TO IX1
SET C TO IX2
```

You can increment or decrement one or more indexes with a value. The *value* can be an integer numeric literal or identifier. It can have a positive or negative value.

```
SET index-1, index-2, ..., index-n UP BY value
SET index-1, index-2, ..., index-n DOWN BY value
SET IX3 UP BY 3
SET IX3, IX4 DOWN BY 5
```

Indexes can appear in relational conditions, such as those in the IF statement, and they participate in the operation as if they were subscripts. If an index is compared to a nonindex item, COBOL automatically converts the index to a subscript value for the operation. Index data items, those not described for a table, cannot be converted to subscripts, because they are not described for a specific table. Therefore, you can compare them only to other indexes or index data items.

Functionally, indexes are a redundant language feature. They permit the compiler writer to make them more efficient than subscripts. The actual contents of the index are compiler-dependent. In VS COBOL II, the index contains the relative byte location of the element within the table. COBOL must convert a subscript to the relative byte location each time the table element is referenced, and indexes eliminate this conversion. However, the gain in efficiency is often minimal. Such scientific programming languages as FORTRAN, PL/I, C, BA-SIC, Pascal, ALGOL, and APL, in which tables are used much more than in COBOL, do not have a special data type for indexes. There is no complaint from them about efficiency.

The restrictions on indexes sometimes lead to convoluted programming that negates some of their efficiency. Index values are defined only for the bounds of the table—1 to the maximum entries in the table. If a table has 20 elements, the index for that table should contain only the values 1 to 20. Zero is not a valid value for an index, and the following statement is in error.

```
SET IX TO ZERO     [Invalid ]
```

In the following statements, VS COBOL II gives a result of 1, but Microsoft COBOL gives a garbage result:

```
SET IX TO 1
SET IX DOWN BY 1  [A zero value is undefined.]
SET IX UP BY 1     [An undefined value plus 1 is still undefined.]
```

Indexes can be zero or one more than the table size to terminate a PERFORM. The following is typical:

```
01  A-RECORD.
    05  A-TABLE                      OCCURS 1000 TIMES
                                     INDEXED BY AN-INDEX
                                     PIC S9(4) BINARY.

    ■ ■ ■

PERFORM VARYING AN-INDEX FROM 1 BY 1
       UNTIL AN-INDEX > 1000
```

Or:

```
PERFORM VARYING AN-INDEX FROM 1000 BY -1
       UNTIL AN-INDEX < 1
```

The loop will terminate properly when AN-INDEX is set to 1001 or 0. However, once outside the loop, these values are undefined. A value greater than the size of the table generally causes no problem, but zero values can. Consequently, don't use indexes if you decrement a loop and need to test the index for a value of zero; use an identifier as a subscript instead.

Indexes make debugging harder, because they cannot appear in DISPLAY statements. If IX is an index, the following statement is illegal:

```
DISPLAY IX
```

You must set a normal numeric data item to the index and then display the data item:

```
SET SOMETHING TO IX
DISPLAY SOMETHING
```

These examples illustrate some of the problems in the use of indexes. The
SEARCH statement requires that tables have indexes, but give careful consideration in using them for other purposes.

COBOL compilers generally don't check indexes or subscripts to see if they
fall within the bounds of a table. (The VS COBOL II SSRANGE compile and run-
time options and the Microsoft COBOL BOUND compile option, all described
in Chapter 17, cause subscripts to be checked.) The result is that indexing
or subscripting beyond the bounds of a table will cause errors. If an item is
moved from a table with an incorrect subscript, its contents are unpredictable,
and this may not be discovered until later. If an item is moved to a table with
an incorrect subscript, it may be moved into another data item or even wipe out
code within the program. The error may not manifest itself until later, when the
other data item is used or the code is executed. If TABLE-X has 100 elements,
the following statement might wipe out parts of the program itself:

```
MOVE 10000 TO A-NUM
MOVE ZEROS TO TABLE-X(A-NUM)
    [Zeros are moved to somewhere in the program, but not within TABLE-X.]
```

II. VARIABLE-LENGTH TABLES

COBOL can describe tables in which the number of table elements is specified
by a data item. For example, a census record for a person might contain a
data item specifying the number of children, followed by a variable-length
table containing their names. You use variable-length tables for variable-size
I/O records, in which the record itself specifies the number of table elements
to be transmitted. Such variable-size records reduce the record size and may
increase the I/O efficiency. You also use variable-length tables when the number
of elements in a table may vary. Once you set the table length, a SEARCH
statement referencing the table knows the table length and will search only the
current size of the table. Chapter 20 describes how to use variable-length tables
as variable-length character strings.

The OCCURS DEPENDING ON *size* clause describes variable-length tables.
The *size* is a numeric integer data item that contains the current table length.
COBOL allocates storage for variable-length tables for the maximum occurrences that the table can have. Thereafter, the occurrences of the table vary
depending on the contents of the *size* data item. When the table is written,
only the number of table elements specified by the *size* data item are transmitted. The general form for the description of variable-length tables is as
follows:

```
01  record-name .
      05  size                        PIC ...
      05  table                       OCCURS min  TO max TIMES
                                      DEPENDING ON size.
```

- *min:* The minimum occurrences of the table. It must be a numeric integer literal of value zero or larger, but less than *max*. The zero value permits a table to have zero entries, allowing the SEARCH statement to work properly for an empty table. VS COBOL II and Microsoft COBOL let you omit the *min* TO *max,* assuming a value of 1 for them.
- *max:* The maximum occurrences of the table. It must be a numeric integer literal greater than *min*.
- *size:* A numeric integer data item set to values from *min* to *max* to specify the current number of occurrences of the table. It cannot lie within the table being defined. That is, it cannot be within or subordinate to the item with the OCCURS DEPENDING ON. The *size* must also be in a fixed portion of the record. This means that it cannot follow an OCCURS DEPENDING ON within the same structure.

The following example describes TABLE-X as a table with a maximum of 100 elements, and it makes the current occurrences of TABLE-X depend on the contents of IX:

```
01  A-RECORD.
    05  IX                        PIC S9(4) BINARY.
        [Must appear before TABLE-X in the record, because TABLE-X has an OCCURS
        DEPENDING ON.]
    05  TABLE-X                    OCCURS 1 TO 100 TIMES
                                   DEPENDING ON IX
                                   PIC S9(5) PACKED-DECIMAL.
```

When IX is assigned a value, the table acts as if it were described to be that size. If IX is set to 75 and the record is written out, only 75 elements of table TABLE-X are written.

```
    MOVE 75 TO IX
    WRITE OUT-X FROM A-RECORD
    [A-RECORD consists of IX and 75 occurrences of TABLE-X.]
```

Items containing the DEPENDING ON clause and items subordinate to them can be assigned initial values. The initial values are assigned for the maximum number of occurrences.

In the ANSI Standard, a group item containing a DEPENDING ON clause may be followed, within that record, only by items subordinate to it. Thus, a group item containing a DEPENDING ON clause must be the last group item of its level or higher in the record. For example, the following are not permitted in the ANSI Standard:

```
01  A-TABLE.
    05  SIZE-1                     PIC S9(4) BINARY.
    05  SIZE-2                     PIC S9(4) BINARY.
```

```
    05  PART-1                     OCCURS 1 TO 5 TIMES
                                   DEPENDING ON SIZE-1.
        10  PART-2                 OCCURS 1 TO 5 TIMES
                                   DEPENDING ON SIZE-2
                                   PIC X(4).
```
    [*Invalid*—OCCURS DEPENDING ON *can't be subordinate to the* OCCURS *in* PART-1.]
```
    05  PART-3                     PIC X(30).
```
    [*Invalid*—OCCURS DEPENDING ON *must be followed only by subordinate items.*]

In VS COBOL II and Microsoft COBOL, subordinate items can contain the OCCURS DEPENDING ON clause in their descriptions. You can also follow the OCCURS DEPENDING ON with nonsubordinate items. The preceding example would be valid in VS COBOL II and Microsoft COBOL.

Nonrelational data base management systems make extensive use of varying-size records. Each related portion of a record is termed a *segment*. In a variable-length table, the segment may be repeated—termed a *repeating segment*. There may be several repeating segments within a record, and the repeating segments may themselves contain repeating segments. For example, the record for a school might have a repeating segment for each administrator and a repeating segment for each teacher. Then, for each teacher segment, there may be a repeating segment for each student. VS COBOL II and Microsoft COBOL permit several DEPENDING ON phrases to be described for items subordinate to group items with the DEPENDING ON phrase. This gives some of the facility required for data bases, but data base systems generally require a specialized language. However, COBOL serves as a host language to many generalized data base management systems.

III. **THE** SEARCH **STATEMENT**

The SEARCH statement searches a table for a specific entry. The simplest and most efficient way of retrieving elements from a table is to use a subscript or index to address the table directly. However, in many applications this is not possible. Suppose that a table representing a calendar contains 12 elements, for the number of days per month. Then, suppose that we are to read in transactions containing a date and retrieve the number of days in the month. A date containing the month as a number from 1 to 12, such as 12/21/96, would allow us to subscript the table directly. But what if the month is in text form, such as JANUARY or FEBRUARY? Then we must store the month name in the table, along with the days, and search the table for the matching month. The two usual means of doing this are a sequential search and a binary search. One further technique, the hash search, is described in the next section, and is used less often.

COBOL provides the SEARCH statement to perform a sequential or binary search to locate elements in a table. It functions like the IF/THEN/ELSE statement: SEARCH searches a table for a specified element; if found, take one action; if not found, take another action.

A *sequential search* examines each element of a table serially and may be used regardless of the order of the table elements. A *binary search* requires the elements of the table to be arranged in ascending or descending order. The binary search begins in the middle of the table. It continues to the middle of the lower or upper half of the table, depending on whether the current element was high or low. This continues until the element is found or the table is exhausted.

A binary search is more efficient for large tables than is a sequential search, although it requires the table to be in sort order. Suppose that we are trying to guess a number from 1 to 100, and that the number is 64. With a sequential search we would guess 1, 2, 3, ..., 64, requiring a total of 64 tries. With a binary search, our first guess is 50 (too low). But we now know that the number must be in the range from 51 to 100. With the first guess we have cut the size of the table we need to search in half. Our next guess is 74 (too high), 62 (too low), 68 (too high), 65 (too high), 63 (too low), 64 (found). Thus, the 64 is found with only 7 searches. Notice that with each guess, we cut the size of the table that must be searched in half. The larger the table, the more efficient the binary search becomes. To locate the number 643 in a table of 1000 elements would require 643 sequential searches, but only 9 binary searches.

To locate an element in a table with a sequential search, the number of searches is on the order of $N/2$, where N is the number of entries in the table. For a binary search, the number of searches is on the order of $N \log_2 N$. Note also that this assumes that the entry is in the table to find. If the entry is not in the table to find, the number of sequential searches is N, whereas the number of binary searches is still $N \log_2 N$.

A sequential search is slightly faster for small tables than is a binary search. A binary search becomes more efficient than a sequential search when there are roughly 60 elements in the table,[1] excluding the time it may take to place the table in sort order for the binary search. Use a binary search if the table is in ascending or descending order. If a large, unordered table is searched often, sort it and use a binary search.

A. Sequential Search

You write the sequential SEARCH statement as follows:

```
SET index TO start
SEARCH table
  AT END imperative-statements
  WHEN condition
        imperative-statements
  ⋮
  WHEN condition
        imperative-statements
END-SEARCH
```

Set the *index* of *table* to an initial value, usually 1, before executing the SEARCH statement. If table has several indexes, set the first index listed in the OCCURS clause, because it is used in the search. The search begins with this element, and COBOL applies the WHEN phrases in the order in which you code them. If any *condition* is true, the search terminates with the *index* pointing to the element satisfying the WHEN phrase, and the *imperative-statements* are executed. If no *condition* is true, the *index* is incremented by 1, and the search continues. If the entire table is searched without a *condition* being met, the AT END phrase executes, and the *index* has no predictable value.

- *table:* A table that must have the OCCURS clause and INDEXED BY phrase in its description. The *table* cannot be subscripted or indexed in SEARCH— SEARCH A(IX) is invalid. If the initial *index* value exceeds the size of *table,* the AT END phrase is immediately executed.

- AT END *imperative-statements:* An optional phrase that causes the *imperative-statements* to execute if the entire table is searched without finding the element. Unless one of the *imperative-statements* is a GO TO, execution then continues with the next executable statement following the SEARCH statement. Execution also continues there if the AT END phrase is omitted. In either case, the *index* has no predictable value.

- WHEN *condition imperative-statement: The condition* may be a compound condition connected by the logical operations AND, OR, or NOT. The *imperative-statements* execute when a condition is true, and unless they contain a GO TO, execution then continues with the next executable statement following the SEARCH statement. The *index* points to the table element found. CONTINUE may be coded as the *imperative-statements,* and execution immediately continues with the next executable statement when an element is found.

The following table is set up to contain the names and ages of people:

```
01  PERSON-RECORD.
    05  PERSON                      OCCURS 1000 TIMES
                                    INDEXED BY IP.
        10  SURNAME                 PIC X(5).
        10  AGE                     PIC S9(3) PACKED-DECIMAL.
```

The following statements search the table for a person named SMITH:

```
SET IP TO 1
SEARCH PERSON
  AT END DISPLAY "SMITH NOT FOUND."
  WHEN SURNAME(IP) = "SMITH"
      PERFORM A20-FOUND-SMITH
END-SEARCH
```

The following statements find the first person less than 21 years old:

```
SET IP TO 1
SEARCH PERSON
  AT END DISPLAY "NO ONE UNDER 21"
  WHEN AGE(IP) < 21
       DISPLAY SURNAME(IP)
END-SEARCH
```

Suppose we wanted to search the table to find all people less than 21 years old. For this, we begin the search with the first element of the table and perform the search within a loop:

```
SET IP TO 1
MOVE "N" TO QUIT-FLAG
PERFORM UNTIL QUIT-FLAG = "Y"
  SEARCH PERSON
    AT END
       DISPLAY "NO MORE UNDER 21"
       MOVE "Y" TO QUIT-FLAG
    WHEN AGE(IP) < 21
       DISPLAY SURNAME(IP)
       IF IP = 1000
          THEN MOVE "Y" TO QUIT-FLAG
          ELSE SET IP UP BY 1
       END-IF
       [This prevents setting IP to greater than the table size.]
  END-SEARCH
```

Suppose now that we wish to read in a list of names and add each unique name to the end of the PERSON table. There will be a varying number of elements in the PERSON table. One way to do this is to code the DEPENDING ON phrase in the PERSON table. Another method is to set the first element of the table to some unique characters, such as HIGH-VALUES. As each name is read, the table is searched for the name. If the name is found in the table, it is not stored, because it is already in the table. Another WHEN clause also looks for HIGH-VALUES and, if found, stores the name at that point in the table and sets the next element to HIGH-VALUES. The following example illustrates this technique:

```
MOVE HIGH-VALUES TO SURNAME(1)
```

Now assume that a record is read in, and the person's surname is contained in THE-NAME:

```
SET IP TO 1
SEARCH PERSON
```

```
      AT END DISPLAY "PERSON TABLE FULL."
      WHEN SURNAME(IP) = HIGH-VALUES
          MOVE THE-NAME TO SURNAME(IP)
          IF IP < 1000
             THEN MOVE HIGH-VALUES TO SURNAME(IP + 1)
          END-IF
      WHEN SURNAME(IP) = THE-NAME
             CONTINUE
   END-SEARCH
```

Now here is the same example, this time using the OCCURS DEPENDING ON:

```
01  PERSON-RECORD.
    05  NO-PEOPLE                  PIC S9(4) BINARY.
    05  PERSON                     OCCURS 0 TO 1000 TIMES
                                   DEPENDING ON NO-PEOPLE
                                   INDEXED BY IP.
        10  SURNAME                PIC X(5).
        10  AGE                    PIC S9(3) PACKED-DECIMAL.
        ▪ ▪ ▪
    MOVE ZERO TO NO-PEOPLE
```

NO-PEOPLE is the number of occurrences in the table. Now if we assume that THE-NAME contains a name, we can add it to the table by coding

```
   SET IP TO 1
   SEARCH PERSON
     AT END
       IF NO-PEOPLE = 1000
          THEN DISPLAY "PERSON TABLE FULL."
          ELSE ADD 1 TO NO-PEOPLE
               MOVE THE-NAME TO SURNAME(NO-PEOPLE)
       END-IF
     WHEN SURNAME(IP) = THE-NAME
          CONTINUE
   END-SEARCH
```

If you search a table containing a variable number of entries, you must always limit the search to the number of entries in the table. Otherwise, you would continue the search past the entries stored in the table, and since these entries contain unpredictable values, the results too are unpredictable. The DEPENDING ON phrase limits the search. If you don't code it, limit the search with a WHEN clause by testing when the index exceeds the table size. Or, if you are using HIGH-VALUES to mark the end of the table, look for them.

```
   SET IP TO 1
   SEARCH PERSON
```

```
      AT END DISPLAY "NOT FOUND IN TABLE."
      WHEN SURNAME(IP) = HIGH-VALUES
          DISPLAY "NOT FOUND IN TABLE."
      WHEN ...
   END-SEARCH
```

A sequential search is more efficient if the most frequently retrieved elements are placed at the front of the table. The sequential search can also search a portion of a table. The following example searches elements 100 to 200 of the PERSON table to see if there is a person named "SMITH". The AT END phrase is omitted, because the search will stop before it reaches the end of the table.

```
   SET IP TO 100
   SEARCH PERSON
     WHEN IP > 200
          DISPLAY "SMITH NOT FOUND."
     WHEN SURNAME(IP) = "SMITH"
          DISPLAY "SMITH FOUND."
   END-SEARCH
```

You can append a VARYING *count* phrase to SEARCH to increment a *count* as each element is searched. Then *count* must first be set to an initial value, usually zero.

```
   MOVE ZERO TO count
   SET index TO start
   SEARCH table  VARYING count
     AT END imperative-statements
     WHEN condition imperative-statements
     ⋮
     WHEN condition imperative-statements
   END-SEARCH
```

• *count:* An index of this or another table, or a numeric integer identifier. If *count* is an index of this *table,* it, not the first index of the *table,* is incremented. If *count* is an index from another table or an identifier, it along with the first index of the *table* is incremented. If SEARCH terminates without finding an element, *count* has no predictable value.

The VARYING phrase allows indexes or subscripts for other tables to be incremented in the SEARCH. This saves having to set them when the element is found.

B. Binary Search

The binary SEARCH statement requires that the table being searched be arranged in ascending or descending order based on selected data items (termed *keys*) of the table. Specify the keys in the data description as follows:

```
   ASCENDING KEY IS key-1, key-2, ..., key-n
```

Or:

```
DESCENDING KEY IS key-1, key-2, ..., key-n
```

Each *key* must be the name of a table element. The *key* can name the table
itself, and then there can only be one *key*. If the *key* does not name the table,
there can be several keys. However, they must be subordinate to *table* and
not be subordinate to, or follow, any other entries in the table that contain an
OCCURS clause.

If more than one *key* is listed, list them in decreasing order of significance.
The *keys* can be DISPLAY, BINARY, PACKED-DECIMAL, COMP-1, or COMP-2
items. The following table indicates that PERSON is in ascending order based
on SURNAME and that the child of each PERSON is in descending order based
on the contents of CHILD.

```
01  PERSON-RECORD.
    05  PERSON                     OCCURS 1000 TIMES
                                   INDEXED BY PX
                                   ASCENDING KEY IS SURNAME.
        10  SURNAME               PIC X(5).
        10  AGE                   PIC S9(5) PACKED-DECIMAL.
        10  CHILDREN              OCCURS 5 TIMES
                                   INDEXED BY CX
                                   DESCENDING KEY IS CHILD.
            15  CHILD             PIC X(5).
```

There cannot be more than 12 keys per table in VS COBOL II, and their
combined length cannot be greater than 256 bytes.

Code the binary SEARCH statement as follows:

```
SEARCH ALL table
    AT END imperative-statements
    WHEN key (index) = expression
        imperative-statement
    ⋮
    WHEN key (index) = expression
        imperative-statement
END-SEARCH
```

- *table:* A table that has the OCCURS INDEXED BY clause and KEY phrase in
  its description. The first index listed in the INDEXED BY phrase of *table* is
  used for the search if there are several, and if an element is found, the *index*
  points to that element. If an element is not found, the *index* has no predictable
  value.
- AT END *imperative-statements:* An optional phrase that causes the *imperative-
  statements* to execute if the element is not found in *table*. Unless it is a GO
  TO, execution then continues with the next executable statement following
  the SEARCH statement. Execution also continues there if the AT END phrase
  is omitted. In either case, the *index* has no predictable value.

- WHEN *key(index)* = *expression imperative-statements:* You must describe the *key* in the KEY phrase for *table.* The *index* must be the first index listed in the INDEXED BY phrase, along with any other subscripts or literals you want. The *expression* may be a literal, identifier, or an arithmetic expression. The logical operation AND can join several comparisons. Any *keys* in the KEY clause may be tested, but if several *keys* are described, all preceding *keys* must be tested. The *imperative-statements* execute when the condition is true, and unless it is a GO TO, execution then continues with the next executable statement following the SEARCH statement. The *index* points to the table element found. CONTINUE may be coded as the *imperative-statements,* and execution immediately continues with the next executable statement if an element is found. VS COBOL II allows a maximum of 12 WHEN clauses.

The following example searches the PERSON table for the age of a person named "SMITH".

```
SEARCH ALL PERSON
   AT END MOVE ZERO TO ANS
   WHEN SURNAME(PX) = "SMITH"
         MOVE AGE(PX) TO ANS
END-SEARCH
```

A table may contain duplicate entries; that is, elements with identical *keys.* This does not affect the search, but which entry it finds of a duplicate entry is unpredictable. It will not necessarily be the first of the duplicate entries in the table.

The binary search can also search a variable-length table. It is best to use the DEPENDING ON phrase to specify the current size of the table, and the SEARCH statement will not search beyond this. If you are not using the DEPENDING ON phrase, fill beyond the last entry in the table with HIGH-VALUES (table in ascending order) or LOW-VALUES (table in descending order). This enables the binary search to work properly.

Both the sequential and binary forms of the SEARCH statement can also search multidimensional tables; the table may be subordinated to an item containing an OCCURS clause. You must set the *index* of the higher-level OCCURS clause before searching the lower levels. For example, if we code SEARCH ALL CHILDREN in the previously described PERSON table, PX must first be set, and all table elements, CHILDREN(PX, 1 to 5), are searched. The following example searches all the CHILDREN of each PERSON and prints the SURNAME if a CHILD named "BOBBY" is found:

```
PERFORM VARYING PX FROM 1 BY 1
         UNTIL PX > 1000
   SEARCH ALL CHILDREN
     WHEN CHILD(PX, CX) = "BOBBY"
         DISPLAY SURNAME(PX)
   END-SEARCH
END-PERFORM
```

You can also use the sequential and binary SEARCH statements in combination to search a multidimensional table. The following example searches for each PERSON whose AGE is greater than 50 and who also has a CHILD named "BETTY". Note that ALL-DONE is used as a flag to terminate the search.

```
        MOVE "N" TO ALL-DONE
        SET PX TO 1
        PERFORM WITH TEST BEFORE UNTIL PX > 1000 OR ALL-DONE = "Y"
            SEARCH PERSON
*               A sequential search finds the next person over 50.
            AT END DISPLAY "ALL DONE."
                    MOVE "Y" TO ALL-DONE
            WHEN AGE(PX) > 50
                SEARCH ALL CHILDREN
*                   A binary search finds any child named "BETTY".
                    WHEN CHILD(PX, CX) = "BETTY"
                        DISPLAY SURNAME(PX)
                END-SEARCH
            END-SEARCH
            SET PX UP BY 1
        END-PERFORM
```

IV. HASH TABLES

Sometimes it is impractical to use a sequential or binary search. Perhaps we must add to the table while it is being searched. We could still use a sequential search by adding new entries to the end of the table. For a binary search, we would locate where to add the new entry and move all the elements from there on down one slot to make room. However, the sequential search or updating the table for a binary search may be too slow.

An alternative is to use what is termed a *hash table*. Rather than searching the table for a match key, we compute a subscript to the table and use it instead. Suppose that we are using a table to retrieve a person's name, given a Social Security number. Suppose further that there are also transactions to add new employees. Assuming that there are 1000 employees to store, we need a technique that will convert the nine-digit Social Security numbers into numbers ranging from 1 to 1000.

The simplest method is to divide the Social Security number by 1000 and use the remainder, which will have a value from 0 to 999. Then add 1 to the remainder to bring it into the subscript range of 1 to 1000. The remainders are more evenly distributed if we divide by the largest prime number less than 1000. (A *prime number* is a number divisible only by 1 and itself, such as 7 and 11.) The largest prime number less than 1000 is 997. If you do not have access to a prime number table, select the largest odd number less than 1000 that does not end in 5. For our example, we shall use 999.

Now to see how this works in practice. The number 520-44-1461 yields a remainder of 423 when divided by 999, and the number 520-44-1462 yields a remainder of 424. So far so good, but the number 558-56-0304 also yields a remainder of 423, the same as 520-44-1461. This raises the problem of *collisions*—when two numbers yield the same remainder. This means that we cannot use the subscript directly. Instead, we use it as the location at which to begin looking for a place to store the entry. This requires that we initialize the table, probably with zeros, so that we can tell if an element contains an entry. We should also increase the size of the table to provide room for the collisions, perhaps to 1500 elements, and then divide by 1499 to compute the subscripts. The larger the table, the less chance of collisions and the more efficient it becomes. The efficiency begins to drop off when the table becomes more than about 70 percent full.

There is still a problem at the end of the table. What if several Social Security numbers yield a subscript of 1500? We solve this by wrapping around to the beginning of the table. To retrieve an entry from the table, we compute the subscript from the Social Security number. Then we use this as the location at which to begin looking for the Social Security number in the table.

To illustrate a hash table, we shall use the Social Security example to add and retrieve a person's name from a table given the person's Social Security number. We shall define the table and write procedures to add new entries to the table and to search it. The table is defined as follows:

```
 01  SS-TABLE.
     05  SS-NAME                 PIC X(25).
*                                Name of person for storing
*                                and retrieval.
     05  SS-NO                   PIC 9(9).
*                                Social Security number for
*                                storing and retrieval.
     05  SS-DIV                  PIC S9(9) PACKED-DECIMAL
                                 VALUE 1499.
*                                Largest odd number not
*                                ending in 5 that is less
*                                than SS-MAX-SIZE.
     05  SS-TEMP                 PIC S9(9) PACKED-DECIMAL.
*                                Scratch storage to store
*                                dividend.
     05  SS-MAX-SIZE             PIC S9(4) BINARY SYNC
                                 VALUE 1500.
*                                Size of person array.
     05  SS-SUBSCRIPT            PIC S9(9) PACKED-DECIMAL.
*                                Computed subscript.
     05  SS-PERSON               OCCURS 1500 TIMES
                                 INDEXED BY IP.
         10  SS-PERSON-NO        PIC 9(9).
*                                Social Security number.
         10  SS-PERSON-NAME      PIC X(25).
```

```
*                                        Name of person.
    ■ ■ ■
*    First zero out the SS-PERSON-NO elements.
     PERFORM VARYING IP FROM 1 BY 1 UNTIL IP > SS-MAX-SIZE
        MOVE ZEROS TO SS-PERSON-NO(IP)
     END-PERFORM
```

Next, we must write a procedure to add entries to the table. The person's name must first be moved to SS-NAME, and the Social Security number to SS-NO. We perform the procedure as follows:

```
     MOVE Social-Security-number  TO SS-NO
     MOVE person's-name TO SS-NAME
     PERFORM C10-ADD-NAME
```

The procedure is written as follows:

```
C10-ADD-NAME.
***************************************************************
* PROCEDURE TO ADD ENTRIES TO PERSON TABLE.                  *
* IN:  SS-NO contains social security number.                *
*      SS-NAME contains person's name.                       *
* OUT: IP points to where SS-NO stored.                      *
*      SS-NO stored in SS-PERSON-NO(IP).                     *
*      SS-NAME stored in SS-PERSON-NAME(IP).                 *
***************************************************************
*    Convert social security number to value from 1 to SS-DIV.
     DIVIDE SS-NO BY SS-DIV GIVING SS-TEMP REMAINDER SS-SUBSCRIPT
     ADD 1 TO SS-SUBSCRIPT
     SET IP TO SS-SUBSCRIPT
*    Search from SS-SUBSCRIPT forward.
     SEARCH SS-PERSON
        AT END
*          *************************************************
*          * Not found from SS-SUBSCRIPT to end of table. *
*          * Wrap around to search from 1 up to SS-SUBSCRIPT. *
*          *************************************************
           SET IP TO 1
           SEARCH SS-PERSON
             WHEN IP = SS-SUBSCRIPT
*                We wrapped around to SS-SUBSCRIPT.  It is not in table.
                 DISPLAY
                     "ERROR - SS-PERSON TABLE FULL, RUN TERMINATED."
                 DISPLAY
             "INCREASE SS-PERSON- SS-DIV, SS-MAX-SIZE AND RECOMPILE."
                 GO TO Z90-STOP-RUN
             WHEN SS-PERSON-NO(IP) = ZEROS
```

```
*                 We found an empty slot.  Store SS-NO and SS-NAME.
                  MOVE SS-NO TO SS-PERSON-NO(IP)
                  MOVE SS-NAME TO SS-PERSON-NAME(IP)
            END-SEARCH
        WHEN SS-PERSON-NO(IP) = ZEROS
*            We found an empty slot.  Store SS-NO and SS-NAME.
             MOVE SS-NO TO SS-PERSON-NO(IP)
             MOVE SS-NAME TO SS-PERSON-NAME(IP)
        END-SEARCH
        SET SS-SUBSCRIPT TO IP
            .
**** Exit
```

We also need a procedure to retrieve a person's name given the Social Security number. The Social Security number is first moved to SS-NO, and the name is returned in SS-NAME. If the name is not found, SS-NAME contains spaces. The procedure is invoked as follows:

```
    MOVE Social-Security-number  TO SS-NO
    PERFORM C20-RETRIEVE-NAME
```

The procedure is written as follows:

```
 C20-RETRIEVE-NAME.
 **************************************************************
 * PROCEDURE TO RETRIEVE A PERSON'S NAME.                    *
 * IN:   SS-NO contains Social Security number.              *
 * OUT:  If found:                                           *
 *          SS-SUBSCRIPT points to entry in table.           *
 *          SS-NAME contains person's name.                  *
 *       Not found:                                          *
 *          SS-SUBSCRIPT contains ZERO.                      *
 *          SS-NAME contains SPACES.                         *
 **************************************************************
 *     Convert Social Security number to value from 1 to SS-DIV.
       DIVIDE SS-NO BY SS-DIV GIVING SS-TEMP REMAINDER SS-SUBSCRIPT
       ADD 1 TO SS-SUBSCRIPT
       SET IP TO SS-SUBSCRIPT
 *     Search from SS-SUBSCRIPT forward.
       SEARCH SS-PERSON
          AT END
 *            ************************************************
 *            * Not found from SS-SUBSCRIPT to end of table.  *
 *            * Wrap around to search from 1 up to SS-SUBSCRIPT. *
 *            ************************************************
```

```
            SET IP TO 1
            SEARCH SS-PERSON
              WHEN IP = SS-SUBSCRIPT OR SS-PERSON-NO(IP) = ZERO
*                  We wrapped around to SS-SUBSCRIPT or found an
*                  empty slot.  It is not in table.
                   MOVE SPACES TO SS-NAME
                   MOVE ZERO TO SS-SUBSCRIPT
              WHEN SS-NO = SS-PERSON-NO(IP)
*                  We found person.
                   MOVE SS-PERSON-NAME(IP) TO SS-NAME
                   SET SS-SUBSCRIPT TO IP
            END-SEARCH
        WHEN SS-PERSON-NO(IP) = ZERO
*            We reached an empty slot.  It is not in table.
             MOVE SPACES TO SS-NAME
             MOVE ZERO TO SS-SUBSCRIPT
        WHEN SS-NO = SS-PERSON-NO(IP)
*            We found person.
             MOVE SS-PERSON-NAME(IP) TO SS-NAME
             SET SS-SUBSCRIPT TO IP
      END-SEARCH
            .
**** Exit
```

There still remains a problem if the key is alphanumeric rather than numeric. We solve this by moving the alphanumeric item to another alphnumeric item redefined as a BINARY data item. (It cannot exceed nine digits.) The following example illustrates this. The person's name, not the Social Security number, is used to compute the subscript.

```
    05  SS-NAME                    PIC X(25).
    05  SS-SHORT-NAME              PIC X(8).
    05  SS-CONVERT REDEFINES SS-SHORT-NAME
                                   PIC S9 (9) BINARY.
    ■ ■ ■
    MOVE SS-NAME TO SS-SHORT-NAME
    DIVIDE SS-CONVERT BY SS-DIV GIVING SS-TEMP
           REMAINDER SS-SUBSCRIPT
```

Fortunately, hash tables are not often needed. For a table with few entries, a sequential search would be simpler and more efficient. If only a few entries are added to the table but we search it often, we might use a binary search. We would move all the entries in the table down to make room for a new entry. The hash table technique is also used for relative files, in which the entries are records stored in a file rather than elements of a table in memory.

V. READING TABLES IN

You often read a table in from a file. In the following example, a personnel file is
read and the employee IDs are stored in a table, perhaps to validate transactions
with a binary search. There are several things to note in this example. First,
the payroll file has 1000-byte records, but we will need to save only the 10-
byte employee ID. The table is a variable-size table, because the number of
employees will change. If the table overflows, a message is printed telling
how to change the program. The payroll file must be sorted in ascending order
on the employee ID, and the program checks to ensure that this has been
done.

```
WORKING-STORAGE SECTION.
 77  OLD-ID                          PIC X(10).
 *                                      OLD-ID checks the sort
 *                                      order of INPUT-FILE.
 **** Employee file.  Record length = 1000.
  01  EMPLOYEE.
      05  EMPLOYEE-ID               PIC X(10).
      05  FILLER                    PIC X(990).
 **** Table of employee IDs.
  01  ID-RECORD.
      05  ID-MAX                    PIC S9(4) BINARY VALUE 1000.
 *                                      Maximum number of IDs in table.
      05  ID-NO                     PIC S9(4) BINARY VALUE ZERO.
 *                                      Current size of table.
      05  ID-TABLE                  OCCURS 0 TO 1000 TIMES
                                    DEPENDING ON ID-NO
                                    INDEXED BY IDX
                                    ASCENDING KEY IS ID-ID.
          10  ID-ID                 PIC X(10).
      ■ ■ ■
      OPEN INPUT PAY-IN
      MOVE LOW-VALUES TO EMPLOYEE-ID, OLD-ID
      PERFORM B20-STORE-IDS WITH TEST AFTER
              UNTIL EMPLOYEE-ID = HIGH-VALUES
      CLOSE PAY-IN
      ■ ■ ■
 B20-STORE-IDS.
 ******************************************************************
 * PROCEDURE TO READ IDS AND STORE THEM IN THE TABLE.         *
 * IN:  PAY-IN file open.                                     *
 *      ID-NO points to last entry in table.                  *
 *      OLD-ID contains previous ID.                          *
 * OUT: PAY-IN file open.  One record read.                   *
 *      ID-NO increased by 1.                                 *
```

```
*       EMPLOYEE-ID stored in OLD-ID, ID-ID(ID-NO).        *
*       EMPLOYEE-ID contains HIGH-VALUES if EOF.           *
***************************************************************
      READ PAY-IN INTO EMPLOYEE
        AT END
          MOVE HIGH-VALUES TO EMPLOYEE-ID
        NOT AT END
          IF EMPLOYEE-ID < OLD-ID
            THEN DISPLAY
              "ERROR - PAYROLL FILE NOT IN SORT, RUN TERMINATED."
                DISPLAY "OLD ID: ", OLD-ID, " CURRENT ID: ",
                        EMPLOYEE-ID
                GO TO Z90-STOP-RUN
          END-IF
          MOVE EMPLOYEE-ID TO OLD-ID
          ADD 1 TO ID-NO
          IF ID-NO > ID-MAX
            THEN DISPLAY
                "ERROR - ID-TABLE OVERFLOW, RUN TERMINATED."
                DISPLAY "PAYROLL RECORD: ", EMPLOYEE-ID
                DISPLAY
                "INCREASE ID-MAX, ID-TABLE AND RECOMPILE PROGRAM."
                GO TO Z90-STOP-RUN
          END-IF
          MOVE EMPLOYEE-ID TO ID-ID(ID-NO)
      END-READ

**** Exit
```

Now whenever an ID is to be validated, the following can be coded:

```
      SEARCH ALL ID-TABLE
        AT END
          statements-if-not-found
        WHEN ID-ID(IDX) = id
          statements-if-found
      END-SEARCH
```

VI. TREE STRUCTURES

Tree structures are sometimes required in COBOL to represent hierarchical data. For example, a company may be divided into several divisions, with each division further subdivided. We can represent this organization with a tree structure. Figure 9.1 shows a company's organization chart, in which each box represents an organizational unit, which is assigned a unique number.

One way to represent such a tree structure is to let the department numbers themselves specify the hierarchy. In Figure 9.1, the first digit represents level

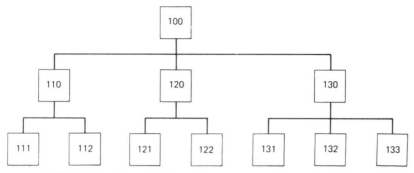

FIGURE 9.1 **Organization chart represented by a tree structure.**

1 of the organization, the second digit level 2, and the third digit level 3. The department table for such a numbering convention would be as follows:

Department Number	Department Name
100	Computer Division
110	Operations Department
111	Computer Operators
112	Distribution
120	Programming Department

If the department table is sorted on the department number, it is also placed in hierarchical order. The COBOL statements necessary to contain this department table are as follows:

```
01  DEPARTMENT.
    05  DEPT-SIZE              PIC S9(4) BINARY.
    05  DEPT-TABLE             OCCURS 0 TO 100 TIMES
                               DEPENDING ON DEPT-SIZE
                               INDEXED BY X-DEPT.
        10  DEPTH-NO           PIC X(3).
        10  DEPT-NAME          PIC X(25).
```

The table has a varying size, because departments are likely to be added or deleted. If the department table were contained in a file, each record would contain a department, and the records could be read into the DEPT-TABLE.

Tree structures must often be searched, but the search is usually to locate all the entries above or below a specific entry in the hierarchy. For example, if we were adding a new department, we would want to make sure that the departments above it in the hierarchy exist. The number itself contains the hierarchy, so that if department 113 is added, we would search for departments 110 and 100. If we delete a department, we may want to delete all departments below it in the hierarchy. To search down in the hierarchy, we must find all records whose high-order digits match this one. For example, if we delete department 110, we could search the table to find all departments that are numbered 11*n* and delete them too.

The disadvantage of this technique, in which the numbers themselves specify the hierarchy, is that you may run out of numbers. Or you may want to transfer one number to be under another. For example, we may want to transfer department 111 to be under department 120. For this, we must store the full upward hierarchy for each record. Such a table would look as follows:

Department Number	Level	Upward Hierarchy	Department Name
100	1	100	Computer Division
110	2	100 110	Operations Department
111	3	100 110 111	Computer Operations
112	3	100 110 112	Distribution
120	2	100 120	Programming Department

The department numbers are arbitrary and signify nothing. To transfer department 111 under department 120, we change the record for department 111 as follows:

111	3	100 110 111	Computer Operations

Notice that the department number is stored twice in each record. This is redundant data, but it is necessary for sorting the department table on the department numbers into hierarchical order. The COBOL statements to contain the table would be as follows:

```
01  DEPARTMENT.
    05  DEPT-SIZE               PIC S9(4) BINARY.
    05  DEPT-TABLE              OCCURS 0 TO 100 TIMES
                                DEPENDING ON DEPT-SIZE
                                INDEXED BY X-DEPT.
        10  DEPTH-NO            PIC X(3).
        10  DEPTH-LEVEL         PIC 9.
        10  DEPT-UP-HIER.
            15  DEPT-1          PIC X(3).
            15  DEPT-2          PIC X(3).
            15  DEPT-3          PIC X(3).
        10  DEPT-NAME           PIC X(25).
```

It is easy to find all the departments above any department in the hierarchy, because the upward hierarchy is contained in each record. To find all the departments below a given department, search the table for those records whose hierarchy points to this department. For example, to find all departments belonging to department 110, which is a level 2 department, look for all records whose DEPT-2 is "110".

Tracing down in the tree structure is more complicated if the entire table cannot be contained in memory. We could read the entire department file sequentially to find the records below a given record in the hierarchy, but this is slow if the file is large. An alternative is to store for each department all those departments that belong to it in the hierarchy. The record for such a file would look as follows:

Department Number	Level	Upward Hierarchy	Next-Level-Down Hierarchy
100	1	100	120 130
110	2	100 110	111 112
111	3	100 110 111	
112	3	100 110 112	
120	2	100 120	121 122

The COBOL statements to describe the records in the file would be as follows:

```
01  DEPT-RECORD.
    05  DEPT-NO                PIC X(3).
    05  DEPT-LEVEL             PIC 9.
    05  DEPT-UP-HIER.
        10  DEPT-1             PIC X(3).
        10  DEPT-2             PIC X(3).
        10  DEPT-3             PIC X(3).
    05  DEPT-DOWN-COUNT        PIC S9(3) PACKED-DECIMAL.
    05  DEPT-DOWN-HIER         OCCURS 0 TO 100 TIMES
                               DEPENDING ON DEPT-DOWN-COUNT
                               INDEXED BY X-DOWN.
        10  DEPT-DOWN          PIC X(3).
```

This record would be especially useful for relative or indexed files, in which records can be accessed directly. To read all records above a given department, we would use the upward hierarchy as the key and read these records directly. To read all records below a given department, we would use the downward hierarchy and read these records directly. If necessary, we could use the downward hierarchy of the records that are read to go down to the next level in the hierarchy. This could continue until we have read all the records.

An alternative way of tracing down the tree structure is to keep only one downward pointer and then keep a side pointer. (Such a structure is termed a *binary tree,* because each element has only two pointers.) Thus, you can go down one level in the hierarchy with the down pointer and then look at all items at this level with the side pointers. The table would look as follows:

Department Number	Level	Upward Hierarchy	Down Pointer	Side Pointer
100	1	100	110	—
110	2	100 110	111	120
111	3	100 110 111	—	112
112	3	100 110 112	—	—
120	2	100 120	121	130

To find all the level 2 entries in the table given the department 100, we would use the down pointer to locate 120. Then we would use the side pointer to locate 120, then the side pointer of 120 to locate 130. The advantage of this type of organization over the previous one is that we need not guess the maximum number of entries at each level. Only one down pointer and one side pointer are needed. On the other hand, it is slower and more complicated to find all the entries at the next level down if the records reside in a file.

The COBOL statements to describe the records in the file would be as follows:

```
01  DEPT-RECORD.
    05  DEPT-NO                PIC X(3).
    05  DEPT-LEVEL             PIC 9.
    05  DEPT-UP-HIER.
        10  DEPT-1             PIC X(3).
        10  DEPT-2             PIC X(3).
        10  DEPT-3             PIC X(3).
    05  DEPT-DOWN-PTR          PIC X(3).
    05  DEPT-SIDE-PTR          PIC X(3).
```

This completes the discussion of records and tables. There are many other sophisticated record and data structures used in computing that generally require dynamic storage allocation and a facility for operating on storage addresses. Chapter 23 describes some of these. The next chapter describes the ACCEPT and DISPLAY statements, which are handy for entering and displaying data.

EXERCISES

1. Define a table to contain numbers with a maximum magnitude of 999.99. The table is to contain 100 elements. Write the statements necessary to fill the table with the numbers from 1 to 100.

2. Define two numeric tables named HOURS and SALARY with dimensions 50 by 20. Multiply the corresponding elements of each table together and store the results in a table named WAGES having the same dimensions. All elements are to have precision S9(7)V9(2).

3. Define a numeric table named TABLES containing 200 elements. The largest number the table is to contain is 999.9999. Assume that the table is unordered and write the statements necessary to count the number of times the number 3.6257 appears in the table. Then write the statements to see if the number 0.7963 is in the table. Finally, assume that the table is in ascending numeric order and write the statements necessary to determine if the number 2.1537 is in the table.

4. Define a table named CITY to contain the population of each of 3 cities within each county, 30 counties within each state, and 50 states. What is the size of the table? Write the statements necessary to sum the total population for all states.

5. A single-dimensional table named POPULATION contains 100 numeric elements. Define the table and sort the values of the table into ascending numerical order, writing your own sort.

6. Declare and initialize a table named CALENDAR containing 12 elements of nine characters each to contain the names of the months. The first element would contain "JANUARY", and so on.

7. A table named LOTS has 100 elements, and each element contains four characters. Count the occurrences of the characters "ABCD" and "CDBA" in the table.

8. Define a table named TEXT-A containing 50 elements of 9 characters each. Define two character data items named EVEN and ODD containing 225 characters each. Create two character strings from TEXT-A by concatenating all the even and all the odd elements and store them in EVEN and ODD.

9. A table named AMOUNT has 100 elements. Sum the even elements from 2 up to and including element 50, and every third element from 15 to 100, but stop the summation if the total exceeds 1000.

REFERENCE

1. William Gear, *Computer Organization and Programming,* New York: McGraw-Hill Book Company, 1974, pp. 383, 384.

10

ACCEPT **and** DISPLAY **Statements**

The ACCEPT and DISPLAY statements provide an easy way of entering data and displaying it. They can accept data from the input stream or a terminal and print it or display it on a terminal. They are especially handy for testing and debugging programs.

I. **THE** ACCEPT **STATEMENT**

The ACCEPT statement accepts input from the system input device or the operator's console:

```
ACCEPT identifier  FROM source
```

- *identifier:* A group item, an elementary alphabetic, alphanumeric, alphanumeric edited, numeric edited, or external decimal numbers. ACCEPT stores the input in *identifier*.
- *source:* Specifies where the data is to come from.

In VS COBOL II and Microsoft COBOL, the *source* can be one of the following:

CONSOLE:	The operator's console in VS COBOL II and the PC keyboard in Microsoft COBOL.
SYSIN:	The system logical input—the input stream. You can also code SYSIPT rather than SYSIN. You must include a SYSIN or SYSIPT DD statement.
menmonic-name:	You can use any mnemonic-name defined in the SPECIAL-NAMES paragraph, as described in Chapter 13.

The following *source* is available in Microsoft COBOL only:

COMMAND-LINE: *The input comes from the command line.*

When you code FROM CONSOLE, VS COBOL II displays an AWAITING REPLY message on the operator's console and suspends program execution until the operator responds. Be careful about using FROM CONSOLE. MVS operators are very busy and dislike responding to messages. Most installations carefully control who can request input from the operators and under what circumstances.

VS COBOL II limits the CONSOLE input to a maximum length of 114 characters. It transmits the input when the operator presses the ENTER key or enters 114 characters of data. It truncates or pads the input on the right with blanks, if necessary, to match the length of *identifier*. If 114 characters are entered and the *identifier* is still not filled, as it would be if it were defined to contain more than 114 characters, VS COBOL II requests more data from the console.

For CONSOLE, use a DISPLAY statement to tell what is expected before executing an ACCEPT. DISPLAY is described below. The following example displays a message to the operator and suspends program execution until the operator responds by typing a message in on the console keyboard. COBOL then stores this message in ANSWER.

```
77  ANSWER                      PIC X(114).
    ■ ■ ■
    DISPLAY "WHAT IS YOUR NAME?" UPON CONSOLE
    ACCEPT ANSWER FROM CONSOLE
```

If you omit the FROM phrase or code FROM SYSIN, VS COBOL II reads input from the system input device (the input stream) and Microsoft COBOL accepts input from the PC keyboard. VS COBOL II input consists of an 80-character line read in from the standard SYSIN file, automatically opening and closing the file. The characters in the line are transmitted into the *identifier* and truncated or padded with blanks on the right to match the length of the *identifier*. In the following example, assume the standard input file SYSIN contains the following line:

```
//GO.SYSIN DD *
244CONTINUE
```

You could then write an ACCEPT statement to read the line:

```
01  RUN-CONTROL.
    05  RUN-NO                  PIC 999.
    05  RUN-TYPE                PIC X(5).
    ■ ■ ■
    ACCEPT RUN-CONTROL
```
   [*The line is read, and* RUN-NO *contains 244.* RUN-TYPE *contains* "CONTI".]

The Microsoft COBOL ACCEPT statement has many additional features for full-screen terminal input, beyond the scope of this book.

The ACCEPT statement can also retrieve the date and time when coded as follows:

```
                                 TIME
                                 DATE
                                 DAY
                                 DAY-OF-WEEK
        ACCEPT identifier  FROM _____
```

- TIME: Returns a PIC 9(8) external decimal number in the form "hhmmsstt": *hh*-hour (00 to 23), *mm*-minute, *ss*-second, *tt*-hundredths of a second.
- DATE: Returns a PIC S9(6) external decimal number date in the form "yymmdd": *yy*-year, *mm*-month, *dd*-day.
- DAY: Returns a PIC S9(5) external decimal number date (year and day of year) in the form "yyddd": *yy*-year, *ddd*-day of year, 001 to 366.
- DAY-OF-WEEK: Returns a PIC 9(1) external decimal number representing the day of week with a value of 1 (Monday) through 7 (Sunday).

```
 01  WEEK-DAY                        PIC 9.
     ■ ■ ■
     ACCEPT WEEK-DAY FROM DAY-OF-WEEK
```

II. **THE** DISPLAY **STATEMENT**

DISPLAY displays alphanumeric literals and the value of data items on the standard output file, SYSPRINT in MVS. COBOL automatically opens and closes the output file. The general form is as follows:

```
     DISPLAY item , item ,  . . ., item UPON device
```

- *item* must not be an index, but it may be any other type of item or a literal. A figurative constant such as SPACES displays as a single character. Numeric literals must be unsigned (1 but not −1) in the ANSI Standard and Microsoft COBOL but not in VS COBOL II. Group items display as alphanumeric. COBOL converts numeric items to external decimal for display. Each DISPLAY statement starts on a new line, and the display continues onto the next line if more than 120 characters are displayed.
- *device* specifies where to display.

The following *devices* are permitted in VS COBOL II and Microsoft COBOL:

CONSOLE:	The operator's console in VS COBOL II and the PC screen in Microsoft COBOL.
SYSOUT:	The system logical output—the printer. You can also code SYSLIST or SYSLST rather than SYSOUT. You must include a SYSOUT, SYSLIST, or SYSLIST DD statement.
menmonic-name:	You can use any mnemonic name described in the SPECIAL-NAMES paragraph, as described in Chapter 13.

The following *device* is available in Microsoft COBOL only:

COMMAND-LINE:	The display overwrites the command line. You can later retrieve the command line with an ACCEPT statement, as described in Chapter 18.

In VS COBOL II, the maximum line length is 120 characters. If the line is shorter than the line of the device, the display is padded on the right with blanks; if longer, it is truncated.

Each DISPLAY statement displays at the current line position and positions to the start of the next line at the end. (The printer spaces before printing.) If you want to leave the display at the end of the displayed line, add the WITH NO ADVANCING clause:

```
DISPLAY "THIS IS A LINE." UPON SYSOUT
   WITH NO ADVANCING
DISPLAY "THIS IS A CONTINUATION." UPON SYSOUT
```

The display will be "THIS IS A LINE.THIS IS A CONTINUATION.", and the display will then be positioned to the start of the next line.

If you omit the UPON phrase, UPON SYSOUT is assumed:

```
DISPLAY "THIS IS A MESSAGE"
```

is the same as

```
DISPLAY "THIS IS A MESSAGE" UPON SYSOUT
```

"THIS IS A MESSAGE" displays on the next line.

Identifiers display according to their descriptions in the PIC clause. An item of PIC X(10) would display 10 characters, and PIC S9(5)V99 would display 7 characters (regardless of whether described as DISPLAY , BINARY, or PACKED-DECIMAL) with leading zeros and no decimal point.

The sign is displayed differently in VS COBOL II and Microsoft COBOL. In VS COBOL II, a minus value is indicated in the rightmost digit, as shown in Table 10.1 (see the discussion of the SIGN clause for external decimal numbers in Chapter 6).

TABLE 10.1 Display of Minus Sign in Right Digit in VS COBOL II

Digit	Displayed As	Digit	Displayed As
0	}	5	N
1	J	6	O
2	K	7	P
3	L	8	Q
4	M	9	R

If VALUE-A is declared S9(5)V99 and contains 23 and VALUE-B is declared S9(3)V9(4) and contains −23.2345, they display as follows:

```
DISPLAY VALUE-A   [Displays as "0002300".]
DISPLAY VALUE-B   [Displays as "023234N".]
```

In Microsoft COBOL, the sign displays to the right of the item for USAGE DISPLAY and to the left for BINARY and PACKED-DECIMAL. If VALUE-A and VALUE-B were BINARY , they would display as follows:

```
DISPLAY VALUE-A   [Displays  as "+0002300".]
DISPLAY VALUE-B   [Displays  as "− 0232345".]
```

Blanks are not inserted between displayed items, as shown in the following example:

```
DISPLAY VALUE-A, VALUE-B
   [Displays as "0002300023234N" in VS COBOL II and as "+0002300-0232345" in
   Microsoft COBOL.]
```

To make numbers readable, separate numeric values with literal blanks. Since only the values of items are displayed, include some text to describe what they signify:

```
DISPLAY "VALUE-A = ", VALUE-A, " VALUE-B = ", VALUE-B
   [Displays as: "VALUE-A =  0002300 VALUE-B =  023234N"
   in VS COBOL II.]
```

Microsoft COBOL has extensive features for displaying output for full-screen output with color, highlighting, reverse video, and so on, which are beyond the scope of this book.

This completes the discussion of ACCEPT and DISPLAY . The next chapters go on to describe input/output in COBOL.

11

Input/Output Concepts and Devices

Input/output (I/O), the transmission of data between memory and an input/output device, is often the most complex part of programming. It requires a knowledge of the data to be transmitted, the hardware devices, and the language features. The logic is deceptively complex, and the external hardware devices have physical limitations, such as capacity, that can cause problems. Input/output also depends on the specific implementation, and this chapter describes IBM mainframe and PC input/output.

COBOL applications are usually heavily I/O-oriented, and you should carefully select the proper I/O device for each file. Specify as little about the I/O device as possible within the program, leaving such details to system commands (JCL, DOS, or OS/2). By doing this, you can use a different I/O device or, on the mainframe, change a blocking factor without modifying the program. Then, if a disk file grows in size, requiring it to be moved to tape, or if a tape unit is changed to one of higher density, or if a program is tested with data on disk and then used to process records on tape during production, the program does not need to be recompiled.

COBOL input/output is record-oriented, in that each READ or WRITE statement transmits a single logical record. A *logical record* is a logical unit of data and may contain several items of differing data types. For example, a personnel record for a company might contain all the personnel data relating to an individual, such as name, age, and length of service. The words *record* and *logical record* are used interchangeably in the context of input/output.

The IBM mainframe blocks records. A *block,* sometimes termed a *physical record,* consists of one or more records stored as a unit on the I/O device for efficiency. Blocks are described in more detail later in this chapter.

I. RECORD FORMATS

A. MVS Record Formats and Blocking

MVS (and thus VS COBOL II) records have three forms: fixed-length, variable-length, and undefined-length. *Fixed-length* records all have the same length. For example, a file containing card images is fixed-length, because each card originally could contain 80 characters. Figure 11.1 illustrates fixed-length records.

LRECL = BLKSIZE

FIGURE 11.1 Fixed-length records.

Variable-length records, as their name implies, may have varying lengths. MVS appends four bytes to the front of the record to specify the record length and four additional bytes to specify the block size. For example, a personnel file containing employee names and the names of their dependents might be variable-length, because people have a varying number of dependents. Figure 11.2 illustrates variable-length records.

Undefined-length records also have varying lengths, but the record length is not contained in the record. The hardware separates records with a physical gap on the storage device called an *interrecord gap* (IRG). The computer is able to recognize this gap when transmitting a record, and thus it can distinguish between records. Undefined-length records cannot be blocked; each record constitutes a block. Undefined-length records are used when the record length is not known until after the entire record is written, as, for example, data transmitted from an on-line terminal. They are also used to read files when you do not know the record format or even the record length of the records in a file. You can read the record as undefined and then display it to see what it contains. Figure 11.3 illustrates undefined-length records.

The system transfers data between memory and I/O devices in *blocks;* each block is separated by an interrecord gap. Several fixed- or variable-length records may be contained in a single block. Blocks of fixed-length records all have the same number of records in each block, except possibly for the last block. Blocks of variable-length records may have a varying number of records in each block. Only one undefined-length record can be contained in a block. A block, then, consists of one or more records to be transmitted at a time and stored on the I/O device as a physical record. Figure 11.4 illustrates blocked records.

You can also *span* records across several blocks. Spanned records allow the record length to exceed the block length so that the logical record is contained in two or more physical records. (In MVS, the maximum block length is 32,767 bytes.) Spanned records are not a separate record format but a special form of either fixed- or variable-length records. (Undefined records cannot be spanned.) You specify spanned records by appending S to the RECFM parameter

m = BLKSIZE

l = LRECL

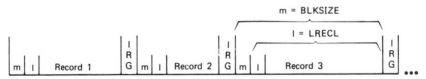

FIGURE 11.2 Variable-length records.

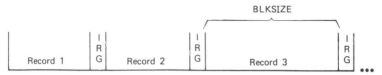

FIGURE 11.3 Undefined-length records.

for example: RECFM=FS, FBS, VS, or VBS. Figure 11.5 illustrates spanned records.

The hardware can transmit data very quickly between memory and direct-access devices or magnetic tapes once the transmission of data begins. However, it may take quite long, relative to the computer's speed, to start the transmission, because of mechanical inertia. For direct-access devices, time is needed to position the access arm over the proper track and rotate it around to the start of the block. Blocking allows large, efficient groups of data to be transmitted at one time. Many installations charge on the basis of blocks transmitted, and large blocks can significantly reduce the run costs. Blocking also conserves storage space on the I/O device by limiting the number of inter-record gaps. For example, if 80-byte records are stored on an IBM 3390 disk, a single track will contain only 78 records when unblocked, but 698 records when blocked 349 records per block.

The number of records per block is termed the *blocking factor*. The system reads a block of data into an area of memory called a *buffer*. When the last record of a block is processed, the system reads another block. The reverse occurs when data is written. The system provides several internal buffers so that while data is being processed in one buffer, the system can read the next block of data into another. This results in considerable efficiency, because the I/O is overlapped; that is, data can be read or written simultaneously with computations being done in memory. Blocking is done only for hardware efficiency and is unrelated to the way you want to process the data. The system does all blocking and unblocking in COBOL, and there is no programming effort to block

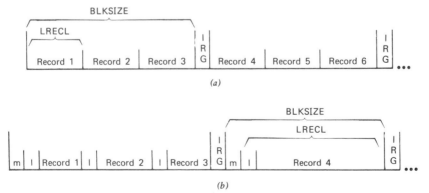

FIGURE 11.4 Blocked records.

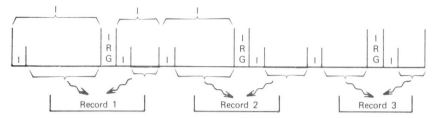

FIGURE 11.5 Spanned records.

files. Consequently COBOL programs can be compatible between VS COBOL II and Microsoft despite their using entirely different blocking techniques.

The blocking factor for sequential files is likely to have more impact on the efficiency of the program than any other easily controlled factor. Block as high as possible within the constraints of the memory size and the I/O devices. If a record containing 100 characters is blocked at 50 records per block, each block contains 5000 characters. Two buffers require 10,000 bytes. Besides these memory constraints, VS COBOL II limits the block size to a minimum of 18 bytes and a maximum of 32,767 bytes. It is best not to specify the blocking in the JCL to let the system select an optimum size. If you select an efficient block size yourself, when your installation installs new disk units with a different track size your blocking will suddenly become inefficient.

B. Microsoft COBOL Record Formats

Microsoft COBOL can read and write two types of records:

- LINE SEQUENTIAL, which is a standard ASCII file for the PC. Each line is terminated by ASCII characters that represent a carriage return and a new line. You can also manipulate these files with a PC text editor or other PC languages.
- RECORD SEQUENTIAL, which is similar to a blocked file in MVS. The data is stored as a single stream of data. It is left up to the program to know how long a record is. You can't manipulate these files with a text editor.

1. LINE SEQUENTIAL *Files*

The standard ASCII files on the PC are essentially undefined, which means that they are fixed-length if the records all have the same length and variable if the lengths differ. These files are easily created, viewed, and modified by any text editor that can operate on ASCII files. These files are LINE SEQUENTIAL in Microsoft COBOL. However, they are not the default files written by Microsoft COBOL. To read or write LINE SEQUENTIAL files, you must either code the SEQUENTIAL "LINE" compile option or code the ORGANIZATION IS LINE SEQUENTIAL clause in the SELECT statement.

At first glance, it would appear that you should make all Microsoft COBOL files be LINE SEQUENTIAL unless you want the faster processing of RECORD

SEQUENTIAL. LINE SEQUENTIAL files also have the advantage of variable-length files in minimizing the amount of file storage space required. Microsoft COBOL stores LINE SEQUENTIAL files as variable-length records and pads them out to fixed-length records as you read them. When you write records, COBOL removes any trailing blanks and transmits only the remaining characters. COBOL writes the ASCII characters representing a carriage return (H"0D") and new line (H"0A") at the end of each record. When the line is read, COBOL removes the H"0D0A" characters at the end of the line and pads the records on the right with blanks to make them fixed-length again. COBOL writes a single H"1A" character at the end of a file as the end-of-file character. (All PC text editors also do this.)

However, you may want to write the same variable-length records on the PC that you write on the mainframe. For them, a data item specifies the length of the record when it is written or contains the record length when a record is read (the RECORD VARYING clause). RECORD SEQUENTIAL does this on the PC.

2. RECORD SEQUENTIAL *Files*

RECORD SEQUENTIAL files are similar to MVS blocked files. The system collects records into a large block and writes them together. Unfortunately, no PC text editor will know the block size, and so no text editor can view, enter, or modify such files. This can be a real inconvenience in debugging. RECORD SEQUENTIAL files can be read and written faster than LINE SEQUENTIAL files. In the best case for LINE SEQUENTIAL, where most of the rightmost characters are blank, it will be faster than RECORD SEQUENTIAL. In the worst case for LINE SEQUENTIAL, where the rightmost character is nonblank, reading can be twice as slow as RECORD SEQUENTIAL, and writing can be up to three times slower.

You must use RECORD SEQUENTIAL files in these instances:

• Where you want the same variable-length records as in VS COBOL II.
• When your data might contain the hex characters H"0D" (carriage return), H"0A" (line feed), or H"1A" (end-of-file). This is always the case when you write BINARY or floating-point data.
• When you need the fastest I/O.

You get RECORD SEQUENTIAL as the default, or you can code the SEQUENTIAL "RECORD" compile option or code the ORGANIZATION IS RECORD SEQUENTIAL clause in the SELECT statement.

II. FILES

You must open files before they can be used, and you should close them after processing is completed. (MVS calls a file a *data set*.) When a file is *opened*, the system creates all the internal tables needed to keep track of the

I/O. It allocates storage for buffers, positions the file to the starting point, and generally readies the file for processing. *Closing* a file releases all buffers and tables associated with the file. It frees any tape drives no longer needed, deletes direct-access storage no longer needed, and generally cleans up after processing the file.

Perhaps the most complicated part of COBOL input/output is the terminology. First, COBOL has three file organizations: sequential, relative, and indexed. The file organization determines how the records are stored. For a file with *sequential* organization, records are stored consecutively on the I/O device and can only be retrieved serially, in the order that they are stored. In a file with *relative organization,* records are stored in what is essentially a table. You read or write records based on their relative position in the file—1st, 2nd, 3rd, and so on. For a file with *indexed* organization, the system stores records so that you can read or write them based on the record key. A *record key* is a portion of the record that uniquely identifies it. For example, in a personnel file, the employee ID might be the record key.

COBOL also has three *access methods,* or means by which records in a file are read or written. *Sequential access* transmits the records one after the other in the order in which they are physically stored in the file. To transmit the last record, all the previous records must be transmitted.

Random access, often termed *direct access,* permits a single record to be transmitted in a file without disturbing the other records, and irrespective of its position in the file. (The term *random* means that any record can be read regardless of the previous record read, not that a record is selected at random when the file is read.) Thus, with random access you can read the last record in a file without having to read all the preceding records. Visualize a deck of playing cards. To locate the ace of hearts with sequential access, you deal one card at a time off the top of the deck until the card is found. For random access, you spread out the entire card deck, face up, so that you can see each card. Then you can select the ace of hearts directly.

A third access method, *dynamic,* allows you to switch back and forth between sequential and random. For example, you can use random access to retrieve a specific record, and then switch to sequential to read all the records that follow it.

Sequential files are often sorted before processing to arrange the records in the necessary sequence. Relative and indexed files have a key with each record. For files with *relative* organization, the *key* is the record's relative position in the file and is usually not a part of the record. For files with *indexed* organization, the *key* is a part of the record. Records are stored in ascending order based on this key, and the system maintains a set of indexes to locate the record on the direct-access storage device.

In VS COBOL II, a tape reel or a direct-access storage device unit is termed a *volume.* The volume may have a volume label, and each file stored on the volume may also have a file label. Direct-access storage volumes must have volume labels; volume labels are optional on tape. The computer operators write the *volume label,* containing the volume serial number, on each volume. The system matches it against the VOL=SER=*volume* parameter in the JCL to ensure that the operator has mounted the proper volume. Files stored on direct-access devices must also have file labels; file labels are optional for tape, but most tapes have them. When the file is created, the system writes a *file label* that contains the file name, record type, record length, and block size. From then on, the DSN=*file-name* parameter specified in the JCL is matched with that in the file label to ensure that the proper file is requested. The system can obtain the DCB (Data Control Block) information from the file label rather than you having to code it in the JCL.

The hardware devices for I/O include tape drives, direct-access storage devices (disk units), and printers. There are other devices, such as graphic displays and magnetic card readers, but they are specialized and less widely used.

III. INPUT STREAM DATA

The input stream is the source of the instructions directing the processing to be done on the computer. It may consist of keyboard input, but more often it is a file that is submitted to the computer by entering a command. In MVS, you submit most files through ISPF commands.

On the mainframe, 80-character lines in the input stream are the most universal I/O medium, because the primary computer input at one time was the 80-column punched card. Today, most terminals have 80-character lines, and so the standard remains.

In MVS, lines are first queued on disk by the operating system. When the program reads a line, the system reads it from disk. This process, termed *spooling,* is necessary because several programs may be reading input lines concurrently.

Input stream input is sequential, and you can update it with a text editor, eliminating complex file update programs for simple applications.

In VS COBOL II, input stream input is specified by the DD * statement. (Microsoft COBOL requires input to be stored in a separate file. It doesn't have the equivalent of DD * input.)

```
//ddname   DD *
  [Lines of data immediately follow.]
```

Microsoft COBOL doesn't have input stream input. Instead, you can store the data in a file and read it.

IV. MAGNETIC TAPES

Mainframe tapes usually consist of either 2400-foot tape reels or 505-foot tape cartridges. A full 2400-foot reel of tape contains roughly 138 million bytes, whereas an IBM 3390 disk pack contains 946 million bytes. You can also attach tape drives to a PC. However, tapes on a PC are rare; on the PC, you generally use diskettes where tape would be used on a mainframe.

The hardware stores a byte of data in a column across the width of the tape; the position of each bit across the width is called a *track*. The *density* is the distance between successive bits along the length of the tape. The 2400-foot tape reels usually have a density of 6250 bits per inch (*bpi*), although some are 1600-bpi. Tape cartridges have 38,800-bpi density.

You can store a single file across several tape volumes, so that an unlimited amount of information can be stored. Tapes can contain only sequential files. You can store several files on a single tape volume by separating them with file marks. You do this with the LABEL=*file-number* parameter in MVS JCL. The following example writes onto file 2 of the tape. (This requires that file 1 already exist on the tape.)

```
//INFILE DD DSN=PAYROLL,LABEL=2,DISP=(NEW,KEEP),UNIT=TAPE,...
```

LABEL=1 is assumed if the LABEL parameter is not coded. If any file is rewritten, all subsequent files on that tape reel are destroyed and must be rewritten. Thus, if a tape contains three files and the second file is rewritten, the first file is unchanged, but the third file is destroyed. You regenerate tapes by reading the old tape and applying any changes to produce a new tape. You create an automatic backup by keeping the old tape and the changes.

In MVS, blocks can range in size from 18 bytes to 32,767 bytes. The hardware separates blocks written on a tape with *interrecord gaps,* which are lengths of blank tape. The end-of-file is marked by another gap followed by a special block written by the hardware, called a *file* or *tape mark*. The following formula shows how to compute the length of tape required to store a given number of records:

$$\text{Length in feet} = \text{Records}\frac{(\text{Block size/Density}) + k}{12(\text{Block size/Record length})}$$

where   *Length in feet* = length of tape in feet required to store the records; tape reels are 2400 feet and tape cartridges are 505 feet

Records = number of records in file

Block size = length of the block in bytes

Record length = record length in bytes; for variable-length records, use the average record length

Density = bits/inch: 1600, 6250, or 38,800

k = interrecord gap in inches: 0.6 for 1600-bpi tapes, 0.3 for 6250-bpi, and 0.08 for 38,800-bpi

For example, if 400-byte records with a block size of 4000 are stored on a 9-track, 6250-bpi tape, the length required to store 400,000 records is computed as follows:

$$\text{length} = 400,000\frac{(4000/6250) + 0.3}{12(4000/400)} = 3,133.3 \text{ feet}$$

Since a single tape reel contains 2400 feet, two tape reels would be required to contain this file.

The system reads tapes by moving the tape past the read head to transmit the data. If an error is detected, the system attempts to reread the block several times before signaling an I/O error. The system notifies your program of the end-of-file if the file mark is read. The system writes a tape by transmitting data from memory onto the tape as it passes the write head. The data is immediately read back as it passes the read head to ensure that it is recorded correctly. The start of the tape contains a marker, which denotes the load point and allows a leader for threading. There is another marker at the end of the reel to mark the end-of-volume with enough space to allow unfinished blocks to be completely transmitted.

In MVS JCL, you specify multiple-volume tapes in the DD statement by listing the volumes. The following example requests a file contained on volumes 214 and 125:

```
//INFILE DD DSN=PAYROLL,UNIT=TAPE,VOL=SER=(000214,000125),
//          DISP=OLD
```

You may rewrite tapes many times, erasing the old data on tape as you write the new data. For safety, computer operators must insert a small plastic ring into a circular groove in the tape reel before the tape can be written upon. Removing this ring allows the tape to be read, but protects it against being written. You must tell the operator whether to write-enable a tape or not, because JCL cannot specify this. Your installation will have a procedure for this.

Tape makes excellent long-term storage, because it is inexpensive (as little as $10 a reel) and can contain vast amounts of information in a small storage space. Tapes may be faster or slower than direct-access storage, depending on the particular device. Automatic devices are available to load tape cartridges, but an operator must mount tape reels, and this may increase the turnaround time of the job.

V. DIRECT-ACCESS STORAGE DEVICES

Direct-access storage devices are more versatile than tape. They have large capacity and fast access. They can contain sequential, relative, and indexed files. Direct-access storage derives its name from the way data is accessed. Unlike tape, you need not read the first nine records to get to the tenth. Direct-access storage devices today are all disk units. PCs have both hard disks and diskettes. They differ in speed and capacity, but not in how you program for them.

A. Disks

A disk device consists of a stack of rotating recording surfaces similar to a stack of compact discs. Each disk surface contains many concentric tracks, each containing the same amount of data. A set of electronic read/write heads is connected to an access arm positioned on top of each disk surface. When a specific track is read or written, the hardware moves the access arm to position the read/write head over the track. This arm movement is called a *seek*. The read/write head looks for a special marker on the rotating track to tell it where the track begins. Thus, there are two physical delays in accessing a specific track: a *seek delay,* which depends on how far the access arm must be moved, and a *rotational delay,* which averages out to be one-half revolution.

Since there is a read/write head for each disk surface, several tracks can be read without arm movement. The tracks that lie one above the other on different surfaces form an imaginary *cylinder,* in which all the tracks are accessible without arm movement once the cylinder has been found.

B. Using Direct-Access Storage

Disks may be rewritten many times. Files can be deleted, allowing the space to be reallocated and reused. Alternatively, you may overwrite the data in an existing file. Disk is relatively expensive storage compared to tape. It gives immediate access, important in on-line applications. You often use it for temporary files and frequently used files. You must use it for relative and indexed files.

In VS COBOL II, you must specify the amount of disk space to allocate to each file. The system terminates the program if the requested space is unavailable or if the program needs more space than requested. You allocate space with the SPACE parameter on the DD statement. With tape, the entire tape reel is always available, and you need not code the SPACE parameter. Estimating the disk space is a difficult task, particularly when a file tends to grow over time. In an MVS system, many users share the same disk packs. There is no easy way to tell whether enough space will be available on a disk to run the program.

Take special care in MVS production jobs to set up the JCL to reduce the risk of terminating because disk storage is not available. Also consider what is needed to restart the job if it terminates. If a job creates temporary files in one step and terminates in a subsequent step, temporary files are deleted. This means that the job must be restarted from the step that created them. This can be expensive. Catalog all such temporary files and delete them in the last step to use them.

To ensure that there is enough space for all steps within a job, allocate all the space in the first step. MVS has a special IEFBR14 null program that you can use to allocate space as follows:

```
//step-name  EXEC PGM=IEFBR14
//ddname  DD  all-parameters-to-create-the-file
```

Include a DD statement for each file for which space is to be allocated. The following example allocates space for the PAYROLL file.

```
//JR964113 JOB (24584),'JONES',CLASS=A
//STEP1 EXEC PGM=IEFBR14
//A DD DSN=A1000.PAYROLL.DATA,DISP=(NEW,CATLG),
//    UNIT=DISK,
//    DCB=(DSORG=PS,RECFM=FB,LRECL=80),AVGREC=U,SPACE=(80,(20000,500))
```

Subsequent steps can now write the A1000.PAYROLL.DATA file by coding the DD statement as follows:

```
//ddname  DD DSN=A1000.PAYROLL.DATA,DISP=OLD
```

Delete all disk files in the last step in which they are used, to free up space for subsequent steps and for other jobs. If a production job has difficulty obtaining disk space, you might permanently allocate space for all the files, even temporary ones. Although this reduces the disk space available to the installation, it guarantees that this job will not be terminated for lack of disk space.

The mainframe problems of allocating space don't exist on a PC. The PC allocates space to files on demand. This is one reason the PC is so much easier to use than the mainframe.

VI. FILE INTEGRITY

In crucial applications, such as an accounting or payroll system, many safe-guards may need to be built in for file integrity. You need to ensure that the proper files are used and that the data they contain is correct. One way to ensure that the proper files are used and to protect their integrity is to write a header and trailer record in addition to the header and trailer labels written by the operating system. The header record might contain a date. This lets the program read the first record and check to see that the current file is supplied by comparing the data in the header record against a transaction date. The trailer record can contain any hash totals and record counts. (Hash totals are described later in this section.) It also gives positive proof that the file contains the last record it was intended to contain.

An additional safeguard of the file's integrity is to check the sequence of the records as they are read in. If a transaction is made up of multiple records, you can ensure that all the parts are present and that they too are in the proper order.

You should always validate source data entering a system to ensure that it is correct, or at least as correct as you can logically ensure it to be. The validation might include batch totals, hash totals, and field validation.

Do all validation in a single place. This makes the data consistent. You won't accept a transaction in one part of the program and reject it in another. This often happens when validation is done in several places. If the validation is changed, all the validation is in one place to change. Also, if you want to know what validation is done, it is all in one place to see.

Do not stop with the first error discovered in a transaction. Check for all possible errors before rejecting the transaction. This may result in some redundant error messages, but each pass through an editor should catch all possible errors.

A. Batch Totals

Batch totals are frequently used to ensure that the input is entered correctly. With each group of transactions, generally all those on a single input form, critical numeric fields are totaled by hand. This batch total and a transaction count are entered with the transactions, so that if a transaction is lost or keyed improperly, the error can be detected. You can also add all the individual batch totals to obtain a grand total and a batch count. This gives an additional safeguard against losing an entire batch.

B. Hash Totals

The batch total is not so much a check against the computer doing something wrong as it is to ensure that transactions are not lost or entered improperly through human error. The usual internal safeguard against the computer making an error or dropping a record or transaction is the hash total. You create a *hash total* when the file is written by summing a numeric field within the record. You write this total as the last record in the file. Then, whenever the file is read, you sum the fields again and check this against the total in the last record. If the totals do not match, either a record was lost or a field was changed.

C. Field Validation

Batch and hash totals do not ensure that the data is correct—only that it is present. To ensure that the data is correct, you must validate individual fields. The secret of validating is to make few assumptions about the data. If a field is to contain numeric data, do not assume that it is numeric; it may contain invalid characters. The following validation checks may be made on individual fields and combinations of fields.

- *Character checking*. You can ensure that fields that are to contain blanks do contain blanks and that nonblank fields are nonblank. Validate numeric fields to ensure that they contain only numeric data, and alphabetic fields only alphabetic data.
- *Field checking*. You can perform a range check on numeric and alphanumeric fields to ensure that the data is within an acceptable range. Note that there may be two ranges—a range that is reasonable and a range that is valid. You can test a field to see that it contains only specific values by looking them up in a table or file. You can check fields for consistency. For example, if a

person's age is less than 18 and he or she shows as a registered voter, there is likely to be an error. The Internal Revenue Service uses this technique extensively.

Alphanumeric fields are more difficult to validate. You may be able to look them up in a table if there are relatively few possible values. When there can be many combinations of characters, as in names and text, it is almost impossible to validate the data with the computer. You can sometimes use the ALPHABETIC test, but character data, such as a name, often contains nonalphabetic characters. You can also check the presence or absence of alphanumeric data, its length, and that it is left-justified. But humans are much better at validating text, and so to validate text, display it so that it can be proofread.

D. File Backup

In designing a system with files, give careful thought to recovering each file in the event that it is destroyed. Disk files can be deleted and tape files can be overwritten. The usual method of backing up files is to make a copy or to keep the old master file and the transactions. Copying a file takes extra effort and expense, whereas keeping the old master file and transactions requires no extra effort or expense. In the grandfather, father, son (generation data set—sometimes called grandmother, mother, daughter) technique, you retain the master file and transactions for three or more cycles. This way you can go back one, two, or more previous cycles to recreate the new master file. Tapes are generally the most convenient medium for this technique, but MVS provides generation data groups for disk storage to accomplish the same thing.

Commercial applications generally differ from scientific applications in file recovery. In scientific applications, there may be no means of regenerating a file. Telemetry data transmitted from a satellite cannot be recreated if it is lost. Consequently, in scientific applications, programmers often must recover as many records from a bad file as possible. In many instances, such as with telemetry data, it is not critical if some data is missing. In commercial applications, you would rarely try to recover records from a bad file. Rather, you would recreate it, because it is critical that none of the data be missing. The accounting books must balance, and all the employees must get paid.

This completes the discussion of I/O devices and concepts, except for the printer. Chapter 13 describes the printer and printed output. But before we get to this, the next chapter tells how you define files in COBOL and how you use the OPEN, CLOSE, READ, and WRITE statements to program the I/O.

12

Sequential Input/Output

For reference, you must code the various headers and clauses for specifying I/O in the following order:

```
IDENTIFICATION DIVISION.
    PROGRAM-ID.  program-name.
ENVIRONMENT DIVISION.
CONFIGURATION SECTION.
SOURCE-COMPUTER. computer.
OBJECT-COMPUTER. computer.
INPUT-OUTPUT SECTION.
FILE-CONTROL.
    SELECT file-name
       ASSIGN TO
       RESERVE AREAS
       ORGANIZATION IS
       PADDING CHARACTER IS
       RECORD DELIMITER
       ACCESS MODE IS
       PASSWORD IS
       FILE STATUS IS

                .
I-O-CONTROL.
    SAME AREA, RECORD AREA, SORT AREA
    APPLY WRITE ONLY

                .
DATA DIVISION.
FILE SECTION.
FD  file-name
    EXTERNAL [or  GLOBAL]
    BLOCK CONTAINS
    RECORD CONTAINS
    LINAGE IS
    LINES AT TOP [or  BOTTOM]
```

```
        RECORDING MODE IS
        CODE-SET IS

        .
WORKING-STORAGE SECTION.
LINKAGE SECTION.
PROCEDURE DIVISION.
DECLARATIVES.
Section-name SECTION.
        USE AFTER ... PROCEDURE.
paragraphs.
        statements

        .
END DECLARATIVES.
END PROGRAM program-name.
```

For sequential input/output, records are read and written in sequence. This is the simplest and most common form of I/O. You can perform it on all I/O devices, including tapes, disks, and printers.

I. FILE DEFINITION

You must specifically describe all files. COBOL permits several I/O options to be coded in the program that can also be specified in the JCL. COBOL also has several anachronisms in the language, remaining from the past when there was no JCL to specify the I/O devices and their attributes. This book omits these anachronisms unless they are required by the compiler.

Unless you specify otherwise, COBOL assumes files have sequential organization and access. You can code ORGANIZATION SEQUENTIAL and ACCESS SEQUENTIAL if you wish:

```
    SELECT file-name ASSIGN TO ddname.
```

Same as

```
    SELECT file-name ASSIGN TO ddname
        ORGANIZATION IS SEQUENTIAL
        ACCESS MODE IS SEQUENTIAL.
```

For reference, the following lists the clauses of the SELECT. SELECT must be coded first, but after that the order doesn't matter. Note that the last clause must be terminated by a period:

```
FILE CONTROL.
    SELECT file-name
    ASSIGN TO
    RESERVE AREAS
    ORGANIZATION IS
    PADDING CHARACTER IS
```

```
RECORD DELIMITER
ACCESS MODE IS
PASSWORD IS
FILE STATUS IS
```

A. The SELECT Clause

You must name each file, termed a *file-name,* in a separate SELECT clause in the Environment Division. The SELECT clause associates the file with an external name.

1. SELECT *for like QSAM Files in VS COBOL II*

QSAM (Queued Sequential Access Method) is the normal MVS sequential file access method. The external name is a *ddname,* and a DD statement must give the operating system the file name and any necessary information about the file.

```
INPUT-OUTPUT SECTION.
FILE-CONTROL.
    SELECT file-name ASSIGN TO ddname.
    ■ ■ ■
//GO.ddname  DD ...
```

2. SELECT *for VSAM Sequential Files in VS COBOL II*

For VSAM (Virtual Sequential Access Method) sequential files, you must prefix the ddname with AS. (Omit the prefix for VSAM relative and indexed files.)

```
    SELECT file-name ASSIGN TO AS-ddname.
```

You usually create VSAM files with the IDCAMS utility.[1] However, you can also create VSAM files in a COBOL program by coding a JCL DD statement, as follows. RECORG specifies the type of VSAM data set (ES: entry-sequenced; KS: key-sequenced; RR: relative record; LS: linear-space). STORCLAS and DATACLAS are installation-dependent parameters. DATACLAS specifies the unit and volume, and DATACLAS can specify the RECORG, KEYOFF, IMBED, REPLICATE, CISIZE, FREESPACE, and SHAROPTIONS VSAM parameters.[2]

```
//ddname  DD DSN=data-set-name, DISP=(NEW,KEEP),
//           STORCLAS=VSAM,RECORG=ES,DATACLAS=class
```

3. SELECT *for Microsoft COBOL Files*

In Microsoft COBOL, you can specify the file name three ways. The first two ways are not compatible with VS COBOL II:

1. By coding the external DOS file name as a literal in the SELECT statement:

```
    SELECT file-name ASSIGN TO "file-name".
```

For example:

```
SELECT IN-FILE ASSIGN TO "C:\COBOL\TEST\STUFF.XXX".
```

2. By assigning the file to an alphanumeric identifier and moving a value to the item before opening the file. (This lets you obtain the file name during run time.)

```
SELECT file-name ASSIGN TO identifier.
■ ■ ■
MOVE "DOS-file-name" TO identifier
OPEN file-name  ...
```

For example:

```
SELECT IN-FILE ASSIGN TO WHAT-FILE.
■ ■ ■
77    WHAT-FILE                    PIC X(30).
■ ■ ■
MOVE "C:\COBOL\TEST\STUFF.XXX" TO WHAT-FILE
OPEN INPUT IN-FILE
```

3. By coding a symbolic name in the SELECT statement:

```
SELECT file-name ASSIGN TO ddname.
```

Then issue a DOS SET command before program execution to associate the file name with the symbolic name:

```
:> SET ddname  = d:\path\file-name
```

For example:

```
SELECT IN-FILE ASSIGN TO INFILE.
■ ■ ■
:> SET INFILE = C:\COBOL\TEST\STUFF.XXX
```

The default file type is RECORD SEQUENTIAL, as described in Chapter 11. You can specify LINE SEQUENTIAL files either of two ways.

1. Add the SEQUENTIAL "LINE" option to the COBOL command line for compiling. This makes the default for all the files be LINE SEQUENTIAL and thus makes the program compatible with VS COBOL II.
2. Add the ORGANIZATION IS LINE SEQUENTIAL clause to the SELECT. (You can also code ORGANIZATION IS RECORD SEQUENTIAL, if you specified the SEQUENTIAL "LINE" option so that RECORD SEQUENTIAL does not default.) This makes the program incompatible with VS COBOL II.

```
SELECT file-name ASSIGN TO external-file
  ORGANIZATION IS LINE SEQUENTIAL.
  [ or ]
SELECT file-name ASSIGN TO external-file
  ORGANIZATION IS RECORD SEQUENTIAL.
```

B. The File Definition (FD)

You further describe each file in the program with a File Description (FD) entry in the File Section of the Data Division. You must write the files' record description immediately following the FD entry.

```
DATA DIVISION.
FILE SECTION.
FD   file-name
```

> [*You must name the file-name in a* SELECT *statement.*]

BLOCK CONTAINS *integer* RECORDS

> [*Specifies the blocking. In VS COBOL II, always code a length of zero. For writing data sets, this allows MVS to select an optimum block size or allows you to specify the block size with the* DCB = BLKSIZE = *length JCL parameter. For reading, it allows the block size to be obtained from the data set label. Omit* BLOCK CONTAINS *for* SYSIN/SYSOUT *files. Microsoft COBOL ignores* BLOCK CONTAINS, *and you can omit it. If you omit the* BLOCK CONTAINS *clause is VS COBOL II, records are not blocked. You can also code* BLOCK CONTAINS *integer* CHARACTERS, *rather than* RECORDS. *to specify the block size in bytes rather than records.*]

RECORD CONTAINS *integer* CHARACTERS

> [*Specifies the record length. The literal integer should match the length of the record description that follows. COBOL ignores it if it does not. In VS COBOL II, you can code a value of zero and have the JCL specify the record length.*]

01   *record-description.*

> [*The record-description following the* FD *entry describes the record and defines its length. This record description area is termed the record area. Records become available here when they are read, and data is moved to this area before the records are written.*]

There may be several *record-description* entries placed one after the other to describe the same input/output record. That is, each level 01 *record-description* implicitly redefines the previous. (For this reason, you can't code REDEFINES for a level 01 *record-description* here.) Variable-length records often require this, as do records that may have different formats. You reference a *record-description* when you write a record. If more than one file has the same *record-description* name, you must qualify these *record-description* names within the program: *record-description* OF *file-name*. Avoid this problem by making the *record-description* names unique.

```
FD   file-name
     BLOCK CONTAINS integer RECORDS
     RECORD CONTAINS integer CHARACTERS

01   record-1-description.
01   record-2-description.
        .
        .
        .
01   record-n-description.
```

Select file and record names that convey information to the reader. Choose names that make it apparent that the file name, record name, and *ddname* all relate to the same file. You might specify whether the file is input or output, perhaps by appending -I or -0 to the file name. You might precede each record item with the *file-name*. If a file needs further documentation, place the comments immediately following the SELECT clause defining the file. The following example illustrates these suggestions:

```
FILE-CONTROL.
    SELECT PAY-I ASSIGN TO PAY.
*                                   PAY is the current payroll
*                                   file for input.
    SELECT RPT-0 ASSIGN TO RPT.
*                                   RPT prints the payroll
*                                   listing for output.
DATA DIVISION.
FILE SECTION.
FD  PAY-I
    BLOCK CONTAINS 0 RECORDS
    RECORD CONTAINS 80 CHARACTERS
     .
01  PAY-I-REC.
    05  PAY-NAME                 PIC X(20).
*                                   Name of person.
    05  PAY-ADDRESS              PIC X(60).
*                                   Person 's mailing address.
    ■ ■ ■
//GO.PAY DD ...
//GO.RPT DD SYSOUT=A
```

The complete set of FD clauses and the order they must be coded are shown here. Most of the options are described further in this chapter. Note that the last clause must be terminated with a period.

```
FD  file-name
    EXTERNAL [or GLOBAL]        [Described in Chapter 18.]
    BLOCK CONTAINS
    RECORD CONTAINS
    LINAGE IS                   [Described in Chapter 13.]
    LINES AT TOP [or BOTTOM]    [Described in Chapter 13.]
    RECORDING MODE IS
    CODE-SET IS
```

C. **The** RECORDING MODE **Clause**

Records are usually fixed-length, which is the default. You can specify different record formats, either explicitly or implicitly. VS COBOL II and Microsoft

COBOL provide the non-ANSI Standard RECORDING MODE clause to specify
the record format explicitly. The RECORDING MODE clause can specify fixed-
length, variable-length, or undefined-length records. It can also specify spanned
records, which may in turn be fixed or variable-length. (RECORDING MODE is
ignored for a VSAM file.) You code it as follows:

```
FD   file-name
                              F      [ Fixed ]
                              V      [ Variable ]
                              U      [ Undefined ]
                              S      [ Spanned ]
         RECORDING MODE IS __
       .
```

Here is an example:

```
FD   PAY-I
         BLOCK CONTAINS 0 RECORDS
         RECORD CONTAINS 80 CHARACTERS
         RECORDING MODE IS F
       .
```

You shouldn't need to code the RECORDING MODE clause, because the RECORD
CONTAINS clause can tell COBOL whether the file is fixed-length or variable.
(If the RECORD CONTAINS value is larger than the BLOCK CONTAINS value,
the compiler knows you want spanned records.) For U records, it is better to
specify them with the DCB = RECFM = U parameter on the JCL DD statement.

You can also code RECORDING MODE in Microsoft COBOL. However, it
is effective only if ORGANIZATION IS RECORD is coded or implied. For
ORGANIZATION IS LINE, RECORDING MODE is ignored, and trailing blanks
are removed when characters are written.

D. Fixed-Length Records

You can specify fixed-length explicitly by coding RECORDING MODE IS F. If
RECORDING MODE is omitted, which it usually is, fixed-length records result if
any of the following is true:

• RECORD CONTAINS *length* is coded in the FD. (If the RECORD CONTAINS
  length is greater than a nonzero BLOCK CONTAINS length, VS COBOL II
  assumes spanned records.)
• All level 01 record descriptions for the file have the same length.
• None of the record descriptions contains an OCCURS DEPENDING ON.

That is, records are fixed-length unless you do something to make them variable-length:

```
FD  IN-FILE
    BLOCK CONTAINS 0 RECORDS
    RECORD CONTAINS 100 CHARACTERS
    .
01  IN-REC                      PIC X(100).
```
        [*This file is fixed-length.*]

E. Variable-Length Records

You specify variable-length records as follows:

• Explicitly, by coding RECORDING MODE IS V.
• Explicitly, by coding RECORD VARYING FROM *min* TO *max* CHARACTERS instead of a RECORDS CONTAINS clause.
• Explicitly, by coding a record description containing an OCCURS DEPENDING ON clause.
• Implicitly, by coding several level 01 record descriptions for the same record, each having different lengths.

   To determine the length of each record and block, MVS appends a four-byte field, containing the record length, to each record. It also appends a four-byte field, containing the block size, to each block. Exclude these fields in the count for the RECORD and BLOCK CONTAINS clauses, and do not provide space for them in the record descriptions; the operating system does this automatically. However, you must count these fields in coding the LRECL and BLKSIZE DCB parameters in MVS JCL. A typical variable-length record might be described as follows:

```
FD  IN-FILE
    BLOCK CONTAINS 0 RECORDS
```
    [*Always code* BLOCK CONTAINS 0 *in VS COBOL II. Microsoft COBOL ignores* BLOCK
    CONTAINS. *You may also code* BLOCK CONTAINS *min*TO *max* RECORDS *or* CHARACTERS
    to specify the blocking in the program.]
```
    RECORD VARYING FROM min TO max CHARACTERS
```
    [*You specify the smallest and largest record sizes in the form min* TO *max. The min
    cannot be less than one nor greater than max. It doesn't matter what values you code,
    because the compiler determines the record lengths from the length of the level 01 record
    descriptions.*]

```
    .
01  IN-REC.
    05  IN-INFO                 PIC X(98).
    05  IN-SIZE                 PIC S999 PACKED-DECIMAL.
    05  IN-TABLE                OCCURS 0 TO 100 TIMES
                                DEPENDING ON IN-SIZE
                                PIC X(3).
```

The length of the variable-length record written by a WRITE, REWRITE, or
RELEASE statement depends on the length of the record description referenced
by the statement. If the record description is fixed-length, the variable-length
record will have that length. If the record description contains an OCCURS
DEPENDING ON clause, the length of the record will depend on the current size
of the table.

Rather than have the record length depend on a record description, you can
make it depend on a data item. For this, you code the RECORD phrase as

```
RECORD VARYING FROM min TO max CHARACTERS
    DEPENDING ON data-name.
```

The *data-name* must be an elementary unsigned data item. You must store the
number of characters in *data-name* before executing any WRITE, REWRITE, or
RELEASE statement. Execution of any I/O statements leaves the contents of
data-name unchanged. When a READ or RETURN statement is executed, the
length of the record read is stored in *data-name*.

Microsoft COBOL assumes ORGANIZATION IS RECORD SEQUENTIAL un-
less you specify something different. It writes the length of each record in front
of each record, as is done in MVS. This allows the record length to be deter-
mined when the records are read. For ORGANIZATION IS LINE SEQUENTIAL,
COBOL removes trailing blanks from the record and writes the remaining characters. Any RECORD VARYING clause is ignored.

F. Undefined-Length Records

You must explicitly specify undefined-length records by coding RECORDING
MODE IS U. The record description may contain the OCCURS DEPENDING ON
clause, or there may be several level 01 record descriptions having different
lengths. Omit the BLOCK CONTAINS clause, because undefined records cannot
be blocked. COBOL ignores the RECORD CONTAINS clause and uses the record
descriptions to determine the record length. A typical undefined-length record
might be described as follows:

```
FD  IN-FILE
    RECORD CONTAINS 200 CHARACTERS
    RECORDING MODE IS U
    .
01  IN-REC-1                    PIC X(100).
```
   [*The record would probably need to contain a code to indicate which record description
   is applicable.*]
```
01  IN-REC-2                    PIC X(200).
```

G. Spanned Records (VS COBOL II Only)

Spanned records are records in which the logical record length exceeds the
block size, requiring the record to be spanned across more than one block. You
specify spanned records by coding RECORDING MODE IS S. (They also result

if RECORDING MODE is not coded and the RECORD CONTAINS length is greater than the BLOCK length, assuming the BLOCK length is nonzero.) They may be fixed- or variable-length. They are variable-length if

- You code RECORD CONTAINS *min* TO *max*.
- You code several level 01 record descriptions of different lengths for the file.
- You code a record description with the OCCURS DEPENDING ON clause.

In all other cases, the records are fixed-length. A typical spanned record might be described as follows:

```
FD  IN-FILE
     BLOCK CONTAINS 0 RECORDS
       [You must code BLOCK CONTAINS for spanned records.]
     RECORD CONTAINS 0 TO 200 CHARACTERS
       [This will be a variable-length record.]
     RECORDING MODE IS S
       .
01  IN-REC-1                      PIC X(100).
01  IN-REC-2                      PIC X(200).
```

Note that spanned records can also be specified in the JCL by coding DCB = RECFM = VBS or FBS.

H. The CODE-SET **Clause**

For magnetic tapes only, the CODE-SET clause can specify the character codes of the characters on the tape if other than the computer's native mode. (That is, other than EBCDIC for VS COBOL II and ASCII for Microsoft COBOL.) You code CODE-SET as follows:

```
FD  file-name
    ■ ■ ■
    CODE-SET IS alphabet-name
       .
```

You specify the *alphabet-name* in the SPECIAL-NAMES paragraph as follows:

```
ENVIRONMENT DIVISION.
CONFIGURATION SECTION.
SOURCE-COMPUTER.  computer-name.
OBJECT-COMPUTER.  computer-name.
SPECIAL-NAMES.
    ALPHABET alphabet-name IS character-set
       .
```

The *character-set* (see also Chapter 7) can be one of the following:

STANDARD-1	For ASCII-encoded files
STANDARD-2	For ISO y-bit encoded files
EBDIC	For EBCDIC—the default for VS COBOL II

ASCII	Microsoft COBOL only; for ASCII—the default
NATIVE	The computer's native mode; this is the default if CODE-SET is omitted

II. OPENING AND CLOSING FILES

Opening a file allocates the buffers; may load the access routines into memory; creates or checks the file labels; and positions the I/O device to the start of the file. Closing a file writes out any remaining records in the output buffers, writes an end-of-file on output files, and for tape may rewind the tape reel.

MVS allocates each job step a fixed amount of storage, termed a *region*. The program is loaded into the region for execution. Then, as each file is opened during execution, the operating system suballocates buffer storage from the pool of available storage within the region. This process of suballocating storage during program execution is termed *dynamic storage allocation*. When a file is closed, the operating system releases any dynamically allocated storage obtained by the open. Thus, it is possible for a program to be loaded into memory, run for some time, and then open a file and be terminated because there is insufficient storage to allocate to the buffers.

The OPEN statement must open files before being used, and the CLOSE statement should close them after processing completes. (COBOL automatically closes any open files at run termination.) You can open files more than once, as long as you close them before opening them again. That is, open–close–open is valid, but open–open is not.

A. The OPEN Statement

You write the OPEN statement as follows:

```
        INPUT
        OUTPUT
        I-O
        EXTEND
OPEN _____ file-name, file-name, ..., file-name
```

These options affect the opening of the file as follows:

INPUT: The file is opened and positioned to its start point for reading.

OUTPUT: The file is created if necessary and positioned to its start point for writing.

I-O: The file is opened for both input and output. This option is used for updating files.

EXTEND: The file is opened for output. If the file doesn't already exist, COBOL creates it. If it does exist, the system positions just past the last record in the file for writing. This allows you to add records to an existing file. EXTEND can also be accomplished by coding DISP = (MOD, ...) in the MVS JCL.

You can also open multiple files for INPUT, OUTPUT, EXTEND, and I-0 with the same OPEN statement:

```
OPEN INPUT   file-name, file-name,  ..., file-name
     OUTPUT  file-name, file-name,  ..., file-name
     EXTEND  file-name, file-name,  ..., file-name
     I-0     file-name, file-name,  ..., file-name
```

For example:

```
OPEN INPUT  FILE-A, FILE-B
     OUTPUT FILE-C
```

If an OPEN statement is executed for a file that is already open, the USE AFTER EXCEPTION/ERROR procedure described in Chapter 15 is executed if provided.

You can also open a single-reel fixed-length record tape file reversed. The system positions the tape at the end of the file, and then reads the tape backwards so that the records are read in reverse order. This feature is rarely needed, but you might use it to read a tape containing a file sorted into ascending order as if it were in descending order. REVERSED is ignored for anything except tape. You code the OPEN as follows:

```
OPEN INPUT file-name REVERSED
```

Also for single-reel tape files, you can open the file for INPUT or OUTPUT without rewinding it, by coding NO REWIND. COBOL ignores NO REWIND for other than tape. (VS COBOL II and Microsoft COBOL ignore NO REWIND, even for tapes. Don't bother using NO REWIND.)

```
OPEN OUTPUT file-name WITH NO REWIND
```

The following are examples of OPEN statements:

```
OPEN INPUT FILE-A
OPEN OUTPUT FILE-B
OPEN INPUT FILE-C, FILE-D
     OUTPUT FILE-E
```

B. The CLOSE **Statement**

You code the CLOSE statement as follows:

```
CLOSE file-name, file-name,  ..., file-name
```

The system automatically writes labels and an end-of-file marker on an output file when it is closed. If you attempt to close a file that is not open, the USE AFTER EXCEPTION/ERROR procedure described in Chapter 15 is executed if provided.

If the file is contained on a tape reel, the tape is automatically rewound. To close a tape file without rewinding it in VS COBOL II, code a JCL DD statement with either DISP = (. . . , PASS) or VOL = (, RETAIN, . . .). This speeds processing when another file is to be read or written beyond the end of the first file.

You can also close files with LOCK to prevent the file from being opened again by the program during the run. (This is of marginal value but might protect against some programming error, since if you didn't want a file opened a second time, you wouldn't code the program to open it.)

```
CLOSE file-name WITH LOCK
```

For multiple-volume tape files, you can force volume switching to the next volume by coding the REEL clause. The file isn't closed when REEL is coded— only a volume switch occurs. For files not on tape or for single-volume tape files, a CLOSE REEL is ignored. You code it as

```
CLOSE file-name REEL
```

For an input file, there is a volume switch, and the next volume is mounted. If it doesn't contain any records, another volume switch occurs. For an output file, a volume switch occurs; the system mounts the next volume and positions it to its starting point for writing. MVS volume switching is automatic, so there is no need to code REEL in VS COBOL II.

The following are examples of CLOSE statements:

```
CLOSE FILE-A
CLOSE FILE-B,
      FILE-C
```

It is generally more efficient to open and close several files with a single statement. However, the system allocates buffers to each file, and the memory requirement is greater if all files are open concurrently. If the processing permits, you can open each file, process it, and then close it before opening the next file, to reduce the memory requirements. This also permits the same file to be read several times, by closing it and then opening it again. You can also write a file, close it, open it again, and then read it:

```
OPEN INPUT [or  OUTPUT] FILE-A
CLOSE FILE-A
OPEN INPUT FILE-A
```

In MVS, you can delete a data set when you close it, by coding DISP=(. . . ,DELETE) on the JCL DD statement. You can delete both normal and VSAM data sets this way. In Microsoft COBOL, you can delete a file with the DOS DEL command or with the following COBOL statement. The file must be closed.

```
DELETE FILE file-name
```

III. READ **AND** WRITE **STATEMENTS**

Each READ statement reads a single logical record, and each WRITE statement writes a single logical record. There are two ways of reading or writing records. First, you can READ INTO or WRITE FROM an identifier. Or you can omit the INTO or FROM phrases and process the records directly in the record area—in the buffer. The READ INTO and WRITE FROM are less efficient, because the record must be moved from the record area to the identifier, but they are perhaps easier to understand and are described first.

A. READ INTO, WRITE FROM **Forms**

```
READ file-name INTO identifier
    AT END
        imperative-statements
    NOT AT END
        imperative-statements
END-READ
```

- *file-name:* A file name described in an FD entry.
- *identifier:* A record whose length is long enough to contain the record. It can be in the Working-Storage or Linkage Section, or it can be the record description of another open file.
- AT END *imperative-statement:* These imperative statements execute when an end-of-file is encountered—that is, when an attempt is made to read a record after the last record has been read. AT END is required (unless the USE AFTER ERROR procedure described in Chapter 15 is specified for the file). AT END can be omitted in VS COBOL II even without a USE AFTER.
- NOT AT END is optional. Its statements execute if no end-of-file is encountered—if a record is read.

```
WRITE record-description FROM identifier
```

- *record-description:* A record described in the record area following the FD entry.
- *identifier:* A record described in the Data Division that contains the record to write.

Remember that you must READ a *file-name* and WRITE a *record-description*. (The logic of this is that you read from the file and write from the record in memory.) Also remember that the file must be open for INPUT for a READ and OUTPUT or EXTEND for a WRITE. The following example illustrates a single file that is first written and then read:

```
DATA DIVISION.
FILE SECTION.
FD  PAY-FILE
    BLOCK CONTAINS 0 RECORDS
```

```
      RECORD CONTAINS 80 CHARACTERS
      .
01  PAY-REC                      PIC X(80).
WORKING-STORAGE SECTION.
01  DATA-REC                     PIC X(80).
PROCEDURE DIVISION.
A00-BEGIN.
    OPEN OUTPUT PAY-FILE
      [First, the file is opened for output.]
    MOVE SPACES TO DATA-REC
    WRITE PAY-REC FROM DATA-REC
      [Then a record is written.]
    CLOSE PAY-FILE
      [The file is closed.]
    OPEN INPUT PAY-FILE
      [Now the file is opened for input.]
    READ PAY-FILE INTO DATA-REC
      AT END DISPLAY "END OF FILE"
      NOT AT END DISPLAY "RECORD: ", DATA-REC
      [The NOT AT END statements execute, because there is a record to read.]
    END-READ
    READ PAY-FILE INTO DATA-REC
      AT END DISPLAY "END OF FILE"
      [The AT END statements execute, because there are no more records.]
      NOT AT END DISPLAY "RECORD: ", DATA-REC
    END-READ
    CLOSE PAY-FILE
```

When the end-of-file is detected in a READ and the AT END phrase executes, no record is read and the contents of *identifier* are unchanged. Once the end-of-file is detected, a subsequent READ to that file will abnormally terminate the program. (However, you may close the file, open it again, and then read it.)

The result of a READ INTO and WRITE FROM is as if the record were moved to or from the record area. In a READ, if the *identifier* is shorter than the length of the record being read, COBOL truncates the record on the right. If longer, it pads the *identifier* on the right with blanks. For a WRITE, if the *identifier* is shorter than the file's record length, COBOL pads it on the right with blanks; if longer, it truncates it on the right.

B. READ, WRITE **in the Record Area**

You can also process records directly in the record area (the I/O buffers) by omitting the INTO or FROM phrase. You access the records by the record names in the record area. (After a READ, the record is also available in the record area when the INTO phrase is coded.) The following example illustrates this with the previous PAY-FILE.

```
READ PAY-FILE
     [The record is available in PAY-REC.]
   AT END DISPLAY "END-OF-FILE"
   NOT AT END DISPLAY "RECORD: ", PAY-REC
END-READ
MOVE PAY-REC TO DATA-REC
     [The record is moved to DATA-REC.]
```

The WRITE works in the reverse. You must move the data to the record:

```
MOVE DATA-REC TO PAY-REC     [The data is moved to PAY-REC.]
WRITE PAY-REC                [The data in PAY-REC is written.]
```

The concept of processing data in the buffers is confusing. Figure 12.1 illustrates what occurs inside the computer when a READ statement is executed. The buffer is equal in length to the block size, and the figure illustrates a block containing three records. The OPEN, READ, and CLOSE do the following:

- Prior to the OPEN: PAY-REC has no predictable value.
- OPEN: Storage is allocated for the buffer and the first block is read in from the file. The contents of PAY-REC are undefined.
- First READ: No data is transmitted, but PAY-REC is made to point to record 1 in the buffer. An INTO phrase would move record 1 to DATA-REC.

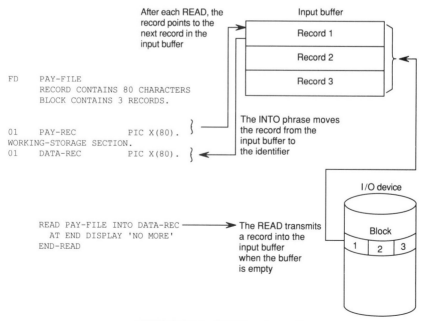

FIGURE 12.1   READ **statements.**

- Second READ: No data is transmitted, but PAY-REC is made to point to record 2 in the buffer. Record 2 is moved to DATA-REC if the INTO phrase is coded.
- Third READ: Same as second READ, but PAY-REC points to record 3 in the buffer.
- Fourth READ: The next block is transmitted into the buffer, PAY-REC is made to point to record 1 in the buffer, and an INTO phrase moves record 1 to DATA-REC.
- CLOSE: Storage for the buffer is released. PAY-REC has no predictable value.

Figure 12.2 illustrates this process for the WRITE. The OPEN, WRITE, and CLOSE do the following:

- Prior to the OPEN: PAY-REC has no predictable value.
- OPEN: Storage is allocated for the buffer, and PAY-REC points to record 1 in the output buffer.
- First WRITE: Any FROM phrase moves DATA-REC to record 1. No data is transmitted, but PAY-REC is made to point to record 2 in the buffer.
- Second WRITE: Same as the first WRITE, but PAY-REC points to record 3 in the buffer.
- Third WRITE: Any FROM phrase moves DATA-REC to record 3. The buffer is transmitted to the I/O device as a block, and PAY-REC is made to point to record 1 in the buffer.

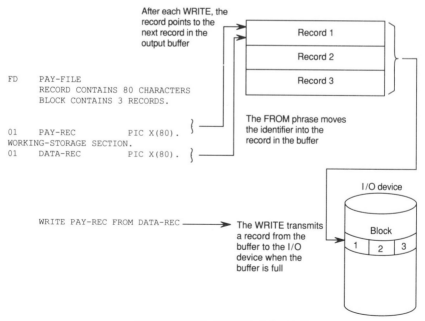

FIGURE 12.2 WRITE **statement.**

• CLOSE: Any partially filled buffer is transmitted, and storage for the buffer is released. PAY-REC has no predictable value.

Processing records in the record area is more efficient, because COBOL does not move the data to another area. However, the READ or WRITE is harder to follow, because you must look back to the FD and locate the record to find out what is read or written. You must also remember the circumstances under which the record becomes unavailable. It is not difficult to write programs with this in mind, but someone can easily forget the restrictions when the program is modified. Records become unavailable under the following circumstances.

For a READ:

• Opening the file does not make the record area available.
• A READ makes a new record available and the old record unavailable.
• An end-of-file makes the current record unavailable.
• Closing the file makes the current record unavailable.

For a WRITE:

• Opening the file makes the current value of the record unpredictable.
• A WRITE makes the current record unavailable.
• Closing the file makes the current record unavailable.

Processing records in the buffers introduces potential problems that are better avoided. The following examples illustrate some common errors:

```
WRITE PAY-REC
MOVE PAY-REC TO SOMETHING
   [Error: PAY-REC contains unpredictable values.]
MOVE FIRST-RECORD TO PAY-REC
OPEN INPUT PAY-FILE
WRITE PAY-REC
   [Error: PAY-REC no longer contains FIRST-RECORD: The OPEN destroyed its contents.]
READ PAY-FILE
   AT END MOVE PAY-REC TO LAST-RECORD
      [Error: PAY-REC contains Unpredictable values.]
END-READ
READ PAY-FILE
   AT END
      CONTINUE
   NOT AT END
      CLOSE PAY-FILE
      MOVE PAY-REC TO LAST-RECORD
         [Error: PAY-REC contains unpredictable values.]
END-READ
```

To summarize, the READ INTO combines reading a *file-name* and moving the record into the *identifier,* and the WRITE FROM moves the *identifier* to the *record* and writes out the record. The following statements are logically equivalent:

```
READ PAY-FILE INTO A-REC    [Same as]  READ PAY-FILE
  AT END                                 AT END
    CONTINUE                               CONTINUE
END-READ                                 NOT AT END
                                           MOVE PAY-REC TO A-REC
                                         END-READ
WRITE PAY-REC FROM A-REC    [Same as]  MOVE A-REC TO PAY-REC
                                       WRITE PAY-REC
```

Keep the number of READ and WRITE statements for each file to a minimum. If a file must be read or written from several places in the program, place the READ or WRITE in a paragraph and PERFORM it. This simplifies program maintenance, because there is only a single place where each file is read or written.

IV. MULTIPLE-FORMAT RECORDS

Sometimes a file may contain several record formats. For example, suppose that a variable-length record contains a 200-byte record when the first byte contains 1, and a 100-byte record when the first byte contains a 2. The following example shows how such a file could be processed:

```
FD  PAY-FILE
    BLOCK CONTAINS 0 RECORDS
    RECORD CONTAINS 100 TO 200 CHARACTERS
    .
01  PAY-REC-1.
    05  PAY-TYPE-1              PIC X.
    05  PAY-1                   PIC X(199).
01  PAY-REC-2.
        [PAY-REC-2 implicitly redefines PAY-REC-1.]
    05  PAY-TYPE-2              PIC X.
    05  PAY-2                   PIC X(99).
    ■ ■ ■
    OPEN INPUT PAY-FILE
    READ PAY-FILE
      AT END
        CONTINUE
      NOT AT END
        EVALUATE PAY-TYPE-1
            WHEN "1"
              MOVE PAY-REC-1 TO BIG-RECORD
              PERFORM A10-PROCESS-BIG-RECORD
            WHEN "2"
              MOVE PAY-REC-2 TO SMALL-RECORD
              PERFORM B10-PROCESS-SMALL-RECORD
```

```
                WHEN OTHER
                   DISPLAY "ERROR-RECORD TYPE NOT 1 OR 2."
             END-EVALUATE
          END-READ
```

V. SEQUENTIAL COPY

The following program illustrates sequential input and output by showing how
to copy a file. The complete program is shown:

```
IDENTIFICATION DIVISION.
    PROGRAM-ID. COPY-PROGRAM.
ENVIRONMENT DIVISION.
INPUT-OUTPUT SECTION.
FILE-CONTROL.
    SELECT IN-FILE ASSIGN TO INPUT.
    SELECT OUT-FILE ASSIGN TO OUTPUT.
DATA DIVISION.
FILE SECTION.
FD  IN-FILE
    RECORD CONTAINS 100 CHARACTERS.
01  IN-REC                PIC X(100).
FD  OUT-FILE
    RECORD CONTAINS 100 CHARACTERS.
01  OUT-REC               PIC X(100).
WORKING-STORAGE SECTION.
01  RECORD-COUNTS.
    05  IN-FILE-NO         PIC S9(9) BINARY VALUE 0.
    05  OUT-FILE-NO        PIC S9(9) BINARY VALUE 0.
PROCEDURE DIVISION.
START-PROGRAM.
    DISPLAY "BEGINNING COPY PROGRAM"
    OPEN INPUT IN-FILE
         OUTPUT OUT-FILE
    MOVE LOW-VALUES TO IN-REC
    PERFORM WITH TEST AFTER
           UNTIL IN-REC = HIGH-VALUES
      READ IN-FILE INTO IN-REC
        AT END
          MOVE HIGH-VALUES TO IN-REC
        NOT AT END
          ADD 1 TO IN-FILE-NO
          WRITE OUT-REC FROM IN-REC
          ADD 1 TO OUT-FILE-NO
      END-READ
    END-PERFORM
    DISPLAY "IN-FILE-NO: ", IN-FILE-NO,
          " OUT-FILE-NO: ", OUT-FILE-NO
```

```
      CLOSE IN-FILE, OUT-FILE
      STOP RUN
      .
END PROGRAM COPY-PROGRAM.
```

VI. UPDATING SEQUENTIAL FILES

A. Sequential Updating

You update a sequential file by reading it sequentially and applying the transactions to it from another sequential file. The file being updated is termed the
old master file, the file containing the transactions is termed the *transaction
file*, and the updated file is termed the *updated master file*. You read the old
master file, and if there is no transaction to update it, you simply write it out.
Otherwise, you apply the transaction and then write it out. You must order the
transactions and the records in the old master file on a record key. You use this
record key to match a transaction in the old master file. A *record key* is a portion of the record that uniquely identifies it, such as the person's Social Security
number in a personnel file. The keys may be composed of several noncontiguous fields within the record. The following example illustrates a sequential
file update in which a MASTER-IN file is updated by a TRANS file to produce
a MASTER-OUT file. For simplicity, the entire record is considered to be the key.

```
WORKING-STORAGE SECTION.
01  MASTER-REC.
    05  MASTER-KEY                PIC X(10).
01  TRANS-REC.
    05  TRANS-KEY                 PIC X(10).
    ■ ■ ■
PROCEDURE DIVISION.
    OPEN INPUT MASTER-IN, TRANS-IN,
        OUTPUT MASTER-OUT
    MOVE LOW-VALUES TO MASTER-KEY, TRANS-KEY
```
*[The record keys are set to HIGH-VALUES to denote an end-of- file. This is convenient
and does not disturb the sort order.]*
```
    PERFORM WITH TEST AFTER UNTIL MASTER-KEY = HIGH-VALUES
```
[All the master file records are read, along with any matching transactions.]
```
      READ MASTER-IN INTO MASTER-REC
        AT END
          MOVE HIGH-VALUES TO MASTER-KEY
        NOT AT END
          PERFORM A20-READ-TRANS WITH TEST BEFORE
              UNTIL TRANS-KEY >= MASTER-KEY
      IF TRANS-KEY = MASTER-KEY
          THEN  ...
```
*[The transaction matches the master file record. Update the master file
record with the transaction.]*

```
                END-IF
                WRITE MASTER-OUT-RECORD FROM MASTER-REC
         END-READ
      END-PERFORM

**** Exit
 A20-READ-TRANS.
      READ TRANS-IN INTO TRANS-REC
         AT END
            MOVE HIGH-VALUES TO TRANS-KEY
         NOT AT END
            IF TRANS-KEY < MASTER-KEY
               THEN DISPLAY "NO MASTER FOR TRANS RECORD."
                    DISPLAY "TRANS-KEY: ", TRANS-KEY
            END-IF
      END-READ

**** Exit
```

The preceding files can only be matched if they are in the same order based on their keys. You often need to check that the files are in the proper order and that there are no duplicate records. The following example shows how the previous MASTER-IN file would be checked for this:

```
  77  OLD-MASTER-KEY                 PIC X(10).
      ■ ■ ■
      MOVE LOW-VALUES TO OLD-MASTER-KEY
      ■ ■ ■
       READ MASTER-IN INTO MASTER-REC
          AT END
             MOVE HIGH-VALUES TO MASTER-KEY
          NOT AT END
             IF MASTER-KEY = OLD-MASTER-KEY
                THEN DISPLAY "DUPLICATE MASTER RECORDS."
                     DISPLAY "MASTER KEY: ", MASTER-KEY
                ELSE IF MASTER-KEY < OLD-MASTER-KEY
                THEN DISPLAY "MASTER OUT OF SORT."
                     DISPLAY "MASTER KEY: ", MASTER-KEY
                     DISPLAY "OLD-MASTER-KEY: ", OLD-MASTER-KEY
             END-IF
             MOVE MASTER-KEY TO OLD-MASTER-KEY
             ■ ■ ■
```

You usually apply transactions to an old master file by allowing records to be deleted, added, or changed. There may also be a *replace,* which is equivalent to a delete and an add. The operation, whether a delete, add, or change, should be specified within the transaction. The advantage of specifying the operation within the transaction is that you can detect errors. With the alternative—adding the transaction if it does not match a record in the old master file, and changing or replacing it if it does match—you couldn't detect the following errors:

- Add: Error if the record already exists in the old master file.
- Delete: Error if the record does not exist in the old master file.
- Change: Error if the record does not exist in the old master file.

If there can be more than one operation on the same old master file record, the order should be add, change, and then delete. This may seem unnecessary. Why add a record and then change it in the same update run? However, transactions are often batched for a periodic update. It may be perfectly logical for one clerk to add a transaction on Monday, another clerk enter a change on Tuesday, and then process all the transactions on a Friday update run.

  The delete and add are straightforward, because you either write or do not write a record, but the change operation is more difficult. With a change, you do not want to update all the fields (that would be a replace), but only certain fields. The usual way of changing a record is to establish a different transaction type for each field to be changed. In critical applications, you can require a change transaction to contain two values. One value can be the current contents of the field being changed to ensure that the proper field is changed, and the second value can be the change. Another way to update individual fields within the old master file records is to use the same transaction format as in the add transaction, but change only the fields that are nonblank in the transaction. The advantage of this is that the same input form used for the add can be used for the update. You simply fill in the record key and the fields to change and leave all the other fields blank. (You can redefine an alphanumeric data item over numeric fields to determine if they are blank.) The disadvantage of this technique is that if you wish to replace a field with blanks, you must indicate this by some means, such as asterisks in the field.

  A common error in updating records is to update the record key and forget that this affects the sort order. In sequential updating, you write the master file out in the same order in which you read it. However, if the record key is updated, the record may no longer be in the proper sort order. Keep in mind that if you update the record key, you should restore the file.

B. Updating Files on Disk with REWRITE

Usually if a single record is changed in a sequential file, you must rewrite the entire file. However, it is possible to rewrite individual records in files that reside on direct-access storage devices (disks). COBOL permits files to be opened for I-0 (input-output), and they can then be both read and written. The REWRITE statement, coded like the WRITE, can rewrite a record that has just been read. The following shows how a sequential file might be updated using REWRITE.

```
FD  PAYROLL-IO
    BLOCK CONTAINS 0 RECORDS
```

```
      RECORD CONTAINS 80 CHARACTERS

01  PAYROLL-RECORD                    PIC X(80).
WORKING-STORAGE SECTION.
01  PAY-REC.
      05  PAY-KEY                     PIC X(20).
      05  PAY-TYPE                    PIC X.
      05  PAY-AMT                     PIC S9(5)V99.
      05  PAY-REST                    PIC X(52).
      ▪ ▪ ▪
      OPEN I-O PAYROLL-IO
        [The file is opened for input/output.]
      PERFORM WITH TEST AFTER UNTIL PAY-KEY = HIGH-VALUES
        READ PAYROLL-IO INTO PAY-REC
          AT END
             MOVE HIGH-VALUES TO PAY-KEY
          NOT AT END
             [A record has been read.]
          IF PAY-TYPE = "A"
             [We may want to update only certain records.]
             THEN MOVE ZERO TO PAY-AMT
                  [We can store any new values in the record.]
                  REWRITE PAYROLL-RECORD FROM PAY-REC
                  [The last record read is rewritten.]
          END-IF
        END-READ
      END-PERFORM
```

The record rewritten must be the same length as the record read, because
REWRITE overwrites the record in the file. Sequential files are often updated
this way by reading a sequential file and executing REWRITE statements for the
records to be rewritten.

REWRITE can also rewrite from the record area by omitting the FROM phrase:

```
REWRITE record-description
```

VII. SEQUENTIAL UPDATE EXAMPLE

The next example shows how a master file is read and updated by a transaction
file to create a new master file. This is a very common process for sequential
files. For brevity, we'll not validate the transactions, but we will print run
statistics. Assume we are given the following information:

1. Old master file

```
[File name:]  OLD-MASTER
[Record is:]  01  MASTER-REC.
```

```
                    05  MASTER-KEY [is record key.]
                    05  MASTER-FIELDS [are the data fields.]
```

In ascending sequence on MASTER-KEY. No duplicate records.

2. Transaction file

```
[File name:]  TRANS-FILE
[Record:]     01  TRANS-REC.
                  05  TRANS-KEY [is record key.]
                  05  TRANS-ACTION [specifies the action:]
                      [D Delete the record.]
                      [I Insert the record.]
                      [U Update the record.]
                  05  TRANS-FIELDS [are the data fields.]
```

Can delete or update an inserted record. Insert must not have matching record in master file. Delete and Change must have a matching record in master file. In ascending order on TRANS-KEY, TRANS-ACTION.

3. New master file

```
[File name:]  NEW-MASTER
[Record:]     01  NEW-MASTER-RECORD
```

4. Hold-area record, to hold an inserted transaction so it can be changed or deleted by another transaction

```
[Record:]  01  HOLD-AREA.
               05  HOLD-KEY [is the record key.]
               05  HOLD-FIELDS [are data fields.]
```

5. Program statistics

OLD-MASTER-COUNT counts master records read.
TRANS-FILE-COUNT counts transactions read.
NEW-MASTER-COUNT counts master records write.
TRANS-CHANGE-COUNT counts records changed.
TRANS-ADD-COUNT counts transactions added.
TRANS-DEL-COUNT counts records deleted.
TRANS-ERROR-COUNT counts transactions in error.

A complete program to perform this update is included here. It is a rather long example, but since it is such a common and important application, it is handy for reference.

```
IDENTIFICATION DIVISION.
    PROGRAM-ID. UPDATE-IT.
ENVIRONMENT DIVISION.
INPUT-OUTPUT SECTION.
FILE-CONTROL.
    SELECT OLD-MASTER ASSIGN TO INPUT.
    SELECT TRANS-FILE ASSIGN TO TRANS.
    SELECT NEW-MASTER ASSIGN TO OUTPUT.
```

```
DATA DIVISION.
FILE SECTION.
FD  OLD-MASTER
    RECORD CONTAINS 100 CHARACTERS.
01  OLD-MASTER-RECORD        PIC X(100).
FD  TRANS-FILE
    RECORD CONTAINS 101 CHARACTERS.
01  TRANS-RECORD             PIC X(101).
FD  NEW-MASTER
    RECORD CONTAINS 100 CHARACTERS.
01  NEW-MASTER-RECORD.
    05  NEW-MASTER-KEY        PIC X(5).
    05  NEW-MASTER-FIELDS     PIC X(95).
WORKING-STORAGE SECTION.
01  MASTER-REC.
    05  MASTER-KEY            PIC X(5).
*       LOW-VALUES:  No record.  HIGH-VALUES:  EOF.
    05  MASTER-FIELDS         PIC X(95).
01  PREV-MASTER-KEY          PIC X(5).
01  TRANS-REC.
    05  TRANS-KEY             PIC X(5).
*       LOW-VALUES:  No record.  HIGH-VALUES:  EOF.
    05  TRANS-ACTION          PIC X.
    05  TRANS-FIELDS          PIC X(95).
01  HOLD-REC.
*     HOLD-REC contains inserted TRANS-REC until written.
    05  HOLD-KEY              PIC X(5).
*       LOW-VALUES:  Record deleted.  HIGH-VALUES:  No record.
    05  HOLD-FIELDS           PIC X(95).
01  PREV-TRANS.
    05  PREV-TRANS-KEY        PIC X(5).
    05  PREV-TRANS-ACTION     PIC X.
01  RECORD-COUNTS.
    05  OLD-MASTER-COUNT      PIC S9(9) BINARY VALUE 0.
    05  TRANS-FILE-COUNT      PIC S9(9) BINARY VALUE 0.
    05  NEW-MASTER-COUNT      PIC S9(9) BINARY VALUE 0.
    05  TRANS-CHANGE-COUNT    PIC S9(9) BINARY VALUE 0.
    05  TRANS-ADD-COUNT       PIC S9(9) BINARY VALUE 0.
    05  TRANS-DEL-COUNT       PIC S9(9) BINARY VALUE 0.
    05  TRANS-ERROR-COUNT     PIC S9(9) BINARY VALUE 0.
PROCEDURE DIVISION.
START-PROGRAM.
    DISPLAY "START OF UPDATE PROGRAM"
    OPEN INPUT OLD-MASTER,
               TRANS-FILE,
         OUTPUT NEW-MASTER
```

```
        MOVE LOW-VALUES TO MASTER-KEY, TRANS-KEY,
                        TRANS-ACTION
        MOVE HIGH-VALUES TO HOLD-KEY
        PERFORM A00-READ-MASTER WITH TEST AFTER
                UNTIL MASTER-KEY = HIGH-VALUES AND
                      TRANS-KEY = HIGH-VALUES
        CLOSE OLD-MASTER,
              TRANS-FILE,
              NEW-MASTER
        DISPLAY "OLD MASTER RECORDS READ:      ", OLD-MASTER-COUNT
        DISPLAY "TRANS RECORDS READ:           ", TRANS-FILE-COUNT
        DISPLAY "NEW MASTER RECORDS WRITTEN: ", NEW-MASTER-COUNT
        DISPLAY "OLD MASTER RECORDS DELETED: ", TRANS-DEL-COUNT
        DISPLAY "OLD MASTER RECORDS CHANGED: ", TRANS-CHANGE-COUNT
        DISPLAY "NEW TRANSACTIONS ADDED:       ", TRANS-ADD-COUNT
        DISPLAY "TRANS ERROR COUNT             ", TRANS-ERROR-COUNT
        DISPLAY "END OF UPDATE PROGRAM EXECUTION"
        STOP RUN


    A00-READ-MASTER.
    ***************************************************************
    * PROCEDURE TO READ ALL MASTER RECORDS.                      *
    * IN:  MASTER, TRANS, NEW-MASTER files open.                 *
    * OUT: MASTER and TRANS file records read.                   *
    *      MASTER-KEY, TRANS-KEY contain HIGH-VALUES when both   *
    *      reach EOF.                                            *
    ***************************************************************
    *      Get a master record.
        PERFORM A10-GET-NEXT-MASTER WITH TEST BEFORE
                UNTIL MASTER-KEY > LOW-VALUES
    *      Process transactions up to the master record.
        PERFORM A30-GET-NEXT-TRANS WITH TEST BEFORE
                UNTIL TRANS-KEY > LOW-VALUES
    *      If we are holding a record less than the transaction record,
    *      write it out.
        IF HOLD-KEY > LOW-VALUES AND < HIGH-VALUES AND < TRANS-KEY
           THEN MOVE HOLD-REC TO NEW-MASTER-RECORD
                PERFORM A50-WRITE-MASTER
                MOVE HIGH-VALUES TO HOLD-KEY
        END-IF
        EVALUATE TRUE
           WHEN TRANS-KEY = HIGH-VALUES AND
                MASTER-KEY = HIGH-VALUES
    *               EOF for both files.
                CONTINUE
           WHEN TRANS-KEY < MASTER-KEY AND
```

```
            HOLD-KEY = HIGH-VALUES OR LOW-VALUES
*             Apply transaction where it doesn't match a master
*             record.
            PERFORM A60-APPLY-TRANS
            MOVE LOW-VALUES TO TRANS-KEY
        WHEN TRANS-KEY < MASTER-KEY AND
            HOLD-KEY NOT = HIGH-VALUES AND LOW-VALUES
*             Apply transaction where we have a record held.
            PERFORM A70-APPLY-TO-HOLD
            MOVE LOW-VALUES TO TRANS-KEY
        WHEN TRANS-KEY = MASTER-KEY
*             Apply transaction to master record.
            PERFORM A80-APPLY-TO-MASTER
            MOVE LOW-VALUES TO TRANS-KEY
        WHEN TRANS-KEY > MASTER-KEY AND MASTER-KEY = LOW-VALUES
*             Delete master file record.
            ADD 1 TO TRANS-DEL-COUNT
            MOVE LOW-VALUES TO TRANS-KEY
        WHEN TRANS-KEY > MASTER-KEY AND
            MASTER-KEY NOT = LOW-VALUES
*             All transactions applied.  Write master record.
            MOVE MASTER-REC TO NEW-MASTER-RECORD
            PERFORM A50-WRITE-MASTER
            MOVE MASTER-KEY TO PREV-MASTER-KEY
            MOVE LOW-VALUES TO MASTER-KEY
     END-EVALUATE
     .
**** Exit
 A10-GET-NEXT-MASTER.
****************************************************************
* PROCEDURE TO READ NEXT MASTER RECORD.                       *
* IN:   MASTER file open.                                     *
* OUT: MASTER-REC contains record.                            *
*      MASTER-KEY contains HIGH-VALUES if EOF.                *
****************************************************************
     READ OLD-MASTER INTO MASTER-REC
       AT END
          MOVE HIGH-VALUES TO MASTER-KEY
       NOT AT END
          ADD 1 TO OLD-MASTER-COUNT
          PERFORM A20-VALIDATE-MASTER
     END-READ
     .
**** Exit
 A20-VALIDATE-MASTER.
****************************************************************
* PROCEDURE TO VALIDATE MASTER RECORD.                        *
```

```
* IN:  MASTER-REC contains record.                               *
* OUT: MASTER-KEY set to LOW-VALUES if invalid.                  *
*****************************************************************
     IF MASTER-KEY < PREV-MASTER-KEY
        THEN DISPLAY "ERROR--MASTER FILE NOT IN SEQUENCE:"
             DISPLAY "PREV-MASTER-KEY: ", PREV-MASTER-KEY,
                     " MASTER-KEY: ", MASTER-KEY
             GO TO Z90-STOP-RUN
     END-IF
     IF MASTER-KEY = PREV-MASTER-KEY
        THEN DISPLAY "ERROR--DUPLICATE MASTER RECORDS:"
             DISPLAY "MASTER-KEY: ", MASTER-KEY
             ADD 1 TO TRANS-ERROR-COUNT
             MOVE LOW-VALUES TO MASTER-KEY
     END-IF
     .
**** Exit
 A30-GET-NEXT-TRANS.
*****************************************************************
* PROCEDURE TO READ NEXT TRANS RECORD.                           *
* IN:  TRANS file open.                                          *
* OUT: TRANS-REC contains record.                               *
*      TRANS-KEY contains HIGH-VALUES if EOF.                    *
*****************************************************************
     MOVE TRANS-KEY TO PREV-TRANS-KEY
     MOVE TRANS-ACTION TO PREV-TRANS-ACTION
     READ TRANS-FILE INTO TRANS-REC
       AT END
          MOVE HIGH-VALUES TO TRANS-KEY
       NOT AT END
          ADD 1 TO TRANS-FILE-COUNT
          PERFORM A40-VALIDATE-TRANS
     END-READ
     .
**** Exit
 A40-VALIDATE-TRANS.
*****************************************************************
* PROCEDURE TO VALIDATE TRANS RECORD.                            *
* IN:  TRANS-REC contains record.                               *
* OUT: TRANS-KEY set to LOW-VALUES if invalid.                   *
*****************************************************************
     EVALUATE TRUE
       WHEN TRANS-KEY < PREV-TRANS-KEY
            DISPLAY "ERROR--TRANS FILE OUT OF SEQUENCE"
            DISPLAY "OLD-KEY: ", PREV-TRANS-KEY,
                    " NEW-KEY: ", TRANS-KEY
            GO TO Z90-STOP-RUN
```

```
          WHEN TRANS-KEY = PREV-TRANS-KEY AND
              TRANS-ACTION < PREV-TRANS-ACTION
              DISPLAY "ERROR--TRANS ACTIONS OUT OF SEQUENCE"
              DISPLAY "OLD-KEY: ", PREV-TRANS-KEY,
                    " OLD-ACTION: ", PREV-TRANS-ACTION,
                    " NEW-KEY: ", TRANS-KEY,
                    " NEW-ACTION: ", TRANS-ACTION
              GO TO Z90-STOP-RUN
       END-EVALUATE
       IF TRANS-ACTION = "I" OR "U" OR "D"
          THEN CONTINUE
          ELSE DISPLAY "ERROR--BAD TRANS-ACTION.  KEY: ",
                       TRANS-KEY,
                       " ACTION: ", TRANS-ACTION
               MOVE LOW-VALUES TO TRANS-KEY
               ADD 1 TO TRANS-ERROR-COUNT
       END-IF
       .
**** Exit
 A50-WRITE-MASTER.
 ****************************************************************
 * PROCEDURE TO WRITE NEW MASTER RECORD.                       *
 * IN:  Record stored in NEW-MASTER-RECORD.                    *
 * OUT: NEW-MASTER-RECORD written.                             *
 ****************************************************************
       ADD 1 TO NEW-MASTER-COUNT
       WRITE NEW-MASTER-RECORD
       .
**** Exit
 A60-APPLY-TRANS.
 ****************************************************************
 * PROCEDURE TO APPLY TRANSACTION WHERE NO MASTER RECORD.      *
 * IN:  TRANS-REC contains record.                             *
 * OUT: TRANS-REC stored in HOLD-REC if insert.               *
 ****************************************************************
       EVALUATE TRANS-ACTION
         WHEN "D"
              DISPLAY "ERROR--DELETE WITH NO MASTER RECORD"
              DISPLAY "IGNORING TRANS-KEY: ", TRANS-KEY
              ADD 1 TO TRANS-ERROR-COUNT
         WHEN "I"
              PERFORM A90-TRANS-ADD
         WHEN "U"
              DISPLAY "ERROR--UPDATE WITH NO MASTER RECORD"
              DISPLAY "IGNORING TRANS-KEY: ", TRANS-KEY
              ADD 1 TO TRANS-ERROR-COUNT
```

```
        END-EVALUATE
        .
**** Exit
 A70-APPLY-TO-HOLD.
 ****************************************************************
 * PROCEDURE TO APPLY TRANS TO HOLD RECORD.                    *
 * IN:   TRANS-REC contains transaction.                       *
 *       TRANS-KEY = HOLD-KEY.                                  *
 *       HOLD-REC contains previous TRANSACTION.               *
 * OUT: Record applied to HOLD-REC.                            *
 *       HOLD-KEY set to HIGH-VALUES if HOLD-REC written.      *
 *                        LOW-VALUES if HOLD-REC deleted.      *
 ****************************************************************
        EVALUATE TRUE
          WHEN TRANS-KEY > HOLD-KEY
               MOVE HOLD-REC TO NEW-MASTER-RECORD
               PERFORM A50-WRITE-MASTER
               MOVE HIGH-VALUES TO HOLD-REC
               PERFORM A60-APPLY-TRANS
          WHEN TRANS-ACTION = "D"
               MOVE LOW-VALUES TO HOLD-KEY
               ADD 1 TO TRANS-DEL-COUNT
          WHEN TRANS-ACTION = "I"
               DISPLAY "ERROR--INSERTING WITH MASTER RECORD"
               DISPLAY "IGNORING TRANS-KEY: ", TRANS-KEY
               ADD 1 TO TRANS-ERROR-COUNT
          WHEN TRANS-ACTION = "U"
               MOVE TRANS-FIELDS TO HOLD-FIELDS
               ADD 1 TO TRANS-CHANGE-COUNT
        END-EVALUATE
        .
**** Exit
 A80-APPLY-TO-MASTER.
 ****************************************************************
 * PROCEDURE TO APPLY TRANS TO MASTER RECORD.                  *
 * IN:   TRANS-REC contains transaction.                       *
 *        TRANS-KEY = MASTER-KEY                               *
 *       MASTER-REC contains master record.                    *
 * OUT: RECORD applied to MASTER-REC.                          *
 *       MASTER-KEY set to LOW-VALUES if deleted.              *
 ****************************************************************
        EVALUATE TRUE
          WHEN TRANS-ACTION = "I" AND MASTER-KEY = LOW-VALUES
               PERFORM A90-TRANS-ADD
          WHEN TRANS-ACTION = "I" AND MASTER-KEY NOT = LOW-VALUES
               DISPLAY "ERROR--ADD WHEN MASTER PRESENT: ",
                       TRANS-KEY
```

```
                 ADD 1 TO TRANS-ERROR-COUNT
         WHEN TRANS-ACTION = "D" AND MASTER-KEY NOT = LOW-VALUES
                 MOVE MASTER-KEY TO PREV-MASTER-KEY
                 MOVE LOW-VALUES TO MASTER-KEY
                 ADD 1 TO TRANS-DEL-COUNT
         WHEN TRANS-ACTION = "D" AND MASTER-KEY = LOW-VALUES
                 DISPLAY "ERROR-DELETING DELETED RECORD: ", TRANS-KEY
                 ADD 1 TO TRANS-ERROR-COUNT
         WHEN TRANS-ACTION = "U" AND MASTER-KEY NOT = LOW-VALUES
                 ADD 1 TO TRANS-CHANGE-COUNT
                 MOVE TRANS-FIELDS TO MASTER-FIELDS
         WHEN TRANS-ACTION = "U" AND MASTER-KEY = LOW-VALUES
                 DISPLAY "ERROR--CHANGING DELETED RECORD: ", TRANS-KEY
                 ADD 1 TO TRANS-ERROR-COUNT
     END-EVALUATE
         .
**** Exit
 A90-TRANS-ADD.
 *************************************************************
 * PROCEDURE TO INSERT A TRANS-REC RECORD.                  *
 * IN:  TRANS-REC contains transaction.                     *
 * OUT: HOLD-REC contains transaction.                      *
 *************************************************************
     ADD 1 TO TRANS-ADD-COUNT
     MOVE TRANS-KEY TO HOLD-KEY
     MOVE TRANS-FIELDS TO HOLD-FIELDS
         .
**** Exit
 Z90-STOP-RUN.
 *************************************************************
 * PROCEDURE TO TERMINATE RUN IF ERROR.                     *
 * IN:  All files open.                                     *
 * OUT: RETURN-CODE set to 16.                              *
 *      All files closed.                                   *
 *************************************************************
     DISPLAY "RUN TERMINATED FOR ERRORS."
     MOVE 16 TO RETURN-CODE
     CLOSE OLD-MASTER,
           TRANS-FILE,
           NEW-MASTER
     STOP RUN
         .
 END PROGRAM UPDATE-IT.
```

This concludes the discussion of sequential input/output, except for the next chapter on printed output. Printed output is discussed in a separate chapter because of the additional considerations in producing output for the printed page.

EXERCISES

1. An input file consists of 80-column lines divided into six fields, each alternating seven and nine characters in length. The last 32 columns of the lines are blank. The first two fields contain integer numbers, the next two fields contain numbers with two digits to the right of the assumed decimal point, and the final two fields contain character data. The numbers may be signed, with a minus sign to the left of the leftmost digit, or they may be unsigned. The numbers also have leading blanks. Write a program to read this file in and store each column in a table. Store the numeric data as PACKED-DECIMAL. Assume that there can be a maximum of 100 records in the file, but print an error message and terminate the job if this number is exceeded. Print out the records as they are read in.

2. Copy a file containing 80 characters per record, and an unknown number of records. Exclude all records that contain the character "I" in the sixty-third character position of the record. Print out the number of records read, number excluded, and the number of records written.

3. Define a record that contains a four-digit project number, a 25-character name, and an overhead percentage of precision PIC S9(5)V99 PACKED-DECIMAL. Read in a file of such records and print the number of duplicate project numbers. Check the sort sequence of the records to ensure that they are in order on the project number.

4. Read in a file containing eight integer numbers per line, 10 columns per number. The numbers are right-justified with leading blanks. Store the numbers in a two-dimensional table with the line number as one dimension and the numbers within the line as the other. Store the data as PIC S9(9) PACKED -DECIMAL. Allow for a maximum of 100 lines, and print an error message and terminate the run if this number is exceeded. Then do the following:

Print the number of records read.
Write out the entire table as a single record.
Read this single record back into an identical table.
Verify that the data was transmitted properly by comparing the first
table with the second.

5. A file must be read that is set up as follows: Column 1 of the first line describes the format of the data contained in the lines that follow. If column 1 contains a 1, the lines following contain integer numbers in columns 1 to 5. If column 1 contains a 2, the lines following contain a decimal number in columns 1 to 10 with two digits to the right of the assumed decimal point. If column 1 contains a 3, the lines following contain integer numbers in columns 1 to 4. Read the file in, edit the data to ensure that it is numeric, and print an error message if any invalid data is found. The numbers may or may not be signed, and there may be leading blanks. Print out the number on each line as it is read.

6. Two files each have records containing 100 characters. Each file is in ascending sort order on the first 10 characters of the records. There may be duplicate records in each file. Read in the two files and merge them to write out a new file containing only records with unique keys.

7. A file contains 80-character lines. The first 10 characters of the record constitute the record key. Write a file containing only unique record keys. The input file is unsorted. Read the records in and store each unique key in a table. Allow for 1000 unique keys, and print an error message if there are more than this. Write the output file from the table.

8. The program listed below was extracted from an actual program, and a very poor one at that. The program reads an old master file and a transaction file and writes out master file records for which there is a matching transaction. The program has been running for some time, but suddenly you are told that the last run did not write out enough records in the output file. The MASTER-IN file is read, and only records that match records in the TRANS-IN file are written out in the MASTER-OUT file. Any record in TRANS-IN is supposed to match a record in MASTER-IN, but the transactions are prepared by hand. Both MASTER-IN and TRANS-IN are in ascending sort order. They are sorted just before being read, so their sort order is likely to be correct. However, the program does not check for the sort order.

Find the error in the program. Since the program has been running for some time, you might suspect that the error is caused by the data's not living up to the program's assumptions. Rewrite the program, following the rules of structured programming, and check for any data errors and print clear error messages.

```
77  ISKIP                    PIC 9.
    ■ ■ ■
    MOVE ZERO TO ISKIP.
A10.  READ MASTER-IN INTO IN-REC AT END GO TO A60.
    IF ISKIP NOT = ZEROS GO TO A20.
    READ TRANS-IN INTO TRANS-REC AT END GO TO A50.
    GO TO A30.
A20.  IF ISKIP = 2 GO TO A10.
    MOVE ZERO TO ISKIP.
A30.  IF TRANS-REC NOT = IN-REC GO TO A40.
    WRITE OUT-REC FROM IN-REC.
    MOVE ZERO TO ISKIP.
    GO TO A10.
A40.  MOVE 1 TO ISKIP.
    GO TO A10.
A50.  MOVE 2 TO ISKIP.
    GO TO A10.
A60.  ...
```

REFERENCES

1. "MVS/370 Integrated Catalog Administration: Access Method Services Reference," Order No. GC26-4051, Poughkeepsie, NY: IBM Corporation, 1991.

2. "MVS/ESA JCL Reference," Order No. GC18-1829, Poughkeepsie, NY: IBM Corporation, 1991.

13

Printed Output

Printed output is the most common form of output, and it can become very complicated. It is read by humans rather than by a computer, and it is two-dimensional, consisting of characters within a line (a line corresponds to a record) and lines on a page. It also requires an aesthetic sense that is not always inherent in the cool logic generally required of programmers. But the most difficult part of printing output is the reaction of the end user to the printed page. Somehow, printed output evokes a response from the reader much like that of newlyweds to a roomful of new furniture. They have definite ideas where each piece should go, but after they see it there, they are apt to change their minds. The same occurs when the reader first sees a report. This is especially true of management reports, which are less standardized and are used for making decisions. It is not necessarily capriciousness on the reader's part to want to make changes to the report. Only by seeing actual numbers and working with them can the reader know what further information is needed. It is hard for a programmer to second-guess the reader. Although readers should be pressed to think about their needs, the needs may not be apparent until the information begins to be used.

The PC has increased the level of expectation for reports. The color graphics display and laser printer, with their pie charts and three-dimensional bar charts, make the typical COBOL report containing rows and columns of numbers look unappealing. Rather than trying to fight this battle using mainframe COBOL, you would be better off to download the data and use PC software to display the reports.

The first thing to come to terms with in designing reports is that they are likely to change. Make them easy to change. There are also various report and graphical packages available on the mainframe and PC that you might consider as an alternative to generating reports with COBOL. Microsoft COBOL and the ANSI Standard have a report writer for generating reports, but since it is not in VS COBOL II, this book does not cover it. The COBOL report writer is very powerful, but somehow it always seems that your particular report needs some special feature not provided.

I. PRINTERS

Most mainframe printers today are laser printers, which print a page of output at a time. The paper is normally 11" wide by $8\frac{1}{2}$" with 66 lines per page and 132 characters per line. However, they can also print 110 and 204 characters per line. Printers can also print 88 lines per page. The paper can be oriented $8\frac{1}{2}$" wide by 11" for letter format. There are also line printers still around that print on continuous-form 14" wide by 11" paper. Other paper sizes are also available, but these are the most common.

There is a wide range of impact and nonimpact printers on PCs. They may or may not have the same capability as the mainframe printers. Their usual paper orientation is $8\frac{1}{2}$" wide by 11", with the ability of some for 11" wide by $8\frac{1}{2}$". Some can also print on 14" wide by 11" paper.

Multiple copies are made by printing the report several times. (Impact printers can print multipart paper.) You can print a file several times with the COPIES subparameter in the DD statement, as follows:

```
//GO.ddname   DD SYSOUT=A,COPIES=copies
```

Special forms can also be made in many sizes and are most widely used to print checks. The special forms can have anything preprinted on them and may come in colors. Never use special forms unless you must, because they are more expensive and an operator must mount and dismount the forms on the printer. They also make reports inflexible, because a report change may require designing a new form, with a lead time to have it made up and delivered.

II. PRINT FILES

A. Specifying the Printer

You must write the SELECT statement for print files, just as for any other file. In VS COBOL II, you specify a *ddname* and then code a DD statement in the JCL, as follows:

```
    SELECT file-name ASSIGN TO ddname .
    ■ ■ ■
//ddname   DD SYSOUT=A
```

The SYSOUT=A specifies the standard printer at most installations, but other output classes may be required or available.

In Microsoft COBOL, you specify the printer by coding PRN as the *ddname:*

```
    SELECT file-name ASSIGN TO PRN.
```

If you don't want the printer hard-wired in the program, specify a symbolic name and then use the DOS SET statement to assign it to the printer. This way is compatible with VS COBOL II:

```
      SELECT file-name ASSIGN TO PRINTIT.
      ■ ■ ■
:> SET PRINTIT PRN
```

B. The FD **Entry**

You describe print files the same as normal files, with the record length set to the number of print positions.

IBM mainframe printers are controlled by the first character position in each line. VS COBOL II automatically accounts for this unless you code the NOADV compile option, described in Chapter 17. If you code NOADV, you must set aside the first character of each line for the carriage control character that controls the printer. You never need to store anything in this position—the VS COBOL II compiler will do this for you. If you accept the default ADV compiler option, VS COBOL II automatically adds an extra byte to the record described in the FD for any file that has the LINAGE clause or for which there are WRITE ADVANCING statements. If you are writing an application to be compatible with Microsoft COBOL, be sure to use the ADV option.

```
FD  file-name
    BLOCK CONTAINS 0 RECORDS
    RECORD CONTAINS 133 CHARACTERS
    .
01  print-line                  PIC X(132).
```

You define the print lines as records and move values to the data items within the record. In VS COBOL II, the WRITE statement moves a carriage control character to the first character position of the record for the file. You must open print files the same as any other file.

C. The WRITE ADVANCING **Statement**

You append the ADVANCING phrase to the WRITE statement to print lines, and VS COBOL II inserts the proper carriage control character in the first character position of the printed line.

```
                                 AFTER
                                 BEFORE
      WRITE record FROM identifier _____ ADVANCING integer LINES
```

The AFTER prints the line after advancing the *integer* lines, and the BEFORE prints the line before advancing the *integer* lines. The *integer* is an integer numeric literal or elementary data item. A value of 0 is valid.

To start a new page before or after printing, you can code

```
                                 AFTER
                                 BEFORE
      WRITE record FROM identifier _____ ADVANCING PAGE
```

If you omit the ADVANCING phrase, lines are written as if you had coded AFTER ADVANCING 1 for single spacing. For single spacing, VS COBOL II appends a blank to the print line. If you code the LINAGE clause, described later in this section, you must not code the ADVANCING clause for the file in Microsoft and ANSI COBOL. VS COBOL II doesn't have this restriction.

You can omit the FROM phrase to write directly from the record area:

```
WRITE PRINT-LINE AFTER ADVANCING PAGE
```

D. Mnemonic Names

ADVANCING may also specify a mnemonic name that is defined in the SPECIAL-NAMES section and is associated with a carriage control character. The mnemonic names for VS COBOL II and Microsoft COBOL are shown here:

```
ENVIRONMENT DIVISION.
CONFIGURATION SECTION.
OBJECT-COMPUTER.   computer-name.
SPECIAL-NAMES.
      CSP IS name-0        [Suppress  spacing.]
      C01 IS name-1        [Eject to a new page.]
      Cnn  IS name-nn      [Skip to channel nn, where nn is 02 through
                            12. The action is installation defined.]
      TAB IS name-t        [Vertical tab. Microsoft COBOL only. Inserts ASCII
                            H"0B" character.]
      FORMFEED IS page      [Skip to new page. Microsoft COBOL only.
                            Inserts ASCII H"0C" character.]
```

The following example uses mnemonic names for suppressing spacing and ejecting to a new page:

```
SPECIAL-NAMES.
    CSP IS OVER-PRINT
    C01 IS NEW-PAGE

    .
    ■ ■ ■
    WRITE RPT-RECORD FROM RPT-LINE
      AFTER ADVANCING NEW-PAGE
    WRITE RPT-RECORD FROM RPT-LINE
      AFTER ADVANCING OVER-PRINT
    WRITE RPT-RECORD FROM RPT-LINE
      AFTER ADVANCING 1 LINE
          [The use of mnemonic names does not preclude the use of integer LINES.]
```

E. The AT EOP Phrase

You can add AT EOP (END-OF-PAGE) and NOT AT EOP phrases to specify imperative statements to execute if an end-of-page occurs or doesn't occur. The LINAGE clause in the FD must be coded for the file. You can't code

EOP with ADVANCING PAGE. In VS COBOL II, but not in Microsoft COBOL or the ANSI Standard, you can code EOP with ADVANCING LINES. Add the END-WRITE scope terminator if you use EOP.

```
WRITE record FROM identifier
   AFTER
   BEFORE
   _____ ADVANCING integer LINES
   AT EOP
       imperative-statements
   NOT AT EOP
       imperative-statements
   END-WRITE
WRITE RPT-RECORD FROM RPT-LINE
   AFTER ADVANCING 1 LINES
   AT EOP PERFORM C20-NEW-PAGE
   END-WRITE
```

F. The LINAGE Clause

Normally, you do not want to print a full 66 lines per page; you want a margin at the top and bottom. You specify top and bottom margins by adding the LINAGE clause to the FD for the print file. LINAGE is also required if you code an EOP phrase in the WRITE statement.

```
FD  RPT-O
    BLOCK CONTAINS O RECORDS
    RECORD CONTAINS 133 CHARACTERS
    LINAGE IS page-lines  LINES
            WITH FOOTING AT footing-line
            LINES AT TOP MARGIN top-margin
            LINES AT BOTTOM MARGIN bottom-margin
```

The four parts of the LINAGE phrase are all optional and have the following effect:

- IS *page-lines* LINES (you can shorten this by coding just *page-lines*): Specifies the number of lines that can be printed on the page (called the page body) and must be greater than zero. It excludes the margins.
- WITH FOOTING AT *footing-line* (you can shorten this by coding just FOOTING *footing-line*): Specifies the first line number of the footing area within the body of the page. The *footing-line* must be greater than zero and less than the last line of the page body *(page-lines)*. If you omit WITH FOOTING, *page-lines* is assumed.
- LINES AT TOP *top-margin* (you can shorting this by coding just TOP *top-margin*): Specifies the number of lines of top margin to leave, and may be zero. Zero is assumed if TOP is omitted.

- LINES AT BOTTOM *bottom-margin* (you can shorten this by coding just BOTTOM *bottom-margin*): Specifies the number of lines of bottom margin, and may be zero. Zero is assumed if BOTTOM is omitted.

Either unsigned literal integers or data items can be used to specify the values. Figure 13.1 shows how the values relate to the page.
Note the following equation:

Logical page size $=$ *top-margin* $+$ *page-lines* $+$ *bottom-margin*

In Microsoft COBOL and the ANSI Standard, you can't code WRITE ADVANCING for files with the LINAGE clause.

The LINAGE clause causes VS COBOL II to append a carriage control character automatically to each line written for the file. Because of this, VS COBOL II allows you to code WRITE ADVANCING for files with the LINAGE clause. However, if you make the file EXTERNAL and use it in several subprograms, you must code LINAGE with the same values in all the subprograms describing the file. Then you can also intermix WRITE and WRITE ADVANCING statements. If you don't code the LINAGE clause for an EXTERNAL file, then if any subprogram uses a WRITE ADVANCING, all the subprograms for the file must use WRITE ADVANCING.

Here is an example of printing a file with the LINAGE clause:

```
FD  RPT-O
    BLOCK CONTAINS O RECORDS
    RECORD CONTAINS 133 CHARACTERS
    LINAGE IS 55 LINES
          LINES AT TOP 5
          LINES AT BOTTOM 6

01  RPT-RECORD                  PIC X(132).
    ■ ■ ■
WORKING-STORAGE SECTION.
01  RPT-LINE.
    05  FILLER                  PIC X(6) VALUE "NAME: ".
    05  RPT-NAME                PIC X(5).
    05  FILLER                  PIC X(3) VALUE SPACES.
    05  RPT-AGE                 PIC 999.
    ■ ■ ■
    OPEN OUTPUT RPT-O
    MOVE "SMITH" TO RPT-NAME
    MOVE 21 TO RPT-AGE
    WRITE RPT-RECORD FROM RPT-LINE
      AT EOP MOVE "Y" TO NEW-PAGE-FLAG
      NOT AT EOP MOVE "N" TO NEW-PAGE-FLAG
    END-WRITE
```

The following line prints with single spacing:

```
NAME: SMITH   021
```

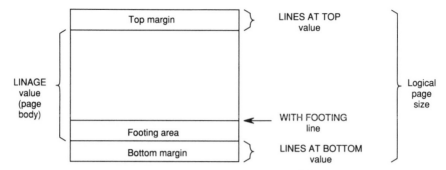

FIGURE 13.1   Phrases of the LINAGE **clause.**

G. The LINAGE-COUNTER **Special Register**

When you code the LINAGE clause in an FD, COBOL automatically creates a LINAGE-COUNTER special register for the file to contain the current line position in the page body. That is, line 1 is the first line below any top margin. COBOL initializes it to a value of one when you open the file and for each new page. If there is more than one FD with a LINAGE clause, you must qualify the LINAGE-COUNTER to specify which file it belongs to by writing LINAGE-COUNTER OF *file-name*. You can retrieve the value of the LINAGE-COUNTER, but you can't change it:

```
MOVE LINAGE-COUNTER OF file-name TO identifier
IF LINAGE-COUNTER OF file-name > 30 THEN ...
```

III. PRINTING NUMERIC DATA

You will usually edit numeric data for printing, to suppress leading zeros and insert commas and decimal points. You edit numbers by defining an item in the print line that specifies the editing and then moving the number to the item to convert and edit it. You specify the editing with special edit characters in the PIC clause. There cannot be more than 30 edit characters in a PIC clause. The maximum length of the edited data item is 249 characters in VS COBOL II.

The 9, S, V, and P edit characters are those for external decimal numbers, and they do not preclude arithmetic operations from being performed on the item. These edit characters were described in Chapter 6, but they are included here again for review. Note that you can write the edit characters in upper or lower case: S9V9 or s9v9.

A. Edit Characters for External Decimal Numbers

1. 9 *(Decimal Digit)*

The 9 edit character in a PIC clause represents a decimal digit (0 to 9) within the number and occupies a character position. The 9 does not imply a signed number; the S, +, −, DB, or CR edit characters do this.

```
77  X                           PIC 9999.
```
   [X *occupies 4 character positions.*]
   ■ ■ ■
```
   MOVE 2 TO X    [X contains "0002".]
   MOVE - 2 TO X  [X contains "0002".]
```

2. S *(Sign)*

The S edit character specifies that the number is signed, but it does not cause the sign to be printed nor to occupy a character position. The sign is carried in the left half of the rightmost byte. In VS COBOL II, a plus sign is a hex "F", and a minus a hex "D". In Microsoft COBOL, a plus is a hex "3" and a minus a hex "7". The S must be the leftmost edit character if included.

```
77  X                           PIC S999.
```
   [X *occupies 3 character positions.*]
   ■ ■ ■
```
   MOVE 2 TO X    [X contains "002" as a positive number.]
   MOVE - 2 TO X  [X contains "002" as a negative number. In VS COBOL II, this would
                  be "00K". In Microsoft COBOL it would be "00r".]
```

3. V *(Decimal Alignment)*

A single V edit character coded in a PIC clause indicates the position of the internal decimal point. If V is not coded, the decimal point is assumed to be to the right of the number. V is not stored as a character and does not occupy a character position.

```
77  X                           PIC S999V99.
```
   [X *occupies 5 character positions.*]
   ■ ■ ■
```
   MOVE 2.3 TO X    [X contains "00230".]
   MOVE - 2.5 TO X  [X contains "00230" as a negative number.]
```

High- or low-order digits are truncated if the value is too large to be contained in the identifier:

```
   MOVE 1234.123 TO X    [X contains "23412".]
```

4. P *(Scaling Factor)*

The P edit character specifies a decimal point outside the range of the number. You code the Ps to the left or right of the 9s. The number of Ps indicates the number of places to the left or right of the number the decimal point lies. (The number is limited to 18 total digits, including the positions specified by the P.)

```
77  X                           PIC SP(3)999.
```
   [X *occupies 3 character positions.*]
   ■ ■ ■
```
   MOVE .000476 TO X
```
   [X *contains* "476" *but is treated as .000476 in arithmetic computations.*]

```
77  Y                              PIC S999P(3).
```
   [Y *occupies 3 character positions.*]
      ■ ■ ■
```
MOVE 476000 TO Y
```
   [Y *contains "476", but is treated as 476,000 in arithmetic computations.*]

The V edit character may be coded, but it is not needed, because the P specifies the assumed decimal point. The X and Y could also be coded as follows:

```
77  X                              PIC SVP(3)999.
77  Y                              PIC S999P(3)V.
```

The next group of edit characters inserts such nonnumeric characters as the comma, decimal point, and blanks for printing numbers. If the data item also contains numeric edit characters, the item is termed a *numeric edited* data item; otherwise it is termed an *alphanumeric edited* data item. (Both types are also referred to as *external* data, because the data is formatted for external display or printing.) You cannot perform arithmetic operations on numeric edited or alphanumeric edited data items.

B. Edit Characters for Numeric Edited Data

The following edit characters are mainly used for numeric edited data. Alphabetic data items may contain the B edit character. Alphanumeric edited data items may contain the 0, B, and / edit characters. Numeric edited data may have a VALUE clause to assign a value to the item, but the VALUE must be an alphanumeric literal or figurative constant—not a number.

```
01  AN-ITEM                        PIC S99V99 VALUE "123K".
```

You can only assign alphanumeric literal initial values to numeric or alphanumeric edited data items. The value is not edited.

```
77  X                              PIC ZZ9 VALUE "006".
```
   [X *contains* "006".]

Numeric edited items may contain any of the following edit characters, subject to their rules of construction, in addition to the edit characters already discussed.

1. Z *(Leading Zero Suppression)*

The Z edit character, like the 9 edit character, represents a decimal digit (0 to 9) within the number. However, the Z causes leading zeros to be replaced with blanks. Each Z occupies a character position and cannot appear to the right of a 9 edit character.

```
77  X                              PIC ZZ9V99.
```
   [X *occupies 5 character positions.*]
      ■ ■ ■
```
MOVE 2.31 TO X        [X contains  "bb231".]
```

```
MOVE 26.3 TO X      [X contains "b2630".]
MOVE .94 TO X       [X contains "bb094".]
```

If the item contains all Zs and no 9 edit characters, COBOL sets the entire item to blanks if you store a value of zero in it. This includes any decimal points, commas, or other editing inserted by other edit characters. Coding all Zs is equivalent to coding the BLANK WHEN ZERO clause, described later in this chapter.

```
77  Y                            PIC ZZZVZZ.
    ■ ■ ■
MOVE ZERO TO Y   [Y contains "bbbbb".]
```

2. * (Leading Asterisks)

The * edit character is identical to the Z edit character, except that it replaces leading zeros with asterisks rather than blanks. It cannot appear in the same PIC clause as the Z, nor can it appear to the right of a 9 edit character.

```
77  X                            PIC **9V99.
    [X occupies 5 character positions.]
    ■ ■ ■
MOVE 26.31 TO X     [X contains "*2631".]
```

If the item contains all *'s and no 9 edit characters, COBOL sets the entire item to blanks, except for any decimal point, if you store a zero value in the item. You cannot code BLANK WHEN ZERO with the * edit character.

```
77  Y                            PIC **.**.
    ■ ■ ■
MOVE ZERO TO Y   [Y contains "bb.bb".]
```

The next group of edit characters, the +, −, DB, and CR, are for signed numbers. Only one can appear in a PIC clause. The S edit character must not be coded in combination with any of these. If the +, −, DB, or CR are not coded, minus numbers print with the minus sign indicated in the rightmost digit, as described earlier in Chapter 10 for the DISPLAY statement. Since no one would like to see −23 print as "2L", use the following edit characters when printing numbers. A string of minus or plus edit characters also suppresses zeros, similar to the Z edit character.

3. − (Minus Sign)

The − edit character indicates a signed number. If the number is negative, a minus sign is inserted where the − appears in the PIC clause; a blank is inserted if the number is positive. The − can be placed to the left or right of all the 9 and V characters in the PIC string. You can code a string of −'s on the left to represent numeric digits and suppress leading zeros in the same manner as the Z edit character. The minus is inserted to the left of the first nonzero digit if the number is negative; a blank is inserted if the number is positive. Each minus sign counts as a character position.

```
77  X                                    PIC − − −9.
```
   [X *occupies four character positions.*]
   ■ ■ ■
```
MOVE − 2 TO X    [X contains "bb− 2".]
MOVE 2 TO X      [X contains "bbb2".]
MOVE 1234 TO X   [X contains "b234"; remember that a blank is inserted, not a digit.
                  Also notice that the leading digit is truncated.]
77  Y                                    PIC 999−.
```
   [Y *occupies four character positions.*]
   ■ ■ ■
```
MOVE − 2 TO Y    [Y contains "002− ".]
MOVE 2 TO Y      [Y contains "002b".]
```

```
77  Z                                    PIC − 999.
```
   ■ ■ ■
```
MOVE 2 TO Z      [Z contains "b002".]
MOVE − 2 TO Z    [Z contains "− 002".]
```

4. + *(Plus Sign)*

The + edit character specifies a signed number and inserts the sign (+ or −) where it appears in the PIC clause. You can place the + to the left or right of all the 9 and V characters in the PIC string. You can code a string of +'s on the left to represent numeric digits and suppress leading zeros in the same manner as the Z edit character. The sign is inserted to the left of the first nonzero digit. Each plus sign counts as a character position.

```
77  X                           PIC +999.
```
   [X *occupies four character positions.*]
   ■ ■ ■
```
MOVE 2 TO X      [X contains "+002".]
MOVE − 2 TO X    [X contains "− 002".]
```

5. CR *(Credit Symbol)*

You can code a single CR edit character in the rightmost position of the PIC clause. If the number is negative, CR is inserted; otherwise two blanks are inserted. CR counts as two character positions.

```
77  X                           PIC 999CR.
```
   [X *occupies five character positions.*]
   ■ ■ ■
```
MOVE − 27 TO X   [X contains "027CR".]
MOVE 27 TO X     [X contains "027bb".]
```

6. DB *(Debit Symbol)*

The DB edit character is identical to the CR edit character, except that the DB is inserted if the number is negative.

```
77  X                                PIC 99DB.
```
   [X *occupies five character positions.*]
   ■ ■ ■
```
MOVE - 1 TO X   [X contains "01DB".]
MOVE 1 TO X     [X contains "01bb"{.}]
```

7. . *(Decimal Point)*

The decimal point edit character is inserted where it appears in the PIC clause, and it occupies a character position. You can only code one decimal point; it specifies the decimal alignment, so the V edit character must not be used. The decimal point cannot be the rightmost character in a PIC clause.

```
77  X                                PIC ZZ9.99.
```
   [X *occupies six character positions.*]
   ■ ■ ■
```
MOVE 22.31 TO X   [X contains "b22.31".]
```

8. , *(Comma)*

The comma edit character is inserted where it appears in the PIC clause, and it counts as a character position. If leading zeros are suppressed, the comma is replaced by a blank if the characters to the left of the comma are all zero. The comma cannot be the rightmost character in the PIC clause.

```
77  X                                PIC 9,999.
```
   [X *occupies five character positions.*]
   ■ ■ ■
```
MOVE 4 TO X       [X contains "0,004".]
MOVE 4000 TO X    [X contains "4,000".]
```

```
77  Y                                PIC Z,ZZ9.
```
   [Y *occupies five character positions.*]
   ■ ■ ■
```
MOVE 4 TO Y       [Y contains "bbbb4".]
MOVE 4000 TO Y    [Y contains "4,000".]
```

```
77  W                                PIC *,**9.
```
   [Y *occupies five character positions.*]
   ■ ■ ■
```
MOVE 4 TO W       [W contains "****4".]
```

```
77  Z                                PIC -- ,-- 9.
```
   [Z *occupies six character positions.*]
       ■ ■ ■
```
MOVE - 4 TO Z       [Z contains "bbbb- 4".]
MOVE - 4000 TO Z    [Z contains "- 4,000".]
```

9. $ *(Dollar Sign)*

A single $ edit character is inserted where it appears in the PIC clause and
counts as a character position. A string of $'s represents numeric digits, sup-
pressing leading zeros in the same manner as the Z edit character. A single $
is inserted to the left of the first nonzero digit. The $ must be to the left of all
9 or V edit characters.

```
77  X                           PIC $999.
```
    [X *occupies four character positions.*]
    ■ ■ ■
```
    MOVE 4 TO X    [X contains  "$004".]
```

```
77  Y                           PIC $$$9.
```
    [Y *occupies four character positions.*]
    ■ ■ ■
```
    MOVE 4 TO Y    [Y contains  "bb$4".]
```
    The edit characters +, −, *, Z, and $, when used as floating edit characters,
cannot appear in the same PIC clause. That is, they are mutually exclusive
(unless there is a single instance of the characters $, −, +).

10. B *(Blank)*

The B edit character causes a blank to be inserted wherever it appears in a PIC
clause, and it counts as a character position.

```
77  X                           PIC B9B9B.
```
    [X *occupies five character positions.*]
    ■ ■ ■
```
    MOVE 21 TO X     [X contains  "b2b1b".]
    MOVE 123 TO X    [X contains  "b2b3b".]
```

11. 0 *(Zero)*

The 0 edit character causes a zero to be inserted wherever it appears in a PIC
clause, and it counts as a character position.

```
77  X                           PIC 0990.
```
    [X *occupies four character positions.*]
    ■ ■ ■
```
    MOVE 21 TO X     [X contains  "0210".]
    MOVE 123 TO X    [X contains  "0230".]
```

12. E *(Floating Point) (VS COBOL II Only)*

You can display floating-point numbers by coding an E separating the number
from its exponent. The E occupies a character position. You can use either a
+ or − sign for both the number and its exponent. A + causes either a plus
or minus sign to be inserted, and a − causes only minus signs to be inserted.
You can't code a BLANK WITH ZERO, JUST, or VALUE clause when you code

the E for floating-point. The exponent must be 99. A V or . can be coded to specify the internal or actual decimal point.

```
77  X                          PIC +9(3)V99E+99.
    [X occupies 10 character positions.]
77  Y                          PIC - ZZ9.99E- 99.
    [Y occupies 11 character positions.]
    ▪ ▪ ▪
    MOVE 2.33E6 TO X    [X contains "+00233E+06".]
    MOVE 2.33E6 TO Y    [Y contains "  2.33E 04".]
```

13. X *(Alphanumeric Character)*

The X edit characters represent any alphanumeric character and occupy character positions.

```
77  Y                          PIC X999X.
    [Y occupies 5 character positions.]
    ▪ ▪ ▪
    MOVE "(234)" TO Y    [Y contains "(234)".]
```

14. A *(Alphabetic Character)*

The A edit characters represent any alphabetic characters or blanks and occupy character positions.

```
77  Y                          PIC A999A.
    [Y occupies 5 character positions.]
    ▪ ▪ ▪
    MOVE "Z234Z" TO Y    [Y contains "Z234Z".]
```

15. / *(Stroke Edit Character)*

The / edit character causes a stroke (slash) character to be inserted wherever it appears in a PIC clause, and it occupies a character position.

```
77  X                          PIC 99/99/9999.
    [X occupies 10 character positions.]
    ▪ ▪ ▪
    MOVE "12251997" TO X    [X contains "12/25/1997".]
```

16. BLANK WHEN ZERO

The BLANK WHEN ZERO clause is not an edit character. You add it to the data description entry to set the entire data item to blanks if a value of zero is stored in it. The * edit character cannot be coded in the PIC character string if BLANK WHEN ZERO is coded.

```
77  X                          PIC ZZ9.9 BLANK WHEN ZERO.
    [X contains five character positions.]
    ▪ ▪ ▪
```

```
MOVE 1 TO X      [X contains "bb1.0".]
MOVE 0 TO X      [X contains "bbbbb".]
```

C. Using the SPECIAL-NAMES Section to Redefine Edit Characters

For reference, you must code the phrases in the SPECIAL-NAMES paragraph in the following order:

```
SPECIAL-NAMES.
    ALPHABET alphabet-name IS name
    SYMBOLIC CHARACTERS symbolic-character IS integer
    CLASS class-name literal THRU literal
    CURRENCY SIGN IS literal
    DECIMAL-POINT IS COMMA

    .
```

The SPECIAL-NAMES Section may specify a symbol other than the $ to be the currency symbol. It may also specify that the roles of the comma and period are to be reversed as edit characters (9,999,99 becomes 9.999,99) to print numbers in the European manner.

```
SPECIAL-NAMES.
    CURRENCY SIGN IS "character"
    DECIMAL-POINT IS COMMA

    .
```

You can code CURRENCY SIGN, DECIMAL-POINT, or both. The *character* may be any character except 0 to 9, A to D, P, R, S, V, X, Z, lower-case a to z, blank, or the special characters * + − / , . ; ( ) = ".

In the following example, the currency sign prints as an "F", and you write and display numbers in the European manner.

```
SPECIAL-NAMES.
    CURRENCY SIGN IS "F"
    DECIMAL-POINT IS COMMA

    .
```

You could then describe an identifier as follows, using F as the currency sign and reversing the roles of the period and comma:

```
77  FRANCS                          PIC FFF.FFF.FF9,99.
```

You must then reverse the comma and period when you write a constant:

```
MOVE 1311,24 TO FRANCS   [FRANCS contains "bbbbbF1.311,24".]
```

D. Underlining Numbers

There are two additional techniques used in printing numbers, although they are not a part of the editing. Sometimes you need to underline a column of numbers to denote a total, and place a double underlined under the total to highlight it.

```
1432
3216
────
5648
════
```

You can create a single underline by printing a row of dashes. (You can also suppress line spacing, to overprint the underscore character (_), if you want the underscore on the same line.) You create the double underline by printing a line of equal signs (=) on the next line.

IV. ANATOMY OF A REPORT

Reports often start out simple—often nothing more than a column listing. The following might represent a report generated for personal finances.

```
JOB      AJAX APPAREL     INCOME                     86.23
TAX      FEDERAL          TAX                  - 17,462.37
RENT     BOB'S BATH HOUSE UTILITIES                 - 0.50
```

Each line represents the lowest level of detail and corresponds to a record in a file. These lines are termed *detail lines* to distinguish them from summary lines, described later in this section.

The only constant in reports is that they change. The first thing we would likely add would be a page heading. Usually a page heading contains titles, a date, and a page number. This means we would need an identifier to contain the page number. We may also need an identifier to contain the line number so that we can determine when a new page is needed, although the LINAGE clause can be used for this. Adding the page heading, the report might look like this:

```
            MONTHLY FINANCE REPORT              PAGE  1
                DATE:  5/1/1994

JOB      AJAX APPAREL     INCOME                     86.23
TAX      FEDERAL          TAX                  - 17,462.37
RENT     BOB'S BATH HOUSE UTILITIES                 - 0.50
```

The date in the heading can be different each time the report is generated, so it must come from an identifier.

In the preceding report, revenue and expenses are printed in the same column, with the sign used to distinguish them. We can make the report clearer by printing descriptions on each line and column heading:

```
CATEGORY  VENDOR         ITEM        TYPE       AMOUNT
JOB       AJAX APPAREL   INCOME      REVENUE     86.23
TAX       FEDERAL        TAX         EXPENSE  17,462.37
RENT      BOB'S BATH HOUSE UTILITIES EXPENSE      0.50
```

Perhaps it would be even better to print the revenue and expense in separate columns:

```
CATEGORY  VENDOR         ITEM        REVENUE    EXPENSE
JOB       AJAX APPAREL   INCOME       86.23
TAX       FEDERAL        TAX                  17,462.37
RENT      BOB'S BATH HOUSE UTILITIES              0.50
```

Next, we would undoubtedly want some summarization, perhaps by category and vendor within category. We would also want a final line of grand totals. For this, we must sort the input file on category and vendor. The body of the report might look as follows:

```
CATEGORY  VENDOR         ITEM        REVENUE    EXPENSE
JOB       AJAX APPAREL   INCOME        86.23
JOB       AJAX APPAREL   INCOME        86.23
          TOTAL                       172.46
JOB       STAN'S PARKING INCOME     1,900.22
          TOTAL                     1,900.22
TOTAL                               2,072.68
TAX       FEDERAL        TAX                  17,462.37
TAX       STATE          TAX            3.23  4,336.34
          TOTAL                         3.23 17,462.37
TOTAL                                        17,462.37
GRAND TOTAL                         2,075.91 35,337,64
```

We would need to define identifiers to contain the column totals for the vendor, category, and grand totals. You might also want an identifier for each total to count the number of items totaled. This enables you to not print a total line when the total is for only one line.

When a new job or vendor is encountered, we have what is termed a *control break,* and we must print a line of subtotals. The summary lines are termed *control footings,* because they occur after a control break; that is, after the value of a key in the sort hierarchy changes. The control footing break occurs after a detail line is printed.

When a control footing break occurs, control breaks must be forced on all lower control items in the hierarchy in minor to major order. That is, if JOB is the category in the previous record and TAX is the category in the current record, we have a control break for the category, but first we must force a control break for the vendor. An end-of-report is treated like a control footing break for the highest-level sort key and forces control breaks in lower to higher order for all other sort keys. Then the grand totals are printed.

Since we have two columns in the report, we might want to add them together and print the total in a separate column. This is termed *cross footing*. The body of the report might look like this:

```
CATEGORY  VENDOR         ITEM     REVENUE    EXPENSE        NET
JOB       AJAX APPAREL   INCOME     86.23                 86.23
JOB       AJAX APPAREL   INCOME     86.23                 86.23
          TOTAL                    172.46                172.46
JOB       STAN'S PARKING INCOME  1,900.22              1,900.22
          TOTAL                  1,900.22              1,900.22
TOTAL                            2,072.68              2,072.68
TAX       FEDERAL        TAX               17,462.37  17,462.37
TAX       STATE          TAX        3.23   4,336.34   4,333.11
          TOTAL                     3.23  21,798.71  21,795.48
TOTAL                               3.23  21,798.71  21,795.48
GRAND TOTAL                      2,072.68 35,337,64  33,264.96
```

Now we might want to clean up the report by eliminating redundant data. The category and vendor names need only be printed the first time they appear. We might also leave a line after the category totals. Printing the category and vendor names requires a control break, and since the information is printed before the detail lines, it is termed a *control heading*. The report body now looks as follows:

```
CATEGORY  VENDOR         ITEM     REVENUE    EXPENSE        NET
JOB       AJAX APPAREL   INCOME     86.23                 86.23
                         INCOME     86.23                 86.23
          TOTAL                    172.46                172.46
JOB       STAN'S PARKING INCOME  1,900.22              1,900.22
TOTAL                            2,072.68              2,072.68


TAX       FEDERAL        TAX               17,462.37  17,462.37
          STATE          TAX        3.23   4,336.34   4,333.11
TOTAL                               3.23  21,798.71  21,795.48
GRAND TOTAL                      2,072.68 35,337,64  33,264.96
```

The report is now less cluttered and looks clearer. To fit more columns across the page, we can print the category and vendor indented on separate lines like

```
CATEGORY  VENDOR    ITEM     REVENUE    EXPENSE        NET
    VENDOR
JOB
    AJAX APPAREL    INCOME     86.23                 86.23
                    INCOME     86.23                 86.23
    TOTAL                     172.46                172.46
    STAN'S PARKING  INCOME  1,900.22              1,900.22
```

```
TOTAL                        2,072.68                  2,072.68
TAX
    FEDERAL        TAX                    17,462.37  17,462.37
    STATE          TAX           3.23     4,336.34   4,333.11
TOTAL                           3.23    21,798.71  21,795.48
GRAND TOTAL               2,072.68  35,337,64  33,264.96
```

The control heading is printed when a control item in the next record to be printed changes value from the previous record. It is printed before the detail line, but it takes its values from the detail record. This is termed a *control heading break*. A control heading break for an item in a hierarchy requires that control breaks also be forced for all lower-level control items in the hierarchy, in major to minor order. Thus, in the previous example, a change in the category causes JOB to be printed, and then a control heading break is forced for the vendor, causing AJAX APPAREL to be printed. The first detail line printed at the start of a report must cause a control heading break for all levels of the hierarchy.

Control breaks occur in the following order:

• Control footings first in minor to major order. Control footings relate to the previous detail line.
• Control headings next in major to minor order. Control headings relate to the next detail line.
• The next detail lines are printed.

Now we can step back and generalize the items that went into the report. There are many different types of reports, but most business applications programmed in COBOL have the form shown in Figure 13.2. You program the report so that when it reads a new record and encounters a new category, it does the following:

• Print the control footing for the old vendor and the vendor totals. Add the vendor column totals to the category totals and reset the vendor totals to zero.
• Print the control footing for the old category and the category totals. Add the category totals to the grand totals, and reset the category totals to zero.
• Print the control heading for the category with the new category.
• Print the control heading for the vendor with the new vendor.
• Print the detail line for the item and add its columns to the vendor totals.

In addition to control breaks, reports also have page breaks. A page break occurs when a page overflows. You may also cause a page break if you want a particular control break to start on a new page. When a page break occurs, you may print a *page footing* at the end of the current page. Then you skip to a new page and print the new *page heading* at the top of the next head. The page heading usually contains titles, a page number, a date, and column headings.

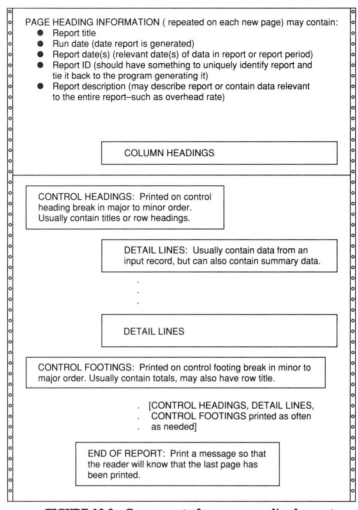

FIGURE 13.2   Components from a generalized report.

V. PRINTING REPORTS

A report should contain a title, describing what it is, and some unique identification in the heading, perhaps the program name, to tie it back to the program
generating it. Paginate reports and date them with the date of the computer
run, the date of the period covered in the report, or both. Print clear column
and row titles to make the report self-descriptive. Repeat the column headings
and at least a portion of the page heading on the second and subsequent pages.
Indent row titles if they have a hierarchical relationship:

```
STATE
    COUNTY
        CITY
```

For columns of numbers, print totals at each level in the hierarchy unless the numbers would have no meaning, as, for example, the ages of people in a personnel report.

Perhaps the most common problem in printing reports is to exceed the columns on a page. What can you do if you need 150 columns and the print page is limited to 132 columns? There are several alternatives.

- Squeeze any blanks from between columns. Don't run columns together, but you can often squeeze several blanks down to one.

```
    23        15         64.7     [Squeezed down to]    23 15 69.7
```

- Eliminate the nonessential. The 132 characters in a print line are a considerable amount of information, and there is likely to be something printed that is nonessential. For example, if three columns contain a starting date, an ending date, and a duration, all the information is contained in any two of the columns. The third column may be convenient, but it is also redundant.
- Print two or more lines, staggering the columns.

```
                          START DATE      FIRST 6-MO
                          END DATE          SECOND 6-MO
        DEPARTMENT 115
           JOE DOE        01/01/76        100,000.00
                          12/31/77          250,000,00
```

- Print two reports, where the second report is a logical continuation of the columns of the first, so that the two reports form a complete report when placed side by side. Print all the page and column headings of the second report, too, so that it can stand by itself. In practice, people will not lay the reports side by side, because it is awkward. You can print the second report on the next page by storing it in a table and printing it from the table after printing the first page. Or you can print it as a separate file so that it forms a completely separate report.

Eliminate unnecessary lines from reports. You might not print a line containing all zeros. Don't print a total line if only one item went into the totals.

```
            HOURS        [Better  as]                      HOURS
ENG DEPT                                  ENG DEPT
   JOHN DOE      0                           MARY ROE    10
   MARY ROE     10
   DEPT TOTAL   10
```

Give careful thought to the credibility of reports. Column totals can be correct but appear wrong through rounding, and they also can be wrong but appear right through truncation. The former diminishes a report's credibility, but the latter shatters it if it is discovered. The first thing many people do when they receive a new report is to add up the columns by hand to check the totals. If people cannot understand how the numbers in a report are derived, they are quite justified in placing little faith in it.

You make reports more credible by printing numbers and totals in a logical sequence, so that a person can see how the totals are derived. This is not difficult with most reports, but it can be a problem in management reports. There, the reader often does not want to see the full detail but only a condensation of it. For example, it is logical to print totals at the bottom of a column of numbers, and this is also easier to program. However, the total may be the most important item to a manager, and you may need to print it at the top of the page.

If a report must print totals at the top of the page before the detail lines, there are three normal solutions. First, you can store the lines of data in a table, total the table, and then print the lines from the table. This does not work when the report becomes large, however, because of the size of the table that would be required. If this happens, you can pass through the file twice—the first time to compute the totals and the second time to print the report. However, this has limitations if there are many subtotals to compute.

The third alternative is to write the lines into a file with a sort key appended containing the report, page, and line number. When the last line is written and the total line is formed, you give it a page and line number so that it sorts in front of the detail lines. After the report is completed, you sort the lines, read the file, drop the sort key, and print the actual report.

In generating a report from a file, you usually must sort the file so that the lines will come out in the proper order. If only certain records are selected to go into the report, the sequence for this should be select, sort, and then report. Sorts are expensive, and selecting before sorting reduces the number of records sorted.

This completes the discussion of printing. The next chapter describes the more advanced I/O of indexed and relative files.

EXERCISES

1. Show what the following numbers will look like in the following statements.

```
77   W                          PIC $$,$$$,$$9.99CR.
     ■ ■ ■
     MOVE 23655.97 TO W
     MOVE - 2 TO W
     MOVE .01 TO W
77   X                          PIC Z,ZZZ,ZZ9.
     ■ ■ ■
     MOVE 26531 TO X
     MOVE - 4 TO X
```

```
77  Y                          PIC - ****9.
    ■ ■ ■
    MOVE - 16 TO Y
    MOVE 327 TO Y
    MOVE - 923945 TO Y


77  Z                          PIC $-- ,- - -,-- 9.99
                               BLANK WHEN ZERO.
    ■ ■ ■
    MOVE 35275.6 TO Z
    MOVE - 247.96 TO Z
    MOVE ZERO TO Z
```

2. Print a table containing the square roots of the integers from 1 to 1000. Print 50 values per page in the following format:

```
SQUARE OF NUMBERS          PAGE xxx

NUMBER        SQUARE
   1             1
   2             4
   .    .   .   .   .  .
 1000      1,000,000
```

3. Print a table containing the square roots of the integers from 1 to 1000. Print the square roots with five significant digits of accuracy to the right of the decimal point. Print 50 lines per page with each line containing two columns of values as shown. Print the page heading at the top of each new page.

```
                TABLE OF SQUARE ROOTS                PAGE xxx

 NUMBER    SQUARE ROOT                  NUMBER    SQUARE ROOT
    1       1.00000                        51      7.14143
    2       1.41421                        52      7.21110
    .   .   .   .   .   .   .   .   .   .   .   .   .   .   .
   50       7.07107                       100     10.00000
```

4. Print a table showing the future value of an amount invested at 8 percent per annum in increments of 1 year for 30 years. The equation for the future value is:

$$\text{Future value} = amount \ (1.08)^n$$

where *n* is the year. Print the table in the format shown for amounts ranging from $100 to $1000 in increments of $200.

```
          FUTURE VALUE TABLE          PAGE xxx

   AMOUNT: $100.00        INTEREST RATE: 8.00%

   YEAR                    FUTURE VALUE
     1                        $103.00
     2                        $116.64

     .   .   .   .   .   .   .   .   .
     30                     $1,006.27
```

5. Write a program to read in a line containing an initial investment, an interest rate, a number of years, and a starting date. The line has the following format:

```
          1|        |     |    |   | 2 |   |    |
 1234567890| 1234   | 56  | 78 | 9 | 01| 2 | 34 |
 aaaaaaa.aa| bb.b   | cc  | mm | / | dd| / | yy |
```

```
aaaaaaa.aa:    The initial investment.
bb.b:          The interest rate.
cc:            The period in years.
mm/dd/yy:      The date.
```

Given this information, you are to produce the following report.

```
                  INVESTMENT ANALYSIS                  PAGE xxx

   PREPARED ESPECIALLY FOR: your name

   INITIAL INVESTMENT: $xxx,xxx.xx     INTEREST = xx.x%   YEARS: xx

     DATE      CURRENT BALANCE   INTEREST EARNED    NEW BALANCE
   YEAR
   xx/xx/xx    $xxx,xxx.xx       $xx,xxx.xx         $xx,xxx.xx      xx
```

Allow 30 lines per page. The interest earned is computed as the current balance times the interest divided by 100. The new balance is the current balance plus the interest earned.

14

Relative and Indexed Files

Relative and indexed files depend heavily on the facilities provided by the computer's operating system. Although they are included in the ANSI Standard, their implementation varies among compilers and operating systems.

The advantage of relative and indexed files is their ability to access records randomly. To see how random access might be used, suppose that payroll transactions contain an employee's Social Security number and department. Suppose further that another file contains all the valid Social Security numbers, and yet another file contains all the valid department numbers. How could the Social Security and department numbers in each payroll transaction be validated against the Social Security file and the department file?

First, we might consider reading the Social Security file and the department file into a table to use the SEARCH statement. This is perhaps the best solution if the table will fit in memory, but the files may be too large for this. Next, we might sort both the payroll transactions and the Social Security file on the Social Security numbers. Then we could write a program to match the two sequential files to see if every Social Security number in the payroll transactions matches one in the Social Security file. Then we must write a similar program to do the same for the department numbers. This is unduly complicated, and if there are only a few payroll transactions and the Social Security or department files are large, the method is inefficient. The problem is compounded if there are additional items to validate in the payroll transactions against other files.

Random access solves the problem. We can read each record irrespective of the previous record read. By making the Social Security and department files random-access, we can read payroll transactions and use the Social Security and department numbers as the key to read records from the Social Security and department files. If a record is found, the payroll transaction is valid. If not found, the payroll transaction is invalid.

This example illustrates the advantage of random access in simplifying the logic where records in a file must be accessed in an unpredictable order. Another advantage of random access is that it is faster to update a few records in a large file than with sequential access. On-line applications usually require random access, because they process relatively few transactions against large files that require fast retrieval or updating. An on-line reservation system could not exist with sequential access, because it would be too slow to update the files sequentially as each reservation is received. Nor can the reservations be batched to run a large group of them together, because any reservation must immediately update the file to avoid overbooking. Random access allows each reservation to update the file as it is received. Random access has the advantage when only a few transactions in a large file are updated. You might also use it when a single transaction must update multiple files or when a file must be immediately accessed or updated.

Random-access files can exist only on direct-access storage devices (termed *mass storage* in the ANSI Standard), but they can be accessed either sequentially or randomly. You can read the records in random-access files sequentially and write them into a sequential file. You can also read records from a sequential file and write them sequentially into a random-access file. Sequential access is often used to backup and restore the random–access files onto tape. You back up the file by reading it sequentially and writing it as a sequential file. You restore it by reading the sequential copy and writing it sequentially as a relative or indexed file.

The two types of random-access files are relative and indexed. For *relative files*, the key is a sequential number that specifies the record's relative position within the file, analogous to the subscript of a table. For *indexed files*, the system sets aside a portion of the file to contain a directory that tells where the records are stored. To retrieve a record randomly, the system first searches the directory, termed the *index area*, to find the area where the record is stored. It then goes to that area to search for a record with a matching key. Indexed files are analogous to the way books are stored in a library. You search an index to find where the book is stored in the shelves.

Relative files, because you go to a record immediately without having to search an index, are faster for random access. Indexed files are easier to use, because the system maintains an index of where the records are stored rather than requiring you to tell where they are stored. Also, the separate index for indexed files makes it easier to expand the file when records are added.

You write relative files when you create them, and you cannot add records from then on, unless you reserved space with dummy records. You supply the operating system with the key when each record is written. To retrieve a record later, you supply the same key. For example, suppose that a personnel record for SMITH is written as the 100th record. For a relative file, you would specify the key of 100 to retrieve the record. Relative files are inconvenient, because to access a given record you must somehow derive the key. Relative files are relatively inefficient for sequential processing, because the records cannot be blocked and the records might not be in a useful order.

Indexed files spare you the effort of determining where the record is stored. The record key is a part of the record. You need not write indexed files in their entirety when you create them. You can add new records later.

You can update relative and indexed files in place, permitting records to be added, deleted, or changed without copying the entire file. Updating records in place simplifies the updating logic but leads to a serious backup problem. When you update a file in place, you change the original version of the file. If you must rerun the job, you must first restore the file from a backup copy, presuming you made a backup copy. Sequential files do not have this problem, because the original version of the file is not changed when it is updated, and you can use it to rerun the job if necessary. Therefore, while it is easy to update relative and indexed files, you must give more thought to backing up the files. The usual technique is to back up the entire file at some point and save all subsequent transactions.

Relative and indexed files are less efficient than sequential files for sequential access, and you shouldn't use them unless random retrieval of records is required. As an alternative to indexed files, you can read a small sequential file into an internal table and retrieve the records with the SEARCH statement. (For a relative file, you don't need the SEARCH. The relative record key is the subscript for the internal table.)

I. STATEMENTS FOR RELATIVE AND INDEXED FILES

The same statements used for sequential files are also used for relative and indexed files, with the following additions.

- SELECT: Contains several additional clauses described later in this chapter. The RESERVE AREAS, PASSWORD, and FILE STATUS clauses described in Chapter 15 can also be coded for relative and indexed files.

```
FILE-CONTROL.
    SELECT file-name ASSIGN TO ddname
                            INDEXED
                            RELATIVE
              ORGANIZATION IS _____
                        DYNAMIC
                        RANDOM
                        SEQUENTIAL
            ACCESS IS _____
                        RECORD
                        RELATIVE
                        _____ KEY IS key
```

- OPEN: In addition to EXTEND, INPUT, and OUTPUT, you can open files for I-O (input/output). This permits records to be updated in place. (Note that files can be opened for EXTEND only with ACCESS IS SEQUENTIAL.)

```
OPEN I-O file-name
```

A. READ and WRITE statements

For ACCESS IS SEQUENTIAL, you write the READ and WRITE statements as for sequential files:

```
READ file-name INTO identifier
  AT END
    imperative-statements
  NOT AT END
    imperative-statements
END-READ
WRITE record-description FROM identifier
```

> [*For* INDEXED *files, you must write the records in ascending order based on their record keys. For* RELATIVE *files, the system assigns a sequential number to each record when it writes it.*]

For ACCESS IS RANDOM, you cannot write the AT END/NOT AT END phrases in the READ. Instead, you write INVALID/NOT INVALID KEY phrases for both the READ and WRITE statements. For a READ, the INVALID KEY phrase executes if a record with the specified key cannot be found. For a WRITE, it executes if the key is invalid. The NOT INVALID KEY phrase is optional and executes for the opposite conditions. You must code the INVALID KEY phrase unless you code the USE AFTER ERROR procedure described in Chapter 15.

```
READ file-name INTO identifier
  KEY IS key
```

> [*Code the* KEY IS *phrase only for* INDEXED *files. Because* INDEXED *files can have several keys, the* KEY IS *phrase names the key within the record that you want to use for retrieving records. You specify which record you want by moving a value to the record key.* RELATIVE *files can have only one key, so you don't code the* KEY IS *clause for them. Instead, you specify the record you want by moving a value to the data item named in the* RELATIVE KEY *clause.*]

```
  INVALID KEY
    imperative-statements
```

> [*These statements execute if the record is not found in the file.*]

```
  NOT INVALID KEY
    imperative-statements
```

> [*These statements execute if the record is found.*]

```
END-READ
```

```
WRITE record-description FROM identifier
```

> [*Before executing the* WRITE, *you must store a value in the record key for the file to identify the record to write.*]

```
  INVALID KEY
    imperative-statements
```

> [*These statements execute if the record is not written because of an invalid key. For* RELATIVE *files, this occurs if the key is outside the limits of the file. For* INDEXED *files, it occurs if a record with the same key exists in the file.*]

```
  NOT INVALID KEY
    imperative-statements
```

> [*These statements execute if the record is written.*]

```
END-WRITE
```

For ACCESS IS DYNAMIC, you have the option of reading sequentially or randomly. To read sequentially, you follow the *file-name* with the keyword NEXT and code the AT END/NOT AT END phrases. (You can code NEXT or NEXT RECORD. You can also code these on a READ for a sequential file, but they have no effect.)

```
READ file-name NEXT INTO identifier
   AT END
      imperative-statements
   NOT AT END
      imperative-statements
END-READ
```

For reading randomly, you code the same READ as for RANDOM access:

```
READ file-name INTO identifier
   KEY IS key
      [Only for INDEXED files.]
   INVALID KEY
      imperative-statements
   NOT INVALID KEY
      imperative-statements
END-READ
```

DYNAMIC only writes randomly. Code the same WRITE as for ACCESS IS RANDOM:

```
WRITE record-description FROM identifier
   INVALID KEY
      imperative-statements
   NOT INVALID KEY
      imperative-statements
END-WRITE
```

B. The REWRITE Statement

The REWRITE statement locates a specified record in the file and replaces it with the contents of *identifier*. You must open the file for I-O to use REWRITE.

For sequential access (ACCESS IS SEQUENTIAL), you first read a record and then execute REWRITE to rewrite it. You can't write sequentially with ACCESS IS DYNAMIC.

For random access (ACCESS IS RANDOM or DYNAMIC), you must move a value to the record key and then execute the REWRITE. The NOT INVALID KEY is optional.

```
REWRITE record-description FROM identifier
   INVALID KEY
```

imperative-statements

[*These statements execute if the specified record is not found in the file. You must code the* INVALID KEY *phrase, unless you code* USE AFTER ERROR PROCEDURE, *described in Chapter 15.*]

NOT INVALID KEY

imperative-statements

[*These statements execute if the record is rewritten.*]

END-REWRITE

You can omit the FROM and INTO phrases and move the data directly to and from the record area in the FILE section.

```
WRITE record-description
   INVALID KEY
      imperative-statements
END-WRITE
```

C. The START Statement

The START statement positions relative and indexed files to a specific record in the file. Then you can begin sequentially reading from that record. START can position to any record in the file, and you can execute START several times to reposition. You write START as

```
                    >
                    =
                    >=
                    NOT <
START file-name KEY _____ key
```

[*You can qualify the key but not subscript it. For relative files, the key must be the data name specified in the* RELATIVE KEY *clause for the file. For indexed files, the key is either the* RECORD KEY *or* ALTERNATE RECORD KEY.]

INVALID KEY

imperative-statements

[*Executed if the record cannot be found. You must code the* INVALID KEY *phrase, unless you code a* USE AFTER ERROR PROCEDURE *for the file, as described in Chapter 15.*]

NOT INVALID KEY

imperative-statements

[*The* NOT INVALID KEY *phrase is optional. It executes if the repositioning is successful.*]

END-START

You can omit the KEY clause, and COBOL will position the file according to the value you store in the data item named in the RELATIVE KEY or RECORD KEY clauses described later:

```
MOVE value TO key     [Same as]   START IN-FILE KEY = value
START IN-FILE                         INVALID KEY . . .
   INVALID KEY . . .
```

START cannot be used for random access. You must also code the RELATIVE KEY clause, for RELATIVE files, or the RECORD KEY clause (or ALTERNATE RECORD KEY clause described later in this chapter) for INDEXED files, even if you code ACCESS IS SEQUENTIAL. That is, you must code

```
FILE-CONTROL.
    SELECT file-name ASSIGN TO ddname
            ORGANIZATION IS RELATIVE   [or INDEXED]
            ACCESS IS SEQUENTIAL [or DYNAMIC]
            RELATIVE KEY IS key      [For RELATIVE files]
            RECORD KEY IS key        [For INDEXED files.]
```

Then you must open the files for INPUT or for I-0 to use START.

```
    OPEN INPUT file-name      [Or:]      OPEN I-0 file-name
```

Next, move a value to the record key and execute the START statement.

```
    MOVE value TO key
    START file-name KEY = key
        INVALID KEY
            DISPLAY "CAN'T POSITION FILE"
    END-START
```

D. The DELETE **Statement**

There is also a DELETE statement to delete records. You must open the file I-0. For ACCESS IS SEQUENTIAL, you must first read the record and then execute the DELETE statement.

```
    READ file-name INTO identifier
    DELETE file-name RECORD
        [DELETE deletes the record just read.]
```

For ACCESS IS RANDOM or DYNAMIC, you first move a value to the record key to indicate the record to delete and then execute the DELETE statement as follows:

```
    DELETE file-name RECORD
        INVALID KEY
            imperative-statements
        NOT INVALID KEY
                [Executed if the file does not contain the record to delete.]
            imperative-statements
                [The NOT INVALID KEY phrase is optional. It executes if the record is deleted.]
    END-DELETE
```

The DELETE statement does not disturb the contents of the record area for the file. Nor does it change the current position in the file. If you follow DELETE with a sequential READ, the deleted record is skipped, and the record following it is read.

E. The ACCESS IS DYNAMIC Clause

You can give files DYNAMIC access, which lets you read them sequentially or randomly, depending on the I/O statement. That is, after a record is located by a random read, the records following it can be read sequentially. Another random read can then be issued to switch back to random access.

```
SELECT ...
        ACCESS IS DYNAMIC
■ ■ ■
OPEN I-0 file-name
```

The WRITE, REWRITE, and DELETE statements access the file randomly, just as they do for ACCESS IS RANDOM. For random reading, you code the READ statement with the INVALID/NOT INVALID KEY phrases rather than the AT END/NOT AT END phrases. To read sequentially, code the READ NEXT statement with the AT END/NOT AT END phrases. You can intersperse sequential and random reads. The following statements position the file:

- OPEN: Positions the file to the first record.
- START: Positions the file to the first record meeting the specified condition.
- READ NEXT: Positions the file to the record following the record read. The WRITE, REWRITE, and DELETE statements have no effect on sequential reading.

The READ NEXT statement has the following format:

```
READ file-name NEXT INTO identifier
    AT END
        imperative-statements
    NOT AT END
        imperative-statements
END-READ
```

COBOL reads the record from the current file position and positions the file to the next record so that you can read it with a subsequent READ NEXT. The AT END phrase executes if there are no more records in the file.

II. RELATIVE FILES

You primarily use relative files when you must access records in random order and you can easily associate the records with a sequential number.

You update a relative file by replacing or deleting records. You replace records by writing the new record over the top of the old one. You assign the records numeric keys ranging in value from 1 to n indicating their relative position in the file. The first record has a key of 1. Thus, COBOL would assign a file containing 500 records keys from 1 to 500. The keys are not a part of the record. You supply them to read or write records.

You use relative files like tables. Their advantage over tables is that their size is limited by the amount of direct-access storage rather than the more limited memory. However, it takes much more time to retrieve an element from a relative file than from a table. Relative files are best for records that are easily associated with ascending, consecutive numbers. For example, years (the years 1960 to 1980 could be stored with keys 1 to 21), months (keys 1 to 12), or the 50 states of the United States (keys 1 to 50).

If the records being stored cannot be easily associated with the keys, as in a personnel file, you can store some unique part of the record, such as the Social Security number, in a table along with the key. Then you can retrieve records by searching the table for the Social Security number to pick up the key. You could write the table as a sequential file and then read it back in when records are to be retrieved from the relative file. This increases the effort required to access the file, and you might instead consider using an indexed file.

A. VS COBOL II VSAM RRDS Files

In VS COBOL II, relative files are VSAM RRDS (Relative Record Data Sets). You usually create the files with the VSAM IDCAMS utility,[1] but you can also create them through JCL.[2] Specify the following parameters when creating the file:

```
//STEP1 EXEC PGM = IDCAMS
//SYSPRINT DD SYSOUT =A
//SYSIN    DD *
  DEFINE CLUSTER -
    (NAME(data-set-name ) -
      [Name the VSAM RRDS data set.]
    VOL(volume,volume . . . , volume ) -
      [Name the volumes the data set is to be stored on.]
    NUMBERED -
      [This identifies it as an RRDS.]
    REC(no-primary   no-secondary) -
      [Specify the number of primary and secondary records for space allocation. Note that
      VSAM data sets can have 123 secondary allocations.]
```

```
        RECSZ(average  maximum) -
          [Specify the average and maximum record length. They are the same for fixed-length
            records.]
        FREESPACE(internal-pct  total-pct) -
          [Specify the percentage of free space within each control interval (internal-pct), and
            the percentage of total control interval to be reserved for free space (total-pct).]
        ) -
    DATA (NAME(control-area-name))
      [You must assign the control area a name, even though the name is seldom used.]
/*
```

VSAM RRDS files normally have only fixed-length records. VSAM can simulate variable-length records by using a KSDS (Keyed Sequential Data Set) rather than a RRDS. VS COBOL II also uses KSDS for indexed files. These are described in more detail later. For variable-length VS COBOL II files, you must do the following:

• Code the SIMVRD run-time option:

```
//  EXEC COBUCLG,PARM.GO=(your-parameters /SIMVRD)
```

• Specify RECORD VARYING in the FD statement for the file.

```
  FD  file-name
        RECORD VARYING FROM min  TO max CHARACTERS.
```

• Define the VSAM file with the following job step:

```
//STEP1 EXEC PGM=IDCAMS
//SYSPRINT DD SYSOUT=A
//SYSIN    DD *
  DEFINE CLUSTER -
    (NAME(data-set-name ) -
    VOL(volume,volume ,...,volume ) -
    INDEXED -
      [This identifies it as a KSDS.]
    KEYS(4    0) -
      [This sets aside the first four bytes of the record for the record key, which will be the
        relative record number.]
    REC(no-primary no-secondary) -
    RECSZ(average  maximum) -
    FREESPACE(internal-pct  total-pct) -
    ) -
    DATA (NAME(control-area-name))
    INDEX (NAME(index-name ))
/*
```

B. Specifying Relative Files

The following statements are required to specify relative files:

```
FILE-CONTROL.
    SELECT file-name ASSIGN TO ddname
           ORGANIZATION IS RELATIVE
                        DYNAMIC
                        RANDOM
                        SEQUENTIAL
           ACCESS IS _____
           RELATIVE KEY IS key
```

> [*The* RELATIVE KEY *clause is required when* ACCESS IS RANDOM *or* DYNAMIC *is coded. You can omit the* RELATIVE KEY *clause for* ACCESS IS SEQUENTIAL, *unless you execute a* START *statement for the file.*]

```
FILE SECTION.
FD  file-name
```

> [*The* BLOCK CONTAINS *clause is not needed.*]

```
    RECORD CONTAINS length  CHARACTERS.
```

> [*For fixed-length records.*]

> [*Or:*]

```
    RECORD VARYING FROM min  TO max CHARACTERS.
```

> [*For variable-length records.*]

> [*Or: *]

```
    RECORD VARYING FROM min  TO max CHARACTERS
       DEPENDING ON data-name.
```

> [*For variable-length record in which a field determines the record length. Remember that the data-name must be contained within the record-description.*]

```
01  record-description.
    05  rest-of-record              PIC . . .
WORKING-STORAGE SECTION.
77  key                             PIC 9(9) BINARY.
```

> [*You must define the key as an unsigned integer whose description does not contain a* P. *You can define it in Working-Storage, in the Linkage Section, or in the* FD *for a record description for another file.*]

The ACCESS MODE is one of the following:

- SEQUENTIAL: Default if ACCESS MODE is omitted. Records are read or written sequentially.
- RANDOM: File is accessed randomly by supplying a key for the record read or written.
- DYNAMIC: Allows both SEQUENTIAL and RANDOM reads for the file. Writing is always RANDOM.

C. Writing Relative Files

In VS COBOL II, you can create VSAM files through JCL, but it is usually easier to create them using the VSAM IDCAMS utility program. In Microsoft COBOL, the system creates relative files when they are opened for OUTPUT (or EXTEND, if the file doesn't already exist). To load a VSAM file for VS COBOL II initially, using the IDCAMS utility, you code the following job step:

```
//STEP1 EXEC PGM=IDCAMS
//SYSPRINT    DD SYSOUT=A
//in-ddname    DD DSN=data-set-name, DISP=SHR
  [Include a   DD statement that names the input data set.]
//out-ddname   DD DSN=data-set-name, DISP=KEEP
  [Include a   DD statement that names the VSAM output data set.]
//SYSIN       DD *
  REPRO -
    INFILE(in-ddname) -
      [Name the normal or VSAM sequential data set containing the records to load. The data
       set must be in the proper sort order.]
    OUTFILE(out-ddname)
/ *
```

The following MVS JCL statement is required for a VS COBOL II to write a relative file. There are other forms, but the following is typical.

```
//GO.ddname   DD DSN=data-set-name, DISP=OLD
```

1. *Writing Sequentially*
The following example shows how to write the records sequentially. COBOL assigns keys from 1 to n.

```
SELECT file-name ASSIGN TO ddname
        ORGANIZATION IS RELATIVE
        ACCESS IS SEQUENTIAL
        RELATIVE KEY IS key
          [You only need to specify the RELATIVE KEY if you will be executing a START
           statement for the file. But it is a good idea always to specify it.]

■ ■ ■
OPEN OUTPUT file-name [or   OPEN I-O file-name]
PERFORM . . .
  WRITE record-description FROM identifier
    INVALID KEY imperative-statements
      [The INVALID KEY phrase executes if there is insufficient space to store the
       record.]
  END-WRITE
END-PERFORM
```

If the RELATIVE KEY phrase is coded for the file, the key of the record written will be stored in the RELATIVE KEY data item.

2. *Writing Randomly*

The following example shows how to write 10 records randomly in a file:

```
SELECT file-name ASSIGN TO ddname
       ORGANIZATION IS RELATIVE
       ACCESS IS RANDOM   [or  ACCESS IS DYNAMIC]
       RELATIVE KEY IS key


■ ■ ■
OPEN OUTPUT file-name  [or OPEN I-O file-name]
PERFORM VARYING key FROM 1 BY 1 UNTIL KEY > 10
   WRITE record-description FROM identifier
      INVALID KEY   imperative-statements
         [This executes if a key is supplied that is outside the range of the file or if the
         record already exists in the file.]
      NOT INVALID KEY imperative-statements
   END-WRITE
END-PERFORM
```

The ten records are written with keys 1 to 10. The next example writes the 11th record with a key of 11.

```
MOVE 11 TO key
WRITE record-description FROM identifier
   INVALID KEY imperative-statements
   NOT INVALID KEY imperative-statements
END-WRITE
```

D. Reading Relative Files

The following MVS JCL statement is required to read a relative file. There are other forms, but the following is typical:

```
//GO.ddname   DD DSN=data-set-name, DISP=SHR
```

1. *Sequential Reading*

The records in relative files are read sequentially in the order that they are stored; that is, in the order of ascending keys.

```
SELECT file-name ASSIGN TO ddname
       ORGANIZATION IS RELATIVE
       ACCESS IS SEQUENTIAL  [or  ACCESS IS DYNAMIC]
       RELATIVE KEY IS key


■ ■ ■
OPEN INPUT file-name  [or OPEN I-O file-name]
READ file-name NEXT INTO identifier
      [You can omit the NEXT for ACCESS IS SEQUENTIAL. You must code it for ACCESS
      IS DYNAMIC.]
```

```
AT END imperative-statements
NOT AT END imperative-statements
END-READ
```

If the RELATIVE KEY clause is coded for the file, the key of the record read is stored in the data item.

The following MVS JCL statement is required to read a relative file sequentially. There are other forms, but the following is typical:

```
//GO.ddname   DD DSN=data-set-name, DISP=SHR
```

2. *Positioning for Sequential Reading*

You can execute the START statement to position to a specific record within a relative file and then begin reading sequentially at that point. You move a value to the RELATIVE KEY data item and then name it in the START statement. You must first open the file INPUT or I-O. For example, if you wanted to begin reading sequentially following the fifth record in a file, you could code the following:

```
FILE-CONTROL.
    SELECT IN-FILE ASSIGN TO INDD
           ORGANIZATION IS RELATIVE
           ACCESS IS SEQUENTIAL [or ACCESS IS DYNAMIC]
           RELATIVE KEY IS IN-KEY

    ■ ■ ■
01  IN-KEY                          PIC S9(9) BINARY.
    ■ ■ ■
    OPEN INPUT IN-FILE
    MOVE 5 TO IN-KEY
    START IN-FILE KEY > IN-KEY
      INVALID KEY
        DISPLAY ''5TH RECORD NOT IN FILE"
        GO TO Z90-STOP-RUN
    END-START
    READ IN-FILE INTO IN-REC
      AT END . . .
         [The fifth record is read.]
```

3. *Random Reading*

```
    SELECT file-name ASSIGN TO ddname
           ORGANIZATION IS RELATIVE
           ACCESS IS RANDOM  [or ACCESS IS DYNAMIC]
           RELATIVE KEY IS key

    ■ ■ ■
    OPEN INPUT file-name [or OPEN I-O file-name]
    MOVE relative-record-number TO key
```

```
READ file-name INTO identifier
   INVALID KEY imperative-statements
      [Executed if the record doesn't exist in the file.]
   NOT INVALID KEY imperative-statements
      [Executed if the record is read.]
END-READ
```

E. Updating Relative Files

1. *Updating Sequentially*

You update relative files sequentially just as you would a sequential file. You first read a record and then execute the REWRITE statement to rewrite it. The record written need not have the same length as the record read. (In Microsoft COBOL, it must have the same length.) Omit the INVALID KEY clauses for sequential updating. Here is an example:

```
SELECT file-name ASSIGN TO ddname
       ORGANIZATION IS RELATIVE
       ACCESS IS SEQUENTIAL
       RELATIVE KEY IS key
          [You only need to code the RELATIVE KEY phrase if you execute a START
          statement for the file. However, it is a good idea to code it.]

■ ■ ■
OPEN I-O IN-FILE
READ IN-FILE INTO IN-REC
   AT END
      MOVE HIGH-VALUES TO IN-REC-KEY
   NOT AT END
      MOVE new-values TO IN-REC
      REWRITE IN-RECORD FROM IN-REC
END-READ
```

2. *Random Updating*

You must open the file for I-O. The record written need not contain the same number of characters as the record in the file. (In Microsoft COBOL, it must have the same length.)

```
SELECT file-name ASSIGN TO ddname
       ORGANIZATION IS RELATIVE
       ACCESS IS RANDOM  [or  ACCESS IS DYNAMIC]
       RELATIVE KEY IS key

■ ■ ■
OPEN I-O file-name
MOVE relative-record-number TO key
REWRITE record-description FROM identifier
```

```
INVALID KEY imperative-statements
    [Executed if the record does not exist in the file.]
NOT INVALID KEY imperative-statements
    [Executed if the record is rewritten.]
END-REWRITE
```

Quite often, you update by first reading the record and then rewriting it:

```
MOVE relative-record-number  TO key
READ file-name INTO identifier
    INVALID KEY imperative-statements
        [The record to be updated must first be read.]
END-READ
MOVE new-value  TO identifier
REWRITE record-description FROM identifier
    INVALID KEY imperative-statements
END-REWRITE
```

The same DD statement is required as for writing.

The DELETE statement deletes records in a relative file. The file must be open I-O. Don't code the INVALID/NOT INVALID KEY phrases if you code ACCESS IS SEQUENTIAL for the file. DELETE is written as

```
OPEN I-O file-name
MOVE relative-key-number TO key
DELETE file-name RECORD
    INVALID KEY imperative-statements
        [Executed if the file does not contain the record to delete.]
    NOT INVALID KEY imperative-statements
        [Executed if the record is deleted.]
END-DELETE
```

Once the record is deleted, the system logically removes it from the file so that it cannot be read. However, you can write it again. The record deleted depends on the ACCESS MODE of the file:

- ACCESS IS SEQUENTIAL: You must first successfully read a record with a READ statement. This record is then deleted in the file. Don't code INVALID or NOT INVALID KEY phrases for sequential access.
- ACCESS IS RANDOM or DYNAMIC: You must move the value of the record key to the key data item defined by RELATIVE KEY key.

III. INDEXED FILES

The record keys in indexed files are a part of the record. Each record must have a unique record key, and the system stores the records in the file in ascending order based on this key. For example, a personnel file might have the person's name as the record key. You could read the file sequentially to process the records for each person in the file, one at a time in alphabetical order. You could also access records randomly by specifying the record key. You could read the record for Smith by presenting SMITH as the record key. You can position the file to a point in the file other than the first record to begin sequential processing. Thus, you could position the file to the record for SMITH and sequentially read all the following records.

A major advantage of indexed files is that records can be added or deleted. With sequential files, you add or delete records only by rewriting the entire file. You cannot add records to relative files, because the records have consecutive key numbers. Indexed files are slower to read sequentially than are sequential files, and slower to read randomly than are relative files. How much slower depends on the implementation.

The system maintains two files for each indexed file. One file holds the data records, and the other file holds record keys pointing to where the data records are stored. VSAM for VS COBOL II and ISAM for Microsoft COBOL both use this technique, although the details of how the indexed and storage areas are organized are different.

VS COBOL II indexed files are VSAM KSDS (Keyed Sequential Data Set) files. VSAM records may be fixed- or variable-length. The system handles all blocking for VSAM files, automatically blocking them, and you cannot specify the blocking. You can create VSAM files with JCL, but you usually create them using the VSAM IDCAMS utility program.[1]

Microsoft COBOL has its own access method that it calls ISAM (Indexed Sequential Access Method), which is similar to VSAM. (Microsoft's ISAM has nothing to do with the old, now obsolete ISAM in the MVS operating system. Microsoft just happened to choose the same name). Microsoft COBOL names the index file *file-name*.IDX.

You initially fill indexed files by writing them sequentially in the order of the record keys, and the system creates the separate index file containing record keys used to locate the records. It is much faster initially to write indexed files sequentially than it is randomly.

The system retrieves records randomly by searching the index to find the record's location and then using this to retrieve the record. You can update indexed files by replacing, adding, or deleting records. You replace records by overwriting the old record.

The system dynamically reorganizes indexed files as they are updated. This is why it is faster initially to write them sequentially—the record keys are in order and no reorganization is necessary. When a record is deleted, the system physically removes it from the file. When a record is added, the system inserts the record in the data space and updates the index file.

When you update indexed files, the system writes the records into the file and updates the pointers. If the program abnormally terminates when the file is opened for OUTPUT, I-O, or EXTEND, the file may become unusable because the pointers may not get updated. This is a serious problem if you do not have a backup. You should back up the file at some point and save all the transactions entered until a new backup is made.

A. VS COBOL II VSAM KSDS Files

In VS COBOL II, indexed files are VSAM KSDS (Keyed Sequential Data Sets). You usually create the files with the VSAM IDCAMS utility[1], but you can create them through JCL.[2] Specify the following parameters when creating the file:

```
//STEP1 EXEC PGM=IDCAMS
//SYSPRINT DD SYSOUT=A
//SYSIN    DD *
  DEFINE CLUSTER -
    (NAME(data-set-name ) -
      [Name the VSAM data set.]
    VOL(volume,volume , . . . , volume ) -
      [The data set can extend over several volumes.]
    INDEXED -
      [This defines it as a KSDS data set.]
    KEYS(key-length  relative-byte-position) -
      [The relative-byte-position is 0 for the first byte in the record.]
    REC(no-primary  no-secondary) -
      [Specify the number of primary and secondary records for space allocation. Note that
       VSAM data sets can have 123 secondary allocations.]
    RECSZ(average   maximum) -
      [Specify the average and maximum record length. They are the same for fixed-length
       records.]
    FREESPACE(internal-pct  total-pct) -
      [Specify the percentage of free space within each control interval (internal-pct) and
       the percentage of total control interval to be reserved for free space (total-pct).]
    ) -
  DATA  (NAME(control-area-name )) -
  INDEX  (NAME(index-area-name )) 
    [You must assign the control area and index area names even though the names are seldom
     used.]
/*
```

B. Specifying Indexed Files

The following COBOL statements are required to specify indexed files:

```
FILE-CONTROL.
    SELECT file-name ASSIGN TO ddname
            ORGANIZATION IS INDEXED
                    DYNAMIC
                    RANDOM
                    SEQUENTIAL
            ACCESS IS _____
```

```
        RECORD KEY IS prime-record-key
        .
```

> [*The* prime-record-key *is described below. It can be qualified but not indexed.*
> *You can also describe alternate record keys for the file as described later in*
> *this chapter.*]

```
FILE SECTION.
FD  file-name
        [BLOCK CONTAINS is not needed.]
    RECORD CONTAINS length CHARACTERS.
    [For fixed-length records.]
    [or:]
    RECORD VARYING FROM min TO max CHARACTERS.
    [For variable-length records.]
    [or:]
    RECORD VARYING FROM min TO max CHARACTERS
        DEPENDING ON data-name.
```

> [*For a variable-length record in which a field determines the record length. Remember*
> *that the* data-name *must be contained within the* record-description.]

```
01  record-description.
    05  perhaps-some-of-the-record      PIC ...
    05  prime-record-key                PIC X(n ).
```

> [*The* prime-record-key *must be an alphanumeric item within the record*
> *description for the file. It must lie within the fixed portion of the record.*
> *(That is, it cannot be in or follow a variable occurrence data item.) VS*
> *COBOL II allows the key to be numeric (internal or external), alphabetic,*
> *numeric edited, or alphanumeric edited. Record key values must be unique*
> *and you cannot change them directly. (To change a record key, delete the*
> *record with the old key and then insert it with the new key.)*]

```
        05  rest-of-record              PIC ...
```

The ACCESS MODE is one of the following:

- SEQUENTIAL: Default if ACCESS MODE is omitted. Records are read or written sequentially.
- RANDOM: File is accessed randomly by supplying a key for the record read or written.
- DYNAMIC: Allows both SEQUENTIAL and RANDOM reads for the file. Writing is always RANDOM.

If there is more than one record description for the file, you need name the *prime-record-key* in only one record description. However, each record description must have the prime record key in the same byte positions within the record.

If you use the PASSWORD clause described in Chapter 15 to specify a password for the file, you must code it immediately after the RECORD KEY clause.

C. Writing Indexed Files

You can create VSAM files through JCL, but it is usually easier to create them using the VSAM IDCAMS utility program.[1] You do this for indexed files just the same as for relative files described earlier in this chapter. In Microsoft COBOL, the system creates indexed files when they are opened for OUTPUT (or EXTEND, if the file doesn't already exist).

1. *Writing Sequentially*

Indexed files are usually first written sequentially. You often create them from some other file. You sort the other file in the order the record keys are to have in the indexed file, and then sequentially write the relative file. The following example illustrates this:

```
FILE-CONTROL.
    SELECT IN-FILE ASSIGN TO INDD
            ORGANIZATION IS SEQUENTIAL

    SELECT OUT-FILE ASSIGN TO OUTDD
            ORGANIZATION IS INDEXED
            ACCESS IS SEQUENTIAL
            RECORD KEY IS OUT-RECORD-KEY
                [The RECORD KEY is only needed if you will be executing a START statement
                for the file. However, it is a good idea to code it.]


DATA DIVISION.
FILE SECTION.
FD  IN-FILE
    RECORD CONTAINS 100 CHARACTERS.
01  IN-RECORD                     PIC X(100).
FD  OUT-FILE
    RECORD CONTAINS 100 CHARACTERS.
01  OUT-RECORD.
    05  OUT-RECORD-KEY            PIC X(10).
    05  OUT-RECORD-DATA           PIC X(90).
WORKING-STORAGE SECTION.
01  IN-REC.
    05  IN-REC-KEY                PIC X(10).
    05  IN-REC-DATA               PIC X(90).
    ■ ■ ■
    OPEN INPUT IN-FILE,
        OUTPUT IN-FILE
    PERFORM WITH TEST AFTER UNTIL IN-REC-KEY = HIGH-VALUES
      READ IN-FILE INTO IN-REC
        AT END
          MOVE HIGH-VALUES TO IN-REC-KEY
        NOT AT END
          WRITE OUT-RECORD FROM IN-REC
                [Note that the WRITE FROM causes IN-REC-KEY to be moved to
                OUT-RECORD-KEY when the WRITE is executed.]
            INVALID KEY
```

```
                    DISPLAY "BAD KEY: ", IN-REC-KEY
                    GO TO Z90-STOP-RUN
                END-WRITE
            END-READ
        END-PERFORM
```

The INVALID KEY phrase executes if the record keys are not in ascending sort order.

The following MVS JCL statement is required to write an indexed file sequentially. There are other forms, but the following is typical:

```
//GO.ddname   DD DSN=data-set-name,DISP=OLD
```

2. *Writing Randomly*

The following example shows how to write a file randomly. You must store a value in the RECORD KEY IS *prime-record-key* data item.

```
SELECT file-name ASSIGN TO ddname
        ORGANIZATION IS INDEXED
        ACCESS IS RANDOM [or ACCESS IS DYNAMIC]
        RECORD KEY IS prime-record-key
```

■ ■ ■

```
OPEN OUTPUT file-name [or OPEN I-O file-name]
MOVE value TO prime-record-key
WRITE record-description FROM identifier
  INVALID KEY imperative-statements
```
   [*Executed if a key is supplied that is outside the range of the file or if the record already exists in the file.*]
```
  NOT INVALID KEY imperative-statements
```
   [*Executed if the record is written.*]
```
END-WRITE
```

D. Reading Indexed Files

The following MVS JCL statement is required to read an indexed file. There are other forms, but the following is typical:

```
//GO.ddname   DD DSN=data-set-name,DISP=SHR
```

1. *Sequential Reading*

The records in indexed files are read sequentially in the order that they are stored; that is, in the order of their keys.

```
SELECT file-name ASSIGN TO ddname
        ORGANIZATION IS INDEXED
```

```
ACCESS IS SEQUENTIAL  [or ACCESS IS DYNAMIC]
RECORD KEY IS prime-record-key
    [The RECORD KEY is only needed if you will be executing a START statement
    for the file. However, it is a good idea to code it.]


■ ■ ■
OPEN INPUT file-name or [OPEN I-O file-name]
READ file-name NEXT INTO identifier
    [You can omit the NEXT for ACCESS IS SEQUENTIAL. You must code it for ACCESS
    IS DYNAMIC.]
  AT END imperative-statements
  NOT AT END imperative-statements
END-READ
```

The following MVS JCL statement is required to read an indexed file sequentially. There are other forms, but the following is typical.

```
//GO.ddname  DD DSN=data-set-name,DISP=SHR
```

2. *Positioning for Sequential Reading*

You can execute the START statement to position to a specific record within an indexed file and then begin reading sequentially at that point. You must move a value to the RECORD KEY data item (or ALTERNATE RECORD KEY, described later in this section) and then name this data item in the START statement. You must first open the file INPUT or I-O. The identifier specifying the key in the START statement can be qualified but not subscripted. It must have a length less than or equal to the *prime-record-key* for the file.

For example, if you wanted to begin reading sequentially following the record whose key begins "SMI" in a file, such as SMITH or SMITHE, you could code the following:

```
FILE-CONTROL.
  SELECT IN-FILE ASSIGN TO OUTDD
      ORGANIZATION IS INDEXED
      ACCESS IS SEQUENTIAL
      RECORD KEY IS IN-KEY


■ ■ ■
OPEN INPUT IN-FILE
MOVE "SMI" TO IN-KEY
START IN-FILE KEY > IN-KEY
  INVALID KEY
    DISPLAY "NO RECORD IN FILE BEGINS WITH SMI"
    GO TO Z90-STOP-RUN
END-START
READ IN-FILE INTO IN-REC
  AT END ...
```

When fields of unequal length are compared, the longer field is truncated on the right to equal the length of the shorter for the comparison. The comparison ignores any PROGRAM COLLATING SEQUENCE clause.

3. *Random Reading*

```
SELECT file-name ASSIGN TO ddname
       ORGANIZATION IS INDEXED
       ACCESS IS RANDOM  [or  ACCESS IS DYNAMIC]
       RECORD KEY IS prime-record-key
```

■ ■ ■

```
OPEN INPUT file-name [or  OPEN I-O file-name]
MOVE value TO prime-record-key
READ file-name INTO identifier
  KEY IS identifier
     [Names an identifier containing the key of the record to read. It may be qualified but
       not subscripted.]
  INVALID KEY imperative-statements
     [Executed if the record doesn't exist in the file.]
  NOT INVALID KEY imperative-statements
     [Executed if the record is read.]
END-READ
```

As we'll see below, an indexed file can have more than one key. If you want other than the *prime-record-key*, you must add the KEY phrase to name the key. (You can also name the *prime-record-key*, but this is default if you omit the KEY phrase.)

```
READ file-name INTO identifier
  KEY IS alternate-key
     [The alternate-key must specify a key defined for the record. It may be qualified but
       not subscripted.]
  INVALID KEY imperative-statements
     [Executed if the record doesn't exist in the file.]
  NOT INVALID KEY imperative-statements
     [Executed if the record is read.]
END-READ
```

E. Updating Indexed Files

1. *Updating Sequentially*

You update indexed files sequentially, just as you would a sequential file. You first read a record and then execute the REWRITE statement to rewrite it. The record rewritten need not have the same length as the record read. (In Microsoft COBOL, it must have the same length.) The *prime-record-key* rewritten must be the same as that read. Here is an example:

```
SELECT IN-FILE ASSIGN TO ddname
        ORGANIZATION IS INDEXED
        ACCESS IS SEQUENTIAL  [or ACCESS IS DYNAMIC]
        RECORD KEY IS prime-record-key
            [The RECORD KEY is only needed if you will be executing a START statement
            for the file. However, it is a good idea to code it.]
```

■ ■ ■

```
OPEN I/O file-name
READ IN-FILE INTO IN-REC
  AT END
     MOVE HIGH-VALUES TO IN-REC-KEY
  NOT AT END
     MOVE new-values TO IN-REC
     REWRITE IN-RECORD FROM IN-REC
       INVALID KEY
          DISPLAY "CAN'T REWRITE RECORD: ", IN-REC-KEY
          GO TO Z90-STOP-RUN
     END-REWRITE
END-READ
```

2. *Updating Randomly*

You must open the file for I-O, and the record written must contain the same number of characters as the record in the file. (In VS COBOL II, the record can have a different length.) You must not change the record key when you rewrite a record. If you need to change a record key, delete the record and write it with the new key.

```
SELECT file-name ASSIGN TO ddname
        ORGANIZATION IS INDEXED
        ACCESS IS RANDOM [or ACCESS IS DYNAMIC]
        RECORD KEY IS prime-record-key
```

■ ■ ■

```
OPEN I-O file-name
MOVE value TO prime-record-key
REWRITE record-description FROM identifier
  INVALID KEY imperative-statements
     [Executed if the record does not exist in the file.]
  NOT INVALID KEY imperative-statements
     [Executed if the record is read.]
END-REWRITE
```

Quite often, you update by first reading the record and then rewriting it:

```
MOVE value TO prime-record-key
READ file-name INTO identifier
     [The record to be updated must first be read.]
```

```
        INVALID KEY imperative-statements
    END-READ
    REWRITE record-description FROM identifier
        INVALID KEY imperative-statements
    END-REWRITE
```

The same DD statement is required as for writing.

The DELETE statement deletes records in an indexed file. The value in the
prime-record-key specifies the record to delete. The contents of the record
description and the file position are not affected by execution of the DELETE
statement. Don't code the INVALID/NOT INVALID KEY phrases if you code
ACCESS IS SEQUENTIAL for the file. You must open the file for I-0:

```
    OPEN I-0 file-name
    MOVE value TO prime-record-key
    DELETE file-name RECORD
        INVALID KEY imperative-statements
            [Executed if the file does not contain the record to delete.]
        NOT INVALID KEY imperative-statements
            [Executed if the record is deleted.]
    END-DELETE
```

Once the record is deleted, the system logically removes it from the file so that
you cannot read it. However, you may write it again.

F. The ALTERNATE RECORD KEY Clause

You specify alternate record keys for a file by coding the ALTERNATE RECORD
KEY clause, as follows:

```
FILE-CONTROL.
    SELECT file-name ASSIGN TO ddname
            ORGANIZATION IS INDEXED
                        DYNAMIC
                        RANDOM
                        SEQUENTIAL
            ACCESS IS _____
            RECORD KEY IS prime-record-key
            ALTERNATE RECORD KEY IS alternate-record-key
            WITH DUPLICATES

                    [The alternate-record-key is described below. It can be qualified but not in-
                    dexed. If there is more than one record description for the file, you need
                    name the alternate-record-key in only one of the record descriptions. How-
                    ever, each record description must have the alternate record key in the same
                    byte positions within the record.]
FILE SECTION.
FD  file-name
    RECORD CONTAINS ...  [or RECORD VARYING ...]
```

```
01   record-description .
        05   perhaps-some-of-the-record          PIC ...
        05   prime-record-key                    PIC X( n ).
```
        [*The relative position of the prime-record-key and the alternate-record-key doesn't matter.*]
```
        05   alternate-record-key                PIC X( n ).
```
        [*The alternate-record-key must be an alphanumeric item within the record description for the file. It must lie within the fixed portion of the record. (That is, it cannot be in or follow a variable-occurrence data item.) VS COBOL II allows the key to be numeric (internal or external), alphabetic, numeric edited, or alphanumeric edited. Alternate record key values need not be unique if* WITH DUPLICATES *is coded. You can also change alternate record keys.*]
```
        05   rest-of-record                      PIC ...
```

Code the WITH DUPLICATES only if there can be duplicate alternate record key values. You can specify several alternate record keys.

```
SELECT file-name ASSIGN TO ddname
        ORGANIZATION IS INDEXED
        ACCESS IS ...
        RECORD KEY IS prime-record-key
        ALTERNATE RECORD KEY IS alternate-record-key-1
           WITH DUPLICATES
        ALTERNATE RECORD KEY IS alternate-record-key-2
        ALTERNATE RECORD KEY IS alternate-record-key-3
           WITH DUPLICATES
```

In VS COBOL II, you can specify a separate password for each ALTERNATE RECORD KEY. VS COBOL II allows a maximum of 253 ALTERNATE RECORD KEY clauses. You must code any PASSWORD clause (described in Chapter 15) for it immediately following the ALTERNATE RECORD KEY/WITH DUPLICATES phrase. You can code PASSWORD in Microsoft COBOL, but it is ignored.

The ALTERNATE RECORD KEY clause causes one or more additional indexes to be created to contain alternate record keys. Alternate keys allow files to be inverted on some key. If the term *inverted* is unfamiliar, the concept is not. Consider a telephone book. The primary index would be the names of people. You could invert the file using the telephone numbers as the alternate key so that you could look up a person's name given his or her telephone number. Since several people may have the same telephone number, the WITH DUPLICATES clause would be needed. A library is an even more familiar example of an inverted file. Libraries maintain catalogs with the book titles as the primary key. They then invert the file on the author so that a book can be retrieved by either its title or author.

Alternate record keys are a significant feature. They give COBOL the facility for inverting files, a facility generally found only in some generalized data base management systems.

You can use an *alternate-record-key* in the I/O statements as follows:

- DELETE: The DELETE statement doesn't use the *alternate-record-key*.
- START: The START statement can name an *alternate-record-key*. This also makes the *alternate-record-key* the key of reference for any subsequent sequential READ statements. That is, once you use START to position to an *alternate-record-key*, READ statements will then read the file in the order of the *alternate-record-key*.
- READ: The READ statement will read the file sequentially in the order of the *alternate-record-key* if you execute a START statement naming an *alternate-record-key*. For reading randomly based on the *alternate-record-key*, you can name an *alternate-record-key* in the KEY IS phrase. Note that only the first of a duplicate record written can be retrieved randomly when there are duplicate keys.
- REWRITE: The REWRITE statement does not use the *alternate-record-key*. You can change an *alternate-record-key* with a REWRITE, and the system will automatically update the alternate file index.
- WRITE: The WRITE statement does not use the *alternate-record-key*. Just be sure to code WITH DUPLICATES if you will be writing records with duplicate alternate record keys.

When you code ALTERNATE RECORD KEY in VS COBOL II, you must use the IDCAMS utility to define the alternate record keys, as follows:

```
//STEP1 EXEC PGM=IDCAMS
//SYSPRINT DD SYSOUT=A
//SYSIN    DD *
  DEFINE AIX (NAME(index-name  -
    VOL(volume,volume ,....,volume ) -
      [The index can extend over several volumes.]
    RELATE(data-set-name ) -
      [Name the data set for which this is the alternate index.]
    UPGRADE -
      [This is default and causes the alternate index to be updated when the data set is updated.
      Code NOUPGRADE if you don't want the index updated.]
    KEYS(key-length  relative-byte-position) -
      [The relative-byte-position is 0 for the first byte in the record.]
    REC(no-primary  no-secondary) -
      [Specify the number of primary and secondary records for space allocation.]
    FREESPACE(internal-pct  total-pct) -
      [Specify the percentage of free space within each control interval (internal-pct), and the
      percentage of total control interval to be reserved for free space (total-pct).]
    NONUNIQUEKEY -
      [Code this if the data set may have multiple records with the same key. The default is
      UNIQUEKEY, which requires each record to have a unique key.]
    ) -
  DATA (NAME(control-area-name )) -
```

```
INDEX (NAME(index-area-name ))
```
  [*You must assign the control area and index area names even though the names are seldom used.*]
```
/*
```

After defining the alternate index, you must then define the alternate index path to form the connection between the alternate index and the data set.

```
//STEP1 EXEC PGM=IDCAMS
//SYSPRINT DD SYSOUT=A
//SYSIN    DD *
  DEFINE PATH ( -
    NAME(path-name ) -
```
      [*Give the path a name. Usually this is the original data set name with "PATH" appended: data-set-name.PATH.*]
```
    PATHENTRY(index-name ) -
```
      [*Name the alternate index.*]
```
    UPDATE -
```
      [*This causes the alternate index to be updated when the data base is changed. You can code NOUPDATE if you don't want it changed. You usually code this when you code UPGRADE for the alternate index.*]
```
    )
/*
```

After you have defined everything and loaded the data set, you then must execute the following to build the alternate index physically:

```
//STEP1 EXEC PGM=IDCAMS
//SYSPRINT DD SYSOUT=A
//SYSIN    DD *
  BLDINDEX -
    INDATASET(data-set-name ) -
    OUTDATASET(index-name )
/*
```

Code a separate DEFINE AIX, DEFINE PATH, and BLDINDEX statement for each alternate index.

This concludes the discussion of relative and indexed files. They are more complex than sequential files, may be slower to process, and can result in difficult backup problems. Because of this, you shouldn't use either relative or indexed files unless a sequential file proves untenable. The next chapters describe how to detect I/O errors and some special I/O processing.

EXERCISES

1. Describe several applications in which relative and indexed files might each be used.

2. Write a program to read a file, containing a charge number in columns 1 to 6, and create a relative file. Then write a program to read in each transaction, in random order, that contains a charge number in columns 1 to 6. Validate each charge number by looking it up in the relative file. Print an error message on the transaction if the charge number is not found in the file.

3. Repeat Exercise 2 for an indexed file. Assume that the charge number can be any alphanumeric characters.

4. Assume the same file described in Exercise 2. However, the transactions are to be used to update the file. Assume that column 7 of the transaction contains a D to delete the record in the file, an A to add the transaction to the file, and an R to replace the record in the file with the transaction. Any other character in column 7 is an error. Display an error message if the record to be deleted or replaced is not in the file, or if a transaction to be added already exists in the file. Do this exercise for either relative or indexed file organization.

5. Write a program to back up and restore the file described in Exercise 2 sequentially.

REFERENCES

1. "MVS/370 Integrated Catalog Administration: Access Method Services Reference," Order No. GC26-4051, Poughkeepsie, NY: IBM Coporation, 1991.

2. "MVS/ESA JCL Reference," Order No. GC18-1829, Poughkeepsie, NY: IBM Corporation, 1991.

ADDITIONAL READINGS

"Introduction to IBM Direct-Access Storage Devices and Access Methods," Order No. GC20-1684, Poughkeepsie, NY: IBM Corporation, 1991.

V. Y. Lum, P. S. T. Yuen, and M. Dodd, "Key-to-Address Transform Techniques: A Fundamental Performance Study on Large Existing Formatted Files," *Communications of the ACM*, Vol. 14, No. 4 (April 1981), pp. 228–239.

"MVS/370 Access Method Services Reference," Order No. GC26-4051, Poughkeepsie, NY: IBM Corporation, 1991.

15

Special Processing for Input/Output

This chapter describes how to handle I/O errors, obtain file status information, and how to use the special I/O features in COBOL. The information applies to sequential, relative, and indexed files. Most COBOL programs won't use the features described in this chapter.

I. I/O ERRORS AND FILE STATUS

A. The USE AFTER ERROR PROCEDURE

In the Declaratives, which immediately follow the PROCEDURE DIVISION name, you can add sections to be automatically invoked when an I/O error occurs.

```
PROCEDURE DIVISION.
DECLARATIVES.
section-name SECTION.
                                    INPUT
                                    OUTPUT
                                    I-O
                                    EXTEND
                                    file-name
      USE AFTER ERROR PROCEDURE ON _____ , ...

      .
paragraphs.
   statements
      .
section-name SECTION.
      USE AFTER ...
   ■ ■ ■
      .
END DECLARATIVES.
```

The system executes the paragraphs in the section if an I/O error occurs on any of the named files. Coding INPUT, for example, would detect an I/O error on any input file. Coding *file-name* would detect only the errors on the specified file. You can code several USE statements, but if you code a *file-name,* it has priority over any generic specification, such as INPUT or OUTPUT, that would include that file name.

The paragraphs within the sections cannot contain any statements that refer to nondeclarative procedures. Nor can nondeclarative procedures refer to any paragraph in the Declarative Section. Control is returned to the statement causing the error when the exit is made from the section — unless the error causes the program to terminate abnormally.

```
PROCEDURE DIVISION.
DECLARATIVES.
FILE-I-ERROR SECTION.
    USE AFTER ERROR PROCEDURE ON FILE-I.
FILE-I-START.
    DISPLAY "ERROR ON FILE-I"
    ADD 1 TO ERROR-COUNT

    .

FILE-O-ERROR SECTION.
    USE AFTER ERROR PROCEDURE ON FILE-O.
FILE-O-START.
    DISPLAY "ERROR ON FILE-O"
    ADD 1 TO ERROR-COUNT

    .

END DECLARATIVES.
    ■ ■ ■
    READ FILE-I INTO X
      AT END
        MOVE "Y" TO EOF-FILE-I
      NOT AT END
        MOVE FILE-I-REC TO FILE-O-REC
        WRITE FILE-O
    END-READ
```

COBOL invokes a USE AFTER ERROR PROCEDURE for the following conditions:

- An I/O error occurs.
- An end-of-file condition occurs, and the READ statement doesn't contain an AT END clause.
- An invalid key error occurs, and the READ or WRITE statement doesn't contain an INVALID KEY clause.
- An I/O error occurs that causes *key-1* of the FILE STATUS, described later in this section, to be set to 9.

Programs terminate if an open is unsuccessful, unless a USE AFTER ERROR PROCEDURE is coded. The USE AFTER ERROR PROCEDURE can take action when an unsuccessful open occurs.

B. User Labels: The USE AFTER LABEL PROCEDURE (not in ANSI Standard)

VS COBOL II and Microsoft COBOL allow you to create and process user labels for files (very rare). User labels are records written immediately after the standard header or trailer labels. The USE AFTER LABEL PROCEDURE declarative allows you to code paragraphs containing statements to read or write these labels and do whatever processing is needed.

VS COBOL II allows user labels only for QSAM sequential files. Microsoft COBOL allows them for sequential, indexed, and relative files. To specify user labels, you must also code a LABEL RECORDS clause in the FD paragraph for the file. The LABEL RECORDS clause also lets you specify STANDARD labels (the default if you omit the clause), or OMITTED for no labels. The LABEL RECORDS clause is obsolete in the ANSI Standard and is to be removed in the next revision. In VS COBOL II, it is better to code the LABEL parameter in the JCL DD statement to specify nonlabeled data sets, which can only be tape. Consequently, you would need the LABEL RECORDS clause only if you have user labels. You code it as

```
FD IN-FILE
    BLOCK CONTAINS ...
    RECORD CONTAINS ...
                 OMITTED
                 STANDARD
                 record-name
    LABEL RECORDS _____
    .
```

You code *record-name* if you have user labels. (If you have user labels, you must also have standard labels.) The *record-name* is then the name of the record description for the user label, and you describe it as a level 01 entry following the FD. The record length must be 80. Here is an example:

```
FD IN-FILE
    BLOCK CONTAINS ...
    RECORD CONTAINS ...
    LABEL RECORDS MY-LABEL
    .
01  MY-LABEL.
    05  SOME-STUFF              PIC X(60).
    05  MORE-STUFF              PIC X(20).
01  normal-record-name   ...
        [You describe both the regular records in the file and the label records with level 01
        entries.]
```

Next, you code the USE AFTER LABEL PROCEDURE in the Declaratives Section in the same way as you code a USE AFTER ERROR PROCEDURE. You code the USE AFTER LABEL PROCEDURE as

```
PROCEDURE DIVISION.
DECLARATIVES.
section-name SECTION.
                                                    INPUT
                                                    OUTPUT
                         FILE                       I-0
            ENDING    REEL                          EXTEND
            BEGINNING UNIT                          file-name
     USE AFTER _____  ____ LABEL PROCEDURE ON _____
paragraphs.
     statements-to-process-the-user-labels

       .
section-name SECTION.
     USE AFTER ...
       ■ ■ ■

       .
END DECLARATIVES.
```

- BEGINNING/ENDING specifies whether the procedure is executed for the BEGINNING label only, the ENDING label only, or both the beginning and ending labels (if neither BEGINNING or ENDING is coded).
- FILE/REEL/UNIT specify when the procedures are to be executed for the beginning and/or ending labels. If none of these three are specified, the procedures are executed as if both REEL/UNIT and FILE were specified.
- FILE

  For BEGINNING: Executed only at the beginning-of-file for the first volume only.

  For ENDING: Executed at the end-of-file for the last volume only.

- REEL or UNIT

  For BEGINNING: Executed at the beginning-of-volume on each volume except the first.

  For ENDING: Executed at the end-of-volume on each volume except the last. Don't code REEL for disk files.

- INPUT or OUTPUT or I-0 or EXTEND execute the procedures only if the file is opened as specified.
- *file-name* names a file for which user labels are to be processed. You can name several files in different USE AFTER LABEL PROCEDURE declaratives for different combinations of BEGINNING/ENDING and FILE/REEL/UNIT. However, the file must not be simultaneously requested for execution by more than one USE procedure. The file can't be a sort file or have the LABEL RECORDS ARE OMITTED clause coded for it. You can code several *file-names,* separating

them by spaces, so that their user labels are processed by the same statements. Here is an example:

```
TAPE-ERROR SECTION.
    USE AFTER BEGINNING FILE LABEL PROCEDURE ON FILE-1, FILE-2.
```

Normally the system exits the Declarative following the last statement in the section. However, you can code a special GO TO MORE-LABELS statement to execute the procedure again, perhaps to read or write a second user label. The GO TO MORE-LABELS finishes reading or writing the current label and then reenters the procedure. Obviously, you would want to insert code to make the GO TO MORE-LABELS conditional so the program does not go into a loop.

C. The FILE STATUS Clause

The FILE STATUS clause in the SELECT clause directs the system to store a two-character status code in a data item at the completion of each I/O statement. You can test these status codes after completion of the I/O statement, either in a USE AFTER ERROR PROCEDURE or in normal program statements:

```
SELECT file-name ASSIGN TO ddname
    FILE STATUS IS status.
```

You must describe the *status* in the Working-Storage or the Linkage Section as a two-character alphanumeric field:

```
WORKING-STORAGE SECTION.
01  status.
    05  key-1                       PIC X.
    05  key-2                       PIC X.
```

The system stores status code values in *status* before any USE AFTER ERROR procedures are executed. The status codes are shown in Table 15.1.

VS COBOL II and Microsoft COBOL also allow a second identifier to be specified in the FILE STATUS phrase for VSAM I/O errors:

```
SELECT file-name ASSIGN TO ddname
        FILE STATUS IS status, VSAM-status.
```

The *VSAM-status* must be a group item of 6 bytes described as follows:

```
WORKING-STORAGE SECTION.
01  VSAM-status.
    05  key-1                       PIC 9(2) BINARY.
        [VSAM return code in binary notation.]
    05  key-2                       PIC 9(1) BINARY.
        [VSAM function code in binary notation.]
    05  key-3                       PIC 9(3) BINARY.
        [VSAM feedback code in binary notation.]
```

TABLE 15.1.   System Status Codes

key-1	key-2	Cause
Successful completion:		
0	0	No further information
	2	Duplicate key detected
	4	Wrong fixed-length record
	5	File created when opened. With sequential VSAM files, 0 is returned.
	7	CLOSE with NO REWIND or REEL, for nontape.
End-of-file:		
1	0	No further information
	4	Relative record READ outside file boundary
Invalid key:		
2	1	Sequence error
	2	Duplicate key
	3	No record found
	4	Key outside boundary of file
Permanent I/O error:		
3	0	No further information
	4	Record outside file boundary
	5	OPEN and required file not found
	7	OPEN with invalid mode
	8	OPEN of file closed with LOCK
	9	OPEN unsuccessful because of conflicting file attributes
Logic error:		
4	1	OPEN of file already open
	2	CLOSE for file not open
	3	READ not executed before REWRITE
	4	REWRITE of different size record
	6	READ after EOF reached
	7	READ attempted for file not opened I-O or INPUT
	8	WRITE for file not opened OUTPUT, I-O, or EXTEND
	9	DELETE or REWRITE for file not opened I-O.
Specific compiler-defined conditions:		
9	0	No further information
	1	VSAM password failure
	2	Logic error
	3	VSAM resource not available
	4	VSAM sequential record not available
	5	VSAM invalid or incomplete file information
	6	VSAM—no DD statement
	7	VSAM OPEN successful. File integrity verified.

D. The INVALID KEY **Phrase (not in ANSI Standard)**

Files written on direct-access storage devices may exceed the amount of space for the device, or an invalid key may be used to write records in an indexed or relative file. VS COBOL II and Microsoft COBOL permit you to detect these conditions by appending the INVALID KEY phrase to the WRITE statement. (You can do the same thing with the USE AFTER ERROR PROCEDURE and stay within the ANSI Standard.)

```
WRITE record-description FROM identifier
   INVALID KEY
      imperative-statements
         [Executed if an attempt is made to write a record outside the bounds of the file.
         This can occur for a sequential file when there is insufficient storage space for the
         record.]
   NOT INVALID KEY
      imperative-statements
         [Executed if the record is written.]
END-WRITE
```

If neither INVALID KEY or USE AFTER ERROR is provided, the program abnormally terminates when this error occurs.

II. SPECIAL I/O FEATURES

The special I/O features in this section are all optional and seldom required. Some of them are compiler-dependent.

A. The I-O-CONTROL **Paragraph**

You can code the I-O-CONTROL paragraph to specify various I/O options. Terminate the last clause with a period. The options are described below.

```
I-O-CONTROL.
   SAME AREA    [or  RECORD AREA or  SORT AREA]
   APPLY WRITE ONLY
```

1. The SAME AREA *Clause*

The SAME AREA and SAME RECORD clauses in the I-O-CONTROL paragraph illustrate how the desire to squeeze the last bit of efficiency from the system can result in making simple things complex. VS COBOL II treats SAME AREA as documentation for sequential files. You code SAME AREA as follows:

```
I-O-CONTROL.
   SAME AREA file-name,  file-name,   ..., file-name.
```

The SAME AREA clause causes the listed files to share the same storage for their access routines and buffers. You must not have the files open at the same time. In the following example, FILE-A and FILE-B could not be open at the same time, because they share the same storage. MVS allocates storage dynamically with the OPEN and releases it with the CLOSE, so any savings are minimal.

```
SAME AREA FILE-A, FILE-B
```

The SAME RECORD AREA clause allows several files to share the same record area. (In VS COBOL II, you cannot code SAME RECORD AREA for a file that has RECORD CONTAINS 0 CHARACTERS specified.) The files may be open at the same time.

```
SAME RECORD AREA file-name, file-name, ..., file-name.
```

In essence, the records following the FD entry are implicitly redefined to each other for all the files listed. This allows a record to be read from one file and written by another without moving the data. The following example illustrates this.

```
I-O-CONTROL.
    SAME RECORD AREA FOR FILE-A, FILE-B.
DATA DIVISION.
FILE SECTION.
FD  FILE-A ...
01  FILE-A-REC                      PIC X(80).
FD  FILE-B ...
01  FILE-B-REC                      PIC X(80).
    ■ ■ ■
    OPEN INPUT FILE-A, FILE-B
    READ FILE-A
      [Record is read into FILE-A-REC.]
      AT END
         CONTINUE
      NOT AT END
         WRITE FILE-B-REC
           [The record in FILE-A-REC is also the FILE-B-REC record, and it is written
           onto FILE-B.]
    END-READ
```

2. The APPLY WRITE-ONLY Clause (not in ANSI Standard)

VS COBOL II allows the APPLY WRITE-ONLY clause to be written for QSAM files with variable-length output files. (APPLY WRITE-ONLY is treated as a comment in Microsoft COBOL.) It optimizes buffer and device space allocation. The savings are generally marginal. (Presumably, if they were significant,

IBM would not make the clause an option but would make it standard in the compiler.) You code it as

```
I-O-CONTROL.
    APPLY WRITE-ONLY ON file-name, file-name, ..., file-name.
```

B. The SELECT Phrase Options

1. The PASSWORD *Clause (not in ANSI Standard)*

VS COBOL II permits a password to be specified in order to limit access to VSAM files. (Microsoft ignores the PASSWORD clause.) The password is a PIC X(8) item and is written into the file when it is created. You must supply the password thereafter to match the password of the file when the file is opened. The password can be specified only for VSAM files.

```
SELECT file-name ASSIGN TO AS-ddname
    PASSWORD IS password.
```

2. The RESERVE AREAS *Clause for Allocating Buffers*

Buffers provide an area in which to block and unblock records. This allows the operating system to be reading or writing some buffer while the program is processing records in the other buffer, overlapping the I/O with the computations. The VS COBOL II default allocation is usually five buffers, and this is adequate in most instances. The RESERVE clause in the SELECT clause changes the number of buffers allocated to a file. You code it as follows, where the literal *integer* is the number of buffers to allocate, from 1 to 255:

```
SELECT file-name ASSIGN TO ddname
    RESERVE integer AREAS.
```

In VS COBOL II, it is better to specify the number of buffers with the JCL DCB=BUFNO=*number* parameter. (Microsoft COBOL treats the RESERVE clause as a comment.)

```
//ddname  DD DCB=(BUFNO=total ,...
```

3. The PADDING CHARACTER *Cause*

VS COBOL II and Microsoft COBOL treat the PADDING CHARACTER clause as a comment. The ANSI Standard allows a padding character to be specified for padding blocks in sequential files. (VS COBOL II, DOS, and OS/2 don't need this.) It is coded as

```
SELECT file-name ASSIGN TO ddname
    PADDING CHARACTER IS item.
```

The *item* can be a one-character nonnumeric literal or identifier.

4. The RECORD DELIMITER *Clause*

VS COBOL II and Microsoft COBOL treat the RECORD DELIMITER clause as a comment. The ANSI Standard allows you to specify the means of determining the length of variable-length records. You code it as

```
SELECT file-name ASSIGN TO ddname
   RECORD DELIMITER IS name.
```

The *name* can be STANDARD-1 for tape, and other values are installation-dependent.

   This completes the discussion of input/output. The next chapters go on to describe how the COBOL statements are coded in a program. But before this, MVS JCL must be explained, because VS COBOL II programs cannot be run, nor input/output accomplished, without it.

16

MVS/ESA Job Control Language

Job Control Language (JCL) is not a part of COBOL, but you can't do much in MVS/VS COBOL II without it. JCL is closely entwined with many of the COBOL statements, serving as the link between the operating system, the hardware devices, and the COBOL program. JCL applies only to MVS, and those using COBOL with other computers and operating systems will find the references to JCL less useful. Most other computers and operating systems have something comparable, although rarely as complex. MVS is also so widely used that most mainframe programmers will come into contact with it some time in their careers. The following brief introduction to JCL gives its form and purpose, but it is not exhaustive. Other JCL features are described throughout the book where they apply.

JCL consists of a set of statements that direct the execution of the computer programs and describe the input/output devices used.

I. THE JOB STATEMENT

The JOB statement denotes the start of a batch computer job, which may itself consist of several computer programs to be run in sequence. A typical JOB statement is coded as follows, but each installation has its own requirements.

```
//JR964113 JOB (24584),'JONES',CLASS=A
```

JR964113 is the job name, and the (24584) is installation-defined accounting information. The 'JONES' is the programmer name or any text (maximum of 20 characters) to identify the job further. The CLASS=A specifies a job class defined by the installation, and the operating system uses it to schedule the job. For example, there might be a job class for quick turnaround and one for overnight service. There is no need to dwell on the JOB statement in detail, because all installations have specific requirements for it.

II. THE EXEC STATEMENT

Each program within a job executes in what is termed a *job step*, or simply a *step*. A typical job might consist of three steps. First, a compile step converts the COBOL statements into executable code. Then a linkage editor step combines the compiled program with other subprograms in subprogram libraries to create a load module for execution. Finally, an execution step runs the job. This entails the execution of three separate programs—the compiler and linkage editor, which are systems programs, and your program. Each step begins with a single EXEC statement, which specifies the program to execute and may be identified with a step name.

```
//  step-name   EXEC PGM=program
```

- *step-name* is optional and is the name you choose for the job step. It is one to eight alphanumeric (A to Z, 0 to 9) or national (@ $ #) character name you select. It must begin in column 3 with an alphabetic or national (A to Z @ $ #) character. Note that only upper-case characters are allowed in JCL.
- *program* names the program to execute.

```
//STEP1 EXEC PGM=RUN12
```

If the program is in the system library, you need not specify the library containing the program. If the program is in your own library rather than in the system library, specify this library with either a JOBLIB or STEPLIB statement. You place the JOBLIB statement immediately after the JOB statement and place the STEPLIB after the EXEC statement:

```
//JR964113 JOB (24584),'JONES',CLASS=A
//JOBLIB DD DSN=library,DISP=SHR
```
   [*The* JOBLIB *statement applies to all steps within the job. The system will first search this library and then the system library for each program.*]
```
//STEP1 EXEC PGM=RUN12
//STEPLIB DD DSN=library,DISP=SHR
```
   [*A* STEPLIB *applies only to the step it is placed after. It has precedence for that step over any* JOBLIB *statement. The system will search the library specified in the* STEPLIB *statement first, and then the system library, to find* RUN12.]

JCL statements may have several optional keyword parameters, which can be coded in any order.

```
//STEP1 EXEC PGM=RUN12,REGION=104K,PARM='XREF',COND=(4,LT)
```

Same as

```
//STEP1 EXEC PGM=RUN12,PARM='XREF',REGION=104K,COND=(4,LT)
```

Only the essential keyword parameters are described here.

A. The PARM **Parameter**

The PARM parameter passes control information (1 to 100 characters) to the job step when the step is initiated. You code it as

//stepname EXEC PGM=*program* , PARM="*string* "

If PARM is omitted, no values are passed. Programs supplied by IBM, such as the compilers and linkage editors, expect the value to represent various run options. COBOL programs can accept PARM values, as described in Chapter 18.

B. The COND **Parameter**

The COND parameter tests return codes from previous steps and bypasses this step if any test is true. In MVS, each job step may pass a return code to the system when it reaches completion. Consequently, COND permits the execution of steps to depend on the return codes from previous steps. If the COND parameter is omitted, the system makes no tests and the steps execute normally. Chapter 18 describes how to set return codes in COBOL.

Return codes can range from 0 to 4095. The IBM conventions for return code values are as follows:

  0:   No errors or warnings detected.
  4:   Possible errors (warnings) detected but execution should be successful.
  8:   Serious errors detected; execution likely to fail.
 12: Severe error: execution impossible.
 16: Fatal error: execution cannot continue.

You code COND in the EXEC statement as

COND=((*number* ,*comparison*) , . . . , (*number* ,*comparison*))

The system compares each number against the return code from each prior step. If any comparison is true, it bypasses the step. You can also code any of the tests as (*number,comparison,step-name*) to compare the number against the return code of a specific step. Coding COND=(4,GT,STEP2) bypasses the step if 4 is greater than the return code issued by STEP2, a previous step. Code *step-name.procstep* to apply the test to the return code from a specific step within a procedure. (Procedures are described later in this chapter.) Coding COND=(4,LT,STEP2.LKED) bypasses the step if 4 is less than the return code issued by the LKED step of the procedure executed by STEP1. When you don't name a specific step and code only (*number,comparison*), the system makes the comparison against the return codes from all previous steps. The comparisons are

GT Greater Than	LT Less Than
GE Greater Than Or Equal	LE Less Than Or Equal
EQ EQual	NE Not Equal

For example, COND=(8,LT) is read "if 8 is less than the return code from any previous step, bypass this step."

```
//step-name  EXEC PGM=program ,COND=(4,LT)
```
  [*This executes the step if no previous step has issued a return code of greater than 4.*]

C. The IF/THEN/ELSE/ENDIF **Construct**

The COND parameter is extremely difficult to code. Consequently, IBM has provided a replacement in Release 4 or later of MVS/ESA in the form of the IF/THEN/ELSE/ENDIF statement construct. This construct provides a simple way of selectively executing job steps. You code the construct as follows:

```
//   IF (relational-expression) THEN
```
[*JCL statements to execute if the relational expression is true.*]
```
//   ELSE
```
[*JCL statements to execute if the relational expression is false. The*
 ELSE *and its statements are optional.*]
```
//   ENDIF
```

The system evaluates the relational expression to yield a true or false value. You write the relational expression using the same relational operators as for COND. You can also connect expressions with AND, OR, and NOT. Here is an example:

```
// IF (STEPA.RC GE 4 AND STEPA.RC LE 6) THEN
```
[*JCL statements to execute if the return code* (RC) *from* STEPA *is 4, 5, or 6.*]
```
// ELSE
```
[*JCL statements to execute if the return code from* STEPA *is not 4, 5, or 6.*]
```
// ENDIF
```

D. The REGION **Parameter**

REGION = nK specifies the amount of storage a job step can use. A default region size set by the installation is used if the REGION parameter is omitted. The n is the number of 1024-byte areas of storage to allocate. You can also write REGION = nM, where n is in units of 1,048,576 bytes.

```
//STEPA EXEC PGM=ONE,REGION=64K
```
  [STEPA *is allocated 64K bytes of storage.*]
```
// EXEC COB2UCLG,REGION.LKED=128K,REGION.GO=64K
```
  [*The system allocates the* LKED *step of the* COB2UCLG *procedure 128K of storage. It allocates the* GO *step 64K.*]

III. DD **STATEMENTS**

You must include a DD statement to describe each *file* or *data set* (the terms are used interchangeably in MVS).

```
//FILEIN DD DSN=PAYROLL,DISP=(OLD,KEEP),
//           UNIT=3390,VOL=SER=222222
```
   [*To continue a statement, break it at a comma, code* // *in columns 1 and 2, and continue anywhere in columns 4 to 16.*]

The DD statement in this example is assigned the name FILEIN, and defines a file named PAYROLL. PAYROLL is an OLD file that we want to KEEP after it is read. It is contained on a 3390 disk unit with a volume serial number 222222. JCL statements are continued as shown in this example. Breaking the statement at the comma following a parameter, code a // in columns 1 and 2 of the next line, and continue the statement anywhere in columns 4 to 16.

The most-used parameters of the rather complex DD statement are as follows:

```
//ddname   DD DSN=file-name,
//            DISP=(beginning-disposition,ending-disposition),
//            UNIT=device, VOL=SER=volume,
//            SPACE=(direct-access-storage-space),
//            DCB=(record-size-and-blocking)
```

The *ddname* is the 1- to 8-character alphanumeric name (first character alphabetic). This connects the file to the COBOL program with the *ddname* in the SELECT statement.

The DSN=*file-name* parameter specifies the name of the file. A file can consist of several separate names, each 1 to 8 characters; first character alphabetic, separated by periods. An example of such a *qualified* name would be A1000.TEST.DATA or B2235.PROD.COBOL. The various levels of the qualified names serve much the same purpose as directories in other computer systems. Most installations require at least three levels of names. The first level is the user ID of the person to whom the file belongs, the second level is the functional name, and the third level specifies what kind of data the file contains. You specify temporary files that exist only for the duration of the job by prefixing two ampersands to the file name (&&*file-name*).

A. The DISP **Parameter**

DISP specifies the status of the file at the start of the step and the disposition of the file at the end of that step. The *beginning-disposition* can be one of the following:

   NEW: Specifies that a new file is to be written. The system positions the file to its starting point. You must also code UNIT and DCB parameters, and SPACE for files on direct-access storage.

OLD: Specifies an existing file to be read or written. The system gives the program exclusive use of the file, and positions to the start of the file.

SHR: Specifies an existing file that is to be read. Other programs may concurrently read the file. Always use SHR for reading system libraries. The system positions to the start of the file.

MOD: Create the file if it does not exist (same as NEW), or add to the end of the file if it does exist. The system positions to the start of the file if it is created, or to the end of the file if it already exists.

The *ending-disposition* can be one of the following:

KEEP: Keep the file. Retains disk files. Rewinds and dismounts tape files, freeing the tape drive for other jobs.

CATLG: Same as KEEP, but in addition *catalogs* the file in the system catalog. The system stores the file name, unit, and volume serial number in a catalog. This allows you to retrieve the file by name later without the UNIT and VOL parameters. Most installations require this for nontemporary disk files.

UNCATLG: Same as KEEP, except that the file is uncataloged.

DELETE: Delete the file. Uncatalogs the file if it was cataloged, and releases direct-access storage space. Tapes are rewound and dismounted.

PASS: Pass the file on to subsequent job steps and let them determine the final disposition. Tape files are rewound, but not dismounted.

A disposition of NEW is assumed if no beginning disposition is specified. Thus, DISP=(,KEEP) is the same as DISP=(NEW,KEEP). If no ending disposition is given, the system leaves the file as it was at the start of the job step. NEW files become DELETE, and existing files are KEEP (or PASS if the file was passed from a previous step).

B. The UNIT and VOL **Parameters**

UNIT=*device* specifies the device, either by the device number such as 3390, or by an installation-defined name, such as SYSDA.

VOL=SER=*volume* specifies the tape volume or disk pack. You often omit this to allow the system to select an appropriate volume.

C. The DCB **Parameter**

The DCB parameter specifies the record format (RECFM), record length (LRECL), and blocking (BLKSIZE). You often omit the BLKSIZE to let the system select an optimum size.

RECFM specifies the record format. MVS has several types of records and can store several records together in a *block* for reading or writing. This allows a large amount of data be read or written at a time, increasing the throughput of the computer. You must tell the system how long each record is in a block for it to be able to unblock the records.

- RECFM = F denotes fixed-length records: Each record has the same length.
- RECFM = FB denotes fixed-length blocked records.
- RECFM = V denotes variable-length records. Each record can have a different length. The system stores the length of the record in front of the record as part of the data.
- RECFM = VB denotes variable-length blocked records. The system stores the length of a block in front of the block as part of the data.
- RECFM = U denotes undefined-length records. There is only one record in a block, and the records can have differing lengths.

The LRECL=*length* parameter specifies the record length in bytes. For variable-length records, it specifies the longest possible length.

The BLKSIZE=*length* parameter specifies the block length in bytes. For variable-length blocks, it specifies the longest possible length. You usually don't specify the BLKSIZE; leaving it unspecified allows the system to specify an optimum length for the type of I/O device the data set is being written onto.

The DCB information must be supplied when the file is created. The system writes the file name and DCB information into the file label on the storage device. This lets you omit the DCB parameter when you read the file, because the system can obtain the information from the file label.

The DCB information can come from three sources:

- From the program's BLOCK CONTAINS, RECORD CONTAINS, and RECORDING MODE clauses or from the record descriptions in the record area
- From the DCB parameter in the DD statement
- From the file label, if there is one

The DCB information coded in the program overrides that coded in the DCB parameter, and that coded in the DCB parameter overrides that contained in the file label. The DCB information may come from any of the three sources, but it must all be present when the file is opened.

D. The SPACE **Parameter**

SPACE specifies the amount of space to allocate on direct-access storage devices:

```
          CYL
          TRK
          blocksize
SPACE=( _____ , ( primary,secondary ) )
```

- CYL: Allocate space in units of cylinders. This is only for very large data sets, because a cylinder is a considerable amount of space.
- TRK: Allocate space in units of tracks. MVS disks are organized into tracks.
- *blocksize:* allocate space in units of blocks of the length specified. The *blocksize* should equal the BLKSIZE figure in the DCB parameter. The advantage of allocating in units of blocks is that the amount of space allocated is independent of the hardware device. With TRK and CYL, the amount of space allocated depends on the hardware device.
- *primary:* The number of units of primary storage to allocate. The system always allocates this space on a single volume.
- *secondary:* The number of units of space for each secondary allocation. This space is allocated only if the primary space is exceeded. The secondary allocation may occur in subsequent runs. The system will allocate the secondary allocation a total of 15 times if required. The default is allow another 16 extents to be allocated on as many as five additional volumes. Beyond this, the program terminates for lack of space. The total possible allocation on the first volume is *primary* + 15(*secondary*), and 16(*secondary*) on each of the five additional volumes. Table 16.1 shows the track capacity of various direct-access storage devices.

In MVS/ESA release 4 or later, you can also specify the amount of space in units of records, which makes a lot more sense. You code as follows:

```
AVGREC=U,SPACE=(record-length , (no-primary,no-secondary ) )
AVGREC=U,SPACE=(240,(10000,2000))
```
> [*Space is allocated for 10,000 240-byte records. Each secondary amount is for 2,000 records.*]

TABLE 16.1 Direct-Access Storage Device Characteristics

Storage	Device	Volume Capacity (M bytes)	Tracks per Cylinder	Number Cylinders	Avg. Seek Time (ms)	Avg. Rota- tional Delay (ms)	Data Rate (kb/sec)	Bytes per Track
3350		317	30	555	25	8.4	1198	19,069
3380	AD4 BD4 AJ4 BJ4	630	15	885	15	8.3	3000	47,476
3380	AE4,BE4	1260	15	1770	17	8.3	3000	47,476
3380	AK4,BK4	1890	15	2655	15	8.3	3000	47,476
3390	A14 B14 A18 B18 B1C	946	15	1113	9.5	7.1	4200	56,664
3390	A24 B24 A38 B28 B2C	1892	15	2226	12.5	7.1	4200	56,664

You can also code the RLSE subparameter in the SPACE parameter to release unused space.

```
AVGREC=U,SPACE=(record-length ,(no-primary,no-secondary)),RLSE)
SPACE=(TRK,(100,20),RLSE)
```

RLSE releases the unused space when the file is closed. The system releases space in units of cylinders for CYL; otherwise it releases it in units of tracks. For example, the SPACE parameter in the foregoing example allocates 100 primary tracks, but if only 30 tracks are used, the excess 70 tracks are released. Code RLSE for all except temporary files (for which the entire space will be released anyway) and files in which more data will be added later, such as program libraries.

E. File Creation and Retrieval

The following example illustrates the creation of a disk file:

```
//FILEIN DD DSN=A1000.PAYROLL.DATA,DISP=(NEW,CATLG),
//          UNIT=DISK,
//          DCB=(RECFM=FB,LRECL=80),
//          AVGREC=U,SPACE=(80,(10000,2000))
```

The file is retrieved in a subsequent job step or job as follows:

```
//FILEIN DD DSN=A1000.PAYROLL.DATA,DISP=SHR
```

Most MVS installations require you to catalog nontemporary data sets by coding DISP=(NEW,CATLG) when you create the data set. The system writes the data set name, the type of device, and the volume serial number where the data set is stored into another system data set, called the catalog. From then on, you can refer to the data set by name. The system looks in the catalog to find the type of hardware device and the volume on which it is stored.

Most MVS installations also write data sets with standard labels. The system writes the label as data along with the data set. The label contains the data set name and the DCB parameters describing the data set. This means that you don't have to specify any of the DCB information to retrieve the data set. Thus, to read a nontemporary data set, you usually need specify only the DSN and DISP parameters.

You can concatenate several files for input to act as if they were all one file. Do this by coding a DD statement for each file in the order the files are to be read, giving only the first DD statement a *ddname*. To the program, it will appear as if only a single file is being read. The files must all have the same RECFM (and record length, if fixed-length records). The following example concatenates three files for input:

```
//INPUT DD DSN=A1000.CITY.DATA,DISP=SHR
//       DD DSN=A1000.COUNTY.DATA,DISP=SHR
//       DD DSN=A1000.STATE.DATA,DISP=SHR
```

You can specify dummy files with the DUMMY parameter coded immediately following the DD. Dummy files give an immediate end-of-file if read, and the output is ignored if they are written. Dummy files are useful for testing and suppressing unwanted output. Code the DCB=BLKSIZE=*blocksize* parameter for all dummy files:

```
//SYSOUT DD DUMMY,DCB=BLKSIZE=133
```

IV. THE COMMENT STATEMENT

JCL also has comment statements, denoted by a //* in columns 1 to 3, and you can intersperse them with the JCL statements.

```
//* COMMENTS IN COLUMNS 4 TO 80
```

Use comment statements as necessary throughout the JCL to describe what the reader needs to know. A solid line of asterisks as comment statements following each EXEC statement makes the steps easier to locate in the source.

```
//STEP6 EXEC SORT
//*************************************************************
//******** SORT THE PAYROLL MASTER FILE ON ASCENDING
//******** EMPLOYEE NAME
//*************************************************************
```

V. EXAMPLE OF JCL

The next example illustrates cataloged procedures and shows how to code JCL statements to form a complete job. The example is the cataloged procedure for the VS COBOL II compile, linkage editor, and execution step.

```
//COB2UCLG PROC CMP='SYS1.COB2COMP',LIB='SYS1.COB2LIB'
```
   [*The* PROC *statement must be the first statement of a cataloged procedure. The procedure name is* COB2UCLG. *The* CMP = 'SYS1.COB2COMP' *assigns a value (*SYS1.COB2COMP*) to a symbolic parameter (*CMP*). Within JCL, you denote a symbolic parameter by coding & followed by the name. Thus, wherever &CMP appears, the system replaces it with* SYS1.COB2COMP. LIB *is a second symbolic parameter.*]
```
//COB2 EXEC PGM=IGYCRCTL,PARM='OBJECT',REGION=1024K
```
   [*The VS COBOL II compiler is named* IGYCRCTL *and is contained in the* SYS1.COB2COMP *library. Since it is not contained in the system library, a* STEPLIB *statement is needed. The* PARM *supplies values to the program being executed. You can also supply* PARM *values to COBOL programs you write, as described in Chapter 18. The* REGION *size is 1024K.*]
```
//STEPLIB   DD DSN=&CMP,DISP=SHR
```
   [*The VS COBOL II compiler is contained in the* SYS1.COB2COMP *library.*]
```
//SYSPRINT DD SYSOUT=A
```
   [SYSPRINT *describes a print data set.* SYSOUT = A *is the standard printer at most installations.*]
```
//SYSLIN    DD DSN=&&LOADSET,DISP=(MOD,PASS),
//             UNIT=SYSDA,SPACE=(TRK,(3,3)),
//             DCB=(RECFM=FB,LRECL=80)
```

[SYSLIN *describes the data set that is to contain the output produced by the compiler. The compiler output is termed an object module, and it must be link-edited before it can be executed. The two ampersands preceding the file name of* LOADSET *indicate that it is a temporary file. A disposition of* MOD *is used so that if there are several compile steps, the object modules are all placed in one sequential data set. The data set is passed on to the next steps. The* DCB *parameter specifies that the records are Fixed Blocked with a logical record length of 80. The* DCB *information is written in the file label and need not be specified in retrieving the file. The* SPACE *parameter requests space in units of tracks. The primary allocation is 3 tracks, and the secondary allocation is also 3 tracks. The secondary allocation is done only as needed, a total of 15 times if necessary. By default, the data set can extend onto five other disk packs, with 16 secondary allocations on each.*]

```
//SYSUT1    DD UNIT=SYSDA,SPACE=(CYL,(1,1))
//SYSUT2    DD UNIT=SYSDA,SPACE=(CYL,(1,1))
//SYSUT3    DD UNIT=SYSDA,SPACE=(CYL,(1,1))
//SYSUT4    DD UNIT=SYSDA,SPACE=(CYL,(1,1))
//SYSUT5    DD UNIT=SYSDA,SPACE=(CYL,(1,1))
//SYSUT6    DD UNIT=SYSDA,SPACE=(CYL,(1,1))
//SYSUT7    DD UNIT=SYSDA,SPACE=(CYL,(1,1))
```

[*The* SYSUT *n* DD *statements are work data sets used by the compiler.*]

```
//LKED EXEC PGM=IEWL,PARM='LIST,XREF,LET,MAP',COND=(5,LT,COB2),
//           REGION=512K
```

[*This* EXEC *statement executes the linkage editor. The linkage editor combines the compiled program with any subprograms, system I/O routines, and other system routines, to form what is termed a load module that can be executed.* COND *bypasses the link edit step unless the compile step returns a completion code of 5 or less.*]

```
//SYSLIN    DD DSN=&&LOADSET,DISP=(OLD,DELETE)
//          DD DDNAME=SYSIN
```

[SYSLIN *describes the primary input—the output from the compiler concatenated with the input stream. The* DCB *attributes are built-in as* RECFM = FB,LRECL = 80. *The* DISP *is* OLD, *because the file already exists, and* DELETE *to scratch it at the end of the step. For passed or cataloged files, the* UNIT *and* VOL *need not be specified.*]

```
//SYSLMOD   DD DSN=&&GOSET(GO),DISP=(NEW,PASS),
//             UNIT=SYSDA,SPACE=(CYL,(1,1,1))
```

[SYSLMOD *defines the data set to contain the load module produced by the linkage edit step. It is placed in a library or partitioned data set that contains one or more sequential subfiles, termed members. New members can be added or old members replaced in permanent libraries. This library is a temporary file named* GOSET, *and the member name is* GO. *The* DCB *parameter is omitted, indicating that all the* DCB *information is hard-coded in the linkage editor program. The* RECFM = U *attribute is built-in. If the* DCB *information is not hard-coded in a program, you can specify it in the* DCB *parameter. The* SPACE *parameter requests 1 cylinder of primary space, 1 cylinder of secondary space, and 1 directory block. Directory blocks contain the names of the partitioned data set members, and each block can contain roughly five member names.*]

```
//SYSLIB    DD DSN=&LIB,DISP=SHR
```

[SYSLIB *points to the library used for the automatic call lookup. The* DCB *attributes are built-in as* RECFM = FB,LRECL = 80.]

```
//SYSUT1    DD UNIT=SYSDA,SPACE=(CYL,(1,1))
```

[SYSUT1 *defines a scratch data set used by the linkage editor.*]

```
//SYSPRINT DD SYSOUT=A
```

[SYSPRINT *defines a print data set. The* DCB *attributes are built-in as* RECFM = FBA,LRECL = 121.]

```
//GO EXEC PGM=*.LKED.SYSLMOD,COND=((5,LT,COB2),(5,LT,LKED))
```
   [GO *executes the program created by the linkage editor.* COND *bypasses the step unless both the compiler and linkage editor return completion codes of 5 or less.*]
```
//STEPLIB  DD DSN=&LIB,DISP=SHR
```
   [*The* SYS1.COB2LIB *contains subprograms loaded in at run time.*]

These JCL statements may seem formidable, and they are only a part of the statements needed. You can make the JCL into a *cataloged procedure* by placing it in a partitioned data set. Then you can invoke it by its name. If the previous JCL were made into a cataloged procedure named COB2UCLG, you could invoke it as follows:

```
//JR964113 JOB (24584),'JONES',CLASS=A
// EXEC COB2UCLG
//COB2.SYSIN DD *
```
   [*The* COB2.SYSIN *tells the system that the* SYSIN DD *statement is to be added to the* COB2 *step. The* DD* *indicates that input data, COBOL source statements here, immediately follow in the input stream.*]
```
/*
//LKED.SYSIN DD *
```
   [*Any linkage editor control statements.*]
```
/*
//GO.ddname  DD ...
```
   [*Any* DD *statements required by the program are placed here.*]

The cataloged procedure has three steps: a compile step named COB2, a linkage editor step named LKED, and an execution step named GO.

This completes the brief description of JCL and covers most of what is needed for COBOL programming. Several other features are discussed in the chapters that follow on program organization and input/output. JCL is a difficult language, because it deals with a complex subject: the interface between a program and the computer's operating system and hardware. Unlike COBOL, in which many features become easy through constant use, you use many JCL features so seldom that they never become familiar. JCL does simplify many exotic requirements, but it also makes many simple requirements needlessly complex. Thus, it accounts for a large portion of the programming problems.

The next chapter describes the specific compile, link, and run procedures for VS COBOL II and Microsoft COBOL.

ADDITIONAL READINGS

Gary D. Brown, System/370/390 Job Control Language, NY: John Wiley & Sons, Inc., 1991.

"MVS/ESA JCL Reference," Order No. GC18-1829, Poughkeepsie, NY: IBM Corporation, 1989.

"MVS/ESA JCL User's Guide," Order No. GC28-1830, Poughkeepsie, NY: IBM Corporation, 1989.

17

Compile, Link, and Run Procedures

In VS COBOL II, you invoke the COBOL compiler by naming an installation-supplied cataloged procedure that contains the necessary JCL statements. The cataloged procedure name may vary with the installation and with the version of the COBOL compiler. The convention is to append the cataloged procedure name with C to indicate compile, CL to indicate compile and link edit, and CLG to indicate compile, link edit, and go (run the program).

I. COMPILE

The compile procedure finds compilation errors and produces a program listing. It doesn't execute the program.

A. Compiling for VS COBOL II

1. *JCL for Compilation*

In VS COBOL II, you execute the COB2UC cataloged procedure to compile a COBOL program:

```
//JR964113 JOB (24584),'JONES',CLASS=A
// EXEC COB2UC,PARM.COB2='XREF,LIB'
```
   [COB2UC *is the name of the cataloged procedure, but installations may have different names. The* PARM.COB2 = 'XREF,LIB' *specifies the XREF and LIB compiler options. The* PARM.COB2 *indicates that the* PARM *is to apply to the* COB2 *step. The convention is for* COB2 *to be the step name for the compile step,* LKED *for the link edit step, and* GO *for the execution step.*]
```
//COB2.SYSLIB DD DSN=copy-library,DISP=SHR
```
   [*You need* SYSLIB *only if you bring in members from a copy library.*]
```
//COB2.SYSIN DD *
```
   [*Place the COBOL program here.*]

There are several compilation options beyond the scope of this book, but the options you are likely to need to use are these:

• ADV or NOADV: ADV causes COBOL to add one extra byte to each line in the FD file description of a file in which you code WRITE AFTER ADVANCING.

305

ADV is the default and enables you not to worry about the mainframe carriage control byte, described in Chapter 13. NOADV requires you to account for the byte yourself.

- DATA(24) or DATA(31): When a program compiles with RENT, DATA(24) requires the Working Storage and FD area to be acquired below the 16-megabyte line. DATA(31) is the default and allows storage to be acquired above or below the 16-megabyte line.

- DYNAM or NODYNAM: DYNAM causes a separately compiled program invoked with the CALL statement to be dynamically loaded at run time. NODYNAM is the usual default. Don't use DYNAM with CICS.

- FASTSRT or NOFASTSRT: FASTSRT speeds up sorting by having the DFSORT program do all I/O rather than the COBOL program, saving overhead. The default is usually NOFASTSRT.

- FDUMP or NOFDUMP: FDUMP produces a formatted dump if your program abnormally terminates. From this, you can determine which statement caused the termination. NOFDUMP is the usual default.

- LIB or NOLIB: Code LIB if your program uses the COPY, BASIS, or REPLACE statements described in Chapter 18. NOLIB is the usual default.

- MAP or NOMAP: MAP generates a listing of the items in the Data Division. NOMAP is the usual default.

- NAME or NONAME: NAME generates a link edit NAME statement for each object module, so that they can be link-edited as separate load modules for output to a partitioned data set. NONAME is the usual default.

- NUMPROC(PFD), (NOPFD), or (MIG): NUMPROC specifies how the sign is carried in external decimal or packed-decimal numbers. PFD is considerably faster and assumes a single code on the high-order digit for − or +. NOPFD, the default, allows four ways of coding a + and three ways of coding a −, which is the ANSI Standard. MIG is used only to migrate from OS/VS COBOL to VS COBOL II.

- OPT or NOOPT: OPT generates optimized code. NOOPT is the usual default. Note that OPT prevents you from locating the statement causing an abnormal termination in any FDUMP formatted dump.

- QUOTE or APOST: QUOTE indicates you are using the quotation mark (") to enclose literals and is the usual default. APOST specifies that you are using the apostrophe (').

- RENT or NORENT: RENT causes reentrant code to be generated and is required for CICS. NORENT is the usual default.

- RES or NORES: RES allows subprograms to be loaded dynamically at run time rather than being link-edited with the program. (RES is always in effect if DYNAM is specified.) NORES is the default and requires subprograms to be link-edited with the program. CICS requires RES.

- SSRANGE or NOSSRANGE: SSRANGE generates code for run-time checking of index, subscript, reference modification, and variable-length group ranges for valid values. NOSSRANGE is usually default. There is also an

SSRANGE/NOSSRANGE run-time option to turn checking on and off at run time; and SSRANGE is the usual default for it.

- TEST or NOTEST: TEST generates programs to be used with the COBTEST debugging tool, described in Chapter 18. NOTEST is the usual default. Don't code FDUMP, OPTIMIZE, or RES with NOTEST.

- VBREF or NOVBREF: VBREF produces a cross-reference listing of the COBOL verbs with a summary of how many times each verb is used. NOVBREF is the usual default.

- XREF or NOXREF: XREF produces a sorted cross-reference listing. NOXREF is the usual default.

You can pass these options to the compiler with the JCL PARM parameter on the EXEC statement or with the CBL statement, described next.

2. Compiler-Directing Statements

- CBL: Rather than specifying the COBOL compilation options in the PARM of the JCL EXEC statement, you can code them on a CBL statement, placed before the Identification Division header. Code the statement in columns 1 to 72 and include several statements, if necessary, to contain all the options. Separate the options with a comma or space. Code the CBL statement as follows:

```
CBL option, option, . . . , option
CBL LIB,ADV,DYNAM,RENT
```

- *CBL: The *CBL statement selectively generates or suppresses the source, object, and storage map listing for the compilation. The *CBL must begin in column 7 or beyond and be followed by a space. Code the *CBL statement as follows:

```
*CBL option
```

You can code only one option on a statement, but there can be several statements. The options are the following:

SOURCE or NOSOURCE: Generate or suppress the source listing.

LIST or NOLIST: Generate or suppress the object code listing.

MAP or NOMAP: Generate or suppress storage map listing.

- EJECT: The EJECT statement causes the next line to begin at the top of the next page in a listing. EJECT is coded in columns 8 through 72.

```
EJECT
```

- SKIP: You can code SKIP1, SKIP2, or SKIP3 to skip one, two, or three blank lines in the listing. Code SKIP anywhere in columns 8 through 72.

```
SKIP1
```

• TITLE: The TITLE statement gives a title to be printed left-justified at the top of each page of the listing. With no TITLE, COBOL prints the compiler name and current release level at the top of each page. Code TITLE anywhere from column 8 to 72 as follows:

        TITLE   *any-title*

The system automatically displays the PROGRAM-ID name, the page number, the compile date, and the time to the right of the title on each line.

B. Compiling in Microsoft COBOL

In Microsoft COBOL, you compile programs by entering the COBOL command. The complete command is

:> COBOL *program-name, obj-file, list-file, list-obj;*

• *program-name* is the name of the file containing the source program to compile. If the suffix is other than ".CBL", you must code it.
• *obj-file* is the name of the file to contain the compiled object code. If the suffix is to be other than ".OBJ", you must code it. If you omit *obj-file*, *program-name*.OBJ is assumed.
• *list-file* is the name of the file to contain the source code listing. If the suffix is other than ".LST", you must code it. If you omit *list-file*, NUL.LST is assumed, and no output is produced. (Files named NUL are not created.)
• *list-obj* is the name of the file to contain the object code listing, and is rarely needed. If the suffix is other than ".GRP", you must code it. If you omit *list-obj*, NUL.GRP is assumed and no output is produced.

If you omit all the names, the compiler prompts you for them. Usually, you omit *obj-file* and *list-obj* and code

:> COBOL *program-name,, list-file* ;

The compiler displays the error messages on your terminal screen along with the line number of the items in error. If you wish, you can direct these error messages to file, so that you can view them with a text editor, by coding

:> COBOL *program-name,, list-file;* > *file-name*

Often all you need for correcting errors are the error messages, so you could omit the source listing and code something like

:> COBOL *program-name;* > TEMP

You may also wish to add compilation options. For this, you would code

:> COBOL *program-name,, list-file/ option option . . . option;*

or

:> COBOL *program-name/ option option . . . option;* > TEMP

There are many options beyond the scope of this book, but the ones you are most likely to use are the following:

- ANIM or NOANIM: ANIM produces code for ANIMATOR debugging. NOANIM is the default.
- ANS85 or NOANS85: ANS85 assumes the rules for ANSI 85 COBOL. NOANS85 is the default.
- BOUND or NOBOUND: BOUND checks the bounds of subscripts in tables. NOBOUND is the default.
- COMP or NOCOMP: COMP optimizes computations, but should be used only if there is likely to be no overflow. NOCOMP is the default.
- MODEL *"size":* Specifies the model in which to compile. Because of the way the 286-chip PC addresses memory in segments, you are required to choose one of the following models. The smaller models execute slightly faster. The default is MODEL "HUGE".

> MODEL "SMALL"   Small code ($< 64K$), small data ($< 64K$).
> MODEL "MEDIUM" Large code ($> 64K$), small data ($< 64K$).
> MODEL "LARGE"   Large code ($> 64K$), large data ($> 64K$).
> MODEL "HUGE"   Large code ($> 64K$), large data ($> 64K$).

- OPTSIZE or NOOPTSIZE: OPTSIZE optimizes program size at the expense of execution speed. The default is NOOPTSIZE. Don't code OPTSIZE with OPTSPEED.
- OPTSPEED or NOOPTSPEED: OPTSPEED optimizes execution speed at the expense of program size and is the default.
- SEQUENTIAL "LINE" or "RECORD": Specifies that the default file type as described in Chapter 11 is LINE SEQUENTIAL, which is the normal ASCII file on the PC. The default, SEQUENTIAL "RECORD", causes blocked records, similar to those on MVS, to be written.
- TRACE or NOTRACE: TRACE produces a trace of the statements executed within the program. NOTRACE is the default.
- VSC2 or NOVSC2: VSC2 assumes the rules for VS COBOL II. NOVSC2 is the default.
- XREF or NOXREF: XREF produces a cross-reference listing at the end of the source listing. NOXREF is the default.

:> COBOL TEST,,TEST /VSC2 XREF; > TEMP

This could compile the source program in TEST.CBL, write the object program into TEST.OBJ, and write the source listing in TEST.LST. It would not produce an object listing. It would check for VS COBOL II syntax and write the error messages into TEMP.

Rather than coding the options on the command line, you can add them as a line of text in the source code by using the SET statement. Code the "$" in column 7. You can't continue the SET statement, but you can code several SET statements. You usually place the SET statements before the first lines in the program, but you can set some options anywhere.

```
$SET (option option ... option )
$SET (VSC2 XREF)
```

II. COMPILE, LINK EDIT, RUN

A. Compile, Link Edit, Run Procedure for VS COBOL II

The compile, link edit, and run procedure is primarily for test runs. It compiles the program, link edits it to produce an executable load module, and executes this load module. You usually don't save the load module for subsequent runs, although you can. The next section on the compile and link edit procedure explains how to save the load module.

```
//JR964113 JOB (24584),'JONES',CLASS=A
// EXEC COB2UCLG,PARM.COB2='XREF,LIB',PARM.LKED='XREF',REGION.GO=nK
```
[The PARM.COB2 = 'XREF,LIB' *specifies parameters for the compile step.* PARM.LKED *specifies parameters for the linkage editor step. The* REGION.GO = nK *specifies the amount of memory in units of 1024 (K) bytes required by the GO step.* REGION.GO = 104K *requests 104K bytes.]*
```
//COB2.SYSLIB DD DSN=copy-library,DISP=SHR
//COB2.SYSIN DD *
```
[Place the COBOL program here.]
```
//LKED ...
```
[To save the load module, place the link edit DD statements described in the following procedure here.]
```
//GO.ddname  DD ...
```
[Place all DD statements specified in SELECT clauses here.]

There is also a COB2UCG cataloged procedure, which compiles and executes without the linkage editor step. It is faster than COB2UCLG, but since there is no linkage editor step, you can't link in other subprograms from subprogram libraries.

```
//JR964113 JOB (24584),'JONES',CLASS=A
// EXEC COB2UCG,PARM.COB2='XREF,LIB',REGION.GO=nK
//COB2.SYSLIB DD DSN=copy-library,DISP=SHR
```

```
//COB2.SYSIN DD *
```
[*Place the COBOL program here.*]
```
//GO.ddname  DD ...
```
   [*Place all* DD *statements specified in* SELECT *clauses here.*]

1. *Linkage Editor Options*

The linkage editor options that apply specifically to COBOL are the following:

- AMODE *value*: AMODE 24 specifies 24-bit addressing and is the usual default. AMODE 31 specifies 31-bit addressing, allowing programs to run above the 16-megabyte line. AMODE ANY specifies both.
- CALL or NOCALL: NOCALL suppresses resolution of linkage editor references (subprogram calls and global data items) and is used when you are creating a subprogram library. CALL resolves the references and is the default.
- RMODE *value*: RMODE 24 requires the program to reside below the 16-megabyte line and is the usual default. RMODE ANY allows the program to reside above the 16-megabyte line, and requires AMODE 31 or ANY.
- XREF: Produces a sorted cross-reference listing of the linkage editor output. Omit XREF if you don't want the listing.

2. *Run-Time Options*

There are several run-time options. The following are the ones most used:

- DEBUG or NODEBUG: DEBUG compiles lines with a "D" in column 7 and is usually default. NODEBUG doesn't compile the lines.
- SIMVRD/NOSIMVRD: SIMVRD allows a VSAM KSDS data set to be used to simulate variable-length records in a relative data set. NOSIMVRD is the usual default.
- SSRANGE or NOSSRANGE: SSRANGE turns on run-time subscript checking and is the usual default. (You must also code SSRANGE as a compilation option.) NOSSRANGE suppresses the checking.

You specify run-time options on the PARM parameter of the EXEC statement for the program. Code a slash before the first run-time parameter. If the PARM must specify both program and COBOL run-time parameters, code them as follows:

```
// EXEC PGM=program, PARM='program-parameters/run-options'
```

B. Compile, Link Edit, Run Procedure for Microsoft COBOL

Microsoft COBOL has three types of linking: static (the fastest at execution time), soft (a combination), and dynamic (slowest at execution time, but allows memory to be reused).

Static linking corresponds to the way linking is done in VS COBOL II. You compile the subprogram separately and then link it in as part of the main program to create an ".EXE" file containing the main program and its subprograms. You compile each subprogram separately to create ".OBJ" files. Then you link with the main program by naming them in the LINK command. (You can't place the subprograms after the main program in the same file and compile them to create a single ".OBJ" file for linking, as you can with VS COBOL II.) Static linking occurs when either of the following is done:

* You specify the SMALL, MEDIUM, or COMPACT model when you link each of the programs.
* You affix one or two underscore characters to the beginning of the literal subprogram name in the CALL statement.

Dynamic linking links and loads the subprograms when they are called. You compile and link each subprogram separately to create ".EXE" files. However, you don't link them with the main program. When you execute the main program and call a subprogram, the system searches for the proper ".EXE" file first in the current directory and then the directories in the DOS path. This slows execution, but it allows dynamic reuse of memory for subprograms. Dynamic linking occurs when both of the following are true:

* The literal subprogram name in the CALL statement does not begin with an underscore character.
* The subprogram is not linked together with the main program by the LINK command.

Soft linking is a combination of static and dynamic. You can link some subprograms with the main program and dynamically link others at run time. Soft linking occurs when the following is true:

* The literal subprogram name in the CALL statement does not begin with an underscore character.
* All the ".OBJ" files except those to be dynamically linked are linked with the main program by the LINK command.

The LINK command links ".OBJ" files to form ".EXE" files for execution:

```
:> LINK obj-file, run-file, list-file, libraries;
```

* *obj-file:* The file containing object code. If several files are to be linked together, join the names with plus (+) signs: MAIN+SUB1+SUB2, for example. If the suffix is not ".OBJ", you must code it.
* *run-file:* The file to contain the executable program. If the suffix is not ".EXE", you must code it. If you omit *run-file,* the file is named *obj-file*.EXE, where *obj-file* is the first file named in the LINK command.

- *list-file:* The file where the linkage editor listing is stored. If the suffix is not ".MAP", you must code it. If you omit *list-file,* no map is produced.
- *libraries:* The name of run-time modules. If you omit *libraries,* LCOBOL.LIB is assumed for DOS and OS2.LIB+DOSCALLS.LIB are assumed for OS/2.

There are also a few link options that are rarely needed and are beyond the scope of this book. Code them at the end of the LINK command as follows:

:> LINK *obj-file/ option option . . . option;*

If you omit any options, you will be prompted for them. The usual command to link a program is just

:> LINK *program;*

Then you can execute the ".EXE" file by coding just its name:

:> *program*

If you want command-line input, you leave a space and write it:

:> *program command-line-input*

    The following DOS commands can placed in a ".BAT" file to compile, link edit, and execute. The example below assumes the file is named COMP.BAT, but any name could be used as long as the suffix is ".BAT". (Note that in a DOS command line, whatever you type following the name of the ".BAT" file replaces the "%1" parameter marker.)

```
ECHO     Compiling %1 program
COBOL %1; > TEMP
IF ERRORLEVEL 1 GOTO ENDIT
ECHO     No compilation errors.  Linking %1
LINK %1;
ECHO     Executing %1
%1
:ENDIT
```

Now to compile, link edit, and execute a program, you can enter this command:

:> COMP *program*

III. CREATING LIBRARIES

The compilation step creates what is termed an *object module,* which must then be link-edited to include all the necessary system routines and create what is termed a *load module.* The load module is executable, and you can retain it to re-execute the program without the compilation and link edit steps. The following examples illustrate the JCL necessary to link edit a program, save the load module, and later execute it.

A. Creating Object Module Libraries

1. *Creating Object Module Libraries in VS COBOL II*

The following example shows how three COBOL programs, ONE, TWO, and THREE, are compiled and retained in object module form in a partitioned data set named A1000.LIB.OBJ. Partitioned data set member names must be one to eight alphanumeric (A to Z, 0 to 9) or national (@ $ #) characters, beginning with an alphabetic (A to Z) or national character.

The COB2UC cataloged procedure is used to compile the programs and create the library. We must override the SYSLMOD DD statement to create the nontemporary data set.

```
//JR964113 JOB (24584),'JONES',CLASS=A
// EXEC COB2UC,PARM.COB2='LIB'
//COB2.SYSLIB DD DSN=copy-library,DISP=SHR
```
   [*Include* DD *statements for copy libraries as needed.*]
```
//COB2.SYSIN  DD *
```
[ONE *source statements*]
```
        END PROGRAM ONE.
```
[TWO *source statements*]
```
        END PROGRAM TWO.
```
[THREE *source statements*]
```
        END PROGRAM THREE.
//COB2.SYSLIN DD DSN=A1000.LIB.OBJ,DISP=(NEW,CATLG),
//               UNIT=SYSDA,SPACE=(1024,(100,30,10))
```
   [*The* A1000.LIB.MOD *data set is created, and the object modules are added as members named* ONE, TWO, *and* THREE. *The* SPACE *parameter is also overridden to allocate a more precise amount of space and to enlarge the directory space.*]

Now you can include the A1000.LIB.OBJ library as input when you compile any COBOL. The following example shows how this is done:

```
//JR964113 JOB (24584),'JONES',CLASS=A
// EXEC COB2UCLG
//COB2.SYSLIB DD DSN=copy-library, DISP=SHR
//COB2.SYSIN  DD *
```
[*Main COBOL source statements.*]
```
//LKED.DD1     DD DSN=A1000.LIB.OBJ,DISP=SHR
//LKED.SYSIN   DD *
  ENTRY name
```
      [*Even though the main routine is still loaded first, it is a good idea to tell the linkage editor the name of the entry point.*]
```
  INCLUDE DD1
```
      [*The* A1000.LIB.OBJ *library is included as additional input.*]

2. *Creating Object Module Libraries in Microsoft COBOL*

To create an object module library in Microsoft COBOL, you compile all the programs to create ".OBJ" files. Then use the LIB command to create the library.

```
:> LIB library+program +program . . .+program ;
```

- *library:* The name of the library. If *library* is to have a suffix other than ".LIB", you must code it.
- *+program:* The + adds the programs named to the library.

Then, to link object modules from this library, code the LINK command as follows:

```
:> LINK obj-file,  run-file, list-file , library;
```

B. Creating Load Module Libraries in VS COBOL II

The next example is the same, except this time ONE, TWO, and THREE are link-edited and stored in load module form in a partitioned data set named A1000.LIB.LOAD. Load module libraries are generally more efficient than object module libraries.

```
//JR964113 JOB (24584),'JONES',CLASS=A
// EXEC COB2UCL,PARM.COB2='NAME,XREF'
```
   [*The compile/link edit procedure is used. The* NAME *parameter causes the COBOL compiler to append linkage editor* NAME *statements to the object modules. This enables them to be link-edited as separate load modules for output in a partitioned data set.* XREF *produces a linkage editor cross-reference listing.*]
```
//COB2.SYSLIB   DD DSN=copy-library ,DISP=SHR
//COB2.SYSIN    DD *
```
[ONE *source statements*]
```
        END PROGRAM ONE.
```
[TWO *source statements*]
```
        END PROGRAM TWO.
```
[THREE *source statements*]
```
        END PROGRAM THREE.
//LKED.SYSLMOD DD DSN=A1000.LIB.LOAD,DISP=(NEW,CATLG),
//              UNIT=SYSDA,SPACE=(1024,(100,30,10))
```
   [*The* A1000.LIB.LOAD *data set is created, and the load modules are added as members named* ONE, TWO, *and* THREE.]

You can also include the A1000.LIB.LOAD library as input when any COBOL program is compiled, as shown in the following example:

```
//JR964113 JOB (24584),'JONES',CLASS=A
// EXEC COB2UCLG
//COB2.SYSLIB DD DSN=copy-library ,DISP=SHR
```

```
//COB2.SYSIN  DD *
```
[*Main COBOL source statements.*]
```
//LKED.DD1 DD DSN=A1000.LIB.LOAD,DISP=SHR
//LKED.SYSIN  DD *
  ENTRY name
```
    [*Although the main routine is still loaded first, it is a good idea to tell the linkage editor the name of the entry point.*]
```
INCLUDE DD1
```
    [*The* A1000.LIB.LOAD *library is included as additional input.*]

C. Creating Load Modules for Program Development in VS COBOL II

For program development, it is usual to compile a COBOL program and its subprograms and link edit them into a single load module. In the example, the library is named A1000.PGM.LOAD, and the load module is named THING. For VS COBOL II, the following JCL does this:

```
//JR964113 JOB (24584),'JONES',CLASS=A
// EXEC COB2UCLG
```
    [*The compile/link edit/go procedure is used.*]
```
//COB2.SYSLIB  DD DSN=copy-library,DISP=SHR
//COB2.SYSIN   DD *
```
[*Main COBOL source statements*]
[*ONE source statements*]
[*TWO source statements*]
[*THREE source statements*]
    [*The absence of any* END PROGRAM *statements causes all the modules being compiled to be placed in a single load module.*]
```
//LKED.SYSLMOD DD DSN=A1000.PGM.LOAD(THING),DISP=(NEW,CATLG),
//               UNIT=SYSDA,SPACE=(1024,(100,30,10))
```
    [*The* A1000.PGM.LOAD *data set is created to contain the load module named THING.*]
```
//GO.IN       DD DSN=A1000.JUNK.DATA,DISP=SHR
```
[*Place any* DD *statements for the* GO *step here.*]

You can also place other programs in the A1000.PGM.LOAD library, as long as you give them different member names. You can now execute the program in a single step:

```
//JR964113 JOB (24584),'JONES',CLASS=A
//GO EXEC PGM=THING
//STEPLIB DD DSN=A1000.PGM.LOAD,DISP=SHR
```
    [*The* STEPLIB DD *statement describes the data set containing the program to execute. The* JOBLIB DD *statement could have been used as well.*]
```
//IN DD DSN=A1000.JUNK.DATA,DISP=SHR
```
    [*Place any* DD *statements for the* GO *step here.*]

The Microsoft COBOL LINK command creates an ".EXE" file, which you can keep and execute repeatedly:

```
:> LINK program;
```

D. **Replacing a Single Subprogram in an Existing Load Module**

One advantage of subprograms is that they can be compiled individually without having to compile the main program or other subprograms. Suppose that the ONE subprogram contains an error and must be replaced. We can compile just the ONE subprogram and replace it in the load module as follows.

1. *Replacing in VS COBOL II*

```
// EXEC COB2UCLG
//COB2.SYSLIB   DD DSN=copy-library,DISP=SHR
//COB2.SYSIN    DD *
[ONE source statements]
//LKED.SYSLMOD DD DSN=A1000.PGM.LOAD(THING),DISP=OLD,SPACE=,UNIT=
```

> [SYSLMOD *is again overridden to describe the data set that is to contain the new load module. Since* THING *is already a member of* A1000.PGM.LOAD, *it is replaced by the new load module. By selecting a different name, we would add the new load module rather than replace the old load module. The* SPACE= *parameter is coded to nullify the* SPACE *parameter on the overridden* SYSLMOD *statement, so that it does not change the secondary allocation specified when* A1000.PGM.LOAD *was created. The* UNIT= *is written, because we want the system to locate the data set from the catalog.*]

```
//LKED.DD1 DD DSN=A1000.PGM.LOAD,DISP=SHR
```

> [*The* DD1 *statement describes the library containing the old load module.*]

```
//LKED.SYSIN   DD *
 ENTRY THING
```

> [*The main routine is no longer loaded first, and so we must tell the linkage editor that* THING *is the entry point.*]

```
INCLUDE DD1(THING)
```

> [*The old load module is included as additional input.*]

```
//GO.IN        DD DSN=A1000.JUNK.DATA,DISP=SHR
```

2. *Replacing in Microsoft COBOL*

In Microsoft COBOL, you recompile the programs to create ".OBJ" files. Then you replace them using the LIB command, coded as follows:

```
:> LIB library - program + program -+ program...;
```

- *library:* The name of the library. If the *library* has a suffix other than ".LIB", you must code it.
- *-program:* Deletes the program from the library.
- *+program:* Adds the program to the library.
- *-+program:* Replaces the program in the library.

Now that the compilation procedures are out of the way, we can discuss program organization in the next chapter.

18

Program Organization

Now we can begin to piece the COBOL statements together to form a complete program. We'll first examine the ways in which individual statements can be grouped.

I. STATEMENT GROUPINGS

COBOL has five groupings of statements: the statement group, sentences, paragraphs, sections, and programs. The *statement group* (not a COBOL term) is one or more statements executed in sequence as if they were a single statement. You place them in the clauses of conditional statements, such as the IF, SEARCH, and READ statements, to form a unit of code. Terminate them with the appropriate END group terminator or other key word, such as ELSE or WHEN. A *sentence* consists of one or more statements and is terminated by a period. Sentences are really vestigial remains in COBOL and serve no purpose today. A *paragraph* consists of all statements following a paragraph name, up to the next paragraph name. It groups statements together, enabling them to be executed by the PERFORM statement. A *section* consists of one or more paragraphs that are to be performed together; additionally, use of sections allows portions of the program to be overlaid, sharing the same storage area. Paragraphs and sections are called *procedures* in COBOL. A *program* is a collection of COBOL statements that are executable.

A. Statement Groups

Statement groups consist of several statements that may be placed wherever a single imperative statement may go. You terminate the group after the last statement with an explicit or implicit scope terminator. The following example shows the use of statement groups in an IF and a SEARCH statement:

```
IF A = B
   THEN MOVE 1 TO I
        COMPUTE J = K * 2
```
        [Statement group implicitly terminated by the following ELSE.*]*

```
        ELSE MOVE 2 TO I
            MOVE ZERO TO J
              [Statement group terminated by END-IF.]
     END-IF
     SEARCH ALL TABLE-A
       AT END
          MOVE 1 TO I
          COMPUTE J = K * 2
            [Statement group implicitly terminated by WHEN.]
       WHEN TABLE-ELEMENT(IX) = B
            MOVE 2 TO I
            MOVE ZERO TO J
              [Statement group terminated by END-SEARCH.]
     END-SEARCH
```

B. Paragraphs

A paragraph consists of a paragraph name and all the statements that follow, up to the next procedure name. A paragraph collects statements into a unit to be executed by the PERFORM statement. A paragraph must end with a period.

```
     PERFORM A10-LABEL-1
     ■ ■ ■
A10-LABEL-1.
     MOVE A TO B        ⎫
                        ⎬  [Paragraph]
     MOVE D TO E        ⎭

A20-LABEL-2.
    [Next procedure delimits the previous paragraph.]
```

C. Sections

A section begins with a section name, followed by a paragraph name. It contains all paragraphs up to the next section name. You can use sections to define the range of the PERFORM statement, similar to paragraphs. Sections are redundant to paragraphs, except to segment programs. They are also required for internal sort procedures. The following example illustrates a section:

```
A10-PART-2 SECTION.
A20-PART-2.
   MOVE A TO B          ⎫
                        ⎪
                        ⎪
A30-PART-2.             ⎬  [Section]
   MOVE C TO D          ⎪
                        ⎪
                        ⎭
A40-PART-2 SECTION.
    [The next section name delimits the previous section.]
```

COBOL requires paragraph names within a section to be unique, but you can use the same paragraph name in different sections. You must then qualify the paragraph name: *paragraph-name* OF *section-name*. Within the section containing a duplicate paragraph name, you need not qualify the paragraph name. Never use duplicate paragraph names, because confusion may result.

Sections can *segment* programs to divide a large program into smaller segments and reduce the memory requirement. With today's computers that have very large memory or virtual storage, there is little need for this. You can assign sections literal priority numbers from 0 to 99. The most frequently used sections should have the lower numbers. Sections having the same priority, termed a *program segment,* are grouped into a single overlay segment by the compiler. Thus, sections that frequently communicate with each other should have the same priority. Sections with priority number 0 to 50, and sections not assigned a priority, constitute a fixed portion and reside permanently in memory during execution. Sections 51 to 99 constitute the *independent segments,* and are loaded into memory when required. You code sections as follows for segmentation.

```
segment-name  SECTION priority.
A10-TASK-A SECTION 55.
```

The system would not bring the code in the A10-TASK-A section into memory until required by it or one of the paragraphs it contains. When the section is brought into memory, it may overlay some other idle section. This reduces the total memory requirement of the program at some cost in extra I/O and slower execution. Because of the extra cost and complexity, don't segment programs unless it is necessary to fit them into the computer.

II. MAIN PROGRAM

Most COBOL programs consist only of the main program, but you should divide larger programs into a main program and subprograms. (Subprograms are described in Chapter 19.) Some COBOL statements serve only as comments. However, if you misspell such a COBOL statement or omit the terminating period, it is an error. It is better to use a comment line denoted by an asterisk in column 7 for a comment, because the compiler does not check these statements for spelling and punctuation.

A. Main Program Divisions and Their Order

The main program is divided into four divisions as follows:

- IDENTIFICATION DIVISION. Contains comments identifying the program, author, and date written.
- ENVIRONMENT DIVISION. Names the source and object computer and describes each file used by the program.

- DATA DIVISION. Describes all data items.
- PROCEDURE DIVISION. Contains the executable program statements.

You code the four divisions as follows in the order shown here.

IDENTIFICATION DIVISION.

[*Required.*]

    PROGRAM-ID. *program-name.*

       [*Required. Specifies a one- to eight-character name for the program, first character alphabetic.*]

    AUTHOR. *comment-entry.*

       [*Optional and obsolete—to be deleted from next ANSI Standard update. Names the program's author. Code any comments in columns 12 to 72, and may continue onto several lines, still in columns 12 to 72, but must terminate with a period. The comments may contain periods in addition to the terminating period. (The comments in the following statements also have the same form.)*]

    INSTALLATION. *comment-entry.*

       [*Optional and obsolete—to be deleted from next ANSI Standard update. Names the installation.*]

    DATE-WRITTEN. *comment-entry.*

       [*Optional and obsolete—to be deleted from next ANSI Standard update. Gives the date the program was written.*]

    DATE-COMPILED. *comment-entry.*

       [*Optional and obsolete—to be deleted from next ANSI Standard update. Prints the compilation date.*]

    SECURITY. *comment-entry.*

       [*Optional and obsolete—to be deleted from next ANSI Standard update. Describes the security level for the program.*]

ENVIRONMENT DIVISION.

[*This entire division is optional.*]

CONFIGURATION SECTION.

[*This entire section is optional.*]

SOURCE-COMPUTER. *computer.*

[*Optional. The computer is the computer on which the program is compiled and is treated as comments in VS COBOL II and Microsoft COBOL. Usual values are* IBM-370, IBM-390, *and* IBM-PC.]

OBJECT-COMPUTER. *computer.*

[*Optional. The computer is the computer upon which the compiled program is to run and is treated as comments in VS COBOL II and Microsoft COBOL. You can also code a* PROGRAM COLLATING SEQUENCE *phrase, as described in Chapter 21.*]

SPECIAL-NAMES.

[*Optional. Specifies a symbol other than the dollar sign ($) to be the currency symbol, and reverses the roles of the comma and period in numbers to enable them to be printed in the European manner. Also specifies mnemonic names used in the* DISPLAY, ACCEPT, *and* WRITE *statements. Described in Chapter 13.*]

INPUT-OUTPUT SECTION.

[*This entire section is optional.*]

FILE-CONTROL.

[*Optional. Specifies the files.*]

```
I-O-CONTROL.
```
[*Optional. Specifies special I/O processing.*]
```
DATA DIVISION.
```
[*This entire division is optional, but it is difficult to conceive of a program without it.*]
```
FILE SECTION.
```
[*Optional. Specifies each file and its records.*]
```
WORKING-STORAGE SECTION.
```
[*Optional. Describes all data items and working storage records.*]
```
LINKAGE SECTION.
```
[*Optional. Describes subprogram parameters in a called subprogram.*]
```
PROCEDURE DIVISION.
```
[*This entire division is optional, but it is difficult to conceive of a COBOL program without it.*]
```
DECLARATIVES.
```
[*Optional. Provides a group of statements to receive control for error or I/O conditions.*]
section-name `SECTION.`
    `USE AFTER ...`
paragraph-name.
    statements

    .
```
END DECLARATIVES.
```
procedure-name.
    statements-in-program

    .
```
END PROGRAM program-name.
```

The END PROGRAM header is optional unless you nest programs or compile several at the same time for batch compilation, as described later in this section. However, *something* should mark the end of a program, so it is a good idea to code it.

B. Usual Statements Needed

The usual statements needed for a complete program are included here for reference. Many programmers keep a file of these lines on disk so that the fixed part of the COBOL program does not need to be rewritten each time.

```
IDENTIFICATION DIVISION.
    PROGRAM-ID.  program-name.
ENVIRONMENT DIVISION.
INPUT-OUTPUT SECTION.
FILE-CONTROL.
DATA DIVISION.
FILE SECTION.
WORKING-STORAGE SECTION.
PROCEDURE DIVISION.
    ■ ■ ■
END PROGRAM program-name.
```

The ANSI Standard requires that the Procedure Division contain paragraphs. This means that there must be a paragraph name before the first statements in the program. VS COBOL II and Microsoft COBOL don't require that a paragraph name precede the first statement in the program.

The ANSI Standard also requires the main program to be divided into sections if a Declaratives Section is written. This means that there must be a SECTION header before a paragraph label before the first statements in the program. VS COBOL II and Microsoft don't require this, and the first line following the DECLARATIVES can be the first program statement.

C. Program Termination

The STOP RUN statement terminates execution, even if executed in a subprogram. It causes all open files to be closed.

```
PROCEDURE DIVISION.
paragraphs.
    STOP RUN
```

perhaps more paragraphs.

The EXIT PROGRAM statement also terminates execution if executed in the main program, but returns control to the calling program if executed in a subprogram. EXIT PROGRAM must appear by itself in a paragraph.

```
paragraph-name.  EXIT PROGRAM.
```

VS COBOL II provides a GOBACK statement, not in the ANSI Standard, that is identical to the EXIT PROGRAM statement except that it need not appear by itself in a paragraph. You can place it wherever an executable statement may go:

```
GOBACK
```

VS COBOL II includes GOBACK for compatibility with previous IBM compilers. (Microsoft COBOL also supports it.) Use EXIT PROGRAM rather than GOBACK.

D. Debugging Aids

The debugging aids in COBOL are obsolete elements that are to be removed from the ANSI Standard when it is next updated. This means that they can be used, but that you should not build your career on them. However, the aids are quite useful, and there is no certainty that they will be removed. The ALTER GO TO has been obsolete through several ANSI Standard updates, and if any statement deserves extinction, it is the ALTER GO TO. The decision to remove the debugging aids from the standard will depend on the politics of the ANSI COBOL committee.

1. *The* DEBUGGING MODE *Clause*

You can mark statements in the Procedure Division as debugging state-
ments by coding a D in column 7. The DEBUGGING MODE clause in the
SOURCE-COMPUTER paragraph determines whether to compile these statements.
You code DEBUGGING MODE as follows:

```
SOURCE-COMPUTER.   computer WITH DEBUGGING MODE.
```

When WITH DEBUGGING MODE is coded, it causes all statements in which a D
is coded in column 7 to be compiled. You usually omit the WITH DEBUGGING
MODE so that COBOL treats any statements with a D coded in column 7 as
comments.

This is a very useful feature of COBOL. Often, debugging statements are
placed in a program during testing and then removed when the program goes
into production. The implicit assumption in this is that once a program is
debugged, bugs never reoccur. Unfortunately, the sad fate of all programs is
that bugs occur during their entire life. Debugging statements should be an
inherent part of any program and never removed. Coding a D in column 7
allows this.

```
D    DISPLAY "THE-VALUE: ", THE-VALUE
```

You can continue debugging statements such as this, but you must code the
D in each continued line. You can place debugging lines anywhere within a
program, following the OBJECT-COMPUTER paragraph.

2. *The* USE FOR DEBUGGING *Statement*

You can code the USE FOR DEBUGGING statement in a Declaratives Section to
receive control when specified actions occur in files, identifiers, and procedures.
Paragraphs placed after the USE statement perform any debugging action or
display debugging information. Upon exit from the section, program execution
continues.

For the USE FOR DEBUGGING statement to become active, you must do two
things:

• Cause them to be compiled by coding the DEBUGGING MODE clause on the
  SOURCE-COMPUTER paragraph. (This also causes any statements with a D
  coded in column 7 to be compiled. If the DEBUGGING MODE clause is omitted,
  any USE FOR DEBUGGING sections and any statements with a D coded in
  column 7 are treated as comments for the compilation.

• Turn on the debugging section during execution. You do this in VS COBOL
  II by coding the DEBUG parameter for the GO step as a PARM. DEBUG is usually
  default, so you must code NODEBUG to turn the debugging off. In Microsoft
  COBOL, you turn debugging on by coding (+D) following the command
  line: :> program (+D). Omit the (+D) if you don't want the debugging
  sections turned on.

The ability to either compile or not compile the debugging sections and turn them on or off during execution is a very good feature. For efficiency during production of a mature system, you may elect not to compile the debugging statements. But early in the life of a system, you may choose to compile the statements but turn them off during production. In either case, the debugging statement can and should be a permanent part of the program.

The USE FOR DEBUGGING sections must immediately follow the DECLARATIVES paragraph header. You code them as follows:

```
PROCEDURE DIVISION.
DECLARATIVES.
section-name SECTION.
     USE FOR DEBUGGING ON event.
paragraph-name.                [There can be several paragraphs.]
     statements

     .
section-name SECTION.
     USE FOR DEBUGGING ON event.
paragraph-name.                [There can be several.]
     statements

     .
END DECLARATIVES.
```

You code the USE FOR DEBUGGING statement as follows:

```
                    file-name          [Not in VS COBOL II]
                    procedure-name
                    ALL PROCEDURES
                    ALL  identifier    [Not in VS COBOL II]
     USE FOR DEBUGGING ON ⎯⎯⎯⎯⎯⎯⎯⎯⎯⎯
```

- *file-name:* Invoked after any OPEN, CLOSE, DELETE, START, or READ statements that reference *file-name* (unless the AT END or INVALID KEY phrases are invoked).
- *procedure-name:* Invoked just before the execution of the named *procedure*. You can't name a procedure that is in a USE FOR DEBUGGING section. That is, you can't debug your debugging.
- ALL PROCEDURES: Invoked before the execution of each procedure within the program. Don't code this if you code a *procedure-name*.
- ALL *identifier:* Invoked after the execution of any statement that references *identifier* during execution. (For WRITE, REWRITE, and GO TO DEPENDING ON, COBOL invokes it just before executing the statement. For a PERFORM VARYING or AFTER, COBOL invokes it immediately after the initialization or evaluation of the data item.)

COBOL executes the USE FOR DEBUGGING only once for a single statement (or a single verb for statement groups), regardless of the number of times a data item is referenced in a statement. This means that it would be executed once for a STRING or UNSTRING statement, regardless of the many steps within these statements.

A special register named DEBUG-ITEM is automatically provided to define a record into which COBOL inserts information identifying the statement and procedure that caused the USE FOR DEBUGGING section to be invoked. COBOL first fills DEBUG-ITEM with SPACES and then moves the relevant information to it. You can only refer to it in a USE FOR DEBUGGING section. COBOL automatically defines it as follows:

```
01  DEBUG-ITEM.
    02  DEBUG-LINE              PIC X(6).
```
[Identifies the statement that caused execution of debugging section.]
```
    02  FILLER                 PIC X VALUE SPACE.
    02  DEBUG-NAME             PIC X(30).
```
[Contains first 30 characters of data item or procedure name that caused execution of debugging section.]
```
    02  FILLER                 PIC X VALUE SPACE.
    02  DEBUG-SUB-1            PIC S9(4) SIGN LEADING SEPARATE.
```
[If the DEBUG-NAME item is subscripted, COBOL stores the subscript of each of the first three levels in DEBUG-SUB-1, DEBUG-SUB-2, and DEBUG-SUB-3. If there are more than three levels of subscripting, don't use these registers. (This is one reason the debugging section is obsolete.)]
```
    02  FILLER                 PIC X VALUE SPACE.
    02  DEBUG-SUB-2            PIC S9(4) SIGN LEADING SEPARATE.
    02  FILLER                 PIC X VALUE SPACE.
    02  DEBUG-SUB-3            PIC S9(4) SIGN LEADING SEPARATE.
    02  FILLER                 PIC X VALUE SPACE.
    02  DEBUG-CONTENTS         PIC X(n).
```
[Contains descriptive information about the item. For example, it might contain "SORT INPUT" when a SORT/MERGE input section executes, and "FALL THROUGH" when execution falls through one procedure into another.]

You can write any statements you wish in paragraphs following the USE FOR DEBUGGING statement to display the contents of DEBUG-ITEM or other identifiers. You can PERFORM paragraphs contained in other USE FOR DEBUGGING procedures. You cannot reference any paragraphs outside the USE FOR DEBUGGING procedures. Nor can statements outside USE FOR DEBUGGING refer to procedures within USE FOR DEBUGGING.

3. *The* COBTEST *Debugging Tool in VS COBOL II*

VS COBOL II has a debugging tool named COBTEST [Ref 1] that is a basic part of the VS COBOL II compiler, although the compiler can be obtained without it. COBTEST lets you execute your program a statement at a time while you view selected variables. You can also execute at full speed and stop at breakpoints you set, examine data, and then either resume full-speed execution or execute a step at a time. You can use COBTEST in batch or on-line from ISPF. Batch is mainly for CICS.

To use COBTEST, first compile your program with the TEST compiler option. Remove any WITH DEBUGGING MODE clause in the SOURCE-COMPUTER paragraph.

```
// EXEC COBUCL,PARM.COB2='TEST'
```

Save the compiler output listing in a cataloged data set on disk and name it *userid.program-id*.LIST so that COBTEST can find it. Before executing COBTEST, you must allocate all the data sets your program reads or writes. (COBTEST automatically allocates SYSABOUT and SYSDBOUT.) Don't forget to allocate SYSOUT for DISPLAY statements. Allocate the data sets using the TSO ALLOC command. Create a CLIST file of the necessary ALLOC commands so that you can quickly allocate the files.

After allocating the files, get into COBTEST by selecting the Foreground Option 4 from the main ISPF menu and then selecting the COBTEST options from the next menu. You will get the first COBTEST menu, on which you name the partitioned data set and member name of your program's load module. Fill in PARM information on the screen (don't enclose it in apostrophes).

Once in COBTEST, you execute it with a series of commands that are beyond the scope of this book. To end COBTEST, enter the QUIT command.

4. *The* ANIMATOR *Debugging Tool in Microsoft COBOL*

Microsoft COBOL has a very powerful debugging tool named ANIMATOR [Ref 2] that lets you execute your program a statement at a time while you view selected variables. You can also execute at full speed and stop at breakpoints you set, examine data, and then either resume full-speed execution or execute a step at a time. To use ANIMATOR, first compile your program with the ANIM compiler parameter.

```
:> COBOL program-name ANIM
```

Then you invoke ANIMATOR and name the program you compiled:

```
:> ANIMATE program
```

You will get a full-screen display of the first statements of your program, with a menu for controlling execution. The menu is fairly self-evident, but see the Microsoft COBOL manuals for a full description.

If your program calls subprograms, compile them with the ANIM option too. (If you don't code the ANIM option for a subprogram, it will work properly, but you won't be able to see its source statements when it is executed.) The LINK command was described in Chapter 17.

```
:> LINK program-name /PROGRAM-NAME;
```

5. *Storage Dumps*

In VS COBOL II, you can code the FDUMP compiler option to obtain a storage dump in source form if your program abnormally terminates. The dump enables you to locate the statement causing the abnormal termination. You must include a SYSDBOUT DD statement if you code FDUMP. If you don't code FDUMP, you get an unformatted dump if you include a SYSUDUMP DD statement. You can also force an abnormal termination within your program by calling the ILBOABNO system subprogram as follows:

```
//STEP1 EXEC COB2UCLG,PARM.COB2='FDUMP'
    ■ ■ ■
 77  SOME-CODE                      PIC S9(4) BINARY.
    ■ ■ ■
    MOVE nnnn  TO SOME-CODE
    CALL "ILBOABNO" USING SOME-CODE
      [The nnnn  appears as Unnnn  in the dump.]
    ■ ■ ■


//GO.SYSDBOUT DD SYSOUT=A
```

In Microsoft COBOL, you can code the TRACE compile parameter to obtain a trace of the statements executed in the program.

E. Main Program Communication with the Operating System

1. *Command Line Input:* PARM *and* ACCEPT *(Not in ANSI Standard)*

VS COBOL II passes parameters to the main program with the PARM parameter on the EXEC JCL statement. You code the EXEC statement as follows to pass a character string containing up to 100 characters to the main program. The qualifier .GO indicates that the parameter is for the GO step.

```
//STEP1 EXEC COB2UCLG,PARM.GO='string '
```

You then code the main program as follows to receive the *string*. You can use any valid data names in place of PARM, PARM-LENGTH, and PARM-VALUE.

```
LINKAGE SECTION.
 01  PARM.
     05  PARM-LENGTH              PIC S9(4) BINARY SYNC.
     05  PARM-VALUE              PIC X(100).
```

COBOL stores the length of *string* in PARM-LENGTH, and moves the *string* itself to PARM-VALUE. Code the USING parameter in the Procedure Division as follows:

```
PROCEDURE DIVISION USING PARM.
```

VS COBOL II also allows you to specify various run-time options to COBOL, such as DEBUG and SSRANGE through PARM. Code a slash (/) after the program parameters and then write the run-time options.

```
//STEP1 EXEC COB2UCLG,PARM.GO='string /DEBUG,SSRANGE')
```

The PARM information is sometimes used in place of data read in from a file, but it is best to reserve it for programming aids, such as debugging flags. The following example illustrates such a use, in which the PARM can trigger a debugging trace or cause an end-of-file after some number of records are read in. If no PARM is coded, the program executes normally. You code the PARM as follows for load module execution:

```
//step-name  EXEC PGM=program ,PARM='tnnnnn '
```
   [*t: debugging flag. Code Y to turn the built-in debugging on. nnnnn: number of input records to read before causing an end-of- file on the input file. Code 99999 to read all records.*]
```
//STEP1 EXEC PGM=RUN12,PARM='Y00020'
```
   [*Debugging is turned on, and 20 records will be read.*]
```
//STEP2 EXEC PGM=RUN12
```
   [*Normal production run with no debugging.*]

The program could then be coded as follows:

```
77  IN-COUNT                    PIC S9(4) BINARY VALUE 0.
*                                   Counts the IN-FILE records.
LINKAGE SECTION.
01  PARM.
    05  PARM-LENGTH             PIC S9(4) BINARY SYNC.
    05  PARM-VALUE.
        10  PARM-DEBUG          PIC X.
*                                   "Y" turns debugging on.
        10  PARM-CUTOFF         PIC 9(5).
*                                   Cutoff count
    05  FILLER                  PIC X(74).
PROCEDURE DIVISION USING PARM.
A00-BEGIN.
```
   [*First, display any debugging information, or set the flags and cutoff count if there is no PARM.*]
```
    IF PARM-LENGTH = ZERO
       THEN MOVE "N" TO PARM-DEBUG
            MOVE 99999 TO PARM-CUTOFF
       ELSE DISPLAY "DEBUG FLAG: ", PARM-DEBUG
            DISPLAY "INPUT RECORD CUTOFF: ", PARM-CUTOFF
```
               [*Then set debugging on if the flag is set.*]
```
    END-IF
```

When the input file is read, the program checks the number of records read and forces an EOF if appropriate:

```
READ IN-FILE INTO IN-REC
   AT END
      MOVE "Y" TO EOF-IN
   NOT AT END
      ADD 1 TO IN-COUNT
      IF (PARM-CUTOFF < 99999) AND
         (IN-COUNT = PARM-CUTOFF)
         THEN MOVE "Y" TO EOF-IN
      END-IF
END-READ
```

Within the program, you could execute various debugging statements when the debugging flag is set on:

```
IF PARM-DEBUG = "Y"
   THEN DISPLAY "THE-VALUE: ", THE-VALUE
END-IF
```

This technique is an alternative to using the COBOL debugging aids, which may someday be removed from the standard.

In Microsoft COBOL, you can place any data on the command line by leaving a blank between it and the program name:

```
:> program  data
```

You define an input area for the data in the Working-Storage or Linkage Section exactly as done for the PARM in VS COBOL II. Then you must execute the following ACCEPT command to move the data from the command line area to the area you define:

```
LINKAGE SECTION.
01  PARM.
    05  PARM-VALUE.
        10  PARM-DEBUG              PIC X.
*                                     "Y" turns debugging on.
        10  PARM-CUTOFF             PIC 9(5).
*                                     Cutoff count.
    ■ ■ ■
    ACCEPT PARM FROM COMMAND-LINE
```

2. *Return Codes (Not in ANSI Standard)*

VS COBOL II and Microsoft COBOL allow a program within a job step to return a completion code to the operating system. You can then test this code in subsequent job steps to determine whether to execute those steps. Thus, if a file to be read by a program in a subsequent job step cannot be written, you can set the return code so that the subsequent job step is not executed.

You set the return code by moving a value to the special register RETURN-CODE, which is automatically defined as PIC S9(4) BINARY.

```
MOVE value TO RETURN-CODE
MOVE 16 TO RETURN-CODE
```

In VS COBOL II, the COND parameter coded on the EXEC statement or the IF/THEN/ELSE/ENDIF construct, described in Chapter 16, tests the return code to determine whether the step should be executed:

```
//step-name  EXEC program ,COND.step-name =(n,comparison )
//STEP2 EXEC PAYROLL,COND.STEP1=(4,LT)
```

In Microsoft COBOL, you code the DOS IF ERRORLEVEL statement in a ".BAT" file to branch around statements to skip execution. You code:

```
IF ERRORLEVEL n  GOTO label
```

The branch is made if the RETURN-CODE value equals *n*.

```
IF ERRORLEVEL 4 GOTO STEP3
[commands]
:STEP3
```

F. Nesting Programs

COBOL 85 allows you to nest one program within another. This feature complicates COBOL without providing any apparent advantage. It is difficult to envision why one would want to nest one program within another. It requires that both programs must be recompiled if either requires recompilation.

Nesting programs simply means that you place one program inside another, just before its END PROGRAM header. The names within the higher-level program and the nested program can be the same, and describe different things without conflict, because the names are known only within the programs. However, names described in the Configuration Section of the higher-level program, including alphabetic names, class names, condition names, mnemonic names, and symbolic characters can be referenced in the nested program.

You write nested programs as follows:

```
IDENTIFICATION DIVISION.             [This begins the higher-level program.]
    PROGRAM-ID.  program-name.
ENVIRONMENT DIVISION.
DATA DIVISION.
PROCEDURE DIVISION.
  [Main program statements.]
```

```
IDENTIFICATION DIVISION.              [This begins the nested program.]
    PROGRAM-ID.  nested-program-name.
ENVIRONMENT DIVISION.
DATA DIVISION.
PROCEDURE DIVISION.
  [Nested program statements.]
END PROGRAM nested-program-name.      [This ends the nested program.]
END PROGRAM program-name.             [This ends the higher-level program.]
```

A higher-level program can contain several nested programs. Likewise, nested programs can have programs nested within them. You must place the nested program directly before the END PROGRAM header of the program in which it is to be nested.

The position of the END PROGRAM header is important, because it can also be used to compile several programs together for batch compilation. Notice the difference here:

Nested program:

```
IDENTIFICATION DIVISION.              [This begins the higher-level program.]
    PROGRAM-ID.  program-name.
  [Main program statements.]
IDENTIFICATION DIVISION.              [This begins the nested program.]
    PROGRAM-ID.  nested-program-name.
  [Nested program statements.]
END PROGRAM nested-program-name.      [This ends the nested program.]
END PROGRAM program-name.             [This ends the higher-level program.]
```

Batch compilation of separate programs:

```
IDENTIFICATION DIVISION.              [This begins the first program.]
    PROGRAM-ID.  program-name.
  [Main program statements.]
END PROGRAM program-name.             [This ends the first program.]
IDENTIFICATION DIVISION.              [This begins the second program.]
    PROGRAM-ID.  program-name.
  [Nested program statements.]
END PROGRAM program-name.             [This ends the second program.]
```

You can call a nested program only by a program in which it is either directly or indirectly nested. (An indirectly nested program is one nested several levels—like the branches of a tree structure.) If you want a nested program to be called by any program, even one on a different branch of the nested tree structure, you code the COMMON clause in the PROGRAM-ID paragraph of the nested program. (Recursive calls are not allowed.) You can code COMMON only for nested programs:

```
    PROGRAM-ID.  program-name COMMON.
```

You can code the GLOBAL phrase for File Definitions (described in Chapter 12) and level 01 data items. (Any subordinate items automatically become global.) This allows them to be referenced in all subprograms directly or indirectly contained within them. (Note that you code COMMON on the PROGRAM-ID of the nested program; on File Descriptions and data items, you code GLOBAL on the higher-level program.)

If a nested program defines the same name as one declared GLOBAL in a higher-level program, COBOL uses the declaration within the nested program. All condition-names, indexes, and lower-level items within the level 01 item declared GLOBAL are also GLOBAL. You cannot use GLOBAL in the Linkage Section.

```
FD   file-name GLOBAL ...
01   data-name GLOBAL ...
```

If the data item contains a REDEFINES clause, GLOBAL must follow it:

```
01   data-name REDEFINES data-name GLOBAL ...
```

G. Sharing Data and Files Among Programs with EXTERNAL

There are three ways to share data and files in COBOL programs:

- By nesting programs and using the GLOBAL phrase, as just described.
- By coding subprograms and passing data as parameters in a CALL statement, as described in Chapter 19. (You can share data but not files this way.)
- By coding the EXTERNAL clause for a File Description or data item, as described here.

You can code EXTERNAL on a File Description (described in Chapter 12) and level 01 data item in Working-Storage. This makes the items external from the program and available to all programs and subprograms in the run. COBOL keeps storage for the EXTERNAL items separate from any program. You cannot code EXTERNAL with COMMON or REDEFINES.

```
FD   file-name EXTERNAL ...
01   data-name EXTERNAL ...
```

Because EXTERNAL items are kept outside any program, any subprogram can use them as if they were part of that subprogram.

H. Writing the Program

There are several ways to make programs easier to update and change and to leave a record of what the program does. Chapter 2 suggested you organize programs into paragraphs and invoke them with PERFORM statements, so that the

PERFORM statements serve as a table of contents to the program. The preceding section illustrated how PARM information could be used to turn debugging statements on and off. The next few paragraphs describe some other techniques, and the sample program that follows illustrates them all.

It is a good practice to build an audit trail into the program so that in a production run you can tell what processing was done in the program. This is especially important later in the program's life when someone less familiar with the program must track down an error. An audit trail is a way of identifying each transaction and tracing its flow through the system—where it came from and where it went. The audit trail should include the following:

- Display any control statements or PARM information read.
- Print a message when program execution begins and when it terminates. Describe the condition under which the program terminates, either normally or for some error condition. If it is a long-running program that operates in several phases, print a message at the end of each phase.
- Count all records read and written for each file, and print these totals at the end of the program. You might also print all input and output transactions themselves, perhaps triggering such detail with a PARM value.

Build the debugging facilities into the program so that production programs can be tested without modification. The most serious bugs occur in production programs, and it is important to be able to quickly track down such errors. Programs are never completely debugged. After thorough testing, they reach a point where bugs are no longer being discovered with the test data, but undiscovered bugs always remain in the program. Devise debugging aids that can be left in a production program at a minimal cost in efficiency. This also eliminates the annoying errors caused by removing debugging aids from a program in preparation for placing it in production.

The following example is a complete program that incorporates these ideas. They are not exhaustive, and you will undoubtedly devise better ones for your own programs.

```
//JR964113 JOB (24584),'JONES',CLASS=A
//STEP1 EXEC COB2UCLG,PARM.GO='00500PT'
//COB2.SYSIN DD *
 IDENTIFICATION DIVISION.
     PROGRAM-ID.   TESTPGM.
 ********************************************************************
 * This program reads in a file and selects records with an       *
 * "X" in column 80.  The selected records are written into an    *
 * output file.  The program serves no purpose but to illustrate  *
 * how a simple COBOL program might be written.                   *
 * RETURN-CODE is ZERO for normal run; 4 for bad PARM field.      *
 ********************************************************************
 ENVIRONMENT DIVISION.
 CONFIGURATION SECTION.
```

```
SOURCE-COMPUTER.  IBM-390 WITH DEBUGGING MODE.
INPUT-OUTPUT SECTION.
FILE-CONTROL.
    SELECT FILEIN ASSIGN TO DDIN.
    SELECT FILEOUT ASSIGN TO DDOUT.
DATA DIVISION.
FILE SECTION.
FD  FILEIN
    BLOCK CONTAINS 0 RECORDS
    RECORD CONTAINS 80 CHARACTERS
    .
01  FILEIN-IMAGE                PIC X(80).
FD  FILEOUT
    BLOCK CONTAINS 0 RECORDS
    RECORD CONTAINS 80 CHARACTERS
    .
01  FILEOUT-IMAGE              PIC X(80).
WORKING-STORAGE SECTION.
77  FILEIN-READ               PIC S9(4) BINARY VALUE ZERO.
77  FILEOUT-WRITTEN           PIC S9(4) BINARY VALUE ZERO.
77  FILEIN-EOF                PIC X.
01  FILE-IMAGE.
*                                This is the line read in.
    05  FILLER                PIC X(79).
*                                Columns 1 to 79 ignored.
    05  CC-80                 PIC X.
*                                Look for "X" in column 80.
LINKAGE SECTION.
************************************************************************
* The PARM field is set up to allow the program to be cut off    *
* after some number of records has been read.  Code the          *
* following on the EXEC statement to cut off early for debugging *
* purposes, where nnnnn is the maximum number of records to      *
* read.  Remember to code the leading zeros.  p is flag to       *
* print input records read and output records written.  Code     *
* "Y" to print, "N" to not print.                                *
*                                                                *
* // EXEC COB2UCLG,PARM.GO='nnnnnp'                              *
*                                                                *
* // EXEC COB2UCLG,PARM.GO='00100Y'   CUTOFF AFTER 100 RECORDS.  *
*                                     PRINT RECORDS.             *
************************************************************************
01  PARM.
    05  PARM-LENGTH           PIC S9(4) BINARY SYNC.
    05  PARM-FIELD.
        10  PARM-CUTOFF       PIC 99999.
```

```
       10   PARM-PRINT              PIC X.
       10   FILLER                  PIC X(94).
PROCEDURE DIVISION USING PARM.
DECLARATIVES.
DEBUG-IT SECTION.
*      This provides a trace of the procedures invoked.
      USE FOR DEBUGGING ON ALL PROCEDURES.
DEBUG-PROCEDURES.
      DISPLAY DEBUG-LINE, DEBUG-NAME, DEBUG-CONTENTS

          .

END DECLARATIVES.
A00-BEGIN.
      DISPLAY "PROGRAM TEST EXECUTION BEGINS."
      PERFORM A10-INITIALIZE
      MOVE "N" TO FILEIN-EOF
      PERFORM A20-READ-ALL-RECORDS WITH TEST AFTER
            UNTIL FILEIN-EOF = "Y"
      PERFORM A40-TERMINATE
      STOP RUN

          .

 A10-INITIALIZE.
 ****************************************************************
 * PROCEDURE TO ADD INITIALIZE FOR RUN.                        *
 * IN:  All files closed.                                      *
 *      PARM fields stored in LINKAGE SECTION.                 *
 * OUT: PARM-CUTOFF contains valid cutoff value.               *
 *      FILEIN opened for input.                               *
 *      FILEOUT opened for output.                             *
 ****************************************************************
      IF PARM-LENGTH NOT = 6
        THEN MOVE 99999 TO PARM-CUTOFF
            MOVE "N" TO PARM-PRINT
        ELSE IF PARM-CUTOFF NOT NUMERIC
                THEN DISPLAY "WARNING--BAD PARM RECORD COUNT: ",
                        PARM-CUTOFF
                  MOVE 4 TO RETURN-CODE
                  MOVE 99999 TO PARM-PRINT
                ELSE DISPLAY "WILL CUTOFF AFTER ", PARM-CUTOFF,
                        "RECORDS READ FOR DEBUGGING"
            END-IF
            IF PARM-PRINT NOT = "Y" AND PARM-PRINT NOT = "N"
                THEN DISPLAY
                    "WARNING--INCORRECT PARM PRINT FLAG: ",
                        PARM-PRINT
                  MOVE 4 TO RETURN-CODE
                  MOVE "N" TO PARM-PRINT
```

```
                    ELSE DISPLAY "PARM PRINT FLAG: ", PARM-PRINT
                END-IF
        END-IF
        OPEN INPUT FILEIN,
             OUTPUT FILEOUT
          .
**** Exit
 A20-READ-ALL-RECORDS.
 ****************************************************************
 * PROCEDURE TO READ ALL THE RECORDS IN FILEIN.               *
 * IN:  FILEIN opened for input.                              *
 *      FILEOUT opened for output.                            *
 *      FILEIN-EOF contains "N".                              *
 * OUT: Records with X in column 80 written into FILEOUT.     *
 *      FILEOUT-WRITTEN bumped by 1 if record written.        *
 ****************************************************************
        MOVE SPACE TO CC-80
        PERFORM A30-SELECT-A-RECORD WITH TEST AFTER
                UNTIL (CC-80 = "X") OR
                      (FILEIN-EOF = "Y")
        IF FILEIN-EOF NOT = "Y"
           THEN WRITE FILEOUT-IMAGE FROM FILE-IMAGE
                ADD 1 TO FILEOUT-WRITTEN
                IF PARM-PRINT = "Y"
                   THEN DISPLAY "FILEOUT: ", FILE-IMAGE
                END-IF
        END-IF
          .
**** Exit
 A30-SELECT-A-RECORD.
 ****************************************************************
 * PROCEDURE TO ADD ENTRIES TO PERSON TABLE.                  *
 * IN:  FILEIN opened for input.                              *
 *      FILEIN-EOF contains "N".                              *
 * OUT: FILEIN-EOF set to "Y" if EOF for FILEIN or            *
 *       PARM-CUTOFF records read.                            *
 *      FILEIN bumped by 1 to count FILEIN record read.       *
 *      FILE-IMAGE contains input record if no EOF.           *
 ****************************************************************
        READ FILEIN INTO FILE-IMAGE
          AT END
             MOVE "Y" TO FILEIN-EOF
          NOT AT END
             IF (PARM-CUTOFF < 99999) AND
                (FILEIN-READ = PARM-CUTOFF)
                THEN MOVE "Y" TO FILEIN-EOF
```

```
                    DISPLAY "CUTOFF FOR DEBUGGING."
               ELSE ADD 1 TO FILEIN-READ
                    IF PARM-PRINT = "Y"
                        THEN DISPLAY "FILE-IMAGE: ", FILE-IMAGE
                    END-IF
             END-IF
      END-READ

**** Exit
 A40-TERMINATE.
 ****************************************************************
 * PROCEDURE TO TERMINATE PROGRAM.                             *
 * IN:  FILEIN-READ contains count of FILEIN records read.     *
 *      FILEOUT-WRITTEN contains count of FILEOUT records      *
 *        written.                                             *
 *      FILEIN and FILEOUT files open.                         *
 * OUT: End message and record counts displayed.               *
 *      FILEIN and FILEOUT files closed.                       *
 ****************************************************************
      CLOSE FILEIN,
            FILEOUT
      DISPLAY "NORMAL COMPLETION OF PROGRAM TESTPGM."
      DISPLAY "RECORDS READ:    ", FILEIN-READ
      DISPLAY "RECORDS WRITTEN: ", FILEOUT-WRITTEN

**** Exit
 END PROGRAM TESTPGM.
//GO.DDOUT DD SYSOUT=A
//******** PLACE INPUT DATA FOLLOWING DDIN DD STATEMENT.
//GO.DDIN DD *
```

III. INCLUSION OF STATEMENTS FROM A LIBRARY

A. The COPY Statement

The COPY statement is an excellent feature that copies source statements into a program from a library. COPY permits a single file description, record description, or paragraph to be used by several programs. This reduces coding and simplifies maintenance by ensuring that all programs use the same data names for files.

COPY is most useful in copying file and record descriptions. Keep all file and record descriptions used by more than one program in a copy library. (Except for source input and printed output, most files are used by more than one program.) Paragraphs are harder to share among programs, because they may use data that has a different data type or names. There is also an inherent difficulty in publicizing and describing paragraphs so that others will know about them and know how to use them. Subprograms also let code be shared, as described in Chapter 19. They have a formal interface that makes them both easier to use and to describe how to be used.

In VS COBOL II, the copy library is a partitioned data set, and the COPY statement specifies a member name. You must specify the LIB parameter for the compile step. You must include a JCL statement in the compile step to name the partitioned data set containing the library members.

```
//STEP1 EXEC COB2UCLG,PARM.COB2='LIB'
//COB2.ddname   DD DSN=library, DISP=SHR
```

There may be several COPY statements within a program, coded as follows. Note that the period is required:

```
COPY member OF ddname.
```

All text contained in the member is copied into the program at the point where COPY appears, replacing the COPY statement and the period following it. You can omit the OF *ddname,* and SYSLIB is assumed.

```
//STEP1 EXEC COB2UCLG,PARM.COB2='LIB'
//COB2.SYSLIB DD DSN=library,DISP=SHR
     COPY member.
```

In Microsoft COBOL, you code the COPY statement as follows:

```
COPY file-name.
```
[*The file-name is the name of the file containing the statements to copy.*]
```
COPY file-name OF library-name.
```
[*The library-name is the name of a library containing the text. If you don't code a suffix, ".LBR" is assumed.*]

The text and lines in the file or member are copied into the program at the point where COPY appears. The COPY statement is replaced in its entirety, including the period, by the copied text. The copied statements can themselves contain a COPY statement, as long as they do not name the member they themselves are in. You can place COPY wherever a word or separator may occur, but you must precede COPY with a space. You should usually place COPY on a line by itself. COBOL treats a COPY statement on a comment line as comments.

```
* COPY STATUS.              [Treated as a comment.]
```

A COPY statement may, however, copy comments in. If a copy library named ENDCOM contained

```
******************
* End of program *
******************
    STOP RUN
```

and you coded this in your program:

```
Z90-END-PROGRAM.
    COPY ENDCOM.
```

the result would be as if you had coded

```
Z90-END-PROGRAM.
******************
* End of program *
******************
    STOP RUN
```

The following example illustrates COPY statements in which two members, PAYFD and PAY, are copied into a program.
Member PAYFD:

```
FD  PAY-IN
    BLOCK CONTAINS 0 RECORDS
    RECORD CONTAINS 80 CHARACTERS

    .

01  PAY-REC                      PIC X(80).
```

Member PAY:

```
01  PAY.
    05  PAY-NAME                 PIC X(25).
    05  PAY-ADDRESS              PIC X(55).
```

The members may then be copied into a program:

```
    COPY PAYFD.
    COPY PAY.
```

Compiled as

```
FD  PAY-IN
    BLOCK CONTAINS 0 RECORDS
    RECORD CONTAINS 80 CHARACTERS

    .

01  PAY-REC                      PIC X(80).
01  PAY.
    05  PAY-NAME                 PIC X(25).
    05  PAY-ADDRESS              PIC X(55).
```

COPY can also edit the text as it is copied into the program. The following example illustrates the need for this. Assume that a member named MFILE is contained in a COPY library as follows.

```
01  DOOR.
    05  Y                        PIC X.
    05  Z                        PIC 9
                                 REDEFINES Y OF DOOR.
```

The library member is copied into the program as follows:

```
COPY MFILE.
```

It would be compiled as

```
01  DOOR.
    05  Y                             PIC X.
    05  Z                             PIC 9
                                      REDEFINES Y OF DOOR.
```

Suppose that DOOR should be renamed REAL-THING. You can do this by coding the COPY statement with the REPLACING phrase to edit the copied text:

```
COPY member REPLACING text  BY new-text
                     text  BY new-text
                            .
                            .
                            .
                     text  BY new-text.
```

The *text* may be any COBOL word (except COPY), a literal, identifier, or pseudotext (explained later in this section). We can now edit the preceding example as it is copied:

```
COPY MFILE REPLACING DOOR BY REAL-THING
                     Y BY FIRST-THING.
```

It is compiled as

```
01  REAL-THING.
    05  FIRST-THING                          PIC X.
    05  Z                         PIC 9
              REDEFINES FIRST-THING OF REAL-THING.
```

Pseudotext consists of text enclosed by ==, the pseudotext delimiters. Pseudotext allows you to change any sequence of words in COBOL statements. Here is an example
   Member MFILE:

```
01  DOOR.
    05  Y                             PIC X.
    05  Z                             PIC 9
                                      REDEFINES Y OF DOOR.
```

Then if you coded

```
COPY MFILE REPLACING ==DOOR== BY ==REAL-THING==
                     ==Y== BY ==FIRST-THING==.
```

the result would be:

```
01  REAL-THING.
    05  FIRST-THING                               PIC X.
    05  Z                          PIC 9
                      REDEFINES FIRST-THING OF REAL-THING.
```

The rules for coding, continuation, searching, and replacement for the REPLACING phrase are the same as for the REPLACE statement, described next.

B. The REPLACE **Statement**

The REPLACE statement allows you to specify a search and replace operation for your program. REPLACE does much the same thing as a global change using a text editor. The main differences are that REPLACE statement operates after any COPY statement has been processed, so that items in a copy library are also changed. REPLACE also compares word by word, not character by character.

You can place a REPLACE statement following any item or statement that you can terminate with a period. (Unless REPLACE is the first statement in the program, precede it with a period. It must also terminate with a period.) The change you specify is made from that point to the end of the item being compiled or until another REPLACE or REPLACE OFF statement is encountered. You code the REPLACE statement as follows:

```
REPLACE ==pseudotext-to-replace == BY ==new-pseudotext ==.
```

- *pseudotext-to-replace* specifies the text you want to replace. You can continue the pseudotext onto another line. The pseudotext to replace must not consist entirely of a comma or semicolon.
- *new-pseudotext* is the replacement text. The change is made only for compilation; the original source code is, of course, not changed. The resulting line after the replacement must not contain a REPLACE statement. That is, REPLACE can't be recursive.

The new pseudotext can be null:

```
REPLACE ==SOURCE-COMPUTER.  IBM-370.== BY ====.
```
  [*Changes all instances of the specified characters to a null, which will result in a blank line.*]

You can specify several replacements with a single REPLACE statement:

```
REPLACE ==DAYS-YR== BY ==DAYS-IN-YEAR==
==DAYS-MO== BY ==DAYS-IN-MONTH==
==PIC S9(4) BINARY== BY ==PIC S9(9) BINARY==.
```

REPLACE and the pseudotext can begin in either area A (column 8) or B (column 12). The pseudotext can be as long as 323 characters, and you can continue it onto another line if necessary. To continue, code the text through column 72, code a hyphen in column 7 of the next line, and continue the text beginning in the B area, column 12. The two pseudotext delimiter characters (==) must appear on the same line.

In matching, COBOL begins matching at the leftmost source program text word following the REPLACE statement, and compares the words in the pseudotext with the words in the COBOL program. For matching, COBOL considers each separator comma, semicolon, or series of spaces to be a single space. If the words match, COBOL replaces the found text with the replacement pseudotext, and continues the search with the next word following the found text. If there is no match, COBOL continues the search with the next word in the source. COBOL ignores comment and blank lines for the search.

If a line becomes too long during replacement, COBOL automatically continues the line.

To terminate the replacement before the end of the program, you can code another REPLACE statement or code the REPLACE OFF statement:

```
REPLACE OFF.
```

C. The BASIS, INSERT, and DELETE Statements (Not in ANSI Standard)

The BASIS statement lets you copy a complete program from a copy library for compilation. INSERT lets you insert lines into the copied program, and DELETE lets you delete lines. Since you can do all this and more with a text editor or a source management system, you are unlikely to need to use BASIS. In VS COBOL II, you code the same JCL for BASIS as you do for COPY, along with the LIB compilation option.

Code the statements anywhere in columns 1 to 72. Just leave at least one space after the statement name.

• BASIS names a program in the copy library you want copied in.

> BASIS *program-name*
> [*Name the program you want copied in. In Microsoft COBOL, write the DOS file name and enclose it in quotations.*]

• DELETE names the six-digit sequence numbers (with leading zeros) in columns 1 to 6 of the lines in the BASIS program to delete. You can write a single number, a series of numbers separated by a comma and space, a range of numbers separated by a hyphen, or a combination of these. The sequence numbers must be in ascending order. If a DELETE line is followed by COBOL statements, the COBOL statements replace the deleted lines.

> DELETE *sequence-numbers*
> [*You can place COBOL source statements here if you wish.*]

• INSERT adds source statements to the BASIS program. You name the six-digit sequence number (with leading zeros) in columns 1 to 6 of a source line in the COBOL program. The COBOL statements that follow INSERT are then inserted in the BASIS program after this line.

```
INSERT sequence-number
[Place COBOL source statements here.]
```

You must place the DELETE and INSERT statements in ascending order of the sequence numbers.

The next chapter describes subprograms, which are another powerful way of organizing a program.

EXERCISES

1. Discuss the advantages and disadvantages of the required statements in COBOL.

2. Discuss the means and limitations of modularizing programs in COBOL.

ADDITIONAL READINGS

"Microsoft® COBOL Optimizing Compiler, Version 3.0 for MS® OS/2 and MS-DOS(R) Operating Guide," Redmond, WA: Microsoft Corporation, 1988.

"VS COBOL II Application Programming: Debugging," Order NO. SC26-4049, Poughkeepsie, NY: IBM Corporation, 1989.

19

Subprograms

Subprograms are self-contained collections of statements that may be compiled separately from the main program and other subprograms. They allow code to be shared among different programs. Subprograms can save compilation time, because each may be compiled separately and, if changes occur, only one subprogram needs to be recompiled and not the remainder of the program. Subprograms can also break up a large program into smaller, more manageable units that are easier to modify and test. Several people can work on a program composed of separate subprograms at the same time without stumbling over one another. The ANSI standard and Microsoft COBOL also have the intrinsic functions described in Appendix D.

Subprograms are used less in COBOL than in other languages. The subprogram feature was added rather late in COBOL. The numeric data of COBOL is harder to pass in subprogram calls, because all programs calling the subprogram must pass the data in the same precision and length. Programmers sometimes find it easier to include the statements as a paragraph than as a subprogram.

I. CALLING SUBPROGRAMS

The CALL statement invokes subprograms.

```
CALL subprogram
```

The *subprogram* can be an alphanumeric data item containing the subprogram name, or it can be a literal:

```
MOVE "SUB2" TO SUB-NAME      [Same as]   CALL "SUB2"
CALL SUB-NAME
```

Usually you pass a subprogram some data. The USING phrase does this by giving a list of data names as *parameters*. For example, the calling program might list three parameters:

```
CALL "TABLEPGM" USING BY REFERENCE A, B, C
```

II. WRITING SUBPROGRAMS

The called subprogram must describe a corresponding list of *parameters* in the Procedure Division paragraph. The parameters correspond item for item to the list of parameters in the calling program, although they may have different names. COBOL makes the parameters available to the subprogram through the parameter names.

```
PROCEDURE DIVISION USING A, B, C.
```

   You write subprograms like a main program, with the addition of the Linkage Section, which describes the parameters in the CALL. The USING phrase of the Procedure Division paragraph must also list these parameters in the order that they appear in the CALL. You write a subprogram as follows:

```
IDENTIFICATION DIVISION.
 PROGRAM-ID.   subprogram-name.
```
   [*The subprogram-name is the name by which the subprogram is called. It has one to eight characters, first character alphabetic.*]
```
ENVIRONMENT DIVISION.
CONFIGURATION SECTION.
INPUT-OUTPUT SECTION.
FILE-CONTROL.                        [Code these only as needed.]
DATA DIVISION.
FILE SECTION.
WORKING-STORAGE SECTION.
```
   [*The subprogram can describe whatever internal data it needs. The items described here in a subprogram are known only within the subprogram, and it doesn't matter if you use the same names as in other programs. COBOL assigns items initial values only once at the start of the run, not each time the subprogram is called. You can reinitialize items by executing the* CANCEL *statement for the subprogram or by coding the* INITIAL *attribute in the Program-ID paragraph. Both are described later on this chapter.*]
```
LINKAGE SECTION.
```
   [*The parameters passed by the calling program must be described here. The data descriptions must each have the same data length and precision as those in the calling program. (They should also have the same data type, but this isn't required.) Items declared in this section cannot be assigned initial values, because they receive their values from the calling program. (However, you can code the* VALUE *clause for level 88 condition names.) COBOL associates the parameters by position and not by name. This means that the names do not need to be the same. VS COBOL II and Microsoft COBOL allow a parameter named in the* PROCEDURE DIVISION USING *to have a* REDEFINES *clause in its description in the Linkage Section. The ANSI Standard does not.*]
```
PROCEDURE DIVISION USING a1, a2, ..., an.
```
   [*You must list a parameter here for each parameter in the* CALL. *Then describe the parameter in the Linkage Section.* COBOL *begins execution at the first executable statement in the subprogram.*]
```
END PROGRAM subprogram-name.
```
   [END PROGRAM *is optional, but you should code it.*]

Subprograms may contain the same statements as a main program. An EXIT PROGRAM statement in the subprogram returns control to the calling program at the next executable statement following the CALL statement. Names described within a subprogram are known only within that subprogram, and you can use these names in the main program or other subprograms for other purposes.

Here is how a calling program might be written:

```
IDENTIFICATION DIVISION.
    PROGRAM-ID. TESTPGM.
DATA DIVISION.
WORKING-STORAGE SECTION.
01  A.
    05  DD                          OCCURS 5 TIMES INDEXED BY IDD
                                    PIC X(20).
77  B                               PIC S9(4) BINARY.
77  C                               PIC X(20).
PROCEDURE DIVISION.
START-PROGRAM.
    MOVE 3 TO B
    MOVE SPACES TO C
    CALL "TABLEPGM" USING A, B, C
```

   [*The structure* A *and two elementary data items,* B *and* C, *are passed to subprogram* TABLEPGM.]

```
    STOP RUN
    .
END PROGRAM TESTPGM.
```

The subprogram might be coded as follows:

```
IDENTIFICATION DIVISION.
    PROGRAM-ID. TABLEPGM.
DATA DIVISION.
WORKING-STORAGE SECTION.
LINKAGE SECTION.
```

   [*Since the parameters are associated by position and not by name, the names do not need to be the same. Thus,* A *in the calling program becomes* X *in the called subprogram,* B *becomes* Y, *and* C *becomes* Z.]

```
01  X.
    05  XX                          OCCURS 5 TIMES INDEXED BY IXX
                                    PIC X(20).
```

   [*Upon entry, the contents of* XX *are undefined, because the calling program didn't assign them values.*]

```
77  Y                               PIC S9(4) BINARY.
```

   [*Upon entry,* Y *contains 3.*]

```
77  Z                               PIC X(20).
```

   [*Upon entry,* Z *contains* SPACES.]

```
PROCEDURE DIVISION USING X, Y, Z.
```

[*The* PROCEDURE DIVISION *header must contain the* USING *phrase and list the parameters being passed by the calling program.*]

```
START-PROGRAM.
    PERFORM VARYING IXX FROM 1 BY 1 UNTIL IXX > Y
        MOVE Z TO XX(IXX)
    END-PERFORM
    MOVE ZERO TO Y
    EXIT PROGRAM
```

[*You can execute* EXIT PROGRAM *anywhere in the subprogram.* EXIT PROGRAM *returns control to the statement following the* CALL *in the calling program. Upon return,* XX(1) *through* XX(3) *will contain* SPACES, *and B will contain* 0.]

```
END PROGRAM TABLEPGM.
```

You can share data by passing it as a parameter in the subprogram call. File names cannot be shared by passing them as parameters to a subprogram. VS COBOL II allows QSAM files (Queued Sequential Access Method—which means a blocked sequential file) to be passed. However, a COBOL subprogram can't process them; only a program written in another language. You can share files by coding EXTERNAL on the FD and record descriptions, as described in Chapter 18.

Since subprograms are separate from the main program, it takes more effort to combine them for execution with other subprograms and to document them.

Sometimes it is not apparent that a functional unit of code is a candidate for being shared with other programs as a subprogram until after the program is written. Then lifting out the code and making it into a subprogram requires maintenance. Subprograms require careful planning to be successful, both in defining the data that is to be shared and in determining the functional units of code that are candidates for being shared. Any data passed as parameters in a calling program must match the parameter data descriptions in the called subprogram. For example, if a subprogram expects a parameter of precision PIC S9(9)V99, but the calling program carries the value with precision S9(5)V99, you must move the item to another item of precision S9(9)V99 in the calling program before it can be used as a parameter in the subprogram call.

III. THE CALL STATEMENT

The general form of the CALL statement is as follows.

```
    CALL subprogram USING a1, a2, ..., an
[or:]
    CALL subprogram USING BY REFERENCE a1, a2, ..., an
[or:]
    CALL subprogram USING BY CONTENT a1 , a2, ..., an
```

• *subprogram.* A literal or alphanumeric data item containing the subprogram. In VS COBOL II, it is one to eight alphanumeric characters, first character alphabetic. If longer than eight characters, only the leftmost eight are used.

- BY REFERENCE means that the address of the data item is passed. This allows the subprogram to change its value in the main program. You cannot pass literals when BY REFERENCE is used.
- BY CONTENT means that only the contents of the parameter are passed. This means that while you can change the value of the parameter within the subprogram, the changed value is not passed back to the calling program. BY CONTENT causes COBOL to move the parameters to temporary storage, so passing large tables with BY CONTENT is less efficient than with BY REFERENCE. In VS COBOL II and Microsoft COBOL, you can use non-numeric literals as parameters when BY CONTENT is coded. (VS COBOL II also permits figurative constants, but Microsoft COBOL does not.) The LENGTH OF special register can also be used as a BY CONTENT parameter. (Remember that is implicitly defined as PIC 9(9) BINARY.)
- *a1, a2, ..., an* are subprogram parameters. They can be any level of data item in the File Section, Working-Storage Section, or Linkage Section. (The ANSI Standard allows them to be only level 01 or 77 or elementary data items.)

If you omit both BY REFERENCE and BY CONTENT, BY REFERENCE is assumed:

```
CALL "SUBMAX" USING X, Y, Z
```

Same as

```
CALL "SUBMAX" USING BY REFERENCE X, Y, Z
```

You can code both BY CONTENT and BY REFERENCE, and they apply only to the parameters following them:

```
CALL "SUBMAX" USING BY REFERENCE X, BY CONTENT Y, Z
    [X is passed by reference and Y and Z by content.]
```

The subprogram called can itself call other subprograms. However, COBOL programs are not recursive. That is, a called subprogram cannot directly or indirectly call the program that called it.

When you pass numeric parameters, COBOL does not convert them if their types don't match. This means that the item in the calling subprogram must match the length, precision, and data type of the item in the called subprogram.

When you pass character data BY CONTENT, the item in the calling subprogram must match the length of the item in the called subprogram. The data type should also match, but it needn't as long as you know what you are doing. That is, you can call a subprogram with an alphabetic item and receive the item as alphanumeric. If you pass the argument BY REFERENCE, the length needn't match as long as you have some means of determining the length. (You could terminate a string with a special character or pass the length as a parameter.) BY CONTENT moves the item to temporary storage, so COBOL must know the length. BY REFERENCE passes the address of the item, which doesn't require COBOL to know its length.

IV. DYNAMIC SUBPROGRAM LOADING

Subprograms can also be loaded into storage dynamically when they are first called. (In VS COBOL II, the DYNAM compiler option, described in Chapter 17, specifies dynamic loading. In Microsoft, dynamic loading occurs when you do dynamic linking.) The ON EXCEPTION phrase specifies imperative statements to execute if the subprogram can't be found or if there is insufficient storage for it. You rarely need to do this in VS COBOL II, because it is better just to let the program terminate and increase the region size.

```
CALL subprogram USING parameters
  ON EXCEPTION
      imperative-statements
  NOT ON EXCEPTION
      imperative-statements
END-CALL
```

You can code ON EXCEPTION, NOT ON EXCEPTION, or both. As a holdover from the previous COBOL version, ON OVERFLOW acts the same as ON EXCEPTION.

```
CALL subprogram USING parameters
  ON OVERFLOW
      imperative-statements
END-CALL
```

V. INITIAL STATE OF SUBPROGRAMS

When a subprogram is loaded into memory, COBOL sets it to its initial state. That is, all the VALUE clauses of the Data Division are set, all the files it describes are closed, and all the PERFORM statements are set to begin with their initial values. Normally, COBOL does not reset subprograms to their initial state each time they are called. You can reset them to their initial state in two ways: by executing a CANCEL statement in the calling program, or by coding the INITIAL clause in the Program-ID for the subprogram.

A. The CANCEL Statement

The CANCEL statement, executed in a program, resets a subprogram to its initial state the next time it is called and closes any files left open in the subprogram. Storage occupied by dynamically loaded subprograms is also made available. CANCEL is ignored if the subprogram has not been called. If the subprogram has been called, EXIT PROGRAM must have been the last statement executed in the subprogram.

A subprogram can execute a CANCEL, but not for itself or a higher-level calling program. CANCEL is coded as follows:

```
CANCEL subprogram , subprogram , ..., subprogram
```

As with CANCEL, the *subprogram* can be an alphanumeric data item or a literal.

```
CANCEL "SUBMAX"
```

B. The INITIAL **Attribute**

Another way of causing a subprogram to put in its initial state when it is called is to code the INITIAL clause in the Program-ID paragraph of the subprogram.

```
PROGRAM-ID. subprogram-name  INITIAL.
```

You can also code the INITIAL clause with the COMMON clause for nested programs:

```
PROGRAM-ID.  program-name INITIAL COMMON.
```

VI. RETURN FROM SUBPROGRAMS

The EXIT PROGRAM statement returns control from a subprogram. On return from the subprogram, COBOL leaves intact all data items within the subprogram, and they retain their values if the subprogram is called again (unless you execute a CANCEL statement or code the INITIAL attribute the Program-ID paragraph).

```
EXIT PROGRAM
```

To terminate execution within a subprogram rather than return to the calling program, execute the STOP RUN statement:

```
STOP RUN
```

VII. MULTIPLE ENTRY POINTS (NOT IN ANSI STANDARD)

VS COBOL II and Microsoft COBOL subprograms can have multiple entry points specified by the ENTRY statement within the subprogram. The ENTRY statement can also list parameters different from those in the PROCEDURE DIVISION USING phrase in number, order, and data type. You code the ENTRY statement as follows:

```
ENTRY "entry-name "
ENTRY "entry-name " USING a1, a2,..., an
```

- *entry-name:* The name of the entry point; one to eight alphanumeric characters, first character alphabetic. A CALL statement can then name this entry point. The CALL has the same format as a call to a subprogram: CALL "entry-name" USING....
- *a1, a2, ..., an:* Subprogram parameters. They must correspond in number and order to the parameters of the CALL and be defined in the Linkage Section.

Execution begins with the first executable statement following ENTRY.

VIII. COMPILATION OF SUBPROGRAMS

You can compile subprograms separately from the main program and other
subprograms so that a change in a single subprogram does not require recompilation of the entire program. VS COBOL II needs an END PROGRAM statement
following each program or subprogram.

```
// EXEC COB2UCLG
//COB2.SYSIN DD *
   [Main program]
        END PROGRAM program-name.            [Begins in column 8.]
   [Subprogram ]
        END PROGRAM subprogram-name.
```

   ■ ■ ■

   This concludes the discussion of subprograms. The next chapter, on advanced character manipulation, contains several examples of the application of
subprograms.

EXERCISES

1. Write a subprogram to compute the future value of an amount invested at
a given interest rate for a given number of years. The formula for this is

$$\text{Future amount} = \text{Investment} \, (1 + i)^n$$

The i is the interest rate [PIC SV9(5)] and n is the years [PIC S9(3)]. Define
the amounts as PIC S9(11)V99. Verify that the subprogram works properly
by checking some results against a table of compound interest.

2. Write a subprogram that is to be called with a parameter consisting of
a one-dimensional PACKED-DECIMAL table with a varying size controlled by
an OCCURS DEPENDING ON clause. The subprogram is to find the minimum,
maximum, and average of the elements in the table. The table is to have a
maximum size of 500, and the elements are to have precision PIC S9(5)V99.

3. Write a subprogram to change a date stored in the form "yyy/mm/dd" to
the form "dd/mm/yyy" or "mm/dd/yyyy", depending on a flag supplied as a
parameter in the call.

4. Write a single subprogram to convert distances into meters. The subprogram is to convert units of inches, feet, yards, and miles. (1 inch = 0.0254
meters, 1 mile = 1609.35 meters.) Assume PACKED-DECIMAL numbers and
choose a suitable precision. Use a parameter as a flag to specify the conversion.
Test the subprogram and verify that it works properly.

5. List at least 10 candidates to be made into general-purpose built-in subprograms or functions for COBOL. Select functions for business data processing
problems similar to the built-in functions provided in FORTRAN, C, or PL/I.

20

Advanced Character Manipulation

The INSPECT, STRING, and UNSTRING statements perform search, replacement, and concatenation operations on character strings. In addition, you can also use the PERFORM statement to operate on character strings. This is illustrated with examples of variable-length character string manipulation. The chapter also illustrates character string manipulation by showing some of the operations that can be done on dates. The ANSI standard and Microsoft COBOL also have intrinsic functions for date and character manipulation, as described in Appendix D.

I. THE INSPECT STATEMENT

The INSPECT statement can both count the number of specific characters or substrings in an identifier and replace them with other characters of the same length. The first form of INSPECT counts characters in an identifier. INSPECT examines the characters in *identifier* from left to right, counting specific characters as specified by the FOR phrase.

```
                                    CHARACTERS
                                    ALL match-string
                                    LEADING match-string
INSPECT identifier  TALLYING count FOR _____
```

- *identifier*: A group item or an elementary USAGE DISPLAY item to examine. COBOL treats it as alphanumeric data and ignores any internal sign for external decimal numbers.
- *count*: An elementary numeric data item to count the number of matches. You must initialize it, because INSPECT adds to it.
- ALL: Count all nonoverlapping characters in *identifier* that match the characters in the *match-string*. (A *match-string* of "AA" counts 2 and not 3 in an *identifier* containing "AAAABAB".)
- LEADING: Count the number of times the *match-string* appears as the leftmost characters in *identifier*. That is, count the number of times the *match-string* appears consecutively at the beginning of the string. (A *match-string* of "THE" counts two in an *identifier* containing "THETHE THE".)

- CHARACTERS: Count the number of characters in *identifier*. (An *identifier* of PIC X(9) counts nine.) This acts the same as the LENGTH OF special register.
- *match-string*: A USAGE DISPLAY elementary data identifier, alphanumeric literal, or figurative constant. INSPECT treats figurative constants as a single instance of the character. (ZEROS is the same as "0".)

```
01 STRING-A                          PIC X(11) VALUE "MISSISSIPPI".
   ■ ■ ■
   MOVE ZEROS TO COUNT-1
   INSPECT STRING-A TALLYING COUNT-1 FOR ALL "S"
      [Adds 4 to COUNT-1; COUNT-1 contains 4.]
   INSPECT STRING-A TALLYING COUNT-1 FOR CHARACTERS
      [Adds 11 to COUNT-1; COUNT-1 contains 15.]
   INSPECT STRING-A TALLYING COUNT-1 FOR LEADING "M"
      [Adds 1 to COUNT-1; COUNT-1 contains 16.]
   INSPECT STRING-A TALLYING COUNT-1 FOR ALL "ISS"
      [Adds 2 to COUNT-1; COUNT-1 contains 18.]
```

A single BEFORE or AFTER phrase (but not both) may follow the FOR phrase to count the characters before or after some other character string is encountered.

```
   BEFORE stop-string [or] AFTER begin-string
```

BEFORE starts the counting with the leftmost character in *identifier* and continues up to but not including the characters matching those in the *stop-string*. If the *stop-string* characters do not appear in *identifier*, the matching terminates with the rightmost characters in *identifier* and BEFORE has no effect. Assume that STRING-A contains "MISSISSIPPI" here:

```
   INSPECT STRING-A TALLYING COUNT-1 FOR ALL "I" BEFORE "IS"
      [Adds 0 to COUNT-1.]
   INSPECT STRING-A TALLYING COUNT-1 FOR CHARACTERS BEFORE "IP"
      [Adds 7 to COUNT-1.]
   INSPECT STRING-A TALLYING COUNT-1 FOR LEADING "M" BEFORE "S"
      [Adds 1 to COUNT-1.]
```

AFTER starts the counting immediately after the *begin-string* characters in *identifier* and continues to the rightmost characters in *identifier*. The FOR phrase is ignored if the *begin-string* characters do not appear in *identifier*. Again, assume (here and in the next five examples) that STRING-A contains "MISSISSIPPI".

```
   INSPECT STRING-A TALLYING COUNT-1 FOR ALL "S" AFTER "IS"
      [Adds 3 to COUNT-1.]
   INSPECT STRING-A TALLYING COUNT-1 FOR CHARACTERS AFTER "IP"
      [Adds 2 to COUNT-1.]
   INSPECT STRING-A TALLYING COUNT-1 FOR LEADING "I" AFTER "S"
      [Adds 0 to COUNT-1.]
```

Both *begin-string* and *stop-string* may be USAGE DISPLAY elementary identifiers, alphanumeric literals, or figurative constants.

There may be several FOR phrases in the INSPECT statement. Notice that you code the FOR only once:

```
INSPECT STRING-A
   TALLYING COUNT-1 FOR ALL "M"
                         [Add 1 to COUNT-1.]
                         ALL "S"
                         [Add 4 to COUNT-1.]
```

LEADING, CHARACTERS, and ALL can all be coded together, but it becomes very difficult to do this correctly. Each successive FOR phrase picks up where the previous one stopped, which may not be the first character position. For example:

```
INSPECT STRING-A
   TALLYING COUNT-1 FOR LEADING "M",
                         [Add 1 to COUNT-1. Now positioned following the leading
                         "M".]
                         ALL "M"
                         [Add 0 to COUNT-C1. No "M" characters follow the leading
                         "M".]
```

Note also that any BEFORE or AFTER clause is performed before any of the other FOR clauses is executed. For example:

```
INSPECT STRING-A
   TALLYING COUNT-1 FOR LEADING "M",
                         [Add 0 to COUNT-1. The following BEFORE "PP" clause
                         is performed first to position before the "PP". The next
                         character is no longer an "M".]
                         CHARACTERS BEFORE "PP",
                         [Add 8 to COUNT-1. This positions at the PP before any
                         FOR phrase is applied.]
                         ALL "S"
                         [Add 0 to COUNT-1. No "SS" characters follow the "PP".]
```

You can write several ALL phrases, but it is best to have only one LEADING or CHARACTERS phrase following a FOR. There may also be separate *counts* for the FOR phrase.

```
INSPECT STRING-A
   TALLYING COUNT-1 FOR ALL "S"
                   [Add 4 to COUNT-1.]
                   COUNT-2 FOR ALL "I"
                   [Add 4 to COUNT-2.]
                   COUNT-3 FOR ALL "P"
                   [Add 2 to COUNT-3.]
```

Be careful combining CHARACTERS and LEADING, because their final position affects following phrases, as shown in this example:

```
INSPECT STRING-A
   TALLYING COUNT-1 FOR CHARACTERS BEFORE "SS",
                     [Add 2 to COUNT-1. This positions to the first "SS".]
                 COUNT-2 FOR LEADING "M",
                     [Add 0 to COUNT-2. The "M" is no longer leading.]
                 COUNT-3 FOR ALL "I"
                    [Add 3 to COUNT-3. There are three "I" characters starting with the "SS".]
```

These forms of INSPECT are complex and make it possible to write statements that are almost indecipherable. INSPECT applies each FOR phrase as follows:

• The first FOR phrase is applied starting from the first character position (or wherever any BEFORE or AFTER phrase would place it).
• If the FOR phrase is not applied because of the BEFORE or AFTER phrase, or if there is no match in the FOR phrase, the next FOR phrase is applied. It starts at the same character as the previous FOR phrase (or wherever any BEFORE or AFTER phrase would place it).
• If a FOR phrase is satisfied, the appropriate count is incremented and the FOR phrases that follow are not applied. The next comparison begins with the first FOR phrase. It begins at the next character in *identifier* that is to the right of the rightmost character that participated in the match.
• If no FOR phrases match, the first FOR phrase is applied starting with the character position in *identifier* to the right of where the last comparison began.

The following example illustrates this form of INSPECT:

```
INSPECT STRING-A
   TALLYING COUNT-1 FOR ALL "AB",
                        ALL "C",
                 COUNT-2 FOR ALL "EFG"
```

Assume that STRING-A contains "ABCDFFGH" and that COUNT-1 and COUNT-2 contain zero. The INSPECT statement then operates as follows:

AB | CDEFGH AB |		FOR ALL "AB" matches the first two characters, and 1 is added to COUNT-1. COUNT-1 now contains 1 and the matching continues to the right of "AB" in STRING-A.

A | B | CDEFGH
  | A | B
  | C |
		FOR ALL "AB" does not match, but ALL "C" matches, and 1 is added to COUNT-1. COUNT-1 now contains 2, and the matching continues to the right of "C" in STRING-A.

ABC	D	EFGH	Neither "AB", "C", nor "EFG" match. The matching
	A	B	continues to the right of "D" in STRING-A.
	C		
	E	FG	

ABCD	EFG	H	Neither "AB" nor "C" match, but FOR ALL "EFG"
	AB		matches, and 1 is added to COUNT-2. COUNT-1
	C		contains 2, COUNT-2 contains 1, and the matching
	EFG		continues to the right of "EFG" in STRING-A.

ABCDEFG	H	Neither "AB", "C", nor "EFG" match. COUNT-1
	AB	contains 2, COUNT-2 contains 1, and the INSPECT
	C	statement has completed execution.
	EFG	

The second form of INSPECT replaces characters:

```
                      CHARACTERS
                      ALL match-string
                      FIRST match-string
                      LEADING match-string
INSPECT identifier  REPLACING _____
  BY replacement-string
```

INSPECT examines the characters in *identifier* as specified by the REPLACING phrase and replaces them with the characters in the *replacement-string*. The *identifier,* ALL, LEADING, and CHARACTERS are exactly as in the first form. FIRST *matching-string* searches *identifier* for the first characters that match the characters in *match-spring*. The *replacement-string* may be a USAGE DISPLAY elementary identifier, an alphanumeric literal, or a figurative constant. It must contain the same number of characters as in *match-string*, or one character for CHARACTERS. In the following examples, assume that STRING-A contains "MISSISSIPPI":

```
    INSPECT STRING-A REPLACING FIRST "SS" BY "XX"
      [STRING-A contains "MIXXISSIPPI".]
    INSPECT STRING-A REPLACING ALL "I" BY "Z"
      [STRING-A contains "MZXXZSSZPPZ".]
    INSPECT STRING-A REPLACING LEADING "M" BY "Y"
      [STRING-A contains "YZXXZSSZPPZ".]
    INSPECT STRING-A REPLACING CHARACTERS BY "W"
      [STRING-A contains "WWWWWWWWWWW". Same as MOVE ALL "W" TO STRING-A.]
```

You can also list several *match-strings* for ALL and LEADING :

```
    INSPECT STRING-A REPLACING ALL "I" BY "Z"
                               ALL "PP" BY "XX"
```

If STRING-A contained "MISSISSIPPI", it would be changed to "MZSSZSSZXXZ".

You can append the BEFORE or AFTER to the REPLACING clause. Again, assume STRING-A contains "MISSISSIPPI".

```
INSPECT STRING-A REPLACING FIRST "SS" BY "XX" AFTER "SS"
  [STRING-A contains "MISSIXXIPPI".]
INSPECT STRING-A REPLACING ALL "I" BY "Z" BEFORE "S"
  [STRING-A contains "MZSSIXXIPPI".]
```

There may be several REPLACING phrases in INSPECT, such as the following. Note that you write the REPLACING only once.

```
INSPECT STRING-A
  REPLACING CHARACTERS BY "Z" AFTER "X",
            ALL "W" BY "Y" BEFORE "T",
                "M" BY "N",
            LEADING "X" BY "Y"
```

INSPECT applies the REPLACING phrases from left to right in the order they are written. The matching occurs the same as for the first format. Each FOR phrase is applied only if its BEFORE or AFTER phrase is satisfied. If any match occurs, the processing begins again with the first phrase immediately after the rightmost character in *identifier* that was replaced. If no match occurs, the comparison begins with the first FOR phrase, one character to the right of where the previous cycle started.

The TALLYING and REPLACING phrases may appear in the same INSPECT statement. The TALLYING phrase is first applied in its entirety, and then the REPLACING phrase is applied. The effect is exactly the same as if two INSPECT statements had been written.

```
INSPECT STRING-A
  TALLYING COUNT-1 FOR ALL "X" AFTER "Y",
  REPLACING ALL "X" BY "Z" AFTER "Y"
```

Same as

```
INSPECT STRING-A TALLYING COUNT-1 FOR ALL "X" AFTER "Y"
INSPECT STRING-A REPLACING ALL "X" BY "Z" AFTER "V"
```

The final form of the INSPECT statement allows you to specify a string of characters, each of which is to be converted to the corresponding character in another string:

```
INSPECT identifier CONVERTING "these-characters" TO "others"
```

For example, if STRING-A contained "MISSISSIPPI" and you executed this statement:

```
INSPECT STRING-A CONVERTING "ISP" TO "XYZ"
```

Any "I" is converted to "X", any "S" to "Y", and any "P" to "Z". STRING-A would contain "MXYYXYYXZZX". Notice that this form of the INSPECT is exactly the same as coding:

```
INSPECT STRING-A REPLACING ALL "I" BY "X"
                              "S" BY "Y"
                              "P" BY "Z"
```

II. THE STRING AND UNSTRING STATEMENTS

The STRING and UNSTRING statements manipulate character strings. *Character string manipulation* is very different from the operations that have been presented so far, and it requires several new concepts. To illustrate character string operations, consider a string such as "MARY HAD A LITTLE LAMB." One operation we might want to perform is to see if the string contains a given substring, such as "LAMB", and where in the string it is located. The location is indicated by the starting character position, such as 19 for "LAMB". Another operation that might be performed is to concatenate two or more strings by appending one to the end of another. Suppose that another string contained " ITS FLEECE WAS WHITE AS SNOW." By concatenating this string to the first, we form a new string containing "MARY HAD A LITTLE LAMB. ITS FLEECE WAS WHITE AS SNOW."

We might also want to break up a string into substrings. This is usually done by specifying the starting character position and the number of characters. By forming a substring of 11 characters, starting at the twelfth character, we form a new string containing "LITTLE LAMB". Next, we might want to replace a substring with another substring. We can do this either by specifying a starting character and the number of characters to replace, or by specifying a substring to locate and a string with which to replace it. In our string, we might replace "LAMB" with "TOFU" so that the string contains "MARY HAD A LITTLE TOFU." If the replacement string is not equal to the length of the substring it is replacing, it is more complicated. If we wanted to replace "LITTLE" with "BIG" in "MARY HAD A LITTLE LAMB.", we would do the following:

- Search the string to find where "LITTLE" begins.
- Form a substring of all characters up to this point and a substring of all characters following the "LITTLE".
- Concatenate the first substring "MARY HAD A" with "BIG" and then with the last substring "LAMB." to form "MARY HAD A BIG LAMB."

You also need substrings when you want to locate all instances of a substring within a string. Suppose we want to replace all instances of "MARY" with "JANE" in the string "MARY HAD A LAMB. MARY ALSO HAD A HORSE." We would first replace the first "MARY" with "JANE" to form "JANE HAD A LAMB. MARY ALSO HAD A HORSE." Then we would examine the substring beginning just beyond where we replaced and replace "MARY" with "JANE" so that "HAD A LAMB. MARY ALSO HAD A HORSE." becomes "HAD A LAMB. JANE ALSO HAD A HORSE." This would continue until no more "MARY" is found to replace.

COBOL is fair as a language for text editing. Its statements are directed more toward examining data items to see if they contain valid numeric or alphabetic characters and toward replacing invalid characters with valid ones. The INSPECT statement already described can locate substrings within a string and can replace substrings with strings of equal length. The STRING and UNSTRING statements described next can concatenate strings, replace substrings with strings, and form strings.

The STRING statement transmits characters from a send string into a receiving string, starting at a specified character position in the receiving string. STRING can transmit multiple send strings into a single receiving string. The UNSTRING statement transmits characters starting at a specified character position in a send string into a receiving string. UNSTRING can separate a single send string into multiple receiving strings. STRING and UNSTRING are both complex and difficult statements—perhaps the most difficult statements to be found in any programming language.

One alternative to STRING and UNSTRING is to use reference modification. For example, if you want to store the characters "AB" into the first two positions of the identifier A, you can code the following:

```
01  A                          PIC X(4) VALUE "WXYZ".
    ▪ ▪ ▪
    MOVE "AB" TO A(2:)   [A contains "ABYZ"]
```

Another alternative to STRING and UNSTRING is to use the REDEFINES clause, described in Chapter 8, which can define one substring to overlay another. The following example also stores the characters "AB" into the first two positions of the identifier A:

```
01  A                          PIC X(4) VALUE "WXYZ".
01  A-2 REDEFINES A            PIC X(2).
    ▪ ▪ ▪
    MOVE "AB" TO A-2   [A contains "ABYZ"]
```

Both these methods work only if a fixed number of characters are to be moved to a fixed position in the identifier. Use them wherever possible rather than STRING and UNSTRING, because they will be both more efficient and more understandable.

A. The STRING Statement

The STRING statement concatenates strings or substrings from one data item into another. The simplest form of the STRING statement transmits the characters in the *send-string* into the *receiving-string*. This acts like a MOVE, except that any characters beyond the length of the *send-string* in the *receiving-string* are not disturbed:

```
STRING send-string DELIMITED SIZE INTO receiving-string
```

- *send-string*: An alphanumeric literal, figurative constant, or USAGE DISPLAY identifier containing the characters to be transmitted. STRING treats figurative constants as single characters. You can reference-modify: *send-string(n:m)*.
- *receiving-string*: The USAGE DISPLAY identifier into which the characters in *send-string* are transmitted. It cannot represent an edited data item or be described with the JUSTIFIED clause. Nor can it be reference-modified. Use the POINTER phrase, described in a subsequent paragraph, instead. Characters in *send-string* are transmitted from left to right into *receiving-string* until the rightmost character in *send-string* is transmitted or *receiving-string* is filled.

```
01  A                        PIC X(4) VALUE "WXYZ".
    ■ ■ ■
    STRING "AB" DELIMITED SIZE INTO A
      [A contains "ABYZ".]
```

Note that this differs from a MOVE in that the STRING does not disturb the "YZ" characters:

```
MOVE "AB" TO A          [A contains "ABbb".]
```

Note also that you can use a MOVE with reference modification to accomplish the same thing:

```
MOVE "AB" TO A(1:2)        [A contains "ABYZ".]
```

The DELIMITED SIZE phrase specifies that all characters in *send-string* are to be transmitted. Alternatively, you can terminate the transmission with *delimiter* characters as follows:

```
STRING send-string DELIMITED delimiter INTO receiving-string
```

- *delimiter*: A figurative constant, alphanumeric literal, or a USAGE DISPLAY elementary identifier containing characters. Transmission terminates if the *delimiter* characters are encountered in *send-string*. All characters in *send-string* are transmitted if *delimiter* is not encountered. If the *delimiter* contains more than one character, they are treated as a unit. That is, a *delimiter* of "AB" terminates when "AB" is encountered, not when an "A" or "B" is encountered. The *delimiter* characters themselves are not transmitted.

```
01  A                       PIC X(4) VALUE "WXYZ".
01  B                       PIC X(4) VALUE "ABCD".
    ■ ■ ■
    STRING B DELIMITED "C" INTO A
      [A contains "ABYZ". ]
```

The specific *position* in *receiving-string* at which transmission is to begin is specified by the POINTER phrase:

```
                                    SIZE
                                    delimiter
    STRING send-string  DELIMITED  _____   INTO  receiving-string
       POINTER position
```

* *position*: A numeric integer data identifier (but not literal) specifying the first character position (the first character is number one) in *receiving-string* into which the *send-string* characters are to be transmitted. It is incremented by one as each character is transmitted. On completion of the statement, it points one character beyond the last character transmitted. The POSITION phrase is optional, and position 1 is assumed if it is omitted.

```
01  A                          PIC X(4) VALUE "WXYZ".
01  B                          PIC S9(4) BINARY VALUE 3.
    ■ ■ ■
    STRING "AB" DELIMITED SIZE INTO A POINTER B
      [A contains "WXAB", and B contains 5.]
```

The STRING statement can also concatenate character strings by listing several *send-strings*. The strings are concatenated by appending one string to the end of another to form a new string. Thus, "AB" concatenated with "CD" yields a new string containing "ABCD". The POINTER clause is optional.

```
                                    SIZE
                                    delimiter
    STRING send-string-1 DELIMITED  _____  ,
                                    SIZE
                                    delimiter
           send-string-2 DELIMITED  _____  ,
                      .
                      .
                      .
                                    SIZE
                                    delimiter
           send-string-n DELIMITED  _____
    INTO  receiving-string  POINTER  position
```

For example:

```
    STRING "AB" DELIMITED SIZE,
           "CD" DELIMITED SIZE
      INTO A
        [A contains "ABCD".]
```

You can detect error conditions by appending the ON OVERFLOW phrase to the end of the STRING statement. The error condition occurs when *position* is less than 1 or greater than the size of *receiving-string*. If the ON OVERFLOW phrase is not coded, execution continues with the next executable statement when an error condition occurs. Code an END-STRING explicit scope delimiter after the ON OVERFLOW phrase. (You can code END-STRING even if you don't code an ON OVERFLOW phrase.)

```
STRING "AB" DELIMITED SIZE INTO A POINTER B
  ON OVERFLOW PERFORM B30-ERROR
END-STRING
```

You can also code a NOT ON OVERFLOW phrase, with or without an ON OVERFLOW phrase:

```
STRING "AB" DELIMITED SIZE INTO A POINTER B
  ON OVERFLOW PERFORM B30-ERROR
  NOT ON OVERFLOW PERFORM C30-PROCESS
END-STRING

STRING "AB" DELIMITED SIZE INTO A POINTER B
  NOT ON OVERFLOW PERFORM C30-PROCESS
END-STRING
```

B. The UNSTRING Statement

The UNSTRING statement selects strings or substrings from one string and stores them in one or more receiving fields. The simplest form of the UNSTRING statement transmits the characters in the *send-string* into the *receiving-string* and is identical to the MOVE statement:

```
UNSTRING send-string INTO receiving-string
```

Same as:

```
MOVE send-string TO receiving-string
```

- *send-string*: An alphanumeric USAGE DISPLAY identifier containing the characters to be transmitted. It cannot be reference-modified. Use the POINTER phrase instead.
- *receiving-string*: The USAGE DISPLAY identifier into which the characters in *send-string* are transmitted. You can reference-modify it: *receiving-string(n:m)*. It cannot be an alphanumeric-edited or numeric edited data item. If numeric, it cannot be floating-point or have a P in its PIC phrase. Characters in *send-string* are transmitted from left to right into *receiving-string* until the rightmost character in *send-string* is transmitted or *receiving-string* is filled. The transmission is performed as if it were a MOVE, so *receiving-string* is padded on the right with blanks if it is not filled.

```
01  A                        PIC X(2) VALUE "AB".
01  B                        PIC X(4) VALUE "WXYZ".
    ■ ■ ■
    UNSTRING A INTO B    [B contains "ABbb".]
```

Note that this form of UNSTRING is identical to a MOVE:

```
MOVE "AB" TO B          [B contains "ABbb".]
```

You can also terminate transmission by *delimiter* characters specified in the DELIMITED phrase.

```
UNSTRING send-string DELIMITED delimiter
    INTO receiving-string
```

• *delimiter*: A figurative constant, nonnumeric literal, or USAGE DISPLAY alphanumeric identifier. (Note that you can't code DELIMITED SIZE for UNSTRING.) Transmission terminates if the *delimiter* characters are encountered in *send-string*. A *delimiter* containing more than one character is treated as a unit. The *delimiter* characters themselves are not transmitted. All characters in *send-string* are transmitted if the *delimiter* is not encountered.

The following example shows how the DELIMITED phrase limits the characters transmitted:

```
01  A                         PIC X(5) VALUE "ABCDE".
01  D                         PIC X(6) VALUE "111111".
    ■ ■ ■
    UNSTRING A DELIMITED "C" INTO D
      [D contains "AB1111". ]
```

You can specify several strings as the delimiter. Just connect them with OR. VS COBOL II allows a maximum of 255 strings.

```
UNSTRING send-string DELIMITED delimiter  OR delimiter  OR ...

UNSTRING A DELIMITED "B" OR "C" INTO D
  [D contains "A1111". Transmission stops if either "B" or "C" is encountered in A.]
```

You specify the *position* in *send-string* at which to begin transmission by coding the POINTER phrase.

```
UNSTRING send-string DELIMITED delimiter  INTO receiving-string
    POINTER position
```

• *position*: A numeric integer identifier specifying the first character position (the first character is position 1) in *send-string* from which transmission is to begin. Note that POINTER applies to the *send-string* in UNSTRING, not to the *receiving-string* as in STRING. It is incremented by 1 as each character is examined. If DELIMITED is coded and the *delimiter* is encountered, this is one character beyond the *delimiter* in *send-string*; otherwise it is one beyond the last character transmitted. The POSITION phrase is optional, and *position* 1 is assumed if omitted.

```
01  A                              PIC X(4) VALUE "WXYZ".
01  B                              PIC X(4) VALUE "1234".
01  C                              PIC S9(4) BINARY VALUE 2.
    ■ ■ ■
    UNSTRING A INTO B POINTER C
      [B contains "YZ34", and C contains  5.]
```

You can also count the number of characters stored in the *receiving-string* by including a COUNT phrase. You must also code the DELIMITED phrase when you code the COUNT phrase. Both the COUNT and POINTER phrases are optional.

```
UNSTRING send-string  DELIMITED delimiter  INTO receiving-string
  COUNT count
  POINTER position
```

- *count*: A numeric integer identifier that is set to the number of characters moved into *receiving-string*. The *count* does not need to contain an initial value, because the count is moved to it as if by a MOVE. (The *delimiter* characters are not counted.)

```
01  A                              PIC X(4) VALUE "WXYZ".
01  B                              PIC X(4) VALUE "1234".
01  C                              PIC S9(4) BINARY VALUE 2.
01  D                              PIC S9(4) BINARY.
    ■ ■ ■
    UNSTRING A DELIMITED SPACE INTO B COUNT D POINTER C
      [B contains "YZ34",  D contains 2, and C contains  5.]
```

The next form of UNSTRING retrieves the delimiter characters:

```
UNSTRING send-string  DELIMITED delimiter  INTO receiving-string
  DELIMITER save-delimiter
  COUNT count
  POINTER position
```

The DELIMITER phrase (not to be confused with the DELIMITED phrase) specifies a USAGE DISPLAY identifier into which a *delimiter* is stored when encountered in *send-string*. The COUNT and POINTER phrases are optional. You must also code the DELIMITED phrase when you code the DELIMITER phrase.

- *save-delimiter*: A USAGE DISPLAY alphanumeric identifier into which the *delimiters* are stored when encountered. When a delimiter is encountered, it is moved to *save-delimiter* as if by a MOVE. If no delimiter is encountered, *save-delimiter* is filled with spaces.

```
01  A                              PIC X(6) VALUE "UVWXYZ".
01  B                              PIC X(6) VALUE "111111".
01  D                              PIC X(6) VALUE SPACES.
```

```
01  COUNT-1                          PIC S9(4) BINARY.
01  POINTER-1                        PIC S9(4) BINARY VALUE 2.
    ■ ■ ■
UNSTRING A DELIMITED "Y" INTO B
  DELIMITER D
  COUNT COUNT-1
  POINTER POINTER-1
```

[*Beginning with the second character in* A, *the three characters up to but not including the* "Y" *are moved to* B. *The delimiter* "Y" *is encountered and is moved to* D. *Since three characters are moved, 3 is moved to* COUNT-1. *At the end of the statement,* B *contains* "VWX111", D *contains* "Ybbbbb", COUNT-1 *contains 3, and* POINTER-1 *contains 5.*]

UNSTRING can separate the *send-string* into several *receiving-strings*. The DELIMITER and COUNT phrases are optional with each *receiving-string*. A TALLYING phrase can specify a numeric integer identifier that is incremented each time a new substring is transmitted.

```
UNSTRING send-string  DELIMITED delimiter
INTO receiving-string-1  DELIMITER save-1  COUNT count-1,
     receiving-string-2  DELIMITER save-2  COUNT count-2,
     ⋮
     receiving-string-n  DELIMITER save-n  COUNT count-n
POINTER position
TALLYING tally
```

• *tally:* A numeric integer identifier that is incremented as each successive *receiving-string* is filled. You must set *tally* to an initial value, usually zero, before executing UNSTRING.

Characters are first transmitted from *send-string,* beginning at the *position* specified, into *receiving-string-1*. When a *delimiter* is encountered, it is moved to *save-1, count-1* is set to the count of characters stored in *receiving-string-1,* and *tally* is incremented by one (assuming that DELIMITER, COUNT, and TALLYING phrases are coded). Characters following the *delimiter* are transmitted into *receiving- string-2* until another *delimiter* is encountered. The *delimiter* is moved to *save-2, count-2* is set to the count of characters moved, and *tally* is incremented by 1. Transmission continues until all *receiving-strings* are filled, or all characters in *send-string* are transmitted. If *receiving-string-n* is filled before a *delimiter* is encountered, blanks are moved to *save-n,* and transmission continues into the next *receiving-string* with the character following the last character transmitted.

You can specify more than one *delimiter* by connecting them with OR. Transmission stops if any *delimiter* is encountered in *send-string*.

```
DELIMITED "A" OR "B" OR "C"
```

If two *delimiters* are encountered in succession, the next *receiving-string* is filled with blanks, and any count for it is set to zero.

You can code ALL before the *delimiter* to treat successive occurrences of the *delimiter* as a single occurrence. For example, DELIMITED ALL "A" OR ALL "B" would treat the *send-string* "WAAXBBBY" as if it were "WAXBY".

You can append the ON OVERFLOW phrase to the end of UNSTRING to detect overflow when *position* has a value less than 1 or greater than the size of *send-string* during execution. ON OVERFLOW also executes when all receiving fields have been filled but not all characters in *send-string* have been examined. If ON OVERFLOW is not coded, execution continues with the next executable statement. You must code END-UNSTRING when you code ON OVERFLOW:

```
UNSTRING send-string DELIMITED delimiter
    INTO receiving-string-1  DELIMITER save-1  COUNT count-1,
         receiving-string-2  DELIMITER save-2  COUNT count-2,
         receiving-string-n  DELIMITER save-n  COUNT count-n
    POINTER position
    TALLYING tally
    ON OVERFLOW imperative-statements
END-UNSTRING
```

You can also code NOT ON OVERFLOW with or without ON OVERFLOW:

```
UNSTRING send-string DELIMITED delimiter
    INTO receiving-string-1  DELIMITER save-1  COUNT count-1,
         receiving-string-2  DELIMITER save-2  COUNT count-2,
         receiving-string-n  DELIMITER save-n  COUNT count-n
    POINTER position
    TALLYING tally
    ON OVERFLOW imperative-statements
    NOT ON OVERFLOW imperative-statements
END-UNSTRING
```

```
UNSTRING send-string DELIMITED delimiter
    INTO receiving-string-1  DELIMITER save-1  COUNT count-1,
         receiving-string-2  DELIMITER save-2  COUNT count-2,
         receiving-string-n  DELIMITER save-n  COUNT count-n
    POINTER position
    TALLYING tally
    NOT ON OVERFLOW imperative-statements
END-UNSTRING
```

The following example illustrates the execution of UNSTRING.

```
MOVE "BALLYbJAZZbTOPAZbA" TO SAVE-IT
UNSTRING SAVE-IT DELIMITED "Z" OR ALL "L"
    INTO B1 DELIMITER S1 COUNT C1,
         B2 DELIMITER S2 COUNT C2,
         B3 DELIMITER S3 COUNT C3,
         B4 DELIMITER S4 COUNT C4
```

```
      TALLYING T
      ON OVERFLOW PERFORM C60-ERROR
   END-UNSTRING
```

Execution proceeds as follows:

- "BA" is stored in B1, "L" is stored in S1, and C1 is set to 2.
- "YbJA" is stored in B2, "Z" is stored in S2, and C2 is set to 4.
- Blanks are stored in B3, "Z" is stored in S3, and C3 is set to 0.
- "bTOPA" is stored in B4, "Z" is stored in S3, and C4 is set to 5.
- T is set to 4.
- The C60-ERROR procedure is performed.

Such a statement constitutes almost an entire program by itself, and you might have to make a flow chart of it to understand what it does. STRING and UNSTRING are difficult statements to write, and they make programs difficult to read. Use them sparingly, and include comments to explain what they are intended to do.

As another, more practical, example, we'll use UNSTRING to take apart a first name, middle initial, and last name:

```
01  NO-FIELDS                    PIC S9(4) BINARY.
01  FIRST-NAME                   PIC X(10) VALUE SPACES.
01  MIDDLE-INIT                  PIC X(10) VALUE SPACES.
01  LAST-NAME                    PIC X(10) VALUE SPACES.
01  THE-NAME                     PIC X(55)
                                 VALUE "LEWIS N. CLARK".
     ■ ■ ■
   MOVE ZERO TO NO-FIELDS
   UNSTRING THE-NAME DELIMITED " "
     INTO FIRST-NAME
          MIDDLE-INIT
          LAST-NAME
     TALLYING NO-FIELDS
        [NO-FIELDS counts how many names we pick up.]
     ON OVERFLOW
          [Here for normal end.]
        PERFORM A10-NORMAL
     NOT ON OVERFLOW
          [Here if characters left to examine.]
        PERFORM A10-MORE-NAMES
   END-UNSTRING
[FIRST-NAME contains "LEWIS", MIDDLE-INIT contains "N.", and LAST-NAME contains
 "CLARK". NO-FIELDS contains 3.]
```

At the beginning of this section, several types of character manipulation were discussed:

- Determine if a string contains "LAMB".
- Concatenate two strings together to form a new string.
- Find the string "LITTLE LAMB" in the concatenated string and move it to another string.
- Replace "LAMB" with "TOFU" in the concatenated string.
- Replace "LITTLE" with "BIG" in the concatenated string.

Here is a program that does each of these:

```
01  POINT-1                    PIC S9(4) BINARY.
01  NO-MOVED                   PIC S9(4) BINARY.
01  POINT-3                    PIC S9(4) BINARY.
01  POINT-4                    PIC S9(4) BINARY.
01  STRING-1                   PIC X(23) VALUE
                               "MARY HAD A LITTLE LAMB.".
01  STRING-2                   PIC X(29) VALUE
                       "ITS FLEECE WAS WHITE AS SNOW.".
01  STRING-3                   PIC X(55).
01  STRING-4                   PIC X(55).
01  STRING-5                   PIC X(55).
■ ■ ■
PROCEDURE DIVISION.
START-PROGRAM.
******************************************************************
* See if STRING-1 contains "LAMB"                                *
******************************************************************
    MOVE ZERO TO POINT-1
    INSPECT STRING-1 TALLYING POINT-1 FOR ALL "LAMB"
```
     [*If* POINT-1 > ZERO, STRING-1 *contains* "LAMB".]

```
******************************************************************
* Concatenate STRING-1 and STRING-2 into STRING-3.              *
******************************************************************
    MOVE SPACES TO STRING-3
```
     [*Clean out* STRING-3 *before we concatenate the strings into it.*]

```
    MOVE 1 TO POINT-1
```
     [POINT-1 *will point to where we want to copy the concatenated strings into* STRING-3.]

```
    STRING STRING-1 DELIMITED "." INTO STRING-3
      POINTER POINT-1
```
     [*Get everything up to the period in* STRING-1. STRING-3 *contains* "MARY HAD A LITTLE LAMB", *and* POINT-1 *now contains 23.*]

```
    STRING ".  " DELIMITED SIZE INTO STRING-3
      POINTER POINT-1
```
     [*Concatenate* ". " *to retain the period and two spaces following it.* STRING-3 *now contains* "MARY HAD A LITTLE LAMB. ", *and* POINT-1 *contains 26.*]

```
    STRING STRING-2 DELIMITED "." INTO STRING-3
```

```
    POINTER POINT-1
```

[*Concatenate everything up the period in* STRING-2 *to the end of* STRING-3.
STRING-3 *now contains* "MARY HAD A LITTLE LAMB. ITS FLEECE WAS WHITE AS
SNOW", *and* POINT-1 *contains 54.*]

```
    STRING "." DELIMITED SIZE INTO STRING-3
      POINTER POINT-1
```

[*Stick a period on the end of* STRING-3. STRING-3 *now contains* "MARY HAD A LITTLE
LAMB. ITS FLEECE WAS WHITE AS SNOW." POINT-1 *now contains 55.*]

```
****************************************************************
*  FIND string "LITTLE LAMB" and move it to STRING-4.         *
****************************************************************
    MOVE SPACES TO STRING-4
```

[*Clear out* STRING-4 *before we move* "LITTLE LAMB" *to it.*]

```
    MOVE 1 TO POINT-3
```

[POINT-3 *points to where* "LITTLE LAMB" *is in* STRING-3.]

```
    STRING STRING-3 DELIMITED "LITTLE LAMB" INTO STRING-5
      POINTER POINT-3
```

[*We don't care what goes into* STRING-5. *We just want to know where* "LITTLE LAMB"
is in STRING-3. POINT-3 *points to it and contains 12.*]

```
    IF POINT-3 > 1
       THEN MOVE STRING-3(POINT-3:11) TO STRING-4
```

[*We found* "LITTLE LAMB". *Move it to* STRING-4.]

```
    END-IF


****************************************************************
* Replace "LAMB" with "TOFU".                                 *
****************************************************************
   INSPECT STRING-3 REPLACING ALL "LAMB" BY "TOFU"
```

[*The* INSPECT *statement does this very simply.*]

```
****************************************************************
* Replace "LITTLE" with "BIG" and store in STRING-4.          *
****************************************************************
    MOVE SPACES TO STRING-4
```

[*Clear out* STRING-4 *before we copy into it.*]

```
    MOVE 1 TO POINT-3
```

[POINT-3 *will point to where we are searching in* STRING-3.]

```
    MOVE 1 TO POINT-4
```

[POINT-4 *will point where we want to move the concatenated characters into* STRING-4.]

```
    PERFORM WITH TEST AFTER UNTIL POINT-3 > LENGTH OF STRING-3
```

[*We continue until we are beyond the end of string* STRING-3.]

```
      UNSTRING STRING-3 DELIMITED "LITTLE" INTO STRING-5
        COUNT NO-MOVED
```

[NO-MOVED *counts how many characters were stored into* STRING-5.]

```
        POINTER POINT-3
```

[POINT-3 *points the starting character in* STRING-3 *that we want to examine.*]

```
        ON OVERFLOW
```

> [*We get to here if we found* "LITTLE" *in* STRING-3. STRING-5 *contains everything from where we started, up to but not including* "LITTLE". NO-MOVED *contains the number of characters moved to* STRING-5.]

```
MOVE STRING-5(1:NO-MOVED) TO
    STRING-4(POINT-4:NO-MOVED)
```

> [*We must move these characters to the end of* STRING-4.]

```
ADD NO-MOVED TO POINT-4
```

> [*Bump* POINT-4 *up by the number of characters we concatenated.*]

```
STRING "BIG" DELIMITED SIZE INTO STRING-4
        POINTER POINT-4
END-STRING
```

> [*Concatenate* "BIG" *to the end of* STRING-4 *and bump*
> POINT-4 *up by 3 for the three characters.*]

```
NOT ON OVERFLOW
```

> [*Here when no* "LITTLE" *found. All the characters from where we started to the end of* STRING-3 *are moved to* STRING-5. NO-MOVED *contains the number of characters moved.*]

```
IF NO-MOVED > ZERO THEN
    MOVE STRING-5(1:NO-MOVED) TO
        STRING-4(POINT-4:NO-MOVED)
```

> [*If we moved any characters to* STRING-5, *concatenate them to the end of*
> STRING-4.]

```
    ADD NO-MOVED TO POINT-4
```

> [*We don't really need to do this, but update* POINT- 4.]

```
    END-IF
  END-UNSTRING
END-PERFORM
```

> [STRING-4 *now contains* "MARY HAD A BIG TOFU. ITS FLEECE WAS WHITE AS
> SNOW."]

```
STOP RUN
```

```
END PROGRAM TEST.
```

III. OPERATIONS ON DATES

For the computer, it is best to carry the date in year/month/day order. This makes sorting much easier, because the entire date field can be sorted as a unit. Most applications carry the year as two digits, which will work wonderfully until the year 2000. Then it will be a disaster, because the year 2000 will suddenly sort in front of all the 19xx dates. This minor detail is going to keep thousands of maintenance programmers busy in the last year of this century. In designing records, keep the year as four digits to prevent this problem.

The ACCEPT statement described in Chapter 10 can retrieve the current time, date, and day of week. Several additional operations frequently performed on dates are shown in this section. For example, the sequential day of the year is often used in data processing, because it makes it easier to calculate the number of days between two dates. The ANSI standard and Microsoft COBOL have intrinsic functions that also operate on dates, as described in Appendix D.

A. Determining Days in Year

To determine the days in a year, we need to know if it is a leap year. For this, we'll write a general subprogram that is passed a year as a parameter in the CALL. It returns the number of days in the year and a value indicating whether it is a leap year:

```
77  THE-YEAR                    PIC 9(4).
77  DAYS-IN-YEAR                PIC S9(4) BINARY.
77  LEAP-YEAR                   PIC S9(4) BINARY.
*                                   0-Leap year.
*                                   1-Not a leap year.
    ■ ■ ■
    CALL "LEAPYR" USING BY CONTENT   THE-YEAR,
                       BY REFERENCE DAYS-IN-YEAR, LEAP-YEAR
```

The subprogram is written as follows:

```
IDENTIFICATION DIVISION.
    PROGRAM-ID. LEAPYR.
*******************************************************************
* SUBPROGRAM TO DETERMINE DAYS IN YEAR AND WHETHER LEAP YEAR. *
* CALL "LEAPYR" USING BY CONTENT   THE-YEAR,                  *
*                     BY REFERENCE DAYS-IN-YEAR, LEAP-YEAR    *
* IN:  THE-YEAR contains the year.  PIC X(4)                  *
* OUT: DAYS-IN-YEAR contains days in year--365 or 356.        *
*        PIC S9(4) BINARY                                     *
*     LEAP-YEAR set to ZERO if it is a leap year.             *
*        PIC S9(4) BINARY                                     *
*******************************************************************
DATA DIVISION.
WORKING-STORAGE SECTION.
77 TEMP-NUM                     PIC S9(4) BINARY.
LINKAGE SECTION.
77  THE-YEAR                    PIC 9(4).
77  DAYS-IN-YEAR                PIC S9(4) BINARY.
77  LEAP-YEAR                   PIC S9(4) BINARY.
*                                   0-Leap year.
*                                   1-Not a leap year.
PROCEDURE DIVISION
    USING THE-YEAR, DAYS-IN-YEAR, LEAP-YEAR.
START-PROGRAM.
    DIVIDE THE-YEAR BY 4 GIVING TEMP-NUM REMAINDER LEAP-YEAR
    IF LEAP-YEAR = ZERO
       THEN MOVE 366 TO DAYS-IN-YEAR
       ELSE MOVE 365 TO DAYS-IN-YEAR
    END-IF
```

```
    EXIT PROGRAM
        .
END PROGRAM LEAPYR.
```

B. Compute Age

The next subprogram computes an age, given a birth date and the current date:

```
01  BIRTH-DATE.
    05  BD-YY                    PIC 9(4).
    05  BD-MM                    PIC 99.
    05  BD-DD                    PIC 99.
01  CURRENT-DATE.
    05  CD-YY                    PIC 9(4).
    05  CD-MM                    PIC 99.
    05  CD-DD                    PIC 99.
77  AGE                         PIC S9(4) BINARY.
    ■ ■ ■
    CALL "THEAGE" USING BY CONTENT   BIRTH-DATE, CURRENT-DATE,
                        BY REFERENCE AGE
```

The subprogram is written as follows:

```
IDENTIFICATION DIVISION.
    PROGRAM-ID. THEAGE.
****************************************************************
* SUBPROGRAM TO COMPUTE AGE GIVEN BIRTH DATE.               *
* CALL "THEAGE" USING BY CONTENT   BIRTH-DATE, CURRENT-DATE, *
*                     BY REFERENCE AGE                       *
* IN:  BIRTH-DATE:  Birth date as yyyymmdd. PIC X(8)        *
*       CURRENT-DATE:  Date as yyyymmdd.    PIC X(8)        *
* OUT: AGE contains the age.                PIC S9(4) BINARY *
****************************************************************
DATA DIVISION.
WORKING-STORAGE SECTION.
LINKAGE SECTION.
01  BIRTH-DATE.
    05  BD-YY                    PIC 9(4).
    05  BD-MM                    PIC 99.
    05  BD-DD                    PIC 99.
01  CURRENT-DATE.
    05  CD-YY                    PIC 9(4).
    05  CD-MM                    PIC 99.
    05  CD-DD                    PIC 99.
77  AGE                         PIC S9(4) BINARY.
```

```
PROCEDURE DIVISION
    USING BIRTH-DATE, CURRENT-DATE, AGE.
START-PROGRAM.
    IF BIRTH-DATE(1:4) >= CURRENT-DATE(1:4)
        THEN COMPUTE AGE = CD-YY - BD-YY
        ELSE COMPUTE AGE = CD-YY - BD-YY - 1
    END-IF
    EXIT PROGRAM
    .
END PROGRAM THEAGE.
```

C. Convert Calendar Date to Year and Day of Year

This subprogram converts a calendar date to a year and day of year (1 to 366):

```
01  YRNDAY-DATE.
    05  YRNDAY-YEAR            PIC 9(4).
    05  YRNDAY-DAYS            PIC S9(4) BINARY.
01  CURRENT-DATE.
    05  CD-YY                  PIC 9(4).
    05  CD-MM                  PIC 99.
    05  CD-DD                  PIC 99.
    ■ ■ ■
    CALL "TOYRNDAY" USING BY CONTENT  CURRENT-DATE,
                    BY REFERENCE YRNDAY-DATE
```

The subprogram can now be written as follows:

```
IDENTIFICATION DIVISION.
    PROGRAM-ID. TOYRNDAY.
****************************************************************
* SUBPROGRAM TO CONVERT CALENDAR DATE TO YEAR AND DAY OF   *
*   YEAR.                                                  *
* CALL "TOYRNDAY" USING BY CONTENT  CURRENT-DATE,          *
*                    BY REFERENCE YRNDAY-DATE              *
* IN:  CALENDAR-DATE contains data as yyyymmdd.  PIC X(8)  *
* OUT: YRNDAY-DATE contains the date described as:         *
*      01  YRNDAY-DATE.                                    *
*          05  YRNDAY-YEAR            PIC 9(4).            *
*          05  YRNDAY-DAYS            PIC S9(4) BINARY.    *
****************************************************************
DATA DIVISION.
WORKING-STORAGE SECTION.
01 MONTH-TABLE.
```

```
    05   MONTH-TBL-VALUES.
         10   MONTH-TBL-JAN          PIC S9(4) BINARY VALUE 31.
         10   MONTH-TBL-FEB          PIC S9(4) BINARY.
         10   MONTH-TBL-MAR          PIC S9(4) BINARY VALUE 31.
         10   MONTH-TBL-APR          PIC S9(4) BINARY VALUE 30.
         10   MONTH-TBL-MAY          PIC S9(4) BINARY VALUE 31.
         10   MONTH-TBL-JUN          PIC S9(4) BINARY VALUE 30.
         10   MONTH-TBL-JLY          PIC S9(4) BINARY VALUE 31.
         10   MONTH-TBL-AUG          PIC S9(4) BINARY VALUE 31.
         10   MONTH-TBL-SEP          PIC S9(4) BINARY VALUE 30.
         10   MONTH-TBL-OCT          PIC S9(4) BINARY VALUE 31.
         10   MONTH-TBL-NOV          PIC S9(4) BINARY VALUE 30.
         10   MONTH-TBL-DEC          PIC S9(4) BINARY VALUE 31.
    05   MONTH-TBL                   REDEFINES MONTH-TBL-VALUES
                                     OCCURS 12 TIMES
                                     INDEXED BY MX
                                     PIC S9(4) BINARY.
77  DAYS-IN-YEAR                     PIC S9(4) BINARY.
77  LEAP-YEAR                        PIC S9(4) BINARY.
LINKAGE SECTION.
01 YRNDAY-DATE.
    05   YRNDAY-YEAR                 PIC 9(4).
    05   YRNDAY-DAYS                 PIC S9(4) BINARY.
01  CURRENT-DATE.
    05   CD-YY                       PIC 9(4).
    05   CD-MM                       PIC 99.
    05   CD-DD                       PIC 99.
PROCEDURE DIVISION
    USING CURRENT-DATE, YRNDAY-DATE.
START-PROGRAM.
* First, determine the number of days in February for
*    MONTH-TBL table.
     CALL "LEAPYR" USING CURRENT-DATE, DAYS-IN-YEAR, LEAP-YEAR
     IF LEAP-YEAR = ZERO
       THEN MOVE 29 TO MONTH-TBL(2)
       ELSE MOVE 28 TO MONTH-TBL(2)
     END-IF
     MOVE ZEROS TO YRNDAY-DAYS
     PERFORM VARYING MX FROM 1 BY 1 UNTIL MX = CD-MM
        ADD MONTH-TBL(MX) TO YRNDAY-DAYS
     END-PERFORM
     ADD CD-DD TO YRNDAY-DAYS
     MOVE CD-YY TO YRNDAY-YEAR
     EXIT PROGRAM
     .

END PROGRAM TOYRNDAY.
```

D. Convert Year and Day of Year to Calendar Date

This subprogram converts a year and day of year to a calendar date.

```
01 YRNDAY-DATE.
    05  YRNDAY-YEAR                 PIC 9(4).
    05  YRNDAY-DAYS                 PIC S9(4) BINARY.
01  CURRENT-DATE.
    05  CD-YY                       PIC 9(4).
    05  CD-MM                       PIC 99.
    05  CD-DD                       PIC 99.
    ▪ ▪ ▪
    CALL "TOCAL" USING BY CONTENT  YRNDAY-DATE,
                       BY REFERENCE CURRENT-DATE
```

The subprogram can now be written as follows:

```
IDENTIFICATION DIVISION.
    PROGRAM-ID. TOCAL.
****************************************************************
* SUBPROGRAM TO CONVERT CALENDAR DATE TO YEAR AND DAY OF   *
*   YEAR.                                                  *
* CALL "TOCAL" USING BY CONTENT  YRNDAY-DATE,              *
*                    BY REFERENCE CURRENT-DATE             *
* IN:  YRNDAY-DATE contains the date described as:        *
*       01  YRNDAY-DATE.                                   *
*           05  YRNDAY-YEAR          PIC 9(4).             *
*           05  YRNDAY-DAYS          PIC S9(4) BINARY.     *
* OUT: CALENDAR-DATE contains date as yyyymmdd.  PIC X(8) *
****************************************************************
DATA DIVISION.
WORKING-STORAGE SECTION.
77  DAYS-IN-YEAR                PIC S9(4) BINARY.
77  LEAP-YEAR                   PIC S9(4) BINARY.
77  TEMP-NUM                    PIC S9(4) BINARY.
01 MONTH-TABLE.
    05  MONTH-TBL-VALUES.
        10  MONTH-TBL-JAN           PIC S9(4) BINARY VALUE 31.
        10  MONTH-TBL-FEB           PIC S9(4) BINARY.
        10  MONTH-TBL-MAR           PIC S9(4) BINARY VALUE 31.
        10  MONTH-TBL-APR           PIC S9(4) BINARY VALUE 30.
        10  MONTH-TBL-MAY           PIC S9(4) BINARY VALUE 31.
        10  MONTH-TBL-JUN           PIC S9(4) BINARY VALUE 30.
        10  MONTH-TBL-JLY           PIC S9(4) BINARY VALUE 31.
        10  MONTH-TBL-AUG           PIC S9(4) BINARY VALUE 31.
        10  MONTH-TBL-SEP           PIC S9(4) BINARY VALUE 30.
        10  MONTH-TBL-OCT           PIC S9(4) BINARY VALUE 31.
```

```
           10   MONTH-TBL-NOV          PIC S9(4) BINARY VALUE 30.
           10   MONTH-TBL-DEC          PIC S9(4) BINARY VALUE 31.
        05   MONTH-TBL                 REDEFINES MONTH-TBL-VALUES
                                       OCCURS 12 TIMES
                                       INDEXED BY MX
                                       PIC S9(4) BINARY.
   LINKAGE SECTION.
   01 YRNDAY-DATE.
       05   YRNDAY-YEAR                PIC 9(4).
       05   YRNDAY-DAYS                PIC S9(4) BINARY.
   01 CURRENT-DATE.
       05   CD-YY                      PIC 9(4).
       05   CD-MM                      PIC 99.
       05   CD-DD                      PIC 99.
   PROCEDURE DIVISION
      USING YRNDAY-DATE, CURRENT-DATE.
   START-PROGRAM.
   * First, determine the number of days in February for
   *    MONTH-TBL table.
        CALL "LEAPYR" USING CURRENT-DATE, DAYS-IN-YEAR, LEAP-YEAR
        IF LEAP-YEAR = ZERO
           THEN MOVE 29 TO MONTH-TBL(2)
           ELSE MOVE 28 TO MONTH-TBL(2)
        END-IF
        MOVE YRNDAY-DAYS TO TEMP-NUM
        PERFORM VARYING MX FROM 1 BY 1
               UNTIL TEMP-NUM <= MONTH-TBL(MX)
          COMPUTE TEMP-NUM = TEMP-NUM - MONTH-TBL(MX)
        END-PERFORM
        MOVE TEMP-NUM TO CD-DD
        SET CD-MM TO MX
        MOVE YRNDAY-YEAR TO CD-YY
        EXIT PROGRAM
          .
   END PROGRAM TOCAL.
```

E. Compute Days Between Two Dates

This subprogram computes the elapsed days between two dates:

```
01   FIRST-DATE.
     05   BD-YY                        PIC 9(4).
     05   BD-MM                        PIC 99.
     05   BD-DD                        PIC 99.
01   LAST-DATE.
     05   CD-YY                        PIC 9(4).
```

```
    05  CD-MM                      PIC 99.
    05  CD-DD                      PIC 99.
01  NO-DAYS                        PIC S9(9) BINARY.
    ■ ■ ■
    CALL "DAYSTWEEN" USING BY CONTENT  FIRST-DATE, LAST-DATE,
                       BY REFERENCE NO-DAYS
```

The subprogram can now be written as follows. To compute the days between
two dates, the program converts the dates to year and day form.

```
IDENTIFICATION DIVISION.
    PROGRAM-ID. DAYSTWEEN.
*******************************************************************
* SUBPROGRAM TO CALCULATE DAYS BETWEEN TWO DATES.               *
* CALL "DAYSTWEEN" USING BY CONTENT   FIRST-DATE, LAST-DATE,    *
*                       BY REFERENCE NO-DAYS                     *
* IN:  FIRST-DATE as yyyymmdd.  PIC X(8)                        *
*        LAST-DATE as yyyymmdd   PIC X(8)                       *
* OUT: NO-DAYS is number of days between the two.               *
*        PIC X9(4) BINARY.                                       *
*******************************************************************
DATA DIVISION.
WORKING-STORAGE SECTION.
01  FIRST-YRNDAY.
    05  FIRST-YEAR                 PIC 9(4).
    05  FIRST-DAYS                 PIC S9(4) BINARY.
01  LAST-YRNDAY.
    05  LAST-YEAR                  PIC 9(4).
    05  LAST-DAYS                  PIC S9(4) BINARY.
77  HOLD-YEARS                     PIC 9(4).
77  DAYS-IN-YEAR                   PIC S9(4) BINARY.
77  LEAP-YEAR                      PIC S9(4) BINARY.
LINKAGE SECTION.
01  FIRST-DATE.
    05  FD-YY                      PIC 9(4).
    05  FD-MM                      PIC 99.
    05  FD-DD                      PIC 99.
01  LAST-DATE.
    05  LD-YY                      PIC 9(4).
    05  LD-MM                      PIC 99.
    05  LD-DD                      PIC 99.
01  NO-DAYS                        PIC S9(9) BINARY.
PROCEDURE DIVISION
    USING FIRST-DATE, LAST-DATE, NO-DAYS.
START-PROGRAM.
*  First, convert the calendar dates to year and day form.
    CALL "TOYRNDAY" USING FIRST-DATE, FIRST-YRNDAY
```

```
      CALL "TOYRNDAY" USING LAST-DATE, LAST-YRNDAY
      IF LAST-YEAR = FIRST-YEAR
         THEN COMPUTE NO-DAYS = LAST-DAYS - FIRST-DAYS
         ELSE MOVE FIRST-YEAR TO HOLD-YEARS
              PERFORM UNTIL HOLD-YEARS = LAST-YEAR
                 CALL "LEAPYR" USING HOLD-YEARS, DAYS-IN-YEAR,
                                     LEAP-YEAR
                 IF HOLD-YEARS = FIRST-YEAR
                    THEN COMPUTE NO-DAYS = DAYS-IN-YEAR + 1 -
                                           FIRST-DAYS
                    ELSE COMPUTE NO-DAYS = NO-DAYS + DAYS-IN-YEAR
                 END-IF
                 ADD 1 TO HOLD-YEARS
              END-PERFORM
      END-IF
      EXIT PROGRAM

 END PROGRAM DAYSTWEEN.
```

IV. CHARACTER MANIPULATION AND VARIABLE-LENGTH CHARACTER STRINGS

COBOL variable-length character strings are defined as a table of characters with an OCCURS DEPENDING ON phrase. The OCCURS DEPENDING ON form allows the INSPECT, STRING, and UNSTRING statements to operate on the current length of the character string.

```
01  S-A-DEF.
    05  S-A-L                    PIC 9(9) BINARY.
    05  S-A.
        10  S-A-ITEM             OCCURS 1 TO 30 TIMES
                                 DEPENDING ON S-A-L
                                 PIC X.
```

You can treat any character string as a variable-length character string by defining a numeric data item for the string that contains the string length. Always define the string length as a PIC 9(9) BINARY data item. The LENGTH OF special register is defined as this, and is often used in subprogram calls.

```
01  S-B-DEF.
    05  S-B-L                    PIC 9(9) BINARY.
    05  S-B                      PIC X(30).
```

When strings in this form are used in the INSPECT, STRING, and UNSTRING statement, you must use reference modification in the statement:

```
    INSPECT S-B(1:S-B-L) ...
```

For our example of variable-length character strings, we'll define a record containing one identifier as a string and another identifier as current length. These items wouldn't have to be in the same structure and can be any level items. It won't matter for the processing we will be doing.

A. Find First Nonblank Character in String

We'll find the first nonblank character position in the string and store the position in T-NUM. ZEROS are stored in T-NUM if there is no nonblank character. We'll define T-NUM as follows.

```
77  T-NUM                        PIC 9(9) BINARY.
```

The first example operates on the variable-length string:

```
MOVE 1 TO T-NUM
INSPECT S-A
  TALLYING T-NUM FOR LEADING SPACES
IF T-NUM > S-A-L
  THEN MOVE ZERO TO T-NUM
END-IF
  [T-NUM contains 3.]
```

The next example operates on the fixed-length string, in which the length of the string is kept in a separate data item:

```
MOVE 14 TO S-B-L
MOVE "  123THE7890  " TO S-B
MOVE 1 TO T-NUM
INSPECT S-B(1:S-B-L)
  TALLYING T-NUM FOR LEADING SPACES
IF T-NUM > S-B-L
  THEN MOVE ZERO TO T-NUM
END-IF
  [T-NUM contains 3.]
```

Reference modification also works for the variable-length string:

```
MOVE 1 TO T-NUM
INSPECT S-A(1:S-A-L)
  TALLYING T-NUM FOR LEADING SPACES
IF T-NUM > S-A-L
  THEN MOVE ZERO TO T-NUM
END-IF
  [T-NUM contains 3.]
```

Since reference modification works for both fixed- and variable-length strings, we'll use it in the following examples, because it is more general.

Rather than using the INSPECT statement, we could also use a PERFORM VARYING statement to look at the characters one at a time to find the first nonblank character. This illustrates how PERFORM VARYING can operate on character strings:

```
PERFORM WITH TEST BEFORE
        VARYING T-NUM FROM 1 BY 1
        UNTIL S-B(T-NUM:1) NOT = SPACE OR
            T-NUM > S-B-L
END-PERFORM
IF T-NUM > S-B-L
   THEN MOVE ZERO TO T-NUM
END-IF
   [T-NUM contains 3.]
```

B. Find Rightmost Nonblank Character in String

To find the rightmost nonblank character position in a string, we must use the PERFORM so we can search the string from right to left:

```
MOVE 14 TO S-B-L
MOVE "  123THE7890  " TO S-B
PERFORM WITH TEST BEFORE
        VARYING T-NUM FROM S-B-L BY -1
        UNTIL S-B(T-NUM:1) NOT = SPACE OR
            T-NUM = ZERO
END-PERFORM
   [T-NUM contains 12.]
```

C. Left-Justify String

We'll left-justify the characters in S-B by finding the first nonblank character and then move the substring starting there to temporary storage. Then we move this result back to S-B:

```
MOVE 1 TO T-NUM
INSPECT S-B(1:S-B-L)
   TALLYING T-NUM FOR LEADING SPACES
      [T-NUM contains 5, the position of the first nonblank character in S-B.]
IF T-NUM > 1 AND <= S-B-L
        [Must account for a null string.]
   THEN MOVE S-B(T-NUM:) TO T-CHAR
        MOVE T-CHAR TO S-B
          [S-B contains "123THE7890".]
END-IF
```

D. Right-Justify String

We'll right-justify the characters in S-B by searching from right to left for the
first nonblank character. We'll then move the string to temporary storage so that
this rightmost character becomes the rightmost character in the target string.
We'll define a string to contain the intermediate results:

```
77  T-CHAR                       PIC X(30).
    ■ ■ ■
    PERFORM WITH TEST BEFORE
            VARYING T-NUM FROM S-B-L BY -1
            UNTIL S-B(T-NUM:1) NOT = SPACE OR
                    T-NUM = ZERO
    END-PERFORM
      [T-NUM now contains 12, the rightmost nonblank character position in S-B.]
    IF T-NUM > ZERO AND < S-B-L
        [Account for a null string.]
      THEN COMPUTE T-NUM = S-B-L - T-NUM + 1
            [T-NUM = 14 - 12 + 1 = 3.]
          MOVE S-B TO T-CHAR(T-NUM:)
            [Move S-B to T-CHAR, starting in byte 3. T-CHAR contains "123THE7890".]
          MOVE T-CHAR TO S-B
            [S-B contains "    123THE7890".]
    END-IF
```

E. Create Substring of Leftmost Characters

We'll move the five leftmost characters of S-B to T-CHAR. T-CHAR will contain
"123TH", and T-NUM will contain 5.

```
    MOVE 5 TO T-NUM
    MOVE S-B(1:T-NUM) TO T-CHAR
```

F. Create Substring of Rightmost Characters

We'll move the four rightmost characters of S-B to T-CHAR. T-CHAR will
contain "7890", and T-NUM will contain 4. We need another numeric variable
to contain a pointer to the first character to move.

```
77  F-NUM                        PIC 9(9) BINARY.
    ■ ■ ■
    MOVE 4 TO T-NUM
    COMPUTE F-NUM = S-B-L - T-NUM + 1
      [F-NUM = 10 - 4 + 1 = 7.]
```

```
MOVE S-B(F-NUM:T-NUM) TO T-CHAR
   [Bytes 7 to 10 are moved to T-CHAR.   T-CHAR contains "7890".]
```

G. Concatenate Characters to End of a Substring

We'll concatenate the characters "THE" to the end of the substring containing bytes 6 to the end of the string S-B and store the results in T-CHAR. It will contain "E7890THE", and T-NUM will contain 8.

```
MOVE 6 TO T-NUM
COMPUTE F-NUM = S-B-L - T-NUM + 1
   [F-NUM = 10 - 6 + 1 = 5.]
MOVE S-B(T-NUM:F-NUM) TO T-CHAR
   [Bytes 6 to 10 are moved to T-CHAR.   It contains "E7890".]
MOVE "THE" TO T-CHAR(T-NUM + 1:3)
   ["THE" is moved to bytes 6 to 8 of S-B.   It contains "E7890THE".]
ADD 3 TO T-NUM
   [T-NUM = 3 + 5 = 8.]
```

H. Find First Instance of a Character in a String

We'll search the S-B string and get the position of the first "T" if it is in the string. T-NUM is to contain the position of the first "T"; it is to contain zero if there is no "T".

```
MOVE 1 TO T-NUM
INSPECT S-B(1:S-B-L)
   TALLYING T-NUM FOR CHARACTERS
   BEFORE "T"
IF T-NUM > S-B-L
   THEN MOVE ZEROS TO T-NUM
END-IF
   [T-NUM contains 4.]
```

I. Find First String in Another String

This is the same as the previous example, but we'll search for the word "THE".

```
MOVE 1 TO T-NUM
INSPECT S-B(1:S-B-L)
   TALLYING T-NUM FOR CHARACTERS
   BEFORE "THE"
IF T-NUM > S-B-L
   THEN MOVE ZEROS TO T-NUM
END-IF
   [T-NUM contains 4.]
```

J. Using Variable-Length Strings in CALL:
Subprogram to Left- or Right-Justify String

For this, we'll write a generalized subprogram to left- or right-justify a variable-length character string. We'll pass the subprogram a flag to tell whether to left- or right-justify the string, along with the string and its length. Although items in a subprogram are supposed to equal the length of the item in a call, it isn't necessary if we pass the length of the item in the CALL.

In the left and right justification above, we used a temporary storage area that was the same length as the string we were converting. In the subprogram, we can't do this, because the length is variable. Instead, we'll move the characters within the string one character at a time. Here's the subprogram:

```
IDENTIFICATION DIVISION.
    PROGRAM-ID. LRJUST.
************************************************************************
* PROCEDURE TO LEFT- OR RIGHT-JUSTIFY CHARACTERS IN STRING.          *
* CALL "LRJUST USING BY CONTENT L-OR-R,                              *
*                     BY REFERENCE S-A,                              *
*                     BY CONTENT S-A-L                               *
* IN:  L-OR-R contains "L":  Left-justify.              PIC X        *
*                      "R":  Right-justify.                          *
*       S-A is the string as PIC X(n).                               *
*       S-A-L is the length of the string as PIC 9(9) BINARY.        *
* OUT: S-A contains the string, left- or right-justified.           *
************************************************************************
DATA DIVISION.
WORKING-STORAGE SECTION.
01  FND-L                          PIC 9(9) BINARY.
*      This points to the leftmost or rightmost character.
01  FROM-L                         PIC 9(9) BINARY.
*      This points to character being sent.
01  TO-L                           PIC 9(9) BINARY.
*      This points to the receiving position.
LINKAGE SECTION.
01  L-OR-R                         PIC X.
*      "L": Convert to lower.  "R": Convert to upper.
01  S-A                            PIC X(1).
01  S-A-L                          PIC 9(9) BINARY.
PROCEDURE DIVISION USING L-OR-R, S-A, S-A-L.
    EVALUATE L-OR-R
      WHEN "L"
*         Left-justify the characters in S-A.
*         Find the leftmost nonblank character.
        MOVE 1 TO FND-L
        INSPECT S-A(1:S-A-L)
          TALLYING FND-L FOR LEADING SPACES
```

```
            IF FND-L <= S-A-L
*                   Move one character at a time, because moved
*                   characters may overlap.
*                   TO-L points to where we move to.
*                   FROM-L points to where we move from.
               THEN MOVE 1 TO TO-L
                    PERFORM VARYING FROM-L FROM FND-L BY 1
                          UNTIL FROM-L > S-A-L
                       MOVE S-A(FROM-L:1) TO S-A(TO-L:1)
                       ADD 1 TO TO-L
                    END-PERFORM
*                   Fill everything to the right with spaces.
*                   FND-L is number of spaces needed + 1.
                    MOVE SPACES TO S-A(TO-L:FND-L - 1)
            END-IF
        WHEN "R"
*           Right-justify the characters in S-A.
*           Find the rightmost nonblank character and
*           store in FND-L.
            PERFORM VARYING FND-L FROM S-A-L BY -1
                    UNTIL S-A(FND-L:1) NOT = SPACE OR
                          FND-L = ZERO
            END-PERFORM
            IF FND-L > ZERO AND < S-A-L
*                   TO-L points to where we move characters
*                   to.  Must move a character at a time,
*                   because they may overlap.
*                   TO-L points to where we move characters to.
               THEN MOVE S-A-L TO TO-L
                    PERFORM VARYING FROM-L FROM FND-L BY -1
                          UNTIL FROM-L = ZERO
                       MOVE S-A(FROM-L:1) TO S-A(TO-L:1)
                       SUBTRACT 1 FROM TO-L
                    END-PERFORM
*                   Now fill the left portion of string with
*                   spaces.
                    MOVE SPACES TO S-A(1:TO-L)
            END-IF
        END-EVALUATE
        EXIT PROGRAM

    END PROGRAM LRJUST.
```

To right-justify some string, we can make the following subprogram call. Notice that the LENGTH OF special register is used to obtain the length of the string for the CALL.

```
CALL "LRJUST" USING BY CONTENT "R",
                    BY REFERENCE SOME-STRING
                    BY CONTENT LENGTH OF SOME-STRING
```

To left-justify the string, we can make this call:

```
CALL "LRJUST" USING BY CONTENT "L",
                    BY REFERENCE SOME-STRING
                    BY CONTENT LENGTH OF SOME-STRING
```

K. Convert Characters to Lower-Case

We'll convert the characters in S-B to lower-case:

```
MOVE 10 TO S-B-L
MOVE "AZ3THe 89ZZZZZ" TO S-B
INSPECT S-B(1:S-B-L)
  CONVERTING "ABCDEFGHIJKLMNOPQRSTUVWXYZ" TO
             "abcdefghijklmnopqrstuvwxyz"
    [S-B contains "az3the 89zZZZZZ"]
```

You can also code the REPLACING ALL form of INSPECT for the conversion as follows. This takes longer to code, but on the PC it executes about 25 percent faster.

```
INSPECT S-B(1:S-B-L)
  REPLACING ALL "A" BY "a", "B" BY "b",
      "C" BY "c", "D" BY "d", "E" BY "e", "F" BY "f",
      "G" BY "g", "H" BY "h", "I" BY "i", "J" BY "j",
      "K" BY "k", "L" BY "l", "M" BY "m", "N" BY "n",
      "O" BY "o", "P" BY "p", "Q" BY "q", "R" BY "r",
      "S" BY "s", "T" BY "t", "U" BY "u", "V" BY "v",
      "W" BY "w", "X" BY "x", "Y" BY "y", "Z" BY "z"
```

L. Convert Characters to Upper-Case

We'll convert the characters in S-B to upper-case:

```
MOVE 10 TO S-B-L
MOVE " az23the78 zTxzzzz" TO S-B
INSPECT S-B(1:S-B-L)
  CONVERTING "abcdefghijklmnopqrstuvwxyz" TO
             "ABCDEFGHIJKLMNOPQRSTUVWXYZ"
    [S-B contains "AZ23THE78 zTxzzzz".]
```

or:

```
INSPECT S-B(1:S-B-L)
  REPLACING ALL "a" BY "A", "b" BY "B",
      "c" BY "C", "d" BY "D", "e" BY "E", "f" BY "F",
      "g" BY "G", "h" BY "H", "i" BY "I", "j" BY "J",
      "k" BY "K", "l" BY "L", "m" BY "M", "n" BY "N",
      "o" BY "O", "p" BY "P", "q" BY "Q", "r" BY "R",
      "s" BY "S", "t" BY "T", "u" BY "U", "v" BY "V",
      "w" BY "W", "x" BY "X", "y" BY "Y", "z" BY "Z"
```

The intrinsic functions in the ANSI standard and Microsoft COBOL described in Appendix D can also convert to upper- or lower-case.

M. Operate on Characters as Numbers: Subprogram to Convert Upper/Lower Case

This example illustrates how we can operate on characters as numbers. For example, we might want to convert the letters A through Z to the numbers 1 through 26 to index a table. For our example, we'll convert to upper- or lower-case by operating on the characters as numbers rather than using the INSPECT statement. On the PC this is about four times faster than the INSPECT REPLACING statement. We'll do this in a general-purpose subprogram.

To convert to upper- or lower-case, we'll add or subtract the difference between the numeric values of the upper-case and lower-case characters. For example, an "A" is hex C1 (decimal 193) and an "a" is hex 81 (decimal 129) in EBCDIC. The difference between them is 64. Thus, we can convert "A through Z" to "a through z" by subtracting 64 from the character. Unfortunately, this won't work on the PC, where an "A" is hex 41 (decimal 65) and an "a" is hex 61 (decimal 97) in ASCII. To be computer-independent, we can compute this constant by storing an "A" in DIF-UC and "a" in DIF-LC and subtract the difference and store it in DIF-NUM. We can also use DIF-UC to perform the conversion. The following subprogram performs the conversion:

```
IDENTIFICATION DIVISION.
  PROGRAM-ID. UPLOW.
*******************************************************************
* SUBPROGRAM TO CONVERT TO UPPER- OR LOWER-CASE.                 *
* CALL "UPLOW" USING BY CONTENT U-OR-L,                          *
*                    BY REFERENCE S-A,                           *
*                    BY CONTENT LEN-STRG                         *
* IN:  U-OR-L contains "L":  Convert to lower-case     PIC X     *
*                      "U":  Convert to upper-case               *
*      S-A is the string as PIC X(n).                            *
*      S-A-L is the length of the string as PIC 9(9) BINARY.     *
* OUT: S-A contains the string with characters converted.        *
*******************************************************************
DATA DIVISION.
WORKING-STORAGE SECTION.
```

```
01 DIF.
   05  DIF-UC-N                        PIC S9(4) BINARY VALUE 0.
   05  DIF-UC REDEFINES DIF-UC-N
                                       PIC X(2).
   05  DIF-LC-N                        PIC S9(4) BINARY VALUE 0.
   05  DIF-LC REDEFINES DIF-LC-N
                                       PIC X(2).
   05  DIF-NUM                         PIC S9(4) BINARY.
01 T-NUM                               PIC 9(9) BINARY.
LINKAGE SECTION.
01 U-OR-L                              PIC X.
*     "L": Convert to lower.  "U": Convert to upper.
01 S-A-L                               PIC 9(9) BINARY.
01 S-A                                 PIC X(30).
PROCEDURE DIVISION
    USING U-OR-L, S-A, S-A-L.
START-PROGRAM.
*    Compute the numeric difference between upper- and lower-
*    case characters.
    MOVE "A" TO DIF-UC(2:1)
    MOVE "a" TO DIF-LC(2:1)
    COMPUTE DIF-NUM = DIF-UC-N - DIF-LC-N
*   DIF-NUM contains -32 for ASCII and 64 for EBCDIC.
    PERFORM VARYING T-NUM FROM 1 BY 1
            UNTIL T-NUM > S-A-L
      EVALUATE U-OR-L
        WHEN "L"
*          Convert to lower case.
           IF S-A(T-NUM:1) >= "A" AND
              S-A(T-NUM:1) <= "Z"
              THEN MOVE S-A(T-NUM:1) TO DIF-UC(2:1)
                   SUBTRACT DIF-NUM FROM DIF-UC-N
                   MOVE DIF-UC(2:1) TO S-A(T-NUM:1)
           END-IF
        WHEN "U"
*          Convert to upper case.
           IF S-A(T-NUM:1) >= "a" AND
              S-A(T-NUM:1) <= "z"
              THEN MOVE S-A(T-NUM:1) TO DIF-UC(2:1)
                   ADD DIF-NUM TO DIF-UC-N
                   MOVE DIF-UC(2:1) TO S-A(T-NUM:1)
           END-IF
      END-EVALUATE
    END-PERFORM
    EXIT PROGRAM
    .
END PROGRAM UPLOW.
```

Now we can convert from upper- to lower-case:

```
MOVE "A23THE789Z" TO SOME-STRING
CALL "UPLOW" USING BY CONTENT "L",
                    BY REFERENCE SOME-STRING,
                    BY CONTENT LENGTH OF SOME-STRING
```

SOME-STRING will now contain "a23the789z". The conversion to upper-case
is accomplished by

```
CALL "UPLOW" USING BY CONTENT "U",
                    BY REFERENCE SOME-STRING,
                    BY CONTENT LENGTH OF SOME-STRING
```

SOME-STRING will now contain "A23THE789Z".

This completes the discussion of character data. The next chapter describes
how sorting is done in COBOL.

EXERCISES

1. Define an identifier named TITLES containing 200 characters. Write the
statements necessary to count the occurrences of the character-strings "ABCD"
and "EFG" in TITLES.

2. Assume that you have read a line into an identifier named INPUT-REC.
The line contains integers enclosed between slashes, and the last number in the
input is terminated by two slashes. The maximum integer is five digits, and
the numbers are unsigned. A typical line would be as follows:

/335/21/4/12562/1956//

Write the statements necessary to retrieve each number from the line and display
its value.

3. Define three identifiers named MONDAY, TUESDAY, and WEDNESDAY containing 10 characters each. Initialize each identifier with the appropriate name of
the day. Then define an identifier named WEEK containing 30 characters. Write
the statements to concatenate the three identifiers and store them in WEEK.

4. Define an identifier named MAXIMUM containing 7 characters. Assume that
the identifier contains characters representing numbers such as -2, $+6.9$,
-43.651, 7, .256426, and 7852390. Write the statements necessary to edit
the number into proper COBOL form, and store it in an identifier defined as
PIC S9(7)V9(7) PACKED-DECIMAL.

5. Assume that an identifier containing 200 characters contains English text.
Change all instances of the abbreviations "MISS" or "MRS." to "bMS.". (Make
sure that words such as "MISSISSIPPI" do not get changed.)

6. Do the same as in the preceding exercise, but change "MISS" or "MRS."
to "MS.". Pad the shortened string with blanks.

21

Sorting

Sorting consists of arranging items in ascending or descending order. The usual case is a sequential file that must be sorted into some order for updating or reporting. For example, a personnel file may be sorted in descending order on age, then in descending order on salary within age, and then in ascending order on name within salary. The sort is performed on three items, termed *sort keys,* within each record: age, salary, and name. The following shows how records in such a file would be sorted:

Before Sorting:			After Sorting:		
Name	Salary	Age	Name	Salary	Age
ABLE	19000	65	JONES	20000	65
BAKER	19000	65	ABLE	19000	65
JONES	20000	65	BAKER	19000	65
NOBEL	25000	50	SMITH	30000	50
SMITH	30000	50	NOBEL	25000	50
WATTS	21000	50	WATTS	21000	50

Sorting can be deceptively complex. For example, it should not be hard to sort names in a personnel file into alphabetic order—as long as you remember to sort on the last name first and then on the first name or initials. Then, it is customary to sort names such as O'Brian as if they were spelled OBrian. Also, names that begin with Mc, such as McDonald, should sort after the Ma's. Thus, something as simple as sorting names into alphabetic order does present problems. The usual solution is to carry the name twice in the file, once as it is (O'Brian), and once as it is to act in a sort (OBrian).

Perhaps the most common error in sorting is to confuse the sort order. For example, if a file is sorted on state and city, one may try to use it to produce a report by cities. After all, the file was sorted on cities. But this is in error, because the file is in sort by cities within state, not by cities. Thus, all the cities for Alabama will come first, then all the cities for Alaska. So to produce a report by cities, the file must be sorted again on just cities.

There are three methods of sorting for COBOL programs: the COBOL SORT verb, an external sort, and writing your own sort. Writing your own sort, usually a last resort when the COBOL or external sorts cannot be used, is described at the end of this chapter. The external sort, invoked as a separate job step in MVS, is not a part of COBOL but a part of the operating system. It is simpler than the COBOL sort, because you need not write a COBOL program to invoke it. You can change an external sort without recompiling the program, and the sort program does not reside in memory with the COBOL program, reducing the maximum storage requirement. It may also make it easier to isolate errors when the sort is a separate job step. External sorts for MVS and Microsoft COBOL are described later in this chapter. The COBOL sort, invoked by the SORT statement, is most useful sorting an internal table or in sorting a file generated within a program. It is also useful when the records to be sorted must be selected or manipulated before being sorted or if only a single program is to read the sorted file.

MVS requires several JCL statements for a step containing a sort. Check your installation's operating system requirements to obtain the exact coding of the JCL statements. The required JCL statements are as follows for a VS COBOL II sort:

```
//GO.SYSOUT DD SYSOUT=A
//GO.SORTLIB D DSN=SYS1.SORTLIB,DISP=SHR
//GO.SORTWK01 DD ...
//GO.SORTWK02 DD ...
//GO.SORTWK03 DD ...

      .

      .

      .

//GO.SORTWKnn DD ...
```
   [*The sort requires a minimum of three* SORTWK *DD statements.*]

COBOL sorts should be simple, but they depend on the operating system, and there can be surprises. If you are using the IBM DFSORT Sort Program Product[1], the sort messages overwrite any DISPLAY output on the SYSOUT file, resulting in lost output. To prevent this, specify a special *ddname* for the sort as follows when using the IBM Sort Program Product. The IBM DFSORT Program Product may also require a STEPLIB DD statement, depending on the particular installation:

```
      MOVE "ddname" TO SORT-MESSAGE
      ■ ■ ■
//GO.STEPLIB D DSN=SYS1.SORT,DISP=SHR
//GO.ddname   DD SYSOUT=A
//GO.SYSOUT   DD SYSOUT=A
//GO.SORTLIB  DD DSN=SYS1.SORTLIB,DISP=SHR
//GO.SORTWKnn DD ...
```

I. SIMPLE SORT

A simple sort consists of sorting an input file to produce a sorted output file.
You must specify the input and output files with SELECT and FD entries. In
addition, you must specify the name of a sort file with a SELECT clause. Then
you must write a Sort Definition (SD) entry to describe the records to be sorted
and establish their sort keys. The SELECT and SD entries describing the sort
file do not define a physical file. They just provide a way of describing the
fields within the record of the file that is to be sorted. There may be several
sort files within a program.

You must also write SELECT clauses and FD entries to describe the input file
you want to sort and the output file to write:

```
FILE-CONTROL.
     SELECT sort-file  ASSIGN TO SORTWK.
     SELECT sort-in ASSIGN TO ddin .
     SELECT sort-out  ASSIGN TO ddout .
DATA DIVISION.
FILE SECTION.
SD    sort-file  .
01    record-description .
      05  data-item  . . .
                  [The record-description describes the records being sorted. The SORT statement
                   names data-items in the record-description upon which to sort.]
FD  sort-in  . . .
         [You must write an FD for the input and output files as you would any other file.]
FD    sort-out   . . .
■ ■ ■
//GO.STEPLIB   DD DSN=SYS1.SORT,DISP=SHR
//GO.ddin       DD . . .
//GO.ddout      DD . . .
//GO.ddname     DD SYSOUT=A
//GO.SYSOUT     DD SYSOUT=A
//GO.SORTLIB    DD DSN=SYS1.SORTLIB,DISP=SHR
//GO.SORTWKnn DD . . .
```

You invoke the sort in the Procedure Division by the SORT statement. There
may be several SORT statements within a program, coded as follows:

```
SORT  sort-file
          ASCENDING
          DESCENDING
      ON _____ KEY key, key, ..., key
          ASCENDING
          DESCENDING
      ON _____ KEY , key, key, ..., key
      USING sort-in, sort-in, ..., sort-in
      GIVING sort-out
```

- *sort-file:* The name in an SD entry describing the records to be sorted.
- ON ASCENDING or DESCENDING: Specifies an ascending or descending order of the sort *keys*. List the *keys* from left to right in decreasing order of significance. You can write several ON phrases, but you must place them in decreasing order of significance in the sort.
- *key:* One or more data items in the *record-description* of the *sort-file* on which the file is to be sorted, listed from left to right in decreasing order of significance. For variable-length records, the keys must be in the fixed portion of the record. In VS COBOL II, all keys must be in the first 4092 bytes of the record.
- USING: Specifies the input file to sort. In MVS, the JCL can concatenate several input files for the sort, and the concatenated files can reside on different device types. The blocking may also be different, as may the record length for variable-length files. As an alternative to concatenating the files through JCL, you can specify several *sort-in* files in the USING phrase. VS COBOL II allows a maximum of 16 files.
- GIVING: Specifies the output file into which the sorted output is to be written. Neither *sort-in* nor *sort-out* may be open when the sort is invoked. SORT automatically opens and closes them.

The following example sorts the FILE-I input file on ascending order on PART-X and SIZE-X, on descending order on NAME-X, and on ascending order on COST-X. The sorted records are written into FILE-O:

```
SORT SORT-A
  ON ASCENDING KEY PART-X, SIZE-X
  ON DESCENDING KEY NAME-X
  ON ASCENDING KEY COST-X
  USING FILE-I
  GIVING FILE-O
```

The entire *sort-in* file is read before the sorting begins, and only after the sorting is completed is the output written onto the *sort-out* file. This enables the *sort-in* and *sort-out* files to be the same physical file. Remember, though, that if you write the *sort-out* file over the top of the *sort-in* file and the sort is unsuccessful, both your *sort-in* and *sort-out* files will contain unpredictable data. In sorting files on tape, you can also sort one file and write the output onto the same or a following file on the same tape reel. For example, you might sort file 1 of a tape and write the output onto file 2. This is often done to minimize tape mounts, but it should not be done for important files, because the tape file protect ring must be present to write-enable the tape. This increases the element of risk.

Records in the input file with duplicate keys are sorted together, but not necessarily in the same order in which they are read. To preserve the order in which they are read, you can add the WITH DUPLICATES phrase.

```
SORT sort-file
   ON ...
   WITH DUPLICATES
   USING sort-in
   GIVING sort-out
```

Although it is not in the ANSI Standard, the VS COBOL II and Microsoft COBOL SORT stores a return code in a special register named SORT-RETURN upon completion of the sort. A value of zero is successful, and a value of 16 means an unsuccessful sort. You can store the number of bytes of memory to allocate to the sort in the special register SORT-CORE-SIZE to change it. (The sort operates more efficiently with large amounts of memory, because it reduces the I/O.) The next example sorts an input file on SORT-AGE in descending order and on SORT-NAME in ascending order.

```
FILE-CONTROL.
    SELECT SORT-IT ASSIGN TO SORTWK.
    SELECT FILE-I ASSIGN TO SORTIN.
    SELECT FILE-O ASSIGN TO SORTOUT.
FILE SECTION.
SD  SORT-IT.
01  SORT-REC.
    05  SORT-NAME                 PIC X(25).
    05  SORT-AGE                  PIC S9(3)V99 PACKED-DECIMAL.
    05  FILLER                    PIC X(30).
FD FILE-I ...
FD FILE-O ...
PROCEDURE DIVISION.
A00-BEGIN.
    MOVE "SORTMSG" TO SORT-MESSAGE
    [This prevents DISPLAY messages from being overwritten.]
    MOVE 44000 TO SORT-CORE-SIZE
    [The sort is given 44K bytes of memory.]
    SORT SORT-IT
      ON DESCENDING KEY SORT-AGE
      ON ASCENDING KEY SORT-NAME
      USING FILE-I
      GIVING FILE-O
    IF SORT-RETURN = 16
      THEN DISPLAY "UNSUCCESSFUL SORT."
    END-IF
```

II. SORT INPUT PROCEDURE

You can write an input procedure to supply records to the sort by coding an INPUT PROCEDURE phrase in place of the USING phrase in the SORT statement.

You can read the records from a file, selecting specific records or modifying them before the sort. You can also obtain them from an internal table or from data generated within the program. The input procedure is a normal procedure, such as one written for a PERFORM statement, although it must be one or more sections rather than a paragraph. You can only invoke the input procedure with the SORT statement. The input procedure cannot refer to procedure names outside itself. A RELEASE statement within the procedure, usually executed within a loop, passes a record to the sort each time it executes.

```
SORT sort-file
    ON ...
    INPUT PROCEDURE IS section-name
        [Can also specify section-name-1 THRU section-name-2.]
    GIVING sort-out
    ■ ■ ■
section-name SECTION.
paragraph-name.
    statements to create each record
    RELEASE record-description FROM variable
        [The RELEASE statement passes each record to the sort.]
    perhaps more statements
    .
paragraph-name. EXIT.
```

The sort will invoke the section once to receive all the records. You execute the RELEASE statement to pass each record to the sort. After the last record has been passed, exit the procedure to allow the sort to proceed. You code the RELEASE statement as follows:

```
RELEASE record-description FROM identifier
```

- *record-description*: A record description in the record area specified for the *sort-file* in the SD entry.
- *identifier*: A record or data item containing the data to be passed to the sort. (You can omit the FROM phrase if you move the data directly to the *record-description* in the record area of the *sort-file*.)

The following example sorts an internal table:

```
FILE SECTION.
SD  SORT-A.
01  SORT-REC.
    05  SORT-AGE            PIC S9(3)V99 PACKED-DECIMAL.
    05  SORT-NAME           PIC X(25).
WORKING-STORAGE SECTION.
01  TABLE-DEF.
    05  TABLE-A             OCCURS 100 TIMES
                            INDEXED BY TABLE-X.
```

```
        10   TABLE-AGE       PIC S9(3)V99 PACKED-DECIMAL.
        10   TABLE-NAME      PIC X(25).
    ■ ■ ■
    SORT SORT-A
      ON ASCENDING KEY SORT-NAME
      INPUT PROCEDURE IS P20-SORT-INPUT
      GIVING FILE-O
    ■ ■ ■
P20-SORT-INPUT SECTION.
P30-SORT-START.
    PERFORM VARYING TABLE-X FROM 1 BY 1
            UNTIL TABLE-X > 100
      RELEASE SORT-REC FROM TABLE-A(TABLE-X)
    END-PERFORM
    .
P50-EXIT. EXIT.
```

III. SORT OUTPUT PROCEDURE

COBOL also permits a procedure to be written to receive the sorted records
from the sort rather than having the sort write them out into a file. This permits
the sorted records to be modified or selected before they are written, or to
be stored in an internal table. You specify the output procedure in the SORT
statement by coding an OUTPUT PROCEDURE phrase in place of the GIVING
phrase. A RETURN statement, usually executed inside a loop, returns the next
sorted record each time it executes.

```
    SORT sort-name
      ON...
      USING sort-in
      OUTPUT PROCEDURE IS section-name
          [Can also specify section-name-1 THRU section-name-2.]
    ■ ■ ■
section-name SECTION.
paragraph-name.
    statements to prepare to receive sorted records
    RETURN sort-file  INTO identifier
    [The RETURN statement retrieves each sorted record.]
      AT END
          imperative-statements
      NOT AT END
          imperative-statements
    END-RETURN
    more  statements
    .
  paragraph-name. EXIT.
```

COBOL invokes the output procedure only once when the sorting is completed. You code the RETURN statement, executed to receive each record, as follows. The NOT AT END is optional.

```
RETURN sort-file   INTO identifier
   AT END
       imperative-statements
          [Executed when there are no more statements to return.]
   NOT AT END
       imperative-statements
          [Executed when a record is returned.]
END-RETURN
```

- *sort-file:* The sort file specified in the record area for an SD entry.
- *identifier:* A record or data item into which the sorted record is to be moved. You can omit the INTO phrase so that the data is available only in the *record-description* in the record area of the *sort-file*.

You terminate the output procedure by exiting the section, and control returns to the next executable statement following the SORT. (To stop passing records even if more remain to be passed, simply exit the procedure.) The following example stores sorted output into the TABLE-A used in the previous example:

```
    SORT SORT-A
       ON ASCENDING KEY SORT-NAME
       USING FILE-I
       OUTPUT PROCEDURE IS P60-GET-RECORD
    ■ ■ ■
 P60-GET-RECORD SECTION.
 P70-START.
    PERFORM VARYING TABLE-X FROM 1 BY 1
             UNTIL TABLE-X > 100
        RETURN SORT-A INTO TABLE-A(TABLE-X)
          AT END
             DISPLAY "ERROR--NO RECORDS SORTED."
             GO TO P90-EXIT
                [Exit the procedure when the AT END is reached.]
        END-RETURN
      END-PERFORM

**** Exit
 P90-EXIT. EXIT.
```

IV. SORT INPUT AND OUTPUT PROCEDURES

You can supply both an input and output procedure for the sort by coding both the INPUT and OUTPUT PROCEDURE phrases:

```
SORT sort-file
  ON ...
  INPUT PROCEDURE IS input-section-name
  OUTPUT PROCEDURE IS output-section-name
```

To illustrate the use of sort input and output procedures, along with some other sorting techniques, consider the following sort problems.

• A file contains more than one record type, and each type must be sorted on a key that appears in a different place in each record type.
• A file contains more than one record type, and each record type is to be sorted on different sort keys into the same output file for later processing.
• A variable-length record is to be sorted on a key that is in the variable portion of the record.

You can do all these items by appending a sort key to the front or end of the record. The sort keys must have the same length, and you control the sort order by placing the appropriate items in the appropriate fields of the sort key. The following example illustrates the sort key technique in which two record types are sorted into ascending order on state and town. Notice that state and town appear in different places in each record type.

```
01  REC-A.
    05  REC-A-TYPE              PIC X.
*                               "A" for REC-A.
    05  REC-A-STATE             PIC X(20).
    05  REC-A-TOWN              PIC X(10).
    05  REC-A-REMAINDER         PIC X(100).
01  REC-B                       REDEFINES REC-A.
    05  REC-B-TYPE              PIC X.
*                               "B" for REC-B.
    05  REC-B-TOWN              PIC X(10).
    05  REC-B-STATE             PIC X(20).
    05  REC-B-REMAINDER         PIC X(100).
```

To sort such a file, we can define a sort record as follows, with a sort key appended:

```
SD  SORT-FILE.
01  SORT-RECORD.
    05  SORT-ORIGINAL           PIC X(131).
    05  SORT-KEY.
        10  SORT-STATE          PIC X(20).
        10  SORT-TOWN           PIC X(10).
```

We then write the SORT statement with a sort input procedure to move the

record to the sort record and build the sort key. An output procedure strips off
the sort key and writes the record:

```
    SORT SORT-FILE
      ON ASCENDING KEY SORT-STATE, SORT-TOWN
      INPUT PROCEDURE IS B10-GET-RECORDS
      OUTPUT PROCEDURE IS C10-WRITE-RECORDS
    ■ ■ ■
  B10-GET-RECORDS SECTION.
  B20-FIRST.
      MOVE LOW-VALUES TO REC-A-TYPE
      PERFORM UNTIL REC-A-TYPE = HIGH-VALUES
        READ FILE-I INTO REC-A
          AT END
             MOVE HIGH-VALUES TO REC-A-TYPE
          NOT AT END
             MOVE REC-A TO SORT-ORIGINAL
             EVALUATE REC-A
               WHEN "A"
                     MOVE REC-A-STATE TO SORT-STATE
                     MOVE REC-A-TOWN TO SORT-TOWN
                     RELEASE SORT-RECORD
               WHEN "B"
                     MOVE REC-B-STATE TO SORT-STATE
                     MOVE REC-B-TOWN TO SORT-TOWN
                     RELEASE SORT-RECORD
               WHEN OTHER
                     DISPLAY "BAD RECORD IGNORED"
             END-EVALUATE
        END-READ
      END-PERFORM
                         .
  B50-EXIT.  EXIT.
  C10-WRITE-RECORDS SECTION.
  C20-FIRST.
      MOVE LOW-VALUES TO SORT-KEY
      PERFORM UNTIL SORT-KEY = HIGH-VALUES
        RETURN SORT-FILE
          AT END
             MOVE HIGH-VALUES TO SORT-KEY
          NOT AT END
             WRITE FILE-O-REC FROM SORT-ORIGINAL
        END-RETURN
      END-PERFORM
      .
  C40-EXIT.  EXIT.
```

V. SORT SEQUENCE

The SORT statement specifies the sort keys left to right in decreasing order of significance, and each ON phrase in decreasing order of significance:

```
SORT SORT-FILE
   ON ASCENDING KEY STATE, COUNTY
   ON DESCENDING KEY CITY
   ON ASCENDING KEY PRECINCT
   USING FILE-I
   GIVING FILE-O
```

This statement sorts states into ascending order, the counties within a state into ascending order, each city in a county into descending order, and each precinct within a city into ascending order. Numeric fields sorted in order of their algebraic values, taking into consideration the sign. Alphanumeric fields sort from left to right, with each character compared according to the collating sequence of the character set. The EBCDIC character set has the following collating sequence:

> Low to high:
> blank
> ¢ . < (+ ¦ & ! $ *) ; ¬ - / , % _ > ? : # @ ' = "
> a through z
> A through Z
> 0 through 9

The ASCII character set has the following collating sequence:

> Low to high:
> blank
> ! " # $ % & ' ( ) * + , - . /
> 0 through 9
> : ; < = > ? @
> A through Z
> [\ ] ^ _ `
> a through z
> { ¦ } ~

If you want a collating sequence other than that native to the computer (EBCDIC in VS COBOL II and ASCII in Microsoft COBOL), you can code the COLLATING SEQUENCE clause:

```
SORT file-name
   ON...
   WITH DUPLICATES
   COLLATING SEQUENCE IS alphabet-name
   USING [or INPUT PROCEDURE] ...
   GIVING [or OUTPUT PROCEDURE] ...
```

The *alphabet-name* can be one of the following:

- STANDARD-1: Specifies the ASCII collating sequence.
- NATIVE: Specifies the collating sequence native to the computer: EBCDIC for VS COBOL II and ASCII for Microsoft COBOL. It is the default if COLLATING SEQUENCE is omitted.
- EBCDIC: Specifies the EBCDIC collating sequence.
- STANDARD-2: Specifies the International Reference Version of the ISO 7-bit code defined in International Standard 646, 7-bit Coded Character Set for Information Processing Interchange.
- *literal:* Specifies a collating sequence defined by the compiler writer.

You can also specify the collating sequence for a program in the COLLATING SEQUENCE clause of the OBJECT-COMPUTER paragraph. Coding the collating sequence there affects the entire program, including comparison operations in IF statements, condition-name conditions, and the sequence of the keys of random-access files, in addition to SORT statements. (Coding COLLATING SEQUENCE in a SORT statement overrides any COLLATING SEQUENCE coded in the OBJECT-COMPUTER paragraph.) The *alphabet-name* is the same as that in the SORT statement.

```
OBJECT-COMPUTER. computer-name.
    COLLATING SEQUENCE IS alphabet-name.
```

VI. SORT EFFICIENCY

Sorts are relatively expensive and can account for a large portion of the running cost of a system. Sorting and merging may consume 25 percent of today's computing capacity.[2] In searching for ways to reduce a system's running costs, look carefully at the sorts. Are all the sorts necessary? Sorts are heavily I/O-bound, so you should block the sort input and output as high as possible. The manufacturer may provide ways to optimize a sort's performance. The cost of a sort increases exponentially with the number of records sorted; it costs more than twice as much to sort 1000 records as 500 records. The cost of a sort also increases proportionally to the record length and number of sort keys; it costs more to sort a 1000-byte record than a 400-byte record.

You can often reduce the number of records and shorten the record length for a sort. Suppose that a file containing 10,000 fixed-length records of 1000 bytes must be sorted to produce a report. However, only 5000 records are selected for the report, with 100 bytes of each record containing relevant data. Such a file would be relatively expensive to sort. It would require reading 10,000 records into the sort, sorting 10,000 records, writing out the 10,000 records, and reading the 10,000 records back into the report program. Each record contains 1000 bytes, resulting in a total of 30 million bytes transmitted, and 10,000 records of 1000 bytes sorted. To reduce this, read in the 10,000 records in a sort input procedure and select only the 5000 records needed. Then move the 100 bytes that go into the report to the sort record, sort the 5000 records with an internal sort, and write the report in a sort output procedure. The result is 10 million bytes read and 5000 records of 100 bytes sorted.

The sort is also sensitive to the amount of memory allocated to it. The default memory size is set by the installation. The sort will operate more efficiently if more memory is allocated by moving the memory size in bytes to the SORT-CORE-SIZE special register. The larger amount of memory reduces the I/O. Generally, you should give the sort a relatively large amount of memory. You can also move values to the SORT-FILE-SIZE and SORT-MODE-SIZE to estimate the number of records and their size. Finally, you can use the FASTSRT compile option to have DFSORT rather than COBOL do all the I/O.

A. SORT **Special Registers (Not in ANSI Standard)**

The special registers for the sort are:

- SORT-CORE-SIZE: Sets the number of bytes memory for the sort. It is defined as

```
01 SORT-CORE-SIZE              PIC S9(8) BINARY VALUE ZERO.
```

- SORT-FILE-SIZE: Estimates the number of records to be sorted. It is defined as

```
01 SORT-FILE-SIZE              PIC S9(8) BINARY VALUE ZERO.
```

- SORT-MODE-SIZE: Contains an estimate of the most-frequent record length of variable-length records. It is defined as

```
01 SORT-MODE-SIZE              PIC S9(5) BINARY VALUE ZERO.
```

- SORT-CONTROL: Ignored in Microsoft COBOL. In VS COBOL II, it contains the *ddname* of a sort control file containing control statements to optimize the sort. (The statements do the same as the aforementioned special registers. If you specify both, the sort control file takes precedence.) The sort attempts to open the file with the *ddname* and uses any control statements it contains. You can include a DD statement with the *ddname* to point to a file containing the statements. SORT-CONTROL is defined as

```
01 SORT-CONTROL               PIC X(8) VALUE "IGZSRTCD".
```

- SORT-RETURN: Sets the return code for a sort. It is defined as

```
01 SORT-RETURN                PIC S9(4) BINARY VALUE ZERO.
```

- SORT-MESSAGE: Ignored in Microsoft COBOL. In VS COBOL II, it specifies the *ddname* of a data set the sort program is to use in place of the SYSOUT data set. If you change this, you must include a DD statement with the *ddname* for the output. It is defined as

```
01 SORT-MESSAGE              PIC X(8) VALUE "SYSOUT".
```

B. The SAME SORT AREA **Clause**

There is a SAME SORT AREA in the ANSI Standard to optimize memory. VS COBOL II and Microsoft COBOL check it for syntax but otherwise treat it as a comment, because the system automatically optimizes memory. You code it in the I-0-CONTROL paragraph as

```
I-0-CONTROL.
    SAME SORT AREA FOR file-name,  file-name,  ...,  file-name.
```

The *file-names* can be SORT or MERGE file names.

VII. **THE** MERGE **STATEMENT**

MERGE allows several input files having identical record formats and arranged in the same sort order to be merged into a single output file in this same sort order. Merging yields the same results as if the several files were concatenated as input to a normal sort. Merging is more efficient, because the input files are already in the proper sort order.

The MERGE statement is similar to the SORT statement. You must describe all input and output files as you would normal files, with SELECT and FD entries. Like the sort file, you must describe the *merge-file* with an SD entry. You write the MERGE statement as follows. The phrases are the same as for the SORT, and COLLATING SEQUENCE is optional.

```
MERGE merge-file
      ASCENDING
      DESCENDING
   ON _____  KEY key, key, ..., key
      ASCENDING
      DESCENDING
   ON _____  KEY key, key, ..., key
   COLLATING SEQUENCE IS alphabet-name
   USING merge-in-1, merge-in-2, ..., merge-in-n
   GIVING merge-out
```

- *merge-file:* The merge file described in an SD entry.
- *merge-in:* Two or more file names to be merged based on the order specified in the ON phrases. The files must be sequential or dynamic access mode. Records with identical keys in several files are merged in the order the files are listed

in the USING phrase. The files must contain records of the same record type. In VS COBOL II for variable-length files, the second and following files must not be specified for records shorter or longer than the minimum and maximum records described for the first file.

- *merge-out*. An output file name to contain the merged files. Neither the *merge-in* nor *merge-out* files may be open when MERGE is executed. MERGE automatically opens and closes the files.

The *merge-in* files and the single *merge-out* file are normal files, and you must specify them with SELECT and FD entries. You can replace the GIVING phrase with the OUTPUT PROCEDURE phrase and write a procedure to receive the merged records. The output procedure must contain RETURN statements to retrieve the merged records. (No input procedure is permitted.)

```
MERGE SORT-A
   ON ASCENDING KEY PART-X, SIZE-X
   USING FILE-1, FILE-2, FILE-3
   OUTPUT PROCEDURE C30-STORE-MERGE
```

The SORT-CONTROL, SORT-MESSAGE, and SORT-RETURN special registers also apply to a merge.

VIII.   EXTERNAL SORT

External sorts are not a part of COBOL, but they are used in combination with many COBOL programs. An external sort is often simpler and more convenient than a COBOL sort. You can change the sort order with a control statement, whereas a COBOL sort requires the COBOL program to be recompiled. However, if you change the sort order of a file, you must recompile the program reading it anyway.

A.   IBM DFSORT SORT/MERGE Program

You invoke MVS external sorts as a separate job step. The JCL is a cataloged procedure like the one following, but check with your installation as there may be differences:

```
//SORT1 EXEC SORTD
//SORT.SORTIN DD DSN=sort-input-file,DISP=SHR,...
  [SORTIN specifies the input file to sort.]
//SORT.SORTOUT DD DSN=sort-out-file, DISP=(NEW,...
  [SORTOUT specifies the output file to contain the sorted records.]
//SORT.SYSIN DD *
 SORT FIELDS=(1,4,CH,A,20,10,CH,D),FILSZ=E1000
```

The SORT statement specifies the sort order. The FILSZ = E1000 is an estimate of the number of records in the file, 1000 in this example. The sort order is as follows:

- 1,4,CH,A: Starting in character position 1, sort 4 CHaracters in Ascending order.
- 20,10,CH,D: Starting in character position 20, sort 10 CHaracters in Descending order.

 The general form of the sort control statement is as follows:

```
SORT FIELDS=(sort-key,sort-key, . . . ,sort-key),FILSZ=En
```

- FILSZ = En: An estimate of the number of records to be sorted, which enables the sort to be more efficient. You may omit it and the sort will proceed with a slight performance degradation.
- *sort-key:* Specifies the fields within the record upon which to sort, their data type, and whether they are to be sorted in ascending or descending order. List the keys from left to right in major to minor order in which they are to be applied in the sort. Each *sort-key* has four parts, as follows:

 start, length, format, order

- *start:* The starting byte position in the record. The first byte is number 1. For binary fields, you can specify *start* in the form *byte.bit,* where *byte* is the byte number and *bit* is the bit number within the byte. (The first bit is number 0.) For example, 4.2 indicates that the key begins in the third bit of the third byte.
- *length:* The length of the field in bytes. For binary fields, you can specify the length in the form *bytes.bits,* where *bytes* is the number of bytes and *bits* is the number of bits. For example, 0.3 indicates that the key is three bits long.
- *format:* The format of the sort field. It must be one of the following:

CH	Character (PIC X)
ZD	Zoned decimal (external decimal number, PIC 9)
PD	Packed decimal (PACKED-DECIMAL)
FI	Fixed-point (BINARY)
BI	Binary (treated as a string of bits without a sign)
FL	Floating-point (COMP-1 or COMP-2)
AC	ASCII character

- *order:* The sort order

A	Ascending
D	Descending

The following example sorts records into ascending order with two sort keys:

```
SORT FIELDS=(4,6,ZD,A,12,3,PD,D)
```

The sort order is as follows:

- 4,6,ZD,A: Bytes 4 to 9 as zoned decimal in ascending order.
- 12,3,PD,D: Bytes 12 to 14 as packed decimal in descending order.

To continue the SORT statement, break it after a comma and continue it columns 2 to 16 of the following line:

```
SORT FIELDS=(4,6,ZD,A,
   12,3,PD,D)
```

The MERGE statement, coded like the SORT statement, merges files. Additionally, there may be up to 16 SORTIN*nn* statements, with the *nn* ranging in consecutive values from 01 up to 16:

```
//JR964113 JOB (24584),'JONES',CLASS=A
// EXEC SORTD
//SORT.SORTIN01 DD ...
//SORT.SORTIN02 DD ...
   ⋮
//SORT.SORTIN16 DD ...
//SORT.SORTOUT  DD ...
//SORT.SYSIN    DD *
 MERGE FIELDS=(1,4,CH,A,20,10,CH,D),FILSZ=E1000
```

B. DOS Sort for Microsoft COBOL

On the PC, you can use the DOS SORT command to sort files. The following command sorts the file in ascending order using the entire record as the key:

```
:> SORT < input-file > output-file
```

To sort in ascending order where the key begins in other than column 1, specify the starting the *column* as follows:

```
:> SORT /+column < input-file > output-file
```

You can't specify a key length—just a starting column, with the key always being the remainder of the line. To sort in descending order, code:

```
:> SORT /R < input-file > output-file
:> SORT /R /+column < input-file > output-file
```

IX. PROGRAMMING A SORT

The SORT verb or the external sort is likely to be more efficient and simpler than writing your own sort. However, there may be situations where you must write your own sort, perhaps to sort a table in which memory is severely limited. There are many techniques for internal sorts, but the *bubble sort* is the simplest and is reasonably efficient for small numbers of records. In the bubble sort, you compare the first table element to each successive element. For an ascending sort, you switch the two elements if the first element is greater than the second. This bubbles the largest value to the top of the table. You repeat this for the second through the next-to-last element until the entire table is in the desired order. The following example illustrates a bubble sort in which the 1000 elements of table AMOUNT are sorted into ascending order.

```
77  SWAP                         PIC S9(7)V99 PACKED-DECIMAL.
    [SWAP is a data item used to swap table elements.]
01  A-TABLE.
    05  AMOUNT                   OCCURS 1000 TIMES
                                 INDEXED BY X-AMT, Y-AMT
                                 PIC S9(7)V99 PACKED-DECIMAL.
    [AMOUNT is the table to sort. Two subscripts are needed for the sort.]
    ■ ■ ■
B10-BUBBLE-SORT.
***************************************************************
* PROCEDURE TO PERFORM BUBBLE SORT.                          *
* IN: AMOUNT is table to sort.                               *
* OUT: AMOUNT table is sorted in ascending order.            *
***************************************************************
    PERFORM VARYING X-AMT FROM 1 BY 1
        UNTIL X-AMT > 999
      PERFORM VARYING Y-AMT FROM X-AMT BY 1
          UNTIL Y-AMT > 1000
        IF AMOUNT(X-AMT) > AMOUNT(Y-AMT)
          THEN MOVE AMOUNT(Y-AMT) TO SWAP
               MOVE AMOUNT(X-AMT) TO AMOUNT(Y-AMT)
               MOVE SWAP TO AMOUNT(X-AMT)
        END-IF
      END-PERFORM
    END-PERFORM
**** Exit
```

The bubble sort is not recommended for large files, because the number of operations it must perform increases as the square of the number of records. See Reference 2 for further discussion of sorts.

   This concludes the chapter on sorting. External sorts are the simplest. COBOL sorts are often convenient, especially when records are selected before sorting. Rarely would you need to program your own sort. The next two chapters describe the facilities for double-byte characters and features needed for CICS. If you will not be using these, you should skip the chapters and go to the concluding chapters.

EXERCISES

1. Assume that a file contains 80-character records. Use the SORT statement to sort the file in ascending order on the first 8 characters and in descending order on the next 12 characters. Write the sorted output into a file.

2. Assume the same file as in Exercise 1. Write a sort input procedure to read the file and select for the sort only records with an "X" in column 40. Write the sorted output into a file.

3. Assume the same file as in Exercise 1. Write a sort output procedure to print the keys of the sorted records, but do not write the sorted output into a file; store it in an internal table.

4. Assume the same file as in Exercise 1. Write a sort input procedure to read the file and select for the sort only records with an "X" in column 40. Write a sort output procedure to print the keys of the sorted records. Also, since only the sort keys are used for output, shorten the record for the sort to a 20-character record containing just the sort keys.

5. Assume that a file contains 80-character records. Sort the file on the first 3 characters so that the records come out in the order shown.

```
991
992
999
981
982
989
891
899
```

6. Assume that you are called upon to develop a set of standards for the use of the sort. Give guidelines for the use of an external sort, an internal sort, and hand-coded sorts.

7. Write an internal bubble sort to sort a table into descending order.

REFERENCES

1. "DFSORT Application Programming: Guide," Program NO. 5740-SM1, San Jose, CA: IBM Corporation, 1985.

2. Donald E. Knuth, *The Art of Computer Programming,* Volume 3, *Sorting and Searching,* Reading, MA: Addison-Wesley Publishing Company, 1973.

22

Double Byte Character Set
(Not in ANSI Standard)

The double-byte character set (DBCS) is used for character sets in which more than eight bits (256 separate characters) are needed to store the characters. Although this is used in some graphic applications, where COBOL is rarely used, the primary use is for the Japanese Kanji alphabet, which has around two thousand characters.

DBCS data is alphanumeric data in which each character occupies two bytes, or 16 bits. This allows a character set of 32,767 characters. The value for a DBCS character can range from X"0000" through X"FFFF". A DBCS blank is defined as X"4040". (Blanks are blanks, whether in the Roman alphabet or Kanji.)

DBCS data can be specified in one of the following:

- Literals. You can write them using hexadecimal notation or use a Kanji keyboard.
- PIC character strings. DBCS data is PIC DISPLAY-1 . You specify a DBCS character in a PIC string as a G , similar to the way EBCDIC are specified with an X .
- COBOL words. These can be data names, paragraph names, or other COBOL words. You usually use a Kanji keyboard to write these, although you can also use hexadecimal notation.

I. SHIFT-OUT, SHIFT-IN CHARACTERS

Because you can mix EBCDIC or ASCII and DBCS characters in a string, you need two special characters. A *shift-out* character, the EBCDIC character X"0E" in VS COBOL II, shifts out of EBCDIC into DBCS. That is, when an X"0E" is encountered in a string, the system knows that thereafter in the item each two characters represent a DBCS character. To terminate DBCS and go back to EBCDIC, there is a *shift-in* character, the EBCDIC character X"0F" in VS COBOL II. In Microsoft COBOL, the shift-out character is an "A" and the shift-in is "Z".

II. DBCS COMPILER OPTIONS

A. VS COBOL II

For the shift-out and shift-in characters to be recognized in a DBCS string, you must code the DBCS compiler option. You can use the following compiler options for DBCS:

- LANGUAGE(JA) lists the compiler output in the Japanese language using the Japanese character set. You can also write LANGUAGE(JP).
- DBCS tells the compiler to recognize X"0E" and X"0F" as shift-out and shift-in characters in the double-byte portion of a nonnumeric literal. The default is NODBCS , which causes the compiler to treat these characters as any other.

B. Microsoft COBOL

You can change the shift-out and shift-in characters by coding the DBCSSOSI compiler option:

    DBCSSOSI *"shift-out-integer"* *"shift-in-integer"*

The integer is the ASCII code for the character. The default is DBCSSOSI "65" "90" , the ASCII codes for "A" and "Z" .

For the shift-out and shift-in characters to be recognized, you must code the DBCS compiler option. You code DBCS literals as you would any alphanumeric literal, except that you begin the literal with the shift-out character and end it with the shift-in. This is the extent of DBCS support in Microsoft COBOL. The remainder of this chapter pertains only to VS COBOL II.

III. WRITING DBCS LITERALS

In writing the shift-out and shift-in characters in a literal, you use the "<" character to represent the shift-out (X"0E") and the ">" to represent the shift-in (X"0F"). Then you precede the literal with a "G" so that the system will know to look for the shift-out and shift-in characters. Here is a typical DBCS literal:

    G"<42C142C2>"

Here is another DBCS literal containing both EBCDIC and DBCS characters:

    G"AB<42C142C2>CD"

The first two characters are an EBCDIC "A" and "B". Then there are two DBCS characters, an X"42C1" and an X"42C2". These might be Kanji characters. However, they can also be DBCS EBCDIC characters. You form a DBCS EBCDIC character by coding the first byte as X"42" and the second byte as the hex code for the EBCDIC character. Thus, the "42C142C2" is the DBCS representation of "AB".

The ‹ and › notation works fine in a literal, but not in other circumstances. For this reason, there are SHIFT-OUT and SHIFT-IN special registers, implicitly defined as follows:

```
01  SHIFT-OUT GLOBAL            PIC X VALUE X"0E".
01  SHIFT-IN  GLOBAL            PIC X VALUE X"0F".
```

These are also in Microsoft COBOL. You can use them as you would any other special register. You can't use them in place of the ‹ and › when defining DBCS literals and user-defined words. Nor can you use them as receiving items. The following is an example of their use to create a DBCS string:

```
01  DBCS-GROUP.
    05  S-OUT                   PIC X.
    05  DBCS-ITEM               PIC G(2) DISPLAY-1.
         [This defines the DBCS item as two DBCS characters.]
    05  S-IN                    PIC X.
    ■ ■ ■
    MOVE SHIFT-OUT TO S-OUT
      [Same as  MOVE X"0E" TO S-OUT.]
    MOVE G"‹42456667›" TO DBCS-ITEM
    MOVE SHIFT-IN TO S-IN
      [Same as MOVE X"0F" TO S-IN.]
    DISPLAY DBCS-GROUP
      [You can display DBCS characters if the output device supports them—as is true for most
      devices in Japan.]
```

You define DBCS literals as follows:

```
G"‹d1d2d3d5 ...d8d9 ›"
```

G" must be followed immediately by the shift-out character, which you code in a literal as "‹". The string must end with a shift-in character, the "›". Enclose the entire literal in quotations, unless the APOST compiler option is specified—then code apostrophes rather than quotations. The DBCS characters represented by d1d2 can be written in hexadecimal with two byes or four hex characters representing each DBCS character. If you have a Kanji keyboard, you can type the character directly.

```
G"‹42456667›"
```

The length of the literal includes bytes for the control characters. The literal above would be six bytes. The maximum length of a literal is 28 DBCS characters.

You can mix EBCDIC and DBCS by enclosing the DBCS characters in the shift-out, shift-in characters, as shown in this example:

```
G"ABC‹D1D2D1D2›DEF‹D1D2›GHI"
  [The literal would be 19 bytes.]
```

The hexadecimal characters representing the DBCS characters can be X"00" through X"FF", but they must not be the shift-out or shift-in characters (X"0E" or X"0F"). You cannot continue DBCS literals across lines.

A nonnumeric DBCS literal is considered alphanumeric, and you can use it as you would any alphanumeric literal. You can use DBCS literals as follows in the Data Division:

- In a VALUE clause
- For data items described as USAGE DISPLAY-1
- With the JUST RIGHT clause

You can use DBCS literals in the Procedure Division as follows:

- As the sending item when a DBCS item or group item is the receiving item
- In a relation condition when the item being compared is a DBCS or group item
- As the figurative constant SPACES. That is, you can move SPACES to a DISPLAY-1 DBCS data item. This is the only figurative constant that can be used with DBCS data items.

You can code DBCS literals wherever nonnumeric literals are allowed, except in the following:

- ALPHABET clause
- ASSIGN clause
- BASIS statement basis-name
- CALL statement program-ID
- CANCEL statement
- CLASS clause
- COPY statement text-name or library-name
- CURRENCY SIGN clause
- END PROGRAM statement
- ENTRY statement
- PADDING CHARACTER clause
- PROGRAM-ID paragraph
- STOP statement

IV. USER-DEFINED WORDS

You can use DBCS characters to name items in COBOL. These include:

- *alphabet-name*
- *class-name*
- *condition-name*
- *data-name* or *identifier*
- *record-name*

- *file-name*
- *index-name*
- *mnemonic-name*
- *paragraph-name*
- *section-name*
- *symbolic-character*

You cannot use them for the following:

- *program-name*
- *subprogram-name*
- *library-name*
- *text-name*

You normally enter user-defined words from a Kanji keyboard. However, you must remember to enter the shift-in and shift-out characters. The following rules apply to DBCS user-defined words:

- They must begin with a shift-out character and end with a shift-in character.
- They can have 1 to 14 DBCS characters.
- They may contain characters whose values range from X"41" to X"FE" in both bytes.
- They can contain both double-byte EBCDIC and non-EBCDIC characters. You represent double-byte EBCDIC characters by an X"42" in the first byte. The only double-byte EBCDIC characters are -, A to Z, a to z, and 0 to 9. The hyphen cannot appear as the first or last character of the word.
- They must contain at least one non-EBCDIC double-byte character.
- You cannot continue them across lines.
- Lower-case double-byte EBCDIC characters are considered to be the same as upper-case characters.

Comment statements can, of course, contain DBCS characters or a combination of EBCDIC and DBCS characters. The compiler doesn't look at what is on a comment statement

V. DBCS DATA ITEMS

You describe a DBCS data item as USAGE DISPLAY-1, and the PIC string can contain only the B and G:

B   Causes DBCS blank (X"4040") to be inserted.
G   Represents a DBCS character of 2 bytes. Only B can be coded with G.

The VALUE clause, if coded, must specify either a DBCS literal or the figurative constant SPACES. For example:

```
77 DBCS-ITEM              PIC GGBBGG DISPLAY-1
                          VALUE G"<42C142C2404042C342C4>".
```

You can't code BLANK WHEN ZERO for DBCS items. SYNC is ignored for DBCS items.

A level 66 DBCS item with RENAMES can specify a DISPLAY-1 target item if the target item is also a DBCS item and THRU is not specified. For example:

```
01  AN-ITEM                      PIC G(10) DISPLAY-1.
66  NEW-ITEM RENAMES AN-ITEM     PIC G(4)BBG(4) DISPLAY-1.
```

In a level 88 condition-name data item, the THRU literals must be DBCS if the associated condition variable is DBCS. The range of the THRU for DBCS is based on the binary collating sequence of the hex values of DBCS characters.

VI. PROGRAMMING CONSIDERATIONS WITH DBCS DATA

Subject to the restrictions already given, you can use DBCS literals and data as just as you would alphanumeric data. DBCS data is treated the same as alphanumeric data. For example, in a MOVE, the DBCS characters are padded DBCS blanks on the right or truncated on the right to fit the receiving item if necessary.

• The PROGRAM COLLATING SEQUENCE clause is not applied to DBCS data.

• If you use DBCS data items, the CURRENCY SIGN literal can't contain a "G".

• In the CLASS *class-name* IS literal clause, the *class-name* may be a DBCS-defined word. The *literal* cannot be DBCS.

• In the ALPHABET clause, you cannot use DBCS items in specifying the collating sequence.

• In the RECORD KEY and ALTERNATIVE RECORD KEY clauses, the *key* can be a DBCS data item. If the *key* is a DBCS item, then the KEY IS phrase in a READ statement must also be a DBCS item.

• DBCS and KANJI are class names. This allows you to test a DISPLAY-1 for contents of DBCS or Kanji as a class. You can code:

```
identifier  IS DBCS
identifier  IS NOT DBCS
identifier  IS KANJI
identifier  IS NOT KANJI
```

The *identifier* must be DISPLAY-1. The test is performed as follows:

```
DBCS:    Item may contain X"0000" through X"FFFF"
         Tested for X"41" through X"FE" in both characters
            or X"4040" as blank.
KANJI:   May contain X"0000" through X"FFFF"
         Tested for X"41" through X"7F" for first byte.
            X"41" through X"FE" in second byte
            or X"4040" as blank.
```

• You can compare DBCS data items and literals in relational operations. However, you can only compare a DBCS item with another DBCS item. They are compared based on the binary collating sequence of the hex values. If the DBCS items are not the same length, the shorter is padded on right with DBCS spaces for the comparison.

- DISPLAY: Can list DBCS identifiers and literals and can intermix them with non-DBCS items. However, the output device must be able to recognize the shift-out and shift-in characters—which most Japanese terminals and printers do. In sending a line to an output device, DISPLAY splits lines only on a double-byte boundary if it is necessary to split them. It leaves space for a shift-in character to be automatically inserted at the end of the line and a shift-out character inserted at the beginning of the next line.

- INITIALIZE: Can initialize DBCS data items. Code the REPLACING phrase as shown. The *identifier* would be a DBCS item, and *item* must be a DBCS identifier or literal.

```
INITIALIZE identifier
  REPLACING DBCS BY G"<406162>"
```

- MOVE: If either item is DBCS, both must be DBCS. SPACE can be a sending item. The DBCS field sent is truncated or padded with DBCS blanks on the right if necessary to match the length of the receiving field.

- INSPECT/STRING/UNSTRING: If any character item is DBCS, all items, including literals, must be DBCS. The DBCS string must not contain a mixture of single-character EBCDIC and DBCS characters, because these statements operate on a character at a time. SPACE is the only figurative constant allowed. The POINTER phrase points to relative DBCS character position, not the relative byte position. The COUNT IN and TALLYING phrases count the number of DBCS characters, not bytes.

- Reference modification: Not allowed.

VII. CONVERSION TO AND FROM DBCS

If you have identifiers that contain EBCDIC or mixed EBCDIC and DBCS characters, you can convert them to DBCS and back to mixed mode using IBM-supplied subprograms.

A. Converting EBCDIC or Mixed EBCDIC/DBCS to DBCS

To convert from alphanumeric to DBCS, you call the IGZCA2D subprogram as follows:

```
CALL "IGZCA2D" USING BY REFERENCE char-item, dbcs-item
       BY CONTENT LENGTH OF char-item, LENGTH OF dbcs-item
```

- *char-item:* An alphanumeric or mixed EBCDIC/DBCS item.
- *dbcs-item:* The field to receive the item after it is converted to pure DBCS. It cannot have reference modification: *dbcs-item(n:m)* not allowed.

For example, suppose you had these data items described:

```
77 CHAR-ITEM                     PIC X(4) VALUE "ABCD".
77 MIXED-ITEM                    PIC X(12) VALUE "AB <D1D2D3D4>CDE".
77 DBCS-ITEM                     PIC G(20) DISPLAY-1.
```

To convert CHAR-ITEM to DBCS and store it in DBCS-ITEM you could code the following:

```
CALL "IGZCA2D" USING BY REFERENCE CHAR-ITEM, DBCS-ITEM
    BY CONTENT LENGTH OF CHAR-ITEM, LENGTH OF DBCS-ITEM
```

DBCS-ITEM would then contain ".A.B.C.Dbbbbbbbbbbbb"; the "." represents the X"42" character that is the left-most byte of an EBCDIC character when converted to DBCS. An EBCDIC blank is converted to X"4040".

To convert MIXED-ITEM to pure DBCS and store it in DBCS-ITEM, you could code the following:

```
CALL "IGZCA2D" USING BY REFERENCE MIXED-ITEM, DBCS-ITEM
    BY CONTENT LENGTH OF MIXED-ITEM, LENGTH OF DBCS-ITEM
```

DBCS-ITEM would then contain ".A.BbbD1D2D3D4.C.D.E".

B. Converting DBCS to Single-Character Alphanumeric

To convert from DBCS to alphanumeric, you call the IGZCD2A subprogram as follows:

```
CALL "IGZCD2A" USING BY REFERENCE dbcs-item, char-item
    BY CONTENT LENGTH OF dbcs-item, LENGTH OF char-item
```

When the *dbcs-item* is converted, shift-out and shift-in characters are inserted before and after any DBCS characters. EBCDIC and DBCS blank characters are converted to single-byte EBCDIC. If DBCS-ITEM contained ".A.BbbD1D2D3D4.C.D.E", you could convert DBCS-ITEM back to AN-ITEM with the following call:

```
77  AN-ITEM                      PIC X(16).
    ■ ■ ■
    CALL "IGZCD2A" USING BY REFERENCE DBCS-ITEM, AN-ITEM
        BY CONTENT LENGTH OF DBCS-ITEM, LENGTH OF AN-ITEM
```

AN-ITEM would then contain "AB <D1D2D3D4>CDEbbbb".

Note that for the conversion, the converted item is truncated or padded on the right with blanks as necessary to match the length of the receiving item.

23

Pointer Data
(Not in ANSI Standard)

VS COBOL II and Microsoft COBOL allow POINTER data to be defined. Pointer data consists of data items that contain the storage (memory address) location of other data items. COBOL pointer data is rather limited and doesn't have the full ability of address manipulation found in languages such as C or PL/I. The primary purpose for POINTER data is for subprogram calls and interface to CICS (Customer Information Control System).

I. DEFINING POINTER DATA

A POINTER is a four-byte data item that can contain either zero (NULLS) or the storage address of another data item. You describe it as USAGE POINTER with no PIC clause:

```
01  AN-ITEM                    POINTER.
```

You can code a VALUE of NULLS for a POINTER item. This is the only initial value permitted:

```
01  ANOTHER-ITEM              POINTER VALUE NULLS.
```

Other than not coding the PIC clause, you describe a POINTER item like any other data item. You can code it for any level except level 88. It can be the subject or object of a REDEFINES, it can contain an OCCURS, and you can code SYNC to align it on a full-word boundary.

If POINTER items are part of a group, the group still acts like an alphanumeric item. You can read or write pointers within group items. However, since POINTER items contain memory addresses, which will likely change each time a program is run, it wouldn't make sense to write POINTER items into a data set for later use in another run.

Because POINTER is not alphanumeric or numeric, you can't code BLANK WHEN ZERO and JUST RIGHT with it.

II. PROGRAMMING WITH POINTER DATA

POINTER data items can only appear in the following statements in the Procedure Division:

- Relational condition: You can compare POINTER items to NULLS or other POINTER items for equality only. That is, you can only compare POINTER items with = or NOT =. A POINTER item either is described as USAGE POINTER or is an ADDRESS OF special register item. Relational conditions are allowed in IF, PERFORM, EVALUATE, and sequential SEARCH (but not a binary SEARCH statement).
- Procedure Division header: The USING phrase may list POINTER items as subprogram parameters.
- CALL or ENTRY statements: Either a POINTER item or ADDRESS OF may appear in the USING phrase. Both may be BY CONTENT or BY REFERENCE.
- EVALUATE: Can have POINTER identifiers.
- SET: The SET statement can store POINTER data items. This will be described subsequently.

POINTER items have the following limitations:

- Class test: There is no class test for POINTER.
- CORR: USAGE POINTER does not participate in CORR operations.
- MOVE: Cannot name a POINTER item. Use SET instead.
- SORT ASCENDING/DESCENDING KEY: Cannot be a POINTER item.

You can also set a value of NULLS into a POINTER item with the SET statement. NULLS (or NULL) is a figurative constant that can be used only with POINTER data. NULLS has a zero value and represents a null address for data items defined with USAGE IS POINTER or ADDRESS OF:

```
SET AN-ITEM TO NULLS
```

ADDRESS OF is a special register, implicitly defined as USAGE POINTER, that is used to obtain the address of level 01 and 77 items in the Linkage Section. An ADDRESS OF *record* exists for every 01 or 77 level data item in the Linkage Section, except those records that redefine others (then ADDRESS OF is similarly redefined). You code ADDRESS OF as follows:

```
ADDRESS OF record
```

where *record* is a level 01 or 77 data item in the Linkage Section. (In Microsoft COBOL, the item can also be defined in Working Storage or be a record description as a sending field.)

The SET statement for POINTER is as follows:

```
                               NULL [or NULLS]
      pointer-identifier       pointer-identifier
      ADDRESS OF identifier    ADDRESS OF identifier
SET _____ TO _____
```

Notice that the ADDRESS OF can be a sending or receiving item. You can pass it in a CALL statement both BY CONTENT and BY REFERENCE. When passed BY REFERENCE, you can use it to set the address of a level 01 or 77 item in the Linkage Section. This lets subprograms manipulate an item, given a pointer containing the item's address. You assign the pointer to a description of the item in the Linkage Section, and then you can manipulate it.

An example will make this clearer. Suppose we have a subprogram that is called as follows:

```
01  NUM-BLANKS                   PIC 9(9) BINARY.
    ■ ■ ■
    CALL "NOBLANKS" USING BY CONTENT   A-POINTER,
                                       LENGTH OF LEN-ITEM,
                          BY REFERENCE NUM-BLANKS
```

The NOBLANKS subprogram is to count all the blanks in the item pointed to it by A-POINTER. The length of the item is stored in LEN-ITEM. (We won't worry now how A-POINTER and LEN-ITEM came to contain their contents.) The number of blanks is to be stored in NUM-BLANKS. The subprogram could be written as follows:

```
IDENTIFICATION DIVISION.
    PROGRAM-ID. NOBLANKS.
*********************************************************************
* SUBPROGRAM TO COUNT NUMBER OF BLANKS IN AN ITEM.                 *
* CALL "NOBLANKS" USING BY CONTENT  A-POINTER, LEN-ITEM,           *
*                       BY REFERENCE NUM-BLANKS                    *
* IN:  A-POINTER points to data item.          POINTER            *
*      LEN-ITEM contains length of data item.  PIC 9(9) BINARY     *
* OUT: NUM-BLANKS contains count of blanks in data item.          *
*                                              PIC 9(9) BINARY     *
*********************************************************************
DATA DIVISION.
WORKING-STORAGE SECTION.
77  NUM-ITEM                  PIC S9(4) BINARY.
       [This is used as a subscript.]
LINKAGE SECTION.
01 A-POINTER                  POINTER.
```

```
01 LEN-ITEM                          PIC 9(9) BINARY.
01 NUM-BLANKS                        PIC 9(9) BINARY.
01 THE-ITEM                          PIC X(1).
```
   [THE-ITEM *isn't passed as a parameter. It is included in the Linkage Section so that we can*
   refer to the item pointed to by A-POINTER *as a character string. We give it a length of 1 in the*
   description, but its real length is contained in LEN-ITEM, *which is passed as a parameter.*]
```
PROCEDURE DIVISION USING A-POINTER, LEN-ITEM, NUM-BLANKS.
    SET ADDRESS OF THE-ITEM TO A-POINTER
```
      [*This makes any reference to* THE-ITEM *reference the item pointed to by* A-POINTER.
       Now we can treat THE-ITEM *as if it were a data item passed as a parameter.*]
```
    MOVE ZEROS TO NUM-BLANKS
```
      [*Set up to count nonblanks in* NUM-BLANKS.]
```
    PERFORM VARYING NUM-ITEM FROM 1 BY 1
            UNTIL NUM-ITEM > LEN-ITEM
```
         [*We'll look at each character and count it if it is blank.*]
```
      IF THE-ITEM(NUM-ITEM:1) = SPACE
         THEN ADD 1 TO NUM-BLANKS
      END-IF
    END-PERFORM
    EXIT PROGRAM
      .
**** Exit
 END PROGRAM NOBLANKS.
```

You can use ADDRESS OF to obtain the address of an item only in the Linkage Section in VS COBOL II. It would be useful to be able to obtain the address of any data item to get around this limitation. We can write a subprogram to do this. We can call the GETADD subprogram that follows and pass it an identifier (BY REFERENCE, so we get its address) and a POINTER variable in which the subprogram is to store the address of the identifier. Since the identifier will be defined in the Linkage Section, we can store its address in the POINTER item.

```
IDENTIFICATION DIVISION.
    PROGRAM-ID. GETADD.
****************************************************************
* SUBPROGRAM TO OBTAIN THE ADDRESS OF AN ITEM.                *
* CALL "GETADD" USING BY REFERENCE A-REC, A-POINTER           *
* IN:  A-REC is any data item:  DISPLAY, BINARY, PACKED, etc. *
* OUT: A-POINTER contains the address of A-REC.  POINTER      *
****************************************************************
DATA DIVISION.
LINKAGE SECTION.
01  A-REC                     PIC X(1).
01  A-POINTER                 POINTER.
PROCEDURE DIVISION USING A-REC, A-POINTER.
* Store the address of A-REC in A-POINTER.
```

```
        SET A-POINTER TO ADDRESS OF A-REC
        EXIT PROGRAM
        .
**** Exit
 END PROGRAM GETADD.
```

To illustrate the use of pointers further, we can provide a subprogram that stores an item in another item, given a pointer to the other item. The following subprogram does this:

```
 IDENTIFICATION DIVISION.
     PROGRAM-ID. STOREADD.
**********************************************************************
* SUBPROGRAM TO STORE ITEM IN IDENTIFIER, GIVEN ITEM'S ADDRESS. *
* CALL "STOREADD" USING BY CONTENT A-POINTER, LEN-ITEM,         *
*                       BY REFERENCE A-REC                      *
* IN:  A-POINTER contains address of item to store.   POINTER  *
*      LEN-ITEM contains the length of item.  PIC 9(9) BINARY   *
* OUT: A-REC contains the contents of item pointed to.         *
*           Should be same PIC as data item, but data is       *
*           moved to it without conversion regardless of       *
*           its format.                                        *
**********************************************************************
 DATA DIVISION.
 WORKING-STORAGE SECTION.
 01 NUM-ITEM                    PIC 9(9) BINARY.
 LINKAGE SECTION.
 01 A-REC                       PIC X(1).
 01 LEN-ITEM                    PIC 9(9) BINARY.
 01 A-POINTER                   POINTER.
 01 THE-ITEM                    PIC X(1).
 PROCEDURE DIVISION USING A-POINTER, LEN-ITEM, A-REC.
* Set address of A-POINTER so we can access it as THE-ITEM.
     SET ADDRESS OF THE-ITEM TO A-POINTER
* Move the item a character at a time.  Doesn't matter
* what kind of data the item contains.
     PERFORM WITH TEST AFTER
             VARYING NUM-ITEM FROM 1 BY 1
             UNTIL NUM-ITEM > LEN-ITEM
       MOVE THE-ITEM(NUM-ITEM:1) TO A-REC(NUM-ITEM:1)
     END-PERFORM
     EXIT PROGRAM
     .
**** Exit
 END PROGRAM STOREADD.
```

To show how the GETADD and STOREADD subprograms use POINTER data, the following example defines two records. It will use GETADD to get the address of the PART-1 record and then to use STOREADD to copy the PART-1 record to PPART-1. (This accomplishes exactly the same thing as MOVE PART-1 TO PPART-1, and so the example is not particularly useful. The intent is just to show how POINTER data is used. A CICS subprogram or a subprogram written in another language can perform far more exotic operations using POINTER data.)

```
01  AN-ADDRESS                    POINTER.
01  PART-1.
    05  PART-A                     PIC X(4) VALUE "1234".
    05  PART-B                     PIC S9(4) BINARY VALUE 10.
    05  PART-C                     PIC S9(6) PACKED-DECIMAL
                                   VALUE 20.
    05  PART-D                     PIC X(2) VALUE "YZ".
01  PPART-1.
    05  PPART-A                    PIC X(4).
    05  PPART-B                    PIC S9(4) BINARY.
    05  PPART-C                    PIC S9(6) PACKED-DECIMAL.
    05  PPART-D                    PIC X(2).
    ■ ■ ■
*       Get the address of PART-1 and store it in AN-ADDRESS.
    CALL "GETADD" USING BY REFERENCE PART-1, AN-ADDRESS
*       Copy PART-1 to PPART-1
    CALL "STOREADD" USING BY CONTENT AN-ADDRESS, LENGTH OF PART-1
                         BY REFERENCE PPART-1
```

To give a flavor of how POINTER data can be used, we can now use the GETADD and STOREADD subprograms to manipulate data. We'll first use GETADD to obtain the address of a table of alphanumeric items and store the addresses in another table. Data for the program is defined as follows:

```
01  REC-TABLE.
    05  REC-1                      PIC X(10) VALUE "1111111111".
    05  REC-2                      PIC X(10) VALUE "2222222222".
    05  REC-3                      PIC X(10) VALUE "3333333333".
    05  REC-4                      PIC X(10) VALUE "4444444444".
    05  REC-5                      PIC X(10) VALUE "5555555555".
    05  REC-NO     PIC S9(4) BINARY VALUE 5.
*       This is the number of items in REC-TABLE.
01                                 REDEFINES REC-TABLE.
    05  REC-ITEM                   OCCURS 5 TIMES
                                   INDEXED BY REC-X
                                   PIC X(10).
*       This redefines the record as a table.
```

```
 01   PTR-TABLE.
      05  PTR-ENTRY                     OCCURS 10 TIMES
                                        INDEXED BY PTR-X
                                        POINTER.
 *        This is a table of pointers.
 01   NEXT-REC                          PIC X(10).
 *        This is used to obtain the contents of the REC-TABLE
 *        items.
      ■ ■ ■
 * Store the addresses of the REC-TABLE entries into PTR-ENTRY.
      PERFORM WITH TEST BEFORE VARYING REC-X FROM 1 BY 1
                UNTIL REC-X > REC-NO
        SET PTR-X TO REC-X
        CALL "GETADD" USING BY REFERENCE REC-ITEM(REC-X),
                                        PTR-ENTRY(PTR-X)
      END-PERFORM
 *      Store NULLS in the next entry to mark the last address.
      SET PTR-ENTRY(REC-NO + 1) TO NULLS
 *  To show some use for this, we'll get each record pointed to
 *  by the PTR-ENTRY TABLE and store it in NEXT-REC where we can
 *  display it.  Notice how we use the value of NULLS to end the loop.
      MOVE SPACES TO NEXT-REC
      PERFORM WITH TEST BEFORE VARYING PTR-X FROM 1 BY 1
                UNTIL PTR-ENTRY(PTR-X) = NULLS
        CALL "STOREADD" USING BY CONTENT   PTR-ENTRY(PTR-X),
                                        LENGTH OF REC-1,
                            BY REFERENCE NEXT-REC
        DISPLAY "NEXT REC: ", NEXT-REC
      END-PERFORM
```

III. CICS CONSIDERATIONS

A full description of the use of COBOL for CICS is beyond the scope of
this book. See References 1 and 2 for this. COBOL programs communicate
with CICS through subprogram calls. CICS permits only CICS I/O, and CICS
I/O is all done through subprogram calls. Because all the I/O under CICS is
done through subprogram calls, a COBOL program running under CICS cannot
contain any of the following:

• Environment Division: No FILE-CONTROL allowed.
• Data Division: No FILE SECTION allowed. No DBCS data allowed.
• Linkage Section: No JCL PARM input allowed.
• Procedure Division:

  • DECLARATIVES: Only USE allowed is USE FOR DEBUGGING.
  • CALL statement: No ON OVERFLOW or ON EXCEPTION phrases.

Following statements not allowed:

```
ACCEPT    FD              I-O-CONTROL   REWRITE   WRITE
CLOSE     FILE            MERGE         SD
DELETE    FILE-CONTROL    READ          SORT
DISPLAY   INPUT-OUTPUT    RERUN         START
```

• Reserved Words. The following additional words are reserved for CICS:

```
CICS  DLI  EXEC  END-EXEC
```

• Compiler Options: The following compiler options must be used when the program is to run under CICS:

```
NODBCS                       RENT
NODYNAM                      RES
LIB [If program has a        TRUNC(BIN) recommended
    COPY or BASIS statement
    in it.]
```
The CICS translator always inserts a CBL statement as follows:

```
CBL RES,RENT,NODYNAM,LIB
```

There is also a WORD compiler option to specify either CICS or an installation-defined list of statements to be flagged at compile time. Coding WORD (CICS) flags any COBOL statements not supported by CICS. The default is NOWORD for no statements to be flagged.
• The CICS preprocessor also generates a SERVICE LABEL statement and places it in the Procedure Division at a point where all registers that may no longer be valid are to be reloaded.

REFERENCES

1. "CICS/ESA Application Programmer's Reference," Order No. SC33-0676, Poughkeepsie, NY: IBM Corporation, 1990.
2. "CICS/OS/VS Application Programmer's Reference (Command Level)," Order No. SC33-0241, Poughkeepsie, NY: IBM Corporation, 1989.

24

Reading Programs

Reading programs for debugging and maintenance is an important skill. For debugging, you will probably be familiar with the program because you wrote it, but for maintenance you may know nothing about the program. Begin by trying to understand generally what the program does. A user's manual, if one exists, is perhaps the best source. There may be an overview in the program documentation, and the introductory remarks in the program are another source. A system flow chart or a JCL listing also tells a great deal about the program.

The next step is to identify the input and output: what is read and written. If you know what goes into a program and what comes out of it, you can make some fairly accurate assumptions about what must be going on inside the program. Get samples of the input and reports, if possible; study file layouts, input forms, and even data entry instructions. Locate the files used within a COBOL program by looking at the File Section, where they must all be listed.

At this level, the understanding depends on the documentation that is available. Do not depend only on formal documentation; use whatever is available. Talk to the people who receive the output of the program and who prepare the input. They often know more about the program than anyone if the original programmer is not available. Although they may not know programming, they know what the program does. They can often answer detailed questions from their long experience that might take days to discover by poring over the code.

Now, let's read a program. It is an actual program, not a good one, but typical, and we shall use it as an example of how to read a program. It is not a structured program, but this will be typical of many programs you will read. First, look at the Identification Division:

```
000001 IDENTIFICATION DIVISION.
000002     PROGRAM-ID.  PAYYE.
000003* REMARKS.
000004* THIS PROGRAM COPIES THE PAY FILE AND EXCLUDES THOSE PERSONNEL
000005* RECORDS WHICH ARE NOT NEEDED IN THE NEW FISCAL YEAR.  RECORDS
000006* ARE NOT NEEDED FOR THE NEW FISCAL YEAR IF THE PERSON IS
000007* INACTIVE, DOES NOT HAVE A COST IN THE COST FILE, AND DOES
```

```
000008* NOT APPEAR AS A PERSON RESPONSIBLE FOR A PROJECT IN THE
000009* PROJ FILE.
000010 ENVIRONMENT DIVISION.
000011 CONFIGURATION SECTION.
000012 SOURCE-COMPUTER.  IBM-370.
000013 OBJECT-COMPUTER.  IBM-370.
```

The remarks are useful, and from them we can expect there to be four files: the PAY file in, the PAY file out, a COST file, and a PROJ file. The main loop within the program is probably controlled by reading the PAY file. Next, look at the Input-Output Section, which lists the files:

```
000014 INPUT-OUTPUT SECTION.
000015 FILE-CONTROL.
000016     SELECT IN-PAY-FILE ASSIGN TO PAY.
000017     SELECT IN-COST-FILE ASSIGN TO SCOST.
000018     SELECT IN-PROJ-FILE ASSIGN TO PROJ.
000019     SELECT OUT-PAY-FILE ASSIGN TO PAYOUT.
```

The FILE-CONTROL paragraph lists each file, and as we expected, there are four files. Evidently IN-PAY-FILE is the PAY input file, IN-COST-FILE is the COST file, IN-PROJ-FILE is the PROJ file, and OUT-PAY-FILE is the PAY file written out.

Next, we shall look at the Data Division and the File Section, where the files are further described:

```
000020 DATA DIVISION.
000021 FILE SECTION.
000022 FD IN-PAY-FILE
000025     BLOCK CONTAINS 0 RECORDS
000024     RECORD CONTAINS 80 CHARACTERS
000025     LABEL RECORDS ARE STANDARD.
000026***** PAY FILE RECORD LAYOUT.  RECORD LENGTH = 80.
000027***** RELATIVE BYTE POSITION IN COLUMNS 75-77.
000028 01  PAY-RECORD.
00002      04  PAY-KEY.
000030*                        RECORD KEY.
000031         10  PAY-EMP-ID   PIC X(9).
000032*                        PERSONS ID
000035     05  PAY-NAME         PIC X(25).
000034*                        PERSONS NAME.
000035     05  PAY-ORGP         PIC X(3).
000036*                        ORG OF PERSON.
000037     05  PAY-SALARY       PIC S9(9)V9(2).
000038*                        ANNUAL SALARY IN DOLLARS.
000039     05  PAY-STATUS       PIC X(1).
```

```
000040*                               PERSONS STATUS.
000041*                               A-ACTIVE- I-INACTIVE.
000042     05  PAY-DATE-UPDATED   PIC X(6).
000043*                               DATE RECORD LAST UPDATED.
000044*                               YYMMDD
000045     05  FILLER             PIC X(25).
000046*                               AVAILABLE SPACE.
000047 FD  IN-COST-FILE
000048     RECORD CONTAINS 80 CHARACTERS
000049     BLOCK CONTAINS 0 RECORDS
000050     LABEL RECORDS ARE STANDARD.
000051***** COST FILE RECORD LAYOUT.  RECORD LENGTH = 80.
000052***** RELATIVE BYTE POSITION IN COLUMNS 73-77.
000053  01  COST-RECORD.
000054     05  COST-KEY.
000055         10  COST-EMP-ID    PIC X(9).
000056*                               ID or PERSON.
000057     05  COST-CHG           PIC X(4).
000058*                               CHARGE NUMBER.
000059     05  COST-OBJ           PIC X(3).
000060*                               OBJECT CODE OF PERSON.
000061     05  COST-TO-DATE.
000062*                               CUMULATIVE AMOUNTS TO DATE
000065         10  COST-AMT       PIC S9(9)V99.
000064*                               DOLLAR AMOUNT EXCLUDING FRINGE
000065*                               AND OVERHEAD
000066         10  COST-DAYS      PIC S9(9)V99.
000067*                               DAYS WORKED
000065         10  COST-FRINGE    PIC S9(9)V99.
000069*                               DOLLAR AMOUNT OF FRINGE.
000070         10  COST-OVERHEAD  PIC S9(9)V99.
000071*                               DOLLAR AMOUNT OF OVERHEAD.
000072     05  COST-DATE-UPDATED  PIC X(6).
000075*                               DATE RECORD LAST UPDATED.
000074*                               YYMMDD
000075     05  FILLER             PIC X(14).
000076*                               AVAILABLE SPACE.
000077 FD  IN-PROJ-FILE
000078     BLOCK CONTAINS 0 RECORDS
000079     RECORD CONTAINS 80 CHARACTERS
000080     LABEL RECORDS ARE STANDARD.
000081***** PROJ FILE RECORD LAYOUT.  RECORD LENGTH = 80.
000082***** RELATIVE BYTE POSITION IN COLUMNS 73-77.
000085  01  PROJ-RECORD.
000084     05  PROJ-KEY.
000085*                               RECORD KEY
```

```
000086          10  PROJ-CHG          PIC X(4).
000087*                               CHARGE NUMBER.
000088      05  PROJ-CHG-TITLE        PIC X(25).
000089*                               PROJECT TITLE.
000090      05  PROJ-ACT-TYPE         PIC X(1).
000091*                               ACTIVITY TYPE.
000092*                               D-DIRECT
000093*                               I-INDIRECT
000094      05  PROJ-PERSON           PIC X(9).
000095*                               ID OF PERSON RESPONSIBLE.
000096      05  PROJ-AMOUNT           PIC S9(9)V9(2).
000097*                               TOTAL CONTRACT AMOUNT.
000098      05  PROJ-START-DATE.
000099*                               CONTRACT START DATE.
000100          10  PROJ-START-YR     PIC 9(2).
000101          10  PROJ-START-MO     PIC 9(2).
000102          10  PROJ-START-DAY    PIC 9(2).
000103      05  PROJ-END-DATE.
000104*                               CONTRACT END DATE.
000105          10  PROJ-END-YR       PIC 9(2).
000106          10  PROJ-END-MO       PIC 9(2).
000107          10  PROJ-END-DAY      PIC 9(2).
000108      05  PROJ-ACTIVE-FLAG      PIC X(1).
000109*                               ACTIVE FLAG.
000110*                               A - ACTIVE.
000111*                               I - INACTIVE.
000112      05  PROJ-DATE-UPDATED     PIC X(6).
000113*                               DATE RECORD LAST UPDATED.
000114*                               YYMMDD.
000115      05  FILLER                PIC X(11).
000116*                               AVAILABLE SPACE.
000117 FD OUT-PAY-FILE
000118     BLOCK CONTAINS 0 RECORDS
000119     RECORD CONTAINS 80 CHARACTERS
000120     LABEL RECORDS ARE STANDARD.
000121  01  OUT-PAY-REC.
000122      05  OUT-PAY-KEY           PIC X(9).
000123      05  FILLER                PIC X(71).
```

From this we can tell that all the files are sequential. The record descriptions are well documented, and we can easily tell what the files contain.

Now, let us look at the Working-Storage Section, which will describe other data items used within the program:

```
000124 WORKING-STORAGE SECTION.
000125  01  FILLER COMP SYNC.
000126      05  IN-COUNT              PIC S9(4) VALUE 0.
```

```
000127       05  OUT-COUNT          PIC S9(4) VALUE O.
000128       05  DROP-COUNT         PIC S9(4) VALUE O.
000129  01  FILLER.
000150       05  PROJ-TABLE-SIZE    PIC S9(4) COMP SYNC VALUE 1000.
000131       05  PROJ-TABLE OCCURS 1000 DEPENDING ON PROJ-TABLE-SIZE
000132           INDEXED BY PROJX  PIC X(6).
```

IN-COUNT, OUT-COUNT, and DROP-COUNT are evidently counters, and we
might guess that they count the PAY records read, dropped, and written. The
PROJ-TABLE is a variable-size table, and we will have to see how it is used.
There are no input/output records described in Working-Storage, and so the
READ INTO form cannot be used. The program processes the data in the buffers.
As we read the program, we should keep this in mind for the potential problems
it can cause.

Now, let us look at the Procedure Division:

```
000133 PROCEDURE DIVISION.
000134 A10-BEGIN.
000135     OPEN INPUT IN-PROJ-FILE.
000136     SET PROJX TO 1.
000137 A20-READ-PROJ.
000138     READ IN-PROJ-FILE AT END GO TO A30.
000139     MOVE PROJ-PERSON TO PROJ-TABLE (PROJX).
000140     SET PROJX UP BY 1.
000141     GO TO A20-READ-PROJ.
000142 A30.
```

The program begins with a paragraph name. We need to know if this is the
start of a loop and how control gets back to A10-BEGIN. For this, we need the
cross-reference list of paragraph names:

```
THE LETTER PRECEDING A PROCEDURE-NAME REFERENCE INDICATES THE CONTEXT
IN WHICH THE PROCEDURE-NAME IS USED.   THESE LETTERS AND THEIR MEANINGS
ARE:
    A = ALTER (PROCEDURE-NAME)
    B = GO TO (PROCEDURE-NAME) DEPENDING ON
    E = END OF RANGE OF (PERFORM) THRU (PROCEDURE-NAME)
    O = GO TO (PROCEDURE-NAME)
    P = PERFORM (PROCEDURE-NAME)
    T = (ALTER) TO PROCEED TO (PROCEDURE-NAME)
    U = USE FOR DEBUGGING (PROCEDURE-NAME)

DEFINED    CROSS-REFERENCE OF PROCEDURES    REFERENCES
000134     A10-BEGIN
000137     A20-READ-PROJ. . . . . . . . .   G000141
000142     A30. . . . . . . . . . . . . .   G000138
000150     B10-READ-PAY . . . . . . . . .   G000163   G000167
```

```
000160      B20-DROP-PAY
000164      B30-KEEP-PAY . . . . . . . . .   G000153   G000155   G000159
000168      C10-LEVEL-COST . . . . . . . .   P000154   G000173
000174      C20-EXIT . . . . . . . . . . .   E000154   G000169   G000172
000175      D10-END. . . . . . . . . . . .   G000151
```

A10-BEGIN is not used, and so the beginning code does not start a loop, but
is executed only once. The first statement following A10-BEGIN opens the
IN-PROJ-FILE. Then we set PROJX to 1. PROJX indexes the PROJ-TABLE,
and so we can expect to store values in it. Next, we pass through the
A20-READ-PROJ label, and we might expect this to be the start of a loop.
Again, the cross-reference list tells us that only statement 141 refers to it, and
it is apparent that it is a loop to read IN-PROJ-FILE. The file is read, and
on encountering an end-of-file we go to A30. (We also note that this is the
only way we can get to A30.) PROJ-PERSON from IN-PROJ-FILE is stored in
PROJ-TABLE, with PROJX used as the index. Then we set PROJX up by 1 and
go to A20-READ-PROJ to read the next record. We do not know the sort order
of IN-PROJ-FILE, and we must check to see whether there is an assumption
of a sort order when PROJ-TABLE is used.

   Now we should examine the extreme cases within the loop. What happens if
IN-PROJ-FILE is empty? We will immediately go to A30 with PROJX set to 1.
Notice that we always go to A30 with PROJX set to 1 greater than the number
of records read. We should keep this in mind, because it is a potential source of
error. Now look at the other extreme, when more than 1000 records are read.
There is no check to see if the table overflows, and this is a potential error
that should be corrected. We might now expect the program to search for the
person's employee ID in the PROJ-TABLE rather than by reading the PROJ file.

   Now let us see what happens next in the program:

```
000143      SET PROJX DOWN BY 1.
000144      SET PROJ-TABLE-SIZE TO PROJX.
000145      CLOSE IN-PROJ-FILE.
000146      OPEN INPUT IN-PAY-FILE.
000147      OPEN INPUT IN-COST-FILE.
000148      OPEN OUTPUT OUT-PAY-FILE.
```

PROJX is set down by 1, because it contains one more than the number of
records read. Then PROJ-TABLE-SIZE, the item that controls the size of
PROJ-TABLE, is set to PROJX. This appears correct, but it contains a potential error. If IN-PROJ-FILE contains no records, PROJX will contain 1, and
setting it down by 1 yields a value of zero, but zero is not a valid value for an
index. We can correct the error by first setting PROJ-TABLE-SIZE to PROJX
and then subtracting 1 from it.

   The next statement closes the IN-PROJ-FILE. Lines 135 to 145 encompass
the statements to read records from IN-PROJ-FILE into PROJ-TABLE, and
we might set them off with comments. Next, we open the IN-PAY-FILE and

IN-COST-FILE for input and the OUT-PAY-FILE for output. Now to read some more of the program:

```
000149     MOVE LOW-VALUES TO COST-EMP-ID.
000150 B10-READ-PAY.
000151     READ IN-PAY-FILE AT END GO TO D10-END.
000152     ADD 1 TO IN-COUNT.
000153     IF PAY-STATUS = "A" GO TO B30-KEEP-PAY.
000154     PERFORM C10-LEVEL-COST THRU C20-EXIT.
```

First, we move LOW-VALUES to COST-EMP-ID. It is not apparent what this is for, and we shall have to see. The programmer may not have realized it when he or she placed the MOVE here, but if it had preceded the OPEN for IN-COST-FILE, it would be in error. COST-EMP-ID is in the record area, and there is no record area until the file is opened. Quirks such as this are the reason that it is bad to read and write from the record area.

Next, we pass through the B10-READ-PAY label and read IN-PAY-FILE. Since IN-PAY-FILE is the master file, we would expect B10-READ-PAY to be the start of the main loop of the program. We note from the cross-reference list that we can get back to here from statements 163 and 167. Let us remember this when we examine those statements. On encountering an end-of-file, we go to D10-END, where we would expect the program to be terminated. If an end-of-file is not encountered, we add 1 to IN-COUNT. We expected IN-COUNT to count the IN-PAY-FILE records, and apparently it did. Since we have not moved an initial value to IN-COUNT, we should check to see that it is assigned an initial value in the Working-Storage Section. On checking, we see that it is assigned a value of zero, as are OUT-COUNT and DROP-COUNT.

The next IF statement goes to B30-KEEP-PAY if the PAY-STATUS is "A". We are to keep records whose pay status is "A", and so B30-KEEP-PAY should write out the record. Let us look at the B30-KEEP-PAY paragraph:

```
000164 B30-KEEP-PAY.
000165     WRITE OUT-PAY-REC FROM PAY-RECORD.
000166     ADD 1 TO OUT-COUNT.
000167     GO TO B10-READ-PAY.
```

We write the OUT-PAY-REC from PAY-RECORD. We are writing the output record from the record area; is this permitted? It turns out to be correct, but it is a bad practice. Then we add 1 to OUT-COUNT, which we know has an initial value of zero, and this confirms our belief that OUT-COUNT counts the OUT-PAY-FILE records. Next, we go to B10-READ-PAY to read the next record. This GO TO is one of the two references to B10-READ-PAY.

Now let us get back to the main line of the code where we perform C10-LEVEL-COST THRU C20-EXIT. Let us see what this paragraph does:

```
000168 C10-LEVEL-COST.
000169     IF COST-EMP-ID NOT < PAY-EMP-ID GO TO C20-EXIT.
```

```
000170     READ IN-COST-FILE AT END
000171        MOVE HIGH-VALUES TO COST-EMP-ID
000172        GO TO C20-EXIT.
000173        IF COST-EMP-ID < PAY-EMP-ID GO TO C10-LEVEL-COST.
000174 C20-EXIT.  EXIT.
```

First, we compare the COST-EMP-ID of the IN-COST-FILE with the
PAY-EMP-ID of the current IN-PAY-FILE record. If it is not less than (greater
than or equal to), we go to C20-EXIT and exit the paragraph. Otherwise,
we read in the next IN-COST-FILE record, and if an end-of-file is encountered, move HIGH-VALUES to COST-EMP-ID and go to C20-EXIT to exit the
paragraph. The first time we enter C10-LEVEL-COST, COST-EMP-ID contains
LOW-VALUES, and this will cause the first IN-COST-FILE record to be read.
Now it is clear why we moved LOW-VALUES to COST-EMP-ID: to force the first
record to be read. If an end-of-file is not encountered, we check to see if the
COST-EMP-ID is less than the PAY-EMP-ID, and if so, we go to C10-LEVEL
to read another record. In essence, we read IN-COST-FILE until we have a
record whose key is equal to or greater than the key of the current IN-PAY-FILE
record. Moving HIGH-VALUES to COST-EMP-ID ensures that the first IF statement in the C10-LEVEL-COST paragraph will immediately go to C20-EXIT
without attempting to read more records.

Now, let us get back to the main line of code following the PERFORM:

```
000155     IF PAY-EMP-ID = COST-EMP-ID GO TO B30-KEEP-PAY.
000156     SET PROJX TO 1.
000157     SEARCH PROJ-TABLE
000158        WHEN PAY-EMP-ID = PROJ-TABLE (PROJX)
000159             GO TO B30-KEEP-PAY.
000160 B20-DROP-PAY.
000161     ADD 1 TO DROP-COUNT.
000162     DISPLAY "PAY-KEY: ", PAY-KEY.
000163     GO TO B10-READ-PAY.
```

We return from the C10-LEVEL-COST paragraph with the next IN-COST-FILE
record equal to or greater than the current IN-PAY-FILE record, or
HIGH-VALUES if there are no more IN-COST-FILE records. Then, if the
PAY-EMP-ID of the IN-COST-FILE record equals the COST-EMP-ID of the
current IN-PAY-FILE, we go to B30-KEEP-PAY to keep the record. This is
correct, but notice the assumptions that the program makes about the order of
the IN-PAY-FILE and the IN-COST-FILE. They must both be in ascending
order on the PAY-EMP-ID and COST-EMP-ID, respectively. The program does
not check the sort orders, and this too is a potential source of error. What if
there are duplicate records in IN-PAY-FILE or IN-COST-FILE? We do not
know if they are permitted, but the logic will work correctly if they exist. This
is comforting.

   If the PAY-EMP-ID does not equal the COST-EMP-ID, we set PROJX to 1
and search the PROJ-TABLE sequentially for an entry equal to PAY-EMP-ID.

Since it is a sequential search, the program makes no assumption about the order of PROJ-TABLE, and duplicate entries will not cause a problem. If PAY-EMP-ID is found in PROJ-TABLE, we go to B30-KEEP-PAY to keep the record. If not found, we pass through the unused B20-DROP-PAY label, add 1 to DROP-COUNT, display the key of the record dropped, and go to B10-READ-PAY to read the next record. This is the second place from which we go to B10-READ-PAY, and we have looked at all the statements in the loop. The statements to read the IN-PAY-FILE encompass statements 146 through 174, and we should enclose them in comments to show their beginning and end.

The last thing is to look at D10-END, where we go when there are no more IN-PAY-FILE records to read:

```
000175 D10-END.
000176     DISPLAY "PAY IN =" IN-COUNT.
000177     DISPLAY "PAY OUT =" OUT-COUNT.
000175     DISPLAY "PAY DROP =" DROP-COUNT.
000179     CLOSE IN-PAY-FILE.
000180     CLOSE OUT-PAY-FILE.
000181     CLOSE IN-COST-FILE.
000182     STOP RUN.
000183*** END OF PROGRAM ***
```

We display the count of records in, out, and dropped. Then we close the three files and stop the run. This concludes the program. We have read the entire program, and it appears to be correct, although we did discover some potential errors. Notice how invaluable the cross-reference listing was to reading the program. This was a small program, but the same techniques apply to large ones.

As you read a program, you will encounter important data items, such as tables, flags, and counters. If the names do not adequately describe their contents, note where the items are declared and your assumption of their use. Again, the cross-reference listing is essential to find all the places in the program where they are used. They let you see if your assumptions are correct and whether they are reused for some other purpose. When you are sure what they contain, insert a comment where they are defined to explain their use.

Often at a particular place in the program, you will want to know what value a data name contains. By using the cross-reference listing to find all references to the data name, and by knowing the major flow of control, you can usually discover what value the data name contains. Let us use the cross-reference listing to verify that IN-COUNT counts the IN-PAY-FILE records. The cross-reference listing tells where it is defined and where it is used:

```
AN "M" PRECEDING A DATA-NAME REFERENCE INDICATES THAT THE DATA-NAME
IS MODIFIED BY THIS REFERENCE.
DEFINED    CROSS-REFERENCE OF DATA NAMES    REFERENCES
000126     IN-COUNT.  .  .  .  .  .  .  .  M000152  000176
```
   [It is defined in statement 000126.]

```
00125   01  FILLER COMP SYNC.
00126       05  IN-COUNT              PIC S9(4) VALUE 0.
```
[It is used in statement 152.]
```
00151       READ IN-PAY-FILE AT END GO TO D10-END.
00152       ADD 1 TO IN-COUNT.
```
[It is also used in statement 176.]
```
00175   D10-END.
00176       DISPLAY "PAY IN =" IN-COUNT.
```

IN-COUNT is used only to count IN-PAY-FILE records, and the count is displayed at the end of the program. As you read a program, annotate the source listing as you discover things. Later, you should insert some of these annotations as comments in the program, so that the next time the program is read it will be easier. These comments are often the best of all comments, because they tell the reader what was not obvious when you read the program.

As you read the program, look closely for errors. Just because the program has run correctly does not mean that there are no errors. We found several potential errors in the program we just read. The following items suggest things that should be checked:

- In a division, look for a possible division by zero or a loss of precision.
- Look for expressions such as A * (B / C) that should be changed to (A * B) / C.
- In a nested IF statement, look for a misplaced period or END-IF.
- In an arithmetic expression, check the accuracy, especially if it contains a division.
- Look at the compiler error listing, because there may be error or warning messages. This is especially important when you recompile an old production program, because a new compiler may discover previously undetected errors, or there may be changes in the language since the last compilation. If you are link editing to place a load module in a library, check the linkage editor listing to ensure that the module was added or replaced correctly.
- Be suspicious of conditional expressions. If NOT and OR appear in the same logical expression, they are usually coded incorrectly.
- Look for exceptional conditions for which there is no detection. If items are stored in a table, check to see that the table does not overflow. Check for indexes having the potential of being set to a zero value.
- Look for off-by-1 errors. In the PERFORM VARYING, check that the loop executes the proper number of times. A PERFORM VARYING X FROM 1 BY 1 UNTIL X = 10 executes the loop 9 times, not 10 times as one might at first expect.
- Identify each file, where it is opened, read or written, and closed. Note any assumptions the program makes about the file's order.
- If you discover an error, do not be misled into believing that it is the last error. That makes it even more likely that there are more errors.

25

Beyond COBOL

This chapter contains a collection of topics that are not a part of the COBOL language but are a part of programming. They include production computing, efficiency, maintenance, programming for change, and testing and debugging. Techniques for these have been discussed throughout the book where they apply to individual language statements, and they are brought together here for a complete discussion.

I. PRODUCTION COMPUTING

Many computer programs are written to be run only once to solve a particular problem. However, this is not the world of COBOL. It is not a good language for quick, one-time programs, but it is an excellent language for production programs. Most COBOL programs are run repeatedly in production. This is perhaps the most significant fact about COBOL, and the one that makes it difficult for many in computing to understand and appreciate it. The production environment of COBOL leads to many considerations, some not at all obvious.

Production programs exist for a long time. This provides time for the environment, the operating system, the compiler, and the ANSI Standard to change. The I/O devices will change, as will the computer. The requirements will change. Laws will change; new information will be legally required, and old information will be legally prohibited. The users will change, as will the organization.

Latent errors will come to life. A single run of the program might not discover some errors, but when the program is run often, those latent errors will occur. Most programs contain errors that lie dormant until a particular combination of data brings them to life. The longer the program's life, the more that can go wrong with the program.

The program must run on schedule. A schedule must be prepared, input must be coordinated, and conditions that would affect the schedule must be anticipated. Errors require immediate attention, and the pressures are intense.

Information is retained. This is an enormously complicating factor, because errors are cumulative. When an error introduces bad data in a file, correcting the program does not correct the error. The file must be purged of the bad data. Also, other programs will be affected if they read the file with bad data.

Someone else will run the program. The organization may set up a separate run group to collect the input, schedule the runs, submit the job, and check and distribute the output. The run group must know how to run the job and keep track of files. They must also be able to tell if the program ran successfully, and they must know what to do if the run was unsuccessful. They may have to learn and program an entire Job Entry System (JES2 or JES3 for VS COBOL II) that directs the program, its files, and the output through a network of computers.

Someone else will modify the program. The original programmer may be reassigned or even leave the company. Someone completely unfamiliar with the program must locate errors and make modifications.

Someone else will read the output. Reports must be carefully formatted with row and column titles and page headings. It is not enough just to print the information; it must be organized and presented to be clear. Managers will wonder why they can't have the reports on their PC terminals so that they can manipulate the data with their spreadsheet tools and display three-dimensional color graphics.

Sheer volume will cause problems. The program may run too long, the files may be too large, and too much may be printed. A production program may encounter limitations in memory size, CPU time, elapsed running time, tape and disk capacity, and lines of output. You must consider backup and recovery. The volume will tend to grow over time, and this may suddenly cause the program to stop running if the maximum capacity is exceeded.

II. EFFICIENCY

A. Why Efficiency Is Still Important

Concern for efficiency permeates computing. Programming classes emphasize it, and techniques for improving efficiency are learned long before techniques for writing correct and easily modified programs are mastered.

Efficiency was critical early in programming, when the storage was small, the CPU relatively slow, and the I/O devices equally limited. It made no difference that a program was clear, if it would not fit on the computer. Many of these restrictions have now been eased. New computers and virtual storage systems provide large amounts of storage, CPUs are an order of magnitude faster, and so are tapes and disks. Why, then, worry about efficiency?

There is a strange effect at work that is almost an inverse law of expectations for computing. *The faster the computer, the more attention that must be paid to efficiency.* The reason is that faster computers raise our expectations of what a computer should do. When the computer's speed is increased by an order of magnitude, a relational data base system is installed, the application is put on-line, and the output is bit-mapped, full-color, moving graphics. The result is that the application takes twenty times the computer power, so that the response is now twice as slow. This isn't always the case, but the rising demand on an application and the increased appetite of the operating system means that the concern for efficiency hasn't changed much since the 1960s.

We need to worry about efficiency for three reasons. First, the operating system's consumption has kept pace with the increased hardware capacity, so that the amount of computer available to work on a program is heavily diluted. The computing power of large computers is further diluted, because many programs are run concurrently and a single program receives only a portion of the computer's resources.

Second, most large mainframe systems charge for use of the computer's resources, and if fewer resources are used, the job will cost less. If you can cut a $200 job down to $50, that is $150 saved, and it is irrelevant that such a job might have cost $1000 to run 10 years ago. (This is the overwhelming reason to use a PC wherever you can. Once the PC is purchased, the run cost is zero.)

The final reason is to guard against Parkinson's law—that the size of the program will expand to use all the computer's resources. Constraints still exist, but perhaps it is good that they do, because they give discipline to programming. People tend to get sloppy when things are too easy. This also guards against the unexpected. For example, with MVS/ESA, there is generally no need to worry about the program's size. But if the company wants to move the application to a PC, program size could become critical.

B. Techniques for Efficiency

Still, while efficiency is important, it doesn't have to be dumb. More dumb things have probably been done for the sake of efficiency than for any other reason. All installations have their tale of a person spending weeks to optimize a program that is run only once. This is not intelligent. Nor is it wise to mount an effort to optimize a program whose biweekly run cost is $2. Even if the run cost were cut to zero, the cost of optimizing would exceed the savings. We should be selective and intelligent in our approach.

The first step in efficiency is to decide what you want to optimize. Efficiency is usually measured by run cost on a mainframe and elapsed time on a PC. Both generally depend on some combination of CPU, memory, and I/O. These items may conflict. Increasing the blocking factor on a mainframe to reduce the number of I/Os can cost more in memory. However, the three may interact in surprising ways. One application used an indexed file for editing, and the program ran slowly. It was changed to read the indexed file into a table, and a binary search rather than random file access was then used for the editing. This saved I/O as expected, CPU time rather surprisingly, and memory totally unexpectedly. (The random access routines required more memory than storing the table.) This points out something else; the results of optimizing can be unexpected and counterintuitive. Unless you can measure the results of optimization, you could end up increasing the run cost or elapsed time.

We often optimize in the wrong place—at the detail level, where the results are rarely measurable, instead of at the design level, where the results can be significant. For example, one may labor long over whether it is more efficient to open all files with a single OPEN statement or several OPEN statements. This may or may not save a few milliseconds in a computer run, but you usually open files only once in a run, and this is bound to have little effect on cost. One may neglect to increase the blocking factor of the files, which might cut the run cost in half.

Begin optimizing during the design. Programs cost little to change there, but they are expensive to change after they have been coded. Bad design cannot be rescued by efficient coding. The best way to optimize is to eliminate something entirely. This saves designing, programming, documenting, and run costs. For example, do not sort a file that is already in the proper sort sequence.

One of the most important determiners of efficiency is the file organization and access. Sequential organization is fastest when most of the records must be processed. Indexed organization and random access are fastest when only a small portion of the records must be processed. Relative organization is even faster than indexed for random access, but it is limited for applications, because the record key is not a part of the record. Internal tables are significantly faster than relative file organization for table lookup.

Program simply and clearly, with an eye toward efficiency so that a separate effort is not required for optimization. It generally requires no more effort to program for efficiency than to program in any other way. If any significant inefficiencies occur, they are likely to be localized to a few places within the program, and you can concentrate on these. The 80:20 rule applies to programs—80 percent of the program's execution time is concentrated in 20 percent of the statements.

Concentrate your effort where there will be a payoff, as in the 20 percent of the statements that constitute 80 percent of the run time. Do not attempt to optimize the compilation of the program with techniques such as crowding many statements onto a line. Such savings are both insignificant and counter-productive. To save compilation time, reduce the number of times that you must recompile the program, by writing it correctly. Then find as many errors as possible in each test run—or compile on a PC.

One of the most significant things you can do to reduce the cost of program development is to do as much as possible on a PC. The savings are the same for production runs, but the choice of a mainframe or PC for production often depends on capacity, access to files, and other things besides run cost. Do as much of the testing as you can on the PC. At a minimum, you can keep your COBOL source on a PC and always make any program changes there. Compile it on the PC to catch all the compilation errors. Then upload it to the mainframe and compile it. This reduces the number of times you have to compile on the expensive mainframe to a minimum.

Optimize where there is repetition, such as in loops, in processing high-volume transactions, and in programs that are run often. Do only what is necessary within a loop. The following techniques should become automatic:

- Move all computed values outside the loop if the value doesn't change with each loop iteration. For example, if COMPUTE A = B + C appears within a loop and the values of B and C do not change, move the COMPUTE outside the loop.

- Choose the data type that is the most efficient. Use PIC X whenever data is not used in computations, BINARY for integer counters, and PACKED-DECIMAL for most other data.
- Use BINARY data items or indexes for subscripting within loops. Indexes are the most efficient. COBOL must compute the position of an element at run time from its length for a data item used as a subscript. For an index, it knows the element length and doesn't have to do this computation.
- COBOL evaluates table subscripts in left to right order to locate an element within a table. COBOL doesn't have to do as many calculations when the leftmost subscripts are constants. If you can, design your tables so that the leftmost subscripts are constant and the rightmost do most of the varying.
- Use BINARY for an OCCURS DEPENDING ON item. It requires more effort for COBOL to operate on an OCCURS DEPENDING ON table than one with fixed length.
- Floating-point is more efficient for most exponentiation.
- Don't do unnecessary conversion. Make sure that your data types are compatible, so that the computer doesn't have to perform needless conversions. You can't specify the data type of numeric constants. They are all external decimal. You might define numeric constants as identifiers and assign initial values to them. You can make them whatever type is needed so that the item doesn't have to be converted.
- For critical loops where you might be concerned whether a COMPUTE is faster or slower than the equivalent ADDs, SUBTRACTs, MULTIPLYs, and DIVIDEs, create a test case and time the loop. See which is faster, or if the difference is significant. The example program later in this section shows how to time a program on the PC.
- Select the compiler options for optimization. Optimizing requires no effort, and you need not sacrifice clarity. Don't use it for testing, because it compiles slower than the ordinary compiler. It is best used to recompile the production version of the program.
- In VS COBOL II, code the OPT (for optimized compilation), NOSSRANGE (to suppress subscript range checking), and NUMPROC(PFD) (if there is a single way of signing numbers). Also code AWO (Apply Write Only), FASTSRT (for optimizing sorting), NOFDUMP (for no debugging dump), and TRUNC(OPT) (for truncating BINARY in a MOVE in the optimum way rather than based on the number of decimal digits). In Microsoft COBOL, code the OPTSIZE or OPTSPEED, COMP, and NOBOUND for optimized compilation.
- Don't make the computer do unnecessary work. For example, COMPUTE A = B * 4 / 2 forces an unnecessary division, which you can eliminate by coding COMPUTE A = B * 2.
- Use a binary search wherever possible in searching a table.
- Do not waste memory. However, if the computer has a fixed memory size allocated to each program, such as on a PC, and the program fits in the computer, you gain nothing by expending effort to conserve storage. Memory is the hardest resource to optimize; its requirements are usually fixed.

Some things may have no effect on the run cost but may affect the efficiency of the operating system. For example, if several files are being written consecutively onto the same tape, each CLOSE will rewind the tape to the load point. Then, when the next file is opened, the tape spaces forward to the proper position on the tape. It is unlikely that this would be reflected in the computer system's charging equation, but as a matter of professional pride, do not let this happen. (This also saves you from the wrath of the computer operators.)

On the mainframe, the cost of I/O depends primarily on the blocking and to a lesser extent on the record size. Block as high as permitted within the constraints of storage and the I/O device. Do this by not coding the BLKSIZE subparameter in your JCL, so that the system will select an optimum block size for the device.

Sorts are a heavy user of I/O. Eliminate any redundant sorts. If a job consists of sorting a file, selecting records, and then producing a report, select the records first, sort them, and then generate the report to reduce the number of sorted records.

Do not be foolish in saving I/O. It saves I/O to compile parameters into a program rather than reading them in from control statements, but it costs little to read a control statement. It might take 100 years of reading in a control statement to equal the cost of one compilation to change a parameter built into the program.

C. Timing Portions of a Program

You can use the following statements to time the execution of portions of a program. The timings will only be accurate on a PC, because the elapsed time is clock time, not CPU time. On a mainframe, where the computer may be serving hundreds of concurrent users, clock time can vary widely with each run.

```
01  START-TIME.
    05   START-HR     PIC 99.
    05   START-MIN    PIC 99.
    05   START-SEC    PIC 99.
    05   START-HUN    PIC 99.
01  END-TIME.
    05   END-HR       PIC 99.
    05   END-MIN      PIC 99.
    05   END-SEC      PIC 99.
    05   END-HUN      PIC 99.
01  TIME-DIFF.
    05   TIME-START   PIC S9(9) BINARY.
    05   TIME-END     PIC S9(9) BINARY.
    05   TIME-DELTA   PIC S9(9) BINARY.
    ■ ■ ■
    ACCEPT START-TIME FROM TIME
```

```
COMPUTE TIME-START = START-HUN + START-SEC * 100 +
   START-MIN * 6000 + START-HR * 360000
```

Place portion of program to time here.

```
ACCEPT END-TIME FROM TIME
COMPUTE TIME-END = END-HUN + END-SEC * 100 +
   END-MIN * 6000 + END-HR * 360000
COMPUTE TIME-DELTA = TIME-END - TIME-START
DISPLAY "ELAPSED TIME (HUNDREDTHS OF A SECOND): ", TIME-DELTA
```

Even if a program runs at an acceptable cost, it will still be necessary to change it. Changing an existing program is maintenance, and it is the subject of the next section.

III. MAINTENANCE

A computer program cannot wear out, and from this one might assume that maintenance is not required for computer software as it is for hardware. But, surprisingly, computer software has as much need for maintenance as hardware. The difference between the two is that preventive maintenance works well for hardware but is usually counterproductive for software maintenance. This is the "If it isn't broken, don't fix it." rule.

There are several reasons for software maintenance. First, no computer program of any size can be tested for all possible combinations of data, and there will be undetected errors that can be triggered by new data. Then, although the computer program does not change, the environment does. Perhaps a new department is added, and the department table overflows. Perhaps the company opens a field office in another state that has a state income tax, and the payroll system must be changed. Perhaps a file being written on tape will no longer fit on a single tape reel. All of this requires maintenance. The computer, its operating system, or the COBOL compiler may also change, which may either introduce new errors or bring to light old, dormant errors in the program.

Maintenance on computer programs is a constant need, as it is for hardware. Because computer programs are not subject to physical wear, they do not require preventive maintenance. However, some installations collect several changes and schedule them together, and the result is much like scheduling preventive maintenance. Maintenance becomes more important over time. Programs age and need more maintenance. More applications are written, and the number of programs that are candidates for maintenance grows. Today, perhaps 80 percent of programming effort goes into maintenance.

There are several benefits to the professional programmer in doing maintenance. It provides an opportunity to learn both good and bad practices and to distinguish between them. It also gives a person feedback on systems design. Some systems designers never learn about their mistakes by revisiting the project. In the rush to meet deadlines and stay within budget, much is sacrificed. The result is often a product developed somewhat on time and within budget, but which costs an inordinate amount to maintain over its life. If systems designers were forced to see and correct their mistakes, we would have better systems.

Maintenance includes fixing errors and making modifications. When an error is discovered or a change is requested, the programmer must locate the necessary materials, including the source listing, source programs, file descriptions, test data, test JCL, and documentation. Then he or she must make the change, test it, update the documentation, and place the new version of the program in production.

The first step in maintenance is to locate the materials. The programmer should be provided with some means of locating them. The second step is to decide what documentation to trust. There needs to be some way of making sure that the documentation is current. Sometimes changes are made to old versions of the source program, with unfortunate results. Once the program change is made, the testing is similar to that of a new program, except that there is now real data with which to test. You must also be more on guard against side effects. Correcting an error does no good if it introduces another error. The trickiest part of maintenance is in implementing the change. It should be done with little risk and disturbance. Often you can make a parallel run with the new program version to ensure that it is working properly with real data.

Don't allow maintenance changes to destroy the integrity of the design. Don't try to minimize the effort with quick and dirty changes, whose cumulative effect is often to make a program unmaintainable. Modifications should be as carefully thought out as the original design.

Some formal control must usually be established for maintenance. This allows changes to be evaluated, assigned priorities, and scheduled. It also gives the people doing maintenance a way of measuring their progress, and it lets managers know what they are doing. Control must also be established over the source program, listing, documentation, and run libraries. This is critical when the efforts of several people must be coordinated.

One problem many companies have in controlling change is that they make it too bureaucratic. The result is that to get things done, programmers avoid the procedures rather than working with them. Maintenance control should be streamlined with the goal of facilitating changes, not making them unnecessarily difficult.

Maintenance in systems that retain data in files must account for the bad data that may remain in the files after the error is corrected in the program. For example, if a program improperly added an employee's current salary to the year-to-date total, you can correct the program. However, the employee's W-2 income tax form will still be wrong at the end of the year unless you correct the data in the file.

When making changes, leave a record of who made the change, when it was made, and what was changed. One way to do this is by comment lines within the program that indicate the specific change. This information helps if some other error crops up, because you can tell what was changed, but do not try to use this history as program documentation. A history is important as an audit trail but poor as documentation. It is too difficult to read through pages of changes, some of which may supersede others, to learn what a program is supposed to be doing today.

Good error messages and an audit trail are also essential in maintenance. They can tell what caused an error and what data was involved. The error messages should tell the following:

- What the error is
- The transaction, and field within the transaction, in error
- The severity of the error (catastrophic, serious, warning, or simply a note)
- What the program will do with the error (assume a value for the field, reject the transaction, or terminate the program)
- What, if anything, should be done outside the program (such as increase a table size and recompile)

There are four major categories of errors, and the program should be written to anticipate each:

- Catastrophic error: The program cannot continue execution. There should be very few errors of this type. For example, a person missing from the payroll file might be thought to be catastrophic. But it may be better to continue processing the payroll so that everyone else gets paid, and then write the check for the missing person by hand. An out-of-date payroll file would be a catastrophic error. A program should never terminate abnormally. Write the program to detect conditions that cause abnormal termination, such as processing nonnumeric data when numeric data is expected.
- Serious error: A transaction must be corrected before the run can be successful or the data accepted. A person missing from the payroll file might be a serious error.
- Warning: The data looks wrong and is not accepted, but it may actually be valid. A transaction entered with a salary of $500,000 might result in a warning. There must be a way of overriding the warning if the transaction is verified as correct.
- Note: The data is accepted, and an informational message is printed. This is more of a "you told me to let you know when this happened" thing than an error. An employee receiving overtime might merit a note.

An audit trail is also essential for maintenance. The audit trail consists of listings of all data read and written by the program and telling the progress of the program's execution. Some of the audit trail may consist of the files themselves, if programs are available to print their contents. Alternatively, you might print all the transactions read or written by the program if there are few, or print the transactions on request if there are many. The latter is handy for debugging but less useful in production. Once the program is run and an error is discovered, it is too late to request an audit trail from the program unless it is rerun. Programs should always print at least the following:

• Number of records read and written for each file
• Number of records selected if there is selection logic
• Any relevant totals, such as the total dollar amount of the transactions read or written
• The progress of the program's execution through its major phases; as a minimum, print when the program begins and ends execution

Perhaps the greatest aid in maintenance is to write programs that are easy to change. The next section describes techniques for this.

IV. PROGRAMMING FOR CHANGE

Programming is much easier if you know beforehand what to program. This is the basis of top-down design and programming, and the alternative of waltzing into something and immediately starting to program is unthinkable, although it is often done. However, the only time when you can know completely what is to be programmed beforehand is when you have just finished programming it. Unfortunately, most systems are not immediately reprogrammed after they are completed, and for those that are, the person who wrote the first version is usually not invited to write the next.

Although the ideal is to know in full detail what should be programmed, in practice you cannot, for several reasons. First, programming requires a complete specification of the details, with nothing left ambiguous. Humans have a high tolerance for ambiguity, and many questions that must be answered will not be raised until one sits down to code. (This was an early and unexpected requirement of programming. The detail required to program a solution had never been needed before, but to program the solution, the detail had to be obtained.)

Another reason for change is that the end users cannot know in full detail what is needed. You must elicit from the users all the known requirements, but not until they have been receiving the reports for some time will they really know in full detail what is wanted. This is not a communication problem. Managers who program often write their own little systems for themselves, and these systems go through iterations just as they do when the end user and the programmer are different people.

The final reason that you can't know everything the customer wants in advance is that the needs change. If the customer were able to tell you exactly what was needed, by the time the program was written and readied for production, the need would have changed.

Write the program with change in mind. Some try to achieve this by incorporating every conceivable requirement. But a program that has attempted to incorporate every conceivable situation would be a monster to change. Anyway, it is usually not the conceivable changes that give problems, but the inconceivable ones. The tradeoff between being comprehensive and being flexible is difficult, but do not confuse the two by choosing one and assuming you have the other. They usually conflict.

The best way to make programs easy to change is to write clear, understandable programs and to drive the program with data where possible. For example, in a billing program it would be bad to code the prices as constants directly in the Procedure Division statements. They would be hard to find when they must be changed, especially if a price appears in several places in the program. In addition, you must recompile the program to make the change, and this is a slow maintenance task. If the rate is parametrized as a data item and assigned an initial value, it is easy to find, and there is only one place in which the price must be changed. But you must still recompile the program. The best way is to read the price in from a control statement or file. Then, to change a price, only this line needs to be changed, and you can leave the program intact.

Minimize the impact of outside forces. Never read in a table without checking to see that the table does not overflow. In reading any file, be prepared to handle an excessive number of records or no records at all. Protect programs against incorrect data. Validate the input data before accepting it. Validate it all in one place. The code required for validation is a potential source of error, and you minimize this code by validating only once in one place.

Safety factors are used in engineering designs so that each component can withstand greater forces than the maximum expected. Computer programs should also have safety factors built into them to accommodate greater growth than expected. Each file and transaction in the system should have some unused space that is carried as filler. Then, if new data is required in the file or transaction, there is space for adding it without recompiling all the programs that read it.

V. DEBUGGING AND TESTING

Debugging consists of attempting to discover the cause of known bugs and fixing them. Testing consists of running the job to discover unknown bugs. Debugging and testing consume an inordinate amount of the program development time, often around 50 percent.[1]

Programmers are often accused of not testing enough, especially after bugs are discovered in production. However, testing cannot be exhaustive, and undiscovered bugs will always remain in production programs. Testing can only prove the presence of errors; it cannot prove their absence. Dijkstra points out that to check all possible combinations in multiplying two numbers might take 10,000 years on a computer.[2] Boehm[1] notes that a simple flow chart with two loops and a few IF statements would take 2000 years on a modern computer to follow all the possible paths.[1] Since testing cannot be exhaustive, you can only test up to the point where the potential cost of undiscovered bugs is less than the cost of additional testing. Unfortunately, this crossover point is never clear. In practice, testing is a bad place to try to save money.

You can reduce the amount of testing by checking only a few values, and make the assumption that the program will work for all values. For example, if the computer adds 10 and 20 correctly, we can safely assume that it will add 5 and 10 correctly. However, we might not so safely assume that it will add 5 and 1000 correctly, because the resultant item may be too small to contain the result. We need to include the extreme values in our testing. If a computation is tested for the smallest, the largest, and a representative value, we can assume that it is correct, even though an infinite number of values have not been tested. We can ensure that the values will be within the allowable range by editing the input data.

Debugging and testing should begin during the design. Design the system and the programs to be easy to test. For example, three separate programs that each run half an hour are easier to test than one gigantic program that runs for one and a half hours. Start with a test plan for the program or system. You may even go so far as to generate test data before the programming begins. Writing the test data before you write the program also forces you to think up the exceptional cases before you begin programming. In effect, this allows you to do your desk checking while you are writing the program. The test data should be expandable to enable new situations to be tested, but then keep old test data to ensure that old errors do not creep back in.

Although it may be hard to generate test data, it is even harder to verify it. The program's authors often do a poor job of finding errors, because they do not expect to find them. Seeing that so much of the program did work to produce any output, they sometimes assume that the numbers must be correct. If someone else verifies the output, he or she will make fewer assumptions about the results being correct. End users are perhaps the best people for verification, because they know what the numbers mean. They can also catch specification errors, in which the program is doing what the programmer intended, but the intent is not what they want.

Validating the test runs also serves to debug the specifications. They too may be wrong or may not be what the users want. Often when users are given a fully tested first version of a report, they will say something like "These numbers don't look right. Didn't you exclude the field offices?" No, you did not, because the users did not tell you to, and even though it was their fault, the report is still wrong. They may have seen a mockup of the report, perhaps even with representative numbers, but after they receive the report with real data, they may want changes. This is a major reason programs take longer to implement than planned. Those last few "minor" changes seem never to end, and they are often difficult changes to make. Some discipline must be imposed on the user so that the changes are not unending.

Testing usually goes in three phases—unit testing to test each program or subprogram, system testing to test several programs and their interactions, and the final testing with real data. Each phase will turn up new errors. The final testing with real data is the most important, because it is here that the unanticipated situations will turn up.

Errors range in seriousness. The least serious errors are those that are discovered, and the most serious are those that are undiscovered. Compilation errors are not serious, because the compiler always catches them. You can minimize them by desk checking, but it is wasteful to spend the painstaking effort to eliminate all compilation errors. The compiler is better at catching them than are humans. Abnormal terminations are not serious during testing, because they too are always discovered. Abnormal terminations are serious in production runs, but not as serious as undiscovered errors in production runs that contaminate the data.

Errors may be undiscovered because they do not show themselves with the test data or because they are overlooked. You can overcome the latter by more careful checking. To detect errors that do not manifest themselves with the test data or even with real data, the best tool is desk checking. Exhaustive desk checking is wasteful in catching compilation errors, because the compiler will catch them. Save your effort to catch logical and arithmetic errors that are not found by the test data. The structured walk-through is a variation on this in which several people go through a program as a group. This is an excellent debugging tool, but very difficult to arrange.

Desk checking consists of reading the program statement by statement to see if it works properly and to detect potential errors. The preceding section on reading a COBOL program illustrated desk checking. Desk checking can also thwart many errors in production programs caused by the environment. It is difficult to generate test cases to tell when a tape reel will be exceeded, when a disk file will overflow, or when the time limit will be exceeded. It is difficult to test a hardware error, an operator error, or operating system errors. With desk checking, you can foresee these errors and determine how the program can recover from them.

Debugging brings out some interesting aspects of our human nature. You may not see these quirks in yourself, but if you ever have the opportunity to do consulting where programmers bring you their problems, you will quickly spot them. As humans, we do not expect to make errors, and we are always amazed when they occur in our programs. Programmers often fail to see even the error messages produced by the program or the operating system. The first reaction when a programmer discovers an error is something like "It didn't run. There must be a hardware problem or something wrong with the operating system." Well, yes, there could be, but the problem usually is in the person's program.

It is surprising even to experienced programmers how often a program may run with no problems and then fail when run again with no change made. "It worked last time, and I didn't change anything! Well, yes, I did make one trivial change, but that couldn't have done anything. Oh my goodness, I just didn't think about the OPEN when I moved the WRITE there." The fact is that test runs are never made without something being changed.

Debugging is a little like detective work. First, establish that there was an error and get concrete evidence of it. Then look at what happened in the program and what did not happen. For example, a program might terminate while searching a table, indicating that the table contained bad data. But the table was read in from a file. The same termination would have occurred when the data was moved to the table if the bad data had been in the file. This might lead you to check to see if you are searching beyond the current end of the table; perhaps the table size was set incorrectly. If a report produces bad output, look at where the output is bad and where it is good.

Look for clues as to what went wrong and what the program was doing when the error occurred. Look at the CPU seconds consumed, the I/O performed, the output produced, the completion codes issued by the operating system, and any error messages. Look at the data. Was the program changed recently, or were changes made in the data? Was anything special done for this run? All of these can give an indication of what the program was doing and what caused the problem.

Next, make some assumptions about what must be causing the error, and track these down. Just because you discover an error, do not stop. It may not be the error for which you are looking, or there may be more errors. If you have a particularly perplexing problem, find someone with whom you can discuss the problem. Often you will discover the cause while you are describing the problem to someone else. If not, someone else may catch some obvious things that you overlooked or may make suggestions on how to locate the cause of the error.

Compilers can help in detecting errors. If a program terminates, they can tell where in the program the termination occurred. They may also tell which files are open and the last input and output records transmitted for each file. This is usually enough to track down all except the most difficult errors. (Unfortunately, not all compilers provide these—VS COBOL II with the FDUMP option does, but Microsoft COBOL doesn't.) You can also use the COBTEST or ANIMATOR debugging tools. These debugging tools are excellent, because they are passive, requiring no programming effort. You can also leave them in production programs. Debugging compilers can give additional help by checking for invalid subscripts and other error conditions. They can also reformat the listing to place a single statement on a line and to indent structures and conditional statements to show the hierarchy.

Beyond this, you may have to trace the execution of the program and print out the values of important data items as the program executes. The problem with these debugging tools is that they require effort, they may introduce errors themselves, and they also require rerunning the program. You can code a "D" in column 7 of the debugging statements to leave them in the program and compile or not compile them.

Try to do your debugging at the source level, the level at which you program. If you must look at the machine language code generated by the compiler or look at hexadecimal storage dumps, debugging is an order of magnitude harder. Use storage dumps only as a last resort, because they take so long to read and are so far removed from the way we think about programming. Storage dumps may be necessary to locate difficult errors, especially if the compiler does not provide you with adequate debugging information. But often a problem that takes half a day to find from reading a storage dump can be located in minutes by just thinking about what must be causing the problem. Your most important debugging tool is your reasoning.

One final word on testing: Test all program changes, however trivial. There are just too many things that can go wrong to forgo testing. The following example from a real situation is typical. To reduce the run cost of a program, the blocking factor was increased. Later a separate program that read the file failed. The programmer discovered that the BLOCK CONTAINS clause specified the blocking, which no longer matched that of the file. To prevent the problem from recurring, the programmer changed the statement to BLOCK CONTAINS 0 RECORDS and recompiled the program, but this resulted in a compilation error. The original programmer had coded the SAME AREA clause, and BLOCK CURTAINS 0 cannot be coded when SAME AREA is coded. (Avoid the SAME AREA clause, because it causes obscure problems like this.)

The programmer removed the SAME AREA clause and the program compiled with no errors, but then it terminated when it was run—the increased blocking required more memory. The region size was increased in the JCL, and the program was run again. Again it failed, this time because the new region size was larger than that allowed by the installation for the job class. The job class was changed, but now the schedule had to be revised because the new job class gave slower turnaround. Ultimately, the old blocking factor was restored, and all the programs were changed back. For the programmer under pressure to get a program running again, these problems are an exquisite form of torture.

This chapter has emphasized that errors may exist in any program, even one that has run correctly in production for years. This does not mean that we should accept or tolerate errors, but only that we must acknowledge that they can exist. This is a large part of the battle in debugging, because if you expect errors to be present, you will look for them and find a surprising number. But if you do not expect errors to exist, human nature is such that you will never find them.

And now, on to the last chapter. It describes considerations in developing on both the mainframe and the PC.

REFERENCES

1. Dr. Barry W. Boehm, "Software and Its Impact; a Quantitative Assessment," *DATA-MATION,* May 1973.

2. O. J. Dahi, E. W. Dijkstra, and C. A. R. Hoare, *Structured Programming,* London and New York: Academic Press, Inc., 1972.

3. Gary D. Brown, *Beyond COBOL: Survival in Business Applications Programming,* New York: John Wiley & Sons, 1981.

26

Mainframe/PC Application Considerations

This chapter describes some of the considerations in developing applications on a PC for a mainframe environment (or perhaps the reverse, or even applications that run in both environments).

I. ADVANTAGES OF CROSS-SYSTEM DEVELOPMENT

The advantages of developing on a PC include the following:

- The mainframe cost per MIPS (million instructions per second) may be 200 to 500 times more than a PC, depending on whether one counts the cost of the raised floor, water cooling, operators, and systems programmers. The incremental cost of computing on a PC is close to zero—about the cost of burning a 60-watt light bulb. The incremental cost of adding capacity with a PC is somewhere from $500 to $5,000. On a mainframe, it is in the $50,000 to $5,000,000 range.
- The PC response is usually faster and always more consistent. Although a typical mainframe computer may be 20 times faster than a PC, it usually supports more than 20 concurrent users, so that its effective response time is slower than a PC.
- PC software is often better than that on a mainframe. And of course, the PC has DOS, OS/2, or Windows, which are more productive and less frustrating than JCL.

II. SAA

IBM has developed System Application Architecture (SAA) as a way of connecting different computers together and enabling applications to run on different computers. SAA has four components:

1. Common User Access: to make all applications look alike to the user
2. Common Programming Interface: to provide the same computer languages and program services on the various IBM platforms

3. Common Communications Support: to allow IBM computers to communicate with each other
4. Common Applications: to allow application programs to run on the various IBM platforms

For item 4, IBM has established an SAA subset of COBOL. Those wishing to write programs using the SAA COBOL subset should obtain a copy of Reference 1. While SAA is an excellent idea, it has limitations:

• SAA doesn't address the main problems of compatibility: writing applications that run on both IBM and non-IBM computers (even Microsoft COBOL on the PC ignores SAA); resolving the differences between character sets (EBCDIC on IBM mainframes and ASCII used by the rest of the world); and accommodating differences in operating systems.
• It is difficult to see the need for IBM to impose a standard when there is an ANSI Standard. In the past, an IBM standard often had more force than an ANSI Standard, but that is no longer true.
• It is extremely difficult to write applications using subsets of languages. It always turns out that a feature not provided on some other computer is vital for writing the application. This is not just bad luck. You often choose to write an application for a particular computer because of the computer's unique capabilities, and it is just these capabilities that are unlikely to exist on other computers.

III. MAINTAINING SOURCE

To make programming and maintenance easier, you should design the program to be easily maintained using the facilities of a text editor. A strange phenomenon occurs when you do most of your programming on a PC. Because the run cost is zero, you can make much more intensive use of the computer, and this changes the way you program. I first noticed this when I hired a young PC programmer and tried to use a printed listing to describe the workings of a program to him. It was as if he couldn't see the listing. Only when he viewed the program on his PC screen could he "read" it. A printed listing was outside his range of experience, and he couldn't relate it to programming. I mentioned this to a friend, saying I thought it was weird behavior. My friend, who had worked with PCs for years, said: "He's not weird. You're out of date. He's the future."

It took two years for me to unconsciously make the transition. Eventually, I found I never printed a listing. Using the windowing facility of a good PC text editor was faster than paging back and forth through a listing. The text editor's global search facility eliminated the need for a cross-reference list. I now work much faster with the text editor than I ever worked with printed listings. There is also something ecologically satisfying in not sacrificing all those trees to make the paper I had been generating.

This technique doesn't work well on a mainframe. A text editor puts heavy demands on the computer's CPU, and you can quickly generate large costs. I once generated a $500 cost in a day on a mainframe using such techniques. With a PC, the only cost of putting a heavy demand on the CPU is in response time.

Use consistent data names in designing your programs. If you use the same data names in the Linkage Sections as you use in the calling programs, a global search can easily locate all references to the data items.

Prefix the level 01 group name to the elementary data items within it. Although this means you can't use CORR (which you usually can't use anyway), it eliminates the need to qualify elementary data names. It also makes it much easier to locate data items with the search facility of a text editor.

Another useful feature, when your program consists of several subprograms, is to concatenate them all into a single file. This lets you easily make global changes, such as names. If you want to see where a data item is used throughout all the subprograms, this too is easy when they are all in a single file. Of course, you also need a way to break the single file back out into the separate subprograms.

All this is easily done on a PC. The following DOS command concatenates several separate files into a single file:

```
:> COPY file-1 + file-2 +...+file-n new-file
```

Deconcatenating is more difficult. You need a program for this, such as the following. It prompts you for a file name and then writes each program in it into a separate file:

```
IDENTIFICATION DIVISION.
    PROGRAM-ID. DECONCAT.
****************************************************************
* PROGRAM TO READ A FILE CONTAINING SEVERAL PROGRAMS AND    *
* WRITE EACH PROGRAM IT CONTAINS INTO A SEPARATE FILE.      *
* IN:  You will be prompted for the file name containing    *
*        the programs.                                      *
*        Note:  This program will not work with nested      *
*               programs.                                   *
* OUT: Each program, as begun by an IDENTIFICATION          *
*        DIVISION header, is written into a separate file.  *
*        The file name is formed from the PROGRAM-ID name,  *
*        truncated to 8 characters if necessary.  A ".CBL"  *
*        suffix is appended to the name.  Any dash (-) in   *
*        the name is replaced by an underline (_).          *
****************************************************************
ENVIRONMENT DIVISION.
INPUT-OUTPUT SECTION.
FILE-CONTROL.
    SELECT IN-FILE ASSIGN TO IN-NAME
        ORGANIZATION IS LINE SEQUENTIAL.
    SELECT OUT-FILE ASSIGN TO OUT-NAME
        ORGANIZATION IS LINE SEQUENTIAL.
DATA DIVISION.
```

```
 FILE SECTION.
 FD  IN-FILE
     RECORD CONTAINS 80 CHARACTERS.
 01  IN-RECORD                   PIC X(80).
 FD  OUT-FILE
     RECORD CONTAINS 80 CHARACTERS.
 01  OUT-RECORD                  PIC X(80).
 WORKING-STORAGE SECTION.
 01  IN-FILE-FIELDS.
     05  IN-REC                  PIC X(80).
     05  IN-NAME                 PIC X(30).
*        Name of input file.
     05  IN-X                    PIC S9(4) BINARY.
*        Subscript used to examine IN-REC characters.
     05  IN-REC-NO               PIC S9(9) BINARY VALUE 0.
*        Count of input records read.
     05  IN-SAVE-REC             PIC X(80).
 01  OUT-FILE-FIELDS.
     05  OUT-FILE-OPEN           PIC X VALUE "N".
*                                "N": Output file closed.
*                                "Y": Output file open.
     05  OUT-NAME                PIC X(30).
*        Name of output file.
     05  OUT-REC-NO              PIC S9(9) BINARY VALUE 0.
*        Count of output records written in file.
     05  OUT-TOTAL-NO            PIC S9(9) BINARY VALUE 0.
*        Count of total output records written.
     05  OUT-FILE-NO             PIC S9(9) BINARY VALUE 0.
*        Count of output files written.
 01  HOLD-RECS.
     05  HOLD-NO                 PIC S9(4) BINARY VALUE 0.
*                                Number of records held.
     05  HOLD-MAX-NO             PIC S9(4) BINARY VALUE 10.
*                                Maximum lines held.
     05  HOLD-LINE               OCCURS 10 TIMES
                                 INDEXED BY HOLD-X
                                 PIC X(80).
*                                Table to hold lines until
*                                we read PROGRAM-ID line.
 01  EIGHT-CHAR                  PIC X(8).
*                                Used to chop off name to 8
*                                chars.
 PROCEDURE DIVISION.
 START-PROGRAM.
     DISPLAY "BEGINNING DECONCAT PROGRAM"
     DISPLAY "ENTER INPUT PROGRAM NAME: ", IN-NAME
```

```
      ACCEPT IN-NAME
      IF IN-NAME = SPACES
         THEN DISPLAY "ERROR--YOU ENTERED BLANK NAME."
              GO TO Z90-STOP-RUN
      END-IF
*     Open the input file and read all its records.
      DISPLAY "OPENING INPUT: ", IN-NAME
      OPEN INPUT IN-FILE
      PERFORM WITH TEST AFTER UNTIL IN-REC = HIGH-VALUES
        READ IN-FILE INTO IN-REC
          AT END
             MOVE HIGH-VALUES TO IN-REC
          NOT AT END
             ADD 1 TO IN-REC-NO
             PERFORM A10-PROCESS-LINES
        END-READ
      END-PERFORM
      IF OUT-FILE-OPEN = "Y"
         DISPLAY "CLOSING: ", OUT-NAME,
                 " RECORDS WRITTEN: ", OUT-REC-NO
         CLOSE OUT-FILE
         ADD OUT-REC-NO TO OUT-TOTAL-NO
         MOVE ZERO TO OUT-REC-NO
      END-IF
      CLOSE IN-FILE
      DISPLAY "LINES READ:    ", IN-REC-NO
      DISPLAY "LINES WRITTEN: ", OUT-TOTAL-NO
      DISPLAY "FILES CREATED: ", OUT-FILE-NO
      DISPLAY "TERMINATING RUN NORMALLY"
      STOP RUN
          .
 **** Exit
 A10-PROCESS-LINES.
 ****************************************************************
 * PROCEDURE TO PROCESS A LINE IN INPUT FILE.              *
 * IN:  IN-REC contains input line.                        *
 * OUT: Line is stored or written in file.                 *
 ****************************************************************
 *    Copy the line to save area and left-justify it.
      IF IN-REC NOT = SPACES
 *         Find first nonblank character in line.
         THEN PERFORM WITH TEST BEFORE
                   VARYING IN-X FROM 1 BY 1
                   UNTIL IN-REC(IN-X:1) NOT = SPACE
                      OR IN-X = 72
              END-PERFORM
```

```
*                     Move from first nonblank character.
              MOVE IN-REC(IN-X:) TO IN-SAVE-REC
*                 For blank line, copy entire line.
           ELSE MOVE IN-REC TO IN-SAVE-REC
        END-IF
        EVALUATE TRUE
*           See if this is the start of a new program.
          WHEN IN-SAVE-REC(1:1) = "$" OR
               IN-SAVE-REC = "IDENTIFICATION DIVISION." OR
               IN-SAVE-REC = "ID DIVISION."
*                It is a new program.  Close previous file if open.
               IF OUT-FILE-OPEN = "Y"
                   THEN DISPLAY "CLOSING: ", OUT-NAME,
                        " RECORDS WRITTEN: ", OUT-REC-NO
                        CLOSE OUT-FILE
                        MOVE "N" TO OUT-FILE-OPEN
                        ADD OUT-REC-NO TO OUT-TOTAL-NO
                        MOVE ZERO TO OUT-REC-NO
               END-IF
*                Save this line.
               PERFORM A15-SAVE-LINE
*           Not a new program line.  See if it is PROGRAM-ID
*           line.
          WHEN IN-SAVE-REC(1:11) = "PROGRAM-ID."
*                It is a PROGRAM-ID line.
               PERFORM A20-PROGRAM-ID
          WHEN OTHER
*                If not PROGRAM-ID line, save the line if
*                output file is not open.
               IF OUT-FILE-OPEN = "N"
                   THEN PERFORM A15-SAVE-LINE
*                   Otherwise, write the line.
                   ELSE WRITE OUT-RECORD FROM IN-REC
                        ADD 1 TO OUT-REC-NO
               END-IF
        END-EVALUATE
          .
**** Exit
 A15-SAVE-LINE.
*****************************************************************
* PROCEDURE TO SAVE A LINE IN HOLD-LINE TABLE.                 *
* IN:  IN-REC contains input line.                            *
*      HOLD-NO contains number already stored.                *
* OUT: Line is stored in HOLD-LINE.                           *
*      HOLD-NO increased by one.                              *
*****************************************************************
     ADD 1 TO HOLD-NO
```

```
     IF HOLD-NO > HOLD-MAX-NO
        THEN DISPLAY "ERROR--TOO MANY LINES TO SAVE"
               DISPLAY
               "INCREASE HOLD-LINE AND HOLD-MAX-NO AND RECOMPILE"
               GO TO Z90-STOP-RUN
     END-IF
     MOVE IN-REC TO HOLD-LINE(HOLD-NO)

**** Exit
 A20-PROGRAM-ID.
****************************************************************
* PROCEDURE TO PROCESS A PROGRAM-ID LINE.                     *
* IN:  IN-REC contains PROGRAM-ID line.                       *
*      HOLD-NO contains number stored.                        *
* OUT: New output file is opened.                             *
*      IN-REC and HOLD-LINES written into output file.        *
****************************************************************
*      If file is open, we have an error.
     IF OUT-FILE-OPEN = "Y"
         THEN DISPLAY
       "ERROR--PROGRAM ID LINE INCORRECTLY PLACED: ", IN-REC
               GO TO Z90-STOP-RUN
     END-IF
*      Find first nonblank character on line following
*      PROGRAM-ID.  This starts the program name.
     PERFORM WITH TEST BEFORE
               VARYING IN-X FROM 12 BY 1
               UNTIL IN-SAVE-REC(IN-X:1) NOT = SPACE
               OR IN-X = 72
     END-PERFORM
*      Move from first nonblank character in name.
     MOVE IN-SAVE-REC(IN-X:) TO EIGHT-CHAR
*       Get rid of any trailing period.
     INSPECT EIGHT-CHAR REPLACING ALL "." BY SPACE
                               ALL "-" BY "_"
*      Concatenate ".CBL" to EIGHT-CHAR and store in PGM-NAME.
     PERFORM WITH TEST BEFORE
               VARYING IN-X FROM 8 BY -1
               UNTIL EIGHT-CHAR(IN-X:1) NOT = SPACE OR
                 IN-X = 1
     END-PERFORM
*      IN-X contains the length of the name.
     MOVE EIGHT-CHAR TO OUT-NAME
     MOVE ".CBL" TO OUT-NAME(IN-X + 1:)
*      Open this file.
     DISPLAY "OPENING OUTPUT FILE: ", OUT-NAME
     OPEN OUTPUT OUT-FILE
```

```
      ADD 1 TO OUT-FILE-NO
      MOVE "Y" TO OUT-FILE-OPEN
*       Write all the saved lines.
      PERFORM WITH TEST BEFORE
              VARYING HOLD-X FROM 1 BY 1
              UNTIL HOLD-X > HOLD-NO
        WRITE OUT-RECORD FROM HOLD-LINE(HOLD-X)
        ADD 1 TO OUT-REC-NO
      END-PERFORM
      MOVE ZERO TO HOLD-NO
*       Write the PROGRAM-ID line.
      WRITE OUT-RECORD FROM IN-REC
      ADD 1 TO OUT-REC-NO
      .
**** Exit
 Z90-STOP-RUN.
 **************************************************************
 * PROCEDURE TO TERMINATE LINE ABNORMALLY.                   *
 * IN:   Nothing.                                            *
 * OUT: Message displayed and run terminated.                *
 *       RETURN-CODE set to 16.                              *
 **************************************************************
      DISPLAY "MUST TERMINATE BECAUSE OF ERROR."
      MOVE 16 TO RETURN-CODE
      STOP RUN
      .
**** Exit
END PROGRAM DECONCAT.
```

IV. DEVELOPING FOR BOTH THE MAINFRAME AND PC

There are two reasons for developing applications to run on both the PC and mainframe. First, the application may run in production on both computers. Even if there isn't a need for this today, one may develop in the future. The second reason is to allow you to do as much development as possible before moving to the mainframe.

Obviously, you need to keep in mind the differences in the two compilers. Microsoft COBOL has virtually all the features of VS COBOL II. The statements that control the compiler are different. Don't use the VS COBOL II NOADV compiler option. You define hexadecimal literals differently in Microsoft COBOL. However, these are all minor items that shouldn't cause problems. Microsoft COBOL has many features not in VS COBOL II, and most of these aren't discussed in this book. You'll know not to use these if you are going to be uploading and downloading applications.

One minor difference in almost all VS COBOL II and Microsoft COBOL programs will be the SELECT clause. RECORD SEQUENTIAL defaults in Microsoft COBOL, but you usually want LINE SEQUENTIAL if you are testing on the PC. Rather than coding LINE SEQUENTIAL in the SELECT clause, which is incompatible with VS COBOL II, code the SEQUENTIAL "LINE" compiler parameter in the COBOL.DIR file, in a $SET command, or on the command line when you compile the program to make LINE SEQUENTIAL the default:

```
:> COBOL MYPGM SEQUENTIAL "LINE";
```

Likewise, always use the DOS SET statement to associate the file name with the SELECT clause:

```
    SELECT IN-FILE ASSIGN TO INFILE.
    ■ ■ ■
:> SET INFILE = C:\TEST\PART.ONE
```

Isolate items that are likely to be different on the different computers, and write comments to explain them. Since I/O is often different, place the READ and WRITE statements in a paragraph and perform the paragraph. This isolates the code, and the program should contain only a single READ and WRITE statement per file.

Maintain only one set of source code for the application, if possible. Maintaining two sets of source is a nightmare. The difficulties are expressed in the old saying: "Someone who has only one watch always knows the time. Someone who has two watches is never sure of the time."

The problem in maintaining only one set of source comes when you must write different code for the PC and the mainframe, such as for hexadecimal constants. It is best to write both statements, enclosing them in comments with some unique character combination coded to mark them. Later, when you compile on a particular computer, you can search the source for these characters. Then you can comment out the statements that aren't needed. Unfortunately, COBOL doesn't let you set a flag and then code IF/ THEN/ ELSE control statements to selectively compile statements. This is the single most important tool in writing cross-system applications, and COBOL requires you to do it manually with comment statements and a text editor.

The problems of cross-systems apply to more than just computers. They also apply to environments. If your program goes international, it will use the "$" in the US and the "£" in the UK. The numeric digits you allow for the pound may be insufficient to contain comparable amounts in dollars. In the next decade, cross-environment systems will likely be as important as cross-computer systems.

Most installations have a way of uploading ASCII files to the mainframe and converting them to EBCDIC files, and the inverse. The problems start after this has been done.

The main differences between COBOL applications on the PC and the mainframe are the files and their contents. The mainframe uses VSAM for relative and indexed files. Microsoft COBOL has its own equivalent on the PC. However, the COBOL statements to process both are the same, so you should be able to write and test applications on the PC for most mainframe applications. (Applications for IMS are an exception.)

The problem of the file's contents is perhaps more difficult. The PC uses the ASCII character set and the mainframe uses EBCDIC. You can process ASCII on the mainframe, but normally, your application must cope with EBCDIC characters. The problems you will encounter are the following:

- Variable-length records, the sign in external decimal numbers, binary and packed-decimal numbers, and indexed and relative files are all handled differently on the PC and mainframe. It may be better to recreate a file on the PC or mainframe than to try to upload or download it.
- The collating sequences differ. ASCII sorts a through z before A through Z before 0 through 9. EBCDIC sorts 0 through 9 before A through Z before a through z. This is a significant difference. It affects sorts, comparisons, and binary searches.
- The ASCII/EBCDIC difference has other surprises. One application converted the letters A through Z to the numbers 1 through 26 to index a table. It worked fine on the PC but fell apart on the mainframe. The conversion was done by subtracting the ASCII numeric code for an A plus 1 from each letter, which converted A through Z to 1 through 26. But on the mainframe, it converted A through Z to 1 through 9, 17 through 25, and 34 through 41. The EBCDIC codes for A through Z aren't consecutive. A gap of 7 exists between I and J and a gap of 8 between R and S. You can program around this, but the differences between EBCDIC and ASCII always seem to have some nasty surprise.
- The keyboard characters differ as follows:

On 3270, not on PC	On PC, not on 3270
¢ cent	^ carat
¬ not	\ backslash
¦ solid line	[left bracket
	] right bracket

When you use the typical IRMA-type board to upload and download files, characters are interchanged as follows:

$$
\begin{array}{ccc}
\wedge & \text{and} & \neg \\
[& \text{and} & ¢ \\
] & \text{and} & ¦
\end{array}
$$

These characters are not in the COBOL character set, so they shouldn't be a problem for COBOL source statements. However, they may appear in your data, and you have to be careful with them.

V. PROCESSING ASCII ON THE MAINFRAME

The following facilities are provided in COBOL to process ASCII data on the mainframe:

1. Specify the *alphabet-name* clause of the SPECIAL-NAMES paragraph as STANDARD-1 or STANDARD-2. You then use this *alphabet-name* in other statements.

2. To change the collating sequence for relational conditions, condition-name conditions, and nonnumeric sort/merge keys, code the `PROGRAM COLLATING SEQUENCE` clause of the `OBJECT-COMPUTER` paragraph. Specify the *alphabet-name* from step 1.
3. To change only the collating sequence for sort/merge, code the `COLLATING SEQUENCE` phrase of the `SORT` or `MERGE` statement. Name the *alphabet-name* from step 1.
4. For ASCII-encoded files, code the `CODE-SET` clause in the FD entry. Name the *alphabet-name* specified in step 1.
5. For signed external decimal numbers, code the `SIGN SEPARATE CHARACTER` phrase.
6. Code only `DISPLAY` for all ASCII items.
7. Don't code the `RERUN` clause for an ASCII-encoded file.
8. To have the system automatically convert ASCII to EBCDIC while reading or convert EBCDIC to ASCII while writing, code `DCB = OPTCD = Q` on the DD statement.

VI. PROCESSING EBCDIC ON THE PC

Microsoft COBOL has the following facilities for processing EBCDIC data on the PC:

1. Specify the *alphabet-name* clause of the `SPECIAL-NAMES` paragraph as `EBCDIC`. You then use this *alphabet-name* in other statements.
2. To change the collating sequence for relational conditions, condition-name conditions, and nonnumeric sort/merge keys, code the `PROGRAM COLLATING SEQUENCE` clause of the `OBJECT-COMPUTER` paragraph. Specify the *alphabet-name* from step 1.
3. To change only the collating sequence for sort/merge, code the `COLLATING SEQUENCE` phrase of the `SORT` or `MERGE` statement. Name the *alphabet-name* from step 1.
4. For EBCDIC files, code the `CODE-SET` clause in the FD entry. Name the *alphabet-name* specified in step 1. Alternatively, code the `NATIVE "EBCDIC"` compiler parameter.
5. Code only `DISPLAY` for all EBCDIC items.
6. For external decimal numbers whose sign is the EBCDIC convention, code the `SIGN "EBCDIC"` compiler parameter.
7. If the source statements are in EBCDIC, code the `CHARSET "EBCDIC"` compiler parameter.

REFERENCE

1. "Systems Application Architecture; Common Programming Interface; COBOL," Order No. GC26-4051, San Jose, CA: IBM Corporation, 1988.

Appendix A

COBOL Reserved Words

VSC2: VS COBOL II
MSC: Microsoft COBOL
CODASYL: Reserved for future use by CODASYL Committee

Word	Not in ANSI	VSC2 Only	MSC Only	CODASYL Only	For CICS
(	x		x		
)	x		x		
*					
**					
+					
-					
/					
;	x		x		
<					
<=					
=					
>					
>=					
ACCEPT					
ACCESS					
ADD					
ADDRESS	x				
ADVANCING					
AFTER					
ALL					
ALPHABET					
ALPHABETIC					
ALPHABETIC-LOWER					
ALPHABETIC-UPPER					

Word	Not in ANSI	VSC2 Only	MSC Only	CODASYL Only	For CICS
ALPHANUMERIC					
ALPHANUMERIC-EDITED					
ALSO					
ALTER					
ALTERNATE					
AND					
ANY					
APPLY	X				
ARE					
AREA					
AREA-VALUE	X		X		
AREAS					
ARITHMETIC	X			X	
ASCENDING					
ASSIGN					
AT					
AUTHOR					
AUTO	X		X		
AUTO-SKIP	X		X		
AUTOMATIC	X		X		
B-AND	X			X	
B-EXOR	X			X	
B-LESS	X			X	
B-NOT	X			X	
B-OR	X			X	
BACKGROUND-COLOR	X		X		
BACKGROUND-COLOUR	X		X		
BACKWARD	X		X		
BASIS	X				
BEEP	X		X		
BEFORE					
BEGINNING	X				
BELL	X		X		
BINARY					
BIT	X			X	
BITS	X			X	
BLANK					
BLINK	X		X		
BOOLEAN	X			X	
BOTTOM					
BY					
CALL					
CANCEL					

Word	Not in ANSI	VSC2 Only	MSC Only	CODASYL Only	For CICS
CBL	x				
CD					
CF					
CH					
CHAIN	x		x		
CHAINING	x		x		
CHARACTER					
CHARACTERS					
CICS	x				x
CLASS					
CLOCK-UNITS					
CLOSE					
COBOL					
CODE					
CODE-SET					
COL	x		x		
COLLATING					
COLOR	x		x		
COLUMN					
COM-REG	x				
COMMA					
COMMIT	x			x	
COMMON					
COMMUNICATION					
COMP					
COMP-0	x		x		
COMP-1	x	x			
COMP-2	x	x			
COMP-3	x				
COMP-4	x				
COMP-5	x		x	x	
COMP-6	x			x	
COMP-7	x			x	
COMP-8	x			x	
COMP-9	x			x	
COMP-X	x		x		
COMPUTATIONAL					
COMPUTATIONAL-0	x		x		
COMPUTATIONAL-1	x	x			
COMPUTATIONAL-2	x	x			
COMPUTATIONAL-3		x			
COMPUTATIONAL-4		x			
COMPUTATIONAL-5	x		x	x	

Word	Not in ANSI	VSC2 Only	MSC Only	CODASYL Only	For CICS
COMPUTATIONAL-6	x			x	
COMPUTATIONAL-7	x			x	
COMPUTATIONAL-8	x			x	
COMPUTATIONAL-9	x			x	
COMPUTATIONAL-X	x		x		
COMPUTE					
CONFUGURATION					
CONNECT	x			x	
CONTAINED	x			x	
CONTAINS					
CONTENT					
CONTINUE					
CONTROL					
CONTROLS					
CONVERTING					
COPY					
CORR					
CORRESPONDING					
COUNT					
CRT	x		x		
CRT-UNDER	x		x		
CURRENCY					
CURRENT	x			x	
CURSOR	x		x		
DATA					
DATE					
DATE-COMPILED					
DATE-WRITTEN					
DAY					
DAY-OF-WEEK					
DB	x			x	
DB-ACCESS-CONTROL-KEY	x			x	
DB-DATA-NAME	x			x	
DB-EXCEPTION	x			x	
DB-RECORD-NAME	x			x	
DB-SET-NAME	x			x	
DB-STATUS	x			x	
DBCS	x	x			
DE					
DEBUG-CONTENTS					
DEBUG-ITEM					
DEBUG-LINE					
DEBUG-NAME					

Word	Not in ANSI	VSC2 Only	MSC Only	CODASYL Only	For CICS
DEBUG-SUB-1					
DEBUG-SUB-2					
DEBUG-SUB-3					
DEBUGGING					
DECIMAL-POINT					
DECLARATIVES					
DEFAULT	x			x	
DELETE					
DELIMITED					
DELIMITER					
DEPENDING					
DESCENDING					
DESTINATION					
DETAIL					
DISABLE					
DISCONNECT	x			x	
DISK	x		x		
DISPLAY					
DISPLAY-1	x				
DISPLAY-2	x			x	
DISPLAY-3	x			x	
DISPLAY-4	x			x	
DISPLAY-5	x			x	
DISPLAY-6	x			x	
DISPLAY-7	x			x	
DISPLAY-8	x			x	
DISPLAY-9	x			x	
DIVIDE					
DIVISION					
DLI	x				x
DOWN					
DUPLICATE	x			x	
DUPLICATES					
DYNAMIC					
EGCS	x				
EGI					
EJECT	x				
ELSE					
EMI					
EMPTY	x			x	
EMPTY-CHECK	x		x		
ENABLE					
END					

Word	Not in ANSI	VSC2 Only	MSC Only	CODASYL Only	For CICS
END-ACCEPT	x		x		
END-ADD					
END-CALL					
END-COMPUTE					
END-DELETE					
END-DISABLE	x			x	
END-DIVIDE					
END-ENABLE	x			x	
END-EVALUATE					
END-EXEC	x				x
END-IF					
END-MULTIPLY					
END-OF-PAGE					
END-PERFORM					
END-READ					
END-RECEIVE					
END-RETURN					
END-REWRITE					
END-SEARCH					
END-SEND	x			x	
END-START					
END-STRING					
END-SUBTRACT					
END-TRANSCEIVE	x			x	
END-UNSTRING					
END-WRITE					
ENDING	x				
ENTER					
ENTRY	x				
ENVIRONMENT					
EOP					
EQUAL					
EQUALS	x			x	
ERASE	x		x	x	
ERROR					
ESCAPE	x		x		
ESI					
EVALUATE					
EVERY					
EXACT	x			x	
EXCEEDS	x			x	
EXCEPTION					
EXCESS-3	x		x		

Word	Not in ANSI	VSC2 Only	MSC Only	CODASYL Only	For CICS
EXCLUSIVE	x		x	x	
EXEC	x		x		x
EXECUTE	x		x		
EXIT					
EXTEND					
EXTERNAL					
FALSE					
FD					x
FETCH	x			x	
FILE					x
FILE-CONTROL					x
FILE-ID	x		x		
FILLER					
FINAL					
FIND	x			x	
FINISH	x			x	
FIRST					
FIXED	x		x		
FOOTING					
FOR					
FOREGROUND-COLOR	x		x		
FOREGROUND-COLOUR	x		x		
FORMAT	x			x	
FREE	x			x	
FROM					
FULL	x		x		
FUNCTION	x			x	
GENERATE					
GET	x			x	
GIVING					
GLOBAL					
GO					
GOBACK	x				
GREATER					
GRID	x		x		
GROUP					
HEADING					
HIGH-VALUE					
HIGH-VALUES					
HIGHLIGHT	x		x		
I-O					
I-O-CONTROL					x
ID	x				

Word	Not in ANSI	VSC2 Only	MSC Only	CODASYL Only	For CICS
IDENTIFICATION					
IF					
IN					
INDEX					
INDEX-1	X			X	
INDEX-2	X			X	
INDEX-3	X			X	
INDEX-4	X			X	
INDEX-5	X			X	
INDEX-6	X			X	
INDEX-7	X			X	
INDEX-8	X			X	
INDEX-9	X			X	
INDEXED					
INDICATE					
INITIAL					
INITIALIZE					
INITIATE					
INPUT					
INPUT-OUPUT					X
INSERT	X				
INSPECT					
INSTALLATION					
INTO					
INVALID					
IS					
JAPANESE	X		X		
JUST					
JUSTIFIED					
KANJI	X				
KEEP	X			X	
KEPT	X		X		
KEY					
KEYBOARD	X		X		
LABEL					
LAST					
LD	X			X	
LEADING					
LEFT					
LEFT-JUSTIFY	X		X		
LEFTLINE	X		X		
LENGTH					
LENGTH-CHECK	X		X		

Word	Not in ANSI	VSC2 Only	MSC Only	CODASYL Only	For CICS
LESS					
LIMIT					
LIMITS					
LINAGE					
LINAGE-COUNTER					
LINE					
LINE-COUNTER					
LINES					
LINKAGE					
LOCALLY	x			x	
LOCK					
LOW-VALUE					
LOW-VALUES					
MANUAL	x		x		
MEMBER	x			x	
MEMORY					
MERGE					
MESSAGE					
MODE					
MODIFY	x			x	
MODULES					
MORE-LABELS	x				
MOVE					
MULTIPLE					
MULTIPLY					
NAME	x		x		
NATIVE					
NEGATIVE					
NEXT					
NO					
NO-ECHO	x		x		
NONE	x			x	
NOT					
NULL	x				
NULLS	x				
NUMBER					
NUMERIC					
NUMERIC-EDITED					
OBJECT-COMPUTER					
OCCURS					
OF					
OFF					
OMITTED					

Word	Not in ANSI	VSC2 Only	MSC Only	CODASYL Only	For CICS
ON					
ONLY	x			x	
OPEN					
OPTIONAL					
OR					
ORDER					
ORGANIZATION					
OTHER					
OUTPUT					
OVERFLOW					
OVERLINE	x		x		
OWNER	x			x	
PACKED-DECIMAL					
PADDING					
PAGE					
PAGE-COUNTER					
PALETTE	x		x		
PARAGRAPH	x			x	
PASSWORD	x				
PERFORM					
PF					
PH					
PIC					
PICTURE					
PLUS					
POINTER					
POSITION					
POSITIVE					
PRESENT	x			x	
PREVIOUS	x		x		
PRINTER	x		x		
PRINTER-1	x		x		
PRINTING					
PRIOR	x			x	
PROCEDURE					
PROCEDURES					
PROCEED					
PROCESSING	x				
PROGRAM					
PROGRAM-ID					
PROMPT	x		x		
PROTECTED	x			x	
PURGE					

Word	Not in ANSI	VSC2 Only	MSC Only	CODASYL Only	For CICS
QUEUE					
QUOTE					
QUOTES					
RANDOM					
RANGE	x		x		
RD					
READ					
READY	x				
REALM	x			x	
RECEIVE					
RECONNECT	x			x	
RECORD					
RECORD-NAME	x			x	
RECORDING	x				
RECORDS					
REDEFINES					
REEL					
REFERENCE					
REFERENCES					
RELATION	x			x	
RELATIVE					
RELEASE					
RELOAD	x				
REMAINDER					
REMOVAL					
RENAMES					
REPEATED	x			x	
REPLACE					
REPLACING					
REPORT					
REPORTING					
REPORTS					
REQUIRED	x		x		
RERUN					
RESERVE					
RESET					
RETAINING	x			x	
RETRIEVAL	x			x	
RETURN					
RETURN-CODE	x				
REVERSE-VIDEO	x		x		
REVERSED					
REWIND					

Word	Not in ANSI	VSC2 Only	MSC Only	CODASYL Only	For CICS
REWRITE					
RF					
RH					
RIGHT					
RIGHT-JUSTIFY	x		x		
ROLLBACK	x		x	x	
ROUNDED					
RUN					
SAME					
SCREEN	x		x		
SD					x
SEARCH					
SECTION					
SECURE	x		x		
SECURITY					
SEGMENT					
SEGMENT-LIMIT					
SELECT					
SEND					
SENTENCE					
SEPARATE					
SEQUENCE					
SEQUENTIAL					
SERVICE		x			
SESSION-ID	x			x	
SET					
SHARED	x			x	
SHIFT-IN	x	x			
SHIFT-OUT	x	x			
SIGN					
SIZE					
SKIP1	x				
SKIP2	x				
SKIP3	x				
SORT					x
SORT-CONTROL	x				
SORT-CORE-SIZE	x				
SORT-FILE-SIZE	x				
SORT-MERGE					
SORT-MESSAGE	x				
SORT-MODE-SIZE	x				
SORT-RETURN	x				
SOURCE					

Word	Not in ANSI	VSC2 Only	MSC Only	CODASYL Only	For CICS
SOURCE-COMPUTER					
SPACE					
SPACE-FILL	x		x		
SPACES					
SPECIAL-NAMES					
STANDARD					
STANDARD-1					
STANDARD-2					
STANDARD-3	x			x	
STANDARD-4	x			x	
START					
STATUS					
STOP					
STORE	x			x	
STRING					
SUB-QUEUE-1					
SUB-QUEUE-2					
SUB-QUEUE-3					
SUB-SCHEMA	x			x	
SUBPROGRAM	x		x		
SUBTRACT					
SUM					
SUPPRESS					
SYMBOLIC					
SYNC					
SYNCHRONIZED					
TABLE					
TALLY	x				
TALLYING					
TAPE					
TENANT	x			x	
TERMINAL					
TERMINATE					
TEST					
TEXT					
THAN					
THEN					
THROUGH					
THRU					
TIME					
TIMES					
TITLE	x				
TO					

Word	Not in ANSI	VSC2 Only	MSC Only	CODASYL Only	For CICS
TOP					
TRACE	x				
TRAILING					
TRAILING-SIGN	x		x		
TRANSCEIVE	x			x	
TRUE					
TYPE					
UNDERLINE	x		x		
UNEQUAL	x			x	
UNIT					
UNLOCK	x		x		
UNSTRING					
UNTIL					
UP					
UPDATE	x		x	x	
UPON					
USAGE					
USAGE-MODE	x			x	
USE					
USER	x		x		
USING					
VALID	x			x	
VALIDATE	x			x	
VALUE					
VALUES					
VARIABLE	x		x		
VARYING					
WAIT	x			x	
WHEN					
WHEN-COMPILED	x				
WITH					
WITHIN	x			x	
WORDS					
WORKING-STORAGE					
WRITE					
WRITE-ONLY	x				
ZERO					
ZERO-FILL	x		x		
ZEROES					
ZEROS					

Appendix B

Answers to Selected Exercises

Every computer problem usually has several correct solutions, each one perhaps better than the others judged by a particular criterion. A solution may be tightly coded to be very efficient, but it may be complex and inflexible and may make the program difficult to debug and maintain. One thing is clear—any acceptable solution must give correct results. They must be correct not merely with a set of test data, but with the wide range of values and unexpected data that may occur in real situations.

Chapter 4

1.
```
MOVE 1 TO A, B                     A = 1, B = 1
COMPUTE B = A + 1                  A = 1, B = 2
ADD B TO A                         A = 3, B = 2
MULTIPLY B BY A                    A = 6, B = 2
DIVIDE A BY 5 GIVING C            A = 6, B = 2, C = 1, D = 1
  REMAINDER D
```

3.
```
MULTIPLY A BY 2
```
   [*The 2 must be an identifier.*]
```
ADD "125" TO B
```
   [*An alphanumeric literal cannot participate in an arithmetic expression.*]
```
DIVIDE BUDGET-REMAINING BY PERIODS-REMAINING
```
   [*From the context of the names,* PERIODS-REMAINING *will contain zero in the last period, resulting in a division by zero.*]
```
MOVE ZERO TO A, B, C
```
   [*Should be a comma rather than a period after B.*]
```
COMPUTE A = B * C ROUNDED
```
   [*Should be* COMPUTE A ROUNDED = B * C.]
```
IF A = 2 = B
  THEN ADD 1 TO A
END-IF
```

475

Should be coded as

```
IF A = 2 AND B ...          [Or]            IF A = 2 AND A = B ...
```

12.
```
        PERFORM VARYING X FROM 1 BY 1 UNTIL X > 9
            MOVE ZERO TO A(X)
        END-PERFORM
        IF (B > 6) OR (B < ZERO) OR (C = ZERO)
            THEN MOVE ZERO TO E
                    IF (X + Y) <= ZERO
                        THEN ADD 1 TO G
                    END-IF
                    ADD 1 TO F
        ELSE IF B > 3
                    THEN ADD 1 TO G
                    ELSE ADD 1 TO B
                        ADD 1 TO F
            END-IF
        END-IF
```

Or:

```
        PERFORM VARYING X FROM 1 BY 1 UNTIL X > 9
          MOVE ZERO TO A(X)
        END-PERFORM
        EVALUATE TRUE
          WHEN (B > 6) OR (B < ZERO) OR (C = ZERO)
                MOVE ZERO TO E
                IF (X + Y) <= ZERO
                    THEN ADD 1 TO G
                END-IF
                ADD 1 TO F
          WHEN B > 3
                ADD 1 TO G
          WHEN OTHER
                ADD 1 TO B
                ADD 1 TO F
        END-EVALUATE
```

Chapter 5

6. You should ask what the basis is for measuring productivity. What is
measured? What are the units of measurement? What is the basis for the
comparison? What caused the increase in productivity? Could something
other than the listed techniques have caused part or all the postulated increase in productivity? For example, the project might have selected only the
top programmers for the experiment, and they might have been affected by
the *Hawthorne effect*, which occurs when the results on an experiment are in-
fluenced by watching it: If people know they are being watched to see if they do

better, they will do better because they know they are being watched rather than because variables are changed in the experiment.

It is impossible to predict accurately what would occur if programmer productivity were increased tenfold. At one extreme, 9 out of 10 programmers might be laid off. At another extreme, the programming population might produce 10 times the number of computer programs they do now. But perhaps there would be little change, because programming itself doesn't occupy that significant a part of a programmer's time. There are social and technical considerations to these extremes and to the entire spectrum in between.

Chapter 6

3.   COMPUTE E = A * D

[*A is converted to* PACKED-DECIMAL *and then to* COMP-1. *The* A * D COMP-1 *intermediate result is converted to* COMP-2 *and stored in* E.]

COMPUTE A = D * B * C

[B *and* C *are converted to* COMP-1. *The* COMP-1 *intermediate result is converted to* USAGE DISPLAY *and stored in* A.]

ADD 1 TO C

[*Conversion depends on compiler. Literal constants in VS COBOL II are* PACKED-DECIMAL, *and so the* 1 *would be converted to* BINARY *and be added to* C.]

MOVE B TO A

[PACKED-DECIMAL *is converted to* USAGE DISPLAY.]

4.   COMPUTE A = 3.5

[A = 3 (4V0)]

COMPUTE A ROUNDED = 3.5

[A = 4 (4V0)]

COMPUTE B = 1254.6 * 3.3235 / 6.43229 + 12.1136

[1254.6 (4V1) * 3.3235 (1V4) = 4169.66310 (5V5)
4169.66310 (5V5) / 6.43229 (1V5) = 648.23928 (4V5)
645.23928 (4V5) + 12.1136 (2V4) = 660.35288 (5V5)
660.35288 (5V5) *stored in* B *as* 660.352 (6V3)]

MOVE 12.211 TO B

[B = 12.211 (6V3)]

COMPUTE B = B / 4.395 * 6.4 + 7.1135

[12.211 (6V3) / 4.395 (1V3) = 2.77838 (3V5)
2.77838 (3V5) * 6.4 (1V1) = 17.781623 (4V6)
17.781623 (4V6) + 7.1135 (1V4) = 24.895123 (5V6)
24.895123 (5V6) *stored in* B *as* 24.895 (6V3)]

COMPUTE A = (12 + .1) / 7

[12 (2V0) + .1 (0V1) = 12.1 (3V1)
12.1 (3V1) / 7 (1V0) = 1.7 (3V1)
1.7 (3V1) *stored in* A *as* 1 (4V0)]

COMPUTE A = (12 / 7) + .1

[12 (2V0) / 7 (1V0) = 1 (2V0)
1 (1V0) + .1 (0V1) = 1.1 (2V1)
1.1 (2V1) *stored in* A *as* 1 (4V0)]

Chapter 7

1. A - "000000"

B - "MARYQU" with compilation warning

C - "ABC"

D - "121212"

E - "123bbbbb"

P - "ABCbbb"

G - "000000"

4.
```
77   THE-NUM PIC S9(5).
77   IX                   PIC S9(5) BINARY.
     ■ ■ ■
     IF THE-NUM = ZERO
        THEN PERFORM VARYING IX FROM 1 BY 1
                      UNTIL IX > LENGTH OF THE-NUM
               MOVE SPACE TO THE-NUM(IX:1)
             END-PERFORM
     END-IF
```

Chapter 8

3.   The technique is termed *rippling a character*. A single character is moved to the first position of an identifier, and then the identifier is moved to itself, one character position beyond the first character. On some computers, this propagates the character through the entire identifier. This is efficient, but it is an abominable practice. First, it is not clear that all that code simply moves blanks to the identifier. Second, it violates the ANSI Standard and does not work in Microsoft COBOL. It did work on IBM System/360 computers, but it no longer works on System/370 and 390 computers.

Chapter 9

3.
```
01   COUNT-IT                PIC S9(4) BINARY.
01   SOMETHING.
     05  TABLES              OCCURS 200 TIMES
                             ASCENDING KEY IS TABLES-VAL
                             INDEXED BY IX.
         10  TABLES-VAL      PIC S9(3)V9(4) PACKED-DECIMAL.
```

Unordered, number of times 3.6257 occurs:

```
MOVE ZEROS TO COUNT-IT
PERFORM VARYING IX FROM 1 BY 1
        UNTIL IX > 200
```

```
    IF TABLES-VAL(IX) = 3.6257
       THEN ADD 1 TO COUNT-IT
    END-IF
END-PERFORM
DISPLAY "3.6257 OCCURS THIS MANY TIMES: ", COUNT-IT
```

Unordered, see if 0.7963 is in table:

```
SET IX TO 1
SEARCH TABLES
  AT END DISPLAY "0.7963 NOT IN TABLES-VAL"
  WHEN TABLES-VAL(IX) = 0.7963
       DISPLAY "0.7963 IS FOUND IN TABLES-VAL"
END-SEARCH
```

Ordered, see if 2.1537 is in table:

```
SEARCH ALL TABLES
  AT END DISPLAY "2.1537 NOT IN TABLES-VAL"
  WHEN TABLES-VAL(IX) = 2.1537
       DISPLAY "2.1537 IS FOUND IN TABLES-VAL"
END-SEARCH
```

5. Chapter 19 contains an example showing how to write a program to sort a table.

Chapter 12

3.
```
IDENTIFICATION DIVISION.
     PROGRAM-ID. VALIDATE-PROGRAM.
ENVIRONMENT DIVISION.
INPUT-OUTPUT SECTION.
FILE-CONTROL.
     SELECT FILE-IN ASSIGN TO INFILE.
DATA DIVISION.
FILE SECTION.
FD  FILE-IN
    BLOCK CONTAINS 0 RECORDS
    RECORD CONTAINS 33 CHARACTERS
    .
01  REC-IN                      PIC X(33).
WORKING-STORAGE SECTION.
01  IN-REC.
    05  IN-PROJ                 PIC X(4).
    05 IN-NAME                  PIC X(25).
    05 IN-OHD                   PIC S9(5)V99 PACKED-DECIMAL.
01 IN-DUP-PROJ                  PIC X(4).
01 IN-NO-DUP                    PIC S9(4) BINARY.
PROCEDURE DIVISION.
```

```
START-PROGRAM.
    DISPLAY "BEGINNING VALIDATE PROGRAM"
    OPEN INPUT FILE-IN
    MOVE LOW-VALUES TO IN-REC, IN-DUP-PROJ
    MOVE ZEROS TO IN-NO-DUP
    PERFORM UNTIL IN-REC = HIGH-VALUES
       READ FILE-IN INTO IN-REC
          AT END
             MOVE HIGH-VALUES TO IN-REC
          NOT AT END
             PERFORM B10-CHECK-RECORDS
       END-READ
    END-PERFORM
    CLOSE FILE-IN
    DISPLAY "NUMBER OF DUPLICATES: ", IN-NO-DUP
    DISPLAY "END VALIDATE PROGRAM"
    STOP RUN
       .

B10-CHECK-RECORDS.
    IF IN-PROJ < IN-DUP-PROJ
        THEN DISPLAY "RECORD OUT OF SORT: "
             DISPLAY IN-REC
        ELSE IF IN-PROJ = IN-DUP-PROJ
                THEN DISPLAY "DUPLICATE PROJECT NUMBER:"
                     DISPLAY IN-REC
                     ADD 1 TO IN-NO-DUP
        END-IF
    END-IF
    MOVE IN-PROJ TO IN-DUP-PROJ
       .

**** Exit
END PROGRAM VALIDATE-PROGRAM.
```

8. The program will work improperly if either the MASTER-IN or TRANS-IN files are out of sequence or if they contain duplicate records. Section VIII in this chapter is essentially a solution to this problem.

Chapter 13

1.

```
MOVE 23655.97 TO W      "bbb$23,658.97bb"
MOVE -2 TO W            "bbbbbbbb$2.00CR"
MOVE .01  TO W          "bbbbbbbb$0.01bb"
MOVE 26531 TO X         "bbb26,531"
MOVE -4 TO X            "bbbbbbbb4"
MOVE -16 TO Y           "-***16"
MOVE 327 TO Y           "b**32?"
MOVE -923945 TO Y       "-23945"
```

```
MOVE 35275.6 TO Z          "$bbbb35,275.60"
MOVE -247.96 TO Z          "$bbbbbb-247.96"
MOVE ZERO TO Z             "bbbbbbbbbbbbb"
```

Chapter 19

3.
```
    IDENTIFICATION DIVISION.
        PROGRAM-ID. STATS.
    DATA DIVISION.
    WORKING-STORAGE SECTION.
    01  TABLE-TOTAL              PIC S9(9)V99 PACKED-DECIMAL.
    LINKAGE SECTION.
    01  TABLE-DEFN.
        05  TABLE-SIZE           PIC S9(4) BINARY.
        05  TABLE-VAL            PIC S9(5)V99 PACKED-DECIMAL
                                 OCCURS 0 TO 500 TIMES DEPENDING ON
                                 TABLE-SIZE INDEXED BY TBL-X.
        05  TABLE-MIN            PIC S9(5)V99 PACKED-DECIMAL.
        05  TABLE-MAX            PIC S9(5)V99 PACKED-DECIMAL.
        05  TABLE-AVG            PIC S9(5)V99 PACKED-DECIMAL.
    PROCEDURE DIVISION USING TABLE-DEFN.
    START-PROGRAM.
        MOVE ZEROS TO TABLE-TOTAL
        MOVE -99999.99 TO TABLE-MAX
        MOVE 99999.99 TO TABLE-MIN
        PERFORM VARYING TBL-X FROM 1 BY 1
                UNTIL TBL-X > TABLE-SIZE
          ADD TABLE-VAL(TBL-X) TO TABLE-TOTAL
          IF TABLE-VAL(TBL-X) > TABLE-MAX
             THEN MOVE TABLE-VAL(TBL-X) TO TABLE-MAX
          END-IF
          IF TABLE-VAL(TBL-X) < TABLE-MIN
             THEN MOVE TABLE-VAL(TBL-X) TO TABLE-MIN
          END-IF
        END-PERFORM
        COMPUTE TABLE-AVG = TABLE-TOTAL / TABLE-SIZE
        EXIT PROGRAM
          .
    END PROGRAM STATS.
```

Chapter 20

1.
```
    01  TITLES                   PIC X(200).
    01  COUNT-IT                 PIC S9(5) BINARY.
        ■ ■ ■
        MOVE ZERO TO COUNT-IT
        INSPECT TITLES TALLYING COUNT-IT FOR ALL "ABCD"
                                            ALL "EFG"
```

Chapter 21

1.
```
IDENTIFICATION DIVISION.
     PROGRAM-ID. SORT-PROGRAM.
INPUT-OUTPUT SECTION.
FILE-CONTROL.
     SELECT SORT-FILE ASSIGN TO SORTWK.
     SELECT SORT-IN ASSIGN TO SORTIN.
     SELECT SORT-OUT ASSIGN TO SORTOUT.
DATA DIVISION.
FILE SECTION.
SD   SORT-FILE.
01   SORT-REC.
     05   SORT-KEY-1              PIC X(8).
     05   SORT-KEY-2              PIC X(12).
     05   FILLER                 PIC X(60).
FD   SORT-IN
     BLOCK CONTAINS 0 RECORDS
     RECORD CONTAINS 80 CHARACTERS
     .
01   IN-REC                      PIC X(80).
FD   SORT-OUT
     BLOCK CONTAINS 0 RECORDS
     RECORD CONTAINS 80 CHARACTERS
     .
01   OUT-REC                     PIC X(80).
PROCEDURE DIVISION.
START-PROGRAM.
     DISPLAY "BEGINNING SORT PROGRAM"
     SORT SORT-FILE
       ON ASCENDING KEY SORT-KEY-1
       ON DESCENDING KEY SORT-KEY-2
       USING SORT-IN
       GIVING SORT-OUT
     DISPLAY "END OF SORT PROGRAM"
     STOP RUN
     .
END PROGRAM SORT-PROGRAM.
```

5.   Sort the number as follows:

- Leftmost digit in descending order.
- Second digit in descending order.
- Third digit in ascending order.

Appendix C

Obsolete and Obsolescent COBOL Items

I. OBSOLETE ITEMS TO BE DELETED NEXT ANSI REVISION

ALL (When used with numeric items)

ALTER GO TO

AUTHOR

DATA RECORDS clause

DATE-COMPILED

DATE-WRITTEN

DEBUGGING MODULE

  READY TRACE

  RESET TRACE

ENTER STATEMENT

INSTALLATION

LABEL RECORDS clause

MEMORY SIZE

MULTIPLE FILE TAPE

OPEN REVERSED

RERUN clause of I-O-CONTROL paragraph

SECURITY

SEGMENTATION MODULE

  SEGMENT-LIMIT IS *number*.

STOP "*literal*"

VALUE OF clause in LABEL RECORDS

II. OBSOLESCENT ITEMS

COBOL allows you to specify condition flags in the SPECIAL-NAMES paragraph of the Environment Division. You can then test the value of the flag in the Procedure Division:

```
ENVIRONMENT DIVISION.
CONFIGURATION SECTION.
SPECIAL-NAMES.
     environment-name
       ON STATUS IS on-name
       OFF STATUS IS off-name
     environment-name IS ON STATUS IS on-name
     environment-name IS OFF STATUS IS off-name
```

VS COBOL II uses these to set what are termed UPSI switches. They are a holdover from the distant past, when a computer operator could flip console switches that a program could test. Today, this feature is entirely redundant, and there is no reason to use it. The *environment-name* can be UPSI-0 through UPSI-7. For example:

```
SPECIAL NAMES.
     UPSI-0 ON STATUS IS YEAR-END

     .
     ■ ■ ■
     IF YEAR-END THEN . . .
```

You set the switches at run time with the UPSI parameter, coded as follows:

```
//STEP1 EXEC COB2UCLG,PARM.GO='UPSI(nnnnnnnn )'
```
   [*Each n represents one of the eight UPSI switches—*UPSI-0 *through* UPSI-7. *A value of 0 is off and 1 is on. The default is* UPSI(0000000).]

III. ANSI ITEMS IGNORED IN VS COBOL II AND MICROSOFT COBOL

```
     PADDING CHARACTER
     RECORD DELIMITER
     SAME SORT AREA
```

IV. ITEMS DROPPED FROM PREVIOUS COBOL COMPILERS

```
     CURRENT-DATE  (Use ACCEPT DATE statement)
     EXAMINE  (Use INSPECT statement)
```

```
EXHIBIT  (Use DISPLAY statement)
ISAM and BDAM files  (Use indexed files)
   ACTUAL KEY
   APPLY CORE-INDEX
   APPLY KEY
   APPLY RECORD OVERFLOW
   APPLY REORG-CRITERIA
   NOMINAL KEY
   TRACK-AREA
   TRACK-LIMIT
NOTE  (Use comment)
ON/THEN/ELSE  (Use D in column 7 or USE AFTER)
OTHERWISE  (Use ELSE)
REMARKS  (Use comment)
TIME-OF-DAY  (Use ACCEPT TIME statement)
TRANSFORM  (Use INSPECT statement)
WRITE POSITIONING  (Use WRITE ADVANCING statement)
```

V. ITEMS IN ANSI AND MICROSOFT COBOL NOT IN VS COBOL II

Report Writer Module:

```
CODE
COLUMN
CONTROL
GENERATE
INITIATE
LINE
LINE-COUNTER
NEXT GROUP
PAGE
PAGE-COUNTER
```

PRINT-SWITCH

REPORT clause of FD

REPORT SECTION

SOURCE

SUM

TERMINATE

TYPE

Communications Module:

COMMUNICATION SECTION

DISABLE

ENABLE

RECEIVE

SEND

Appendix D

COBOL Intrinsic Functions

The intrinsic functions are a part of COBOL 85, as revised in 1989. They are supported in Microsoft/Micro Focus COBOL, but as of this writing have not yet been implemented in VS COBOL II. Functions are written in the form:

```
FUNCTION function-name(arguments)
```

For example, the function named FACTORIAL computes the factorial of an integer.

```
COMPUTE T-VAL = FUNCTION FACTORIAL(6)
```

The function computes the factorial of 6 and returns the value, 720, which is then stored in T-VAL. The following rules apply to intrinsic functions.

- The arguments can be identifiers, literals, or, for numeric functions, arithmetic expressions.

```
COMPUTE MIN-S = FUNCTION MIN(0,LOW-S,HIGH-S / 10)
```

- You can code a function wherever an identifier of that data type is permitted, except the function cannot be a receiving field.

```
COMPUTE T-VAL = FUNCTION RANDOM *
               STAT-POP(FUNCTION MIN(1, IDX))
```

The following is in error because the function is a receiving field.

```
COMPUTE FUNCTION FACTORIAL(6) = T-VAL
```

- The arguments must be of the proper data type for the function. When a series of arguments are listed, they must all have the same data type: numeric, or alphanumeric/alphabetic. (That is, you can mix alphanumeric and alphabetic.)

- Several of the numeric functions allow you to list multiple items as arguments. For these, you can also process all the elements of a table by naming the table and coding ALL rather than a subscript. For example

```
COMPUTE T-VAL = FUNCTION MAX(STAT-POP(ALL))
```

would examine all the elements of the STAT-POP table and return the maximum value.
- The function has a data type that determines the value returned. For example, the data type of FACTORIAL is integer numeric.
- You can reference modify character data when coded as an argument.
- A function can be an argument of a function, and the functions can be recursive. Functions are evaluated from left to right, taking into account any parentheses. For example,

```
COMPUTE T-VAL = FUNCTION FACTORIAL(FUNCTION FACTORIAL(3))
```

first computes the factorial of 3, which is 6. Then it calculates the factorial of 6, which is 720, and this value is stored in T-VAL

I. DATE FUNCTIONS

The date functions use the Gregorian calendar for conversion to other forms. Monday, January 1, 1601 is day 1 of this calendar. The integer Gregorian date is the number of days, beginning on 1/1/1601 — or the number of days following 12/31/1660. Thus, the integer Gregorian date 144,270 is December 31, 1995.

CURRENT-DATE: Get current date.
WHEN-COMPILED: Get compilation date.
Argument: None.
Returns: PIC X(21) as yyyymmddhhmmsstt±hhmm
       yyyy: Year
       mm: Month (01 to 12)
       dd: Day of month (01 to 31)
       hh: Hour (01 to 23)
       mm: Minutes (00 to 59)
       ss: Seconds (00 to 59)
       tt: hundreths of seconds (00 to 99)
   ±hhmm: Hours and minutes ahead (+) or behind (−) Greenwich Mean Time
       (00000 if system does not have the facility)
    FUNCTION CURRENT-DATE and FUNCTION WHEN-COMPILED might return "199510220832171200000".

DATE-OF-INTEGER: Get calendar date from integer Gregorian date.
Argument: DATE-OF-INTEGER *(integer-Gregorian-date)*
Returns: Integer containing digits: yyyymmdd.
    FUNCTION DATE-OF-INTEGER (144270)
    returns 19951231.

DAY-OF-INTEGER: Get year and day of year from integer Gregorian date.
Argument: DAY-OF-INTEGER *(integer-Gregorian-date)*
Returns: Integer containing digits: yyyyddd, where ddd is the
    day of year (1 to 366).
    FUNCTION DAY-OF-INTEGER(144270) returns
    1995365.

INTEGER-OF-DATE: Get integer Gregorian date from date in integer
    form.
Argument: INTEGER-OF-DATE(*integer* in form yyyymmdd)
    The *integer* = (yyyy $\times$ 10,000) + mm $\times$
    100 + dd
Returns: Integer Gregorian date.
    FUNCTION INTEGER-OF-DATE(19951231) returns
    144,270.

INTEGER-OF-DAY: Get integer Gregorian date from date in integer
    form.
Argument: INTEGER-OF-DAY (*integer* in form yyyyddd)
    The *integer* = (yyyy $\times$ 10,000) + ddd
Returns: Integer Gregorian Date.
    FUNCTION(1995365) returns 144,270.

II. CHARACTER FUNCTIONS

CHAR: Convert character to ordinal position of character in
    collating sequence.
Argument: CHAR (*integer*)
    The *integer* is the ordinal position of the character
    in the collating sequence and must be 1 to 256. Note
    that this is one greater than the ASCII or EBCDIC code
    for the character.
Returns: Single character as PIC X.
    FUNCTION CHAR(110) returns "m" in ASCII and
    "%" in EBCDIC.

LENGTH: Get length of a data item.
Argument: LENGTH (*item*)
Returns: Integer length of *item*.
    FUNCTION LENGTH ("ABCD") returns 4.

LOWER-CASE:	Convert characters to lower case.
UPPER-CASE:	Convert characters to upper case.
Argument:	LOWER-CASE (*string*)
Argument:	UPPER-CASE (*string*)
	The *string* can be alphanumeric or alphabetic.
Returns:	A character string of the same length *string*. The new string contains the characters converted to lower or upper case. FUNCTION LOWER-CASE("123aBCD+−") returns "123abcd+−".

NUMVAL:	Convert a string to numeric.
Argument:	NUMVAL (*string*)
	The string contains characters representing numbers in the form: "+nnn,nnn,nnn.nn " There can be a leading sign ($\pm$) or training sign ($\pm$, CR, or DB). Blanks may optionally separate the sign and the groups of digits. The commas and decimal point are optional.
Returns:	The numeric value of the string. FUNCTION NUMVAL("+100,233.56") returns numeric 100,233.56.

NUMVAL-C:	Convert a string with a currency symbol to numeric.
Argument:	NUMVAL-C(string)
	NUMVAL-C(*string, currency-symbol*)
	Same as NUMVAL, except the currency symbol can be placed to the left of the left-most digit (and to the right of any leading sign). If you specify the currency sign as a literal or identifier containing a single character, it and not the normal currency sign is assumed for the string.
Returns:	The numeric value of the string. FUNCTION NUMVAL-C("+£100,233.56", "£") returns numeric 100,233.56.

ORD:	Get the ordinal position of a character in the collating sequence.
Arugment:	ORD (*character*)
Returns:	The ordinal position of the character in the collating sequence. Note that this is one greater than the ASCII or EBCDIC code for the character. FUNCTION ORD("A") returns 66 in ASCII and 194 in EBCDIC.

ORD-MAX:	Get the number of the character in as string having the highest value in the collating sequence.
Argument:	ORD-MAX (*item, item,...,item*)
	The *items* must all be of the same class. Alphanumeric and alphabetic can be mixed.
Returns:	The number of the *item* having the maximum value. FUNCTION ORD-MAX("A","B","C","D","Z", "M","N") returns 5.

REVERSE:	Reverse the characters in a string.
Argument:	REVERSE (*string*)
Returns:	A string (same length as *string*) containing all the characters in reverse order.
	FUNCTION REVERSE("ABCD") returns "DCBA".

III. NUMERIC FUNCTIONS

ACOS:	Compute arccosine in radians.
ASIN:	Compute arcsine in radians.
ATAN:	Compute arctangent in radians.
COS:	Compute cosine in radians.
SIN:	Compute sine in radians.
TAN:	Compute tangent in radians.
Argument:	ACOS (*radians*) Any numeric value from -1 through $+1$
	ASIN (*radians*) Any numeric value from -1 through $+1$
	ATAN (*radians*)
	COS (*radians*)
	SIN (*radians*)
	TAN (*radians*)
Returns:	The value in radians.
	FUNCTION COS(0) returns 1.

ANNUITY:	Calculate the annuity value of 1 for an interest rate and a number of periods.
Argument:	ANNUITY (*interest-rate*, *integer-periods*)
	The *interest rate* is the percentage/100 and must be $\geq$ 0. The *integer-periods* must be $>$ 0.
Returns:	The anniuty for an initial investment of one, assuming the interest is applied at the end of each period.
	FUNCTION ANNUITY(.1,1) = 1.1.

FACTORIAL:	Compute factorial of an integer.
Argument:	FACTORIAL (*integer*)
	The *integer* must be $\geq$ 0.
Returns:	Integer factorial.
	FUNCTION FACTORIAL(6) returns $6 \times 5 \times 4 \times 3 \times 2 \times 1 = 720$.

INTEGER:	Get the greatest integer value that is less than or equal to a number.
INTEGER-PART:	Get the integer part of a number.
Argument:	INTEGER (*number*)
	INTEGER-PART (*number*)
Returns:	FUNCTION INTEGER(23.5) returns 23.
	FUNCTION INTEGER(-23.5) returns -24.
	FUNCTION INTEGER-PART(23.5) returns 23.
	FUNCTION INTEGER-PART(-23.5) returns -23.

LOG:	Get logarithm to the base e.
LOG10:	Get logarithm to the base 10.
Argument:	LOG (*number*) The *number* must be $\geq$ 0.
	LOG10 (*number*) The *number* must be $\geq$ 0.
Returns:	Number representing the logarithm to the base e or base 10.
	FUNCTION LOG10(100) returns 2.

MAX:	Get the maximum value of a series of values.
MIN:	Get the minimum value of a series of values.
Argument:	MAX (*item, item, ..., item*)
	MIN (*item, item, ..., item*)
	The *items* must all have the same data class. They can be alphabetic/alphanumeric, integer, or numeric.
Returns:	The value of the *item* having the maximum or minimum value.
	FUNCTION MAX(10,33,4,6) returns 33.
	FUNCTION MIN(10,33,4,6) returns 4.

MEAN:	Calculate the mean of a series of numbers.
Argument:	MEAN (*number, number, ..., number*)
Returns:	The arithmetic mean of the *numbers*.
	FUNCTION MEAN(10,33,4,6) returns $(10 + 33 + 4 +6)/4 = 13.25$.

MEDIAN:	Calculate the median of a series of numbers.
Argument:	MEDIAN (*number, number, ..., number*)
Returns:	The median value of the *numbers*.
	FUNCTION MEDIAN(10,33,4,6) returns $(10 + 6)/2 = 8$. (If the number of items is even, the median is the average of the middle two numbers.)
	FUNCTION MEDIAN(10,33,4,6,12) returns 10.

MIDRANGE:	Calculate the middle range value of a series of numbers.
Argument:	MIDRANGE (*number, number, ..., number*)
Returns:	The average of the minimum and maximum values of the series of *numbers*.
	FUNCTION MIDRANGE(10,33,4,6) returns $(33 + 4)/2 = 18.5$.

MOD:	Get the modulo value.
Argument:	MOD(*integer-1, integer-2*)
Returns:	The value of *integer-1* modulo *integer-2*. The calculation is *integer-1* $-$ (*integer-2* $\times$ FUNCTION INTEGER(*integer-1/integer-2*)).
	FUNCTION MOD(36,5) returns $36 - (5 \times (36/5))$ $= 36 - (5 \times 5) = 7$.
	FUNCTION MOD(-27,5) returns $-27 - (5 \times (-27/5))$ $= -27 - (5 \times -6) = 3$.

PRESENT-VALUE: Calculate the present value given a discount rate and a series of future values.

Argument: PRESENT-VALUE (*discount-rate*, *amount*, *amount*, ..., *amount*) The *discount-rate* is the percentage/100 and must be greater than −1.

Returns: The present value of the series of future period-end amounts.
FUNCTION PRESENT-VALUE(.1,100,100) returns 248.685.

RANDOM: Get pseudo-random number.

Argument: RANDOM
RANDOM (*starting-integer*)
If no *starting-integer* is given the first time invoked, a value of zero is assumed. When the *starting-integer* is specified, even after the first time invoked, it is used to calculate the beginning of the random number sequence. Usually you code FUNCTION RANDOM (*starting-integer*) first to start a series of random numbers and then code FUNCTION RANDOM thereafter.

Returns: A pseudo-random number having a value from 0 to 1.
FUNCTION RANDOM returns .470, .799, etc. (Actual values depend on implementation.)
FUNCTION RANDOM(9) always returns .523. (Actual value depends on implementation.)

RANGE: Calculate the range of a series of numbers.

Argument: RANGE(*number*, *number*, ..., *number*)
If any of the *numbers* are integer, all must be integer.

Returns: The value of the maximum value of the series minus the minimum value.
FUNCTION RANGE(10,33,4,6) returns $33 − 4 = 29$.

REM: Calculate the remainder.

Argument: REM (*number-1*, *number-2*)
The *number-2* cannot be zero.

Returns: The remainder of *number-1/number-2*.
FUNCTION REM(36,5) returns 1.
FUNCTION REM(-27,5) returns −2.

SQRT: Compute the square root of a number.

Argument: SQRT (*number*)
The *number* must be ≥ 0.

Returns: The square root of *number*.
FUNCTION SQRT(9) returns 3.

STANDARD-DEVIATION: Calculate the standard deviation of a series of numbers.

Argument: STANDARD-DEVIATION (*number*, *number*, ..., *number*)

Returns: The standard deviation of the *numbers*.
FUNCTION STANDARD-DEVIATION (10,33,4,6) returns 11.605.

SUM: Sum a series of numbers.
Argument: SUM (*number*, *number*, ..., *number*)
Returns: The arithmetic sum of the *numbers*. The value is
                     integer only if all the arguments are integer.
                     FUNCTION SUM(10,33,4,6) returns 53.

VARIANCE: Compute the statistical variance of a series of
                     numbers.
Argument: VARIANCE (*number*, *number*, ..., *number*)
Returns: The statistical variance of the numbers.
                     FUNCTION VARIANCE(10,33,4,6) returns 134.678

Index